Successful
College Writing

www. galileo.usg.edu

password: tenfold

BRIEF FOURTH
EDITION

Successful
College Writing

SKILLS | STRATEGIES | LEARNING STYLES

KATHLEEN T. McWHORTER
Niagara County Community College

Why type a racial
History Discrim
Why is it still
occuring to day

BEDFORD/ST. MARTIN'S
Boston • New York

For Bedford/St. Martin's

Senior Developmental Editor: John Elliott
Senior Production Editor: Harold Chester
Production Supervisor: Andrew Ensor
Senior Marketing Manager: Karita France dos Santos
Marketing Manager: Molly Parke
Art Director: Lucy Krikorian
Text Design: Brian Salisbury
Copy Editor: Jamie Nan Thaman
Photo Research: Connie Gardner
Cover Design: Donna Lee Dennison
Cover Art: Richard Kalina, *The Abduction from Siena,* Courtesy of Lennon, Weinberg, Inc.
Composition: Pre-Press PMG
Printing and Binding: RR Donnelley and Sons

President: Joan E. Feinberg
Editorial Director: Denise B. Wydra
Editor in Chief: Karen S. Henry
Director of Development: Erica T. Appel
Director of Marketing: Karen R. Soeltz
Director of Editing, Design, and Production: Marcia Cohen
Assistant Director of Editing, Design, and Production: Elise S. Kaiser
Managing Editor: Shuli Traub

Library of Congress Control Number: 2009929649 (with Handbook)
2009929904 (without Handbook)

Manufactured in the United States of America.

3 2 1 0 9
e d c b

For information, write: Bedford/St. Martin's, 75 Arlington Street, Boston, MA 02116   (617-399-4000)

ISBN-10:   0-312-60339-8 (Student Edition with Handbook; MLA Update)
ISBN-13:   978-0-312-60339-7 (Student Edition with Handbook; MLA Update)

ISBN-10:   0-312-60338-X (Student Edition without Handbook; MLA Update)
ISBN-13:   978-0-312-60338-0 (Student Edition without Handbook; MLA Update)

ISBN-10:   0-312-53280-6 (Instructor's Annotated Edition)
ISBN-13:   978-0-312-53280-2 (Instructor's Annotated Edition)

Acknowledgments

Acknowledgments and copyrights appear at the back of the book on pages 711–14, which constitute an extension of the copyright page.

My goal in writing *Successful College Writing* was to create a first-year composition text that covers the skills other college-level texts assume students already possess. The overwhelmingly positive response from instructors who have used the first three editions confirms my own experience: Many students today need a review of basic writing conventions before they can be equipped with college-level skills in writing, reading, or critical thinking. *Successful College Writing* in its fourth edition continues to address this reality.

Through its unique, highly visual, student-centered approach, *Successful College Writing* teaches students essential skills while guiding them through the writing strategies and activities that form the core of composition instruction. With this revision, I sought to provide more guidance for students in critical reading and paragraph writing, to strengthen coverage of topics that are integral to students' success in college, and to make the reading selections even more appealing to students and instructors.

PROVEN FEATURES OF *SUCCESSFUL COLLEGE WRITING*

True to its goal of offering more coverage of essential skills, *Successful College Writing* provides abundant guidance and support for inexperienced writers along with thorough help with reading and study skills.

Extensive Support for Inexperienced College Writers Throughout

Every chapter of *Successful College Writing* provides practical, student-oriented instruction, along with extra help for those students who need it.

Detailed coverage of each stage of the writing process. Part Two of the text, "Strategies for Writing Essays," consists of six chapters that cover each stage of the writing process in detail, with plenty of skill-building exercises, many of them collaborative; a running student example; and Essay in Progress activities that lead students through each step in writing an essay.

Appealing, helpful visuals. Because inexperienced writers often are more comfortable with images than with text, *Successful College Writing* employs a visual approach to writing instruction. The Quick Starts at the beginning of each chapter provide engaging images for students to respond to. In addition, Graphic Organizers—maps that display relationships among ideas—present students with an alternative to traditional outlines. Students

v

are encouraged to use the Graphic Organizers as tools both for analyzing readings and for planning and revising their own essays. Revision Flowcharts help students systematically read their own essays with a critical eye and revise them as well as review those of their peers, and other figures and boxes reinforce points made in the text and summarize information. Finally, new Visualizing the Reading activities following one of the readings in each chapter in Parts Two and Three give students a clear, simple way to chart key features of the reading, with the first part of each chart done for them to provide guidance.

Practical, step-by-step writing assignments. Each chapter in Part Three covers one of the patterns of development that students will frequently encounter in college and on the job. The chapters in Part Three, as well as the chapter on writing arguments in Part Four and on writing a literary analysis in Part Six, include Guided Writing Assignments that lead students step by step through the process of writing an essay. These guided assignments give student writers the support they need, whether they are working in class or on their own. The assignments will also appeal to faculty members who often have limited time to become familiar with a complex textbook.

Comprehensive coverage of research and documentation. Because many students are called upon to work with sources early in their college careers and because technological advancements and the Internet have made such source-based writing increasingly difficult, *Successful College Writing* provides three full chapters on writing with sources, covering both electronic and print sources. Students learn to locate sources and take effective notes, evaluate a source's relevancy and reliability, synthesize and integrate sources, avoid plagiarism, and properly use MLA and APA documentation formats, including updated MLA guidelines.

Unique emphasis on learning styles. Because students learn in different ways, they learn to write in different ways as well, yet most writing texts do not take these differences into account. *Successful College Writing* encourages students to explore alternative writing strategies and provides the tools to approach writing as a flexible, multifaceted process, alleviating some of the frustration students often feel.

In this text, I focus on four learning styles that are relevant for writing: verbal versus spatial learning, creative versus pragmatic learning, concrete versus abstract learning, and social versus independent learning. A brief questionnaire in Chapter 2 enables students to assess their learning styles. Recognizing that no one strategy works for every student, the text includes a variety of strategies for generating ideas and revising an essay. Alternative strategies are identified by the "Learning Style Options" icon *Learning Style Options* found in the margins throughout the text.

Emphasis on Reading and Study Skills

Over the years, my work with students has convinced me that skills taught in isolation are seldom learned well or applied. Because reading and study skills are essential to successful writing, instruction in these skills is integrated throughout *Successful College Writing*. By becoming proficient, enthusiastic readers, students learn to be better writers and improve their chances for success not only in the writing classroom but also in their other courses as well.

Complete chapter on active, critical reading. To provide students with solid, proven strategies for working with text, the Guide for Active Reading in Chapter 3 helps students improve their comprehension and build skills that they can apply to the readings within this text as well as to those that they encounter in their other college classes.

Thorough coverage of reading skills throughout. The reading skills that are taught in Chapter 3 are reinforced in each of the chapters on the patterns of development. As students develop their writing skills by writing a particular type of essay, they simultaneously learn practical strategies for reading that type of essay. In addition, Chapter 18, "Reading Arguments," gives students guidelines for analyzing and evaluating arguments.

High-interest readings. Students who enjoy what they are reading become more proficient readers. Therefore, the professional and student readings in this text were carefully chosen to interest students as well as to function as strong rhetorical models. The professional readings come from a wide range of sources, including newspapers, popular magazines, special-interest magazines, blogs, other Web sites, textbooks, and scholarly journals, representing the diverse texts students encounter in both their personal and academic lives. Authors include such well-known writers as Amy Tan, William Safire, Barbara Ehrenreich, Dorothy Allison, and Ilan Stavans.

Attention to study skills. *Successful College Writing* gives students practical survival strategies that they can use not only in their writing course but in all their college courses. In addition to guidelines for reading different types of texts, *Successful College Writing* includes excerpts from college textbooks in marketing, biology, and communication; practical advice on study strategies in Chapter 24 on essay examinations, and useful, often interactive advice on college life, self-assessment, and study skills in Chapter 1, which incorporates much of the former Keys to Academic Success section.

NEW TO THE FOURTH EDITION

The main goals of the revision—based on feedback from instructors and students who used the text—were to strengthen the book's advice for succeeding in college, especially the coverage of academic reading and writing; to give students more help with paragraph writing; and to update the book with current and engaging professional readings and student writing. We also set out to make it more engaging and easier to use by tightening the prose; reducing duplication of advice within chapters; and developing a new, more contemporary, and more navigable design.

Greater emphasis on college "survival skills" and academic reading and writing. The early chapters of the book have been significantly changed and expanded to give students the thorough grounding in academic expectations they need for college success. A new Chapter 1, "Succeeding in College," incorporates new advice on topics such as procrastination and plagiarism with advice on time management and study skills formerly in the "Keys to Academic Success" section in the front of the book and material on classroom communication skills formerly in a chapter at the end of the book. The chapter now presents a prominent, unified, and consolidated approach to student success. Chapters 2 and 3 include new discussions of academic reading and writing, their distinctive demands, and the importance of mastering them as a requirement for success in college.

New chapter on writing effective paragraphs. This new Chapter 7, which follows the chapter on drafting (from which some of its content was drawn), presents guidance on paragraph structure, topic sentences, supporting details, and transitional words and phrases. A student essay-in-progress illustrates the skills taught in this chapter.

New annotations for student essays. Most of the student essays in the book have been annotated, with color-coded screening added to emphasize the writer's rhetorical strategies (and important features of the writing such as thesis statements, topic sentences, transitions, and source citations) as well as the distinctive features of the mode taught in the chapter. In addition, many of the brief examples of student and professional writing throughout the book are annotated to help students immediately see key points.

Eighteen new readings. Many of the new readings deal with issues close to students' lives. The fourteen new selections by professional writers include a classification of excuses for turning in college assignments late and a favorable comparison of *The Onion* with mainstream media; the four new student essays include a description of working in a fast-paced restaurant kitchen, an analysis of the lengths Americans go to in their quest to look good, and an explanation of how to make chili for a crowd. A number of the new essays demonstrate effective use of sources.

New design. A completely new design using a brighter palette makes the book more visually engaging and easier to navigate. For example, marginal tabs, rules, and graphic elements make it easier to locate reading selections and exercises within chapters; and, as noted earlier, color screens help to highlight annotated elements in student essays.

New e-book. The e-book, available for packaging or separate purchase, offers the complete text of the print book, with state-of-the-art tools and multimedia built in. Students can highlight and annotate the readings, respond to writing prompts directly in the book, and bookmark sections to be used for reference. Instructors can add their own materials—models, notes, assignments, course guidelines—and even reorganize chapters. The e-book also offers links to **new peer-review resources**, confidence-building activities that teach best practices for peer review; these include *Peer Factor*, an interactive simulation game, along with models, exercises, and assignments.

Correlation to the Council of Writing Program Administrators' Outcomes Statement. *Successful College Writing* helps students build proficiency in the four categories of learning that writing programs across the country use to assess their work: rhetorical knowledge; critical thinking, reading, and writing; writing processes; and knowledge of conventions. For a table that correlates WPA outcomes to features of *Successful College Writing,* see p. xvi. For a more detailed correlation, see the Instructor's Resource Manual or visit bedfordstmartins.com/successfulwriting.

USEFUL ANCILLARIES FOR INSTRUCTORS AND STUDENTS

The print and electronic ancillaries that accompany *Successful College Writing* offer plenty of support for both students and instructors. The Instructor's Annotated Edition and the Instructor's Resource Manual are valuable resources for all instructors but are especially helpful for adjunct instructors, who often don't receive their teaching assignments until the last minute.

Print Ancillaries for Instructors

- **Instructor's Annotated Edition,** with annotations prepared by Kathleen McCoy, Adirondack Community College. This useful volume provides abundant teaching tips, including suggestions for collaborative activities and applying learning styles to the writing classroom; computer hints; notes on additional resources; and answers to exercises and questions following readings. ISBN-10: 0-312-53280-6; ISBN-13: 978-0-312-53280-2.
- **Instructor's Resource Manual,** by Kathleen T. McWhorter; Michael Hricik, Westmoreland County Community College; Mary Applegate, D'Youville College; Rebecca J. Fraser, Nassau Community College; and Lucy MacDonald, Chemeka Community College. This extensive collection of materials provides extra support for adjuncts and new instructors. It includes sample syllabi along with chapters on teaching with *Successful College Writing,* helping underprepared students in the first-year writing classroom, evaluating student writing, and using the writing center. It also provides a bibliography of books and articles in rhetoric and composition. ISBN-10: 0-312-53281-4; ISBN-13: 978-0-312-53281-9.

Print Ancillaries for Students

- **Additional Exercises for *Successful College Writing,*** by Carolyn Lengel and Jess Carroll. Available free with the text, these exercises are keyed specifically to the handbook available in the full version of the book. ISBN-10: 0-312-53283-0; ISBN-13: 978-0-312-53283-3.
- ***The Bedford/St. Martin's ESL Workbook.*** This comprehensive exercise workbook covers grammar issues for multilingual students with varying English-language skills and cultural backgrounds. To reinforce each lesson, instructional introductions are

followed by illustrative examples and exercises. Answers are provided at the back. ISBN-10: 0-312-44503-2; ISBN-13: 978-0-312-44503-4.

- *The Bedford/St. Martin's Planner with* **Grammar Girl's** *Quick and Dirty Tips.* This resource includes everything that students need to plan and use their time effectively, with advice on preparing schedules and to-do lists and blank schedules and calendars (monthly and weekly) for planning. Integrated into the planner are tips from the popular *Grammar Girl* podcast; quick advice on fixing common grammar errors, note-taking, and succeeding on tests; an address book; and an annotated list of useful Web sites. The planner fits easily into a backpack or purse, so students can take it anywhere. ISBN-10: 0-312-48023-7; ISBN-13: 978-0-312-48023-3.
- *From Practice to Mastery.* This study guide for the Florida Basic Skills Exit Tests in reading and writing gives students all the resources they need to practice for—and pass—these tests. It includes pre- and post-tests, abundant practices, and clear instruction in all the skills covered on the exams. ISBN-10: 0-312-41908-2; ISBN-13: 978-0-312-41908-0.

Premium Electronic Ancillaries

- *CompClass* **for Successful College Writing.** In *CompClass*, the first online course space shaped by the needs of composition students and instructors, students can read assignments, do their work, and see their grades all in one place; and instructors can easily monitor student progress and give feedback right away. Along with the *Successful College Writing e-Book* (described below), *CompClass* comes preloaded with the innovative digital content that Bedford/St. Martin's is known for. ISBN-10: 0-312-56029-X; ISBN-13: 978-0-312-56029-4.
- *Successful College Writing e-Book.* In addition to the free resources described below, the Book Companion Site offers access to the new e-book version of *Successful College Writing.* As noted above under "New to the Fourth Edition," the e-book can be packaged for free with the print book or purchased separately; it integrates the complete text of the print book with state-of-the-art tools and multimedia, including the *Peer Factor* interactive simulation game to teach best practices for peer review. ISBN-10: 0-312-56031-1; ISBN-13: 978-0-312-56031-7.
- *Re:Writing Plus,* **bedfordstmartins.com/rewritingplus.** This collection brings together a variety of our premium digital content into one online library for composition. In addition to *Make-a-Paragraph Kit, i·cite,* and *Exercise Central to Go* (all described below), *Re:Writing Plus* includes hundreds of model documents.
- *Exercise Central to Go:* **Writing and Grammar Practices for Basic Writers.** This CD-ROM for basic writers has hundreds of practice items for writing and editing skills. Drawn from the popular *Exercise Central* resource, the exercises provide audio instructions and instant feedback and have been extensively class-tested. No Internet connection is necessary.
- *iX.* This CD-ROM allows students to analyze and manipulate the elements of visuals, giving them a more thorough understanding of how visual rhetoric works. Available free with *Successful College Writing.*

- *i·claim.* This CD-ROM features six tutorials on fundamental qualities good arguments share. An illustrated glossary defines fifty key terms from argument theory and classical rhetoric, and a visual index provides direct access to more than seventy multimedia arguments on the CD-ROM. Available free with *Successful College Writing*.
- *i·cite.* This CD-ROM brings research and documentation to life with animation and four interactive tutorials that explore fundamental concepts about working with sources. A gallery of sources provides concrete practice recognizing, evaluating, incorporating, and citing a wide range of real-life sources from across the disciplines. Available free with *Successful College Writing*.
- *Make-a-Paragraph Kit.* This interactive CD-ROM includes an "Extreme Paragraph Makeover" animation teaching students about paragraph development as well as activities that guide them through creating their own paragraphs. Additionally, it offers a set of audiovisual tutorials on fragments, run-ons and comma splices, subject-verb agreement problems, and verb problems. Grammar exercises are also included. ISBN-10: 0-312-45332-9; ISBN-13: 978-0-312-45332-9.

Free Electronic Resources

- **Book Companion Site with *Re:Writing*, bedfordstmartins.com/successfulwriting.** The Web site provides a grammar diagnostic, an online version of the book's Learning Styles Inventory, reading comprehension quizzes, and downloadable versions of the print ancillaries. The site also provides access to *Re:Writing*, an online collection of free, open, and easy-to-access resources for the writing class. Here you'll find plagiarism tutorials, model documents, style and grammar exercises, visual analysis activities, research guides, bibliography tools, and much more.
- *Exercise Central.* This extensive collection of interactive online grammar exercises is easy to use and convenient for students and instructors alike. Multiple exercise sets on every grammar topic ensure that students get as much practice as they need. Customized feedback turns skills practice into a learning experience, and the reporting feature allows both students and instructors to monitor and assess the students' progress. *Exercise Central* can be accessed through the Book Companion Site for *Successful College Writing*.
- *Testing Tool Kit: A Writing and Grammar Test Bank.* This CD-ROM allows instructors to create secure, customized tests and quizzes to assess students' writing and grammar competency and gauge their progress during the course. The CD includes nearly 2,000 test items on 47 writing and grammar topics, at two levels of difficulty, as well as ten pre-built diagnostic tests. Scoring is instantaneous when tests and quizzes are administered online. ISBN-10: 0-312-43032-9; ISBN-13: 978-0-312-43032-0.
- *Just-in-Time Teaching,* **at bedfordstmartins.com/justintime.** Looking for last-minute course materials from a source you can trust? We've culled the best handouts, teaching tips, assignment ideas, and more from our print and online resources and put them all in one place.

Ordering Information

To order any of the ancillaries, please contact your Bedford/St. Martin's sales representative, e-mail sales support at sales_support@bfwpub.com, or visit our Web site at bedfordstmartins.com. Note that activation codes are required for the e-book and *CompClass*. Codes can be purchased separately or packaged with the print book at a significant discount.

When ordering an access card for premium Web site content (the e-book) packaged with the book, use these ISBNs:

- Full edition with e-book: ISBN-13: 978-0-312-57182-5; ISBN-10: 0-312-57182-8.
- Brief edition with e-book: ISBN-13: 978-0-312-57176-4; ISBN-10: 0-312-57176-3.

When ordering an access card for *CompClass* packaged with the book, use these ISBNs:

- Full edition with *CompClass*: ISBN-13: 978-0-312-57177-1; ISBN-10: 0-312-57177-1.
- Brief edition with *CompClass*: ISBN-13: 978-0-312-57181-8; ISBN-10: 0-312-57181-X.

When ordering the book with *Additional Exercises*, use these ISBNs:

- Full edition with *Additional Exercises*: ISBN-13: 978-0-312-57176-4; ISBN-10: 0-312-57176-3.
- Brief edition with *Additional Exercises*: ISBN-13: 978-0-312-57180-1; ISBN-10: 0-312-57180-1.

When ordering an access card for *Re:Writing Plus* packaged with the book, use these ISBNs:

- Full edition with *Re:Writing Plus*: ISBN-13: 978-0-312-57175-7; ISBN-10: 0-312-57175-5.
- Brief edition with *Re:Writing Plus*: ISBN-13: 978-0-312-57178-8; ISBN-10: 0-312-57178-X.

ACKNOWLEDGMENTS

A number of instructors and students from across the country have helped me to develop and revise *Successful College Writing*. I would like to express my gratitude to the following instructors, who served as members of the advisory board for the first edition. They provided detailed, valuable comments and suggestions about the manuscript as well as student essays and additional help and advice during its development: Marvin Austin, Columbia State Community College; Sarah H. Harrison, Tyler Junior College; Dan Holt, Lansing Community College; Michael Mackey, Community College of

Denver; Lucille M. Schultz, University of Cincinnati; Sue Serrano, Sierra College; Linda R. Spain, Linn-Benton Community College; and Jacqueline Zimmerman, Lewis and Clark Community College. I would also like to thank the following instructors and their students, who class tested chapters from *Successful College Writing* and provided valuable feedback about how its features and organization worked in the classroom: Mary Applegate, D'Youville College; Michael Hricik, Westmoreland County Community College; Lee Brewer Jones, DeKalb College; Edwina Jordan, Illinois Central College; Susan H. Lassiter, Mississippi College; Mildred C. Melendez, Sinclair Community College; Steve Rayshich, Westmoreland County Community College; Barbara J. Robedeau, San Antonio College; and Deanna White, University of Texas at San Antonio.

I am indebted to the valuable research conducted by George Jensen, John DiTiberio, and Robert Sternberg on learning-style theory that informs the pedagogy of this book. For their comments on the coverage of learning styles in this text, I would like to thank John DiTiberio, Saint Louis University; Ronald A. Sudol, Oakland University; and Thomas C. Thompson, The Citadel. My thanks go to Mary Jane Feldman, Niagara County Community College, for designing the field test of the Learning Styles Inventory and conducting the statistical analysis of the results. I would also like to thank the instructors and students who participated in a field test of the Learning Styles Inventory: Laurie Warshal Cohen, Seattle Central Community College; Lee Brewer Jones, DeKalb College; Edwina Jordan, Illinois Central College; Jennifer Manning, John Jay College; Mildred Melendez, Sinclair Community College; Paul Resnick, Illinois Central College; and Deanna M. White, University of Texas at San Antonio.

I benefited from the experience of those instructors who reviewed the third edition, and I am grateful for their thoughtful comments and helpful advice: Irene Anders, Indiana University–Purdue University Fort Wayne; Gloria Brooks, Tyler Junior College; Charles F. Burm, Southeastern Community College; Margaret Burnett, Metropolitan Community College; Anna Maria Cancelli, Coastal Carolina Community College; Uzzie T. Cannon, Johnson & Wales University; Kathy Chrismon, Northeastern A&M College; Leah Creque, Morehouse College; Susan Muaddi Darraj, Harford Community College; Deborah Doolittle, Coastal Carolina Community College; Sohn Enis, University of Central Arkansas; Laura L. Fox, Harford Community College; Melissa Fry, Gateway Community and Technical College; Monica Konarski Fusetti, Montreat College, School of Professional Adult Studies; Emily Golson, University of Colorado; Laura Reed Goodson, Montreat College; George V. Griffith, Chadron State College; Katie Kalisz, Grand Rapids Community College; Evelyn M. Keable, Plattsburgh State University; Beata Levin, Pace University; Amy Locklear, Auburn University at Montgomery; Donna Mayes, Blue Ridge Community College; Rock Neely, University of Cincinnati, Raymond Walters Campus; Laurie Novy, Chadron State College; Dianne Perkins, Community College of Philadelphia; Debra Stevens, Las Positas College; Bill M. Stiffler, Harford Community College; Joan Stottlemyer, Carroll College; Karen Szudzik, University at Buffalo, Millard Fillmore College; Rodica Vasiliu, St. Clair College; Patricia Ventura, Spelman College; Gail Waller, Auburn University at Montgomery; Jamie J. Weaver, Northeastern Oklahoma A&M College; Pat West, Armstrong Atlantic State University; and Sally Padgett Wheeler, Georgia Perimeter College.

I am grateful to the following students whose essays appear in this text: Tracey Aquino, Andrew Decker, Sunny Desai, Nicholas Destino, Stanford DeWinter, Robin Ferguson, Heather Gianakos, David Harris, Christine Lee, Eric Michalski, Maria Rodriguez, Nick Ruggia, Ted Sawchuck, Harley Tong, and Aphonetip Vasavong. I also want to thank Elizabeth Gruchala-Gilbert for her research assistance, Lucy MacDonald for her thoughtful updating of the Instructor's Resource Manual, and Kathleen McCoy for her insightful and creative revision of the Instructor's Annotated Edition of the book. Brian Salisbury deserves special praise for creating a new striking and effective design.

Many people at Bedford/St. Martin's have contributed to the creation and development of *Successful College Writing*. Each person with whom I have worked is a true professional; each demonstrates high standards and expertise; each is committed to producing a book focused on student needs.

To Chuck Christensen, former president of Bedford/St. Martin's, I attribute much of my success in writing college textbooks. Twenty-seven years ago, I signed a contract for my first textbook with Chuck. Under his guidance, it became a bestseller. From Chuck I learned how to translate what I teach to the printed page. Joan Feinberg, current president, has become another trusted adviser. I value her editorial experience and appreciate the creative energy she brings to each issue and to each conversation. I also must thank Erica Appel, director of development in Bedford's New York office, for her forthright advice and for valuable assistance in making some of the more difficult decisions about the book. Special thanks to Kim White, new media editor, for her careful and talented work on the new e-book version.

I also appreciate the advice and guidance that Karen R. Soeltz, Karita dos Santos, and their colleagues in the marketing department at Bedford/St. Martin's have provided at various junctures in the revision of this text. Cecilia Seiter, editorial assistant, has helped prepare the manuscript in innumerable ways. Harold Chester, senior project editor, deserves special recognition for guiding this revision through the production process.

I owe the largest debt of gratitude to John Elliott, senior development editor, for his valuable guidance and assistance in preparing this revision. His awareness of the book's audience, his creative revision suggestions, his help in identifying appropriate professional readings, his careful editing, and his attention to detail have strengthened the fourth edition significantly. He helped me to reinforce the book's strengths and to retain its focus on providing extra help to the student. I particularly value his knowledge of the freshman composition field and appreciate his analytical and organizational skills. He is an editor from whom I have learned a great deal and with whom I am pleased and fortunate to have worked.

Finally, I must thank the many students who inspired me to write this book. From them I have learned how to teach, and they have shown me how they think and learn. My students, then, have made the largest contribution to this book, for without them I would have little to say and no reason to write.

Kathleen T. McWhorter

Features of *Successful College Writing*, Fourth Edition, Correlated to the WPA Outcomes Statement

Desired Student Outcomes	Relevant Features of *Successful College Writing*
Rhetorical Knowledge	
Focus on a purpose	Each writing assignment chapter in Parts Three and Four offers extensive discussion of the purpose(s) for the rhetorical pattern of development covered in that chapter.
Respond to the needs of different audiences	Each chapter in Parts Three and Four discusses the need to consider one's audience for the rhetorical pattern of development covered in that chapter. In Chapters 18 and 19, which cover argument, there is also extensive discussion of the need to anticipate opposing viewpoints and to analyze the audience's existing views about the claim and adjust one's argument accordingly.
Respond appropriately to different kinds of rhetorical situations	Each chapter in Parts Two and Three gives detailed advice on responding to a particular rhetorical situation, from narration (Chapter 10) to argument (Chapters 18 and 19). The book also includes advice about writing using sources (Part Five) and about writing about literature, taking essay examinations, and giving oral presentations (Part Six).
Use conventions of format and structure appropriate to the rhetorical situation	Chapter 7 gives general advice about organizing the details in an essay and writing an appropriate introduction and conclusion. Each chapter in Parts Two and Three as well as Chapter 23 on writing about literature points out features of effectively structured writing using a particular pattern of development and includes a Guided Writing Assignment to help students systematically develop their own effective structures. Chapter 20 teaches students appropriate formats for writing a paper using sources.

Adopt appropriate voice, tone, and level of formality	Appropriateness of voice is addressed in the Handbook. Advice about tone appears in several of the chapters in Parts Three and Four, such as those on description and argument, as well as in Chapter 7 on editing, where levels of diction are also discussed. Also, see purpose and audience coverage mentioned previously.
Understand how genres shape reading and writing	Chapters 18–24 explain how the genres of argument, source-based writing, literary analysis, and essay examinations require specialized kinds of reading and writing, with Chapter 18 entirely devoted to teaching how to read argument.
Write in several genres	In addition to the overall general guidance for writing in the earlier part of the book, Chapters 19–24 explain how to write in the specific genres of argument, source-based writing, literary analysis, and essay examinations
Critical Thinking, Reading, and Writing	
Use writing and reading for inquiry, learning, thinking, and communicating	The entire book is informed by an emphasis on the connection between reading and writing in a particular genre. Part One explains the importance of reading and writing for college success and the distinctive qualities and demands of academic reading and writing. Each chapter in Parts Three and Four teaches students to read and write essays using a particular pattern of development and includes a group of readings whose apparatus introduces students to thinking about the features of the genre. Each of these chapters also includes a section on thinking critically about characteristic flaws in the chapter's pattern.

Understand a writing assignment as a series of tasks, including finding, evaluating, analyzing, and synthesizing appropriate primary and secondary sources	The Guided Writing Assignments in each chapter in Parts Three and Four break writing assignments down into doable focused thinking and writing activities that engage students in the recursive process of invention and research to find, analyze, and synthesize information and ideas. Part Five, "Working with Sources," offers detailed coverage of finding, evaluating, using, and acknowledging primary and secondary sources.
Integrate their own ideas with those of others	Chapter 20 offers detailed advice on how to integrate and introduce quotations, paraphrases, and summaries so as to distinguish them from the writer's own ideas, and how to avoid plagiarism.
Understand the relationships among language, knowledge, and power	A recurring section in each chapter in Parts Two and Three poses questions that encourage students to think critically about possible flaws in the pattern of development covered in the chapter.
Processes	
Be aware that it usually takes multiple drafts to create and complete a successful text	The need for a critical reading of a draft and for revision is emphasized in Part Two, especially Chapters 6 and 8, as well as in the Guided Writing Assignments in Chapters 10–17, 19, and 23.
Develop flexible strategies for generating ideas, revising, editing, and proofreading	General advice about generating and researching ideas, getting a critical reading of a draft, revising, editing, and proofreading is given in Chapters 4, 8, and 9. The Guided Writing Assignments in Chapters 10–17, 19, and 23 offer pattern-specific coverage of these topics.
Understand writing as an open process that permits writers to use later invention and rethinking to revise their work	General advice about revision is found in Chapter 8. The Guided Writing Assignments in Chapters 10–17, 19, and 23 offer extensive pattern- and genre-specific advice on revising.

Understand the collaborative and social aspects of writing processes	Many of the exercises in the book call for students to work with classmates or give them the option of doing so, and the Instructor's Annotated Edition provides many more options for having students work collaboratively.
Learn to critique their own and others' works	The Guided Writing Assignments in Chapters 10–17, 19, and 23 offer extensive pattern- and genre-specific advice on peer review and revision. A Revision Flowchart in each of these chapters as well as Chapters 8, 9, and 22 guides students step by step through critical review and revision of a particular part of the writing process or kind of essay.
Learn to balance the advantages of relying on others with the responsibility of doing their part	A section in Chapter 1, "Work with Classmates," gives advice about being a committed and productive member of a collaborative group and getting one's group work done on time. This goal is also implicit in many of the collaborative activities, especially the ones that ask students to pair off, with each member of the pair taking responsibility for a specific task.
Use a variety of technologies to address a range of audiences	Chapter 21 discusses how to responsibly use the Internet, email, and online communities for research, and Chapter 24 offers advice on using visuals such as CDs and PowerPoint in making oral presentations.
Knowledge of Conventions	
Learn common formats for different kinds of texts	Formatting of research papers is covered in Chapter 22.
Develop knowledge of genre conventions ranging from structure and paragraphing to tone and mechanics	Each chapter in Parts Four and Five develops such knowledge for a specific genre, including argument, source-based writing, literary analysis, and essay examinations.

Practice appropriate means of documenting their work	Chapter 20 offers detailed advice on how to integrate and introduce quotations, paraphrases, and summaries so as to distinguish them from the writer's own ideas, and how to avoid plagiarism. This chapter also offers coverage of MLA and APA documentation in addition to an annotated sample student research paper.
Control such surface features as syntax, grammar, punctuation, and spelling	The Handbook provided in the longer version of the book covers all of these issues. Pattern- and genre-specific advice about editing and proofreading is given at the end of each Guided Writing Assignment in Chapters 10–17, 19, and 23.

CONTENTS

PART 2   Strategies for Writing Essays   75

4   Prewriting: How to Find and Focus Ideas   77

5   Developing and Supporting a Thesis   99

8 Revising Content and Organization 155

11 Description: Portraying People, Places, and Things 233

14 Comparison and Contrast: Showing Similarities and Differences   339

MEN, WOMEN, AND INTERPERSONAL RELATIONSHIPS

CURRENT ISSUES

NATURE AND THE ENVIRONMENT

US racist

Although has come a long way in racial American act racist Discrimined.

Racial Discrimination

As a college student, you probably have many responsibilities. You may need to balance the demands of college with the needs of your family and the requirements of your job. In addition, you are probably attending college to make a change in your life—to better your prospects. You may not have chosen a specific career path yet, but you eventually want a rewarding, secure future. Consequently, you are ready to pursue a course of study that will lead you there.

I have been teaching students like you for over thirty years in numerous colleges. I have written this book to help you achieve your goals by becoming a successful college writer. In writing the book, I have taken into account your busy lifestyle and made this book practical and easy to read. As simply and directly as possible, the text explains what you need to know to sharpen your writing skills. You will also find it easy to locate the information you need within the text. You can use the brief contents on the inside front cover, the detailed contents, or the comprehensive index to locate information. In addition, numerous flowcharts, boxes, and other visual aids appear throughout to help you quickly find the information or writing assistance you need. I also show how the writing strategies you are learning apply to other college courses and to the workplace. Throughout the book you will find tips for completing reading and writing assignments in your other college courses, and Chapters 1–3 contain useful study-skills advice, as well.

HOW THIS BOOK CAN HELP YOU SUCCEED

There are no secrets to success in writing—no tricks or miracle shortcuts. Rather, becoming a successful student writer requires hard work, guidance and feedback, and skills and strategies. You must provide the hard work; your instructor and classmates will provide you with the guidance and feedback. This book introduces you to the skills and strategies that successful writers need to know. Specifically, this book will help you succeed in your writing course in the following ways.

- **By emphasizing the connection between reading and writing.** You have been reading nearly your entire life. You could probably read sentences and paragraphs before you could write them. This book shows you how reading and writing are connected and how to use your reading skills to improve your writing.
- **By including readings on topics and issues of interest and concern to college students.** The readings in this book have been selected from a wide range of sources—including newspapers, popular magazines, special-interest magazines, blogs, other Web sites, textbooks, and scholarly journals—that represent the diverse texts you will encounter in both your personal life and your academic life.
- **By offering you both professional and student models of good writing.** As you work with the essays in this book, you will discover that both professional writers and

student writers follow the same principles in organizing and presenting their ideas. You will also have opportunities to examine, react to, and discuss the ideas presented in these essays and to relate those ideas to your own life.

- **By helping you discover the writing strategies that work best for you.** You may have noticed that you don't learn in the same way as your best friend or the person who sits next to you in class. For example, some students learn better by listening, while others learn better by reading. Because not all students learn in the same way, Chapter 2 includes a Learning Style Inventory that will help you discover how you learn. As you work through the writing assignments throughout the book, you will find lists of Learning Style Options that suggest different ways that you can approach a given writing task. Feel free to experiment with these options; try one and then another. You will probably discover some techniques that work better or take less time than those you are currently using.

- **By helping you identify and eliminate frequently occurring problems with sentence structure, grammar, punctuation, and mechanics.** Sections in Chapter 6, "Drafting an Essay," and in Chapter 9, "Editing Sentences and Words," provide strategies for fixing errors that students commonly make. In addition, Chapters 10–17 and 19 all provide editing and proofreading tips particular to the type of essays you will be writing in each chapter. Part 7, "Handbook: Writing Problems and How to Correct Them" (not included in the brief version of the book), covers important grammar rules and provides exercises that allow you to practice applying those rules. For more help, a student workbook, *Additional Exercises for Successful College Writing*, is available, and *Exercise Central*, available on the companion Web site, offers online grammar practice.

HOW TO USE THIS BOOK

In writing this book, I have included many features that I use when I am actually teaching a class. Each is described below along with suggestions for how the feature can help you become a skilled, successful writer.

A Guide to Active Reading

Chapter 3, "Reading and Writing about Text," includes specific, practical strategies that will help you get the most out of the selections in this book as well as the reading assignments in your other courses. The Guide to Active Reading on page 46 explains, step by step, how to improve your comprehension and build your critical reading skills.

Detailed Coverage of Each Stage of the Writing Process

Part 2 of the text, "Strategies for Writing Essays," includes six chapters (Chapters 4–9) that cover each stage of the writing process in detail. Each step in the process is illustrated by the example of a student, Christine Lee, as she generates ideas for, drafts, and revises an essay. Chapter 8, "Revising Content and Organization," includes an important section on working with classmates to revise an essay (p. 162), with plenty of practical suggestions for you to use both as a writer seeking advice and as a peer reviewer.

Annotated Student Essay

Students Write

READING

Eric Michalski wrote the following essay in response to an assignment that asked him to explain a process that he had mastered. As you read the essay, consider if the steps described in the essay clearly explain the process of making chili.

Feed Your Friends . . . and Their Friends . . . and Their Friends: Chili for Fifty

Eric Michalski

Cooking up chili for a large crowd is only a tad more difficult than whipping up a fraction- 1 ally smaller batch. It's quite useful being the person who can feed a full hotel floor/campsite/ election office/family reunion on a trip to the grocery store and a few hours' time. If this recipe is followed accurately, it'll result in a deeply flavorful mud-brown sludge that tastes much better than it looks.

When you're feeding a crowd, though, things do get complicated. The key is following a 2 strict sequence. It's like learning a dance--you've got to follow the steps until you know it well enough to freestyle. All ingredients require some type of processing, which has to be done at a specific time to build the right flavor and texture while preserving the integrity of the in- dividual components. Order is important, even though "precision" and "chili" don't share too many sentences.

Title: Michalski identifies the process to be explained.

Introduction: Michalski explains the value of learning to make chili. His thesis statement reveals his attitude toward the topic.

As he often does throughout the essay, Michalski uses a transition to keep readers on track and a topic sentence to preview a paragraph's content. Here he also uses a figure of speech to warn that following the steps in order is crucial.

Annotated Student Essays

Throughout the text, student essays illustrate different types of writing or different writing strategies. These student examples are usually found in sections titled "Students Write," and most of them have been annotated to call your attention to particular writing features. Within the annotations and the text that they refer to, color-coded highlighting is used for features like the thesis statement, topic sentences, and source citations as well as features distinctive to the particular kind of writing, such as sensory details in description. A sample annotated student essay appears above.

A section in Chapter 3, "How to Approach Student Writing," explains how to read and examine student essays and apply what you learn to improve your writing. In addition, use the questions following these student essays to help you discover how other students apply the techniques you are learning to their writing.

Computer Tips

Today more than ever before, computers affect every aspect of the writing process. Using a computer at home or at a computer lab on campus can help you write and revise your papers more efficiently, and using the Internet for research opens up an almost unlimited number of sources for you to consider. Throughout the text, I suggest particular ways that computers, and specifically word processing programs, can be especially helpful as you write and revise an essay. This advice is designated by the icon ▢ .

Graphic Organizer

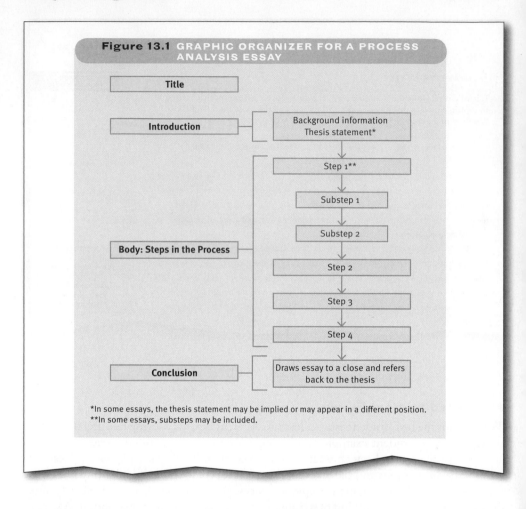

Figure 13.1 GRAPHIC ORGANIZER FOR A PROCESS ANALYSIS ESSAY

Title

Introduction — Background information / Thesis statement*

Body: Steps in the Process —
Step 1**
↓
Substep 1
↓
Substep 2
↓
Step 2
↓
Step 3
↓
Step 4

Conclusion — Draws essay to a close and refers back to the thesis

*In some essays, the thesis statement may be implied or may appear in a different position.
**In some essays, substeps may be included.

Graphic Organizers

Throughout the text you will find Graphic Organizers—diagrams that offer a visual approach to organizing and revising essays. A sample Graphic Organizer appears above. As you draft and revise, you can refer frequently to the graphic organizer for the particular type of essay you are writing. The text also demonstrates how to draw your own organizers to help you analyze a reading, structure your ideas, and write and revise drafts.

Guided Writing Assignments

Chapters 10–17, 19, and 23 contain writing guides that "walk you through" a writing assignment step by step. The Guided Writing Assignments are shaded, as in the sample on page xlix. You can refer to this guide as often as you need to while you complete the assignment in the chapter or other similar assignments. Think of it as a tutorial to which you can always turn for tips, examples, and advice.

Part of a Guided Writing Assignment

A GUIDED WRITING ASSIGNMENT

The following guide will help you write a process analysis essay. It may be either a how-to or a how-it-works essay. Although you will focus on process analysis, you may need to integrate one or more other patterns of development in your essay.

The Assignment

Write a process analysis essay on one of the following topics or one of your own choosing. Be sure the process you choose is one that you know enough about to explain to others or can learn about through observation or research. Your audience consists of readers who are unfamiliar with the process, including your classmates.

How-To Essay Topics

1. How to improve _____ (your study habits, your wardrobe, your batting average)
2. How to be a successful _____ (diver, parent, gardener)
3. How to make or buy _____ (an object for personal use or enjoyment)
4. How to prepare for _____ (a test, a job interview, an oral presentation)

How-It-Works Essay Topics

1. How your college _____ (spends tuition revenues, hires professors, raises money)
2. How _____ works (an answering machine, a generator, email, a cell phone)
3. How a decision is made to _____ (accept a student at a college, add or eliminate a local or state agency)
4. How _____ is put together (a quilt, a news broadcast, a football team, a Web site)

As you develop your process analysis essay, you will probably use narrative strategies, description (for example, to describe equipment or objects), or illustration (such as to show an example of part of the process).

For more on narration, description, and illustration, see Chapters 10–12.

Selecting a Process

The following guidelines will help you select a process to write about. You may want to use one of the prewriting techniques discussed in Chapter 14. Consider your learning style when you select a prewriting technique. You might try questioning, group brainstorming, or sketching a diagram of a process. Be sure to keep the following tips in mind.

- For a how-to essay, choose a process that you can visualize or perform as you write. Keep the equipment nearby for easy reference. In explaining how to scuba dive, for example, it may be helpful to have your scuba equipment in front of you.

Part of a Revision Flowchart

Figure 11.3 Flowchart for Revising a Descriptive Essay

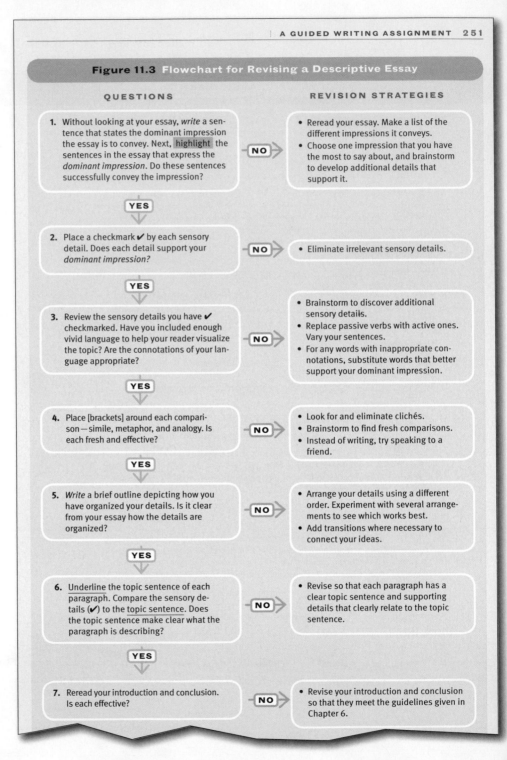

QUESTIONS

REVISION STRATEGIES

1. Without looking at your essay, *write* a sentence that states the dominant impression the essay is to convey. Next, highlight the sentences in the essay that express the *dominant impression*. Do these sentences successfully convey the impression?

NO

- Reread your essay. Make a list of the different impressions it conveys.
- Choose one impression that you have the most to say about, and brainstorm to develop additional details that support it.

YES

2. Place a checkmark ✔ by each sensory detail. Does each detail support your *dominant impression?*

NO

- Eliminate irrelevant sensory details.

YES

3. Review the sensory details you have ✔ checkmarked. Have you included enough vivid language to help your reader visualize the topic? Are the connotations of your language appropriate?

NO

- Brainstorm to discover additional sensory details.
- Replace passive verbs with active ones. Vary your sentences.
- For any words with inappropriate connotations, substitute words that better support your dominant impression.

YES

4. Place [brackets] around each comparison—simile, metaphor, and analogy. Is each fresh and effective?

NO

- Look for and eliminate clichés.
- Brainstorm to find fresh comparisons.
- Instead of writing, try speaking to a friend.

YES

5. *Write* a brief outline depicting how you have organized your details. Is it clear from your essay how the details are organized?

NO

- Arrange your details using a different order. Experiment with several arrangements to see which works best.
- Add transitions where necessary to connect your ideas.

YES

6. Underline the topic sentence of each paragraph. Compare the sensory details (✔) to the topic sentence. Does the topic sentence make clear what the paragraph is describing?

NO

- Revise so that each paragraph has a clear topic sentence and supporting details that clearly relate to the topic sentence.

YES

7. Reread your introduction and conclusion. Is each effective?

NO

- Revise your introduction and conclusion so that they meet the guidelines given in Chapter 6.

Documentation Diagram

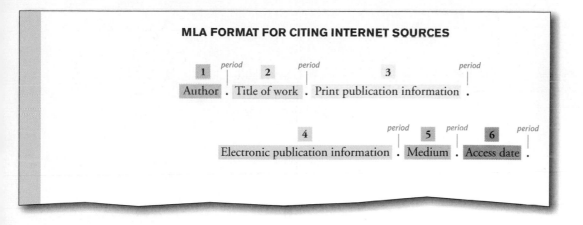

Revision Flowcharts

Many chapters include flowcharts that will help you identify what you need to revise in a first draft. Each flowchart lists key questions to ask about a draft and offers suggestions for how to revise to correct any weaknesses you uncover. (See the sample on page l.) You can also use the questions in the appropriate revision flowchart to guide classmates who are reviewing your essay.

Writing Using Sources

Often, as you write and revise an essay you will find that you need facts, statistics, or the viewpoint of an expert to strengthen your own ideas. Chapter 20, "Planning a Paper with Sources," shows you where to start and gives helpful advice for evaluating different types of sources. Chapter 21, "Finding Sources and Taking Notes," explains how to locate sources in the library and on the Internet and how to extract the information you need. Chapter 22, "Writing a Paper Using Sources," demonstrates how to use, integrate, and document information from sources within an essay. For your convenience, this book includes guidelines for using two widely recommended styles for documenting sources: MLA (green-bordered pages) and APA (orange-bordered pages). In addition, color-coded visuals provide clear models for documenting books, articles, and Web sites.

A Final Word

In my high school and early college years, I was an OK writer but never a skilled writer. I certainly never imagined myself writing a textbook, and yet *Successful College Writing* is my tenth college textbook. How did I learn to write well? I learned from my college writing courses and from my instructors, both in English classes and in other disciplines as well. I learned from my husband, who used to read and comment on my papers while we were in college. I learned from friends and classmates; I continue to learn from colleagues, editors, and most important from my own students, who deserve clear and concise expression. Never stop learning: I know I will not. I wish you success.

Kathleen T. McWhorter

Successful College Writing

PART 1

Academic Quick Start

CHAPTER 1

Succeeding in College

The photographs on the opposite page show two first-year college students. One is a successful student, and the other is a very frustrated one. Why is one student successful and the other not?

Write a paragraph, based on your experience with education up to this point, that explains what factors you think contribute to academic success and/or frustration. Be specific; discuss tasks that students need to know how to perform to be successful. You might offer tips or identify pitfalls or troublespots, as well. You might also consider what nonacademic factors, such as jobs and family responsibilities, may play a crucial role in student success.

What skills did you identify as contributing to college success? You may have mentioned being motivated and organized, performing well in class, knowing how to read and study, or knowing how to write papers and exams. All these skills, and many others, contribute to academic success. This chapter will present numerous strategies for success; it is intended to help you develop the skills you need for a successful college career.

Strategies for Success

You can start preparing for college success even before you enter the classroom. To begin, make sure you

- focus on success;
- manage your time effectively;
- organize a writing and study area;
- develop effective study strategies;
- learn to manage stress.

Focus on Success

No doubt you are enthusiastic about jumping into your college studies, but you may be concerned about how you will juggle a job, your family life, and school. You also may be wondering whether you have the skills and abilities necessary to get the grades you want. Having doubts and concerns is normal, but it is important to think positively and to focus on success. Here are a few success strategies.

- **Define success.** *Success* means different things to different people, and you need to decide what it means to you. Is a rewarding career your highest priority? Are relationships with family and friends important? What about helping others? Define what *success* means to you, and decide how college fits into your definition of success.
- **Develop long-term goals that will lead to success.** Once you have defined *success*, you need to determine the long-term goals that will get you there. What do you intend to accomplish this term? This year? In the next four years? Complete Exercise 1.1 to help you define your goals. List where you would like to be and what you would like to be doing at each of the times listed. You may have multiple goals, so list as many as apply.
- **Take responsibility for achieving those goals.** Only you are in charge of your own learning and reaching your goals. You can do as little or as much as you want to achieve your goals, but you take the responsibility either way.
- **Visualize success.** To keep your goals in mind, close your eyes and imagine yourself achieving your goals. For example, picture yourself finishing your first year of college with high marks or walking across the stage at graduation. Never visualize failure.
- **Develop essential skills that will help you achieve success.** Success is not a matter of luck; it is a matter of specific skills, such as communicating effectively and visualizing success, that will help you achieve success.

Exercise 1.1

List what you expect to accomplish in the next two weeks.	1. 2.
List what you expect to have accomplished by the end of this semester.	1. 2. 3.
List what you will accomplish within the next year.	1. 2. 3.
List what you will have accomplished upon graduation.	1. 2. 3.
Where do you see yourself five years after you graduate?	1. 2. 3.

Exercise 1.2

Write a paragraph describing your academic and professional goals. Include the specific steps you need to take to achieve those goals.

Manage Your Time

Examine the two student schedules shown in Figures 1.1(below) and 1.2 (on the next page). Which student is more likely to meet his or her deadlines? Why?

FIGURE 1.1 Planner with Due Dates

NOVEMBER	NOVEMBER
10 Monday	Thursday 13 *10 am Essay 3 due*
11 Tuesday *3 pm History exam*	Friday 14 *1 pm Anthro quiz*
12 Wednesday	Saturday 15
	Sunday 16

FIGURE 1.2 Planner with Detailed Schedule

NOVEMBER	NOVEMBER
10 Monday	Thursday 13
am—outline English Essay 3 *6 pm History study group*	*10 am Essay 3 due* *5–8 pm Work* *9–10 pm Study Anthro chapters*
11 Tuesday	Friday 14
am—Draft Essay 3 *3 pm History exam* *6–8 pm Work* *Read Anthro Ch. 20*	*am—Review Anthro notes and* *chapter highlighting* *1 pm Anthro quiz*
12 Wednesday	Saturday 15
10 am Writing Center—review *Essay 3* *Read Anthro Chs. 21–22*	*9–4 Work*
	Sunday 16
	Read Bio Ch. 17 *Review Bio lab* *Read History Ch. 15*

The student planner in Figure 1.1 shows only test dates and assignment deadlines. Figure 1.2 shows a planner that details how and when the student will meet those deadlines. The student who uses the planner in Figure 1.2 is likely to complete his or her work with less stress and worry.

The biggest challenge for most first-year college students is managing time. The most successful students spend two hours outside of the classroom for every hour spent in the classroom (more for reading- or writing-intensive courses). College students are required to spend only twelve to eighteen hours per week in class or lab. For many students, the remainder of their time is unstructured, and as a result, they never seem to get organized. Others are overwhelmed by the workload and the challenge of integrating college study into already busy lives. Still others tend to study nonstop: by never finding free time for relaxation, they set themselves up for burnout.

To avoid these traps and manage your time effectively, you need to establish goals and plan your activities.

Establish Positive, Realistic, Short-Term Goals

The first step in managing your time is establishing goals that are positive and realistic. Keep in mind a broad, long-term goal, like earning a bachelor's degree in elementary education in four years, before setting short-term goals that you can achieve more quickly. A short-term goal could be finishing an assigned paper by next Friday. Setting a time frame is a critical step toward accomplishing each of your goals.

Plan Your Activities

If you let days "just happen," you're not likely to accomplish much. You need to plan your activities. You may prefer a tightly structured or loosely structured plan—or something in between. Consider the following three types of plans—term, weekly, and daily—and choose the one that works best for you. If you are not sure, experiment by trying out all three.

The term plan. Once you have a sense of the work that you will need to complete for each of your courses, block out four to six hours per week for each course. Remember, the rule of thumb is that for every hour spent in class you should plan to work two hours outside of class. Study for each course during the same time period each week. For instance, you might reserve Monday, Wednesday, and Thursday evenings between 8:00 and 10:00 P.M. for your writing course. This plan establishes a routine for study. The tasks you work on each week will vary, but you will always be certain you have enough time to get everything done. If you have trouble starting on assignments, this plan may be the best one for you.

The weekly plan. Take ten minutes at the beginning of each week to specify when you'll work on each course, taking into account upcoming assignments. Figure 1.2 is a good example of how to organize a weekly plan.

Regardless of which plan you choose, you need to purchase a student planner or pocket calendar for recording assignments, due dates for papers, and upcoming exams. You'll also want to schedule time to work on your coursework, whether you schedule this time daily, weekly, or across the term. Keep this planner or calendar with you at all times and check it daily. It will help you get and stay organized.

Each time you begin studying, assess what needs to be done and determine the order in which you will do these tasks. Although you may be tempted to tackle short or easy tasks first, it is usually best to work on the most challenging assignments first, when your concentration is at its peak.

Avoid Procrastination

Procrastination is putting off things that need to be done; you know you should work on an assignment, but you do something else instead. To avoid procrastination, divide the task into manageable parts. Don't attempt to do the whole task, but do plan to complete one part. Avoid making excuses. It is easy to say you don't have enough time to get everything done, but often that is not true. Also avoid escaping into routine tasks such as shopping, cleaning, or washing your car rather than completing the task.

Organize a Writing and Study Area

You don't need a lot of room to create an appropriate space for studying and writing. Use the following suggestions to organize an efficient work area.

- **Work in the same location daily.** As you become accustomed to working in the same spot each day, your mind will focus on academic tasks as soon as you enter this area.

- **Choose a setting that is conducive to writing and studying.** Your work area should be relatively free of distractions, well lit, comfortable, and equipped with all the tools you need—a clock, a computer, a calculator, pens, pencils, paper, a pencil sharpener. Be sure to keep a dictionary and a thesaurus nearby as well.
- **Find a quiet area.** If you live on campus, your dormitory room probably includes a desk or work area. If your dorm is noisy, consider studying in the library or another quiet place. Libraries offer free carrel space where you can work without distractions. Many also offer study rooms for group work or secluded areas with upholstered chairs if you do not need a desk.

  If you live off campus, find a place where you won't be disturbed by family or roommates. Your work area need not be a separate room, but it should be a place where you can spread out your materials and find them undisturbed when you return. Otherwise, you may waste a great deal of time setting up your work, figuring out where you left off, and getting started again. In addition, you should find a quiet place on campus where you can study between classes.

> ### Exercise 1.3
>
> *Using the suggestions listed above and those you learned through discussion with your class-mates, write a paragraph describing what you can do to organize an area that is conducive to writing and studying.*

"Study Smarter"

Does either of these situations sound familiar?

"I just read a whole page, and I can't remember anything I read!"
"Every time I start working on this assignment, my mind wanders."

If so, you may need to improve your concentration. No matter how intelligent you are or what skills or talents you possess, if you cannot keep your mind on your work, your classes, including your writing class, will be unnecessarily difficult. Try the following concentration skills to help you "study smarter," not harder.

- **Work at peak periods of attention.** Find out the time of day or night that you are most efficient and least likely to lose concentration. Do not try to work when you are tired, hungry, or distracted by others.
- **Work on difficult assignments first.** Your mind is freshest as you begin to work. Putting off difficult tasks until last may be tempting, but you need your fullest concentration when you begin challenging assignments.
- **Vary your activities.** Do not complete three reading assignments consecutively. Instead, alternate assignments: for example, read, then write, then work on math problems, then read another assignment, and so on.
- **Use writing to keep you mentally and physically active.** Highlight and annotate as you read. These processes will keep you mentally alert.

- **Approach assignments critically.** Ask questions as you read. Make connections with what you have already learned and with what you already know about the subject.
- **Challenge yourself with deadlines.** Before beginning an assignment, estimate how long it should take and work toward completing it within that time limit.
- **Keep a list of distractions.** When you are working on an assignment, stray thoughts about other pressing things are bound to zip through your mind. You might remember that your car has to be inspected tomorrow or that you have to buy your mother's birthday present next week. When these thoughts occur to you, jot them down so that you can unclutter your mind and focus on your work.
- **Reward yourself.** Use fun activities, such as emailing a friend or getting a snack, as a reward when you have completed an assignment.

Exercise 1.4

Not all students study the same way, and most students study differently for different courses. List below the courses you are taking this semester. For each, identify a study strategy that works for that course. Compare your list with those of other students and add useful techniques you have discovered.

Course	Study Strategies to Try
1.	
2.	
3.	
4.	
5.	

Manage Stress

The pressures and obligations of school lead many students to feel overwhelmed and overstressed. As a successful student, you need to monitor your stress. Take the quiz on page 10 to assess your stress level.

Stress is a natural reaction to the challenges of daily living, but if you are expected to accomplish more or perform better than you think you can, stress can become overwhelming. You can respond to stress either positively or negatively. For example, you can use stress to motivate yourself and start a project or assignment, or you can let it interfere with your ability to function mentally and physically. Here are some effective ways to change your thinking and habits and reduce stress.

- **Establish your priorities.** Decide what is more and less important in your life. Let's say you decide college is more important than your part-time job, for example. Once you have decided this, you won't worry about requesting a work schedule to accommodate your study schedule because studying is your priority.

Exercise 1.5

Complete the following Stress Mini Quiz. If you answered "Always" or "Sometimes" to more than two or three items, identify at least two ways you can begin to reduce your stress level.

	Always	Sometimes	Never
1. I worry that I do not have enough time to get everything done.	❏	❏	❏
2. I regret that I have no time to do fun things each week.	❏	❏	❏
3. I find myself losing track of details and forgetting due dates, promises, and appointments.	❏	❏	❏
4. I worry about what I am doing.	❏	❏	❏
5. I have conflicts or disagreements with friends or family.	❏	❏	❏
6. I lose patience with small annoyances.	❏	❏	❏
7. I seem to be late, no matter how hard I try to arrive on time.	❏	❏	❏
8. I have difficulty sleeping.	❏	❏	❏
9. My eating habits have changed.	❏	❏	❏
10. I find myself needing a cigarette, drink, or prescription drug.	❏	❏	❏

- **Be selfish and learn to say no.** Many people feel stress because they are trying to do too many things for too many people—family, friends, classmates, and coworkers. Allow your priorities to guide you in accepting new responsibilities.
- **Simplify your life by making fewer choices.** Avoid simple daily decisions that needlessly consume time and energy. For example, instead of having to decide what time to set your alarm clock each morning, get up at the same time each weekday morning. Choose fixed study times and adhere to them without fail.
- **Focus on the positive.** Do not say, "I'll never be able to finish this assignment on time." Instead ask yourself, "What do I have to do to finish this assignment on time?"
- **Separate work, school, and social problems.** Create mental compartments for your worries. Don't spend time in class thinking about a problem at work. Leave work problems at work. Don't think about a conflict with a friend while attempting to write a paper. Deal with problems at the appropriate time.
- **Keep a personal journal.** Writing is not just for school. Taking a few minutes to write down details about your worries and your emotions can go a long way toward relieving stress. Be sure to include your goals and how you plan to achieve them.

Exercise 1.6

Using the guidelines on page 10, write a brief paragraph listing ways you successfully manage stress or ways you could improve how you manage stress.

Classroom Skills

What you do within the classroom largely determines your success in college. Make sure that you

- polish your academic image;
- demonstrate academic integrity;
- communicate effectively with your instructors;
- listen carefully and critically;
- ask and answer questions appropriately;
- work with classmates;
- take effective notes in class.

Polish Your Academic Image

Your academic image is the way you are seen and thought of as a student by your instructors and other students. How you act and respond in class plays a large part in determining this image.

Do ...

Make thoughtful contributions to class discussions

Maintain eye contact with instructor

Ask questions if information is unclear to you

Refer to assigned readings in class

Be courteous to classmates when you speak

Don't ...

Work on homework during class

Sleep or daydream in class

Remain silent during class discussion

Interrupt others or criticize their contributions

Once you see yourself as a serious student, you are ready to project that positive academic image to your instructors and classmates. Don't underestimate the value of communicating daily—through your words and actions—that you are a hardworking student who takes your college experience seriously. A student who takes his or her studies seriously is more likely to be taken seriously and to find the assistance he or she needs.

Exercise 1.7

Rate your academic image by checking "Always," "Sometimes," or "Never" for each of the following statements.

	Always	Sometimes	Never
I arrive at classes promptly.	❑	❑	❑
I sit near the front of the room.	❑	❑	❑
I look and act alert and interested in the class.	❑	❑	❑
I make eye contact with instructors.	❑	❑	❑
I complete reading assignments before class.	❑	❑	❑
I ask thoughtful questions.	❑	❑	❑
I participate in class discussions.	❑	❑	❑
I complete all assignments on time.	❑	❑	❑
I turn in neat, complete, well-organized papers.	❑	❑	❑
I refrain from carrying on conversations with other students while the instructor is addressing the class.	❑	❑	❑
I say "hello" when I meet my instructors on campus.	❑	❑	❑

To project a positive image, you must actively participate in class at every opportunity. Keep in mind the following suggestions.

- **Prepare to participate.** As you read an assignment, make notes and jot down questions to use as a starting point for class participation.
- **Organize your remarks.** Plan in advance what you will say or ask in class. Work on stating your ideas clearly.
- **Say something early in a discussion.** The longer you wait, the more difficult it will be to say something that has not already been said.
- **Keep your comments brief.** You will lose your classmates' attention if you ramble. Your instructor may ask you to explain your ideas further.
- **Be sensitive to the feelings of others.** Make sure that what you say does not offend or embarrass other class members.

Participation in class involves more than just speaking out. It also involves making a serious effort to focus on the discussion and to record important ideas that others may have. Be sure to take notes on class discussions, record whatever the instructor writes on the chalkboard, keep handouts from PowerPoint presentations, and jot down ideas for future writing assignments.

Exercise 1.8

Write a brief statement about how you think others perceive you as a student. Refer to the list of tips about building a positive academic image on page 12. What tips do you normally follow? Which do you most need to work on?

Demonstrate Academic Integrity

Academic integrity—conducting yourself in an honest and ethical manner—is important in the college classroom. It involves avoiding the obvious forms of dishonesty such as copying homework, buying a paper on the Internet, and cheating on exams or helping others do so.

But it also involves avoiding intellectual dishonesty, either deliberate or unintentional, in which you use the ideas or language of others without giving credit to the author. This form of academic dishonesty is known as plagiarism. An example of intentional plagiarism is cutting and pasting information into your paper from the Internet without indicating that it is borrowed. Unintentional plagiarism occurs when you use language too similar to that of the original source or forget to place quotation marks around a quotation. To learn how to avoid these various forms of plagiarism, refer to Chapter 21, p. 591.

Communicate with Your Instructors

Meeting regularly with your instructor will help you understand and meet the course objectives. Take advantage of your instructor's office hours, or speak to him or her after class. Use the following tips to communicate with your instructors.

- **Don't be afraid to approach your instructors.** At first, some of them may seem distant or unapproachable. In fact, they enjoy teaching and working with students. They may not become your best friends, but they can answer questions you have about a reading, help you with problems you may experience with an assignment, and suggest directions to take with a topic for a paper or research project. You will find that most instructors are happy to help you and to serve as valuable sources of information on research, academic decisions, and careers in their respective fields.
- **Learn your instructors' contact information.** Most instructors keep office hours—times during which they are available and ready to talk with you and answer your questions. Some instructors also give out their email addresses. In either case, though, you have to take the initiative to contact them.
- **Prepare for meetings with your instructor.** Write out specific questions in advance. If you need help with a paper, be sure to bring along all the work (drafts, outlines, research sources) you have done so far.
- **Stay in touch with your instructor.** If you absolutely cannot attend class for a particular reason, be sure to notify your instructor and explain. Unexcused absences generally lower your grade and suggest that you are not taking your studies seriously. In addition, if personal problems interfere with your schoolwork, let your instructors know. They can refer you to the counseling services on campus and may grant you an extension for work missed for an emergency.

Exercise 1.9

Using the chart below, list the name of each of your instructors; also include the course he or she teaches. Considering factors such as class size and organization, subject matter, assignments, tests and exams, and so forth, identify at least one opportunity to communicate with each of your instructors.

Instructor and Course	Opportunities to Communicate
1.	
2.	
3.	
4.	
5.	

Listen Carefully and Critically

Of the most common ways people communicate—reading, writing, speaking, and listening—listening is the skill that you perform most frequently in a classroom. Think about the classes you attended this week; you probably spent far more time listening than reading, writing, or speaking. Because you spend so much time doing it, you need to listen carefully and critically—grasping what is said and questioning and reacting to what you hear.

Becoming a Careful Listener

Did you know that you can process information faster than speakers can speak? As a result, your mind has time to wander while listening. Try using the following suggestions to maintain your attention in the classroom.

- **If you are easily distracted by sights and sounds, sit in the front of the room** so you can focus more easily on the speaker.
- **Take notes.** Writing will help focus and maintain your attention.
- **Try to anticipate the ideas the speaker will address next.** This activity keeps your mind active.
- **Sit comfortably but do not sprawl.** A serious posture puts your mind in gear for serious work.
- **Maintain eye contact with the speaker.** You will feel more personally involved and will be less likely to drift off mentally.
- **Avoid sitting among groups of friends.** You will be tempted to talk to or think about them, and you risk missing information that the speaker is presenting.

Listening Critically

In many classes, you are expected not only to understand what the speaker is saying but also to respond to it. Here are a few suggestions for developing your critical-listening skills.

Maintain an open mind. It is easy to shut out ideas and opinions that do not conform to your values and beliefs. Try to avoid evaluating a message either positively or negatively until it is complete and understandable.

Avoid selective listening. Some listeners hear what they want to hear; they do not remember ideas with which they disagree. This is dangerous, since you may miss important points in a discussion. Make a deliberate attempt to understand the speaker's viewpoint, and distract yourself from disagreeing by taking notes or creating an informal outline of the speaker's main points.

Avoid oversimplification. When listening to difficult, unpleasant, emotional, or complex messages, it is tempting to simplify them by eliminating their details, reasons, and supporting evidence. For example, if you are listening to a speaker describe his wartime experiences in Iraq, the speaker's details may be unpleasant but are important to understanding his experience.

Focus on the message, not the speaker. Try not to be distracted by the speaker's clothing, mannerisms, speech patterns, or annoying quirks.

Exercise 1.10

Working with a classmate, identify at least five topics that you would need to listen to critically to avoid the pitfalls listed above.

Ask and Answer Questions

You can learn more from your classes if you develop or polish your questioning skills. This means asking questions when you need information and clarification, and answering questions posed by the instructor to demonstrate and evaluate your knowledge and express interest in the class. Use the following tips to strengthen your questioning and answering skills.

- **Conquer your fear of speaking in class.** Stop worrying what your friends and classmates will think: Speak out.
- **While reading an assignment, jot down questions as they occur to you.** Bring your list to class, and use it when your instructor invites questions.
- **Form your questions concisely.** Don't apologize for asking, and don't ramble.
- **Don't worry if your questions seem unimportant or silly.** Other students probably have the same questions but are reluctant to ask them.

- **Focus on critical questions.** Instead of asking factual questions, think about questions that focus on how the information can be used, how ideas fit together, how things work, what might be relevant problems and solutions, or what the long-term value and significance of the information are.
- **Think before responding.** When answering questions, try to compose your response before volunteering to answer.

> ### Exercise 1.11
>
> *Working with a classmate, brainstorm a list of questions you could ask about the content presented in this chapter.*

Work with Classmates

Many college assignments and class activities involve working with other students. For example, in this book, many chapters contain a box titled "Trying Out Your Ideas on Others" that asks you to work with other students. Group projects vary, and therefore your approach may vary depending on the discipline, the course, and the instructor. Some groups may be assembled to discuss problems; others may carry out an activity, such as examining a piece of writing; others may research a topic and present their findings.

Understanding the Purpose

Many students expect to learn from their instructors but do not realize they can learn from one another as well. Group projects enable students to share experiences, understand classmates' thinking, and evaluate new ideas and approaches to completing a task. For example, if you are working with several classmates to prepare a panel discussion, you may observe that different classmates approach the task differently. Some may begin by brainstorming about the topic; others may begin by asking questions; still others may start by reading about or researching the topic. To benefit most from group projects, be sure you understand the task and then analyze it. Ask yourself, "What can I learn from this?" You will get more out of an assignment if you are focused on outcomes.

Keeping Groups Functioning Effectively

Some students complain that group projects are time-consuming and often unproductive. If you feel that way about a project, take a leadership role and make it work. Here are some suggestions for making groups work more effectively.

Do ...	*Don't ...*
Set a good example as a committed and productive group member.	Take a passive role by allowing others in the group to do the bulk of the planning and work.
Work with serious, energetic, and creative classmates, if you have a choice.	Work with people who will be easily distracted and less likely to get their work done.

As a group, decide on an action plan, distribute responsibilities, and establish a firm schedule.	Work haphazardly, so that some tasks do not get done and others are duplicated.
Stay focused on the project during group meetings.	Waste time by allowing group discussions to wander off topic or turn into a social situation.
Do the best work you can, and get it done on time, since each member's work affects the grade for the project.	Complain about your workload or hold up the group by completing your part late or insufficiently.
Assign tasks wisely and equitably in a way that best uses members' strengths.	Assign important preliminary tasks to a member who works slowly or is disorganized.
Address potential problems quickly.	Allow interpersonal problems or other conflicts to get in the way of productivity.

Managing conflicts. Despite your best efforts and those of other group members, not all groups function effectively. Conflicts may arise; members may complain; a group member may not do his or her share. Since your grade on the project may depend on every other member's work, your best interests require you to address these problems quickly and effectively if they occur. Use the following suggestions to do so.

- If members miss meetings, offer to contact everyone to remind them of the time and place.
- Establish a more detailed timetable if the work is not getting done.
- Offer to take on a greater share of the work if it will help get the assignment done.
- Ask questions that may stimulate unproductive members' ideas and interest.
- Suggest that uncommunicative members share their ideas in written form.
- Encourage the students who are causing the problem to propose solutions.

If you are unable to resolve problems or conflicts, discuss them with your instructor.

Take Effective Notes in Class

To become a successful student, you also need to take careful notes on your classes and review those notes. Plan on reviewing notes at least once each week. Researchers have shown that most people retain far more information when they interact with it using more than one sense. For instance, if a student only listens to a lecture or discussion, he or she will probably forget most of it within a couple of weeks, well before the next exam. However, if a student takes accurate notes and reviews them regularly, then he or she is likely to retain the main points and supporting details needed to understand the concepts discussed in the class. Following are some useful note-taking tips.

Note-Taking Tips

Use the following tips to take more effective notes:

- **Read assignments before the lecture.** Whenever possible, read any textbook material to which the lecture corresponds *before* the lecture. Familiarity with the topic will make note-taking easier.
- **Don't attempt to record everything.** Record only main ideas and key details. Avoid writing in complete sentences; instead use words and phrases. Develop a system of abbreviations, signs, and symbols, as well.
- **Pay attention to your instructor's cues to what is important.** These cues include repetition of points, changes in voice or rate of speech, listing or numbering of points, and the use of the chalkboard or visuals.
- **Avoid tape-recording the class.** Tapes takes too long to play back and encourage you to not pay full attention during class.
- **Don't plan to recopy your notes.** Your time is valuable; recopying is time-consuming. You can better use the time reviewing and studying your notes.
- **Leave plenty of blank space.** Use this space to fill in information you missed during the lecture or to add in examples.
- **When you must miss a class, borrow notes from a classmate who you know is a good student.**
- **Review and study your notes immediately after the lecture.** While the class is still fresh in your mind, you can fill in missed information, clarify relationships, and add examples. If you wait a day or more, your memory of the class will fade. See below for a system that facilitates study of your notes.

Here are two of the most popular and efficient methods of taking notes on class lectures, discussions, and readings.

Two-Column Method

This note-taking method is valuable for all learners. Draw a vertical line from the top of a piece of paper to the bottom. The left-hand column should be about half as wide as the right-hand column.

In the wider, right-hand column, record ideas and facts as they are presented in a lecture or a discussion. In the narrower, left-hand column, note your own questions as they arise during the class. When you go home and review your notes, add summaries of major concepts and sections to the left-hand margin. This method allows you to quickly review an outline or overview of a lecture by reading the left-hand column and to study specific information and examples in the right-hand column. See the figure on the next page.

Modified Outline Method

The modified branch or outline method uses bullets for main ideas and dashes for detailed information within a section. The more detailed the information gets, the farther to the right you indent your outline entries.

Good note-taking is a hallmark of a successful student. It gets easier with practice, and developing your own symbols over time will help make note-taking quicker and more consistent for you. When you take good notes and review them regularly, you are replacing the inefficient and exhausting strategy of cramming for exams—a strategy that loads information into your memory only temporarily—with a system of learning that allows deeper, longer-term retention of information.

THE TWO-COLUMN METHOD OF NOTE-TAKING

Writing process	*Prewriting—taking notes, writing ideas, drawing a cluster diagram, researching, writing questions, noting what you already know, outlining, etc.*
	Writing—drafting
(How many drafts does the average writer complete?)	*Rewriting—revision = "to see again"* *2 types: global = major rehaul (reconsidering, reorganizing)* *local = rewording, correcting grammar (editing for correctness & style)*
NOT linear	*Writing is not a linear process. May go back to prewriting after writing, etc.*

THE MODIFIED OUTLINE METHOD OF NOTE-TAKING

Writing is a process.
- *Prewriting*
  - *Taking notes*
  - *Writing ideas*
  - *Drawing a cluster diagram*
  - *Researching*
  - *Writing questions*
  - *Noting what you already know*
  - *Outlining*
- *Writing*
  - *First drafts*
    - *On paper*
    - *On cards*
    - *On computer*
  - *Later drafts*
- *Rewriting, or revision (means "to see again")*
  - *Global*
    - *Major revision*
    - *Reconsidering ideas*
    - *Reorganizing*
  - *Local*
    - *Rewording for style*
    - *Rewriting for correct grammar, spelling, punctuation*

CHAPTER 2

Writing in College

The photographs on the opposite page show several situations in which college students use writing. In these photographs, the students are using writing to record information. Brainstorm a list of other situations—both academic and nonacademic—in which you use writing. You might consider on-the-job writing and personal writing, for example. You might also consider purposes other than to record information, such as to entertain or to express feelings.

What did your list reveal about the importance of writing? Did you discover a variety of purposes and situations in which writing is useful? Some kinds of writing help you explore ideas and learn information; others help you learn about yourself and your values. You will learn more about these and other kinds of writing throughout college.

Most, if not all, college classes require some form of writing—exams, essays, journals, reports, and so forth. Strong writing skills are essential to college success. So the time and effort you will spend in improving your writing skills is certainly worthwhile. The main purpose of this chapter—and of this entire book—is to help you succeed in your writing class as well as in other classes that involve writing.

In this chapter, you will learn what is expected of you as a college writer. You will learn about the importance of improving your writing skills and discover useful strategies for doing well in your writing class. This chapter will also help you learn and write more effectively by analyzing your learning style.

Academic Writing: What to Expect

In college you will probably do more writing than you did at previous educational levels. You will be expected to write not only in your writing class but in most other classes as well. Instructors consider writing a means of learning—not just a means of testing and evaluating what students have already learned. The following section explains what you can expect about writing in college.

Expect Your Writing to Move from More Personal to Less Personal

Much of your writing up to now may have been about yourself and your experiences. In college you can expect to write less about yourself and more about ideas. You will still often be asked to share your personal perspective when expressing ideas. For example, in a communications class you might write a film review. In other cases you will be writing to inform—to present information about a subject in an objective, nonpersonal way. For example, in a sociology class you might write an essay explaining what the 1.5 generation is. Or you may be writing to persuade—to convince your readers to think or act a certain way. For example, you might write an essay for your criminal justice class arguing that the penalties for drunk driving should be increased, or a proposal to convince college officials that more security is needed on campus. In doing so, you might draw on your personal knowledge or experience, but you would need to depend mostly on objective evidence to persuade your readers. In general, therefore, you will find that in college much less writing is done in the first person (*I, me*) and much more is done in the third person (*it, they, he, she*). When given a writing assignment, make sure it is clear how much of your personal experience and personal opinion, if any, are appropriate for the assignment.

Expect Your Writing to Take Different Forms

In college you will write much more than essays and exam answers. Depending on your field of study, you may also be required to write in a variety of specialized *genres,* such as logs, case reports, abstracts, patient observation charts, and diagnostic evaluations. Each genre has its own set of conventions and expectations. A lab report is a good example. It has a specific purpose (to report the results of a laboratory experiment), follows a specific format (Introduction, Materials and Methods, Observation), has an expected style of writing (brief, factual, and concise), and uses technical and specialized language (names of instruments, names of chemicals, names of procedures).

As you encounter new genres, it is helpful to read samples written in that form. Be sure to ask questions so you understand exactly what your instructor expects.

Expect to Use the Language of the Discipline

Each academic discipline has its own language—words and phrases that are used only or primarily in that discipline. The words *photosynthesis* and *homeostasis,* for example, are used primarily in biology-related fields, and the words *allegory, symbolism,* and *mythology* are used in literary fields. When you write in a particular discipline, you are expected to use the language of that discipline. In doing so, the first step is to learn the language. See Chapter 3 for suggestions on learning vocabulary. When you write a paper, concentrate first on expressing your ideas, but as you revise, check to be sure you have used the appropriate language of the discipline.

Expect to Use Standard American English

While nonstandard English (slang, incorrect grammar, misspellings) may be appropriate in some settings (such as informal conversation, or text messages and emails to friends), you are expected to use standard, correct American English for academic writing. As you revise and proofread your writing, concentrate on correctness. Refer to a grammar handbook or consult an online writing resource that offers help with particular problems. You can also refer to Chapter 9 of this book (for help with sentence-level problems) and—unless you are using the Brief Edition—the handbook at the back of the book.

Expect to Use and Document Scholarly Sources

Although you have probably written research papers in high school, more college writing assignments will require you to use library or Internet sources to acquire needed information or to support your own ideas. Depending on the assignment, you will need to summarize, paraphrase (express in your own words), and quote the sources you use.

In college, writers are often required to use scholarly sources rather than popular sources such as newsstand magazines and personal Web sites. Scholarly sources are those written by experts in the field and published by professional organizations in the field. In many cases popular sources may not be appropriate in that they may not offer expert, trustworthy opinion. In other cases they may not be sufficient—they may not offer enough detail or provide enough background information, for example. Chapters 20 and 21 of this book offer help in locating and using scholarly sources. Be sure to consult your reference librarian if you need additional help.

It is important in college writing to give credit to all sources that you use in your writing. This includes not just language that you quote but also information that you borrow and express in your own words. Chapter 22 of this book will show you how to correctly document the sources you use.

Expect to Collaborate with Classmates

More often than in high school, college instructors expect student writers to collaborate, or work together, on a piece of writing. Collaboration is a form of learning about a subject as well as a means of improving your writing by learning from others. In an environmental studies class, for example, you may be asked to work with classmates on a report on a local air-quality problem. Because collaboration on writing projects is expected in a wide variety of career fields, many instructors consciously build collaborative activities into their courses. To learn to collaborate successfully, refer to Chapter 8, p. 162.

Why Strive to Improve Your Writing Skills?

Most college students ask themselves the following two questions:

- How can I improve my grades?
- How can I improve my chances of getting a good job?

The answer to both questions is the same: Improve your writing, reading, and thinking skills. The following sections explain how these skills, especially writing, are essential to your success in college and on the job.

Writing Skills Help You Succeed in College and in Your Career

College courses such as psychology, biology, and political science demand that you read articles, essays, reports, and textbooks and then react to and write about what you have read. In many courses, you demonstrate what you have learned by writing exams, reports, and papers.

Writing is important on the job, as well. In most jobs, workers need to communicate effectively with supervisors, coworkers, patients, clients, and customers. You can expect to write plenty of letters, email messages, memos, and reports. The 2000–2001 study performed by the Collegiate Employment Research Institute found that employers consistently want the "total package" in recent college graduates. Employers want job candidates who have not only the technical knowledge to work but also strong oral and written communication skills.*

Because your writing course offers both immediate and long-range benefits, it is one of the most important college courses you will ever take. You will learn how to express your ideas clearly, structure convincing arguments, prepare research papers, and write essay exams. Your writing course will also help you improve your reading and thinking skills. As you read, respond to, and write about the readings, you will learn how to analyze, synthesize, and evaluate ideas.

Writing Helps You Learn and Remember Things

Taking notes, outlining, summarizing, or annotating focuses your attention on the course material and gets you thinking about the subject matter as you connect and define ideas. In addition, writing facilitates learning by engaging two senses at once. Whereas you take in information visually by reading or aurally by listening, writing engages your sense of touch as you put your pen to paper or your fingers on a keyboard. In general, the more senses you use in a learning task, the more easily learning occurs and the more you remember about the task later on. You can often remember something more easily if you write it down.

---

* Betsy Stevens, "What Communication Skills Do Employers Want? Silicon Valley Recruiters Respond," *Journal of Employment Counseling* 42 (March 2005): 2–9.

Writing Helps You Think More Clearly

Writing forces you to think through a task. Getting your ideas down on paper or on a computer screen helps you evaluate them. Writing, then, is a means of sorting ideas, exploring relationships, weighing alternatives, and clarifying values.

Writing Helps You Solve Problems

When you solve problems, you identify possible actions that may change undesirable situations (your car won't start) to desirable ones (your car starts). Writing makes problem solving easier by helping you define the problem. By describing the problem in writing, you can often see new aspects of it.

One student, for example, had a father-in-law who seemed hostile and uncooperative. The student described her problem in a letter to a friend: "He looks at me as if I'm going to take his son to the end of the earth and never bring him back." When she reread this statement, the student realized that her father-in-law might resent her because he was afraid of losing contact with his son. She began to think of ways to reassure her father-in-law and strengthen their relationship. Writing about the problem helped the student define it and discover ways to solve it. Similarly, writing can help you think through confusing situations and make difficult decisions.

Developing Strategies for Writing

Establishing a study area, planning your time, and using academic services such as the writing center are all strategies that will help you succeed in your courses. Other strategies will also make a big difference in your writing: starting with a positive attitude, keeping a journal, and planning to get the most out of conferences with your writing instructor.

Start with a Positive Attitude

You have the potential and ability to be a successful writer. To approach your writing course positively and to get the most out of it, use the following suggestions.

1. **Think of writing as a process.** Writing is not a single act of getting words down on paper. Instead, it is a series of steps—planning, organizing, drafting, revising, and editing and proofreading. In addition, most writers go back and forth among these steps. Chapters 4 to 9 cover these steps of the writing process.
2. **Be patient.** Writing is a skill that improves gradually. Don't expect to see dramatic differences in your writing immediately. As you draft and revise your essays, your writing will improve in small ways that build on one another.
3. **Expect writing to take time, often more time than you planned.** Realize, too, that on some days writing will be easier than on other days.
4. **Focus on learning.** When you are given a writing assignment, ask, "What can I learn from this?" As you learn more about your own writing process, write down your observations (see the section on journal writing below).

5. **Use the support and guidance available to you.** Your instructor, your classmates, and this book can all help you become a better writer. In Parts 3 and 4 of the text, Guided Writing Assignments will lead you, step-by-step, through each chapter assignment. You will find tips, advice, and alternative ways of approaching the assignment.

6. **Look for ideas in the readings.** The essays in this book have been chosen to spark your interest and to touch on current issues. Think of every assigned reading as an opportunity to learn about a topic that you might not otherwise have the time to read or think about. Chapter 3 provides a Guide to Active Reading and a Guide to Responding to Text that offer helpful strategies for getting the most out of the reading assignments in this book and responding to what you have read.

7. **Attend all classes.** Writing is a skill, not a set of facts you can read about in a book; it is best learned through interactions with your instructor and classmates.

Use Your Course Syllabus

The syllabus is the most important document you will receive in your first week of class. Some instructors place the syllabus on the course's Web site as well. A syllabus usually describes how the course operates. It includes information on the required texts, attendance policy, grading system, course objectives, weekly assignments or readings, due dates of papers, and dates of exams. Think of a syllabus as a course guide or course

FIGURE 2.1 Excerpted Sample Syllabus for a College Writing Course

I. General Information

Course Title: English Composition I	*Course Number:* ENG 161
Prerequisite: English 070 or placement test	*Semester:* Fall
Instructor: John Gillam	*Phone:* (724) 555-7890
Email: gillam@indiana.edu	*Office Hours*
	& Location: MWF 3-5
	English Department offices
	in Ryan Hall

A good way to ········· contact your instructor.

Important—
···be sure
to use them.

II. Text

McWhorter, Kathleen T. *Successful College Writing*, 4th Edition: New York: Bedford, 2009.

III. General Course Objectives

1. The student will learn to organize his or her thoughts into a meaningful written work.
2. The student will easily recognize grammar mistakes.
3. The student will be familiar with different types of writing.
4. The student will be able to use several different writing styles.

Planning and organizing are expected.

Grammar is ·············· important.

IV. Specific Course Objectives

1. The student will write papers using the following strategies: description, illustration, process analysis, comparison and contrast, classification and division, and cause and effect.

What you will ·········· be graded on.

Learn these strategies.

Read assign- ·············· 2. The student will edit and proofread for errors in grammar,

Read assign- ·············· punctuation, mechanics, and spelling.

ments carefully. ·········· 3. The student will be tested on reading comprehension.

4. The student will write a research paper using appropriate documentation.

Learn about ············· 5. The student will critically analyze readings that use specific writing strategies.

documentation. 6. The student will use the Internet as a tool for research.

Correctness counts: Allow time for proofreading.

V. Classroom Procedures

Attendance is ··········· *Absences*: The student is responsible for attendance. Attendance affects per-

essential. formance, and all students are expected to take part in class discussions and

peer-review editing sessions. Each student is expected to be present and is re-

sponsible for class notes and assignments. If absent, the student is responsible

for arranging an appointment with the instructor to discuss the notes and assign-

ments missed.

Format for papers: Papers must be typed double-spaced using a 12-point font. Be sure to keep a copy of each assignment for yourself.

Keep a copy of assignments.

VI. Disability Statement

If you need to have special arrangements made due to a physical or learning disability, please notify the instructor as soon as possible. (Disclosure of the type of disability is not required.)

Don't hesitate to ask for needed services.

VII. Grading

All papers must be turned in on the due date. Late papers will be lowered one letter grade. No papers will be accepted after the last day of class. If you do not understand the grade assigned to a paper, see me immediately. You are encouraged to save all papers in a folder to enable you to keep track of progress and compute your own grade.

Meeting deadlines is essential.

The instructor encourages questions.

VIII. Tentative Schedule

Week of Sept. 5:	Course Introduction
	Ch. 1 (Succeeding in College)
	Ch. 2 (Writing in College)
Week of Sept. 12:	Writing Assessments
	Ch. 3 (Reading and Writing about Text)
	Ch. 4 (Prewriting)
	Ch. 5 (Developing and Supporting a Thesis)
Week of Sept. 19:	Ch. 6 (Drafting an Essay)
	Ch. 10 (Narration)
	Draft of Essay #1 due
Week of Sept. 26:	Ch. 12 (Illustration)
	Draft of Essay #2 due

Read these chapters the first week. Your instructor may not remind you of reading assign-ments, so check the syllabus weekly.

Assignment due dates

planner that directs you through your writing class. Examine the accompanying excerpt from a sample syllabus illustrating how an instructor might organize a writing course.

A course syllabus can be prepared in various styles. Some instructors prefer to use a weekly format for a syllabus and then give specific assignments in class. The sample syllabus in Figure 2.1 is formatted this way. Some instructors avoid dates by using a general outline of assignments and requirements and then craft the assignment schedule as the class masters each topic. Still other instructors prefer a highly structured syllabus that lists daily assignments as well as required readings, long-term writing assignments, and group work. Whatever format the syllabus takes, be sure to read it carefully at the beginning of the course and to check it regularly so that you are prepared for class. Mark all deadlines on your calendar. Ask your instructor any questions you may have about the syllabus, course structure, deadlines, and his or her expectations about course objectives. Note his or her answers on your syllabus or in your course notebook.

Pay particular attention to the course objectives section of the syllabus, where your instructor states what he or she expects you to learn in the course. Objectives also provide clues about what the instructor feels is important and how he or she views the subject matter. Since the course objectives state what you are expected to learn, papers and exams will measure how well you have met these objectives.

Make a copy of each course syllabus. Keep one syllabus in the front of your notebook for easy reference during class or while you are studying. Keep another syllabus in a file folder at home in case you lose your notebook on campus.

Exercise 2.1   Getting the Most from Your Syllabus

Review the syllabus that your writing class instructor distributed. Write a paragraph describing your expectations and concerns about your writing course based on the syllabus. Be sure to include information on the questions listed below. If the syllabus does not contain the information, consult your college catalog for general policies and your instructor for specific questions.

1. What are you expected to learn in the course?
2. What kinds of essays will you write?
3. What are the grading and attendance policies?
4. Is class participation expected and required? Is it part of your grade?
5. Is research required? Is Internet use required or expected?

Use the Right Learning Tools

How often do you need to look up a word in a dictionary? Have you ever used an online dictionary? (If not, visit www.m-w.com.) Do you prefer using a hard-bound or online dictionary? Each has its advantages, and which dictionary you use depends on your purpose and your personal preferences.

To be successful in college, you will need the right learning tools. Your textbooks are essential, but you will also need quick access to other sources of information. Be sure you have each of the following handy in your writing and study area.

- The URL of an online dictionary (such as www.bartleby.com/61 for the *American Heritage Dictionary*, shown on the next page)
- A reliable hard-bound collegiate dictionary, such as *Merriam-Webster's Collegiate Dictionary* or *Webster's New World Dictionary*
- A paper-bound pocket dictionary to carry to class or to the library
- A thesaurus (dictionary of synonyms), such as *Roget's Thesaurus*. You may have a thesaurus as part of your word-processing program.
- The URLs of Internet search engines. See Chapter 21, page 582, for suggestions.

- The URL of an online reference desk, such as www.refdesk.com, for factual information
- CDs or USBs for saving and transporting your work
- Classmates' and instructors' email addresses
- Specialized accessories your classes may require, such as a graphing calculator or a foreign language dictionary

Exercise 2.2

Record below the online reference sources that you have found useful or helpful. Compare your list with lists of other students, and add any sources that seem useful to your list.

Online Reference Sources

1.

2.

3.

4.

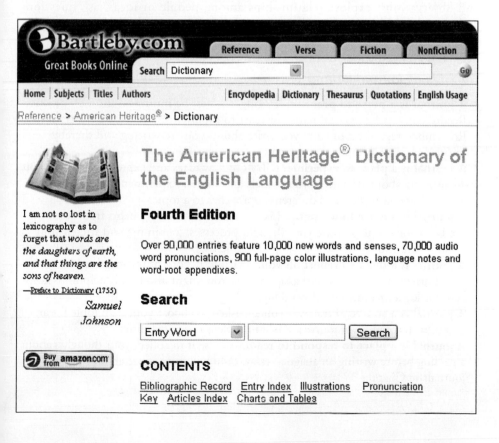

Use the College Writing Center

Many colleges have a writing center that offers individualized help with any college writing assignment—not just assignments for your writing class. The center uses student tutors as well as professional staff to help you; some centers offer online tutorial services as well. Some function on a walk-in basis; others require an appointment. Computers may be available for your use as well.

You can expect the writing center staff to help you with an assignment, but do not expect them to write or "fix" your paper for you, or to correct all of its errors. The staff can help you understand an assignment, come up with ideas, organize your ideas, revise, use appropriate format and documentation, and understand errors on a graded paper.

When you visit the writing center, be sure to bring your assignment, all drafts of your essay, and any articles or essays to which the assignment refers. Also bring paper and pen or pencil.

Keep a Writing Journal

Use a **writing journal** in either a notebook or a computer file to record daily impressions, reflect on events or on reading assignments, comment on experiences and observations, explore relationships among people or ideas, ask questions, and test ideas. You should write in your journal frequently; write every day, if possible.

Benefits of Journal Writing

- **A journal is a place to practice.** Writing can best be improved through practice. Record conversations, summarize or react to experiences, or release frustrations. Remember, regardless of what you write about, you are writing and thereby improving your skills.
- **A journal is a place to experiment.** Try out new ideas and express things that you are learning about yourself—your beliefs and values. Experiment with different voices, different topics, and different approaches to a topic.
- **A journal is a place to warm up.** Like an athlete, a writer benefits from warming up. Use a journal to activate your thought processes, loosen up, and stretch your mind before you tackle your writing assignments.
- **A journal is a place to reflect on your writing.** Record problems, strategies you have learned, and ways to start assignments. You might also find it helpful to keep an error log and a misspelled word log.
- **A journal is a source of ideas.** If you are asked to choose your own topic for an essay, leaf through your journal. You'll find plenty of possibilities.
- **A journal is a place to respond to readings.** Use it to collect your thoughts about a reading before writing an assigned essay. (You will learn more about response journals in Chapter 3.)

How to Get Started

Your first journal entry is often the most difficult one to write. Once you've written a few entries, you'll begin to feel more comfortable. Here's how to get started.

1. **Write in a spiral-bound notebook or create a computer file.** Be sure to date each entry.
2. **Set aside five to ten minutes each day for journal writing.** "Waiting times" at the bus stop, at the laundromat, or in long lines provide opportunities for journal writing, as do "down times," such as the ten minutes before a class begins or the few minutes between finishing dinner and studying.
3. **Concentrate on capturing your ideas—not on being grammatically correct.** Try to write correct sentences, but do not focus on grammar and punctuation.
4. **If you are not sure what to write about, consult Figure 2.2.** Coding your entries as shown in the figure will make you more aware of your thought processes and help you distinguish different types of entries.
5. **Reread your journal entries on a regular basis.** By doing so, you will discover that rereading entries is similar to looking at old photographs: They will bring back vivid snippets of the past for reflection and appreciation.

> **Writing Activity 1**
> Write a journal entry describing your reaction to one or more of your classes this semester. For example, you might write about which classes you expect to be most or least difficult, most or least enjoyable, and most or least time-consuming.

Get the Most out of Writing Conferences

Many writing instructors schedule periodic writing conferences with individual students. These conferences are designed to give you and your instructor an opportunity to discuss your work and your progress in the course. Such conferences are opportunities for you to get help with your writing skills. If the conferences are optional, be sure to schedule one. The following tips will help you get the most out of a writing conference.

1. **Arrive on time or a few minutes early.**
2. **Bring copies of the draft essay you are currently working on as well as previously returned papers.** Have them in hand, not buried in your backpack, when your conference begins.
3. **Reread recently returned papers ahead of time,** so that your instructor's comments are fresh in your mind. Review your notes from any previous conferences.
4. **Allow your instructor to set the agenda,** but come prepared with a list of questions you need answered.
5. **Take notes, either during or immediately after the conference.** Include the comments and suggestions offered by your instructor. You might also consider writing a journal entry that summarizes the conference.
6. **Revise the draft essay you and your instructor discussed as soon as possible,** while the suggestions for revision you received are still fresh in your mind.

FIGURE 2.2 Starting Points for Journal Writing

Codes for Your Journal Entries	Type of Writing	Ideas for Subjects
< >	Describing	a daily event a sporting event an object a cartoon or photograph an overheard conversation
!!	Reacting to	a person a world, national, local, or campus event a passage from a book a magazine or newspaper article a film, song, or concert a television program a radio personality a fashion or fad
←	Recollecting	an important event a childhood experience an impression or a dream a favorite relative or friend
?	Questioning	a policy a trend a position on an issue
↔	Comparing or contrasting	two people two events or actions two issues
ex	Thinking of examples of	a personality type a type of teacher, supervisor, or doctor
+ −	Judging (evaluating)	a rule or law a decision a musician or another performer an assignment a radio or television personality a political candidate

Assessing Your Learning Style

Each person learns and writes in a unique way, depending in part on his or her experiences, personality, and prior learning. Discovering your learning style will give you an important advantage in your writing course and in your other courses. In this section and the following one, you will assess how you learn by using a Learning Style Inventory. You will learn specific strategies to learn more effectively, capitalizing on your strengths and overcoming your weaknesses.

What Is Your Learning Style?

Have you noticed that you do better with some types of academic assignments than with others? Hands-on assignments may be easier than conducting research, for example. Have you discovered that it is easier to learn from some instructors than from others? You may prefer instructors who give plenty of real-life examples or those who show relationships by drawing diagrams. Have you noticed differences in how you and your friends study, solve problems, and approach assignments? You may be methodical and analytical, whereas a friend may get flashes of insight. You may be able to read printed information and recall it easily, but a friend may find it easier to learn from class lectures or a videotape. Have you noticed that some students prefer to work alone on a project, while others enjoy working as part of a group?

These differences can be explained by what is known as **learning style**, or the set of preferences that describes how you learn. The following Learning Style Inventory is intended to help you assess your learning style. After you have completed the Learning Style Inventory, you'll find directions for scoring on page 36.

LEARNING STYLE INVENTORY

Directions: Each numbered item presents two choices. Select the one alternative that best describes you. There are no right or wrong answers. In cases in which neither choice suits you, select the one that is closer to your preference. Check the letter of your choice next to the question number on the answer sheet on page 36.

1. In a class, I usually
   a. make friends with just a few students.
   b. get to know many of my classmates.
2. If I were required to act in a play, I would prefer to
   a. have the director tell me how to say my lines.
   b. read my lines the way I think they should be read.
3. Which would I find more helpful in studying the processes by which the U.S. Constitution can be amended?
   a. a one-paragraph summary
   b. a diagram

4. In making decisions, I am more concerned with
   a. whether I have all the available facts.
   b. how my decision will affect others.

5. When I have a difficult time understanding how something works, it helps most if I can
   a. see how it works several times.
   b. take time to think the process through and analyze it.

6. At a social event, I usually
   a. wait for people to speak to me.
   b. initiate conversation with others.

7. I prefer courses that have
   a. a traditional structure (lectures, assigned readings, periodic exams, and assignments with deadlines).
   b. an informal structure (class discussions, flexible assignments, and student-selected projects).

8. If I were studying one of the laws of motion in a physics course, I would prefer to have my instructor begin the class by
   a. stating the law and discussing examples.
   b. giving a demonstration of how the law works.

9. Which set of terms best describes me?
   a. fair and objective
   b. sympathetic and understanding

10. When I learn something new, I am more interested in
    a. the facts about it.
    b. the principles behind it.

11. As a volunteer for a community organization that is raising funds for a hospice, I prefer the following tasks.
    a. stuffing envelopes for a mail campaign
    b. making phone calls asking for contributions

12. I would begin an ideal day by
    a. planning what I want to do during each hour of the day.
    b. doing whatever comes to mind.

13. If I wanted to learn the proper way to prune a rosebush, I would prefer to
    a. have someone explain it to me.
    b. watch someone do it.

14. It is more important for me to be
    a. consistent in thought and action.
    b. responsive to the feelings of others.

15. If I kept a journal or diary, it would most likely contain entries about
    a. what happens to me each day.
    b. the insights and ideas that occur to me each day.

16. If I decided to learn a musical instrument, I would prefer to take
    a. one-on-one lessons.
    b. group lessons.

17. If I worked in a factory, I would prefer to be a
   a. machine operator.
   b. troubleshooter.

18. I learn best when I
   a. write down the information.
   b. form a mental picture of the information.

19. If I gave a wrong answer in class, my main concern would be
   a. finding out the correct answer.
   b. what others in class thought of me.

20. I prefer television news programs that
   a. summarize events through film footage and factual description.
   b. deal with the issues behind the events.

21. Whenever possible, I choose to
   a. study alone.
   b. study with a group.

22. In selecting a topic for a research paper, my more important concern is
   a. choosing a topic for which there is adequate information.
   b. choosing a topic I find interesting.

23. To help me reassemble a complicated toy or machine I took apart to repair, I would
   a. write a list of the steps I followed when taking the toy or machine apart.
   b. draw a diagram of the toy or machine.

24. As a member of a jury for a criminal trial, I would be primarily concerned with
   a. determining how witness testimony fits with the other evidence.
   b. judging the believability of witnesses.

25. If I were an author, I would most likely write
   a. biographies or how-to books.
   b. novels or poetry.

26. A career in which my work depends on that of others is
   a. less appealing than working alone.
   b. more appealing than working alone.

27. When I am able to solve a problem, it is usually because I
   a. worked through the solution step by step.
   b. brainstormed until I arrived at a solution.

28. I prefer to keep up with the news by
   a. reading a newspaper.
   b. watching television news programs.

29. If I came upon a serious auto accident, my first impulse would be to
   a. assess the situation.
   b. comfort any injured people.

30. I pride myself on my ability to
   a. remember numbers and facts.
   b. see how ideas are related.

31. To solve a personal problem, I prefer to
   a. think about it myself.
   b. talk it through with friends.

32. If I had one last elective course to take before graduation, I would choose one that presents
   a. practical information that I can use immediately.
   b. ideas that make me think and stimulate my imagination.

33. For recreation, I would rather do a
   a. crossword puzzle.
   b. jigsaw puzzle.

34. I can best be described as
   a. reasonable and levelheaded.
   b. sensitive and caring.

35. When I read a story or watch a film, I prefer one with a plot that is
   a. clear and direct.
   b. intricate and complex.

Answer Sheet

Directions: Check either *a* or *b* in the boxes next to each question number.

	Column One			Column Two			Column Three			Column Four			Column Five	
	a	*b*		*a*	*b*		*a*	*b*		*a*	*b*		*a*	*b*
1			2			3			4			5		
6			7			8			9			10		
11			12			13			14			15		
16			17			18			19			20		
21			22			23			24			25		
26			27			28			29			30		
31			32			33			34			35		
Total														

Directions for Scoring

1. On your answer sheet, add the checkmarks in each *a* and *b* column, counting first the number of *a*s checked and then the number of *b*s.

2. Enter the number of *a*s and *b*s you checked in the boxes at the bottom of each column.

3. Transfer these numbers to the Scoring Grid on page 37. Enter the number of *a* choices in column one in the blank labeled "Independent," the number of *b* choices in column one in the blank labeled "Social," and so on.

4. Circle your higher score in each row. For example, if you scored 2 for Independent and 5 for Social, circle "5" and "Social."

5. Your higher score in each row indicates a characteristic of your learning style. If the scores in a particular row are close to one another, such as 3 and 4, this suggests that you do not have a strong preference for either approach to learning. Scores that are far apart, such as 1 and 6, suggest that you favor one way of learning over the other.

Interpreting Your Scores

The Learning Style Inventory is divided into five parts; each question in the inventory assesses one of five aspects of your learning style. Here is how to interpret the five aspects of your learning style.

Scoring Grid		
Column	**Number of Checkmarks**	
	Choice a	Choice b
One	_____ Independent	_____ Social
Two	_____ Pragmatic	_____ Creative
Three	_____ Verbal	_____ Spatial
Four	_____ Rational	_____ Emotional
Five	_____ Concrete	_____ Abstract

1. Independent or Social

These scores indicate the level of interaction with others that you prefer. *Independent* learners prefer to work and study alone. They focus on the task at hand rather than on the people around them and are often goal oriented and self-motivated. *Social* learners are more people oriented and prefer to learn and study with classmates. They often focus their attention on those around them and see a task as an opportunity for social interaction.

2. Pragmatic or Creative

These scores suggest how you prefer to approach learning tasks. *Pragmatic* learners are practical and systematic. They approach tasks in an orderly, sequential manner. They like rules and learn step by step. *Creative* learners, in contrast, approach tasks imaginatively. They prefer to learn through discovery or experiment. They enjoy flexible, open-ended tasks and tend to dislike following rules.

3. Verbal or Spatial

These scores indicate the way you prefer to take in and process information. *Verbal* learners rely on language, usually written text, to acquire information. They are skilled in the use of language and can work with other symbol systems as well. *Spatial* learners prefer to take in information by studying graphics such as drawings, diagrams, films, or videos. They can visualize in their minds how things work or how things are positioned in space.

4. Rational or Emotional

These scores suggest your preferred approach to decision making and problem solving. *Rational* learners are objective and impersonal; they rely on facts and information when making decisions or solving problems. Rational learners are logical, often challenging or questioning a task. They enjoy prioritizing, analyzing, and arguing. In contrast, *emotional* learners are subjective; they focus on feelings and values. Emotional decision makers are socially conscious and often concerned with what others think. In making a decision, they seek harmony and may base a decision in part on its effect on others. Emotional decision makers are often skilled at persuasion.

5. Concrete or Abstract

These scores indicate how you prefer to perceive information. *Concrete* learners pay attention to what is concrete and observable. They focus on details and tend to perceive tasks in parts or steps. Concrete learners prefer actual, tangible tasks and usually take a no-nonsense approach to learning. *Abstract* learners look at a task from a broader perspective. They tend to focus on the "big picture" or an overview of a task. Abstract learners focus on large ideas, meanings, and relationships.

A Word about Your Findings

The results of the Learning Style Inventory probably confirmed some things you already knew about yourself as a learner and provided you with some new insights as well. Keep in mind, though, that there are other ways to measure learning style.

- The inventory you completed is an informal measure of your learning style. Other, more formal measures—including Kolb's *Learning Style Inventory,* the *Canfield Instructional Styles Inventory,* and the *Myers-Briggs Type Indicator*—may be available at your college's counseling or academic skills center.
- The inventory you completed measures the five aspects of learning style that are most relevant to the writing process. However, many other aspects of learning style exist.
- You are the best judge of the accuracy of the results of this inventory and how they apply to you. If you think that one or more of the aspects of your learning style indicated by the inventory do not describe you, trust your instincts.

How to Use Your Findings

Now that you have identified important characteristics of your learning style, you are ready to use the findings to your advantage—to make learning easier and improve your writing skills. As you do so, keep the following suggestions in mind.

1. **If you have a strength in one area, you can still act in the opposite way.** For example, if you scored highly on the pragmatic scale, you are still capable of creative thinking.
2. **Learning style tendencies are not fixed, unchangeable characteristics.** Although you may have a higher score on the independent scale, for example, you can learn to function effectively in groups.
3. **Experiment with approaches that are not necessarily suited to your learning style.** Some students find that when they try a new approach, it works better than they expected. A verbal learner, for example, may discover that drawing a diagram of how a process works is an effective learning strategy.
4. **Learning style is not an excuse to avoid learning.** Don't make the mistake of saying, "I can't write poetry because I'm not a creative learner." Instead, use what you know about your learning style to guide your approach to each task. If you are a pragmatic learner, try writing a poem about a tangible object or place or a real event.

Applying Your Learning Style to Your Writing

Writing is a process that involves planning, organizing, drafting, revising, and editing and proofreading. You'll learn more about each of these steps in Chapters 4 to 9. It is important to realize that you can approach each step in the writing process in more than one way. For example, one of the first steps in that process is to select a topic to write about. There are a number of ways to go about this task. A social learner may prefer to brainstorm about possible topics with a friend. A verbal learner may find that flipping through a newsmagazine brings topics to mind. A spatial learner may see a photograph that generates ideas for topics. Someone who is a social as well as a spatial learner may prefer to discuss photographs with a classmate.

Let's consider an example involving two hypothetical students. Yolanda and Andrea, classmates in a first-year writing course, are assigned to write an essay describing an event that has influenced their lives. Yolanda writes a list of possible events and arranges them in order of importance in her life. After selecting one of these events, she draws a diagram showing the circumstances that led up to the event and the effects that the event had on her. Before she begins writing, Yolanda decides on the best way to organize her ideas and creates an outline.

Andrea lets her mind roam freely over various events in her life while she is out jogging. All of a sudden an idea comes to mind, and she knows what she wants to write about. She jots down everything she can recall about the event, in the haphazard order that each remembered detail comes to her. From these notes, she selects ideas and writes her first draft. Andrea writes numerous drafts, experimenting with different organizations. Finally, she produces an essay with which she is satisfied.

Although Yolanda and Andrea approach the same assignment in different ways, they both write effective essays. Yolanda prefers a deliberate and systematic approach because she is a pragmatic learner. Andrea, a creative learner, prefers a less structured approach. Yolanda spends a great deal of time planning before writing, while Andrea prefers to experiment with various versions of her paper.

Because students' learning styles differ, this book presents alternative strategies for generating ideas and for revising your writing. These choices are indicated by the marginal note "Learning Style Options" (see p. 69 for an example). The following advice will help you take advantage of these learning style alternatives.

1. **Select an alternative that fits with how you learn.** If you are writing an essay on insurance fraud and are given the choice of interviewing an expert on insurance fraud or finding several articles in the library on the topic, choose the option that best suits the way you prefer to acquire information.

2. **Experiment with options.** To sustain your interest and broaden your skills, you should sometimes choose an option that does not match your preferred learning style. For example, if you are an independent learner, interviewing the insurance fraud expert may help you strengthen your interpersonal skills.

3. **Don't expect the option that is consistent with your learning style to require less attention or effort.** Even if you are a social learner, an interview must still be carefully planned and well executed.

4. **Keep logs of the skills and approaches that work for you and the ones you need to work on.** The logs may be part of your writing journal (see p. 30). Be specific: Record the assignment, the topic you chose, and the skills you applied. Analyze your log, looking for patterns. Over time, you will discover more about the writing strategies and approaches that work best for you.

Your learning style profile also indicates your strengths as a writer. As with any skill, you should try to build on your strengths, using them as a foundation. Work with Figure 2.3 to identify your strengths. First circle or highlight the characteristics that you scored higher on in the five areas of learning style. Then refer to the right-hand column to see your strengths as a writer in each area.

Writing Activity 2

Write a two-page essay describing your reactions to the results of the Learning Style Inventory. Explain how you expect to use the results in your writing course or other courses.

Writing Activity 3

Using your responses to the Writing Quick Start on page 21 and the results of the Learning Style Inventory, write a two-page profile of yourself as a student or as a writer.

FIGURE 2.3 Your Strengths as a Writer

Learning Style Characteristic	Strengths as a Writer
Independent Social	You are willing to spend time thinking about a topic and are able to pull ideas together easily. You usually find it easy to write from experience. Writing realistic dialogue may be one of your strengths. You tend to have a good sense of who you are writing for (your audience) and what you hope to accomplish (your purpose).
Pragmatic Creative	You can meet deadlines easily. You recognize the need for organization in an essay. You tend to approach writing systematically and work through the steps in the writing process. You tend to enjoy exploring a topic and often do so thoroughly and completely. Your writing is not usually hindered or restricted by rules or requirements.
Verbal Spatial	You may have a talent for generating ideas to write about and expressing them clearly. You can visualize or draw a map of the organization of your paper. Descriptions of physical objects, places, and people come easily.
Rational Emotional	You tend to write logically developed, well-organized essays. You usually analyze ideas objectively. Expressive and descriptive writing usually go well for you. You have a strong awareness of your audience.
Concrete Abstract	You find it easy to supply details to support an idea. You are able to write accurate, detailed descriptions and observations. You can organize facts effectively and present them clearly. You can develop unique approaches to a topic; you can grasp the point to which supporting ideas lead.

CHAPTER 3

Reading and Writing about Text

The photograph on the opposite page is taken from a mass communication textbook. Your mass communication instructor has asked your class to study the photograph and discuss its significance.

Write a paragraph explaining what you think the photograph means and why it might have been included in the mass communication textbook. Be detailed and specific. Evaluate the photograph's content, and then try to discover what statement it makes about communication.

To explain the meaning of the photograph, you had to think beyond the obvious action it portrays. You had to interpret and evaluate the photograph to arrive at its possible meaning. To complete this evaluation, you did two things. First, you grasped what the photograph showed; then you analyzed what it meant.

Reading involves a similar process of comprehension and evaluation. First, you must know what the author *says;* then you must interpret and respond to what the author *means.* Both parts of the process are essential. This chapter will help you succeed with both parts of the reading process.

In this chapter, you will learn to be a more active reader, a reader who becomes engaged and involved with a reading assignment by analyzing, challenging, and evaluating ideas. The chapter contains a Guide to Active Reading (p. 46) in which you will learn what to do before, during, and after reading to strengthen your comprehension and increase your recall. You will also learn how to approach difficult assignments and how to draw a diagram, called a *graphic organizer,* that will help you grasp both the content and the organization of an assignment. The chapter also includes a Guide to Responding to Text (p. 63) that offers several useful strategies for responding to what you read.

As you improve your ability to read and respond thoroughly and carefully, you'll learn more about what you read. You'll also do better on exams and quizzes that ask you to apply, connect, and evaluate ideas.

The examples in the accompanying box demonstrate why active, critical reading and active response are essential to your success in college and on the job.

Reading in College

Reading skill is essential for college success. In some ways, it is a hidden skill, because when you think of college success, what probably comes to mind is attending classes, writing papers, and studying for and taking exams. A closer look at each of these activities reveals, however, that reading is involved in each task. It is the primary means

SCENES FROM COLLEGE AND THE WORKPLACE

- In an *art history* class, your instructor assigns a critical review of a museum exhibit that your class recently visited. She asks you to read the review and write an essay agreeing or disagreeing with the critic's viewpoint and expressing your own views.

- For a *zoology* course, your instructor distributes an excerpt from the book *When Elephants Weep: The Emotional Lives of Animals* and asks you to write a paper summarizing and analyzing the author's position.

- You are working as an *inspector* for the Occupational Safety and Health Administration (OSHA). Part of your job is to read, interpret, and evaluate corporate plans to comply with OSHA safety standards.

through which you acquire ideas and gather information. To use reading as a tool for success, use the following suggestions.

- **Assume responsibility for reading assignments.** In college, you can expect instructors to offer you less help with your reading assignments. They won't remind you to do them, and they often won't check to see if you are keeping up with them. It is tempting to let them go undone, especially when you are pressured to complete other work. Use the time-management suggestions in Chapter 1 (pp. 5–7) to build in time each week to complete all assignments. Instructors will not only assume that you are keeping up with reading assignments but also assume that you are learning the material as you do. Most instructors won't tell you *how* to learn it, either. Consequently, you will have to learn how best to learn each subject. Experiment with different methods: taking notes on assignments, preparing study sheets that summarize important information, highlighting (see p. 53), outlining (see Chapter 6), and annotating (see p. 53).
- **Think and read critically.** Most students expect to learn and memorize information, but in college, reading and understanding the literal content of reading assignments is often not enough. You must go beyond what an article or essay *says*, and focus on what it *means*. You also need to think about how true, useful, and important the information is. Instructors expect you to interpret, evaluate, and respond to the ideas you have read about. They expect you to read and think critically, questioning and challenging ideas as you encounter them. To develop your critical-thinking skills, pay particular attention to the section at the end of Chapters 10–18 titled "Thinking Critically About . . .".
- **Adapt your reading skills to different materials.** In college, you will encounter a wide range of materials, and you will be expected to read each skillfully. Not only will you be reading textbooks, but you may also be reading articles, essays, critiques, field reports, scientific studies, and Internet sources. You will need to use different strategies for reading each type of material. For each type, begin by noticing how it is organized and determining the purpose for which it was written. Then, devise a strategy for identifying what is important to learn and remember.
- **Polish your vocabulary skills.** An extensive vocabulary is a powerful tool and is essential to effective written and oral communication. Don't be satisfied with your current repertoire of words. Notice words; keep track of new ones you encounter by creating a vocabulary log or computer file. Look for new ways in which familiar words are used. Use these new words and new meanings as soon as possible, so they become part of your active vocabulary.
- **Use reading to help you write.** By studying the writing of others, you can improve your own writing. As you read an article, essay, or textbook assignment, take note of the writer's techniques. For example, notice how the writer organizes paragraphs, how he or she uses language to express ideas, and how ideas are developed throughout the work.

Changing Some Misconceptions about Reading

Much misinformation exists about how to read effectively and efficiently. This section dispels some popular misconceptions about reading.

For more on how to read selectively by scanning and skimming, see Working with Text: Reading Sources in Chapter 20 (p. 570).

- **Not everything on a page is equally important.** Whether you are reading an article in a sports magazine, a biography of a president, or an essay in this book, each text contains a mixture of important and not-so-important ideas and information. Your task as a reader is to sort through the material and evaluate what you need to know.

- **You should not read everything the same way.** What you read; how rapidly and how carefully you read; what you pay attention to; and what, if anything, you skip are all affected by your intent. For instance, if your psychology instructor assigns an article from *Psychology Today* as a basis for class discussion, you would read it differently than if you were preparing for a quiz based on the article. Your familiarity with a topic also affects how you read. Effective readers vary their reading techniques to suit what they are reading and why they are reading it.

- **Reading material once is often not sufficient.** In many academic situations, you will need to read chapters, articles, or essays more than once to discover the author's position, summarize the author's key ideas, and analyze the strength of the supporting evidence that he or she provides.

- **Not everything in print is true.** Just as you don't believe everything you hear, neither should you believe everything you read. Be sure to read with a critical, questioning eye and, at times, with a raised eyebrow. To evaluate a text, consider the authority of the author and the author's purpose for writing. As you read, try to distinguish facts from opinions, value judgments, and generalizations. If you were to read an article titled "Woman Loses 30 Pounds in One Week," for example, your critical, questioning eye would probably be wide open. Be sure to keep that eye open when you read scholarly essays as well.

A Guide to Active Reading

When you attend a ball game or watch a soap opera, do you get actively involved? If you are a baseball fan, at ball games you cheer some players and criticize others, evaluate plays and calls, offer advice, and so forth. Similarly, if you are a soap-opera fan, you get actively involved in your favorite program. You react to sudden turns of events, sympathize with some characters, and despise others. By contrast, if you are not a fan of a baseball team or soap opera, you might watch the game or show passively, letting it take its course with little or no personal involvement or reaction. Like fans of a sports team or soap opera, active readers get involved with the material they read. They question, think about, and react to ideas using the process outlined in Figure 3.1.

The chart on p. 48 shows how active and passive readers approach a reading assignment in different ways. As you can see, active readers get involved by using a step-by-step approach. The sections that follow explain each of these active reading steps in more detail.

FIGURE 3.1 The Active Reading Process

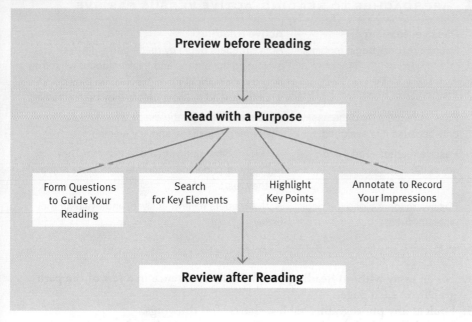

Preview before Reading

You probably wouldn't pay to see a movie unless you knew something about it. Similarly, you should not start reading an essay without checking its content to get a sense of what it is about. **Previewing** is a quick way to familiarize yourself with an essay's content and organization. Previewing also enables you to decide what you need to know from the material. Previewing has a number of other benefits as well.

- It helps you get interested in the material.
- It provides you with a mental outline of the material before you read it.
- It enables you to concentrate more easily on the material because you know what to expect.
- It helps you remember more of what you read.

To preview a reading assignment, use the guidelines in the following list. Remember to read *only* the parts of an essay that are listed.

1. **Read the title, subtitle, and author.** The title and subtitle may tell you what the reading is about. Check the author's name to see if it is one you recognize.
2. **Read the introduction or the first paragraph.** These sections often provide an overview of the essay.
3. **Read any headings and the first sentence following each one.** Headings, taken together, often form a mini-outline of the essay. The first sentence following a heading often explains the heading further.

APPROACHES TO READING: ACTIVE VERSUS PASSIVE

Passive Reading	Active Reading
Passive readers begin reading.	Active readers begin by reading the title, evaluating the author, and thinking about what they already know about the subject. Then they decide what they need to know before they begin reading.
Passive readers read the essay only because it is assigned.	Active readers read the essay while looking for answers to questions and key elements.
Passive readers read but do not write.	Active readers read with a pen in hand. They highlight or underline, annotate, and write notes as they read.
Passive readers close the book when finished.	Active readers review, analyze, and evaluate the essay.

---

4. **For an essay without headings, read the first sentence in a few of the paragraphs on each page.**
5. **Look at any photographs, tables, charts, and drawings.**
6. **Read the conclusion or summary.** A conclusion will draw the reading to a close. If the reading concludes with a summary, it will give you a condensed view of the reading.
7. **Read any end-of-assignment questions.** These questions will help focus your attention on what is important in the reading and on what you might be expected to know after you have read it.

The following essay, "Purse Snatching," has been highlighted to illustrate the parts you should read while previewing. Preview it now.

READING

Purse Snatching

The issue not yet confronted is the barrier to being treated equally when it comes to money.

Donna Lopiano

1   It appears that we are at a crossroads in women's sports. As Jesse Jackson said of the civil rights movement, "We have moved from the battlefield of access to opportunity to the battlefield of access to capital." Through government legislation like Title IX and the pressure of societal sanction and criticism, we have removed the participation barriers that once confronted women in the world of sport, especially sport at government-supported educational institutions. The right to play has been established. However, the issue that has not yet been confronted is the barrier to being treated equally when it comes to money.

2   Few see the fairness, for example, in our 1999 U.S.A. Women's World Cup soccer champions being promised $12,500 if they won compared to the approximately

$300,000 received by male World Cup champs. Now the U.S. women will receive almost $50,000 as a result of the public outcry over how the event's huge profits (estimates hover at $2 to $5 million) would be spent. And few would argue against the position that the women's pro tennis tour is more appealing and interesting to the public than the men's tour and should command equal if not higher salaries for its players. Yet women's professional tennis purses are 25 percent smaller than those of men.

The Women's National Basketball Association (WNBA) players had trouble negotiat-   3
ing minimum salary guarantees of $20,000 to $30,000 a year—a tiny fraction of what most NBA players make. Meanwhile, it took almost 30 years for the NBA to average 10,000 spectators a game and only two years for the WNBA to reach that mark.

Where are the women in auto racing at Indy, NASCAR, or CART events—truly the   4
most lucrative of all professional sports—when it comes to endorsements, winnings, and the profits of team ownership? The answer is nowhere, since virtually no women regularly participate in auto racing. With regard to salaries, profit sharing, or access to significant dollars to begin professional leagues or gain entry into high-stakes sports competition, women are still behind the eight ball.

Instead of paying women athletes what they're worth, there seems to be a concerted   5
effort to sexualize them. By commenting on the looks of the U.S. women's soccer team, the media blatantly suggest that these athletes' physical appearance is more important and of greater interest than their athletic achievements. When Brandi Chastain took her shirt off following the winning goal, displaying considerable muscle as well as a sports bra that more than covered the territory, the media acted like they were looking at a Victoria's Secret catalog as opposed to a world championship soccer match. How many women jog on city streets and work out in health clubs every day wearing less?

The media and the medical establishment, despite evidence to the contrary, are quick   6
to posit that the reason for a spate of anterior cruciate knee injuries in women is because women are physically inferior to men (our knees are ill-constructed and our hormones wreak havoc on our bodies). Are these predominantly male professionals maybe too eager to reinforce the strength and dominance of males and dismiss women in sport?

I travel all over the country as a public speaker. I love talking to high school boys   7
because they reflect the male view before the veil of political correctness disguises their true feelings. Young boys believe that it's terribly important for me to acknowledge that males are better athletes than females. Males jump higher, throw farther, run faster, dunk basketballs better, and are more interesting to watch than female athletes. They listen intently as I ask, "Who is the better athlete, Mike Tyson or Sugar Ray Leonard?" Initially struck silent by the question, they then respond with considerable chagrin, "That's not a fair question! Those are boxers in different weight classes. They don't compete against each other. They are both great boxers." To which I quietly respond, "Exactly." Why the need to affirm male dominance? Why the need to hog the marbles?

Women's sport has proved it has a market. What the marketplace needs is people   8
who are willing to risk and share capital to exploit that market. One would think that sex discrimination would take a backseat to making money and good business decisions. How many more wildly successful events need to occur before people talk positively about an investment in the women's sports market and act to take advantage of this opportunity? When will questioning the physical ability of female athletes go away? When will efforts to undermine the women's sports industry cease? Ultimately, it comes down to a matter of will and being gender blind when exploiting business opportunities. We're not there yet.

Exercise 3.1

Based only on your preview of the essay "Purse Snatching," answer the following questions as either true or false to determine whether you have gained a sense of the essay's content and organization. If most of your answers are correct, you will know that previewing worked. (For the answers to this exercise, see p. 74.)

_____ 1. The reading is primarily about the financial inequity between men's and women's sports.

_____ 2. Auto racing is not a lucrative sport.

_____ 3. The author suggests that women's sports have proven to be sound business opportunities.

_____ 4. In basketball, there is a large discrepancy between men's and women's salaries.

_____ 5. World Cup soccer championships pay men and women equally.

Read with a Purpose

If you tried to draw the face side of a one-dollar bill from memory, you would probably remember little about its appearance. In much the same way, if you read an essay thinking, "Well, it was assigned, so I had better read it," you probably won't remember much of what you read. Why does this happen? According to a psychological principle known as *intent to remember,* you remember what you decide to remember. So if you begin reading an essay without first deciding what you need to know and remember, you won't be able to recall any more about the essay than you could about the dollar bill.

Form Questions to Guide Your Reading

Before you begin reading, you will want to improve your intent to remember. Look again at the guidelines for previewing on page 47. You can use these parts of an essay to form questions. Then, as you read, you can answer those questions and thereby strengthen your comprehension and memory of the material. The following suggestions will help you start devising your questions.

- **Use the title of an essay to devise questions.** Then read to find the answers. Here are a few examples of titles and relevant questions.

Essay Title	*Question*
"Part-time Employment Undermines Students' Commitment to School"	Why does part-time employment undermine commitment to school?
"Human Cloning: Don't Just Say 'No'"	What are good reasons to clone humans?

- **Use headings to devise questions.** For example, in an essay titled "Territoriality," headings include "Types of Territoriality" and "Territorial Encroachment." Each of these headings can easily be turned into a question that becomes a guide as you read: What are the types of territoriality? and What is territorial encroachment and how does it occur?

Not all essays lend themselves to these particular techniques. For some essays, you may need to dig deeper into the introductory and final paragraphs to form questions. Or you may discover that the subtitle is more useful than the title. Look again at your preview of "Purse Snatching." Using the subtitle and the introductory paragraph of that essay, you might decide to look for answers to this question: Why does financial inequity exist between men's and women's sports?

Search for Key Elements

When you know what to look for as you read, you will read more easily, read faster, and do less rereading. When you read assigned articles, essays, or chapters, search for the following key elements.

1. **The meaning of the title and subtitle.** In some cases, the title announces the topic and reveals the author's point of view. In others, the meaning or the significance of the title becomes clear only as you read the text.
2. **The introduction.** The opening paragraph or paragraphs should provide background information, announce the topic, and get the reader's attention.
3. **The author's main point.** Usually, a **thesis statement** directly expresses the one big idea that the piece of writing explains, explores, or supports. The thesis is often placed in the first or second paragraph to let the reader know what lies ahead. But it may at times appear at the end instead. Occasionally, a thesis will be implied or suggested rather than stated directly.

   For more about thesis statements, see Chapter 5, p. 99.

4. **The support and explanation.** The body of the piece of writing should support or give reasons for the author's main point. Each paragraph in the body has a topic sentence, which states what the paragraph is about. Each topic sentence should in some way explain or support the essay's thesis statement.
5. **The conclusion.** The final paragraph or paragraphs should restate the author's main point or offer ideas for further thought.

You'll learn much more about each part of an essay in Chapters 5 to 7.

Now read the entire essay "Purse Snatching" with a purpose—to know and to remember the material. Remember to look for key elements as you read.

Purse Snatching

The issue not yet confronted is the barrier to being treated equally when it comes to money.

Donna Lopiano

Donna Lopiano is the execcutive director of the Women's Sports Foundation. This essay was first published in Ms. *magazine in 1999. As you read, pay attention to the marginal notes that identify and explain various parts of the essay.*

Introductory blurb: summarizes main point of essay

It appears that we are at a crossroads in women's sports. As Jesse Jackson said of the civil rights movement, "We have moved from the battlefield of access to opportunity to the battlefield of access to capital." Through government legislation like Title IX and the

1

Introductory paragraph: suggests importance of sports inequality by comparing it to racial discrimination

pressure of societal sanction and criticism, we have removed the participation barriers that once confronted women in the world of sport, especially sport at government-supported educational institutions. The right to play has been established. However, the issue that has not yet been confronted is the barrier to being treated equally when it comes to money.

Thesis statement

Few see the fairness, for example, in our 1999 U.S.A. Women's World Cup soccer champions being promised $12,500 if they won compared to the approximately $300,000 received by male World Cup champs. Now the U.S. women will receive almost $50,000 as a result of the public outcry over how the event's huge profits (estimates hover at $2 to $5 million) would be spent. And few would argue against the position that the women's pro tennis tour is more appealing and interesting to the public than the men's tour and should command equal if not higher salaries for its players. Yet women's professional tennis purses are 25 percent smaller than those of men.

Support: unfairness in soccer and tennis

The Women's National Basketball Association (WNBA) players had trouble negotiating minimum salary guarantees of $20,000 to $30,000 a year—a tiny fraction of what most NBA players make. Meanwhile, it took almost 30 years for the NBA to average 10,000 spectators a game and only two years for the WNBA to reach that mark.

Support: Compare salaries in men's and women's basketball.

Where are the women in auto racing at Indy, NASCAR, or CART events—truly the most lucrative of all professional sports—when it comes to endorsements, winnings, and the profits of team ownership? The answer is nowhere, since virtually no women regularly participate in auto racing. With regard to salaries, profit sharing, or access to significant dollars to begin professional leagues or gain entry into high-stakes sports competition, women are still behind the eight ball.

Support: Women do not participate in some high-paying sports like auto racing.

Instead of paying women athletes what they're worth, there seems to be a concerted effort to sexualize them. By commenting on the looks of the U.S. women's soccer team, the media blatantly suggest that these athletes' physical appearance is more important and of greater interest than their athletic achievements. When Brandi Chastain took her shirt off following the winning goal, displaying considerable muscle as well as a sports bra that more than covered the territory, the media acted like they were looking at a Victoria's Secret catalog as opposed to a world championship soccer match. How many women jog on city streets and work out in health clubs every day wearing less?

Support: gives reasons for salary inequity

The media and the medical establishment, despite evidence to the contrary, are quick to posit that the reason for a spate of anterior cruciate knee injuries in women is because women are physically inferior to men (our knees are ill-constructed and our hormones wreak havoc on our bodies). Are these predominantly male professionals maybe too eager to reinforce the strength and dominance of males and dismiss women in sport?

Support: explains media and medical bias

I travel all over the country as a public speaker. I love talking to high school boys because they reflect the male view before the veil of political correctness disguises their true feelings. Young boys believe that it's terribly important for me to acknowledge that males are better athletes than females. Males jump higher, throw farther, run faster, dunk basketballs better, and are more interesting to watch than female

Support: Men's and women's sports are distinct and should not be compared.

athletes. They listen intently as I ask, "Who is the better athlete, Mike Tyson or Sugar Ray Leonard?" Initially struck silent by the question, they then respond with considerable chagrin, "That's not a fair question! Those are boxers in different weight classes. They don't compete against each other. They are both great boxers." To which I quietly respond, "Exactly." Why the need to affirm male dominance? Why the need to hog the marbles?

Women's sport has proved it has a market. What the marketplace needs is people who are willing to risk and share capital to exploit that market. One would think that sex discrimination would take a backseat to making money and good business decisions. How many more wildly successful events need to occur before people talk positively about an investment in the women's sports market and act to take advantage of this opportunity? When will questioning the physical ability of female athletes go away? When will efforts to undermine the women's sports industry cease? Ultimately, it comes down to a matter of will and being gender blind when exploiting business opportunities. We're not there yet.

8 Conclusion: affirms thesis statement

Questions that suggest reasons why change is justifiable

Final word on current status

Highlight Key Points

As you read, you will encounter many new ideas. You will find some ideas more important than others. You will agree with some and disagree with others. Later, as you write about what you have read, you will want to return to the main points to refresh your memory. To locate and remember these points easily, it is a good idea to read with a highlighter or pen in hand. Highlighting is an active reading strategy because it forces you to sort and sift important ideas from less important ideas.

Develop a system of highlighting that you can use as you read to identify ideas you plan to reread or review later on. Use the following guidelines to make your highlighting as useful as possible.

1. **Decide what kinds of information to highlight before you begin.** What types of tasks will you be doing as a result of your reading? Will you write a paper, participate in a class discussion, or take an exam? Think about what you need to know, and tailor your highlighting to the particular needs of the task.
2. **Be selective.** If you highlight every idea, none will stand out.
3. **Read first; then highlight.** First read a paragraph or section; then go back and mark what is important within it. This approach will help you control the tendency to highlight too much.
4. **Highlight key elements, words, and phrases.** Mark the thesis statement, the topic sentence in each paragraph, important terms and definitions, and key words and phrases that relate to the thesis.

Annotate to Record Your Impressions

When you annotate, you jot down your ideas about what you are reading in the margins of the essay. Think of your annotations as a personal response to the author's ideas. Your annotations can take several forms, including questions that come to mind, personal reactions (such as disagreement or surprise), or brief phrases that summarize important points. Later on, when you are ready to write about or discuss the reading, your annotations will help you focus on major issues and questions. Following is a partial list of what you might annotate.

- Important points (such as the thesis) to which you react emotionally
- Places where you need further information
- Places where the author reveals his or her reasons for writing
- Ideas you disagree or agree with
- Inconsistencies

Sample annotations for a portion of "Purse Snatching" are shown below.

Exercise 3.2

Reread "Purse Snatching" on page 51. Highlight and annotate the essay as you read.

SAMPLE ANNOTATIONS

Where are the women in auto racing at Indy, NASCAR, or CART events—truly the most lucrative of all professional sports—when it comes to endorsements, winnings, and the profits of team ownership? The answer is nowhere, since virtually no women regularly participate in auto racing. With regard to salaries, profit sharing, or access to significant dollars to begin professional leagues or gain entry into high-stakes sports competition, women are still behind the eight ball.

Why?

Instead of paying women athletes what they're worth, there seems to be a concerted effort to sexualize them. By commenting on the looks of the U.S. women's soccer team, the media blatantly suggest that these athletes' physical appearance is more important and of greater interest than their athletic achievements. When Brandi Chastain took her shirt off following the winning goal, displaying considerable muscle as well as a sports bra that more than covered the territory, the media acted like they were looking at a Victoria's Secret catalog as opposed to a world championship soccer match. How many women jog on city streets and work out in health clubs every day wearing less?

This is one example; are there others?

Interesting comparison

The media and the medical establishment, despite evidence to the contrary, are quick to posit that the reason for a spate of anterior cruciate knee injuries in women is

Why doesn't the author include this evidence?

because women are physically inferior to men (our knees are ill-constructed and our hormones wreak havoc on our bodies). Are these predominantly male professionals maybe too eager to reinforce the strength and dominance of males and dismiss women in sport?

Is medicine still predominantly male?

Review after Reading

Do you simply close a book or put away an article after you have read it? If so, you are missing an opportunity to reinforce your learning. If you are willing to spend a few minutes reviewing and evaluating what you read, you can dramatically increase the amount of information you remember.

To review material after reading, use the same steps you used to preview a reading (see p. 47). You should do your review immediately after you have finished reading. Reviewing does not take much time. Your goal is to touch on each main point one more time, not to embark on a long and thorough study. Pay particular attention to the following elements.

- **The headings**
- **Your highlighting**
- **Your annotations**
- **The conclusion**

As part of your review, it is also helpful to write a brief summary of the essay. See the section on summarizing later in this chapter for detailed suggestions on how to write a summary (p. 63).

Understanding Difficult Text and Visuals

All students experience difficulty with a reading assignment at one time or another. Perhaps this will happen because you just can't "connect" with the author or because you find the topic uninteresting or the writing style confusing. Regardless of the problem, however, you know you must complete the assignment. Table 3.1 lists some typical problems that students experience with difficult reading material and identifies strategies for solving them.

Draw a Graphic Organizer

If you are having difficulty following a long or complicated essay, try drawing a graphic organizer—a diagram of the structure of an essay's main points. Even if you are not a spatial learner, you will probably find a graphic organizer helpful. Think of a graphic organizer as a means of tracking the author's flow of ideas.

TABLE 3.1 Difficult Readings: Specific Problems and Strategies for Solving Them

Problems	Strategies
You cannot concentrate.	1. Take limited breaks. 2. Tackle the assignment at peak periods of attention. 3. Divide the material into sections. Make it your goal to complete one section at a time. 4. Give yourself a reasonable deadline for completing the assignment.
The sentences are long and confusing.	1. Read aloud. 2. Divide each sentence into parts, and analyze the function of each part. 3. Express each sentence in your own words.
The ideas are complicated and hard to understand.	1. Reread the material several times. 2. Rephrase or explain each idea in your own words. 3. Make outline notes. 4. Study with a classmate; discuss difficult ideas. 5. Look up the meanings of unfamiliar words in a dictionary.
The material seems disorganized or poorly organized.	1. Study the introduction for clues to organization. 2. Pay more attention to headings. 3. Read the summary or conclusion. 4. Try to discover the organization by writing an outline or drawing a graphic organizer (see pp. 58 and 59).
You cannot get interested in the material.	1. Think about something you've experienced that is related to the topic. 2. Work with a classmate, discussing each section as you go.
You cannot relate to the writer's ideas or experiences.	1. Find out some background information about the writer. 2. Imagine yourself having the writer's experiences. How would you react differently?
The subject is unfamiliar; you lack background information on the subject.	1. Obtain a more basic text or other source that moves slower, offers more explanation, and reviews fundamental principles and concepts. 2. For unfamiliar terminology, consult a specialized dictionary within the field of study. 3. Ask your instructor to recommend useful references.

The graphic organizer format is shown in Figure 3.2. When you draw a graphic organizer, be sure it includes all the key elements of an essay listed on page 51. An example of a graphic organizer for "Purse Snatching" appears in Figure 3.3. Work through the organizer and reread the essay (pp. 51–53), paragraph by paragraph, at the same time.

To draw detailed graphic organizers using a computer, visit www.bedfordstmartins.com/ successfulwriting.

Read Visuals

Much of what you read is accompanied by visuals—drawings, photographs, diagrams, graphs, charts, and so forth. A writer may use a visual to clarify or emphasize an idea, reveal a trend, condense information, or illustrate a particular point of view. For example, an article espousing the value of a college education may contain a graph comparing lifetime average salaries of college graduates and high school graduates to emphasize the dramatic differences in income. An argument for increased U.S. aid to developing countries may use a photograph of a sickly, emaciated child to emphasize the effects of a recent famine while drawing out feelings of shock or pity to make the reader sympathetic. Writers may also use visuals to help readers visualize a place or setting, understand a complicated process, or remember important information.

Because writers (along with editors of books, magazines, and Web sites) use visuals deliberately and creatively to shape the message they are sending to the reader, it is worthwhile to spend time analyzing visuals that accompany text. To analyze a visual, ask yourself the following questions.

- **What is the background of the visual?** Where is it from? How does it connect to the article or essay?
- **What is the purpose of the visual?** Why has it been included? What does it contribute to the text? Is it intended for illustration or to emphasize a particular point?
- **What does the visual show?** Who or what is in the image? What action is occurring or has occurred? What information is presented? What is emphasized?
- **What does the visual mean?** What is important? What is the intended message?
- **If the visual is accompanied by verbal text, how are the two related?** Is there a caption or other related text? If so, does one explain the other? What is stated and what is left unstated?
- **What does the visual suggest?** How does it make you feel? What should you remember? What questions or issues does it raise?

In "Purse Snatching," Lopiano refers to the various media interpretations of Brandi Chastain's removal of her shirt in a victory pose. The photograph of Chastain on page 60 demonstrates Lopiano's point: The media focuses on sexual issues rather than the skills and competitive nature of female athletes.

Figure 3.2 GRAPHIC ORGANIZER: KEY ELEMENTS TO INCLUDE

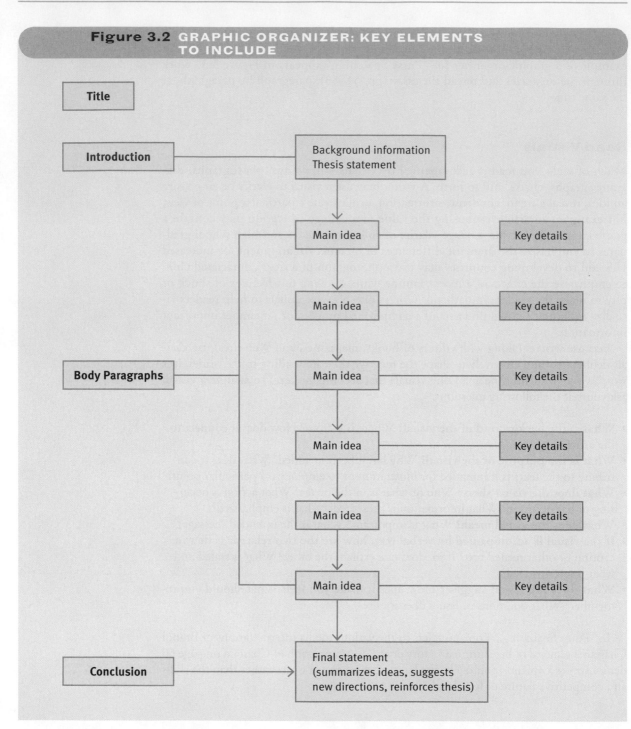

Figure 3.3 GRAPHIC ORGANIZER FOR "PURSE SNATCHING"

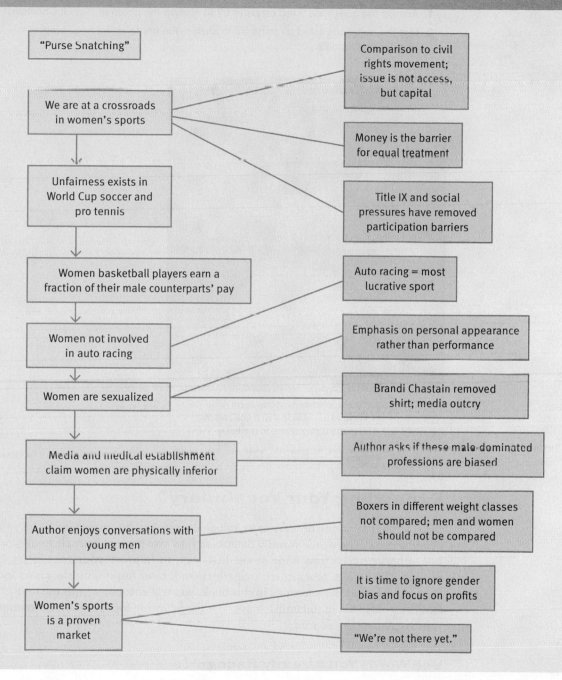

"Purse Snatching"

Comparison to civil rights movement; issue is not access, but capital

We are at a crossroads in women's sports

Money is the barrier for equal treatment

Unfairness exists in World Cup soccer and pro tennis

Title IX and social pressures have removed participation barriers

Women basketball players earn a fraction of their male counterparts' pay

Auto racing = most lucrative sport

Women not involved in auto racing

Emphasis on personal appearance rather than performance

Women are sexualized

Brandi Chastain removed shirt; media outcry

Media and medical establishment claim women are physically inferior

Author asks if these male-dominated professions are biased

Author enjoys conversations with young men

Boxers in different weight classes not compared; men and women should not be compared

Women's sports is a proven market

It is time to ignore gender bias and focus on profits

"We're not there yet."

Exercise 3.3

1. Answer the questions listed on page 57 to analyze the photo of Brandi Chastain.

2. Use the questions listed on page 57 to analyze the photo at the beginning of this chapter on page 42.

Brandi Chastain of the U.S. women's soccer team removes her shirt in triumph after kicking in the final goal, winning the World Cup. This photo is mentioned in the essay "Purse Snatching."

Expanding Your Vocabulary

Your vocabulary is one of your most valuable assets and an important factor in academic success. The words you use determine how you present yourself to others and how others perceive you. One of the best ways to improve your vocabulary is by reading—textbooks; newspapers; magazines; and, most important, the essays in this book. As you read the selections in this book, you will encounter both unfamiliar and familiar words used in unfamiliar ways. Use the following four suggestions to improve your vocabulary as you read.

Use Words You Already Recognize

One of the easiest ways to expand your vocabulary is to concentrate on words that you have seen before but cannot define precisely—and therefore do not use. Practically speaking, your vocabulary is made up of words that you know and *use*. Most college students understand more words than they actually use in their own speech or writing. For example, you probably know the meaning of the words *criteria, implication, legitimate,* and *rationed,* but have you used any of them lately?

To expand your vocabulary, start using the words you already recognize in conversation. Be sure, however, that you are certain of the meanings of the words you decide to use. Writing is ideally suited for expanding your vocabulary because it involves revision. As you draft papers, use whatever language comes to mind to express your ideas. Then, after you have revised the ideas in your writing, take a few minutes to study and evaluate your choice of words.

Pay Attention to Unfamiliar Words

When you find an interesting or unfamiliar word in a reading, mark it in the text. Look up its meaning and record it in a vocabulary log—a notebook or computer file for keeping track of words you want to learn. To help expand your vocabulary, the last question in the "Examining the Reading" section that follows most professional readings requires you to define several words as they are used in the reading. If they are unfamiliar to you, add these words to your vocabulary log.

Figure Out Unfamiliar Words without a Dictionary

If you were to look up every unfamiliar word that you ever came across in a dictionary, you would likely not have enough time to complete all your assignments. You can often figure out the meaning of a word by using one of the following strategies.

- **Look for clues in surrounding text.** You can often figure out a word from the way it is used in its sentence or in surrounding sentences. Sometimes the author may provide a brief definition or synonym, other times a less obvious context clue reveals meaning.

BRIEF DEFINITION	Janice *prefaced,* or introduced, her poetry reading with a personal story. [*Prefaced* means "introduced."]
CONTEXT CLUE	In certain societies young children are always on the *periphery,* and never in the center, of family life. [*Periphery* means "the edges or the fringe," which is far away from the center.]

- **Try pronouncing the word aloud.** Hearing the word will sometimes help you grasp its meaning. By pronouncing the word *magnific,* you may hear part of the word *magnify* and know that it has something to do with enlargement. *Magnific* means "large or imposing in size" and "impressive in appearance."
- **Look at parts of the word.** If you break down the parts of a word, you may be able to figure out its meaning. For example, in the word *nonresponsive* you can see the verb *respond,* which means "act or react." *Non* means "not," so you can figure out that *nonresponsive* means "not acting or reacting."

Use a Dictionary When Necessary

There will be times when you must look up a word in a dictionary. Be sure you have a collegiate dictionary readily available where you read and study, or access to an online dictionary. Do not rely solely on a pocket dictionary because it will not have enough definitions to suit your needs.

RESPONDING TO TEXT

Active reading is one step in understanding a text, but equally important is responding. Once you respond to material, you understand it better.

There are a number of different ways you can respond to something you have read. In your everyday life, you might read an advertisement for a digital camera and respond by taking action—purchasing it. If you read a review of a movie that sounds interesting, you might respond by emailing a friend and suggesting a time to see it. In your college career, you may read a key chapter of your psychology textbook and respond by writing an outline because the material is likely to be on your next exam. Response, then, can take a variety of forms.

When an instructor assigns a reading, some form of response is always expected. You might be expected to participate in a class discussion, summarize the information as part of an essay exam, or research the topic further and report your findings. One of the most common types of response that instructors assign is called a *response paper*. A **response paper** requires you to read an essay, analyze it, and write about some aspect of it. For some assignments, your instructor may suggest a particular direction for the paper. At other times, it will be up to you.

Before beginning any response paper, make sure you understand the assignment. If you are uncertain of what your instructor expects, be sure to ask. You may also want to check with other students to find out how they are approaching the assignment. If your instructor does not mention length requirements, be sure to ask how long the paper should be.

In a response paper, your instructor does not want you simply to summarize an essay, although summarizing may be a useful way to begin planning a response (see the next section). You may include a brief summary as part of your introduction, but you should concentrate on interpreting and evaluating what you have read. Keep in mind, however, that you should not attempt to discuss all of your reactions. Instead, choose one key idea, one question the essay raises, or one issue it explores.

For example, suppose your instructor asks you to read an article titled "Advertising: A Form of Institutional Lying" that tries to show that advertisements deceive consumers by presenting half-truths, distortions, and misinformation. Your instructor asks you to write a two-page paper about the essay but gives you no other directions. In writing this response paper, you might take one of the following approaches.

- Discuss how you were once deceived by an advertisement, as a means of confirming the author's main points.
- Evaluate the evidence and examples the author provides to support his claim; determine whether the evidence is relevant and sufficient.

- Discuss the causes or effects of deception in advertising that the author overlooks (you might need to consult other sources to take this approach).
- Evaluate the assumptions the author makes about advertising or consumers.

For an assignment like this one, or for any response paper, how do you decide on an issue to write about? How do you come up with ideas about a reading? The following guide will help you.

A Guide to Responding to Text

This guide presents a step-by-step process for discovering ideas for response papers, as shown in Figure 3.4. Notice that the guide begins with summary writing to check and clarify your understanding, moves to connecting the ideas to your own experiences, and then offers numerous strategies for analyzing the reading. Each of these steps is discussed below within the context of a reading assignment.

Summarize to Check Your Understanding

A **summary** is a brief statement of major points, and whether or not we recognize it, we all practice summarizing every day. When a friend asks, "What was the movie about?" we reply with a summary of the plot. A summary presents only the main ideas, not details. Your summary of a movie would not include specific scenes or dialogue, for example. When summarizing print text, a summary is about one-fifth of the original, or less, depending on the amount of detail needed.

Summarizing is an excellent way to check whether you have understood what you have read. If you have difficulty writing a summary, this is a sign that you do not

FIGURE 3.4 Active Response to a Reading

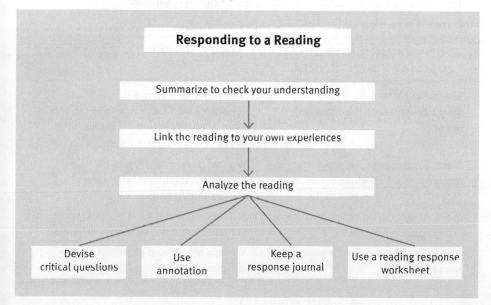

fully know what is important in the reading. Summarizing is also an excellent way to improve your retention of the material. Summaries make it easier for you to keep track of a writer's important ideas and can be reviewed easily and quickly in preparation for a class discussion or exam.

For more on journal writing, see Chapter 2, p. 30.

Many students keep a journal in which they write summaries of essays as well as other responses to what they read. Journal writing is a good way to generate and record ideas about an essay, and your journal entries can serve as useful sources of ideas for writing papers.

To write an effective and useful summary, use the following seven guidelines.

1. **Read the entire essay before attempting to write anything.**
2. **Highlight or annotate as you read.** These markings will help you pick out what is important to include in your summary.
3. **Write your summary as you reread the essay.**
4. **Write an opening sentence that states in your own words the author's thesis, the most important idea the entire essay explains.**
5. **Include the author's most important supporting ideas.** Use either highlighted topic sentences or marginal summary notes as a guide for knowing what to include. Marginal summary notes briefly state the content of each paragraph. If you write notes similar to those on pages 54–55, you can easily convert them into sentences for your summary. Following is a list of the summary notes written for "Purse Snatching" along with sentences that have been generated from the notes, which then become part of the sample summary below.
6. **Present the ideas in the order in which they appear in the original source.** Be sure to use transitions (connecting words) as you move from one supporting idea to another.
7. **Reread your summary to determine if it contains sufficient information.** Would your summary be understandable and meaningful to someone who has not read the essay? If not, revise it to include additional information.

CONVERTING MARGINAL SUMMARY NOTES TO SUMMARY SENTENCES

Marginal Note	Summary Sentence
(para. 2) unfairness in soccer and tennis	In both World Cup soccer and pro tennis, there are vast differences between men's and women's salaries.
(para. 3) compares salaries in men's and women's basketball	Women basketball players (WNBA) earn only a fraction of what men players (NBA) earn.
(para. 4) women do not participate in high-paying auto racing	Auto racing is the most lucrative sport but has almost no women participants.
(para. 6) gives reasons for salary inequity	Women are treated as sexual objects, as shown by the coverage of Brandi Chastain removing her shirt.

Here is a sample summary for the essay "Purse Snatching," written by a student using the preceding seven steps.

Although the right to participate in women's professional sports is now well established, financial equality with men participants does not exist. In both World Cup soccer and pro tennis, there are vast differences between men's and women's salaries. In professional basketball, women players earn a fraction of what men players are paid. Auto racing, the most lucrative of all sports, has few, if any, women participants. Women are at a financial disadvantage not only in salary but also for endorsements, winnings, and profit sharing. Financial inequity may exist because women are treated as sexual objects, as shown by the recent media coverage of Brandi Chastain removing her shirt. The media and the medical profession suggest that women are physically inferior to men. The author contends that boxers in different weight categories are not compared and, likewise, that men and women participating in the same sport should not be compared. Sex discrimination should be less important than financial considerations, but financial inequity still exists.

The writer expresses Lopiano's thesis in her own words.

The order of ideas parallels the order in Lopiano's essay.

The writer continues to use her own words—not those of Lopiano.

Exercise 3.4

Write a summary of the section of this chapter titled Changing Some Misconceptions about Reading, p. 46.

Link the Reading to Your Own Experiences

One way to get ideas flowing for a response paper is to think about how the reading relates to your own experiences. It is a way of building a bridge between you and the author, between your ideas and those expressed by the author.

- **Begin by looking for useful information in the essay and considering how you could apply or relate that information to other real-life situations.** Think of familiar situations or examples that illustrate the subject. For example, while "Purse Snatching" considers inequity in professional sports, you might write a journal entry about inequities that exist among Little League teams or among women in high school or collegiate athletics.
- **Try to think beyond the reading itself.** Recall other material you have read and events you have experienced that are related to the reading. In thinking about "Purse Snatching," for example, you might recall an article about the WNBA or a men's or women's tennis match on television.
- **Use the key-word response method for generating ideas.** Choose one or more key words that describe your initial response, such as *angered, amused, surprised, confused, annoyed, curious,* or *shocked.* For example, fill in the following blank with key words describing your response to "Purse Snatching."

"After reading the essay, I felt _____."

The key-word response you just wrote will serve as a point of departure for further thinking. Start by explaining your response; then write down ideas as they come to you, trying to approach the reading from many different perspectives. Here is the result of one student's key-word response to "Purse Snatching."

For more on freewriting, see Chapter 4, p. 86.

After reading "Purse Snatching," I <u>felt depressed and at the same time somewhat relieved.</u> I had no idea of the extent to which such discrimination existed in professional sports. It is depressing that after all of the reforms and advances required by Title IX, the problem still exists. In a way, though, it was gratifying to know that professional sports are not exempt from sexual discrimination. Everything is always magnified and blown out of proportion in professional sports. Sports have become an unreal fantasy where superathletes perform extraordinary feats, becoming superheroes. The problem of sexual discrimination makes professional sports seem almost human instead of superhuman.

Possible Topic #1: professional sports as fantasy

Possible Topic #2: athletes as superheroes

Exercise 3.5

Review the three preceding techniques for connecting the subject of an essay to your own experiences. Choose one of those techniques, and try it out on the topic of inequity in women's sports.

Analyze the Reading

Analyzing, like summarizing, is a skill we use every day. After you see a movie, you ask a friend, "So, what did you think of it?" In response, your friend may praise the plot, criticize the photography, or comment on the believability of the characters, for example. Analysis of text, then, is a broad opportunity to comment on any aspect of the essay, such as the author's fairness or accuracy, his or her method of presentation, the quality of the supporting evidence provided, or the intended audience. Methods for discovering ideas for analysis include devising critical questions, using annotation, keeping a response journal, and using a reading response worksheet.

Devise Critical Questions

Asking critical questions and then answering them is a useful method for analysis and for discovering ideas for a response paper. Here are three sample questions and the answers that one student wrote in response to them after reading the essay.

Will female athletes ever become as popular as their male counterparts when it comes to team sports?

I think patience is the key here. The degree of popularity, respect, and salaries desired by female team sports athletes won't occur overnight. The all-male major leagues have

Possible topic: general popularity of women's athletics

been around for over a century. Also, we have to remember how African American sports figures had to struggle to fit in and prove themselves worthy of their game.

Why did Brandi Chastain remove her shirt?

Perhaps she did so in the exuberance of the moment, but why choose an action with a sexual connotation? Chastain played into the hands of the media by giving them a controversial behavior to report. She could have thrown her shoes, tossed a soccer ball, or just shouted exuberantly.

Possible topic: behavior of women athletes

Why did the media give so much coverage to Chastain's removal of her shirt?

Perhaps her action was a ploy to draw media attention to the sporting event. Perhaps the media reports what people want to hear and see. Is the public more interested in women as women or as athletes?

Possible topic: media coverage of women athletes

> ### Essay in Progress 1
> Write a list of critical questions about the reading "Purse Snatching" on page 51 or another essay assigned by your instructor. Use *why, how,* and *what* questions to generate ideas about inequity in women's sports.

Use Annotation

In the Guide to Active Reading, you learned to annotate as you read. Annotation can also be used to analyze and respond to a reading after you have read it the first time and while you are preparing to write about it. As you read an essay for the second time, record additional reactions that occur to you. Some students prefer to use a different color of ink to record their second set of annotations. Refer to the sample student annotation shown on p. 54.

> ### Essay in Progress 2
> Reread "Purse Snatching" or the other assigned essay, this time adding annotations that record your reactions to and questions about the essay as you read.

Keep a Response Journal

A response journal is a section of your writing journal (see Chapter 2, p. 30) in which you record your reactions to and questions about readings. There are two ways you can organize a response journal; experiment with each format until you discover the one that works best for you.

The open-page format. On a blank page, write, outline, draw, or create a diagram to express your reactions to an essay. Because the open-page format encourages you to let your ideas flow freely, it may work particularly well for creative and spatial learners. Figure 3.5 shows one student's open-page response journal entry for "Purse Snatching." This entry suggests several possible topics to write about—how women athletes dress, how endorsements affect images of women athletes, how commercials create negative images of women athletes.

FIGURE 3.5 Sample Open-Page Journal Format

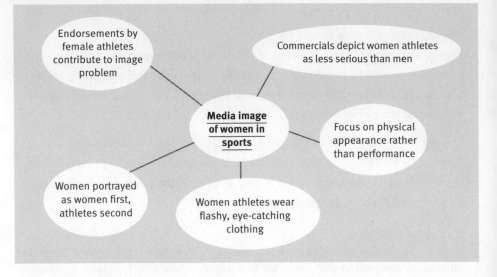

The two-column format. Divide several pages of your journal into two vertical columns. If you journal on a computer, you can insert a table with two columns. Label the left side "Quotations" and the right side "Responses." Under "Quotations," jot down five to ten quotations from the text. Choose remarks that seem important—that state an opinion, summarize a viewpoint, and so forth. In the right column, directly opposite each quotation, write your response to the quotation. You might explain it, disagree with or question it, relate it to other information in the reading or in another reading, or tie it to your own experiences. The two-column format forces you to think actively about an essay while you question what you have read and draw connections. Because it provides more structure than the open-page format, students who tend to be pragmatic or concrete learners may find it effective.

Figure 3.6 follows the two-column format. In this entry, the writer has uncovered several possible topics—the dispersion of available funds for sporting events, the attire and behavior of female athletes, and male viewpoints and political correctness.

For more on paraphrasing, see Chapter 21, p. 589.

You may find it useful to paraphrase the quotation before writing your response. Paraphrasing forces you to think about the meaning of the quotation, and ideas for writing may come to mind as a result. To use paraphrasing, add a "Paraphrases" column to your journal between the "Quotations" column and the "Responses" column.

> **Essay in Progress 3**
> For "Purse Snatching" or another essay, write a response in your journal using the open-page format or the two-column format.

Use a Reading Response Worksheet

An easy way to record all of your ideas about a reading in one place is to use a reading response worksheet. The worksheet guides your response while directing your thinking.

FIGURE 3.6 Sample Two-Column Journal Format

Quotations	Responses
"Why the need to hog the marbles?"	This statement implies that there are only so many marbles. If there is limited money, then the question becomes how it should be divided between men and women. It would seem that the most money should go to the sporting events that are most profitable.
"How many women jog on city streets and work out in health clubs every day wearing less?"	The fact that some women do wear body-revealing sports clothing does not justify an athlete removing clothing during a public sporting event.
"I love talking to high school boys because they reflect the male view before the veil of political correctness disguises their true feelings."	Do men feel the need to veil their feelings? It could be possible that their attitudes have changed instead of being disguised. Are most men concerned with political correctness in expressing their attitudes about sports?

A blank worksheet is shown in Figure 3.7 on p. 70. Notice that it includes space for recording your first impressions, a summary, connections to your own experiences, ideas for analysis, and additional sources.

Using Your Learning Style

If you are a *verbal* learner, a *social* learner, or both, you probably find reading a comfortable and convenient way to obtain information. If you are a *spatial* learner, though, you may prefer the graphic images of video and film to those of printed material. Regardless of your learning style, most of your assignments will be in print form for the foreseeable future. Therefore, it is up to you to use your learning style in a way that enhances your reading and writing. The following guidelines for active reading and response are tailored to the various learning styles.

Learning Style Options

- If you are a *spatial* learner, create mental pictures of people and places. For example, while reading the essay "Purse Snatching," you might create a mental image of a female athlete in a sports competition. In addition, use graphic organizers and diagrams to organize the ideas in an essay. As you annotate, use symbols to connect the ideas within and between paragraphs (for example, see the symbols listed for the reading response journal on p. 32).
- If you are a *social* learner, discuss a reading assignment with a classmate both before and after reading. Preview the essay together, sharing ideas about the topic. After reading the essay, discuss your reactions to it. In both instances, use the Guide to Active Reading in this chapter (p. 46) and the Guide to Responding to Text (p. 63) to get started.

FIGURE 3.7 Sample Reading Response Worksheet

READING RESPONSE WORKSHEET

TITLE: _____

AUTHOR: _____

FIRST IMPRESSIONS: _____

_____

_____

SUMMARY: _____

_____

_____

_____

_____

_____

CONNECTIONS TO YOUR OWN EXPERIENCES: _____

_____

_____

_____

ANALYSIS (issue, aspect, feature, problem)

1. _____

_____

_____

2. _____

_____

_____

_____

ADDITIONAL SOURCES OR VISUALS (if needed)

1. _____

_____

2. _____

_____

3. _____

_____

- If you are an *abstract* learner, a *creative* learner, or both, you may tend to overlook details while focusing instead on the "big ideas" and overall message of a reading. Be sure to highlight important points and to concentrate on facts and supporting details.
- If you are a *concrete* learner, a *pragmatic* learner, or both, you may like to focus on details instead of seeing how ideas fit together and contribute to an author's overall message. Use graphic organizers to help you create a larger picture. Try to make the essay as "real" as possible; visualize events occurring or the author writing. You might visualize yourself interviewing the author, alone or with a panel of classmates.
- If you are an *emotional* learner, you may generally focus on your feelings about people or events in the essay and overlook the way an author uses them to convey an overall message. Keep this question in mind. How does the author use these people or events to get his or her message across?
- If you are a *rational* learner, you may zero in on how logical or clear the presentation of ideas is and overlook more subtle shades of meaning. Be sure to annotate in order to draw out your personal reactions to a piece of writing.

Essay in Progress 4

Discuss "Purse Snatching" with a classmate. Make notes as you discuss. If you chose another essay, pair up with a classmate who also chose that essay, or ask your classmate to read the essay you have chosen.

Essay in Progress 5

Write a two- to four-page paper in response to "Purse Snatching" or the essay you have chosen. Use the following steps to shape the ideas you generated in Essays in Progress 1 to 4.

1. Reread the writing you did in response to the reading. Look for ideas that seem worthwhile and important enough to become the basis of your essay.

2. Look for related ideas. Try to find ideas that fit together to produce a viewpoint or position toward the reading.

3. Do not attempt to cover all your ideas. Your essay should not analyze every aspect of the essay. Instead, you should choose some feature or aspect on which to focus.

4. Write a sentence that states your central point. This sentence will become your thesis statement. It should state what your essay will assert or explain.

5. Collect ideas and evidence from the reading to support your thesis. Your thesis should be backed up by specifics in the reading.

6. Organize your ideas into essay form. Your paper should have a title, introduction, body, and conclusion.

7. Revise your essay. Be sure that you have explained your ideas clearly and have provided support from the reading for each one.

8. Proofread for accuracy and correctness. Use the Suggestions for Proofreading in Chapter 9 (p. 195).

For more on thesis statements, see Chapter 5. For more on organizing your ideas, see Chapter 6. To help you revise your essay, see Chapter 8. For more on editing and proofreading, see Chapter 9.

How to Approach the Student Essays in This Book

Use the following suggestions when reading student essays.

- **Read an essay several times.** During your first reading, concentrate on the writer's message. Then read the essay again as many times as necessary to analyze its writing features. For example, first notice how the writer supported the thesis statement, and then look at the language used to create a particular impression.
- **Read with a pen or marker in hand.** As you discover writing techniques that are emphasized in the chapter, mark or annotate them.
- **Focus on characteristics.** Each chapter in Part 3 presents the characteristics of a particular method of organization. Consider how the student essay demonstrates some or all of that method's characteristics.
- **Focus on techniques.** Each chapter in Part 3 offers specific techniques and suggestions for writing a particular type of essay. Review these techniques and observe how the writer applied them.
- **Focus on what is new and different.** Ask yourself the following questions as you read: What is the writer doing that you haven't seen before? What catches your attention? What works particularly well? What techniques might be fun to try? What techniques would be challenging to try? For example, if a writer begins his or her essay with a striking statistic, consider whether you could use a striking statistic to begin your essay.
- **Use student essays to train your critical eye.** Although student essays are reasonably good models, they are not perfect. Look for ways the essays can be improved. Once you can see ways to improve someone else's essay, you will be better equipped to analyze and improve your own writing.
- **Use graphic organizers to grasp the essay's structure.** In Part 3, a graphic organizer is presented for each method of organization. Compare the essay to the graphic organizer, noticing how the essay contains each element.

Students Write

Tracey Aquino was a student at Johnson & Wales University when she wrote the following essay in response to "Purse Snatching." As you read, notice how Aquino analyzes Lopiano's points about female athletics.

The Games We Play: Inequality in the Pro-Sports Workplace

Tracey Aquino

Donna Lopiano in her article "Purse Snatching" states that professional female athletes   1
are not getting their fair share of salary and respect compared to professional male athletes.
Feminists may cheer upon hearing Lopiano's point of view, and some sports fans may grumble
about it. "Purse Snatching" may justify feminist ways of thinking, but Lopiano's argument does

READING

Introduction: identifies the article Aquino is responding to

In her thesis statement, Aquino states how her ideas differ from those of Lopiano.

not account for the necessary time it will take for the exposure and investment in female team athletics to grow.

Perhaps the question we should ask is *why* this is such a big problem, especially for team sports. Lopiano never asks, Why aren't female team players getting as much pay and respect as their male counterparts? The answer could be only a matter of time. Professional female leagues have only gained media exposure in the past decade, whereas all-male professional leagues have been well known since the late 1800s. After over a century of building a strong relationship with spectators and host cities, male professional team sports have become a prominent part of American culture. Professional female leaguers will have to wait a little longer before they see the money and adoration they want.

Lopiano states that the Women's National Basketball Association averages 10,000 spectators a game—a feat reached in only two years as opposed to the 30 years it took the NBA. After stating this statistic, Lopiano declares that the $30,000-per-year salary of a WNBA player is only a small percentage of what most NBA players make. What she fails to recognize is that not only does attendance matter but that television exposure has a direct effect on investment and salaries. With additional television exposure the WNBA can expect to generate interest and popularity, and with increased popularity will come successful investors willing to field six- or seven-figure salaries for the players.

WNBA games suffer from being aired primarily on the Lifetime television network, a specialty cable channel aimed at women. When a WNBA game is aired only on Lifetime, the WNBA is neglecting male viewers who do not watch cable channels marketed toward women. Compare this audience to the one who watches a sports channel or a major national network. If popularity is the door to a six- or seven-figure salary, exposure via a gender-specific cable channel is not the key. The WNBA and similar female team sporting leagues need to grow their audience to grow their revenue.

Lopiano implies that this problem is based on investment. If new interest can be found from better exposure, however, new investors will be attracted and richly compensated. Women's soccer and basketball players have proven over time to be worthy of their fans, of which they have many. With a comparison to boxing, Lopiano disproves the argument that women are physically inferior to men and therefore men's team sports are better. When women play against women, there is no inferiority because everyone is on equal ground. On the court or on the field, professional female athletes show true stamina and spirit. With the proper media outlets, more fans and investors will be attracted to female team sports. But this will take time.

If Lopiano wants positive action taken for women's rights in sports, she must first realize that fame and fortune happen not overnight but over time. Sexism will always be a factor in the workplace, even if that workplace is a basketball court, a tennis court, or a soccer field. Female athletes have a long road to pave ahead of them in the fight for fairness, but in time, exposure, audiences, investment, and salaries will grow.

2

Aquino considers a question Lopiano never asked.

3

Aquino points out that Lopiano fails to consider the relationship between television exposure and salary level.

4

Aquino explains why WNBA visibility is limited by the cable channel on which games are shown.

5

Aquino addresses Lopiano's idea that female athletes lack investment support.

6

Conclusion: Aquino states that Lopiano should accept that change takes time.

Analyzing the Writer's Technique

1. Express Aquino's thesis (central point) in your own words.
2. What kind of information does Aquino include to support her thesis?
3. What additional information, if any, would you recommend that Aquino include in her essay?

Reacting to the Reading

1. Is television and advertising exposure a result of popularity, or does it build and increase popularity? Explain your answer.
2. Do you agree with Aquino that it may be only a matter of time before the inequity in men's and women's sports is resolved? Explain your answer.
3. Write a journal entry describing a situation in which you observed or experienced women being treated differently than men.
4. What steps not mentioned by Aquino or Lopiano might be effective in increasing equity between men's and women's sports?

Applying Your Skills: Writing about the Reading

Use your highlighting, annotating, and graphic organizers as sources of ideas for the following writing assignments based on "Purse Snatching."

1. Write an essay describing a female athlete that you know personally or that you watch playing professional sports. Describe the traits that make this person a good athlete.
2. Discuss whether it is fair to compare men's and women's performance in areas such as education or in the workplace, given that men and women seem to approach tasks differently and may have different priorities.
3. Discuss whether spending more money on women's sports will make them more popular.

Answers to Exercise 3.1

1. True   2. False   3. True   4. True   5. False

PART 2

Strategies for Writing Essays

CHAPTER 4

Prewriting: How to Find and Focus Ideas

Study the photo on the opposite page. What is happening in the photo? What do you think the man could be reacting to?

Take out a sheet of paper or open a new computer file, and write whatever comes to mind about the photo and what you think might be happening in it. You might write about times when you've felt the same emotions you think the man is expressing, or you might write about times when you've seen others express strong emotions in a public place. Try to write nonstop for at least five minutes, jotting down or typing whatever ideas cross your mind. Don't stop to evaluate your writing or to phrase your ideas in complete sentences or correct grammatical form. Don't worry about correctness; just record your thinking

You have just used *freewriting,* a method of discovering ideas about a topic. Read over what you wrote. Suppose you were asked to write an essay about joy or exuberance. Do you see some starting points and usable ideas in your freewriting? In this chapter, you will learn more about freewriting as well as a number of other methods, in addition to those described in Chapter 3, that will help you find ideas to write about. You will also learn how to focus an essay by considering why you are writing (your purpose), whom you are writing for (your audience), and what perspective you are using to approach your topic (point of view). These steps are all part of the beginning of the process of writing an essay, as illustrated in Figure 4.1.

Choosing and Narrowing a Topic

When you begin an essay assignment, it's a good idea to allow time for choosing a broad topic and then narrowing it to be manageable within the assigned length of your paper. Skipping this step is one of the biggest mistakes you can make in beginning a writing assignment. You can waste a great deal of time working on an essay only to discover that the topic is too large or that you don't have enough to say about it.

Choosing a Topic

In some writing situations, your instructor will assign the topic. In others, your instructor will allow you to write on a topic of your choice. Or you may be given a number of possible topics to choose from, as in the Guided Writing Assignments in Chapters 10 to 17, 19, and 23 of this text. In the latter cases, use the following guidelines to choose a successful topic.

1. **Invest time in making your choice.** It may be tempting to grab the first topic that comes to mind, but you will produce a better essay if you work with a topic that interests you and that you know something about.
2. **Focus on questions and ideas rather than topics.** For example, the question, Do television commercials really sell products? may come to mind more easily than the broad topic of advertising or commercials.
3. **Use your journal as a source of ideas.** Chapter 2 describes how to keep a writing journal, and Chapter 3 explains how to use a response journal. If you have not begun keeping a journal, start one now; try writing in it for a few weeks to see if it is helpful.
4. **Discuss possible topics with a friend.** Conversations with friends may help you discover worthwhile topics and give you feedback on topics you have already thought of.
5. **Consult Table 4.1 (p. 80) or Table 4.3 (p. 95).** A number of specific sources of ideas for essay topics are listed in Table 4.1. Table 4.3 groups topics from this chapter's exercises into broad categories.

FIGURE 4.1 An Overview of the Writing Process

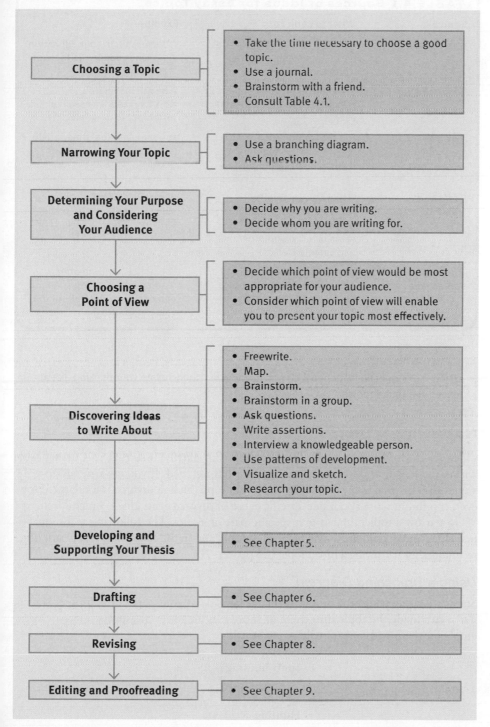

TABLE 4.1 Sources of Ideas for Essay Topics

Source	What to Look For	Example
Your classes	Listen for issues, controversies, and new ideas that might be worth exploring.	A discussion in your education class leads you to the topic of standardized testing.
Daily activities	Take note of incidents at work and at sporting or social events.	A health inspector's visit at work suggests an essay on restaurant food safety.
Newspapers and magazines	Flip through recent issues; look for articles that might lead to promising topics.	You find an interesting article on a hip-hop musician and decide to write about her career.
Radio and television	Listen to your favorite radio station for a thought-provoking song, or look for ideas in television programs and commercials.	Commercials for diet soda suggest an essay on the diet-food industry.
The world around you	Look within your household or outside of it. Notice people, objects, interactions.	You notice family members reading books or newspapers and decide to write about the value of leisure time.

Essay in Progress 1

Using the suggestions on page 78 and in Table 4.1 to stimulate your thinking, list at least three broad topics.

Narrowing a Topic

Once you have chosen a topic, the next step is to narrow it so that it is manageable within the length of the essay your instructor has assigned. If you are assigned to write a two- to four-page essay, for example, a broad topic such as divorce is too large. However, you might write about one specific cause of divorce or its effects on children.

To narrow a topic, limit it to a specific part or aspect. The following techniques—branching and questioning—will help you do so. Later in the chapter, you will learn other techniques for narrowing a broad topic (see pp. 86–91).

Using a Branching Diagram

Start by writing your broad topic at the far left side of your paper or computer screen. Then subdivide the topic into three or more subcategories or aspects. Here is an example for the broad topic of wild game hunting.

■ **Wild-game hunting**
- Sport hunting
- As source of food
- Hunting accidents

Then choose one subcategory and subdivide it further, as shown here.

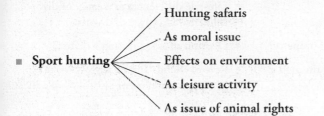

- **Sport hunting**
  - Hunting safaris
  - As moral issue
  - Effects on environment
  - As leisure activity
  - As issue of animal rights

Continue narrowing the topic in this way until you feel you have found one that is both interesting and manageable.

Keep in mind that once you begin planning, researching, and drafting the essay, you may need to narrow your topic even further. The following example shows additional narrowing of the topic "effects on environment."

- **Effects on environment**
  - Prized species may become endangered.
  - Hunters may spoil pristine wilderness areas.
  - Regulated hunting helps control animal populations.

Any one of these narrowed topics would be workable for a two- to four-page essay. Did you notice that as the narrowing progressed, the topics changed from words and phrases to statements of ideas?

Exercise 4.1

Use branching diagrams to narrow three of the following broad topics to more manageable topics for a two- to four-page essay.

1. Divorce
2. Safe transportation
3. Population explosion
4. Military spending
5. Birth control
6. Early childhood education

Essay in Progress 2

Narrow one of the broad topics you chose in Essay in Progress 1 to a topic manageable for a two- to four-page essay.

Asking Questions to Narrow a Broad Topic

Use questions that begin with *who, what, where, when, why,* and *how* to narrow your topic. Questioning will lead you to consider and focus your attention on specific aspects of the topic. Here is an example of questioning for the broad topic of divorce.

Questions	*Narrowed Topics*
Why does divorce occur?	• Lifestyle differences as a cause of divorce • Infidelity as a cause of divorce
How do couples divide their property?	• Division of assets during a divorce
Who can help couples work through a divorce?	• Role of friends and family • Marital counselor's or attorney's role in divorce
What are the effects of divorce on children?	• Emotional effects of divorce on children • Financial effects of divorce on children
When might it be advisable for a couple considering divorce to remain married?	• Couples who stay together for the sake of their children • Financial benefit of remaining married

As you can see, the questions about divorce produced several workable topics. At times, however, you may need to ask additional questions to get to a topic that is sufficiently limited. The topic "emotional effects of divorce on children," for example, is still too broad for an essay. Asking questions such as "What are the most typical emotional effects?" and "How do divorcing parents prevent emotional problems?" would lead to more specific topics.

Exercise 4.2

Use questioning to narrow three of the following subjects to topics that would be manageable within a two- to four-page essay.

1. Senior citizens
2. Mental illness
3. Environmental protection
4. Affirmative action
5. Television programming

Thinking about Your Purpose, Audience, and Point of View

Once you have decided on a manageable topic, you are ready to determine your purpose and consider your audience.

Determining Your Purpose

A well-written essay should have a specific purpose or goal. There are three main purposes for writing—to *express* yourself, to *inform* your reader, and to *persuade* your reader. For example, an essay might express the writer's feelings about an incident of road rage that he or she observed. Another essay may inform readers about the primary causes of road rage. Still another essay might attempt to persuade readers to vote for funding to investigate the problem of road rage in the local community.

As you plan your draft essay, ask yourself two critical questions.

- Why am I writing this essay?
- What do I want this essay to accomplish?

Some essays can have more than one purpose. An essay on snowboarding, for example, could be both informative and persuasive: It could explain the benefits of snowboarding and then urge readers to take up the sport because it is good aerobic exercise.

Considering Your Audience

Considering your **audience**—the people who read your essay—is an important part of the writing process. Many aspects of your writing—how you express yourself (the type of sentence structure you use, for example), which words you choose, what details and examples you include, and what attitude you take toward your topic—all depend on the audience. Your **tone**—how you sound to your audience—is especially important. If you want your audience to feel comfortable with your writing, be sure to write in a manner that appeals to them.

If you were describing a student orientation session to a friend, you would use a different tone and select different details than you would if you were describing the orientation in an article for the student newspaper. Consider the following examples and notice how they differ.

TELLING A FRIEND

Remember I told you how nervous I am about attending college in the fall? Well, guess what? I went to my student orientation over the weekend, and it was much better than I had expected! I even met one of my psych teachers—they call them "instructors" here—and he was so nice and down-to-earth that now I'm starting to get excited about going to college.

Language: casual
Sentence Structure: shorter sentences
Tone: familiar, friendly

WRITING FOR THE STUDENT NEWSPAPER

College student orientations are often thought to be stuffy affairs where prospective students attempt to mix with aloof professors. For this reason, I am pleased to report that the college orientation held on campus last weekend was a major success and not a pointless endeavor after all. Along with my fellow incoming first-year students, I was impressed with the friendliness of instructors and the camaraderie that developed between students and faculty.

Language: more formal
Sentence Structure: longer sentences
Tone: serious, formal

How to Consider Your Audience

As you consider your audience, keep the following points in mind.

- **Your readers are not present and cannot observe or participate in what you are writing about.** If you are writing about your apartment, for example, they cannot visualize it unless you describe it in detail.

- **Your readers do not know everything you do.** They may not have the same knowledge about and experience with the topic that you do, and they may not know what specialized terms mean.
- **Your readers may not necessarily share your opinions and values.** If you are writing about raising children and assume that strict discipline is undesirable, for example, some readers may not agree with you.
- **Your readers may not respond in the same way you do to situations or issues.** Some readers may not see any humor in a situation that you find funny. An issue that you consider only mildly disturbing may make some readers angry.

The following box lists questions you can ask to analyze your audience.

- **What does your audience know or not know about your topic?** If you are proposing a community garden project to an audience of city residents who know little about gardening, you would need to describe the pleasures and benefits of gardening to capture their interest.

- **What is the education, background, and experience of your audience?** If you are writing your garden-project proposal for an audience of low-income residents, you might emphasize how much money they could save by growing vegetables, but if you are proposing the project to middle-income residents, you might stress instead how relaxing gardening can be and how a garden can beautify a neighborhood.

- **What attitudes, beliefs, opinions, or biases is your audience likely to hold?** If, for example, your audience believes that most development is harmful to the environment, and you are writing an essay urging your audience to agree to a new community garden, consider emphasizing how the garden will benefit the environment and decrease development.

- **What tone do your readers expect you to take?** Suppose you are writing to your local city council urging council members to approve the community garden. Although the council has been stalling on the issue, your tone should be serious and not accusatory. As community leaders, the council members expect to be treated with respect.

When Your Audience Is Your Instructor

Instructors occasionally direct students to write for a particular audience, such as readers of a certain magazine or newspaper, but you can usually assume that your audience is your instructor. You should not, however, automatically assume that he or she is an expert on your topic. In most cases, it is best to write as if your instructor were unfamiliar with your topic. He or she wants to see if you understand the topic and can write and think clearly about it. For academic papers, then, you should provide enough information to demonstrate your knowledge of the subject. Include background information, definitions of technical terms, and relevant details to make your essay clear and understandable.

Exercise 4.3

1. Write a one-paragraph description of a current television commercial for a particular product. Your audience is another college student.

2. Write a description of the same commercial for one of the following writing situations.

   a. An assignment in a business marketing class: Analyze the factors that make the advertisement interesting and appealing. Your audience is a marketing instructor.

   b. A letter to the company that produces the product: Describe your response to the advertisement. Your audience is the consumer relations director of the company.

   c. A letter to your local television station: Comment favorably on or complain about the advertisement. Your audience is the station director.

Choosing a Point of View

Point of view is the perspective from which you write an essay. There are three types—*first, second,* and *third person.* In choosing a point of view, consider your topic, your purpose, and your audience.

Think of point of view as the "person" you become as you write. For some essays, you may find first-person pronouns (*I, me, mine, we, ours*) effective and appropriate, such as in an essay narrating an event in which you participated. For other types of essays, second-person pronouns (*you, your, yours*) are appropriate, as in an essay explaining how to build a fence: "First, *you* should measure . . ." At times, the word *you* may be understood but not directly stated, as in "First, measure . . ." Many textbooks, including this one, use the second person to address student readers.

In academic writing, the third-person point of view is prevalent. The third-person point of view is less personal and more formal than both the first person and the second person. The writer uses people's names and third-person pronouns (*he, she, they*). Think of the third person as public rather than private or personal. The writer reports what he or she sees.

Exercise 4.4

Working with a classmate, discuss which point of view (first, second, or third person) would be most appropriate in each of the following writing situations.

1. An essay urging students on your campus to participate in a march against hunger to support a local food drive

2. A description of a car accident on a form that your insurance company requires you to submit in order to collect benefits

3. A paper for an ecology course on the effects of air pollution caused by a local industry

Discovering Ideas to Write About

Many students report that one of the most difficult parts of writing an essay is finding enough to say about a narrowed topic. In the following sections, you will learn a number of useful strategies for discovering ideas to write about. Experiment with each before deciding which will work for you. Depending on your learning style, you will probably discover that some strategies work better than others. You may also find that the technique you choose for a given essay may depend in part on your topic.

Freewriting

When you use **freewriting**, you write nonstop for a specific period of time, usually five to ten minutes. As you learned in the activity that opens this chapter, freewriting involves writing whatever comes to mind, regardless of its relevance to your topic. If nothing comes to mind, just write the topic, your name, or "I can't think of anything to write." Then let your mind run free: Explore ideas, make associations, jump from one idea to another. The following tips will help you.

- **Be sure to write nonstop.** Writing often forces thought.
- **Don't be concerned with grammar, punctuation, or spelling.**
- **Write fast!** Try to keep up with your thinking. (Most people can think faster than they can write.)
- **Record ideas as they come to you** and in whatever form they appear—words, phrases, questions, or sentences.
- **If you are freewriting on a computer, darken the screen** so that you are not distracted by errors, formatting issues, and the words you have already written.

Next, reread your freewriting, and highlight or underline ideas that seem useful. Look for patterns and connections. Do several ideas together make a point; reflect a sequence; or suggest a larger, unifying idea? Here is an excerpt from one student's freewriting on the broad topic of violence in the media.

> There seems to be a lot of violence in the media these days, particularly on TV. For example, last night when I watched the news, the camera man showed people getting shot in the street. What kind of people watch this stuff? I'd rather watch a movie. It really bothered me because people get so turned off by such an ugly, gruesome scene that they won't want to watch the news anymore. Then we'll have a lot of uninformed citizens. There are too many already. Some people do not even know who the vice president of the U.S. is. A negative thing--that is the media has a negative impact on anyone or group who want to do something about violence in the inner city. And they create negative impressions of minority and ethnic groups, too. If the media shows one Latino man committing a crime, viewers falsely assume all Latinos are criminals. It's difficult to think of something positive that can be done when you're surrounded by so much violence. It's all so overwhelming. What we need in the inner city is not more

coverage of violence but <u>viable solutions</u> to the violence we have. The media coverage of violent acts only serves to make people think that this <u>violence is a normal state of affairs and nothing can be done</u> about it.

A number of different subtopics surfaced from this student's freewriting:

The media's graphic portrayal of violence

The negative impact of media violence on viewers

The media's portrayal of minority and ethnic groups

Any one of these topics could be narrowed into a manageable topic for an essay.

If you are a creative learner or feel restricted by organization and structure, freewriting may appeal to you because it allows you to give your imagination free rein.

Learning Style Options

Exercise 4.5

Set a clock or timer for five minutes and freewrite on one of the following broad topics. Then review and highlight your freewriting, identifying usable ideas with a common theme that might serve as a topic for an essay. Starting with this potential topic, freewrite for another five minutes to narrow your topic further and develop your ideas.

1. Rap music
2. Blogs
3. How to be self-sufficient
4. Pressures on college students
5. Job interviews

Mapping

Mapping, or **clustering**, is a visual way to discover ideas and relationships. It is also a powerful tool for some writers. Here is how it works.

1. Write your topic in the middle of a blank sheet of paper, and draw a box or circle around it.
2. Think of ideas that are related to or suggested by your topic. As you think of them, write them down in clusters around the topic, connecting them to the topic with lines (see Figure 4.2). Think of your topic as a tree trunk and the related ideas as branches.
3. Draw arrows and lines or use highlighting to show relationships and connect groups of related ideas.
4. Think of still more ideas, clustering them around the ideas already on your map.
5. If possible, experiment with mapping on a computer, using a graphics program such as the draw function available in Microsoft Word. You can then cut and paste items from your map into an outline or draft of your essay.

The sample map in Figure 4.2 was done by a student working on the topic of the costs of higher education. In this map, the student compared attending a local community college and attending an out-of-town four-year college. A number of different subtopics evolved, including the following.

- Transportation costs
- Social life
- Availability of degree programs
- Room and board costs

FIGURE 4.2 Sample Map

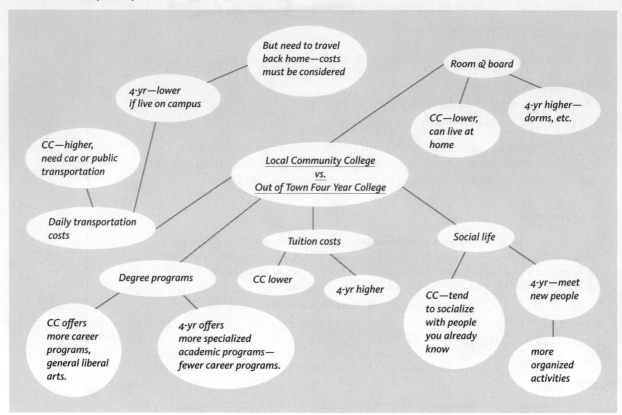

Learning Style Options

Mapping may appeal to you if you prefer a spatial method of dealing with information and ideas. It also appeals to creative learners who like to devise their own structure or framework within which to work.

> ### Exercise 4.6
>
> *Narrow one of the following topics. Then select one of your narrowed topics, and draw a map of related ideas as they come to mind.*
>
> 1. Presidential politics
> 2. Daydreaming
> 3. The function of jewelry
> 4. Radio stations
> 5. Year-round schooling

Brainstorming

When you do **brainstorming**, you list everything that comes to mind when you think about your topic—impressions, emotions, and reactions, as well as facts. Record words or phrases rather than sentences, and give yourself a time limit; it will force ideas to come faster. If you use a computer, you might use bullets or the indent function to brainstorm.

The following example shows a student's brainstorming on the narrowed topic of the disadvantages of home schooling.

Topic: Disadvantages of Home Schooling

- Parent may not be an expert in each subject
- Libraries not easily accessible
- Wide range of equipment, resources not available
- Child may be confused by parent playing the role of teacher
- Child does not learn to interact with other children
- Child does not learn to compete against others
- Parents may not enforce standards
- Parents may not be objective about child's strengths and weaknesses
- Child may learn only parent's viewpoint--not exposed to wide range of opinions
- Special programs (art, music) may be omitted
- Services of school nurse, counselors, reading specialists not available

Three clusters of topics are evident—unavailable services and resources (highlighted in red), limits of parents, and problems of social development (highlighted in tan). Once the student selected a cluster of topics, he did further brainstorming to generate ideas about his narrowed topic.

Brainstorming is somewhat more structured than freewriting because the writer focuses only on the topic at hand instead of writing whatever comes to mind. If you are a pragmatic learner, brainstorming may help you release your creative potential.

Learning Style Options

Brainstorming can also work well when it is done in groups of two or three classmates. Use a chalkboard in an empty classroom, share a large sheet of paper, sit together in front of a computer screen, or use networked computers. Say your ideas aloud as you write. You'll find that your classmates' ideas will trigger more of your own. Group brainstorming often appeals to students who are social learners and who find it stimulating and enjoyable to exchange ideas with other students.

Exercise 4.7

Choose one of the following subjects and narrow it to a manageable topic for a two- to four-page paper. Then brainstorm, either alone or with one or two classmates, to generate ideas to write about.

1. Value of music
2. National parks
3. Credit card fraud
4. Instant messaging
5. Web advertising

Questioning

Questioning is another way to discover ideas about a narrowed topic. Working either alone or with a classmate, write down every question you can think of about your topic. As with other prewriting strategies, focus on ideas, not correctness. Don't judge or evaluate ideas as you write. It may help to imagine that you are asking an expert on your topic anything that comes to mind.

Here is a partial list of questions one student generated on the narrow topic of the financial problems faced by single parents.

Possible Topics:
income disparity

financial planning

Why do many female single parents earn less than male single parents?

How can single parents afford to pay for day care?

Is there a support group for single parents that offers financial advice and planning?

How do single parents find time to attend college to improve their employability?

child support

establishment of credit

employability

How can women force their former husbands to keep up with child support payments?

How can single female parents who don't work outside the home still establish credit?

Are employers reluctant to hire women who are single parents?

Is it more difficult for a working single parent to get a mortgage than for a couple in which only one spouse works?

Beginning a question with "What if . . ." is a particularly good way to extend your thinking and look at a topic from a fresh perspective. Here are a few challenging "What if . . ." questions about the financial situation of single parents:

What if the government provided national day care or paid for day care?

What if single parents were not allowed to deduct more than one child on their income tax?

What if there were financial support groups for single parents?

Learning Style Options

You may find questioning effective if you are an analytical, inquisitive person, and social learners will enjoy using this technique with classmates. Since questions often tend to focus on specifics and details, questioning is also an appealing strategy for concrete learners.

Exercise 4.8

Working either alone or with a classmate, choose one of the following topics, narrow it, and write a series of questions to discover ideas about it.

1. The campus newspaper
2. Learning a foreign language
3. Financial aid regulations
4. Late-night talk radio shows
5. Government aid to developing countries

Writing Assertions

The technique of **writing assertions** forces you to look at your topic from a number of different perspectives. Begin by writing five to ten statements that take a position on or make an assertion about your topic. Here are a few possible assertions for the topic of the growing popularity of health food.

> Supermarkets have increased their marketing of health foods.
>
> Health food is popular because buying it makes people think they are hip.
>
> Health food is popular because it is chemical-free.
>
> Health food tricks people into thinking they have a healthy lifestyle.

Review your list of assertions, choose one statement, and try brainstorming, free-writing, or mapping to generate more ideas about it.

Abstract learners who prefer to deal with wholes rather than parts or who tend to focus on larger ideas rather than details often find this technique appealing.

Learning Style Options

Exercise 4.9

Working either alone or with one or two classmates, write assertions about one of the following topics.

1. Advertising directed toward children
2. Buying a used car from a private individual
3. Needed improvements in public education
4. Characteristics of a good teacher
5. Attempts to regulate speech on campus

Using the Patterns of Development

In Parts 3 and 4 of this book, you will learn nine ways to develop an essay—narration, description, illustration, process analysis, comparison and contrast, classification and division, definition, cause and effect, and argument. These methods are often called *patterns of development*. In addition to providing ways to develop an essay, the patterns of development may be used to generate ideas about a topic. Think of the patterns as doors through which you can gain access to your topic. Just as a building or room looks different depending on which door you enter, so you will see your topic in various ways by approaching it through different patterns of development.

The list of questions in Table 4.2 (p. 92) will help you approach your topic through these different "doors." For any given topic, some questions will work better than others. If your topic is voter registration, for example, the questions listed for definition and process analysis would be more helpful than those listed for description.

As you write your answers to the questions, also record any related ideas that come to mind. If you are working on a computer, create a table listing the patterns

TABLE 4.2 **Using the Patterns of Development to Explore a Topic**

Pattern of Development	Questions to Ask
Narration (Chapter 10)	What stories or events does this topic remind you of?
Description (Chapter 11)	What does the topic look, smell, taste, feel, or sound like?
Illustration (Chapter 12)	What examples of this topic are particularly helpful in explaining it?
Process Analysis (Chapter 13)	How does this topic work? How do you do this topic?
Comparison and Contrast (Chapter 14)	To what is the topic similar? In what ways? Is the topic more or less desirable than those things to which it is similar?
Classification and Division (Chapter 15)	Of what larger group of things is this topic a member? What are its parts? How can the topic be subdivided? Are there certain types or kinds of the topic?
Definition (Chapter 16)	How do you define the topic? How does the dictionary define it? What is the history of the term? Does everyone agree on its definition? Why or why not? If not, what points are in dispute?
Cause and Effect (Chapter 17)	What causes the topic? How often does it happen? What might prevent it from happening? What are its effects? What may happen because of it in the short term? What may happen as a result of it over time?
Argument (Chapters 18 and 19)	What issues surround this topic?

in one column and your questions in another. This way, you can brainstorm ideas about various rhetorical approaches. Pragmatic and creative learners will find this technique helpful.

Learning Style Options

One student who was investigating the topic of extrasensory perception (ESP) decided to use the questions for definition and cause and effect. Here are the answers she wrote:

Definition (How can my topic be defined?)

• ESP, or extrasensory perception, is the ability to perceive information not through the ordinary senses but as a result of a "sixth sense" (as yet undeveloped in most people).

• Scientists disagree on whether ESP exists and how it should be tested.

Cause and Effect (Why does my topic happen? What does it lead to?)

- Scientists do not know the cause of ESP and have not confirmed its existence, just the possibility of its existence.
- The effects of ESP are that some people know information that they would (seemingly) have no other way of knowing.
- Some people with ESP claim to have avoided disasters such as airplane crashes.

Using the patterns of development helps to direct or focus your mind on specific issues related to a topic. The strategy may appeal to you if you are a pragmatic learner who enjoys structured tasks or a creative learner who likes to analyze ideas from different viewpoints.

Learning Style Options

Exercise 4.10

Use the patterns of development to generate ideas on one of the following topics. Refer to Table 4.2 (p. 92) to form questions based on the patterns.

1. Buying only American-made products
2. The increase in incidents of carjacking
3. Community policing in urban areas
4. Effects of labor union strikes on workers
5. Cell phone usage

Visualizing or Sketching

Especially if you enjoy working with graphics, **visualizing** or actually **sketching** your topic may be an effective way to discover ideas. If you are writing a description of a person, for example, close your eyes and visualize that person in your mind. Imagine what he or she is wearing; study facial expressions and gestures.

Here is what one student "saw" when visualizing a shopping mall. Possible subtopics are annotated.

As I walked through the local mall, I crossed the walkway to get to Sears and noticed a large group of excited women all dressed in jogging suits; they were part of a shopping tour, I think. I saw a tour bus parked outside. Across the walkway was a bunch of teenagers, shouting and laughing and commenting on each other's hairstyles. They all wore T-shirts and jeans; some had body adornments--pierced noses and lips. They seemed to have no interest in shopping. Their focus was on one another. Along the walkway came an obvious mother-daughter pair. They seemed to be on an outing, escaping from their day-to-day routine for some shopping, joking, and laughing. Then I noticed a tired-looking elderly couple sitting on one of the benches. They seemed to enjoy just sitting there and watching the people walk by, every now and then commenting on the fashions they observed people wearing.

Possible Subtopics:

tour-group shopping

body piercing

teenage behavior

Visualization is a technique particularly well suited to spatial and creative learners.

Learning Style Options

Exercise 4.11

Visualize one of the following situations. Make notes on or sketch what you "see." Include as many details as possible.

1. A traffic jam
2. A couple obviously "in love"
3. A class you recently attended
4. The campus snack bar
5. A sporting event

Researching Your Topic

For more information on locating, using, and crediting sources, refer to Chapters 20 and 22.

Do some preliminary research on your topic in the library or on the Internet. Reading what others have written about your topic may suggest new approaches, reveal issues or controversies, and help you determine what you do and do not already know about the topic. This method is especially useful for an assigned essay with an unfamiliar topic or for a topic you want to learn more about.

Learning Style Options

Take notes while reading sources. In addition, be sure to record the publication data you will need to cite each source (author, title, publisher, page numbers, and so on). If you use ideas or information from sources in your essay, you must give credit to the sources of the borrowed material. While research may be particularly appealing to concrete or rational learners, all students may need to use it at one time or another depending on their topic.

Exercise 4.12

Do library or Internet research to generate ideas on one of the narrowed topics listed here.

1. A recent local disaster (hurricane, flood)
2. Shopping for clothes on the Internet or on television
3. Preventing terrorism in public buildings
4. Controlling children's access to television programs
5. Advantages or disadvantages of belonging to a health maintenance organization (HMO)

Exercise 4.13

Choose two prewriting techniques discussed in this chapter that appeal to you. Experiment with each method by generating ideas about one of the topics from the previous exercises in the chapter. These topics are listed in Table 4.3. Use a different topic for each prewriting technique you choose.

Essay in Progress 3

Keeping your audience and purpose in mind, use one of the prewriting strategies discussed in this chapter to generate details about the topic you narrowed in Essay in Progress 2.

TABLE 4.3   Broad Topics from Chapter 4 Exercises

Family Matters	Birth control
	Divorce
	Early childhood education
	Senior citizens
	Mental illness
	Year-round schooling
	Controlling children's access to television programs
College Life	Pressures on college students
	The campus newspaper
	Learning a foreign language
	Financial aid regulations
	Characteristics of a good teacher
	Attempts to regulate speech on campus
	A class you recently attended
	The campus snack bar
Community Concerns	Safe transportation
	Needed improvements in public education
	The increase in incidents of carjacking
	Community policing in urban areas
	A traffic jam
	A recent local disaster (hurricane, flood)
National Government	Military spending
	Environmental protection
	Affirmative action
	Presidential politics
	National parks
	Government aid to developing countries
	Effects of labor union strikes on workers
	Preventing terrorism in public buildings
World Issues	Global warming
Consumer Culture	Credit card fraud
	Web advertising
	Advertising directed toward children
	Buying a used car from a private individual
	Buying only American-made products
	Shopping for clothes on the Internet or on television
Entertainment Culture	Television programming
	Rap music
	Radio stations
	Value of music
	Late-night talk radio shows
	A sporting event

(continued on next page)

TABLE 4.3 *(continued)*	
Technology Issues	Blogs Instant messaging Cell phone usage
Everyday Life	How to be self-sufficient Job interviews Daydreaming The function of jewelry A couple obviously "in love" Advantages or disadvantages of belonging to a health maintenance organization (HMO)

Students Write

In this and the remaining five chapters of Part 2, we will follow the work of Christine Lee, a student in a first-year writing course who was assigned to write about a recent trend or fad in popular culture.

Lee decided to use questioning to narrow her topic and freewriting to generate ideas about the topic. Here is an example of her questioning.

SAMPLE QUESTIONING

What are some recent fads or trends?

Freak dancing

Political blogging

Extreme sports

Tattooing and body piercing

Reality TV

Lee decided to explore two of these experiences further: tattooing and body piercing and reality TV. She did so by asking another question.

Why are these trends popular?

1. Tattooing and body piercing

They are forms of self-expression.

They can be considered an art form--body art.

They can be used to commemorate a particular person or event, such as the loss of a loved one.

They can make a fashion statement and identify people as part of a group.

2. Reality TV

   People are more likely to identify with real people, not actors.

   The shows are usually contests, which keep viewers watching until the last episode.

   They are unscripted and often unpredictable.

   Survivor was popular because money was involved.

After looking over the answers to her questions, Lee chose reality TV as her topic, and she decided to focus on its evolution and popularity. The following excerpt from her freewriting shows how she started to develop her topic.

SAMPLE FREEWRITING

When *Survivor* was first on TV everyone was watching and talking about it at school and work. It was new and different, and it was interesting to watch how people started to act when a million dollars was at stake. Everybody had a favorite and someone else they loved to hate. After that season it seemed like every network had two or three reality shows they were trying out. They get more and more ridiculous and less tasteful with every new show. And now they are coming up with shows based on talent and beauty contests, like *American Idol*. Now I'm getting tired of all these "real" people as they defend their pettiness by saying "It's just a game." In the end I'll go back to watching *The Office* because it's funny (which *Big Brother* never is), and *ER* because they talk about serious issues that real people deal with. Maybe we'd all like to think that we wouldn't be as petty and mean as all of these contestants, but with all of these "real" people on TV these days, I can't relate to a single one of them.

As you work through the remaining chapters of Part 2, you will see how Lee develops her tentative thesis statement in Chapter 5, her first draft in Chapter 6, a specific paragraph in Chapter 7, and her final draft in Chapter 8. In addition, in Chapter 9, you will also see a portion of her final draft, edited and proofread to correct sentence-level errors.

Developing and Supporting a Thesis

WRITING QUICK START

Study the cartoon on the opposite page; it humorously depicts a serious situation.

Working alone or with one or two classmates, write a statement that expresses the main point of the cartoon. Your statement should not just describe what is happening in the cartoon but also state the idea that the cartoonist is trying to communicate to his audience.

The statement you have just written is an assertion around which you could build an essay. Such an assertion is called a *thesis statement.* In this chapter, you will learn how to write effective thesis statements and how to support them with evidence. Developing a thesis is an important part of the writing process shown in Figure 5.1, which lists the skills presented in this chapter while placing them within the context of the writing process.

FIGURE 5.1 An Overview of the Writing Process

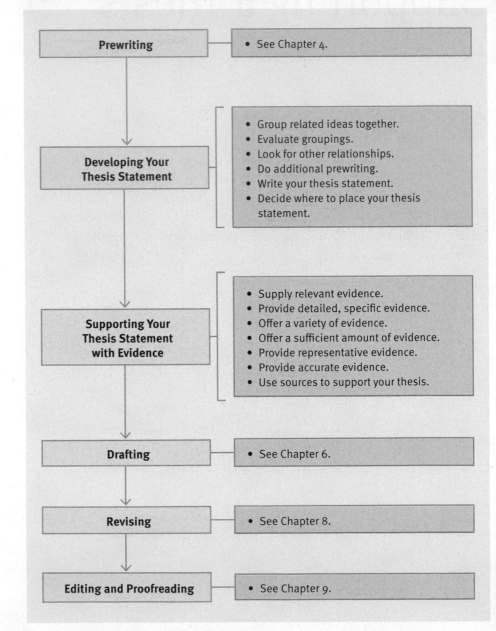

What Is a Thesis Statement?

A **thesis statement** is the main point of an essay. It explains what the essay will be about and expresses the writer's position on the subject. It may also give clues about how the essay will develop or how it will be organized. Usually a thesis statement is expressed in a single sentence. When you write, think of a thesis statement as a promise to your reader. The rest of your essay delivers on your promise.

Here is a sample thesis statement.

> Playing team sports, especially football and baseball, develops skills and qualities that can make you successful in life because these sports demand communication, teamwork, and responsibility.

In this thesis, the writer identifies the topic—team sports—and states the position that team sports, especially football and baseball, equip players with important skills and qualities. After reaching the end of this statement, the reader expects to discover what skills and qualities football and baseball players learn, and how these contribute to success in life.

Developing Your Thesis Statement

A thesis statement usually evolves or develops as you explore your topic during prewriting: Do not expect to be able to sit down and simply write one. As you prewrite, you may discover a new focus or a more interesting way to approach your topic. Expect to write several versions of a thesis statement before you find one that works. For some topics, you may need to do some reading or research to get more information about your topic or tentative thesis. Your thesis may change, too, as you organize supporting evidence and draft and revise your essay.

For more on prewriting, see Chapter 4.

For more on library and Internet research, see Chapter 21.

Your learning style can influence how you develop a thesis statement. Some students find it helpful to generate facts and details about a narrow topic and then write a thesis statement that reveals a large idea that is demonstrated by the details (pragmatic and concrete learners). Other students find it easier to begin with a broad idea, focus it in a thesis statement, and then generate details to support the thesis (creative and abstract learners).

Learning Style Options

Coming Up with a Working Thesis Statement

To come up with a preliminary or working thesis for your paper, reread your prewriting, and look for and highlight groups of details that all have to do with the same subtopic. Write a word or phrase that describes each group of related ideas.

For example, a student working on the topic of intelligence in dogs noticed in her brainstormed list that the details she highlighted could be grouped into two general categories—details about learning and details about instinct. Here is how she arranged her ideas.

<u>Learning</u>

follow commands

perform new tricks

read master's emotions

adapt to new owners

get housebroken

serve as guide dogs for blind people

roll up clothing to carry it more easily

carry empty water dish to owner

<u>Instinct</u>

females deliver and care for puppies

avoid danger and predators

seek shelter

automatically raise hair on back in response to aggression

Once you've grouped similar details together, the next step is to decide which group or groups of ideas best represent the focus your paper should take. In some instances, one group of details will be enough to develop a working thesis for your paper. At other times, you'll need to use the details in two or three groups. The student working on a thesis for the topic of intelligence in dogs evaluated her groups of details and decided that instinct was unrelated to her topic. Consequently, she decided to write about learning.

If you are not satisfied with how you have grouped or arranged your details, you probably don't have enough details to come up with a good working thesis. If you need more details, use prewriting to generate more ideas. Be sure to try a different prewriting strategy than the one you used previously. A new strategy may help you see your narrowed topic from a different perspective. If your second prewriting does not produce better results, consider refocusing or changing your topic.

For more on prewriting, see Chapter 4.

> **Essay in Progress 1**
> If you used a prewriting strategy to generate details about your topic in response to Essay in Progress 3 in Chapter 4 (p. 95), review your prewriting, highlight useful ideas, and identify several sets of related details among those you have highlighted.

Writing an Effective Thesis Statement

A thesis statement should introduce your narrowed topic, revealing what your essay is about, and state the point you will make about that topic. Use the following guidelines to write an effective thesis statement or to evaluate and revise your working thesis.

1. **Make an assertion.** An **assertion**, unlike a fact, takes a position, expresses a viewpoint, or suggests your approach toward the topic.

LACKS AN ASSERTION	Hollywood movies, like *Pearl Harbor* and *A Beautiful Mind*, are frequently based on true stories.
REVISED	Hollywood movies, like *Pearl Harbor* and *A Beautiful Mind*, manipulate true stories to cater to the tastes of the audience.

2. **Be specific.** Try to provide as much information as possible about your main point.

TOO GENERAL	I learned a great deal from my experiences as a teenage parent.
REVISED	From my experiences as a teenage parent, I learned to accept responsibility for my own life and for that of my son.

3. **Focus on one central point.** Limit your essay to one major idea.

FOCUSES ON SEVERAL POINTS	This college should improve its tutoring services, sponsor more activities of interest to Latino students, and speed up the registration process for students.
REVISED	To better represent the student population it serves, this college should sponsor more activities of interest to Latino students.

4. **Offer an original perspective on your topic.** If your thesis seems dull or ordinary, it probably needs more work. Search your prewriting for an interesting angle on your topic.

TOO ORDINARY	Many traffic accidents are a result of carelessness.
REVISED	When a driver has an accident, it can change his or her entire approach to driving.

5. **Avoid making an announcement.** Don't use phrases such as "This essay will discuss" or "The subject of my paper is." Instead, state your main point directly.

MAKES AN ANNOUNCEMENT	The point I am trying to make is that people should not be allowed to smoke on campus.
REVISED	The college should prohibit smoking on campus.

6. **Use your thesis to preview the organization of the essay.** Consider using your thesis to mention the two or three key concepts on which your essay will focus, in the order in which you will discuss them.

Exercise 5.1

Working in a group of two or three students, discuss what is wrong with each of the following thesis statements. Then revise each thesis to make it more effective.

1. In this paper, I will discuss the causes of asthma, which include exposure to smoke, chemicals, and allergic reactions.

2. Jogging is an enjoyable aerobic sport.

3. The crime rate is decreasing in American cities.

4. Living in an apartment has many advantages.

5. Children's toys can be dangerous, instructional, or creative.

Essay in Progress 2
Keeping your audience in mind, select one or more of the groups of ideas you
identified in Essay in Progress 1, and write a working thesis statement based on
these ideas.

Placing the Thesis Statement

Your thesis statement can appear anywhere in your essay, but it is usually best to place
it in the first paragraph as part of your introduction. When your thesis appears at the
beginning of the essay, your readers will know what to pay attention to and what to
expect in the rest of the essay. When your thesis is placed later in the essay, you need to
build up to the thesis gradually in order to prepare readers for it.

Using an Implied Thesis

In some professional writing, especially in narrative or descriptive essays, the writer
may not state the thesis directly. Instead, the thesis may be strongly implied by the
details the writer chooses and the way those details are organized. Although professional writers may use an implied thesis, academic writers—including professors and
students—generally state their thesis. You should always include a clear statement of
your thesis for your college papers.

Supporting Your Thesis Statement with Evidence

Once you have written a working thesis statement, the next step is to develop evidence
that supports your thesis. **Evidence** is any type of information, such as examples, statistics, or expert opinion, that will convince your reader that your thesis is reasonable or correct. This evidence, organized into well-developed paragraphs, makes up the
body of your essay. To visualize the basic structure of an essay, look ahead to Figure 6.2
on p. 117.

Choosing Types of Evidence

Although there are many types of evidence, it is usually best not to use them all.
Analyze your purpose, audience, and thesis to determine which types of evidence
will be most effective. If your audience is unfamiliar with your topic, provide definitions, historical background, an explanation of a process, and factual and descriptive
details. If your purpose is to persuade, use comparison and contrast, advantages and
disadvantages, examples, problems, statistics, and quotations to make your argument. Table 5.1 lists various types of evidence and gives examples of how each type
could be used to support a working thesis on acupuncture. Note that many of the
types of evidence correspond to the patterns of development discussed in Parts 3 and 4
of this text.

Exercise 5.2

1. Working in a group of two to three students, discuss and list the types of evidence that could be used to support the following thesis statement for an informative essay.

   The pressure to become financially independent is a challenge for many young adults and often causes them to develop social and emotional problems.

2. For each audience listed here, discuss and record the types of evidence that would offer the best support for the preceding thesis.

   a. Young adults   **c.** Counselors of young adults

   b. Parents of young adults

TABLE 5.1 Types of Evidence Used to Support a Thesis

Working Thesis	Acupuncture, a form of alternative medicine, is becoming more widely accepted in the United States.
Types of Evidence	**Example**
Definitions	Explain that in acupuncture, needles are inserted into specific points of the body to control pain or relieve symptoms.
Historical background	Explain that acupuncture is a medical treatment that originated in ancient China.
Explanation of a process	Explain the principles on which acupuncture is based and how scientists think it works.
Factual details	Explain who uses acupuncture, on what parts of the body it is used, and under what circumstances it is applied.
Descriptive details	Explain what acupuncture needles look and feel like.
Narrative story	Relate a personal experience that illustrates the use of acupuncture.
Causes or effects	Discuss one or two theories that explain why acupuncture works. Offer reasons for its increasing popularity.
Classification	Explain types of acupuncture treatments.
Comparison and contrast	Compare acupuncture to other forms of alternative medicine, such as massage and herbal medicines. Explain how acupuncture differs from these other treatments.
Advantages and disadvantages	Describe the pros (nonsurgical, relatively painless) and cons (fear of needles) of acupuncture.
Examples	Describe situations in which acupuncture has been used successfully: by dentists, in treating alcoholism, for pain control.
Problems	Explain that acupuncture is not always practiced by medical doctors; licensing and oversight of acupuncturists may thus be lax.
Statistics	Indicate how many acupuncturists practice in the United States.
Quotations	Quote medical experts who attest to the effectiveness of acupuncture as well as those who question its value.

Collecting Evidence to Support Your Thesis

Learning Style Options

Prewriting may help you collect evidence for your thesis. Try a different prewriting strategy from the one you used previously to arrive at a working thesis statement. Depending on your learning style, select one or more of the following suggestions to generate evidence that supports your thesis.

1. Complete the worksheet shown in Figure 5.2. For one or more types of evidence listed in the left column of the worksheet, give examples that support your thesis in the right column. Collect evidence only for those types that are appropriate for your thesis.
2. Visualize yourself speaking to your audience. What would you say to convince your audience of your thesis? Jot down ideas as they come to you.

For more on outlining, see Chapter 6, p. 122.

3. On a sheet of paper or in a computer file, develop a skeletal outline of major headings. Leave plenty of blank space under each heading. Fill in ideas about each heading as they come to you.

See p. 55 in Chapter 3 for instructions on drawing a graphic organizer. For samples of graphic organizers for each pattern of development, see Parts 3 and 4. To draw detailed graphic organizers using a computer, visit www.bedfordstmartins .com/successfulwriting.

4. Draw a graphic organizer of your essay, filling in supporting evidence as you think of it.
5. Discuss your thesis statement with a classmate; try to explain why he or she should accept your thesis as valid.

Essay in Progress 3

Using the preceding list of suggestions for collecting evidence to support a thesis, generate at least three different types of evidence to support the working thesis statement you wrote in Essay in Progress 2.

Choosing the Best Evidence

In collecting evidence in support of a thesis, you will probably generate more than you need. Consequently, you will need to identify the evidence that best supports your thesis and that suits your purpose and audience. Your learning style can also influence

Learning Style Options

the way you select evidence and the kinds of evidence you favor. If you are a creative or an abstract learner, for example, you may tend to focus on large ideas and overlook the need for supporting detail. However, if you are a pragmatic or concrete learner, you may tend to include too many details or fail to organize them logically.

The following guidelines will help you select the types of evidence that will best support your thesis.

1. **Make sure the evidence is relevant.** All of your evidence must clearly and directly support your thesis. Irrelevant evidence will distract your readers and cause them to question the validity of your thesis. If your thesis is that acupuncture is useful for controlling pain, you would not need to describe other, less popular alternative therapies.
2. **Provide specific evidence.** Avoid general statements that will neither engage your readers nor help you make a convincing case for your thesis. For instance, to support the thesis that acupuncture is becoming more widely accepted by patients in the United States, it would be most convincing to cite statistics that demonstrate

FIGURE 5.2 A Worksheet for Collecting Evidence

Purpose: _____

Audience: _____

Point of View: _____

Thesis Statement: _____

_____

Type of Evidence	Actual Evidence
Definitions	
Historical background	
Explanation of a process	
Factual details	
Descriptive details	
Narrative story	
Causes or effects	
Classification	
Comparison and contrast	
Advantages and disadvantages	
Examples	

(continued on next page)

FIGURE 5.2 *(continued)*

Type of Evidence	Actual Evidence
Problems	
Statistics	
Quotations	

an increase in the number of practicing acupuncturists in the United States over the past five years.

To locate detailed, specific evidence, return to your prewriting or use a different prewriting strategy to generate concrete evidence. You may also need to conduct research to find evidence for your thesis.

For more on conducting research, see Chapters 20–22.

3. **Offer a variety of evidence.** Using diverse kinds of evidence increases the likelihood that your evidence will convince your readers. If you provide only four examples of people who have found acupuncture helpful, for example, many of your readers may conclude that these few isolated examples are not convincing. If you provide statistics and quotations from experts along with an example or two, however, more readers will be likely to accept your thesis. Using different types of evidence also shows readers that you are knowledgeable and informed about your topic, thus enhancing your own credibility.

4. **Provide a sufficient amount of evidence.** The amount of evidence you need will vary according to your audience and your topic. To discover whether you have provided enough evidence, ask a classmate to read your essay and tell you whether he or she is convinced. If your reader is not convinced, ask him or her what additional evidence is needed.

5. **Provide representative evidence.** Be sure the evidence you supply is typical and usual. Do not choose unusual, rare, or exceptional situations as evidence. Suppose your thesis is that acupuncture is widely used for various types of surgery. An example of one person who underwent painless heart surgery using only acupuncture without anesthesia will not support your thesis unless the use of acupuncture in heart surgery is routine. Including such an example would mislead your reader and could bring your credibility into question.

For more on choosing reliable sources, see Chapter 20, p. 562.

6. **Provide accurate evidence.** Gather your information from reliable sources. Do not guess at statistics or make estimates. If you are not certain of the accuracy of a fact or statistic, verify it through research. For example, do not estimate the number of medical doctors who are licensed to practice acupuncture in the United States. Instead, find out exactly how many U.S. physicians are licensed to practice.

Choosing Evidence for Academic Writing

For most kinds of academic writing, certain types of evidence are preferred over others. In general, your personal experiences and opinions are not considered as useful as more objective evidence such as facts, statistics, historical background, and research evidence. Suppose you are writing an academic paper on the effects of global warming. Your own observations about climate changes in your city would not be considered adequate or appropriate evidence to support the idea of climatic change as an effect of global warming. Instead, you would need to provide facts, statistics, and research evidence on climatic change in a wide range of geographic areas and demonstrate their relationship to global warming.

Essay in Progress 4
Evaluate the evidence you generated in Essay in Progress 3. Select from it the evidence that you could use to support your thesis in a two- to four-page essay.

Using Sources to Support Your Thesis

For many topics, you will need to research library or Internet sources or interview an expert on your topic to collect enough supporting evidence for your thesis. Chapter 21 provides a thorough guide to locating sources in the library and on the Internet, and it also includes tips for conducting interviews (p. 593). Chapter 22 provides guidelines for integrating and documenting sources. Also see "Using Sources to Add Details to an Essay" on page 555 of Chapter 20.

Essay in Progress 5
Locate and consult at least two sources to find evidence that supports the working thesis statement you wrote in Essay in Progress 2.

Students Write

In the Students Write section of Chapter 4, you saw how student writer Christine Lee narrowed her topic and generated ideas for her essay on a contemporary fad. You also saw how she decided to focus on reality TV.

After reviewing her responses to questions about her topic and her freewriting, Lee decided that reality TV had become less tasteful and less interesting. She then wrote the following working thesis statement.

> As the trend in reality TV wears on, shows are becoming both less interesting and less tasteful.

To generate more details to support her thesis, Lee did more freewriting and brainstorming to help her recall details from shows. Here's an excerpt from what she wrote:

- Early shows: *Cops* and *Candid Camera*
- MTV's *Real World* was first recent reality show to become popular.

- Original Survivor was smart and interesting.
- Big Brother just locked people up together and forced us to watch them bicker.
- The Survivor series continues to be popular, while copycats like Murder in Small Town X and Fear Factor get more graphic and unwatchable.
- People will tire of Fear Factor quickly because there is no plot to follow from one episode to the next and watching people eat worms and hold their breath underwater gets boring.
- Reality TV was popular because it was something different, but now there are dozens of these shows each season and few worth watching.
- Murder in Small Town X opens with a reenactment from the murderer's point of view and ends with the audience watching one of two players getting "attacked" and "killed."
- Shows such as American Idol and America's Top Model are a revival of earlier types of TV shows--the talent show and the beauty contest.

Working with Text

READING

Pet Therapy for Heart and Soul
Kerry Pechter

The following essay by Kerry Pechter was first published in 1985 in *Prevention* magazine, a periodical that focuses on promoting a healthy lifestyle. Later the article appeared in a collection of essays, *Your Emotional Health and Well-Being* (1989). Pechter supports the essay's thesis with a variety of evidence. As you read, underline the thesis statement, and examine the types of evidence that are offered to support it.

It's exercise hour at the Tacoma Lutheran Home in the state of Washington, and P.T., an 1 exotic yellow-crested bird called a cockatiel, is having the time of his life. He's sitting on the foot of 81-year-old Ben Ereth, riding in circles while Ben pedals vigorously on an exercise bicycle. The bird likes it so much that if Mr. Ereth stops too soon, he'll squawk at him.

A bizarre sort of activity to find in a nursing home? Not at Tacoma Lutheran. 2 Three years ago, the nursing home adopted an angora rabbit. Then a puppy. Then tropical birds. The home's elderly residents have taken to these animals with a passion. And, says Virginia Davis, director of resident services, the animals have breathed enthusiasm into what otherwise might have been a listless nursing home atmosphere.

"The animals help in several ways," says Davis. "One of the cockatiels gives a wolf 3 whistle whenever anyone passes its cage. That gives them an unexpected boost in morale. And the birds seem to alleviate the tension associated with exercise. They make exercise more acceptable and relaxing."

What's happening at Tacoma Lutheran is just one example of an increasingly popular 4 phenomenon called pet therapy. Although humans have adopted pets for thousands of years, only recently have social scientists taken a close look at the nature of the relationship that people form with dogs, cats, and other "companion animals."

At places like the Center for the Interaction of Animals and Society in Philadelphia 5
and the Center for the Study of Human Animal Relationships and Environments (CENSHARE) in Minneapolis, they've discovered that there is something mutually therapeutic about these relationships. They say that pets relax us, help us communicate with each other, build our self-esteem, and comfort us when we're feeling down.

In fact, many now believe that pets play a small but very significant role in deter- 6
mining how well, for example, a heart attack survivor recuperates, how a family handles domestic strife, whether a disturbed teenager grows up straight, or even whether a nursing home resident like Mr. Freth enjoys and sticks to his daily exercycle program.

Pet animals, in short, may affect our health. 7

ANIMAL MAGNETISM AT WORK

Pet therapists have put these capacities to work in a variety of ways. Pet therapy is very 8
often used, for example, to combat the isolation and loneliness so common in nursing homes. At the Tacoma Lutheran Home, Davis has found that the pets help many residents break their customary silence.

"Animals are a catalyst for conversation," she says. "Most people can remember 9
a story from their past about a pet animal. And people are more comfortable talking to animals than they are to people. Sometimes a person who hasn't spoken for a long time, or one who has had a stroke and doesn't talk, will talk to an animal."

Animals also seem to draw everyone into the conversation. "Even in a nursing 10
home, there are some people who are more attractive or responsive than others," says Phil Arkow, of the Humane Society of the Pike's Peak Region in Colorado, who drives a "Petmobile" to local nursing homes. "Human visitors try not to do it, but they inevitably focus on those who are most attractive. But animals don't make those distinctions. They focus on everyone equally."

A person doesn't have to live in a nursing home, however, in order to reap the 11
benefits of a pet. Pets typically influence the communication that goes on between family members in a normal household. During a research project a few years ago, University of Maryland professor Ann Cain, Ph.D., discovered that pets help spouses and siblings express highly charged feelings.

"When family members want to say something to each other that they can't say di- 12
rectly," Dr. Cain says, "they might say it to the pet and let the other person overhear it. That also lets the listener off the hook, because he doesn't have to respond directly."

Though it's still in the experimental stage, researchers are discovering that watching 13
or petting friendly animals—not only dogs and cats but almost any pet—can produce the kind of deep relaxation usually associated with meditation, biofeedback, and hypnosis. This kind of relaxing effect is so good that it can actually lower blood pressure.

At the University of Pennsylvania's Center for the Interaction of Animals and Society, 14
for instance, Dr. Katcher and Dr. Friedmann monitored the blood pressure of healthy children while the children were sitting quietly or reading aloud, either with or without a dog in the room. Their blood pressure was always lower when the dog was in the room.

The researchers went on to discover, remarkably, that looking at fish could tempo- 15
rarily reduce the blood pressure of patients with hypertension. In one widely reported study, they found that the systolic and diastolic pressure of people with high blood

pressure dipped into the normal range when they gazed at an aquarium full of colorful tropical fish, green plants, and rocks for 20 minutes.

This calming power of pets has found at least a few noteworthy applications. In Chicago, one volunteer from the Anti-Cruelty Society took an animal to a hospital and arranged for a surgical patient to be greeted by it when he awoke from anesthesia. "It's a comforting way to come back to reality," says one volunteer. "For children, pets can make a hospital seem safer. It's a reminder of home." 16

Animals may also have the power to soften the aggressive tendencies of disturbed adolescents. At Winslow Therapeutic Riding Unlimited, Inc., in Warwick, New York, where horseback riding is used to help handicapped children of all kinds, problem teenagers seem to behave differently when they're put on a horse. 17

"These are kids who fight in school. Some of their fathers are alcoholics," says Mickey Pulis of the nonprofit facility. "But when they come here, they're different. When they groom and tack the horses, they learn about the gentle and caring side of life. 18

"The horse seems to act like an equalizer," she says. "It doesn't care what reading levels these kids are at. It accepts them as they are." 19

Ultimately, researchers like Dr. Friedmann believe that the companionship of pets can reduce a person's risk of dying from stress-related illnesses, such as heart disease. 20

"The leading causes of mortality and morbidity in the United States are stress-related or life-style related," she says. "Pets, by decreasing the level of arousal and moderating the stress response, can help slow the progression of those diseases or even prevent them." 21

PETS ARE COMFORTING

But what is it about pets that make them capable of all this? And why do millions of people go to the trouble and expense of keeping them? Pet therapists offer several answers. 22

For one thing, animals don't talk back to us. Researchers have discovered that a person's blood pressure goes up whenever he talks to another person. But we talk to animals in a different way, often touching them at the same time, which minimizes stress. 23

Another theory holds that pets remind us of our ancestral link with other animals. "By domesticating an animal, man demonstrates his kinship to nature," Dr. Levinson once wrote. "A human being has to remain in contact with all of nature throughout his lifetime if he is to maintain good mental health." 24

Dr. Corson, on the other hand, says that we love pets because they are perpetual infants. Human infants charm us, but they eventually grow up. Pets never do. They never stop being cuddly and dependent. Likewise, pets are faithful. "Pets can offer a relationship that is more constant than relationships with people," says Dr. Cain. "You can count on them." 25

Some argue that the most important ingredient in our relationships with animals is that we can touch them whenever we want to. "Having access to affectionate touch that is not related to sex is important," says Dr. Katcher. "If you want to touch another person, you can't always do it immediately. But with pets you can." 26

Examining the Reading

1. Define the term *pet therapy.*
2. What characteristics do pets possess that make them good therapists?

3. In what situations, other than nursing homes, are pets beneficial?
4. Define each of the following words as it is used in the essay: *bizarre* (paragraph 2), *alleviate* (paragraph 3), *therapeutic* (paragraph 5), *catalyst* (paragraph 9), and *morbidity* (paragraph 21).

Analyzing the Writer's Technique

1. State the author's thesis in your own words. Then, using the guidelines on pages 102–103, evaluate the effectiveness of the thesis.
2. To what audience does Pechter address this essay? What purpose does the essay fulfill? How do you think the audience and purpose affect the author's choice of evidence?
3. What types of evidence does the author use to support the thesis? Which type does the author rely on most? What other types of evidence could the author have used? (Refer to Table 5.1, p. 105, for a summary of the various types of evidence.)
4. Do you think the author provides sufficient evidence for you to accept the thesis? Why or why not?
5. Cite one paragraph from the essay in which you think the author provides detailed, specific information. Explain why you chose it.

Visualizing the Reading

The reading presents numerous reasons why pets are useful and effective for human therapy. Use the chart below to record at least five reasons and the evidence used to support each. The first one has been done for you.

Reasons	Evidence
1. Pets boost morale and make exercise more acceptable	Cockatiel sitting on foot of nursing home residents using an exercise bicycle

Reacting to the Reading

1. How do you think this essay would change if the writer wrote it for readers of *Dog Fancy*, a magazine for dog owners?
2. Most pet owners talk to their pets even though the pets probably do not understand most of what is being said. In what sense is this "talk" therapeutic?
3. In your journal, write about other activities or types of recreation that you find relaxing or comforting because they remind you of your kinship to nature.

CHAPTER 6

Drafting an Essay

WRITING QUICK START

The photographs on the opposite page show a few of the technologies that have reshaped the way we experience the world and interact with others. Study these photographs, and think of other recent technological innovations.

Working alone or with two or three classmates, write a sentence that states your opinion of how electronic media have affected society. Then support this opinion with a list of details (evidence) from the three photographs and from your own knowledge of new technologies. Number your best evidence 1, your second-best evidence 2, and so on. Cross out any details that do not support your opinion, or adjust the sentence if the evidence you gathered disagrees with it. Finally, write a paragraph that begins with the sentence you wrote and includes your evidence in order of importance.

The paragraph you have just written could be part of an essay on the topic of how access to electronic media varies in developed and developing countries. To write an essay you would need to do additional prewriting and research to learn more about this topic. Then you would write a thesis statement, develop supporting paragraphs, write an effective introduction and conclusion, and choose a good title. This chapter will guide you through the process of developing an essay in support of a thesis statement, as part of the writing process shown in Figure 6.1.

The Structure of an Essay

Think of an essay as a complete piece of writing, much as a textbook chapter is. For example, a textbook chapter might have the title "Human Rights in Developing Countries," which gives you a clear idea of the chapter's subject. The first few paragraphs of the chapter would probably introduce and define the concept of human rights. The chapter might then assert that human rights is a controversial global issue of growing importance. The rest of the chapter might explain the issue by tracing its history, examining why it is a world issue, and discussing its current status. The chapter would conclude with a summary.

Similarly, as you can see in Figure 6.2 on page 117, an essay has a title and an introduction. It also makes an assertion (the thesis statement) that is explained and

FIGURE 6.1 An Overview of the Writing Process

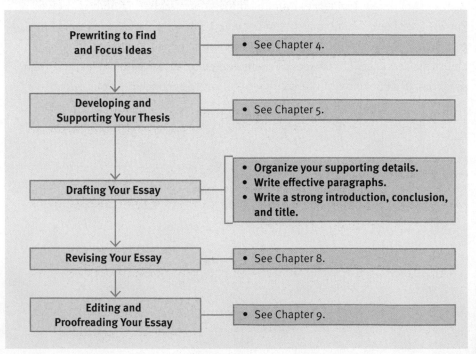

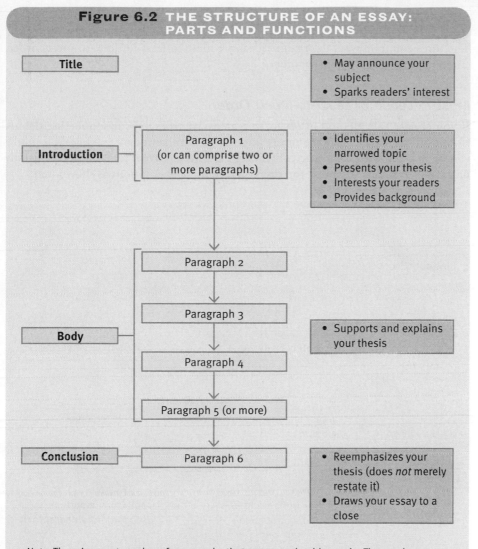

Figure 6.2 THE STRUCTURE OF AN ESSAY: PARTS AND FUNCTIONS

Title
- May announce your subject
- Sparks readers' interest

Introduction
Paragraph 1 (or can comprise two or more paragraphs)
- Identifies your narrowed topic
- Presents your thesis
- Interests your readers
- Provides background

Body
Paragraph 2
Paragraph 3
Paragraph 4
Paragraph 5 (or more)
- Supports and explains your thesis

Conclusion
Paragraph 6
- Reemphasizes your thesis (does *not* merely restate it)
- Draws your essay to a close

Note: There is no set number of paragraphs that an essay should contain. The number depends on your narrowed topic, purpose, and audience.

supported throughout the body of the essay. The essay ends with a final statement, its conclusion.

Organizing Your Supporting Details

The body of your essay contains the paragraphs that support your thesis. Before you begin writing these body paragraphs, decide on the supporting evidence you will use and the order in which you will present your evidence.

For more on developing a thesis and selecting evidence to support it, see Chapter 5.

Selecting a Method of Organization

The three common ways to organize ideas are most-to-least (or least-to-most) order, chronological order, and spatial order.

Most-to-Least (or Least-to-Most) Order

If you choose this method of organizing an essay, arrange your supporting details from most to least (or least to most) important, familiar, or interesting. You might choose to begin with your most convincing evidence or save it for last, building gradually to your strongest point. You can visualize these two options as shown here.

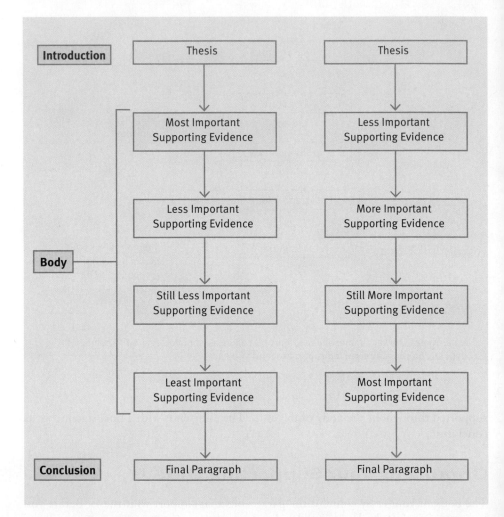

A student, Robin Ferguson, was working on the thesis statement "Working as a literacy volunteer taught me more about learning and friendship than I ever expected" and identified four primary benefits related to her thesis.

BENEFITS

- I learned about the learning process.
- I developed a permanent friendship with my student, Marie.
- Marie built self-confidence.
- I discovered the importance of reading.

Ferguson then chose to arrange these benefits from least to most important and decided that the friendship was the most important benefit. Here is how she organized her supporting evidence.

WORKING THESIS

Working as a literacy volunteer taught me more about learning and friendship than I ever expected.

LEAST	Supporting paragraph 1:	Learned about the learning process
TO	Supporting paragraph 2:	Discovered the importance of reading for Marie
MOST	Supporting paragraph 3:	Marie increased her self-confidence
IMPORTANT	Supporting paragraph 4:	Developed a permanent friendship

---

Exercise 6.1

For each of the following narrowed topics, identify several qualities or characteristics that you could use to organize details in most-to-least or least-to-most order.

1. Three stores in which you shop
2. Three friends
3. Three members of a sports team
4. Three fast-food restaurants
5. Three television shows you watched this week

Chronological Order

When you arrange your supporting details in **chronological order**, you put them in the order in which they happened. When using this method of organization, begin the body of your essay with the first event, and progress through the others as they occurred. Depending on the subject of your essay, the events could be minutes, days, or years apart. Chronological order is commonly used in narrative essays and process analyses. You can visualize this order as follows.

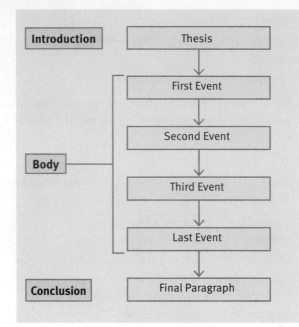

As an example, let's suppose that Robin Ferguson, writing about her experiences as a literacy volunteer, decides to demonstrate her thesis by relating the events of a typical tutoring session. In this case, she might organize her essay by narrating the events in the order in which they usually occur, using each detail about the session to demonstrate what tutoring taught her about learning and friendship.

Exercise 6.2

Working alone or with a classmate, identify at least one thesis statement from those listed below that could be supported by chronological paragraphs. Write a few sentences explaining how you would use chronological order to support this thesis.

1. European mealtimes differ from those of many American visitors, much to the visitors' surprise and discomfort.

2. Despite the many pitfalls that await those who shop at auctions, people can find bargains if they prepare in advance.

3. My first day of kindergarten was the most traumatic experience of my childhood, one that permanently shaped my view of education.

4. Learning how to drive a car increases a teenager's freedom and responsibility.

Spatial Order

When you use **spatial order**, you organize details about your subject according to their location or position in space. Consider, for example, how you might use spatial order to support the thesis that modern movie theaters are designed to shut out the outside world and create a separate reality within. You could begin by describing the ticket booth, then the lobby, and finally the individual theaters. Similarly, you might describe a basketball court from right to left or a person from head to toe. Robin Ferguson, writing about her experiences as a literacy volunteer, could describe her classroom or meeting area from front to back or left to right. Spatial organization is commonly used in descriptive essays as well as in classification and division essays.

You can best visualize spatial organization by picturing your subject in your mind or by sketching it on paper. "Look" at your subject systematically—from top to bottom, inside to outside, front to back. Cut it into imaginary sections or pieces and describe each piece. Here are two possible options for visualizing an essay that uses spatial order.

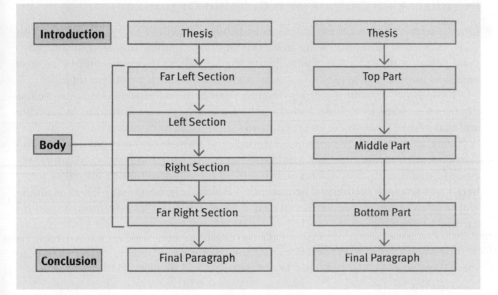

Exercise 6.3

Working alone or with a classmate, identify one thesis statement listed below that could be supported by means of spatial organization. Write a few sentences explaining how you would use spatial order to support this thesis.

1. Our family's yearly vacation at a cabin in Maine provides us with a much needed opportunity to renew family ties.

2. The Civic Theatre of Allentown's set for Tennessee Williams's play *A Streetcar Named Desire* was simple, yet striking and effective.

3. Although a pond in winter may seem frozen and lifeless, this appearance is deceptive.

4. A clear study space can cut down on time-wasting distractions.

Essay in Progress 1
Choose one of the following activities.

1. Using the thesis statement and evidence you gathered for the Essay in Progress activities in Chapter 5, choose a method for organizing your essay. Then explain briefly how you will use that method of organization.
2. Choose one of the following narrowed topics. Then, using the steps in Figure 6.1, An Overview of the Writing Process (p. 116), prewrite to produce ideas, develop a thesis, and generate evidence to support the thesis. Next, choose a method for organizing your essay. Explain briefly how you will use that method of organization.
   a. Positive or negative experiences with computers
   b. Stricter (or more lenient) regulations for teenage drivers
   c. Factors that account for the popularity of action films
   d. Discipline in public elementary schools
   e. Advantages or disadvantages of instant messaging

Preparing an Outline or a Graphic Organizer

Once you have written a thesis statement and chosen a method of organization for your essay, take a few minutes to write an outline or draw a graphic organizer of the essay's main points in the order you plan to discuss them. Making an organizational plan is an especially important step when your essay is long or deals with a complex topic.

Outlining or drawing a graphic organizer can help you plan your essay as well as discover new ideas to include. Either method will help you see how ideas fit together and may reveal places where you need to add supporting information.

There are two types of outlines—informal and formal. An **informal outline**, also called a *scratch outline,* uses key words and phrases to list main points and subpoints. An informal outline does not necessarily follow the standard outline format of numbered and lettered headings. The outline of Robin Ferguson's essay below is an example of an informal outline. Recall that she chose to use a least-to-most-important method of organization.

SAMPLE INFORMAL OUTLINE

Thesis: Working as a literacy volunteer taught me more about learning and friendship than I ever expected.

Paragraph 1: Learned about the learning process
- Went through staff training program
- Learned about words "in context"

Paragraph 2: Discovered the importance of reading for Marie
- Couldn't take bus, walked to grocery store
- Couldn't buy certain products
- Couldn't write out grocery lists

Paragraph 3: Marie increased her self-confidence
- Made rapid progress

- Began taking bus
- Helped son with reading

<u>Paragraph 4</u>: Developed a permanent friendship

- Saw each other often
- Both single parents
- Helped each other baby-sit

<u>Conclusion</u>: I benefited more than Marie did.

Formal outlines use Roman numerals (I, II), capital letters (A, B), arabic numbers (1, 2), and lowercase letters (a, b) to designate levels of importance. Formal outlines fall into two categories: *Sentence outlines* use complete sentences, and *topic outlines* use only key words and phrases. In a topic or sentence outline, less important entries are indented, as in the sample formal outline below. Each topic or sentence begins with a capital letter.

FORMAT FOR A FORMAL OUTLINE

I.   First main topic
   A.   First subtopic of I
   B.   Second subtopic of I
      1.   First detail about I.B
      2.   Second detail about I.B
   C.   Third subtopic of I
      1.   First detail about I.C
         a.   First detail or example about I.C.1
         b.   Second detail or example about I.C.1
      2.   Second detail about I.C
II. Second main topic

Here is a sample outline that a student wrote for an essay for her interpersonal communication class:

SAMPLE FORMAL OUTLINE

I.   Types of listening
   A.   Participatory
      1.   Involves the listener responding to the speaker
      2.   Has expressive quality
         a.   Maintain eye contact
         b.   Express feelings using facial expressions
   B.   Nonparticipatory
      1.   Involves listener listening without talking or responding
      2.   Allows speaker to develop his or her thoughts without interruption
   C.   Critical listening
      1.   Involves listener analyzing and evaluating the message
      2.   Is especially important in college classes
         a.   Listen for instructors' biases
         b.   Evaluate evidence in support of opinions expressed

For more on parallel structure, see Chapter 9, p. 186.

Remember that all items labeled with the same designation (capital letters, for example) should be at the same level of importance, and each must explain or support the topic or subtopic under which it is placed. Also, all items at the same level should be grammatically parallel.

NOT
PARALLEL
	I. Dietary Problems
	   A. Consuming too much fat
	   B. High refined-sugar consumption

PARALLEL	I. Dietary Problems
	   A. Consuming too much fat
	   B. Consuming too much refined sugar

If your instructor allows, you can use both phrases and sentences within an outline, as long as you do so consistently. You might write all subtopics (designated by capital letters A, B, and so on) as sentences and all supporting details (designated by 1, 2, and so on) as phrases, for instance.

Learning Style Options

For more about graphic organizers, see Chapter 3, p. 55.

If you have a pragmatic learning style or a verbal learning style or both, preparing an outline will probably appeal to you. If you are a creative or spatial learner, however, you may prefer to draw a graphic organizer. Whichever method you find most appealing, begin by putting your working thesis statement at the top of a piece of paper or word-processing document. Then list your main points below your thesis. Be sure to leave plenty of space between main points. While you are filling in the details that support one main point, you will often think of details or examples to use in support of a different one. As these details or examples occur to you, jot them down under or next to the appropriate main point of your outline or graphic organizer.

The graphic organizer shown in Figure 6.3 was done for Ferguson's essay. Notice that it follows the least-to-most-important method of organization, as did her informal outline on page 122.

> ### Essay in Progress 2
> For the topic you chose in Essay in Progress 1, write a brief outline or draw a graphic organizer to show the organizational plan of your essay.

Using Transitions and Repetition to Connect Your Ideas

To show how your ideas are related, be sure to use transitions between sentences and paragraphs as well as repetition of key words and the synonyms and pronouns that refer to them. Use transitions and repetition both within your paragraphs (see Chapter 7, p. 149) and between paragraphs.

Coherent Essays Use Transitional Expressions to Connect Ideas

A **transitional expression**—which can be a word, phrase, clause, or sentence—shows the reader how a new sentence or paragraph is connected to the one that precedes it. It may also remind the reader of an idea discussed earlier in the essay.

Figure 6.3 SAMPLE GRAPHIC ORGANIZER

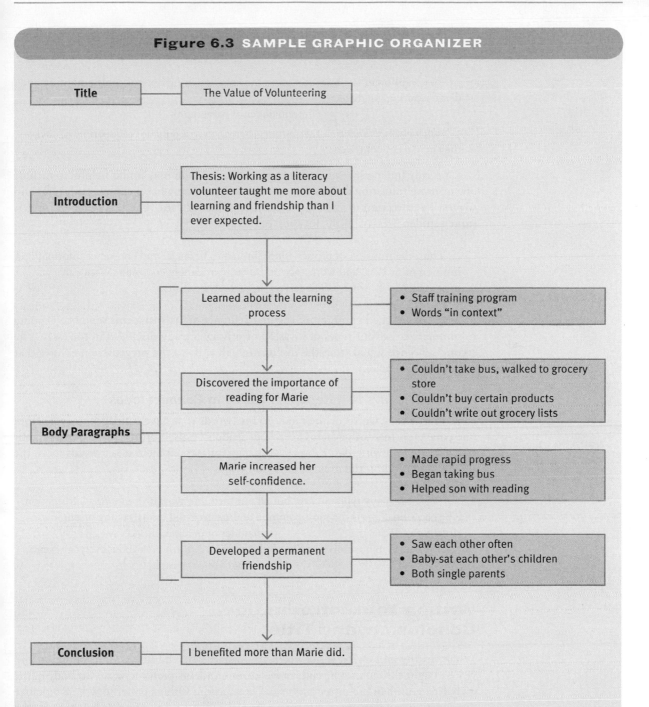

Title — The Value of Volunteering

Introduction — Thesis: Working as a literacy volunteer taught me more about learning and friendship than I ever expected.

Learned about the learning process
- Staff training program
- Words "in context"

Discovered the importance of reading for Marie
- Couldn't take bus, walked to grocery store
- Couldn't buy certain products
- Couldn't write out grocery lists

Body Paragraphs

Marie increased her self-confidence.
- Made rapid progress
- Began taking bus
- Helped son with reading

Developed a permanent friendship
- Saw each other often
- Baby-sat each other's children
- Both single parents

Conclusion — I benefited more than Marie did.

In the example that follows, the italicized transitional clause connects the two paragraphs by reminding the reader of the main point of the first.

> A compliment is a brief and pleasant way of opening lines of communication and demonstrating goodwill. _____
> [remainder of paragraph]
> *Although compliments do demonstrate goodwill,* they should be used sparingly; otherwise they may seem contrived. _____

Especially in lengthy essays (five pages or longer), you may find it helpful to include one or more transitional clauses or sentences that recap what you have said so far and suggest the direction of the essay from that point forward. The following example is from a student's essay on the invasion of privacy.

> Thus, the invasion of privacy is not limited to financial and consumer information; invasion of medical and workplace privacy is increasingly common. What can individuals do to protect their privacy in each of these areas?

The *Thus* at the beginning of the first sentence signals that this sentence is going to summarize the four types of invasion of privacy already discussed in the essay. The second sentence signals that the discussion will shift to the preventive measures that individuals can take.

Coherent Essays Use Repeated Words to Connect Ideas

Repetition of key words or their **synonyms** (words that have similar meanings) from one paragraph to another helps keep your readers focused on the main point of your essay. In the following two abbreviated paragraphs, the italicized key words focus the readers' attention on the topic of liars and lying.

> There are many types of *liars,* but all put forth *dishonest* or *misleading* information. The occasional *liar* is the most common and *lies* to avoid embarrassing or unpleasant situations.   [remainder of paragraph]
> Less common but still dangerous is the habitual *liar,* who *lies* about everyday events.
> [remainder of paragraph]

Writing Your Introduction, Conclusion, and Title

When writing an essay, it is not necessary to start with the title and introduction and write straight through to the end. In fact, some students prefer to write the body of the essay first and then the introduction and conclusion. Others prefer to write a tentative introduction as a way of getting started. Some students think of a title before they start writing; others find it easier to add a title when the essay is nearly finished. Regardless of when you write them, the introduction, conclusion, and title are important components of a well-written essay.

Writing a Strong Introduction

Your introduction creates a first, and often lasting, impression. It focuses your readers on your topic and establishes the tone of your essay—how you "sound" to your readers and what attitude you take toward them. Based on your introduction, your readers will form an expectation of what the essay will be about and the approach it will take. Because the introduction is crucial, take the time to get it right.

For more on tone, see Chapter 9, p. 189.

Two sample introductions to student essays follow. Although they are written on the same topic, notice how each creates an entirely different impression and set of expectations.

INTRODUCTION 1

The issue of sexual harassment has received a great deal of attention in recent years. From the highest offices of government to factories in small towns, sexual harassment cases have been tried in court and publicized on national television for all Americans to witness. This focus on sexual harassment has been, in and of itself, a good and necessary thing. However, when a little boy in first grade makes national headlines for having kissed a little girl of the same age, and the incident is labeled "sexual harassment," the American public needs to take a serious look at the definition of sexual harassment.

INTRODUCTION 2

Sexual harassment in the workplace seems to be happening with alarming frequency. As a woman who works part time in a male-dominated office, I have witnessed at least six incidents of sexual harassment aimed at me and my female colleagues on various occasions during the past three months alone. For example, in one incident, a male co-worker repeatedly made kissing sounds whenever I passed his desk, even after I explained that his actions made me uncomfortable. A female co-worker was invited to dinner several times by her male supervisor; each time she refused. The last time she refused, he made a veiled threat, "You obviously aren't happy working with me. Perhaps a transfer is in order." These incidents were not isolated, did not happen to only one woman, and were initiated by more than one man. My colleagues and I are not the only victims. Sexual harassment is on the rise and will continue to increase unless women speak out against it loudly and to a receptive audience.

In introduction 1, the writer focuses on the definition of sexual harassment. Introduction 2 has an entirely different emphasis—the frequency of incidents of sexual harassment. Each introductory paragraph reveals a different tone as well. Introduction 1 suggests a sense of mild disbelief, whereas introduction 2 suggests anger and outrage. From introduction 1, you expect the writer to examine definitions of sexual harassment and, perhaps, suggest his or her own definition. From introduction 2, you expect the writer to present additional cases of sexual harassment and suggest ways women can speak out against it.

In addition to establishing a focus and tone, your introduction should:

- present your thesis statement
- interest your reader
- provide any background information your reader may need

Introductions are often difficult to write. If you have trouble, write a tentative introductory paragraph and return to it later. Once you have written the body of your essay, you may find it easier to complete the introduction. In fact, as you work out your ideas in the body of the essay, you may think of a better way to introduce them in the opening.

Tips for Writing a Strong Introduction

The following suggestions for writing a strong introduction will help you capture your readers' interest.

1. **Ask a provocative or disturbing question.** Or consider posing a series of short, related questions that will direct your readers' attention to the key points in your essay.

   Should health insurance companies pay for more than one stay in a drug rehabilitation center? Should insurance continue to pay for rehab services when patients consistently put themselves back into danger by using drugs again?

2. **Begin with a story or anecdote.** Choose one that will appeal to your audience and is relevant to your thesis.

   I used to believe that it was possible to stop smoking by simply quitting cold turkey. When I tried this approach, I soon realized that quitting was not so simple. When I did not smoke for even a short period of time, I became so uncomfortable that I started again just to alleviate the discomfort. I realized then that in order to quit smoking, I would need a practical solution that would overcome my cravings.

3. **Offer a quotation.** The quotation should illustrate or emphasize your thesis.

   As Indira Gandhi once said, "You cannot shake hands with a clenched fist." This truism is important to remember whenever people communicate with one another but particularly when they are attempting to resolve a conflict. Both parties need to agree that there is a problem and then agree to listen to each other with an open mind. Shaking hands is a productive way to begin working toward a resolution.

4. **Cite a little-known or shocking fact or statistic.**

   Recent research has shown that the color pink has a calming effect on people. In fact, a prison detention center in western New York was recently painted pink to make prisoners more controllable in the days following their arrest.

   Between 1963 and 1993, there was a 26 percent increase in the proportion of college students who admitted copying academic work from another student. This increase suggests that students' attitude toward cheating changed dramatically during that thirty-year period.

5. **Move from general to specific. Begin with the category or general subject area to which your topic belongs, and narrow it to arrive at your thesis.**

   The First Amendment is the basis for several cherished rights in the United States, and free speech is among them. Therefore, it would seem unlawful—even anti-American—for a disc jockey to be fired for expressing his or her views on the radio, regardless of whether those views are unpopular or offensive.

6. State a commonly held misconception or a position that you oppose. Your thesis would then correct the misconception or state your position on the issue.

Many people have the mistaken notion that only homosexuals and drug users are in danger of contracting AIDS. In fact, many heterosexuals also suffer from this debilitating disease. Furthermore, the number of heterosexuals who test HIV-positive has increased substantially over the past decade. It is time the American public became better informed about the prevention and treatment of AIDS.

7. Describe a hypothetical situation.

Suppose you were in a serious car accident and became unconscious. Suppose further that you slipped into a coma, with little hope for recovery. Unless you had a prewritten health-care proxy that designated someone familiar with your wishes to act on your behalf, your fate would be left in the hands of medical doctors who knew nothing about you or your preferences for treatment.

8. Begin with a striking example.

The penal system is sometimes too concerned with protecting the rights of the criminal instead of the victim. For example, during a rape trial, the victim is often questioned about his or her sexual history by the defense attorney. However, the prosecuting attorney is forbidden by law to raise the question of whether the defendant has been charged with rape in a previous trial. In fact, if the prosecution even hints at the defendant's sexual history, the defense can request a mistrial.

9. Make a comparison. Compare your topic to one that is familiar or of special interest to your readers.

The process a researcher uses to locate a specific piece of information in the library is similar to the process an investigator follows in tracking a criminal; both use a series of questions and follow clues to accomplish their task.

Mistakes to Avoid

The following advice will help you avoid the most common mistakes students make in writing introductions.

1. **Do not make an announcement.** Avoid opening comments such as "I am writing to explain . . ." or "This essay will discuss . . ."
2. **Keep your introduction short.** An introduction that goes beyond two paragraphs will probably sound long-winded and make your readers impatient.
3. **Avoid statements that may discourage your readers from continuing.** Statements such as "This process may seem complicated, but . . ." may make your readers apprehensive.
4. **Avoid a casual, overly familiar, or chatty tone.** Openings such as "Man, did it surprise me when . . ." or "You'll never in a million years believe what happened . . ." are not appropriate.

5. **Be sure your topic is clear or explained adequately for your readers.** Do not begin an essay by stating, for example, "I oppose Proposition 413 and urge you to vote against it." Before stating your position on your topic, you need to explain to readers what that legislation is and what it proposes.

Writing an Effective Conclusion

Your essay should not end abruptly with your last supporting paragraph. Instead, it should end with a conclusion—a separate paragraph that reiterates (without directly restating) the importance of your thesis and that brings your essay to a satisfying close.

Tips for Writing a Solid Conclusion

For most essays, your conclusion should summarize your main points and reaffirm your thesis. For many essays, however, you might supplement this information and make your conclusion more memorable and forceful by using one of the following suggestions.

1. **Look ahead.** Take your readers beyond the scope and time frame of your essay.

   For now, then, the present system for policing the Internet appears to be working. In the future, though, it may be necessary to put a more formal, structured procedure in place.

2. **Remind readers of the relevance of the issue.** Suggest why your thesis is important.

   As stated earlier, research has shown that implementing the seat-belt law has saved thousands of lives. These lives would almost certainly have been lost had this law not been enacted.

3. **Offer a recommendation or make a call to action.** Urge your readers to take specific steps that follow logically from your thesis.

   To convince the local cable company to eliminate pornographic material, concerned citizens should organize, contact their local cable station, and threaten to cancel their subscriptions.

4. **Discuss broader implications.** Point to larger issues not fully addressed in the essay, but do not introduce a completely new issue.

   When fair-minded people consider whether the FBI should be allowed to tap private phone lines, the issue inevitably leads them to the larger issue of First Amendment rights.

5. **Conclude with a fact, a quotation, an anecdote, or an example that emphasizes your thesis.** These endings will bring a sense of closure and realism to your essay.

   The next time you are tempted to send a strongly worded message over email, consider this fact: Your friends and your enemies can forward those messages, with unforeseen consequences.

Mistakes to Avoid

The following advice will help you avoid common mistakes writers make in their conclusions.

1. **Avoid a direct restatement of your thesis.** An exact repetition of your thesis will make your essay seem dull and mechanical.
2. **Avoid standard phrases.** Don't use phrases such as "To sum up," "In conclusion," or "It can be seen, then." They are routine and tiresome.

3. **Avoid introducing new points in your conclusion.** Major points belong in the body of your essay.

4. **Avoid apologizing for yourself, your work, or your ideas.** Do not say, for example, "Although I am only twenty-one, it seems to me . . ."

5. **Avoid weakening your stance in the conclusion.** If, for instance, your essay has criticized someone's behavior, do not back down by saying "After all, she's only human."

Writing a Good Title

The title of your essay should suggest your topic and spark your readers' interest. Depending on the purpose, intended audience, and tone of your essay, your title may be direct and informative, witty, or intriguing. The following suggestions will help you write effective titles.

1. **Write straightforward, descriptive titles for most academic essays.**

   Lotteries: A Game Players Can Little Afford

2. **Ask a question that your essay answers.**

   Who Plays the Lottery?

3. **Use alliteration.** Repeating initial sounds (called alliteration) often produces a catchy title.

   Lotteries: Dreaming about Dollars

4. **Consider using a play on words or a catchy or humorous expression.** This technique may work well for less formal essays.

   If You Win, You Lose

5. **Avoid broad, vague titles that sound like labels.** Titles such as "Baseball Fans" or "Gun Control" provide your reader with too little information.

Exercise 6.4

For each of the following essays, suggest a title. Try to use each of the above suggestions at least once.

1. An essay explaining the legal rights of tenants
2. An essay opposing human cloning
3. An essay on causes and effects of road rage
4. An essay comparing fitness routines
5. An essay explaining how to choose a primary care physician

---

Essay in Progress 3

Using the outline or graphic organizer you created in Essay in Progress 2, write a first draft of your essay.

Students Write

In her first draft the writer concentrated on expressing her ideas. Consequently, it contains errors that she later corrects. See Chapter 8, p. 172, and Chapter 9, p. 196, for later versions of this essay.

The first draft of a narrative essay by Christine Lee follows. Lee used her freewriting (see Chapter 4) and her working thesis (see Chapter 5) as the basis for her draft, adding details that she came up with by doing additional brainstorming (see Chapter 5). Because she was writing a first draft, Lee did not worry about correcting the errors in grammar, punctuation, and mechanics. (You will see her revised draft in Chapter 8 and an excerpt that shows Lee's final editing and proofreading in Chapter 9.)

FIRST DRAFT

The Reality of Real TV

Do you remember life before the reality TV craze? One look at a *TV Guide* today shows an overload of reality-based programming, even with the guaranteed failure of most of these shows. Before reality TV there was mostly situational comedies and serial dramas. When *Survivor* caught every viewer's attention, every network in American believed they must also become "real" to keep up its ratings. Shows that followed it were less interesting and less tasteful in the hopes of finding a show as original, inventive, and engaging as the first *Survivor*.

When *Survivor* began in the summer of 2000, there was nothing else like it on TV. *Survivor* had real people in a contest in an exotic location. It had different kinds of players. There was a certain fascination in watching these players struggle week after week for food and shelter but the million dollar prize kept viewers tuning in week after week. Viewers wanted to find out who was going to win and who was getting "voted off the island." The last contestant on the island wins. Players developed a sense of teamwork and camaraderie, as they schemed and plotted. And we as an audience were allowed to watch every minute of it.

Big Brother started as the first of the reality TV spinoffs but audiences didn't have the same things to respond to. It has never been a success because they took the basic concept of *Survivor* and added nothing new or interesting to it. *Big Brother* locked a bunch of people up together in a house and forced the audience to watch them bicker over nothing. Viewers were forced to watch bored contestants bicker and fight, locked up in a house with nothing else to do. It didn't seem the kind of competition that *Survivor* was, even though there was a cash prize on the line. The cash prize wasn't large enough anyways. We didn't choose favorites because the players weren't up against anything, except fighting off weeks of boredom. *Big Brother* introduced audience participation with the television audience voting off members, which actually only gave the house members less to do and less motive to scheme and plot their allegiances like the castaways on *Survivor*. Voting members off was an arbitrary and meaningless process. But *Big Brother* had the prize component, and it took away the housemates' access to the outside world.

Although nothing seems to capture ratings like the original *Survivor*, networks have continued to use sensational gimmicks to appeal to the audience's basic instincts. Nothing good was carried over from *Survivor*, and the new shows just had extreme situations. There were shows that revolved around flirtation and sex. In shows like *Chains of Love*, *Temptation Island*, and *Love Cruise*, audiences watched as contestants back-stabbed, cheated, lied, and connived in the name of "love." Audiences watched because of sexual intrigue, but these sexually charged shows pushed the limits of taste.

Another type of reality show like *Fear Factor* and *Murder in Small Town X* gets more graphic   5
and unwatchable, trying to push the limit of reality TV to the edge. Like watching a car wreck, viewers hold some interest in watching how far other people will go, but most were repulsed. Most people don't watch *Fear Factor* because watching people eat worms or getting immersed in rats is boring. *Murder in Small Town X* combined a murder mystery with a group of "detective" strangers living together in a small town, it forced contestants to work together in the beginning. Just as survival on a Pacific Island in itself was a new and interesting concept to viewers, the mystery aspect of *Murder in Small Town X* was supposed to hold viewers' attention. The controversy of the show was that it opens with a reenactment from the murderer's point of view and ends with the audience watching one of two players getting "attacked" and "killed." Viewers turned off in disgust.

When these gimmicks did not retain viewers, they turned back to two traditional types   6
of reality TV and put modern twists on them: the talent show and the beauty contest. So were born shows like *American Idol* and *America's Top Model*. Again, there was no built in drama like in *Survivor* so they tried to create drama with the colorful judges and supportive fans. At first, the shows were exciting with the singing and the beauty, but after a while, audiences lost interest. Even showing the long lines that contestants had to wait in, and footage of those who did not make the cut did not help to keep viewers hooked on these types of reality shows. Viewers could only stomach so much loud singing and mascara.

The biggest problem with the shows that followed *Survivor* is that viewers are so over-   7
loaded with reality TV now that it has become as mainstream as sitcoms and dramas were but not as interesting. *Survivor* was popular because it was something different, but now there are dozens of these shows each season and few worth watching. They are less interesting and less tasteful, and people have stopped watching.

Analyzing the First Draft

1. Evaluate Lee's title and introduction.
2. Evaluate Lee's thesis statement.
3. Does Lee provide adequate details for her essay? If not, what additional information might she include?
4. How does Lee organize her ideas?
5. Evaluate her supporting paragraphs. Which paragraphs need more detail?
6. Evaluate the conclusion.

Working with Text

Black Men and Public Space
Brent Staples

Brent Staples is a journalist who has written numerous articles and editorials as well as a memoir, *Parallel Time: Growing Up in Black and White* (1994). Staples holds a Ph.D. in psychology and is currently an editor at the *New York Times*. This essay, first published in *Harper's* magazine in 1986, is a good model of a well-structured essay. As you read the selection, highlight or underline the author's thesis.

My first victim was a woman—white, well dressed, probably in her early twenties. I came upon her late one evening on a deserted street in Hyde Park, a relatively affluent neighborhood in an otherwise mean, impoverished section of Chicago. As I swung onto the avenue behind her, there seemed to be a discreet, uninflammatory distance between us. Not so. She cast back a worried glance. To her, the youngish black man—a broad six feet two inches with a beard and billowing hair, both hands shoved into the pockets of a bulky military jacket—seemed menacingly close. After a few more quick glimpses, she picked up her pace and was soon running in earnest. Within seconds she disappeared into a cross street.

That was more than a decade ago. I was twenty-two years old, a graduate student newly arrived at the University of Chicago. It was in the echo of that terrified woman's footfalls that I first began to know the unwieldy inheritance I'd come into—the ability to alter public space in ugly ways. It was clear that she thought herself the quarry of a mugger, a rapist, or worse. Suffering a bout of insomnia, however, I was stalking sleep, not defenseless wayfarers. As a softy who is scarcely able to take a knife to a raw chicken—let alone hold one to a person's throat—I was surprised, embarrassed, and dismayed all at once. Her flight made me feel like an accomplice in tyranny. It also made it clear that I was indistinguishable from the muggers who occasionally seeped into the area from the surrounding ghetto. That first encounter, and those that followed, signified that a vast, unnerving gulf lay between nighttime pedestrians—particularly women—and me. And I soon gathered that being perceived as dangerous is a hazard in itself. I only needed to turn a corner into a dicey situation, or crowd some frightened, armed person in a foyer somewhere, or make an errant move after being pulled over by a policeman. Where fear and weapons meet—and they often do in urban America—there is always the possibility of death.

In that first year, my first away from my hometown, I was to become thoroughly familiar with the language of fear. At dark, shadowy intersections, I could cross in front of a car stopped at a traffic light and elicit the *thunk, thunk, thunk, thunk* of the driver—black, white, male, or female—hammering down the door locks. On less traveled streets after dark, I grew accustomed to but never comfortable with people crossing to the other side of the street rather than pass me. Then there were the standard unpleasantries with policemen, doormen, bouncers, cabdrivers, and others whose business it is to screen out troublesome individuals *before* there is any nastiness.

I moved to New York nearly two years ago and I have remained an avid night walker. In central Manhattan, the near-constant crowd cover minimizes tense one-on-one street encounters. Elsewhere—in SoHo, for example, where sidewalks are narrow and tightly spaced buildings shut out the sky—things can get very taut indeed.

After dark, on the warrenlike streets of Brooklyn where I live, I often see women who 5 fear the worst from me. They seem to have set their faces on neutral, and with their purse straps strung across their chests bandolier-style, they forge ahead as though bracing themselves against being tackled. I understand, of course, that the danger they perceive is not a hallucination. Women are particularly vulnerable to street violence, and young black males are drastically overrepresented among the perpetrators of that violence. Yet these truths are no solace against the kind of alienation that comes of being ever the suspect, a fearsome entity with whom pedestrians avoid making eye contact.

It is not altogether clear to me how I reached the ripe old age of twenty-two without 6 being conscious of the lethality nighttime pedestrians attributed to me. Perhaps it was because in Chester, Pennsylvania, the small, angry industrial town where I came of age in the 1960s, I was scarcely noticeable against a backdrop of gang warfare, street knifings, and murders. I grew up one of the good boys, had perhaps a half-dozen fistfights. In retrospect, my shyness of combat has clear sources.

As a boy, I saw countless tough guys locked away; I have since buried several, too. 7 They were babies, really—a teenage cousin, a brother of twenty-two, a childhood friend in his mid-twenties—all gone down in episodes of bravado played out in the streets. I came to doubt the virtues of intimidation early on. I chose, perhaps unconsciously, to remain a shadow—timid, but a survivor.

The fearsomeness mistakenly attributed to me in public places often has a perilous 8 flavor. The most frightening of these confusions occurred in the late 1970s and early 1980s, when I worked as a journalist in Chicago. One day, rushing into the office of a magazine I was writing for with a deadline story in hand, I was mistaken for a burglar. The office manager called security and, with an ad hoc posse, pursued me through the labyrinthine halls, nearly to my editor's door. I had no way of proving who I was. I could only move briskly toward the company of someone who knew me.

Another time I was on assignment for a local paper and killing time before an interview. 9 I entered a jewelry store on the city's affluent Near North Side. The proprietor excused herself and returned with an enormous red Doberman pinscher straining at the end of a leash. She stood, the dog extended toward me, silent to my questions, her eyes bulging nearly out of her head. I took a cursory look around, nodded, and bade her good night.

Relatively speaking, however, I never fared as badly as another black male journalist. 10 He went to nearby Waukegan, Illinois, a couple of summers ago to work on a story about a murderer who was born there. Mistaking the reporter for the killer, police officers hauled him from his car at gunpoint and but for his press credentials would probably have tried to book him. Such episodes are not uncommon. Black men trade tales like this all the time.

Over the years, I learned to smother the rage I felt at so often being taken for a crim- 11 inal. Not to do so would surely have led to madness. I now take precautions to make myself less threatening. I move about with care, particularly late in the evening. I give a wide berth to nervous people on subway platforms during the wee hours, particularly when I have exchanged business clothes for jeans. If I happen to be entering a building behind some people who appear skittish, I may walk by, letting them clear the lobby before I return, so as not to seem to be following them. I have been calm and extremely congenial on those rare occasions when I've been pulled over by the police.

> And on late-evening constitutionals I employ what has proved to be an excellent tension-reducing measure: I whistle melodies from Beethoven and Vivaldi and the more popular classical composers. Even steely New Yorkers hunching toward nighttime destinations seem to relax, and occasionally they even join in the tune. Virtually everybody seems to sense that a mugger wouldn't be warbling bright sunny selections from Vivaldi's *Four Seasons*. It is my equivalent of the cowbell that hikers wear when they know they are in bear country.

Examining the Reading

1. Explain what Staples means by "the ability to alter public space" (para. 2).
2. Staples considers himself a "survivor" (para. 7). To what does he attribute his survival?
3. What does Staples do to make himself seem less threatening to others?
4. Explain the meaning of each of the following words as it is used in the reading: *uninflammatory* (para. 1), *unwieldy* (2), *vulnerable* (5), *retrospect* (6), and *constitutionals* (12).

Analyzing the Writer's Technique

1. Evaluate Staples's opening paragraph. Does it spark your interest? Why or why not?
2. Identify Staples's thesis statement. How does the author support his thesis? What types of information does he include?
3. Cite several examples of places in the essay where Staples uses specific supporting details and transitions effectively. Explain your choices.
4. Evaluate Staples's conclusion. Does it leave you satisfied? Why or why not?
5. What is Staples's method of organization in this essay? What other method of organization could he have used?

Visualizing the Reading

Review the reading and supply the missing information in the graphic organizer on page 137.

Reacting to the Reading

1. Why is Staples's whistling of classical music similar to hikers wearing cowbells in bear country?
2. In what other ways can an individual "alter public space"?
3. Do you think Staples should alter his behavior in public to accommodate the reactions of others? Write a journal entry explaining whether you agree or disagree with Staples's actions.
4. **Essay assignment.** Staples describes himself as a "survivor" (para. 7) of the streets he grew up on. In a sense, everyone is a survivor of certain decisions or circumstances that, if played out differently, might have resulted in misfortunes. Write an essay that explains how and why you or someone you know is a survivor.

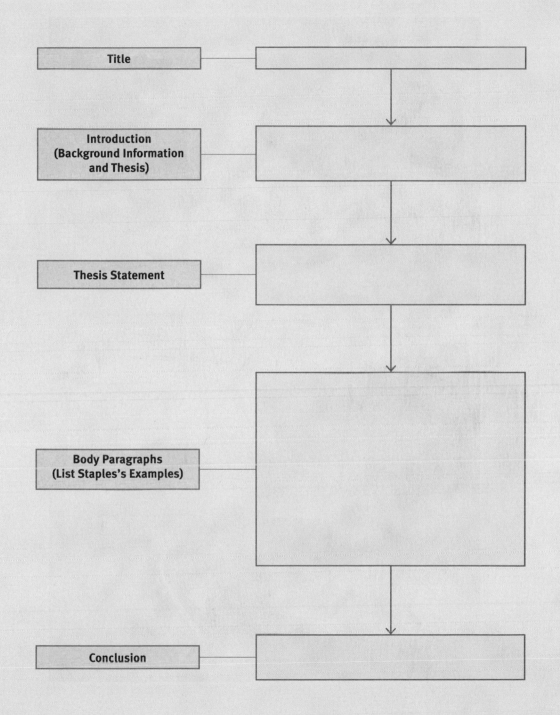

Title

Introduction
(Background Information
and Thesis)

Thesis Statement

Body Paragraphs
(List Staples's Examples)

Conclusion

CHAPTER 7

Writing Effective Paragraphs

Study the photograph on the opposite page. What event does it portray?

Write a sentence that states the main point of the photograph. Then write several more sentences explaining what is happening in the photograph. Describe what details in the photo enabled you to identify the event.

In much the same way as a photograph does, a paragraph makes an overall impression, or point. The first sentence that you wrote functions as a topic sentence, and the remainder of the sentences are the details that support it. This point is expressed in a sentence called the topic sentence. Likewise, both a photograph and a paragraph contain details that support this central idea.

The Structure of a Paragraph

A paragraph is a group of connected sentences that develop an idea about a topic. Each paragraph in your essay should support your thesis and contribute to the overall meaning and effectiveness of your essay. A well-developed paragraph contains

- a well-focused topic sentence
- unified, specific supporting details (definitions, examples, explanations, or other evidence)
- transitions and repetition that show how the ideas are related

Here is a sample paragraph with its parts labeled.

Topic sentence

      Audiences gather with varying degrees of willingness to hear a speaker. Some are anxious to hear the speaker, and may even have paid a substantial admission price. The "lecture circuit," for example, is a most lucrative aspect of public life. But whereas some audiences are willing to pay to hear a speaker, others don't seem to care one way or the other. Other audiences need to be persuaded to listen (or at least to sit in the audience).

Details and transitions

Still other audiences gather because they have to. For example, negotiations on a union contract may require members to attend meetings where officers give speeches.

DeVito, *The Essential Elements of Public Speaking*

Notice also how the writer repeats the words *audience(s)* and *speaker,* along with the synonyms *lecture* and *speeches,* to help tie the paragraph to the idea in the topic sentence.

    To visualize the structure of a well-developed paragraph, see Figure 7.1.

FIGURE 7.1 The Structure of a Paragraph

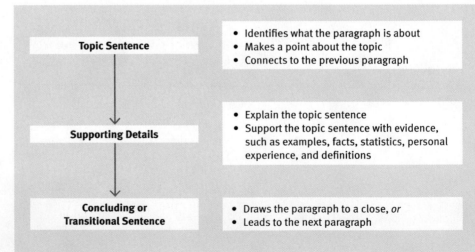

- **Topic Sentence**
  - Identifies what the paragraph is about
  - Makes a point about the topic
  - Connects to the previous paragraph

- **Supporting Details**
  - Explain the topic sentence
  - Support the topic sentence with evidence, such as examples, facts, statistics, personal experience, and definitions

- **Concluding or Transitional Sentence**
  - Draws the paragraph to a close, *or*
  - Leads to the next paragraph

For a paragraph to develop a single idea, it needs to have unity. A unified paragraph stays focused on one idea, without switching or wandering from topic to topic. A paragraph also should be of a reasonable length, neither too short nor too long. Short paragraphs look skimpy and are often underdeveloped; long paragraphs are difficult for your reader to follow.

Writing a Topic Sentence

A topic sentence is to a paragraph what a thesis statement is to an essay. Just as a thesis announces the main point of an essay, a topic sentence states the main point of a paragraph. In addition, each paragraph's topic sentence must support the thesis of the essay. A topic sentence has several specific functions.

A Topic Sentence Should Be Focused

A topic sentence should make clear what the paragraph is about (its topic) and express a view or make a point about the topic.

- *topic*
  Shocking behavior by fans, including rudeness and violent language, has become

  point about the topic
  common at many sporting events.

The topic sentence should tell readers what the paragraph is about in specific and detailed language. Avoid vague or general statements. Compare these examples of unfocused and focused topic sentences.

UNFOCUSED	**Some members of minority groups do not approve of affirmative action.**
FOCUSED	**Some members of minority groups disapprove of affirmative action because it implies that they are not capable of obtaining employment based on their own accomplishments.**
UNFOCUSED	**Many students believe that hate groups shouldn't be allowed on campus.**
FOCUSED	**The neo-Nazis, a group that promotes hate crimes, should not be permitted to speak in our local community college because most students find its members' views objectionable.**

If you have trouble focusing your topic sentences, review the guidelines for writing an effective thesis statement in Chapter 5 (p. 102), many of which also apply to writing effective topic sentences.

A Topic Sentence May Preview the Organization of the Paragraph

A topic sentence may suggest the order in which details are discussed in the paragraph, thereby helping readers know what to expect.

- *first detail*
  Teaching employees how to handle conflicts through **anger management** and *second detail* **mediation** is essential in high-stress jobs.

Readers can expect anger management to be discussed first, followed by a discussion of mediation.

Exercise 7.1

Revise each topic sentence to make it focused and specific. At least two of your revised topic sentences should also preview the organization of the paragraph.

1. In society today, there is always a new fad or fashion in clothing.
2. People watch television talk shows because they find them irresistible.
3. Body piercing is a popular trend.
4. Procrastinating can have a negative effect on your success in college.
5. In our state, the lottery is a big issue.

A Topic Sentence Should Support Your Thesis

Each topic sentence must in some way explain the thesis or show why the thesis is believable or correct. This sample thesis, for example, could be supported by the topic sentences that follow it.

THESIS   **Adoption files should not be made available to adult children seeking their biological parents.**

TOPIC SENTENCES

Research has shown that not all biological parents want to meet with the sons or daughters they gave up many years before.

If a woman gives up a child for adoption, it is probable that she does not ever intend to have a relationship with that child.

Adult children who try to contact their biological parents often meet resistance and even hostility, which can cause them to feel hurt and rejected.

A woman who gave up her biological child because she became pregnant as a result of rape or incest should not have to live in fear that her child will one day confront her.

All of these topic sentences support the thesis because they offer valid reasons for keeping adoption files closed.

Exercise 7.2

For each of the following thesis statements, identify the topic sentence in the list below that does not support the thesis.

1. To make a marriage work, a couple must build trust, communication, and understanding.

   a. Knowing why a spouse behaves as he or she does can improve a relationship.

   b. People get married for reasons other than love.

   c. The ability to talk about feelings, problems, likes, and dislikes should grow as a marriage develops.

   d. Marital partners must rely on each other to make sensible decisions that benefit both of them.

2. Internet sales are capturing a larger market share relative to in-store sales.

   a. Internet retailers that target a specific audience tend to be most successful.

   b. The convenience of ordering any time of day or night accounts, in part, for increased Internet sales.

   c. Many customers use Paypal for online purchases.

   d. Web sites that locate and compare prices for a specified item make comparison shopping easier on the Internet than in retail stores.

A Topic Sentence Should Be Strategically Placed

Where you place the topic sentence will determine the order and structure of the rest of the paragraph. The topic sentence also may have different effects, depending on its placement.

Topic Sentence First

The most common and often best position for a topic sentence is at the beginning of the paragraph. A paragraph that opens with the topic sentence should follow a logical sequence: You state your main point, and then you explain it. The topic sentence tells readers what to expect in the rest of the paragraph, making it clear and easy for them to follow.

> Advertising is first and foremost based on the principle of visibility—the customer must notice the product. Manufacturers often package products in glitzy, even garish, containers to grab the consumer's attention. For example, one candy company always packages its candy in reflective wrappers. When the hurried and hungry consumer glances at the candy counter, the reflective wrappers are easy to spot. It is only natural for the impatient customer to grab the candy and go.

Topic sentence

Explanatory details

Topic Sentence Early in the Paragraph

When one or two sentences at the beginning of a paragraph are needed to smooth the transition from one paragraph to the next, the topic sentence may follow these transitional sentences.

Transitional sentence

Topic sentence

However, visibility is not the only principle in advertising; it is simply the first. A second and perhaps more subtle principle is identity: The manufacturer attempts to lure the consumer into buying a product by linking it to a concept with which the consumer can identify. For instance, Boundaries perfume is advertised on television as the choice of "independent" women. Since independent women are admired in our culture, women identify with the concept and therefore are attracted to the perfume. Once the consumer identifies with the product, a sale is more likely to occur.

Topic Sentence Last

The topic sentence can also appear last in a paragraph. You first present the supporting details and then end the paragraph with the topic sentence, which usually states the conclusion that can be drawn from the details. Common in argumentative writing, this arrangement allows you to present convincing evidence before stating your point about the issue.

Evidence

Topic sentence

The saying "Guns don't kill people; people kill people" always makes me even more certain of my own position on gun control. That statement is deceptive in the same way that the statement "Heroin doesn't kill people; people kill themselves" is deceptive. Naturally, people need to pull the trigger of a gun in order to make the gun kill other people, just as it is necessary for a person to ingest heroin in order for it to kill him or her. However, these facts do not excuse us from the responsibility of keeping guns (or heroin) out of people's hands as much as possible. People cannot shoot people unless they have a gun. This fact alone should persuade the government to institute stiff gun control laws.

Essay in Progress 1

For the first draft you wrote in Essay in Progress 3 in Chapter 6, page 131, evaluate each of your topic sentences for content and placement. Revise to make each more effective, as needed.

Including Supporting Details

In addition to including well-focused topic sentences, effective paragraphs are unified and well developed, and provide concrete details that work together to support the main point.

Effective Paragraphs Have Unity

In a unified paragraph, all of the sentences directly support the topic sentence. Including details that are not relevant to the topic sentence makes your paragraph unclear and distracts your reader from the point you are making. To identify irrelevant details, evaluate each sentence by asking the following questions.

1. Does this sentence directly explain the topic sentence? What new information does it add?
2. Would any essential information be lost if this sentence were deleted? (If not, delete it.)
3. Is this information distracting or unimportant? (If so, delete it.)

The following sample paragraph lacks unity. As you read it, try to pick out the sentences that do not support the topic sentence.

Paragraph Lacking Unity

(1) Much of the violence we see in the world today may be caused by the emphasis on violence in the media. (2) More often than not, the front page of the local newspaper contains stories involving violence. (3) In fact, one recent issue of my local newspaper contained seven references to violent acts. (4) There is also violence in public school systems. (5) Television reporters frequently hasten to crime and accident scenes and film every grim, violent detail. (6) The other day, there was a drive-by shooting downtown. (7) If the media were a little more careful about the ways in which they glamorize violence, there might be less violence in the world today and children would be less influenced by it.

Although sentences 4 and 6 deal with the broad topic of violence, neither is directly related to the idea of the media promoting violence—the main point stated in the topic sentence. Both should be deleted.

Exercise 7.3

Working alone or in a group of two or three students, read each paragraph and identify the sentences that do not support the topic sentence. In each paragraph, the topic sentence is underlined.

1. (a) Today many options and services for the elderly are available that did not exist years ago. (b) My grandmother is eighty-five years old now. (c) Adult care for the elderly is now provided in many parts of the country. (d) Similar to day care, adult care provides places where the elderly can go for meals and social activities. (e) Retirement homes for the elderly, where they can live fairly independently with minimal supervision, are another option. (f) My grandfather is also among the elderly at eighty-two. (g) Even many nursing homes have changed so that residents are afforded some level of privacy and independence while their needs are being met.

2. (a) Just as history repeats itself, fashions have a tendency to do the same. (b) In the late 1960s, for example, women wore miniskirts that came several inches above the knee; some forty years later, the fashion magazines are featuring this same type of dress, and many teenagers are wearing them. (c) The miniskirt has always been flattering on slender women. (d) I wonder if the fashion industry deliberately recycles fashions. (e) Men wore their hair long in the hippie period of the late 1960s and 1970s. (f) Today, some men are again letting their hair grow. (g) Beards, considered "in" during the 1970s, have once again made an appearance.

Effective Paragraphs Are Well Developed

A unified paragraph provides adequate and convincing evidence to explain the topic sentence. Include enough supporting details to demonstrate that your topic sentence is accurate and believable. Evidence can include explanations, examples, or other kinds of information that help the reader understand and believe the assertion in the topic sentence. The following example shows an underdeveloped paragraph that is revised into a well-developed paragraph.

UNDERDEVELOPED PARAGRAPH

Email and instant messaging (IM) are important technological advances, but they have hidden limitations, even dangers. It is too easy to avoid talking to people face to face. Using email can be addictive, too. Plus, they encourage ordinary people to ignore others while typing on a keyboard.

DEVELOPED PARAGRAPH

Email and instant messaging (IM) are important technological advances, but they have hidden limitations, even dangers. While email and instant messaging allow fast and efficient communication and exchange of information, they provide a different quality of human interaction. It is too easy to avoid talking to people. It is easier to click on one's "Buddy List" and check to see if she wants to meet for dinner than it would be to look up her number and actually talk to her. Online you can post a "be right back" message, avoiding an intrusion into your life. In fact, using these services can become addictive. For example, some students on campus are obsessed with checking their email several times throughout the day. They spend their free time talking to email acquaintances across the country, while ignoring interesting people right in the same room. Because computer interaction is not face to face, email and instant messenger addicts are shortchanging themselves of real human contact. There is something to be said for responding not only to a person's words but to their expressions, gestures, and tone of voice.

These two versions of the paragraph differ in the degree to which the ideas are developed. The first paragraph has skeletal ideas that support the topic sentence, but those ideas are not explained. For example, the first paragraph does not explain why email and instant messaging are important or provide any evidence of how or why email can be addictive. Notice that the second paragraph explains how email and instant messaging allow for fast and efficient communication and gives further information about the addictive qualities of email. The second paragraph also explains the qualities of face-to-face interaction that are absent from online communication.

To discover if your paragraphs are well developed, begin by considering your audience. Have you given them enough information to make your ideas understandable and believable? Try reading your essay aloud, or ask a friend to do so. Listen for places where you jump quickly from one idea to another without explaining the first idea. To find supporting evidence for a topic sentence, use a prewriting strategy from Chapter 4. Also, the same types of evidence shown in the table on page 105 to support a thesis can be used to develop a paragraph. You may need to do some research to find this evidence.

Exercise 7.4

Use Table 5.1 (p. 105) to suggest the type or types of evidence that might be used to develop a paragraph based on each of the following topic sentences.

1. Many people have fallen prey to fad diets, risking their health and jeopardizing their mental well-being.
2. One can distinguish experienced soccer players from rookies by obvious signs.
3. To begin a jogging routine, take a relaxed but deliberate approach.
4. The interlibrary loan system is a fast and convenient method for obtaining print materials from libraries affiliated with the campus library.
5. Southwest Florida's rapid population growth poses a serious threat to its freshwater supply.

Exercise 7.5

Create a well-developed paragraph by adding details to the following paragraph.

Although it is convenient, online shopping is a different experience than shopping in an actual store. You don't get the same opportunity to see and feel objects. Also, you can miss out on other important information. There is much that you miss. If you enjoy shopping, turn off your computer and support your local merchants.

Effective Paragraphs Provide Specific Supporting Details

The evidence you provide to support your topic sentences should be concrete and specific. Specific details interest your readers and make your meaning clear and forceful. Compare the following two examples.

VAGUE

Many people are confused about the difference between a psychologist and a psychiatrist. Both have a license, but a psychiatrist has more education than a psychologist. Also, a psychiatrist can prescribe medication.

CONCRETE AND SPECIFIC

Many people are confused about the difference between psychiatrists and psychologists. Both are licensed by the state to practice psychotherapy. However, a psychiatrist has earned a degree from medical school and can also practice medicine. Additionally, a psychiatrist can prescribe psychotropic medications. A psychologist, on the other hand, usually has earned a Ph.D. but has not attended medical school and therefore cannot prescribe medication of any type.

General statements that do not completely explain the topic sentence

Concrete details make clear the distinction between the two terms

To make your paragraphs concrete and specific, use the following guidelines.

1. **Focus on *who, what, when, where, how,* and *why* questions.** Ask yourself these questions about your supporting details, and use the answers to expand and revise your paragraph.

   VAGUE　　　Some animals hibernate for part of the year.
   　　　　　　(What animals? When do they hibernate?)

   SPECIFIC　　Some bears hibernate for three to four months each winter.

2. **Name names.** Include the names of people, places, brands, and objects.

   VAGUE　　　When my sixty-three-year-old aunt was refused a job, she became an angry victim of age discrimination.

   SPECIFIC　　When my sixty-three-year-old Aunt Angela was refused a job at Vicki's Nail Salon, she became an angry victim of age discrimination.

3. **Use action verbs.** Select strong verbs that will help your readers visualize the action.

   VAGUE　　　When Silina came on stage, the audience became excited.

   SPECIFIC　　When Silina burst onto the stage, the audience screamed, cheered, and chanted "Silina, Silina!"

4. **Use descriptive language that appeals to the senses (smell, touch, taste, sound, sight).** Words that appeal to the senses enable your readers to feel as if they are observing or participating in the experience you are describing.

   VAGUE　　　It's relaxing to walk on the beach.

   SPECIFIC　　I walked in the sand next to the ocean, breathing in the smell of the salt water and listening to the rhythmic sound of the waves.

5. **Use adjectives and adverbs.** Including carefully chosen adjectives and adverbs in your description of a person, a place, or an experience can make your writing more concrete.

   VAGUE　　　As I weeded my garden, I let my eyes wander over the meadow sweets and hydrangeas, all the while listening to the chirping of a cardinal.

   SPECIFIC　　As I slowly weeded my perennial garden, I let my eyes wander over the pink meadow sweets and blue hydrangeas, all the while listening absent-mindedly to the chirping of a bright red cardinal.

Exercise 7.6

Working alone or in a group of two or three students, revise and expand each sentence in the following paragraph to make it specific and concrete. Feel free to add new information and new sentences.

I saw a great concert the other night in Dallas. Two groups were performing. The music was great, and there was a large crowd. In fact, the crowd was so enthusiastic that the second group performed one hour longer than scheduled.

Details Are Arranged Logically

The details in a paragraph should follow a logical order to make them easier to follow. You might arrange the details from most to least (or least to most) important, in chronological order, or in spatial order. Refer to Chapter 6, pages 118–121, for more information on each of these arrangements.

> **Essay in Progress 2**
> For the draft you worked with in Essay in Progress 1 on page 144, evaluate the supporting details you used in each paragraph. Revise to make each paragraph unified, coherent, and logically organized. Make sure you have provided concrete, specific details.

Using Transitions and Repetition

All of the details in a paragraph must fit together and function as a connected unit of information. When a paragraph has **coherence**, its ideas flow smoothly, allowing readers to follow its progression with ease. Using one of the methods of organization discussed earlier in this chapter can help you show the connections among details and ideas. Two other useful devices for linking details are transitions between sentences and repetition of key terms.

Coherent Paragraphs Include Transitional Expressions

Transitions are words, phrases, or clauses that lead your reader from one idea to another. Think of transitional expressions as guideposts, or signals, of what is coming next in a paragraph. Some commonly used transitions are shown in the box on page 150, grouped according to the type of connections they show.

In the two examples that follow, notice that the first paragraph is disjointed and choppy because it lacks transitions, whereas the revised version is easier to follow.

WITHOUT TRANSITIONS

Most films are structured much like a short story. The film begins with an opening scene that captures the audience's attention. The writers build up tension, preparing for the climax of the story. They complicate the situation by revealing other elements of the plot, perhaps by introducing a surprise or additional characters. They introduce a problem. It will be solved either for the betterment or to the detriment of the characters and the situation. A resolution brings the film to a close.

WITH TRANSITIONS

Most films are structured much like a short story. The film begins with an opening scene that captures the audience's attention. Gradually, the writers build up tension, preparing for the climax of the story. Soon after the first scene, they complicate the situation by revealing other elements of the plot, perhaps by introducing a surprise or additional characters. Next, they introduce a problem. Eventually, the problem will be solved either for the betterment or to the detriment of the characters and the situation. Finally, a resolution brings the film to a close.

COMMONLY USED TRANSITIONAL EXPRESSIONS

Type of Connection	*Transitions*
Logical Connections	
Items in a series	then, first, second, next, another, furthermore, finally, as well as
Illustration	for instance, for example, namely, that is
Result or cause	consequently, therefore, so, hence, thus, then, as a result
Restatement	in other words, that is, in simpler terms
Summary or conclusion	finally, in conclusion, to sum up, all in all, evidently, actually
Similarity/agreement	similarly, likewise, in the same way
Difference/opposition	but, however, on the contrary, nevertheless, neither, nor, on the one/other hand, still, yet
Spatial Connections	
Direction	inside/outside, along, above/below, up/down, across, to the right/left, in front of/behind
Nearness	next to, near, nearby, facing, adjacent to
Distance	beyond, in the distance, away, over there
Time Connections	
Frequency	often, frequently, now and then, gradually, week by week, occasionally, daily, rarely
Duration	during, briefly, hour by hour
Reference to a particular time	at two o'clock, on April 27, in 2000, last Thanksgiving, three days ago
Beginning	before then, at the beginning, at first
Middle	meanwhile, simultaneously, next, then, at that time
End	finally, at last, eventually, later, at the end, subsequently, afterward

Essay in Progress 3

For the draft you worked with in Essay in Progress 2 on page 149, evaluate your use of transitions within each paragraph, adding them where needed to make the relationship among your ideas clearer.

Exercise 7.7

The following student essay by Robin Ferguson on volunteering in a literacy program was written using the graphic organizer shown in Chapter 6, page 125. Read the essay and answer the questions that follow.

READING

The Value of Volunteering
Robin Ferguson

I began working as a literacy volunteer as part of a community service course I was taking last semester. The course required a community service project, and I chose literacy volunteers simply as a means of fulfilling a course requirement. Now I realize that working as a literacy volunteer taught me more about learning and friendship than I ever expected.   1

When I first went through the training program to become a literacy volunteer, I learned about the process of learning--that is, the way in which people learn new words most effectively. To illustrate this concept, the person who trained me wrote a brief list of simple words on the left side of a chalkboard and wrote phrases using the same words on the right side of the chalkboard. She instructed us to read the words and then asked which words we would be most likely to remember. We all said the words on the right because they made more sense. In other words, we could remember the words in the phrases more easily because they made more sense in context. The trainer showed us several more examples of words in context so we could get a grasp of how people learn new information by connecting it to what they already know.   2

The training I received, though excellent, was no substitute for working with a real student, however. When I began to discover what other people's lives are like because they cannot read, I realized the true importance of reading. For example, when I had my first tutoring session with my client, Marie, a forty-four-year-old single mother of three, I found out she walked two miles to the nearest grocery store twice a week because she didn't know which bus to take. When I told her I would get her a bus schedule, she confided to me that it would not help because she could not read it and therefore wouldn't know which bus to take. She also said she had difficulty once she got to the grocery store because she couldn't always remember what she needed. Since she did not know words, she could not write out a grocery list. Also, she identified items by sight, so if the manufacturer changed a label, she could not recognize it as the product she wanted.   3

As we worked together, learning how to read built Marie's self-confidence, which gave her an incentive to continue in her studies. She began to make rapid progress and was even able to take the bus to the grocery store. After this successful trip, she reported how self-assured she felt. Eventually, she began helping her youngest son, Mark, a shy first grader, with his reading. She sat with him before he went to sleep, and together they would read bedtime stories. When his eyes became wide with excitement as she read, her pride swelled, and she began   4 to see how her own hard work in learning to read paid off. As she described this experience, I swelled with pride as well. I found that helping Marie to build her self-confidence was more rewarding than anything I had ever done before.

5   As time went by, Marie and I developed a friendship that became permanent. Because we saw each other several times a week, we spent a lot of time getting to know each other, and we discovered we had certain things in common. For instance, I'm also a single parent. So we began to share our similar experiences with each other. In fact, we have even baby-sat for each other's children. I would drop my children off at her house while I taught an evening adult class, and in return, I watched her children while she worked on Saturday mornings.

6   As a literacy volunteer, I learned a great deal about learning, teaching, and helping others. I also established what I hope will be a lifelong friendship. In fact, I may have benefited more from the experience than Marie did.

1. Highlight each of the topic sentences in the body of the essay (between the introduction and the conclusion). Evaluate how well each supports the thesis.
2. What type(s) of evidence does Ferguson use to support each topic sentence?
3. What method(s) does Ferguson use to logically arrange her details within paragraphs?
4. Highlight transitions that Ferguson uses to connect her ideas, both within and between paragraphs.

Students Write

Chapters 4–6 show Christine Lee's progress in planning and drafting an essay on reality television. Below you can see her first draft paragraph (also included in Chapter 6 as part of her first draft essay, p. 132) and her revision to strengthen the paragraph.

First Draft Paragraph

Big Brother started as the first of the reality TV spinoffs but audiences didn't have the same things to respond to. It has never been a success because they took the basic concept of *Survivor* and added nothing new or interesting to it. *Big Brother* locked a bunch of people up together in a house and forced the audience to watch them bicker over nothing. Viewers were forced to watch bored contestants bicker and fight, locked up in a house with nothing else to do. It didn't seem the kind of competition that *Survivor* was, even though there was a cash prize on the line. The cash prize wasn't large enough anyways. We didn't choose favorites because the players weren't up against anything, except fighting off weeks of boredom. *Big Brother* introduced audience participation with the television audience voting off members, which actually only gave the house members less to do and less motive to scheme and plot their allegiances like the castaways on *Survivor*. Voting members off was an arbitrary and meaningless process. But *Big Brother* had the prize component, and it took away the housemates' access to the outside world.

REVISED PARAGRAPH

 Big Brother was the first spin-off reality TV show to try and repeat the success of *Survivor*, but it did not offer the drama that *Survivor* did. In *Big Brother*, contestants were locked in a house without any outside contact for weeks. Like *Survivor*, there was a cash prize on the line, but in *Big Brother* there were not any competitions or struggles. Contestants were expelled by a viewer phone poll, but the viewer phone poll gave the house members no motive to scheme and plot allegiances like *Survivor*. In fact, the contestants had little to do, and viewers were forced to watch bored contestants bicker and fight. Viewers were not interested in the players who were not up against anything except fighting off weeks of boredom. In the end, *Big Brother* was simply not interesting.

Analyzing the Writer's Technique

1. How did Lee strengthen her topic sentence?
2. What irrelevant details did she delete?
3. What transitions did she add to provide coherence?
4. What words are repeated that contribute to coherence?
5. What further revisions do you recommend?

Working with Text

In Chapter 6, you read the essay "Black Men and Public Space" by Brent Staples (p. 134). Return to this essay now and examine Staples's use and placement of topic sentences. As you read, highlight each topic sentence and study how each is supported with concrete, specific details.

CHAPTER 8

Revising Content and Organization

Looking at the photo from left to right, list everything that is happening in the picture.

Examine your list, looking for ways to make it more understandable to someone who has not seen the photo. Write a few sentences summarizing what you think is going on in the photo, and then add details to your original list to describe the photo more fully. After you make these changes, will it be easier for a reader who has not seen the photo to understand what is happening in it?

Now, exchange papers with a classmate and examine how your classmate organized ideas. Look for parts that you find confusing and that need more detail. Write down your comments for your classmate. Finally, using your own comments and those of your classmate, make changes to improve your own description of the photograph.

When you changed your list, did you include more details from the photo? Leave some unimportant details out? Change the content of any details? Whatever changes you made improved the content of your writing. In other words, you have *revised* the description of the photo.

Revising an essay works in much the same way. **Revision** is a process of making changes to improve both what your essay says and how it is said. This chapter offers several approaches to revising an essay. It lists some general suggestions, describes how to use a graphic organizer for revision, offers specific questions to guide your revision, and discusses the implications of learning style for the revision process. You will notice in Figure 8.1 that revision is an essential part of the writing process.

Why Revise?

A thorough, thoughtful revision can change a C paper to an A paper! Revising can make a significant difference in how well your paper achieves your purpose and how effectively it expresses your ideas to your intended audience. Although revision takes time and hard work, it pays off and produces results.

FIGURE 8.1 An Overview of the Writing Process

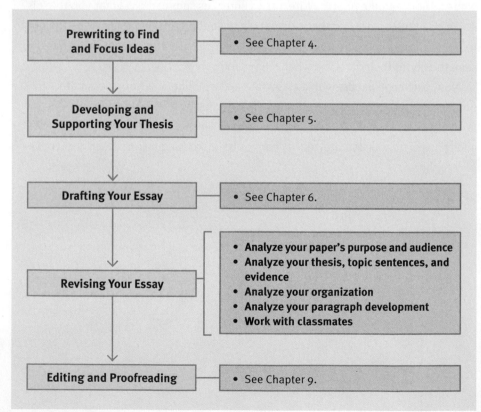

Most professional writers revise frequently and thoroughly, as do successful student writers. Revision is a process of looking again at your *ideas* to make them clearer and easier to understand. It is not merely a process of correcting surface errors. It may mean adding, eliminating, or reorganizing key elements within the essay. It may even mean revising your thesis statement and refocusing the entire essay.

The amount of revision you will need to do will depend, in part, on how you approach the task of writing. Some writers spend more time planning; others spend more time revising. For example, students who tend to be pragmatic learners take a highly structured approach to writing. They plan in detail what they will say before they draft. More creative learners, however, may dash off a draft as ideas come to mind. A well-planned draft usually requires less revision than one that was spontaneously written. However, regardless of how carefully planned an essay may be, any first draft will require at least some revision.

Learning Style Options

Useful Techniques for Revision

The following techniques will help you get the most benefit from the time you spend revising your essays.

- **Allow time between drafting and revising.** Once you have finished writing, set your draft aside for a while, overnight if possible. When you return to your draft, you will be able to approach it from a fresh perspective.
- **Read your draft aloud.** Hearing what you have written will help you discover main points that are unclear or that lack adequate support. You will notice confusing paragraphs, awkward wording, and vague or overused expressions.
- **Ask a friend to read your draft aloud to you.** When your reader hesitates, slows down, misreads, or sounds confused, it could be a signal that your message is not as clear as it should be. Keep a copy of your draft in front of you as you listen, and mark places where your reader falters or seems baffled.
- **Seek the opinions of classmates.** Ask a classmate to read and comment on your paper. This process, called **peer review**, is discussed in more detail later in this chapter (see p. 162).
- **Look for consistent problem areas.** Over the course of writing and revising several essays, many students discover consistent problem areas, such as organization or a lack of concrete details to support main points.
- **Use a typed and printed copy.** Even if you prefer to handwrite your draft, be sure to type and print it before you revise. Because computer-generated, typed copy will seem less personal, you will be able to analyze and evaluate it more impartially. You will also be able to see a full page at a time on a printed copy, instead of only a paragraph at a time on a computer screen. Finally, on a printed copy you can write marginal annotations, circle troublesome words or sentences, and draw arrows to connect details.

Using a Graphic Organizer for Revision

One of the best ways to reexamine your essay is to draw a graphic organizer—a visual display of your thesis statement and supporting paragraphs. A graphic organizer allows you to see how your thesis and topic sentences relate to one another. It will also help you evaluate both the content and the organization of your essay.

For instructions on creating a graphic organizer, see Chapter 3, page 55. If you are working on an assignment in Chapters 10 to 17 or Chapter 19, each of those chapters includes a model graphic organizer for the type of writing covered in the chapter. As you are drawing your graphic organizer, if you spot a detail or an example that does not support a topic sentence or discover any other kind of problem, write notes to the right of your organizer, as shown in Figure 8.2.

Another option, instead of drawing a graphic organizer, is to write an outline of your draft. For more information on outlining, see Chapter 6, page 122.

Figure 8.2 SAMPLE GRAPHIC ORGANIZER FOR REVISION

Introduction: Thesis Statement		Unrelated Details

**Introduction:
Thesis Statement**

↓

**Paragraph 2:
Topic Sentence**

↓

Detail

↓

Detail

↓

**Paragraph 3:
Topic Sentence**

↓

Detail

↓

Detail

↓

Detail

Unrelated Details

1. _____

2. _____

3. _____

Details to Add

1. _____

2. _____

3. _____

Other Problems

1. _____

2. _____

(and so on)

Key Questions for Revision

The five key questions listed below will help you know what to look for when you revise. Use the questions to identify broad areas of weakness in your essay.

- **Does your essay clearly convey a purpose, address an appropriate audience, and state a thesis?**
- **Do you have enough reasons and evidence to support your thesis?**
- **Do the ideas in your essay fit together?**
- **Is each paragraph well developed?**
- **Does your essay have a strong introduction and conclusion?**

After reading your draft or after discussing it with a classmate, try to pinpoint areas that need improvement by answering each of these five questions. Then refer to the self-help flowcharts in the following sections. In addition to the revision suggestions and flowcharts in this chapter, the chapters in Part 3, Chapter 19 in Part 4, and Chapters 21 and 22 in Part 5 provide revision flowcharts tailored to the specific assignments in those chapters.

Analyzing Your Purpose and Audience

For more information about purpose and audience, see Chapter 4, pp. 82–84. For more on developing a thesis, see Chapter 5, p. 101.

First drafts are often unfocused and may go off in several directions rather than have a clear purpose. For instance, one section of an essay on divorce may inform readers of its causes, and another section may argue that it harms children. A first draft may contain sections that appeal to different audiences. For instance, one section of an essay on counseling teenagers about drug abuse might seem to be written for parents; other sections might be more appropriate for teenagers.

To find out if your paper has a clear focus, write a sentence stating what your paper is supposed to accomplish. If you cannot write such a sentence, your essay probably lacks a clear purpose. To find a purpose, do some additional thinking or brainstorming, listing as many possible purposes as you can think of.

To find out if your essay is directed to a specific audience, write a sentence or two describing your intended readers. Describe their knowledge, beliefs, and experience with your topic. If you are unable to do so, try to zero in on a particular audience and revise your essay with them in mind.

Essay in Progress 1

Evaluate the purpose and audience of the draft essay you wrote in Essay in Progress 3 in Chapter 6, page 131, or of any essay that you have written. Make notes on your graphic organizer or annotate your outline.

Analyzing Your Thesis, Topic Sentences, and Evidence

Once your paper is focused on a specific purpose and audience, your next step is to evaluate your thesis statement and your support for that thesis. Use Figure 8.3 to examine your thesis statement, topic sentences, and evidence.

Figure 8.3 Flowchart for Evaluating Your Thesis Statement, Topic Sentences, and Evidence

QUESTIONS

REVISION STRATEGIES

1. Does your essay have a thesis statement that identifies your topic and states your position or suggests your slant on the topic? (To find out, state your thesis aloud without looking at your essay; then highlight the sentence in your draft essay that matches or is close to what you have just said. If you cannot find such a sentence, you have probably not written a well-focused thesis statement.)

- Reread your essay and answer this question: What one main point is most of this essay concerned with?
- Write a thesis statement that expresses that main point.
- Revise your paper to focus on that main point.
- Delete parts of the essay that do not support your thesis statement.

YES

2. Have you given your readers all the background information they need to understand your thesis? (To find out, ask someone unfamiliar with your topic to read your essay, asking questions as he or she reads.)

- Answer *who, what, when, where, why,* and *how* questions to discover more background information.

YES

3. Have you presented enough convincing evidence to support your thesis? (To find out, place checkmarks ✓ beside the evidence in your essay, and compare the evidence against the thesis. Ask yourself this question: Would I accept the thesis, or does it need more evidence to be convincing?)

- Use prewriting strategies or do additional research to discover more supporting evidence.
- Evaluate this new evidence and add the most convincing evidence to your essay.

YES

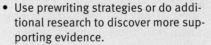

QUESTIONS	REVISION STRATEGIES
4. Does each topic sentence logically connect to and support the thesis? (To find out, <u>underline</u> each topic sentence. Read the thesis, and then read each topic sentence. When the connection between them is not obvious, revision is needed.) **NO**	• Rewrite the topic sentence so that it clearly supports the thesis. • If necessary, broaden your thesis so that it encompasses all your supporting points.

 YES

QUESTIONS	REVISION STRATEGIES
5. Is your evidence specific and detailed? (To find out, go through your draft, and reread where you placed checkmarks ✓. Does each checkmarked item answer one of these questions: *Who? What? When? Where? Why? How?* If you have not placed a checkmark in a particular paragraph or have placed a checkmark by only one sentence or part of a sentence, you need to add more detailed evidence to that paragraph.) **NO**	• Name names, give dates, specify places. • Use action verbs and descriptive language, including carefully chosen adjectives and adverbs. • Answer *who, what, when, where, why,* and *how* questions to discover more detailed evidence.

Essay in Progress 2

Using Figure 8.3, evaluate the thesis statement, topic sentences, and evidence of your essay in progress in Chapter 6, page 131. Make notes on your graphic organizer or annotate your outline.

Analyzing Your Organization

Your readers will not be able to follow your ideas if your essay does not hold together as a unified piece of writing. To be sure that it does, examine your essay's organization. The graphic organizer or outline of your draft (see p. 157) that you completed will help you analyze the draft's organization and discover any flaws.

To determine if the organization of your draft is clear and effective, you can also ask a classmate to read your draft and explain to you how your essay is organized. If your classmate cannot describe your essay's organization, it probably needs further work. Use one of the methods in Chapter 6 (pp. 117–21) or one of the patterns of development described in Parts 3 and 4 to reorganize your ideas.

Analyzing Your Introduction, Conclusion, and Title

Once you are satisfied with the draft's organization, evaluate your introduction, conclusion, and title. Use the following questions as guidelines.

1. **Does your introduction interest your reader and provide needed background information?** If your essay jumps into the topic without preparing readers for it, your introduction needs to be revised. Use the suggestions on pages 128 to 130 to create interest. Ask the *W* questions—*who, what, when, where, why,* and *how*—to determine the background information that you need.
2. **Does your conclusion draw your essay to a satisfactory close and reinforce your thesis statement?** Does the conclusion follow logically from the introduction? If not, use the suggestions for writing conclusions in Chapter 6 (pp. 130–31). Also try imagining yourself explaining the significance or importance of your essay to a friend. Use this explanation to rewrite your conclusion.
3. **Does your title accurately reflect the content of your essay?** To improve your title, write a few words that "label" your essay. Also, reread your thesis statement, looking for a few key words that can serve as part of your title. Finally, use the suggestions in Chapter 6 (p. 131) to help you choose a title.

> **Essay in Progress 3**
> Evaluate the organization of your essay in progress. Make notes on your draft copy.

Analyzing Your Paragraph Development

See Chapter 6 for more on paragraph development.

Each paragraph in your essay must fully develop a single idea that supports your thesis. (Narrative essays are an exception to this rule. As you will see in Chapter 10, in a narrative essay, each paragraph focuses on a separate part of the action.)

In a typical first draft, paragraphs are often weak or loosely structured. They may contain irrelevant information or lack a clearly focused topic sentence. To evaluate your paragraph development, study each paragraph separately in conjunction with your thesis statement. You may need to delete or combine some paragraphs, rework or reorganize others, or move paragraphs to a more appropriate part of the essay. If you need to supply additional information to support your thesis, you may need to add paragraphs to the draft. Use Figure 8.4 to help you analyze and revise your paragraphs.

> **Essay in Progress 4**
> Using Figure 8.4, examine each paragraph of your essay in progress. Make notes on the draft copy of your essay.

Working with Classmates to Revise Your Essay

Increasingly, instructors in writing and other academic disciplines use **peer review**, a process in which two or more students read and comment on each other's papers. Students might work together in class or outside of class, or communicate via email

Figure 8.4 Flowchart for Evaluating Your Paragraphs

QUESTIONS	REVISION STRATEGIES

1. Does each paragraph have a clear topic sentence that expresses the main point of the paragraph? (To find out, underline the topic sentence in each paragraph. Then evaluate whether the topic sentence makes a statement that the rest of the paragraph supports.)

 NO

- Revise a sentence within the paragraph so that it clearly states the main point.
- Write a new sentence that states the one main point of the paragraph.

YES

2. Do all sentences in each paragraph support the topic sentence? (To find out, read the topic sentence, and then read each supporting sentence in turn.)

NO

- Revise supporting sentences to make their connection to the topic sentence clear.
- Delete any sentences that do not support the topic sentence.

YES

3. Does the paragraph offer adequate explanation and supporting details? (To find out, place checkmarks ✓ beside supporting details. Then ask yourself: Is there other information readers will want or need to know?)

NO

- Add more details if your paragraph seems skimpy.
- Use either the *who, what, when, where, why,* and *how* questions or the prewriting strategies in Chapter 4 to generate the details you need.

YES

4. Will it be clear to your reader how each sentence and each paragraph connects to those before and after it? (To find out, read your paper aloud to see if it flows smoothly or sounds choppy.)

NO

- Add transitions where they are needed. Refer to the list of common transitions on page 150.

or a classroom computer network. Working with classmates is an excellent way to get ideas for improving your essays. You'll also have the opportunity to discover how other students view and approach the writing process. The following suggestions will help both the writer and the reviewer get the most out of peer review.

How to Find a Good Reviewer

Selecting a good reviewer is key to getting good suggestions for revision. Your instructor may pair you with another class member or let you find your own reviewer, either a classmate or someone outside of class. Class members make good reviewers, since they are familiar with the assignment and with what you have learned so far in the course. If you need to find someone outside of class, try to choose a person who has already taken the writing course you are taking, preferably someone who has done well. Close friends are not necessarily the best reviewers; they may be reluctant to offer criticism, or they may be too critical. Instead, choose someone who is serious, skillful, and willing to spend the time needed to provide useful comments. If your college has a writing center, you might ask a tutor in the center to read and comment on your draft. Consider using more than one reviewer so you can get several perspectives.

Suggestions for the Writer

To get the greatest benefit from having another student review your paper, use the following suggestions.

1. **Be sure to provide readable copy.** A typed, double-spaced draft is preferred.
2. **Do some revision yourself first.** If your essay is not very far along, think it through a little more, and try to fix at least some obvious problems. The more developed your draft is, the more helpful the reviewer's comments will be.
3. **Offer specific questions or guidelines to your reviewer.** A sample set of Questions for Reviewers is provided below. Give your reviewer a copy of these questions, adding others that you need answered. You might also give your reviewer questions from one of the revision flowcharts in this chapter. If you have

QUESTIONS FOR REVIEWERS

1. What is the purpose of the paper?
2. Who is the intended audience?
3. Is the introduction fully developed?
4. What is the main point or thesis? Is it easy to identify?
5. Does the essay offer evidence to support each important point? Where is more evidence needed? (Be sure to indicate specific paragraphs.)
6. Is each paragraph clear and well organized?
7. Are transitions used to connect ideas within and between paragraphs?
8. Is the organization easy to follow? Where might it be improved, and how?
9. Does the conclusion draw the essay to a satisfying close?
10. What do you like about the draft?
11. What are its weaknesses, and how could they be eliminated? Underline or highlight sentences that are unclear or confusing.

written an essay in response to an assignment in a later chapter, consider giving your reviewer the revision flowchart for that assignment.

4. **Be open to criticism and new ideas.** As much as possible, try not to be defensive; instead, look at your essay objectively, seeing it as your reviewer sees it.

5. **Don't feel obligated to accept all of the advice you are given.** A reviewer might suggest a change that will not work well in your paper or wrongly identify something as an error. If you are uncertain about a suggestion, discuss it with your instructor.

Suggestions for the Reviewer

Be honest but tactful. Criticism is never easy to accept, so keep your reader's feelings in mind. The following tips will help you provide useful comments.

1. **Read the draft through completely before making any judgments or comments.** You will need to read it at least twice to evaluate it.

2. **Concentrate on content; pay attention to what the paper says.** Evaluate the writer's train of thought; focus on the main points and how clearly they are expressed. If you notice a misspelling or a grammatical error, you can circle it, but correcting errors is not your primary task.

3. **Offer some positive comments.** It will help the writer to know what is good as well as what needs improvement.

4. **Be specific.** For instance, instead of saying that more examples are needed, tell the writer which ideas in which paragraphs are unclear without examples, and suggest what kind of example would be most useful in each case.

5. **Use the Questions for Reviewers on page 164 as well as any additional questions that the writer provides to guide your review.** If the essay was written in response to an assignment in one of the chapters in Parts 3 or 4, you might use the revision flowchart in that chapter.

6. **Write notes and comments directly on the draft. Then, at the end, write a note summarizing your overall reaction, pointing out both strengths and weaknesses.** Here is a sample final note written by a reviewer.

   Overall, I think your paper has great ideas, and I found that it held my interest. The example about the judge did prove your point. I think you should organize it better. The last three paragraphs do not seem connected to the rest of the essay. Maybe better transitions would help, too. Also work on the conclusion. It just says the same thing as your thesis statement.

7. **If you are reviewing a draft on a computer, type your comments in brackets following the appropriate passage, or highlight them in some other way.** The writer can easily delete your comments after reading them. Some word-processing programs have features for adding comments.

8. **Do not rewrite paragraphs or sections of the paper.** Instead, suggest how the writer might revise them.

Essay in Progress 5

Give your essay in progress to a classmate to read and review. Ask your reviewer to respond to the Questions for Reviewers. Revise your essay using your revision outline, your responses to Figures 8.3 and 8.4, and your reviewer's suggestions.

Using Your Instructor's Comments

Another resource to use in revising your essays is the commentary your instructor provides. These comments can be used not only to submit a revised version of a particular essay but also to improve your writing throughout the course.

Revising an Essay Using Your Instructor's Comments

Your instructor may want to review a draft of your essay and suggest revisions you can make for the final version. Some instructors allow students to revise and resubmit a paper and then give the students an average of the two grades. Either way, your instructor's comments can provide a road map for you to begin your revision. Review the comments on your essays carefully, looking for problems that recur, so that you can focus on these elements in your future writing.

Different instructors may use different terminology when they mark up writing assignments, but most like to point out several common problems. The marks on your essay will often address spelling and grammar errors, and problems with organization and with the clarity or development of ideas.

Figure 8.5 shows a first draft of an essay by a student, David Harris, that has been read and marked up by his instructor. The assignment was to write an essay defining a specialized term, and the student chose the salary cap in professional football as his subject. Note that the instructor has commented on a range of elements in the essay, including grammar, structure and organization, effectiveness of the introduction, paragraph unity and development, and transitions. Some spelling and punctuation errors have not been marked. Harris read the comments carefully and used them to revise his essay. His final draft appears in Chapter 16 (pp. 431–33).

FIGURE 8.5 Using Your Instructor's Comments to Revise Your Essay

NFL salary cap

In the 1990s sports salaries increased at record-breaking   1
rates. The onset of free agency caused owners to search for ways
to limit the ballooning salaries. [In previous years players were   Run-on
owned by a team, when a players' contract ran out, the players
needed permission to negotiate with other teams.] [Beginning   Run-on
in the 70's and 80's, after a contract expired players were free to
negotiate with any team, this freedom caused bidding wars that
eventually raised salaries dramatically.] A salary cap in sports

List events in order —

is a limit on the amount of money a team can spend on player salaries, either as a per-player limit or a total limit for the team's roster. (http://www.wordiq.com/definition/Salary cap) The NFL (National Football League) instituted a salary cap in 1994. Since that time no team has won more than two super bowls and only the 1998 and 1999 broncos won consecutive Super Bowls; the most appearances by one team is three ("Super Bowl History"). Baseball however, a sport without a salary cap, the New York Yankees have won 4 times and made 6 total appearances (http://www.mlb.com). The salary cap has given every team regardless of revenue a chance to compete for the championship of their respective sport.

The NFL salary cap is a total team limit salary cap; in 2006 the NFL salary cap was $102 million ("2007 NFL Salary Cap Figures"). All NFL teams must bring their total salaries paid down to this $102 million mark. A player's salary is not always the same as their value according to the salary cap. Signing bonuses are distributed over the length of the contract unevenly, if the teams choose to do so. Many teams run into huge salary cap problems because of back-loaded contracts. [A Super Bowl team] one year could have to cut many of its star players to remain under the salary cap. In 2003 the Tampa Bay Buccaneers won the Super Bowl, but failed to make the playoffs the following year. Continued success in the NFL is a product of good management and good scouting. A rookie contract, typically, is much smaller than that of a proven player. Replacing high-priced veterans with low-cost rookies is an excellent way to manage a cap, and translates into more money for other positions.

The NFL salary cap is absolute, but, it does change from year to year. [In 2005 the NFL salary cap was $85.5 million, it increased by 19.3% to $102 million dollars in 2006 ("2007 NFL Salary Cap Figures").] The salary cap is not randomly set. It is a calculation of a percentage of combined revenue of each team divided by the 32 teams in the NFL. This salary cap is in effect for the whole season. If a team exceeds the salary cap at any point in the season the NFL has the right to cut any player starting from the lowest salary until the team is below the set cap. Cut-

---

Marginal comments (left):

Why baseball? Title says "NFL..."

Intro lacks focus and unity. What is your main point?

Subject-pronoun agreement

Connection is unclear

Clarify connection for reader

Run-on

Marginal comments (right):

Central definition is buried here

Too specific for intro

Nice, strong thesis! Need more info at beginning on how caps were started

Subject-pronoun agreement

A team in the Bowl? Or the winner?

Tie this fact in specifically, or omit it

Clarify connection for reader

Commas

Examples?

Paragraph numbers: 2, 3

ting a player from a team eliminates him from team's payroll and

How is this related to subject of paragraph?

any team can acquire him at his current contracted rate. [This is the fate of many players as they reach the twilight years of their careers.]

Need transition

Sports without salary caps have had trouble keeping the level 4 of competition equal. In Major League baseball the largest markets dominate and teams in smaller cities can not compete. The New York Yankees' salary has been the highest in the league since 1996, and since then they have won 4 World Series and finished first in their division almost every year. There is no team even close to this kind of dominance in the NFL. The salary cap keeps smaller city teams, with less revenue like The Buffalo Bills in contention.

Rest of paragraph doesn't follow from first sentence

[There are many reasons that not all sports have salary 5 caps.] The NFL salary cap was first negotiated by the players' union and the owners union in 1994. In the same year baseball owners tried to impose a salary cap. The players' union strongly opposed this action; the union went on strike, canceling the entire postseason for the first time since World War II. It is still a highly contested topic in baseball. The NFL has benefited greatly from its addition of the salary cap. They have created their own network, The NFL Network, and fan interest is at record levels.

This info would be helpful at beginning

The salary cap has had a tremendous impact on the game of 6 football, the fans of football and the owners of football teams. The limit on players' salaries keeps all teams in contention, and for that, the fans are grateful.

Need stronger, more developed conclusion

Exercise 8.1

Working either alone or in small groups, compare the first draft of David Harris's essay with the final version on pages 431–33. Make a list of the changes Harris made to his essay in response to his instructor's comments. Also, put a checkmark next to any problems that recur throughout the first draft of the essay.

Exercise 8.2

If your instructor has returned a marked-up first draft to you, read the comments carefully. Then draw a line down the middle of a blank piece of paper. On the left, write the instructor's comments; on the right, jot down ways you might revise the essay in response to each. Put a checkmark next to any problems that recur throughout your essay; these are areas you will want to pay particular attention to in your future writing.

Using Your Instructor's Comments to Improve Future Essays

When you receive a graded essay back from an instructor, it is tempting to note the grade and then file away the essay. To improve your writing, however, take time to study each comment. Use the following suggestions.

- **Reread your essay more than once.** Read it once to note grammatical corrections, and then read it again to study comments about organization or content. Processing numerous comments on a wide range of topics takes more than one reading.
- **For grammar errors, make sure you understand the error.** Check a grammar handbook or ask a classmate; if the error is still unclear, check with your instructor.
- **Record grammar errors in your error log (see Chapter 9, p. 196).** When you proofread your next essay, be sure to look carefully for each of these errors.
- **If you did not get a high grade, try to determine why.** Was the essay weak in content, organization, or development?
- **Using Figures 8.3 and 8.4, highlight or mark weaknesses that your instructor identified.** When writing your next essay, refer back to these flowcharts. Pay special attention to these areas as you evaluate your next paper.
- **If any of your instructor's comments are unclear, first ask a classmate if he or she understands them.** If not, then ask your instructor, who will be pleased that you are taking time to study the comments.

Considering Your Learning Style

Depending on your learning style, you may tend to focus on some elements of an essay and overlook others. For example, a pragmatic learner tends to write tightly organized drafts, but they may lack interest, originality, or sufficient content. A creative learner may write drafts that lack organization. Writers with different learning styles may need to address different kinds of problems as they revise their drafts.

Learning Style Options

   Following are some revision tips for other aspects of your learning style.

- *Independent* learners, who often need extra time for reflection, should be sure to allow sufficient time between drafting and revising. *Social* learners often find discussing revision plans with classmates particularly helpful.
- *Verbal* learners may prefer to use outlining to check the organization of their drafts, while *spatial* learners may find it more helpful to draw a graphic organizer.
- *Rational* learners should be sure their drafts do not seem dull or impersonal, adding vivid descriptions and personal examples where appropriate. *Emotional* learners, whose writing may tend to be overly personal, should state their ideas directly, without hedging or showing undue concern for those who may disagree.
- *Concrete* learners, who tend to focus on specifics, should check that their thesis and topic sentences are clearly stated. *Abstract* learners, who tend to focus on general ideas, should be sure they have enough supporting details.

Students Write

After writing her first draft, which appears in Chapter 6 (pp. 132–33), Christine Lee used the guidelines and revision flowcharts in this chapter to help her decide what to revise. For example, she decided that she needed to add more details about what happened on the TV show *Survivor*. She also decided that she should emphasize the uninteresting details of the examples of some other reality TV shows.

Lee asked a classmate named Sam to review her essay. A portion of Sam's comments is shown below.

REVIEWER'S COMMENTS

The trend that you have chosen to write about is well-known and interesting. Beginning your introduction with a question piques the reader's interest, and your thesis is clear: Reality TV shows are becoming less interesting and tasteful. You mention why people enjoyed *Survivor* and why they didn't enjoy the other shows. You should also emphasize why television viewers watched *Survivor*. Once that point is clear, many of your ideas might fit better.

I think some specific details about the example reality TV shows you mention would help readers who are not familiar with the shows. It would also help prove your point: These shows are getting worse.

The title and conclusion could better help make this point too. The title doesn't indicate what the reality of reality TV is, and the conclusion could look ahead to what you think the fate of reality TV will be.

Using her own analysis and her classmate's suggestions, Lee created a graphic organizer to help her decide how to revise her draft, using the format for an illustration essay provided in Chapter 12 (on p. 276). Lee's graphic organizer, which includes her notes for revision, is shown in Figure 8.6.

After creating the graphic organizer, Lee revised her first draft. A portion of her revised draft, with her revisions marked, follows.

REVISED DRAFT

A Trend Taken Too Far:
The Reality of Real TV

Do you remember life before the reality TV craze? ~~One look at a *TV Guide* today shows~~

~~an overload of reality-based programming, even with the guaranteed failure of most of these~~

Before reality TV television viewers seemed interested only in the fictional lives of characters in
shows. ~~Before *Survivor* there was only~~ situational comedies and serial dramas. *Survivor* caught

the attention of even more viewers and dominated television ratings. Television
~~every viewers' attention. Every network in American believed they must also become "real" to~~

Survivor was engaging and dramatic, but the shows *, lacking drama and*
~~keep up its ratings.~~ Shows that followed it were less interesting and less tasteful ~~in the hopes~~

relying on gimmicks.
~~of finding a show as original, inventive and engaging as the first *Survivor*.~~

Characters were played by professional actors and the shows were written by professional writers. Except for a few early reality type shows such as Cops *and* Candid Camera, *this simple formula was what network television offered. Then came MTV's* The Real World *in 1992. The high ratings that this cable show garnered made network executives take notice of the genre. Eventually* Survivor *debuted in the summer of 2000.*

networks changed their programming. It seemed that every network acted as though it had to become "real" to compete with Survivor *and maintain viewer interest. The problem with networks trying to copy* Survivor *is that the original* Survivor *offered more interesting elements to its audience than any reality TV show modeled after it.*

Figure 8.6 GRAPHIC ORGANIZER FOR CHRISTINE LEE'S REVISION PLANS

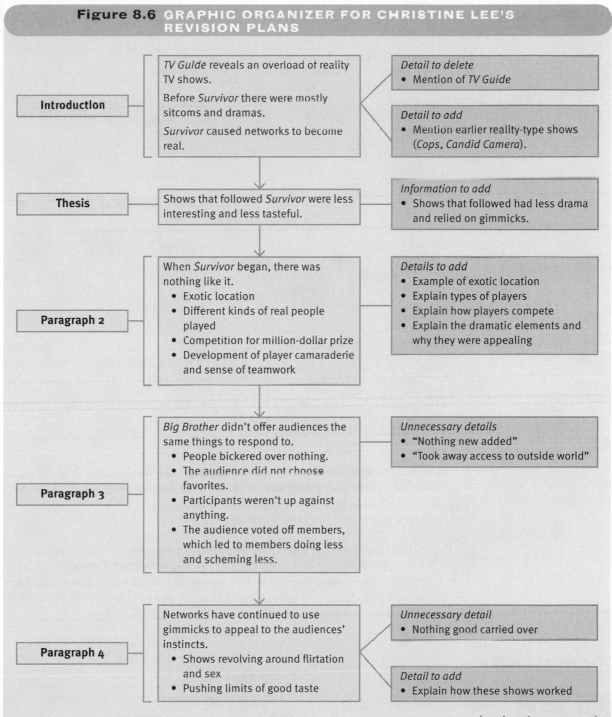

Introduction

TV Guide reveals an overload of reality TV shows.

Before *Survivor* there were mostly sitcoms and dramas.

Survivor caused networks to become real.

Detail to delete
- Mention of *TV Guide*

Detail to add
- Mention earlier reality-type shows (*Cops*, *Candid Camera*).

Thesis

Shows that followed *Survivor* were less interesting and less tasteful.

Information to add
- Shows that followed had less drama and relied on gimmicks.

Paragraph 2

When *Survivor* began, there was nothing like it.
- Exotic location
- Different kinds of real people played
- Competition for million-dollar prize
- Development of player camaraderie and sense of teamwork

Details to add
- Example of exotic location
- Explain types of players
- Explain how players compete
- Explain the dramatic elements and why they were appealing

Paragraph 3

Big Brother didn't offer audiences the same things to respond to.
- People bickered over nothing.
- The audience did not choose favorites.
- Participants weren't up against anything.
- The audience voted off members, which led to members doing less and scheming less.

Unnecessary details
- "Nothing new added"
- "Took away access to outside world"

Paragraph 4

Networks have continued to use gimmicks to appeal to the audiences' instincts.
- Shows revolving around flirtation and sex
- Pushing limits of good taste

Unnecessary detail
- Nothing good carried over

Detail to add
- Explain how these shows worked

(continued on next page)

Figure 8.6 *(continued)*

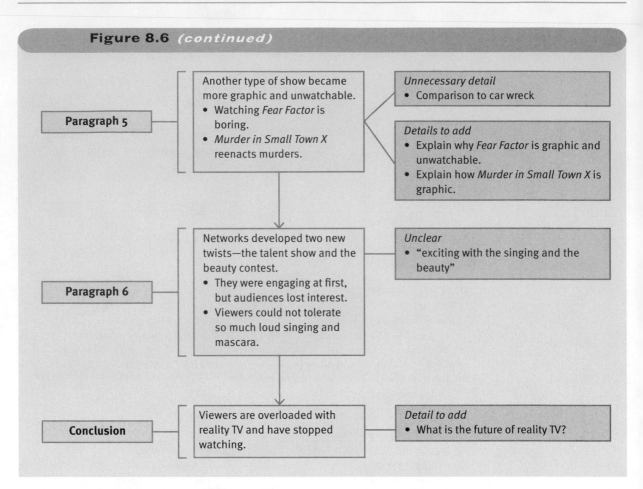

Survivor captured the interest of a wide viewing audience because it was fresh and provocative.

When *Survivor* began in the summer of 2000, there was nothing else like it on TV. *Survivor*

participants. *There was* *where contestants competed against each other*

had real people in a contest in an exotic location.

Before Lee submitted her final draft, she read her essay several more times, editing it for sentence structure and word choice. She also proofread it once to catch errors in grammar and punctuation as well as typographical errors. (A portion of Lee's revised essay, with editing and proofreading changes marked, appears in Chapter 9, pp. 196–97.) The final version of Lee's essay follows.

FINAL DRAFT

Title: a play on words catches the reader's attention

A Trend Taken Too Far: The Reality of Real TV

Christine Lee

Do you remember life before the reality TV craze? Before reality TV, television viewers seemed interested only in the fictional lives of characters in situational comedies and serial dramas. Characters were played by professional actors, and the shows were written by professional writers. Except for a few early reality type shows such as *Cops* and *Candid Camera,* this simple formula was what network television offered. Then came MTV's *The Real World* in 1992. The high ratings that this cable show garnered made network executives take notice of the genre. Eventually *Survivor* debuted in the summer of 2000. When *Survivor* caught the attention of even more viewers and dominated television ratings, television networks changed their programming. It seemed that every network acted as though it had to become "real" to compete with *Survivor* and maintain viewer interest. The problem with networks trying to copy *Survivor* is that the original *Survivor* offered more interesting elements to its audience than any reality TV show modeled after it. *Survivor* was engaging and dramatic, but the shows that followed it were less interesting and less tasteful, lacking drama and relying on gimmicks.

Background information on shows leading up to reality TV

Thesis statement is focused and detailed

Survivor captured the interest of a wide viewing audience because it was fresh and entertaining. *Survivor* introduced real participants in a contest where they competed against each other in an exotic location. The participants on *Survivor* were ethnically and socially diverse and represented a variety of ages including younger, middle aged, and older adults. The location for *Survivor* was fascinating; a South Pacific island was more interesting than any house full of people on a sitcom. However, the most unique feature of *Survivor* was to make the participants compete for a million-dollar prize. Contestants were divided into two camps that had to compete to win everyday supplies, like food and shelter. At the end of each episode, players voted, and one of them was kicked off the show and lost his or her chance for the million dollars. The last contestant on the island won. To win the game, contestants created alliances and manipulated other contestants. All of these unique elements drew television viewers back each week.

2 Topic sentence supports part of thesis statement: "*Survivor* was engaging and dramatic."

Details offer reasons that support the topic sentence.

The television audience responded favorably to the dramatic elements of *Survivor*. The competition gave viewers something to speculate about as the show progressed. Viewers' allegiance to one team over another or one player over another developed from episode to episode. Viewers were fascinated watching these players struggle in primitive situations, compete in tasks of strength and skill, and decide on how to cast their votes. The phrase "getting voted off the island" became a recognizable saying across America. While players displayed positive human traits like teamwork, compassion, and camaraderie, they also schemed and plotted to win the allegiance of their fellow players. This situation made *Survivor* dramatic, and the viewers were attracted to the drama. Reality TV shows that followed *Survivor* had none of the interesting elements that it had.

3 Topic sentence continues to support thesis by explaining engaging aspects of *Survivor*.

Specific details about dramatic elements support the topic sentence.

Big Brother was the first spin-off reality TV show to try and repeat the success of *Survivor*, but it did not offer the drama that *Survivor* did. In *Big Brother,* contestants were locked in a house without any outside contact for weeks. Like *Survivor,* there was a cash prize on the line,

4 Topic sentence supports thesis that later shows were "less interesting."

Concrete details about *Big Brother* contestants

but in *Big Brother* there were not any competitions or struggles. Contestants were expelled by a viewer phone poll, but the viewer phone poll gave the house members no motive to scheme and plot allegiances like *Survivor*. In fact, the contestants had little to do, and viewers were forced to watch bored contestants bicker and fight. Viewers were not interested in the players who were not up against anything except fighting off weeks of boredom. In the end, *Big Brother* was simply not interesting.

Topic sentence identifies one of the "gimmicks" mentioned in the thesis.

Detailed examples support the topic sentence and the "less tasteful" point in the thesis.

Attempts to make reality TV more interesting failed because they relied on sensational gimmicks; the first of these gimmicks was sex. Shows like *Chains of Love, Temptation Island,* and *Love Cruise* revolved around flirtation and sex where contestants competed for prizes by flirting with members of the opposite sex. In every one of these shows, members of the opposite sex were organized in a way to make them grow jealous. For example, *Temptation Island* featured engaged couples living in separate camps, surrounded by attractive members of the opposite sex. The premise of the show was to see if engaged couples could resist temptation and remain engaged. Viewers might have responded to the sexual intrigue, but these sexually charged situations turned viewers away pushing the limits of taste.

Topic sentence identifies another gimmick.

Examples of other shows continue to support the "less tasteful" idea.

After using sex to try and interest viewers, the next wave of reality TV shows tried another gimmick—the use of graphic displays of terror and violence. Examples of this type of reality show include *Murder in Small Town X* and *Fear Factor*. Both feature graphic scenes that repulsed viewers. *Murder in Small Town X* featured a murder mystery where contestants worked together to solve a made-up crime. Just as survival on a Pacific Island interested viewers, the mystery plot in *Murder in Small Town X* was supposed to interest viewers, but the show went too far in its tasteless depiction of violence. The show opens with a reenactment from the murderer's point of view and ends with the viewers watching one of two chosen players getting fictitiously attacked and killed. The randomness of who got killed and the graphic way it was presented turned viewers away. Similarly, *Fear Factor* has its contestants commit all manner of gross and terrifying acts, like eating worms or being immersed in live rats. Some viewers may hold some interest in watching how far the contestants will go, but the majority of viewers regard these acts with disgust. Viewers might tune in once or twice but, disgusted, will not be interested in the long run.

Topic sentence explains additional gimmicks.

Details about talent shows and beauty contests

When these gimmicks did not retain viewers, two traditional types of reality TV were revived with modern twists added--the talent show and the beauty contest. So were born shows like *American Idol* and *America's Top Model*. Again, there was no built-in drama as in *Survivor*, so the shows tried to create drama using colorful judges and supportive fans. At first, these twists provided enough spectacle to engage viewers, but after a while, audiences lost interest. Even footage showing the long lines that contestants had to wait in, and the despair of those who did not make the cut did not help to keep viewers hooked on these types of reality shows. Viewers could only tolerate so much loud singing and mascara.

Viewers understandably were not interested in the tasteless and uninteresting gimmicks that   8 were featured in the reality TV shows that followed *Survivor*. In the end, it is the viewers who determine what gets shown on television. As reality TV becomes less interesting and less tasteful, ratings will drop. One can hope that there will be less reality TV, and viewers can return to their familiar situational comedies and serial dramas, or perhaps to another form of engaging program that may evolve.

Conclusion returns to thesis and looks ahead to better shows.

Analyzing the Revision

1. Identify the major revisions that Lee made from the earlier draft in Chapter 6 (pp. 132–33). How did she carry out the plan indicated in her graphic organizer?
2. Choose one major revision that Lee made and explain why you think it improved her essay.
3. Evaluate Lee's introduction and conclusion. In what ways are they more effective than the introduction and conclusion in her first draft? What additional improvements could she make?
4. Choose one paragraph and compare the details provided in it with those in the corresponding paragraph of the first draft. Which added details are particularly effective, and why?

"Sorry, but I'm going to have to issue you a summons for reckless grammar and driving without an apostrophe."

CHAPTER 9

Editing Sentences and Words

The cartoons on the facing page take a humorous view of language; however, each makes a point about writing as well.

Write a few sentences describing what you think the cartoons suggest about writing and about the focus of this chapter—editing sentences and words.

FIGURE 9.1 An Overview of the Writing Process

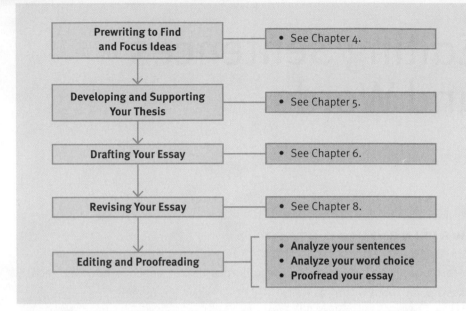

Once you have revised an essay for content and organization, as discussed in Chapter 8, you are ready to edit and proofread the essay. Your task is to examine individual sentences and words with care, to be sure that each conveys your meaning accurately, concisely, and in an interesting way. Even an essay with good ideas will be ineffective if its sentences are vague and wordy or if its words convey an inappropriate tone and level of diction. This chapter will help you sharpen your sentences and refine your word choice.

As shown in Figure 9.1, editing and proofreading are the final steps in the writing process. Because you are almost finished with your assignment, you may be tempted to hurry through these steps or to skip them altogether. Careful editing and proofreading will always pay off in the end, however, because an error-free essay makes a good impression on the reader.

Analyzing Your Sentences

Effective sentences have four important characteristics:

- **They should be clear and concise.**
- **They should be varied.**
- **They should use parallel structure for similar ideas.**
- **They should contain strong, active verbs.**

Use the questions in the next four sections to analyze your sentences, and use the suggestions in each section to create more effective sentences.

Are Your Sentences Concise?

Sentences that are concise convey their meaning in as few words as possible. Use the following suggestions to make your sentences concise.

1. Avoid wordy expressions. Search your essay for sentences with empty phrases that contribute little or no meaning. If the sentence is clear without a particular phrase or if the phrase can be replaced by a more direct word or phrase, take it out or replace it. Here are a few examples.

- ~~In the near future,~~ _Aanother revolution in computer technology is bound to occur. *soon.*

- ~~In light of the fact that~~ *Since* computer technology changes *monthly* ~~every month or so~~, software

  upgrades are *necessary* ~~what everybody has to do.~~

2. Eliminate redundancy. Look for places where you may have repeated an idea unnecessarily by using the same words or different words that have the same meaning. Here are some examples.

- ~~My decision to choose~~ *Choosing* accounting as my major will lead to steady, rewarding employment.

- Teenagers use slang to establish ~~who they are and what~~ their identity ~~is~~.

3. Eliminate unnecessary sentence openings. When you first write down an idea, you may express it indirectly or tentatively. As you revise, look for and edit sentence openings that sound indirect or tentative. Consider these examples.

- ~~It is my opinion that~~ *F*fast-food restaurants should post nutritional information for each menu item.

- ~~Many people would agree that~~ *S*selecting nutritious snacks is a priority for health-conscious people.

4. Eliminate unnecessary adverbs. Using too many **adverbs** can weaken your writing. Adverbs such as *extremely*, *really*, and *very*, known as intensifiers, add nothing and can actually weaken the word they modify. Notice that the following sentence is stronger without the adverb.

An **adverb** modifies a verb, an adjective, or another adverb.

- The journalist was ~~very~~ elated when he learned that he had won a Pulitzer Prize.

Other adverbs, such as *somewhat*, *rather*, and *quite*, also add little or no meaning and are often unnecessary.

- The college president was **quite** disturbed by the findings of the Presidential Panel on Sex Equity.

A **prepositional phrase** is a group of words that begins with a preposition and includes the object or objects of the preposition and all their modifiers: *above the low wooden table.*

5. Eliminate unnecessary phrases and clauses. Wordy phrases and clauses can make it difficult for readers to find and understand the main point of your sentence. This problem often occurs when you use too many **prepositional phrases** and clauses that begin with *who*, *which*, or *that*.

- The complaints ~~of students in the college~~ encouraged the dean to create additional parking spaces. *(students')*

- The ~~teenagers who were~~ mall walkers disagreed with the editorial ~~in the newspaper~~ ~~that supported the~~ shopping mall regulations. *(teenage) (newspaper) (supporting)*

6. Avoid weak verb-noun combinations. Weak verb-noun combinations such as *wrote a draft* instead of *drafted* or *made a change* instead of *changed* tend to make sentences wordy.

- The attorney ~~made an assessment of~~ the company's liability in the accident. *(assessed)*

- The professor ~~gave a lecture~~ on Asian American relations. *(lectured)*

Exercise 9.1

Edit the following sentences to make them concise.

1. Due to the fact that Professor Wu assigned twenty-five math problems for tomorrow, I am forced to make the decision to miss this evening's lecture to be given by the vice president of the United States.

2. In many cases, workers are forced to use old equipment that needs replacing despite the fact that equipment malfunctions cost the company more than the price of new machines.

3. Britney Spears is one of the best examples of an entertainment celebrity being given too much publicity.

4. The president of Warehouse Industries has the ability and power to decide who should and who should not be hired and who should and who should not be fired.

5. The soccer league's sponsor, as a matter of fact, purchased league jerseys for the purpose of advertisement and publicity.

Are Your Sentences Varied?

Sentences that are varied will help hold your reader's interest and make your writing flow more smoothly. Vary the type, length, and pattern of your sentences.

How to Vary Sentence Type

There are four basic types of sentences—*simple, compound, complex,* and *compound-complex.* Each type consists of one or more clauses. A **clause** is a group of words with both a subject and a verb. There are two types of clauses. An **independent clause** can stand alone as a complete sentence. A **dependent clause** cannot stand alone as a complete sentence. It begins with a subordinating conjunction (for example, *because* or *although*) or a relative pronoun (for example, *when*, *which*, or *that*).

Here is a brief summary of each sentence type and its clauses.

Sentence Type	*Clauses*	*Example*
Simple	One independent clause and no dependent clauses	Credit card fraud is increasing in the United States.
Compound	Two or more independent clauses and no dependent clauses	Credit card fraud is increasing in the United States; it is a violation of financial privacy.
Complex	One or more dependent clauses and one independent clause	Because credit card fraud is increasing in America, consumers must become more cautious.
Compound-Complex	One or more dependent clauses and two or more independent clauses	Because credit card fraud is increasing in America, consumers must be cautious, and retailers must take steps to protect consumers.

Use the following suggestions to vary your sentence types.

1. Use simple sentences for emphasis and clarity. A **simple sentence** contains only one independent clause, but it is not necessarily short. It can have more than one subject, more than one verb, and several modifiers.

- Both retailers and consumers have and must exercise the responsibility to curtail fraud by reporting suspicious use of credit cards.

A short, simple sentence can be used to emphasize an important point or to make a dramatic statement.

- Credit card fraud is rampant.

If you use too many simple sentences, however, your writing will sound choppy and disjointed.

- It was a cold, drizzly spring morning. I was driving to school. A teenage hitchhiker stood alongside the road. He seemed distraught.

2. Use compound sentences to show relationships between equally important ideas. A **compound sentence** consists of two or more independent clauses joined in one of the following ways.

Coordinating conjunctions
(*and, but, or, nor, for, so, yet*)
connect sentence elements that
are of equal importance.

A **conjunctive adverb** is a word
(such as *also*, *however*, or *still*)
that links two independent
clauses.

A **correlative conjunction** is a
word pair (such as *not only . . . but
also*) that works together to join
elements within a sentence.

- With a comma and **coordinating conjunction** (*and, but, or, nor, for, so, yet*):
  - Leon asked a question, *and* the whole class was surprised.
- With a semicolon:
  - Graffiti had been scrawled on the subway walls; passersby ignored it.
- With a semicolon and a **conjunctive adverb**:
  - Each year thousands of children are adopted; *consequently*, adoption service agencies have increased in number.
- With a **correlative conjunction**:
  - *Either* the jury will reach a verdict tonight, *or* it will recess until Monday morning.

Notice that in each example, both clauses are equally important and receive equal emphasis.

You can also use compound sentences to explain *how* equally important ideas are related. You can, for example, suggest each of the following relationships, depending on the coordinating conjunction you choose.

Coordinating Conjunction	Relationship	Example
and	additional information	The three teenage vandals were apprehended, *and* their parents were required to pay damages.
but, yet	contrast or opposites	No one wants to pay more taxes, *yet* taxes are necessary to support vital public services.
for, so	causes or effects	Telephone calls can interrupt a busy worker constantly, *so* answering machines are a necessity.
or, nor	choices or options	Quebec may become a separate country, *or* it may settle its differences with the Canadian government.

3. Use complex sentences to show that one or more ideas are less important than (or subordinate to) another idea. A **complex sentence** consists of one independent clause and at least one dependent clause; either type of clause may come first. When the dependent clause appears first, it is usually followed by a comma. When the independent clause comes first, a comma is usually not used.

- Because the dam broke, the village flooded.
- The village flooded because the dam broke.

In the preceding sentences, the main point is that the village flooded. The dependent clause explains *why* the flood happened. A dependent clause often begins with a *subordinating conjunction* that indicates how the less important (dependent) idea is related to the more important (independent) idea. Here is a list of some subordinating conjunctions and the relationships they suggest.

Subordinating Conjunction	Relationship	Example
as, as far as, as soon as, as if, as though, although, even though, even if, in order to	circumstance	*Even though* cable television has expanded, it is still unavailable in some rural areas.
because, since, so that	causes or effects	*Because* the movie industry has changed, the way theaters are built has changed.
before, after, while, until, when	time	*When* prices rise, demand falls.
whether, if, unless, even if	condition	More people will purchase hybrid cars *if* they become less expensive.

Dependent clauses can also begin with a relative pronoun (*that, who, which*).

■ **Many medical doctors** *who are affiliated with a teaching hospital use interns in* **their practices.**

To see how complex sentences can improve your writing, study the following two paragraphs. The first paragraph consists primarily of simple and compound sentences. The revised paragraph uses complex sentences that show relationships.

ORIGINAL

Are you one of the many people who has tried to quit smoking? Well, don't give up trying. Help is here in the form of a nonprescription drug. A new nicotine patch has been developed. This patch will help you quit gradually. That way, you will experience less severe withdrawal symptoms. Quitting will be easier than ever before, but you need to be psychologically ready to quit smoking. Otherwise, you may not be successful.

REVISED

If you are one of the many people who has tried to quit smoking, don't give up trying. Help is now here in the form of a nonprescription nicotine patch, which has been developed to help you quit gradually. Because you experience less severe withdrawal symptoms, quitting is easier than ever before. However, for this patch to be successful, you need to be psychologically ready to quit.

4. Use compound-complex sentences occasionally to express complicated relationships. A compound-complex sentence contains one or more dependent clauses and two or more independent clauses.

■ **If you expect to study medicine, you must take courses in biology and chemistry, and you must prepare for four more years of study after college.**

Use compound-complex sentences sparingly; when overused, they make your writing hard to follow.

Exercise 9.2

Combine each of the following sentence pairs into a single compound or complex sentence.

1. A day-care center may look respectable.
   Parents assume a day-care center is safe and run well.

2. In some states, the training required to become a day-care worker is minimal.
   On-the-job supervision and evaluation of day-care workers are infrequent.

3. Restaurants are often fined or shut down for minor hygiene violations.
   Day-care centers are rarely fined or closed down for hygiene violations.

4. More and more mothers have entered the workforce.
   The need for quality day care has increased dramatically.

5. Naturally, day-care workers provide emotional support for children. Few day-care workers are trained to provide intellectual stimulation.

How to Vary Sentence Length

Usually, if you vary sentence type, you will automatically vary sentence length as well. Simple sentences tend to be short, whereas compound and complex sentences tend to be longer. Compound-complex sentences tend to be the longest. You can, however, use sentence length for specific effect. Short sentences tend to be sharp and emphatic; they move ideas along quickly, creating a fast-paced essay. In the following example, a series of short sentences creates a dramatic pace.

■ **The jurors had little to debate. The incriminating evidence was clear and incontrovertible. The jury announced its verdict with astonishing speed.**

Longer sentences, in contrast, move the reader more slowly through the essay. Notice that the lengthy sentence in this example suggests a leisurely, unhurried pace.

■ **While standing in line, impatient to ride the antique steam-powered train, the child begins to imagine how the train will crawl deliberately, endlessly, along the tracks, slowly gathering speed as it spews grayish steam and emits hissing noises.**

How to Vary Sentence Pattern

A sentence is usually made up of one or more subjects, verbs, and modifiers. **Modifiers** are words (adjectives or adverbs), phrases, or clauses that describe or limit another part of the sentence (a noun, pronoun, verb, phrase, or clause). Here are some examples of modifiers in sentences.

WORDS AS MODIFIERS	The *empty* classroom was unlocked. [adjective]
	The office runs *smoothly*. [adverb]
PHRASES AS MODIFIERS	The student *in the back* raised his hand.
	Schools should not have the right *to mandate community service*.
CLAUSES AS MODIFIERS	The baseball *that flew into the stands* was caught by a fan.
	When the exam was over, I knew I had earned an A.

As you can see, the placement of modifiers may vary, depending on the pattern of the sentence.

1. Modifier last: subject-verb-modifier. In this sentence pattern, the main message (expressed in the subject and verb) comes first, followed by information that clarifies or explains the message.

subject *verb* *modifier*
- The instructor walked into the room.

In some cases, a string of modifiers follows the subject and verb.

subject *verb* *modifiers*
- The salesperson demonstrated the word-processing software, creating and deleting files, moving text, creating directories, and formatting tables.

2. Modifier first: modifier-subject-verb. Sentences that follow this pattern are called **periodic sentences**. Notice that information in the modifier precedes the main message, elaborating the main message but slowing the overall pace. The emphasis is on the main message at the end of the sentence.

modifier *subject* *verb*
- Tired and depressed from hours of work, the divers left the scene of the accident.

Use this sentence pattern sparingly. Too many periodic sentences will make your writing sound stiff and unnatural.

3. Modifier in the middle: subject-modifier-verb. In sentences that follow this pattern, the modifier or modifiers appear between the subject and the verb. The modifier thus interrupts the main message and tends to slow the pace of the sentence. The emphasis is on the subject because it comes first in the sentence.

subject *modifier* *verb*
- The paramedic, trained and experienced in water rescue, was first on the scene of the boating accident.

Avoid placing too many modifiers between the subject and verb in a sentence. Doing so may cause your reader to miss the sentence's key idea.

4. Modifiers used throughout. In this pattern, modifiers are used throughout a sentence.

modifier *subject*
- Because human organs are in short supply, awarding an organ transplant, especially

modifier *verb* *modifier*
hearts and kidneys, to patients has become a controversial issue, requiring difficult

medical and ethical decisions.

By varying the order of subjects, verbs, and modifiers, you can give emphasis where it is needed as well as vary sentence patterns as shown in the paragraphs that follow.

ORIGINAL

monotonous use of same subject-verb-modifier pattern

Theme parks are growing in number and popularity. Theme parks have a single purpose—to provide family entertainment centered around high-action activities. The most famous theme parks are Disney World and Disneyland. They serve as models for other, smaller parks. Theme parks always have amusement rides. Theme parks can offer other activities such as swimming. Theme parks will probably continue to be popular.

REVISED

ideas come alive through use of varied sentence patterns

Theme parks are growing in number and popularity. Offering high-action activities, theme parks fulfill a single purpose—to provide family entertainment. The most famous parks, Disney World and Disneyland, serve as models for other, smaller parks. Parks always offer amusement rides, which appeal to both children and adults. Added attractions such as swimming, water slides, and boat rides provide thrills and recreation. Because of their family focus, theme parks are likely to grow in popularity.

Exercise 9.3

Add modifiers to the following sentences to create varied sentence patterns.

1. The divers jumped into the chilly waters.
2. The beach was closed because of pollution.
3. Coffee-flavored drinks are becoming popular.
4. The dorm was crowded and noisy.
5. The exam was more challenging than we expected.

Are Your Sentences Parallel in Structure?

Parallelism means that similar ideas in a sentence are expressed in similar grammatical form. It means balancing words with words, phrases with phrases, and clauses with clauses. Use parallelism to make your sentences flow smoothly and your thoughts easy to follow. Study the following pairs of sentences. Which sentence in each pair is easier to read?

- The horse was large, had a bony frame, and it was friendly.
- The horse was large, bony, and friendly.

- Maria enjoys swimming and sailboats.
- Maria enjoys swimming and sailing.

In each pair, the second sentence sounds better because it is balanced grammatically. *Large, bony,* and *friendly* are all adjectives. *Swimming* and *sailing* are nouns ending in *-ing.*

The following sentence elements should be parallel in structure.

1. **Nouns in a series should be parallel.**

   - A *clear* thesis statement, ~~that is clear,~~ strong supporting paragraphs, and *an interesting* a conclusion ~~that should be interesting~~ are all elements of a well-written essay.

2. **Adjectives in a series should be parallel.**

   - The concertgoers were rowdy and *noisy.* ~~making a great deal of noise.~~

3. **Verbs in a series should be parallel.**

   - The sports fans jumped and *applauded.* ~~were applauding.~~

4. **Phrases and clauses within a sentence should be parallel.**

   - The parents who supervised the new playground were pleased *that* ~~about~~ the pre-schoolers *played* ~~playing~~ congenially and that everyone enjoyed the sandbox.

5. **Items being compared should be parallel.** When items within a sentence are compared or contrasted, use the same grammatical form for each item.

   - It is usually better to study for an exam over a period of time than *to cram* ~~cramming~~ the night before.

Exercise 9.4

Edit the following sentences to eliminate problems with parallelism.

1. The biology student spent Saturday morning reviewing his weekly textbook assignments, writing a research report, and with lab reports.

2. The career counselor advised Althea to take several math courses and that she should also register for at least one computer course.

3. Three reasons for the popularity of fast-food restaurants are that they are efficient, offer reasonable prices, and most people like the food they serve.

4. Driving to Boston is as expensive as it is to take the train.

5. While at a stop sign, it is important first to look both ways and then proceeding with caution is wise.

Do Your Sentences Have Strong, Active Verbs?

Strong, active verbs make your writing lively and vivid. By contrast, *to be* verbs (*is, was, were, has been,* and so on) and other **linking verbs** (*feels, became, seems, appears*), which connect a noun or pronoun to words that describe it, can make your writing sound dull. Often, these verbs contribute little meaning to a sentence. Whenever possible, use stronger, more active verbs.

"TO BE" VERB	The puppy *was* afraid of thunder.
ACTION VERBS	The puppy *whimpered* and *quivered* during the thunderstorm.
LINKING VERB	The child *looked* frightened as she boarded the bus for her first day of kindergarten.
ACTION VERBS	The child *trembled* and *clung* to her sister as she boarded the bus for her first day of kindergarten.

To strengthen your writing, try to use active verbs rather than passive verbs as much as possible. A **passive verb** is a form of the verb *to be* combined with a past participle (*killed, chosen, elected*). In a sentence with a passive verb, the subject does not perform the action of the verb but instead receives the action. By contrast, in a sentence with an **active verb**, the subject performs the action.

PASSIVE	It *was claimed* by the cyclist that the motorist failed to yield the right of way.
ACTIVE	The cyclist *claimed* that the motorist failed to yield the right of way.

Notice that the first sentence emphasizes the action of claiming, not the person who made the claim. In the second sentence, the person who made the claim is the subject.

Unless you decide deliberately to deemphasize the subject, try to avoid using passive verbs. On occasion, you may need to use passive verbs, however, to emphasize the object or person receiving the action.

■ **The Johnsons' house *was destroyed* by the flood.**

Passive verbs may also be appropriate if you do not know or choose not to reveal who performed an action. Journalists often use passive verbs for this reason.

■ **It *was confirmed* late Tuesday that Senator Kraemer is resigning.**

Exercise 9.5

Edit the following sentences by changing passive verbs to active ones, adding a subject when necessary.

1. Songs about peace were composed by folk singers in the 1960s.
2. The exam was thought to be difficult because it covered thirteen chapters.
3. For water conservation, it is recommended that low-water-consumption dishwashers be purchased.
4. The new satellite center was opened by the university so that students could attend classes nearer their homes.
5. In aggressive telemarketing sales calls, the consumer is urged by the caller to make an immediate decision before prices change.

Essay in Progress 1

For your essay in progress (the one you worked on in Chapters 6–8) or any essay you are working on, evaluate and edit your sentences.

Analyzing Your Word Choice

Each word you select contributes to the meaning of your essay. Consequently, when you are revising, be sure to analyze your word choice, or **diction**. The words you choose should suit your purpose, audience, and tone. This section describes four aspects of word choice to consider as you evaluate and revise your essay.

- Tone and level of diction
- Word connotations
- Concrete and specific language
- Figures of speech

Are Your Tone and Level of Diction Appropriate?

Imagine that as a technician at a computer software company you discover a time-saving shortcut for installing the company's best-selling software program. Your supervisor asks you to write two memos describing your discovery and how it works—one for your fellow technicians at the company and the other for customers who might purchase the program. Would both memos say the same thing in the same way? Definitely not. The two memos would differ not only in content but also in tone and level of diction. The memo addressed to the other technicians would be technical and concise, explaining how to use the shortcut and why it works. The memo directed to customers would praise the discovery, mention the time customers will save, and explain in nontechnical terms how to use the shortcut.

    Tone refers to how you sound to your readers. Your word choice should be consistent with your tone. Your memo to the technicians would have a direct, matter-of-fact tone. Your memo to the customers would be enthusiastic.

Formal Diction

There are three common **levels of diction**—formal, popular, and informal. The **formal** level of diction is serious and dignified. Think of it as the kind of language that judges use in interpreting laws, presidents employ when greeting foreign dignitaries, or speakers choose for commencement addresses. Formal diction is often written in the third person, tends to include long sentences and multisyllabic words, and contains no slang or contractions. It has a slow, rhythmic flow and an authoritative, distant, and impersonal tone. Here is an example taken from *The Federalist, No. 51*, a political tract written by James Madison in 1788 to explain constitutional theory.

> It is of great importance in a republic, not only to guard the society against the oppression of its rulers, but to guard one part of the society against the injustice of the other part. Different interests necessarily exist in different classes of citizens. If a majority be united by a common interest, the rights of the minority will be insecure.

Formal diction is also used in scholarly publications, in operation manuals, and in most academic fields. Notice in the following excerpt from a chemistry textbook that the language is concise, exact, and marked by specialized terms, called *jargon*, used within the particular field of study. The examples of jargon are in italics.

A *catalyst* is classified as *homogeneous* if it is present in the same *phase* as that of the *reactants*. For reactants that are *gases*, a *homogeneous catalyst* is also a *gas*.

Atkins and Perkins, *Chemistry: Molecules, Matter, and Change*

Popular Diction

Popular, or casual, diction is common in magazines and newspapers. It sounds more conversational and personal than formal diction. Contractions may be used, and sentences tend to be shorter and less varied than in formal diction. The first person (*I, me, mine, we*) or second person (*you, your*) may be used. Consider this example taken from a popular newsmagazine, *Newsweek*.

Pop quiz: What percentage of 18- to 25-year-olds can correctly identify the vice president? The answer, according to a Pew survey released last week, is 51 percent. (Older Americans do about 15 points better.) Maybe Dick Cheney should come out of hiding after all.

Jonathan Alter, "Give the Pols a Gold Star"

In this excerpt, the writer conveys a light, casual tone.

Informal Diction

Informal diction, also known as *colloquial language*, is the language of everyday speech and conversation. It is friendly and casual. Contractions (*wasn't, I'll*), slang expressions (*cops, chill out, What up?*), sentence fragments, and first-person and second-person pronouns are all common in informal diction. This level of diction should not be used in essays and academic writing, except when it is part of a quotation or a block of dialogue. Here is an example of informal diction.

This guy in my history class is a psycho. He doesn't let anybody talk but him. I mean, this guy interrupts all the time. Never raises his hand. He drives us nuts—what a loser.

Notice the use of the first person, slang expressions, and a loose sentence structure.

Diction in Academic Writing

When you write academic papers, essays, and exams, be sure to use somewhat formal diction, avoiding flowery or wordy language. To point you in the right direction, use the following guidelines.

- Use the third person (*he, she, it*) rather than the first person (*I, we*), unless you are expressing a personal opinion.
- Use standard vocabulary, not slang or a regional or an ethnic dialect.
- Use correct grammar, spelling, and punctuation.
- Aim for a clear, direct, and forthright tone.

One of the biggest mistakes students make in academic writing is trying too hard to sound "academic." Be sure to avoid writing stiff, overly formal sentences; using big words just for the sake of it; and expressing ideas indirectly.

INAPPROPRIATE DICTION

Who among us would be so bold as to venture to deny that inequities are rampant in our ailing health- and medical-care system? People of multiethnic composition overwhelmingly receive health care that is not only beneath the standard one would expect, but even in some cases threatening to their very lives. An abundance of research studies and clinical trials prove beyond a doubt that a person of non-European descent residing in the United States of America cannot rely on doctors, nurses, physician assistants, nurse practitioners, and other health-care workers to provide treatment free of invidious discrimination.

REVISED DICTION

Who can deny that inequities are common in our ailing medical care system? Racial and ethnic minorities receive health care that is not only substandard but even in some cases life-threatening. An abundance of research studies and clinical trials demonstrate that minorities in the United States cannot rely on doctors, nurses, physician assistants, nurse practitioners, and other health-care workers to provide unbiased treatment.

Exercise 9.6

Revise the following informal statement by giving it a more formal level of diction.

It hadn't occurred to me that I might be exercising wrong, though I suppose the signs were there. I would drag myself to the gym semi-regularly and go through the motions of walking (sometimes jogging) on the treadmill and doing light weight training. But I rarely broke a sweat. I just didn't have the energy. "Just doing it" wasn't cutting it. My body wasn't improving. In fact, certain areas were getting bigger, overly muscular. I needed someone to kick my butt—and reduce it too.

Wendy Schmid, "Roped In," *Vogue*

Do You Use Words with Appropriate Connotations?

Many words have two levels of meaning—a denotative meaning and a connotative meaning. A word's **denotation** is its precise dictionary definition. For example, the denotative meaning of the word *mother* is "female parent." A word's **connotation** is the collection of feelings and attitudes the word evokes—its emotional colorings or shades of meaning. A word's connotation may vary, of course, from one person to another. One common connotation of *mother* is a warm, caring person. Some people, however, may think of a mother as someone with strong authoritarian control. Similarly, the phrase *horror films* may conjure up memories of scary but fun-filled evenings for some people and terrifying experiences for others.

Since the connotations of words can elicit a wide range of responses, be sure the words you choose convey only the meanings you intend. In each pair of words that follows, notice that the two words have a similar denotation but different connotations.

artificial/fake
firm/stubborn
lasting/endless

Exercise 9.7

Describe the different connotations of the three words in each group of words.

1. crowd/mob/gathering
2. proverb/motto/saying
3. prudent/penny-pinching/frugal
4. token/gift/keepsake
5. display/show/expose

Do You Use Concrete Language?

Specific words convey much more information than general words. The following examples show how you might move from general to specific word choices.

General	Less General	More Specific	Specific
store	department store	Sears	Sears at the Galleria Mall
music	popular music	country and western music	Garth Brooks's "Friends in Low Places"

Concrete words add life and meaning to your writing. In each of the following sentence pairs, notice how the underlined words in the first sentence provide little information, whereas those in the second sentence provide interesting details.

GENERAL	Our <u>vacation</u> was <u>great fun</u>.
CONCRETE	Our <u>rafting trip</u> was filled with <u>adventure</u>.
GENERAL	The <u>red flowers</u> were blooming in our yard.
CONCRETE	<u>Crimson and white petunias</u> were blooming in our yard.

Suppose you are writing about a shopping mall that has outlived its usefulness. Instead of saying "a number of stores were unoccupied, and those that were still in business were shabby," you could describe the mall in concrete, specific terms that would enable your readers to visualize it.

The vacant storefronts with "For Rent" signs plastered across the glass, the half-empty racks in the stores that were still open, and the empty corridors suggested that the mall was soon to close.

Exercise 9.8

Revise the following sentences by adding concrete, specific details.

1. The book I took on vacation was exciting reading.
2. The students watched as the instructor entered the lecture hall.
3. The vase in the museum was an antique.
4. At the crime scene, the reporter questioned the witnesses.
5. Although the shop was closed, we expected someone to return at any moment.

Do You Use Fresh, Appropriate Figures of Speech?

A **figure of speech** is a comparison between two things that makes sense imaginatively or creatively, but not literally. For example, if you say "the movie was *a roller coaster ride,*" you do not mean the movie was an actual ride. Rather, you mean it was thrilling, just like a ride on a roller coaster. This figure of speech, like all others, compares two seemingly unlike objects or situations by finding one point of similarity.

Fresh and imaginative figures of speech can help you create vivid images for your readers. However, overused figures of speech can detract from your essay. Be sure to avoid **clichés** (trite or overused expressions) such as *blind as a bat, green with envy, bite the bullet,* or *sick as a dog.*

Although there are many kinds of figures of speech, the most useful types are simile, metaphor, and personification. In a **simile**, the word *like* or *as* is used to make a direct comparison of two unlike things.

> The child acts *like a tiger.*

> The noise in a crowded high school cafeteria is as deafening *as a caucus of crows.*

A **metaphor** also compares unlike things, but does not use *like* or *as.* Instead, the comparison is implied.

> That child is a tiger.

> If you're born in America with black skin, you're born in prison.
>
> Malcolm X, "Interview"

Personification describes an idea or object by giving it human qualities.

> A sailboat, or any other pleasure vehicle, devours money.

In this example, the ability to eat is ascribed to an inanimate object, the sailboat.

When you edit an essay, look for and eliminate overused figures of speech, replacing them with creative, fresh images. If you have not used any figures of speech, look for descriptions that could be improved by using a simile, a metaphor, or personification.

For more on figures of speech, see Chapter 11, p. 250.

Exercise 9.9

Invent fresh figures of speech for two items in the following list.

1. Parents of a newborn baby
2. A lengthy supermarket line or a traffic jam
3. A relative's old refrigerator
4. A man and woman obviously in love
5. Your team's star quarterback or important player

Evaluating Your Word Choice

Use Figure 9.2 to help you evaluate your word choice. If you have difficulty identifying which words to revise, ask a classmate or friend to read and evaluate your essay by using the flowchart as a guide and marking any words that may need revision.

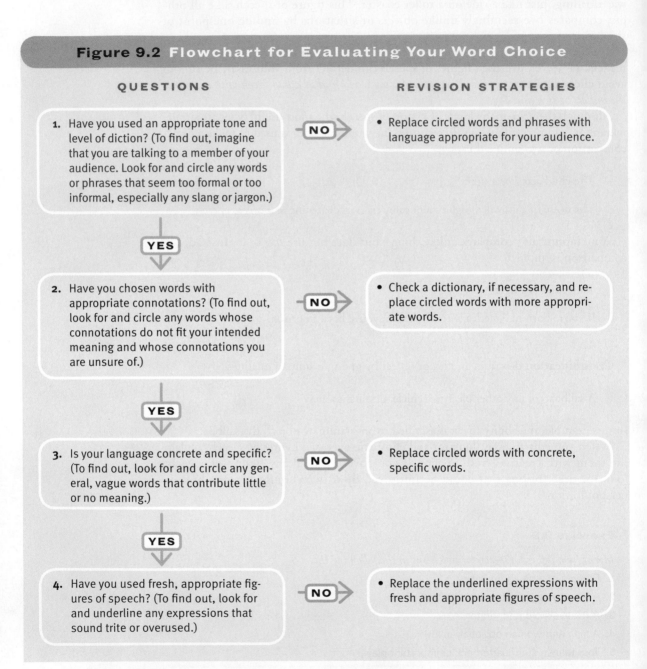

Figure 9.2 Flowchart for Evaluating Your Word Choice

QUESTIONS

REVISION STRATEGIES

1. Have you used an appropriate tone and level of diction? (To find out, imagine that you are talking to a member of your audience. Look for and circle any words or phrases that seem too formal or too informal, especially any slang or jargon.)

   NO ▷ • Replace circled words and phrases with language appropriate for your audience.

   YES

2. Have you chosen words with appropriate connotations? (To find out, look for and circle any words whose connotations do not fit your intended meaning and whose connotations you are unsure of.)

   NO ▷ • Check a dictionary, if necessary, and replace circled words with more appropriate words.

   YES

3. Is your language concrete and specific? (To find out, look for and circle any general, vague words that contribute little or no meaning.)

   NO ▷ • Replace circled words with concrete, specific words.

   YES

4. Have you used fresh, appropriate figures of speech? (To find out, look for and underline any expressions that sound trite or overused.)

   NO ▷ • Replace the underlined expressions with fresh and appropriate figures of speech.

A word-processing program is a useful editing tool. For example, you might experiment with several different word choices in a paragraph, print out all versions, and make comparisons. Because it is difficult to spot ineffective word choices on a computer screen, print a copy of your essay and work with the print copy, circling words or phrases that may need revision.

> **Essay in Progress 2**
> For the essay you worked on in Essay in Progress 1, use Figure 9.2 to evaluate and edit your word choice.

Suggestions for Proofreading

Once you are satisfied with your sentences and words and your edited essay as a whole, you are ready for the final step of the writing process—*proofreading*. When you proofread, you make sure your essay is error-free and is presented in acceptable manuscript format. Your goals are to catch and correct surface errors — such as errors in grammar, punctuation, spelling, and mechanics—as well as keyboarding or typographical errors. Making sure your essay is free of surface errors will help create a favorable impression in readers—of both the essay and of you as its writer. Careless proofreading is a sign of a careless writer, and if you are writing for a class, careless mistakes will cause your instructor to give you a lower grade. The guidelines in this section will help you become a careful proofreader.

For information on manuscript format, see Chapter 22, p. 615.

If you are using a computer, print out a clean copy of your essay for proofreading. Do not attempt to work with a previously marked-up copy or on a computer screen. Spotting errors in grammar, spelling, punctuation, and mechanics is easier when you work with a clean printed copy. Be sure to double-space the copy to allow room to mark corrections between lines.

Use the following suggestions to produce an error-free essay.

1. **Review your paper once for each type of error.** Because it is difficult to spot all types of surface errors simultaneously during a single proofreading, you should read your essay several times, each time focusing on *one* error type—errors in spelling, punctuation, grammar, mechanics, and so on.
2. **Read your essay backwards, from the last sentence to the first.** Reading in this way will help you concentrate on spotting errors without being distracted by the flow of ideas.
3. **Use the spell-check and grammar-check functions cautiously.** The spell-check function can help you spot some spelling and keyboarding errors, but you cannot rely on it to catch all spelling errors. For example, it cannot detect the difference in meaning between *there* and *their* or *to* and *too*. Similarly, the grammar-check function can identify only certain kinds of errors and is not a reliable substitute for a careful proofreading.
4. **Read your essay aloud.** By reading aloud slowly and deliberately, you can catch certain errors that sound awkward, such as missing words, errors in verb tense, and errors in the singular or plural forms of nouns.
5. **Ask a classmate to proofread your paper.** Another reader may spot errors you have overlooked.

FIGURE 9.3 Sample Error Log

Type of Error	Assignment 1	Assignment 2	Assignment 3
Subject-verb agreement	X	XX	XX
Spelling	XXXX	XXX	XXX
Verb tense	XX	XX	XXX
Word choice	X		X
Parallelism			X

Keeping an Error Log

You may find it helpful to keep an error log as part of your writing journal. Start by recording errors from several graded or peer-reviewed papers in the log. Then look for patterns in the types of errors you tend to make. Once you identify these types of errors, you can proofread your essays specifically for them.

In the sample error log in Figure 9.3, notice that the student kept track of five types of errors in three writing assignments. By doing so, she discovered that most of her errors fell into the categories of subject-verb agreement, spelling, and verb tense. She was then able to proofread for those errors specifically. The error log also allowed the student to keep track of her progress in avoiding these types of errors over time.

Essay in Progress 3

For the essay you edited in Essay in Progress 2, use one or more of the proofreading tips on page 195 to catch and correct errors in spelling, punctuation, grammar, and mechanics.

Students Write

Recall that Christine Lee's essay, "A Trend Taken Too Far: The Reality of Real TV," was developed, drafted, and revised in the Students Write sections of Chapters 5 to 8. Printed here are the first two paragraphs of Lee's essay with Lee's final editing and proofreading changes. Each revision has been numbered. The list following the excerpt explains the reason for each change. The final draft of Lee's essay, with these changes incorporated into it, appears in Chapter 8, on pages 172–75.

A Trend Taken Too Far: The Reality of Real TV

Do you remember life before the reality TV craze? Before reality TV television viewers

seemed interested only in the fictional lives of characters in situational comedies and se-

rial dramas. Characters were played by professional actors and the shows were written by professional writers. Except for a few early reality type shows such as *Cops* and *Candid Camera,* this simple formula was what network television offered. Then came MTV's *The Real World* in 1992. The high ratings that this cable show garnered made network executives take notice of the genre. Eventually *Survivor* debuted in the summer of 2000. When *Survivor* caught the attention of even more viewers and dominated television ratings. Television networks changed their programming. It seemed that every network acted as though it had to become "real" to compete with *Survivor* and maintain viewer interest. The problem with networks trying to copy *Survivor* is that the original *Survivor* offered more interesting elements to its audience than any reality TV show modeled after it. *Survivor* was engaging and dramatic, but the shows that followed it were less interesting and less tasteful, lacking drama and relying on gimmicks.

Survivor captured the interest of a wide viewing audience because it was fresh and entertaining and provocative. *Survivor* introduced real participants in a contest where they competed against each other in an exotic location. The participants on *Survivor* were ethnically and socially diverse and represented a variety of ages including younger, middle aged, and older adults. The location for *Survivor* was fascinating. A South Pacific island was more interesting than any house full of people on a sitcom. However, the most unique feature of *Survivor* was to make the participants compete for a million-dollar prize. Contestants were divided into two camps that had to compete to win everyday supplies, like food and shelter. At the end of each episode, players voted, and one of them was kicked off the show and lost his or her chance for losing the million dollars. The last contestant on the island won. To win the game, contestants created alliances and manipulated other contestants. All of these unique elements drew television viewers back each week.

Notice that in editing and proofreading these paragraphs, Lee improved the clarity and variety of her sentences; chose clearer, more specific words; and corrected errors in punctuation.

1. A comma was needed to separate the opening phrase from the rest of the sentence.
2. A comma was needed between two independent clauses joined by *and.*
3. *Viewers* is a plural noun but is not possessive. The apostrophe should not follow the word.

4. Lee combined the two sentences to emphasize the cause-and-effect relationship between the two ideas. (For more on combining sentences and sentence variety, see p. 180.)

5. The word *provocative* suggests something that arouses or stimulates. This connotation was not intended nor supported in the paragraph, so Lee changed the word to *entertaining*. (For more on connotation of words, see p. 191.)

6. Lee replaced the verb *had* with *introduced* because the latter is more descriptive. (For more on using descriptive verbs, see p. 187.)

7. A *contest* with *contestants* is redundant, so Lee eliminated the redundancy. (For more on redundancy, see p. 179.)

8. Lee combined the two sentences to tie the two ideas more closely together and to indicate that the second idea more fully explains the first. (For more on varying sentence patterns, see p. 180.)

9. Lee clarified that the contestant lost the *chance* to win the million dollars.

10. Lee replaced the slang term *messed with* with more acceptable language. (For more on slang, see p. 190.)

11. Lee eliminated the cliché *glued to their sets* and replaced it with a fresher expression. (For more on clichés and figures of speech, see p. 193.)

Patterns of Development

CHAPTER 10

Narration: Recounting Events

The photograph on the opposite page shows a tragic scene. Imagine what series of events led up to this tragedy. Who died? What events led up to the person's death? Who are the mourners? How are they related to the deceased? What is the significance of the objects left at the scene?

Working by yourself or with a classmate, construct a series of events leading up to this tragedy, culminating with the scene shown in the photograph. Write a brief summary of the events you imagined.

WRITING A NARRATIVE

As you imagined the events that led up to the tragic scene, you constructed the beginnings of a narrative. You began to describe a series of events or turning points, and you probably wrote them in the order in which they occurred. In this chapter, you will learn how to write narrative essays as well as how to use narratives in essays that rely on one or more other patterns of development.

What Is Narration?

A narrative relates a series of events, real or imaginary, in an organized sequence. It is a story, but it is *a story that makes a point.* You probably exchange family stories, tell jokes, read biographies or novels, and watch television situation comedies or dramas—all of which are examples of the narrative form. In addition, narratives are an important part of the writing you will do in college and in your career, as the examples in the accompanying box illustrate.

Narratives provide human interest and entertainment, spark our curiosity, and draw us close to the storyteller. In addition, narratives can create a sense of shared history, linking people together, and provide instruction in proper behavior or moral conduct.

The following narrative relates the author's experience with racial profiling. As you read, notice how the narrative makes a point by presenting a series of events that build to a climax.

SCENES FROM COLLEGE AND THE WORKPLACE

- Each student in your *business law course* must attend a court trial and complete the following written assignment: Describe what happened and what the proceedings illustrated about the judicial process.

- In a *sociology* course, your class is scheduled to discuss the nature and types of authority figures in U.S. society. Your instructor begins by asking class members to describe situations in which they found themselves in conflict with an authority figure.

- Your job in *sales* involves frequent business travel, and your company requires you to submit a report for each trip. You are expected to recount the meetings you attended, your contacts with current clients, and new sales leads.

Right Place, Wrong Face
Alton Fitzgerald White

This narrative was first published in the *Nation* in October 1999. Alton Fitzgerald White is an actor, singer, and dancer and has appeared in several Broadway shows. He is the author of *Uncovering the Heart Light* (1999), a collection of poems and short stories.

As the youngest of five girls and two boys growing up in Cincinnati, I was raised to believe that if I worked hard, was a good person, and always told the truth, the world would be my oyster. I was raised to be a gentleman and learned that these qualities would bring me respect.   1

While one has to earn respect, consideration is something owed to every human being. On Friday, June 16, 1999, when I was wrongfully arrested at my Harlem apartment building, my perception of everything I had learned as a young man was forever changed—not only because I wasn't given even a second to use the manners my parents taught me, but mostly because the police, whom I'd always naively thought were supposed to serve and protect me, were actually hunting me.   2

I had planned a pleasant day. The night before was a payday, plus I had received a standing ovation after portraying the starring role of Coalhouse Walker Jr. in the Broadway musical *Ragtime*. It is a role that requires not only talent but also an honest emotional investment of the morals and lessons I learned as a child.   3

Coalhouse Walker Jr. is a victim (an often misused word, but in this case true) of overt racism. His story is every black man's nightmare. He is hardworking, successful, talented, charismatic, friendly, and polite. Perfect prey for someone with authority and not even a fraction of those qualities. On that Friday afternoon, I became a real-life Coalhouse Walker. Nothing could have prepared me for it. Not even stories told to me by other black men who had suffered similar injustices.   4

Friday for me usually means a trip to the bank, errands, the gym, dinner, and then off to the theater. On this particular day, I decided to break my pattern of getting up and running right out of the house. Instead, I took my time, slowed my pace, and splurged by making strawberry pancakes. Before I knew it, it was 2:45; my bank closes at 3:30, leaving me less than 45 minutes to get to midtown Manhattan on the train. I was pressed for time but in a relaxed, blessed state of mind. When I walked through the lobby of my building, I noticed two light-skinned Hispanic men I'd never seen before. Not thinking much of it, I continued on to the vestibule, which is separated from the lobby by a locked door.   5

As I approached the exit, I saw people in uniforms rushing toward the door. I sped up to open it for them. I thought they might be paramedics, since many of the building's occupants are elderly. It wasn't until I had opened the door and greeted them that I recognized that they were police officers. Within seconds, I was told to "hold it"; they had received a call about young Hispanics with guns. I was told to get against the wall. I was searched, stripped of my backpack, put on my knees, handcuffed, and told to be quiet when I tried to ask questions.   6

With me were three other innocent black men who had been on their way to their   7
U-Haul. They were moving into the apartment beneath mine, and I had just bragged
to them about how safe the building was. One of these gentlemen got off his knees,
still handcuffed, and unlocked the door for the officers to get into the lobby where
the two strangers were standing. Instead of thanking or even acknowledging us, they
led us out the door past our neighbors, who were all but begging the police in our
defense.

The four of us were put into cars with the two strangers and taken to the precinct   8
station at 165th and Amsterdam. The police automatically linked us, with no questions
and no regard for our character or our lives. No consideration was given to where we
were going or why. Suppose an ailing relative was waiting upstairs, while I ran out for
her medication? Or young children, who'd been told that Daddy was running to the corner store for milk and would be right back? My new neighbors weren't even allowed to
lock their apartment or check on the U-Haul.

After we were lined up in the station, the younger of the two Hispanic men was iden-   9
tified as an experienced criminal, and drug residue was found in a pocket of the other.
I now realize how naive I was to think that the police would then uncuff me, apologize
for their mistake, and let me go. Instead, they continued to search my backpack, questioned me, and put me in jail with the criminals.

The rest of the nearly five-hour ordeal was like a horrible dream. I was handcuffed,   1
strip-searched, taken in and out for questioning. The officers told me that they knew
exactly who I was, knew I was in *Ragtime,* and that in fact they already had the men
they wanted.

How then could they keep me there, or have brought me there in the first place?   1
I was told it was standard procedure. As if the average law-abiding citizen knows
what that is and can dispute it. From what I now know, "standard procedure" is
something that every citizen, black and white, needs to learn, and fast.

I felt completely powerless. Why, do you think? Here I was, young, pleasant, and   1
successful, in good physical shape, dressed in clean athletic attire. I was carrying a
backpack containing a substantial paycheck and a deposit slip, on my way to the bank.
Yet after hours and hours I was sitting at a desk with two officers who not only couldn't
tell me why I was there but seemed determined to find something on me, to the point
of making me miss my performance.

It was because I am a black man!   1

I sat in that cell crying silent tears of disappointment and injustice with the realiza-   1
tion of how many innocent black men are convicted for no reason. When I was handcuffed, my first instinct had been to pull away out of pure insult and violation as a
human being. Thank God I was calm enough to do what they said. When I was thrown
in jail with the criminals and strip-searched, I somehow knew to put my pride aside,
be quiet, and do exactly what I was told, hating it but coming to terms with the fact
that in this situation I was a victim. They had guns!

Before I was finally let go, exhausted, humiliated, embarrassed, and still in shock,   1
I was led to a room and given a pseudo-apology. I was told that I was at the wrong
place at the wrong time. My reply? "I was where I live."

Everything I learned growing up in Cincinnati has been shattered. Life will never be   1
the same.

Characteristics of a Narrative

As you can see from "Right Place, Wrong Face," a narrative does not merely report events; a narrative is *not* a transcript of a conversation or a news report. Instead, it is a story that conveys a particular meaning. It presents actions and details that build toward a climax, the point at which the conflict of the narrative is resolved. Most narratives use dialogue to present portions of conversations that move the story along.

Narratives Make a Point

A narrative makes a point or supports a thesis by telling readers about an event or a series of events. The point may be to describe the significance of the event or events, make an observation, or present new information. Often a writer will state the point directly, using an explicit thesis statement. Other times a writer may leave the main point unstated, using an implied thesis. Either way, the point should always be clear to your readers. The point also determines the details the writer selects and the way they are presented.

The following excerpt from a brief narrative written by a student is based on a photo of a homeless family on a street corner. After imagining the series of events that might have brought the family to homelessness, the student wrote this final paragraph.

Jack and Melissa are kind, patient people who want nothing more than to live in a house or an apartment instead of camping out on a street curb. Unfortunately, their unhappy story and circumstances are not uncommon. Thousands of Americans, through no fault of their own, share their hopeless plight. The homeless can be found on street corners, in parks, and under bridges in the coldest months of winter. Too often, passersby shun them and their need for a helping hand. They either look away, repulsed by the conditions in which the homeless live, and assume they live this way out of choice rather than necessity, or they gaze at them with disapproving looks, walk away, and wonder why such people do not want to work.

Notice that the writer makes a point about the homeless and about people's attitudes toward them directly. Note, too, how the details support the writer's point.

Narratives Convey Action and Detail

A narrative presents a *detailed* account of an event or a series of events. In other words, a narrative is like a camera lens that zooms in and makes readers feel as if they can see the details and experience the action.

Writers of narratives can involve readers in several ways—through *dialogue,* with *physical description,* and by *recounting action.* In "Right Place, Wrong Face," both physical description and the recounting of events help build suspense and make the story come alive. Readers can easily visualize the scene at White's apartment building and the scene at the police station.

For more on descriptive writing, see Chapter 11.

Narratives Present a Conflict and Create Tension

An effective narrative presents a **conflict**—such as a struggle, question, or problem—and works toward its resolution. The conflict can be between participants or between a participant and some external force, such as a law, value, tradition, or act of nature. **Tension** is the suspense created as the story unfolds and as the reader wonders how the conflict will be resolved. In "Right Place, Wrong Face," for example, tension is first suggested in the third paragraph with "I had planned a pleasant day," suggesting that what was planned did not materialize. The tension becomes evident in paragraphs 7 to 14, and the conflict is resolved in paragraph 15, when White is released. The point just before the conflict is resolved is called the **climax**. The main point of the story—how White's life is changed by the incident of racial profiling—concludes the narrative.

Exercise 10.1

Working alone or with a classmate, complete each of the following statements by setting up a conflict. Then for one of the completed statements, write three to four sentences that build tension through action or dialogue (or both).

1. You are ready to leave the house when . . .
2. You have just turned in your math exam when you realize that . . .
3. You recently moved to a new town when your spouse suddenly becomes seriously ill . . .
4. Your child just told you that . . .
5. Your best friend phones you in the middle of the night to tell you . . .

Narratives Sequence Events

The events in a narrative must be arranged in an order that is easy for readers to follow. A narrative often presents events in chronological order—the order in which they happened. "Right Place, Wrong Face," for example, uses this straightforward sequence. At other times writers may use the techniques of flashback and foreshadowing to make their point more effectively. A **flashback** returns the reader to events that took place in the past, whereas **foreshadowing** hints at events in the future. Both of these techniques are used frequently in drama, fiction, and film. A soap opera, for instance, might open with a scene showing a woman lying in a hospital bed, flash back to a scene showing the accident that put her there, and then return to the scene in the hospital. When used sparingly, flashback and foreshadowing can build interest and add variety to a narrative, especially a lengthy chronological account.

Narratives Use Dialogue

Just as people reveal much about themselves by what they say and how they say it, dialogue can reveal much about the characters in a narrative. Dialogue is often used to dramatize the action, emphasize the conflict, and reveal the personalities or motives of the key participants in a narrative. Keep in mind that dialogue should resemble everyday speech; it should sound natural, not forced or formal. Consider these examples.

TOO FORMAL   Maria confided to her grandfather, "I enjoy talking with you. I especially like hearing you tell of your life in Mexico long ago. I wish I could visit there with you."

NATURAL   Maria confided to her grandfather, "Your stories about Mexico when you were a kid are great. I'd like to go there with you."

Exercise 10.2

For one of the following situations, imagine what the person might say and how he or she would say it. Then write five or six sentences of natural-sounding dialogue. If your dialogue sounds forced or too formal, try saying it out loud into a tape recorder.

1. An assistant manager is trying to explain to a supervisor that an employee offends customers.

2. A man or a woman has just discovered that he or she and a best friend are dating the same person.

3. A babysitter is disciplining an eight-year-old girl for pouring chocolate syrup on her brother's head.

Narratives Are Told from a Particular Point of View

Many narratives use the first-person point of view, in which the key participant speaks directly to the reader ("*I* first realized the problem when . . ."). Other narratives use the third-person point of view, in which an unknown storyteller describes what happens to the key participants ("The problem began when Saul Overtone . . ."). The first person is used in "Right Place, Wrong Face."

Both the first person and third person offer a distinct set of advantages. The first person allows you to assume a personal tone and to speak directly to your audience. You can easily express your attitudes and feelings and offer your interpretation and commentary. When you narrate an event that occurred in your own life, for example, the first person is probably your best choice. In "Right Place, Wrong Face" the first person allows White to express directly his anger, humiliation, and outrage.

One drawback to using the first person, however, is that you cannot easily convey the inner thoughts of other participants unless they are shared with you. The third person gives the narrator more distance from the action and often provides a broader, more objective perspective.

Exercise 10.3

For each of the following situations, decide which point of view would work best. Discuss with your classmates the advantages and disadvantages of using the first- and third-person points of view for each example.

1. The day you and several friends played a practical joke on another friend

2. An incident of sexual or racial discrimination that happened to you or someone you know

3. An incident at work that a coworker told you about

Visualizing a Narrative: A Graphic Organizer

Whether or not you are a spatial learner, it is often helpful to see the content and organization of an essay in simplified, visual form. The graphic organizer shown in Figure 10.1 is a visual diagram of the basic structure of a narrative. A graphic organizer can help you structure your writing, analyze a reading, and recall key events as you generate ideas for an essay.

For more on graphic organizers, see Chapter 3, p. 55.

Use Figure 10.1 as a basic model, but keep in mind that narrative essays vary in organization and may lack one or more of the elements included in the model.

The following selection, "Selling Civility," is an example of a narrative. Read it first, and then study the graphic organizer for it in Figure 10.2 (on p. 210).

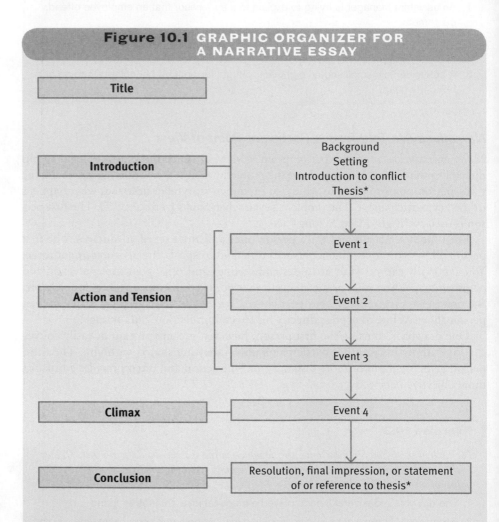

Figure 10.1 GRAPHIC ORGANIZER FOR A NARRATIVE ESSAY

Title

Introduction — Background / Setting / Introduction to conflict / Thesis*

Action and Tension — Event 1 / Event 2 / Event 3

Climax — Event 4

Conclusion — Resolution, final impression, or statement of or reference to thesis*

*The thesis may be stated directly at the beginning or at the end of a narrative, or it may be implied.

Selling Civility
Peter Scott

This essay first appeared in 2001 at OpinionJournal.com, the online edition of the *Wall Street Journal* editorial page. Peter Scott is an independent writer and film producer living in Washington, D.C. As you read the selection, look for the elements of a narrative essay. Compare your findings with the graphic organizer shown in Figure 10.1. Then study the graphic organizer for this reading in Figure 10.2.

For some time now, a general incivility has made its way into everyday life. It is noticeable 1 in a thousand different ways, not least in the small exchanges between buyer and seller, customer and clerk. In the small-town America of yesteryear, such exchanges might have been governed by a genial familiarity. But the shop around the corner has given way to sprawling franchises and large corporate identities. With them, it seems, has come an impersonality and indifference that adds stinging little indignities to simple transactions.

What is the answer to this problem? For a growing number of companies, it's a secret. 2 That is, it involves sending in a secret shopper—a "mole" posing as a customer—to see what's going on. Few companies have been using secret shoppers longer than Giant Supermarkets of Landover, Maryland, which instituted the practice back in 1958. Giant's secret shoppers work undercover, using code names and a shifting matrix of routes and "drops" to conceal their identities. Toiling in near total isolation, they receive weekly voice-mail instructions from headquarters to visit stores and observe specific employees. Last-minute changes are communicated through a field commander.

On a steamy Friday afternoon, secret shopper "N" sets out on store checks with me 3 in tow. Arriving at store 215, she evaluates the parcel-pickup area even before killing the ignition of her battered minivan. While there is plenty of hustle, a baghoy named Ryan is wearing his hat backward, one of several offenses for which he'll later be written up. Seconds later, a more serious 10-point "courtesy error" is assessed against Caprice from the produce department when we "hover" near her and she fails to greet us.

At a service counter, N spots a woman chewing gum, a definite no-no. Attempting to 4 read her nametag, we sprint to the hydroponic tomatoes for a better view. Sorry, Tanita, you're busted. These and other scores will be delivered to the store manager in the next 10 days, a time lag designed to protect the shopper's identity.

As we shop, N describes her favorite tactics. In addition to "hovering" to see if 5 she'll be greeted, N likes to watch the deli and service counters. After Bobby from the meat department practically bowls us over ("no acknowledgement"), we ask Gerald about shrimp for an imaginary party ("no closing") and see Valentina about special-ordering an ice-cream cake ("customer had to ask for assistance").

Exiting checkout, N asks if I noticed anything unusual about our cashier's performance. 6 I don't. N calmly shares her findings, later written up as "no greeting"; "does not keep bills separate/sideways"; and an "incorrect price code." The store earns a respectable final score, but "nobody went the extra mile," N notes.

Ten days later, I arrange a parking lot rendezvous with "P," a fit and energetic 68-year- 7 old now in his eighth year as a Giant secret shopper. "I think of it very much as a mission," says the former nuclear-sub commander. Laughing, he concedes that his former career "kind of prepared me in a lot of respects for this job."

P buzzes through each store like an efficiency expert conducting a time-and-motion   8
study. He gathers duplicate orders so he can check two different cashiers without leaving the store. Leaving cart number two in the calm of the pet-food aisle, we march to checkout, where the cashier spots our "cashier challenge," a bottle of spring water we've stashed under the cart, a signature secret-shopper move.

The cashiers fare admirably, but the big winner is Chris, an eager produce clerk who   9
practically carries us to the California avocados. Later, P will nominate him for a commendation and possible cash reward. He'll phone in his findings and, leaving nothing to chance, spell the young man's name using naval phonetics: Charlie, Hotel, Romeo, India, Sierra. For P, today's mission ended in victory.

In such a way, modern commerce—whether Giant or just gigantic—can police it-   10
self into the conscientiousness and civility of mom-and-pop stores.

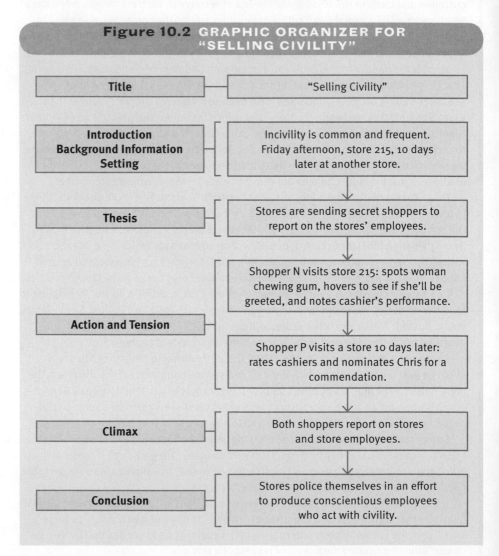

Figure 10.2 GRAPHIC ORGANIZER FOR "SELLING CIVILITY"

Title	"Selling Civility"

Introduction Background Information Setting	Incivility is common and frequent. Friday afternoon, store 215, 10 days later at another store.

| Thesis | Stores are sending secret shoppers to report on the stores' employees. |

| Action and Tension | Shopper N visits store 215: spots woman chewing gum, hovers to see if she'll be greeted, and notes cashier's performance. |
| | Shopper P visits a store 10 days later: rates cashiers and nominates Chris for a commendation. |

| Climax | Both shoppers report on stores and store employees. |

| Conclusion | Stores police themselves in an effort to produce conscientious employees who act with civility. |

To draw detailed graphic organizers using a computer, visit www.bedfordstmartins .com/successfulwriting.

Exercise 10.4

Using the graphic organizers in Figures 10.1 and 10.2 as models, draw a graphic organizer for "Right Place, Wrong Face" (pp. 203–204).

Integrating a Narrative Into an Essay

In many of your essays, you will want to use a narrative along with one or more other patterns of development to support your thesis effectively. In much of the writing you encounter in newspapers, magazines, and textbooks, the patterns of development often mix and overlap. Similarly, although "Right Place, Wrong Face" is primarily a narrative, it also uses cause and effect to explain why White was detained despite evidence that he was a respectable, law-abiding citizen. "Selling Civility" is a narrative that contains descriptions of grocery store employees.

Although most of your college essays will not be primarily narrative, you can often use stories to illustrate a point, clarify an idea, support an argument, or capture readers' interest in essays that rely on another pattern of development or on several patterns. Here are a few suggestions for using narration effectively in the essays you write.

For more on description and cause and effect, see Chapters 11 and 17.

1. **Be sure that your story illustrates your point accurately and well.** Don't include a story just because it's funny or interesting. It must support your thesis.
2. **Keep the narrative short.** Include only relevant details—those facts that are necessary to help your reader understand the events you are describing.
3. **Introduce the story with a transitional sentence or clause that indicates you are about to shift to a narrative.** Otherwise, your readers may wonder, "What's this story doing here?" Your transition should also make clear the connection between the story and the point it illustrates.
4. **Use descriptive language, dialogue, and action.** These elements make narratives vivid, lively, and interesting in any essay.

In "Another Mother's Child: A Letter to a Murdered Son" on page 229, Norma Molen incorporates narration into a persuasive essay.

A GUIDED WRITING ASSIGNMENT

Learning Style Options

The following guide will lead you through the process of writing a narrative essay. Although your essay will be primarily a narrative, you may choose to use one or more other patterns of development as well. Depending on your learning style, you might decide to start at various points and move back and forth within the process. If you are a spatial learner, for example, you might begin by visualizing and sketching the details of your narrative. If you are a social learner, you might prefer to start out by evaluating your audience.

The Assignment

Write a narrative essay about an experience in your life that had a significant effect on you or that changed your views in some important way. Choose one of the following topics or one that you think of on your own. The readers of your campus newspaper are your audience.

1. An experience that caused you to learn something about yourself
2. An incident that revealed the true character of someone you knew
3. An experience that helped you discover a principle to live by
4. An experience that explains the personal significance of a particular object
5. An incident that has become a family legend, perhaps one that reveals the character of a family member or illustrates a clash of generations or cultures
6. An incident that has allowed you to develop an appreciation or awareness of your ethnic identity

For more on description and comparison and contrast, see Chapters 11 and 14.

As you develop your narrative essay, be sure to consider using one or more of the other patterns of development. You might use description to present details about a family member's appearance, for example, or comparison and contrast to compare your attitudes or ideas to those of a parent or child.

Generating Ideas

Use the following steps to help you choose a topic and generate ideas about the experience or incident you decide to write about.

Choosing an Experience or Incident That Leads to a Working Thesis

Be sure that the experience you write about is memorable and vivid and that you are comfortable writing about it. When a draft is nearly complete, no student wants to discover that he or she cannot remember important details about the experience or that it does not fulfill the requirements of the assignment.

For more on formulating a working thesis, see Chapter 5, p. 101.

The following suggestions will help you choose an experience. Experiment and use whatever suggestions prove helpful to you. After you have chosen one, make sure that you can develop it by formulating a working thesis.

1. You can probably eliminate one or more broad topic choices right away. List those that remain across the top of a piece of paper or on your computer screen—for example, *Learn about Self*, *A Principle to Live By*, and *Family Legend*. Then brainstorm about significant experiences or incidents in your life, and write each one beneath the appropriate heading.
2. Brainstorm with another student, discussing and describing experiences or incidents that fit one or more of the suggested topics.
3. Flip through a family photo album, or page through a scrapbook, diary, or yearbook. Your search will remind you of people and events from the past.
4. Work backwards. Think of a principle you live by, an object you value, or a family legend. How did it become so?
5. Using freewriting or another prewriting technique, write down any experiences or incidents that come to mind. The memory of one incident will trigger memories of other incidents. Then sort your list to see if any of these experiences or incidents fulfill the assignment.

Learning Style Options

For more on prewriting strategies, see Chapter 4.

Essay in Progress 1

For the assignment given on page 212, use one or more of the preceding suggestions to choose an experience or incident to write about, and formulate a working thesis for your choice.

Considering Your Purpose, Audience, and Point of View

Once you have chosen an experience or incident to write about, the next step is to consider your purpose, audience, and point of view. Recall from Chapter 4 that most essays have one of three possible purposes—to inform, to express thoughts or feelings, or to persuade. Thinking about your audience may help you clarify your purpose and decide what to include in your essay. For this Guided Writing Assignment, your audience consists of readers of your campus newspaper. You should also decide on a point of view. In most cases, you will use the first person to relate a personal experience.

For more on purpose, audience, and point of view, see Chapter 4, pp. 82–85.

Learning Style Options

Gathering Details about the Experience or Incident

This step involves recollecting as many details about the experience or incident as possible and recording them on paper or in a computer file. Reenact the story, sketching the scene or scenes in your mind. Identify key actions, describe key participants, and describe your feelings. Here are a few ways to generate ideas.

1. Replay the experience or incident in your mind. If you have a strong visual memory, close your eyes and imagine the incident or experience taking place. Jot down what you see, hear, smell, and feel—colors, dialogue, sounds, odors, and sensations— and how these details make you feel.
2. Write the following headings on a piece of paper, or type them on your computer screen: *Scene, Key Actions, Key Participants, Key Lines of Dialogue,* and *Feelings.* Then list ideas under each heading.

3. Describe the incident or experience to a friend. Have your friend ask you questions as you retell the story. Jot down the details that the retelling and questioning help you recall.
4. Consider different aspects of the incident or experience by asking *who*, *what*, *when*, *where*, *how*, and *why* questions. Record your answers.

In addition, as you gather details for your narrative, be sure to include the types of details that are essential to an effective narrative.

For more on sensory details, see Chapter 11, p. 247.

- *Scene:* **Choose relevant sensory details.** Include enough detail about the place where the experience occurred to allow your readers to feel as if they are there. Details that appeal to the senses work best. Also try to recall important details that direct your readers' attention to the main points of the narrative, and avoid irrelevant details that distract readers from the main point.
- *Key actions:* **Choose actions that create tension, build it to a climax, and resolve it.** Be sure to gather details about the conflict of your narrative. Answer the following questions.
  Why did the experience or incident occur?
  What events led up to it?
  How was it resolved?
  What were its short- and long-term outcomes?
  What is its significance now?
- *Key participants:* **Concentrate only on the appearance and actions of those people who were directly involved.** People who were present but not part of the incident or experience need not be described in detail or perhaps even included.
- *Key lines of dialogue:* **Include dialogue that is interesting, revealing, and related to the main point of the story.** To make sure the dialogue sounds natural, read the lines aloud, or ask a friend to do so.
- *Feelings:* **Record your feelings before, during, and after the experience or incident.** Did you reveal your feelings then? If so, how? How did others react to you? How do you feel about the experience or incident now? What have you learned from it?

> **Essay in Progress 2**
> For the experience or incident you chose in Essay in Progress 1 (p. 213), use one or more of the preceding suggestions to generate details.

Evaluating Your Ideas

Evaluate the ideas you have gathered about your topic before you begin drafting your narrative. You want to make sure you have enough details to describe the experience or incident vividly and meaningfully.

Begin by rereading everything you have written with a critical eye. As you do, add dialogue, descriptions of actions, or striking details as they come to mind. Highlight the most relevant material, and cross out any material that does not directly support your main point. Some students find it helpful to read their notes aloud. If you are working on a computer, highlight usable ideas by making them bold or moving them to a separate page or document for easy access when drafting.

Trying Out Your Ideas on Others

Once you are satisfied with the details you have generated about your incident or experience, you are ready to discuss your ideas with others. Working in a group of two or three students, each student should narrate his or her experience and state the main point of the narrative. Then work together to answer the following questions about the narrative.

1. What more do you need to know about the experience or incident?

2. What is your reaction to the story?

3. How do the events of the narrative support or not support the main point?

Essay in Progress 3

Gather your prewriting and any comments you have received from your classmates or instructor, and evaluate the details you have developed so far. Based on your findings, generate additional details. Highlight the most useful details, and omit those that do not support the main point.

Developing Your Thesis

Your thesis should make clear the main point of your narrative. You should already have a working thesis in mind. Now is the time to focus it. For example, a student who brainstormed a list of ideas and decided to write about her family's antique silver platter wrote the following focused thesis statement for her narrative.

For more on thesis statements, see Chapter 5, p. 101.

> The silver serving platter, originally owned by my great-grandmother, became our most prized family heirloom after a robbery terrorized our family.

Notice that the thesis identifies the object, introduces the experience that made the object a valuable family possession, and expresses the main point of the narrative.

A thesis statement may be placed at the beginning of a narrative essay. In "Right Place, Wrong Face" (p. 203), for example, the thesis appears near the beginning of the essay. A thesis may also be placed at the end of a narrative, as in "Selling in Minnesota" (p. 225).

Essay in Progress 4

Develop a thesis statement for the narrative you worked on in Essays in Progress 1–3. Make sure the thesis expresses the main point of the incident or experience you have chosen to write about.

Once you have a thesis, you may need to do some additional prewriting to collect evidence for the thesis, including dialogue, action, and details. Your prewriting at this stage may involve elaborating on some of the details you've already collected. Be sure your events and details contribute to the tension or suspense of the narrative.

See Chapter 5, p. 104, for more on supporting a thesis with evidence.

Organizing and Drafting

For more on drafting an essay, see Chapter 6.

Once you are satisfied with your thesis and your support for it, you are ready to organize your ideas and write your first draft. Use the following suggestions for organizing and drafting your narrative.

Choosing a Narrative Sequence

As noted earlier in the chapter, all of the events of a narrative may follow a chronological order from beginning to end, or some events may be presented as flashbacks or foreshadowing for dramatic effect. Try one of the following strategies to help you determine the best sequence for your narrative.

Learning Style Options

1. Write a brief description of each event on an index card. Be sure to highlight the card that contains the climax. Experiment with various ways of arranging your details by rearranging the cards. When you have chosen a sequence, prepare an outline of your narrative.
2. Draw a graphic organizer of the experience or incident (see p. 208).

3. Use a word-processing program to create a list of the events. Rearrange the events using the cut-and-paste function, experimenting with different sequences.

> **Essay in Progress 5**
> Using one or more of the preceding suggestions, plan the order of the events for your narrative essay.

Drafting the Narrative Essay

Now that you've determined your narrative sequence, you are ready to begin drafting your essay. As you write, use the following guidelines to help keep your narrative on track.

For more on writing effective paragraphs, including introductions and conclusions, see Chapter 6.

The Introduction.   Your essay's introduction should catch your reader's attention, provide useful background information, and set up the sequence of events. Your introduction may also contain your thesis, if you have decided to place it at the beginning of the essay.

The Story.   The story should build tension and follow a clear order of progression. As you draft your narrative, be conscious of your paragraphing, devoting a separate paragraph to each major action or distinct part of the story. Use transitional words and phrases—such as *during*, *after dinner*, and *finally*—to connect events and guide readers along.

For more on transitions, see Chapter 6, p. 124.

In addition, be consistent in your use of verb tense. Most narratives are told in the past tense ("Yolanda discovered the platter . . ."). Fast-paced, short narratives, however, are sometimes related in the present tense ("Yolanda discovers the platter . . ."). Avoid switching between the past and present tenses unless the context of the narrative clearly requires it.

The Ending.   Your final paragraph should conclude the essay in a satisfying manner. A summary is usually unnecessary and may detract from the impact of the narrative. Instead, try ending in one of the following ways.

- **Make a final observation about the experience or incident.** For an essay on part-time jobs in fast-food restaurants, a writer could conclude by writing: "Overall, I learned a lot more about getting along with people than I did about how to prepare fast food."
- **Ask a probing question.** For an essay on adventure travel, a writer could conclude: "Although the visit to Nepal was enlightening for me, do the native people really want or need us there?"
- **Suggest a new but related direction of thought.** For an essay on racial profiling, a writer could conclude by suggesting that police sensitivity training might have changed the outcome of the situation.
- **Refer to the beginning**, as White does in the final paragraph of "Right Place, Wrong Face" (p. 204).
- **Restate the thesis in different words.**

Essay in Progress 6

Using the narrative sequence you developed in Essay in Progress 5 and the preceding guidelines for drafting, write a first draft of your narrative essay.

Analyzing and Revising

If possible, set your draft aside for a day or two before rereading and revising it. As you reread your draft, focus on improving the overall effectiveness of your narrative. Will it interest readers and make them want to know what happens next? Does it make your point clear? To discover weaknesses in your draft, try the following strategies.

1. Reread your paper aloud or ask a friend to do so as you listen. Hearing your essay read out loud may help you identify parts in need of revision.

2. Write an outline or draw a graphic organizer, or review the one you created earlier. Does your narrative follow the intended sequence?

Learning Style Options

As you analyze your narrative, be on the lookout for dialogue that doesn't support your thesis, events that need further explanation or description, and details that contribute nothing to the overall impression you want to convey. Use Figure 10.3 on page 218 to help you discover the strengths and weaknesses of your narrative. You might also ask a classmate to review your essay. Your reviewer's comments and impressions may reveal strengths and weaknesses that you had overlooked.

For more on the benefits of peer review, see Chapter 8, p. 162.

Essay in Progress 7

Revise your narrative essay, using Figure 10.3 on page 218 and the suggestions of your classmate to guide you.

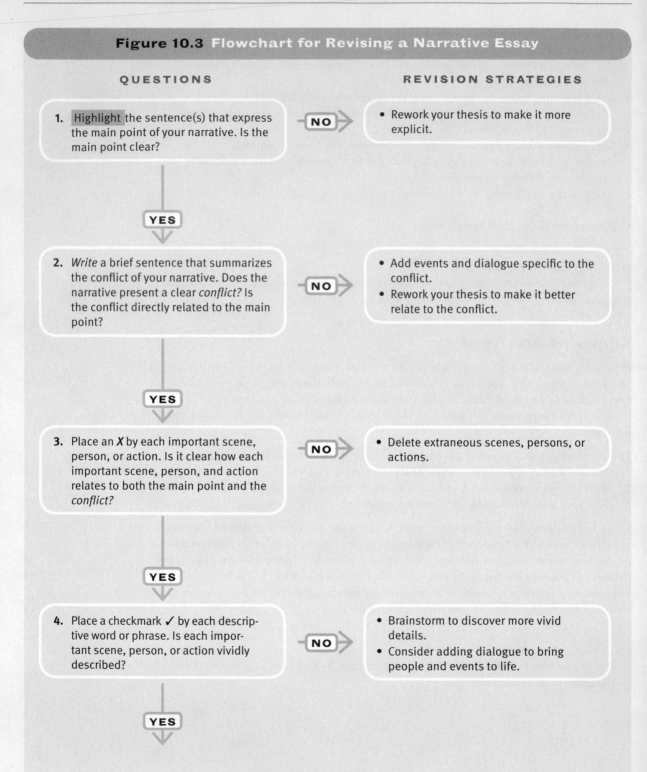

Figure 10.3 Flowchart for Revising a Narrative Essay

QUESTIONS

REVISION STRATEGIES

1. Highlight the sentence(s) that express the main point of your narrative. Is the main point clear?

NO

- Rework your thesis to make it more explicit.

YES

2. *Write* a brief sentence that summarizes the conflict of your narrative. Does the narrative present a clear *conflict?* Is the conflict directly related to the main point?

NO

- Add events and dialogue specific to the conflict.
- Rework your thesis to make it better relate to the conflict.

YES

3. Place an *X* by each important scene, person, or action. Is it clear how each important scene, person, and action relates to both the main point and the *conflict?*

NO

- Delete extraneous scenes, persons, or actions.

YES

4. Place a checkmark ✓ by each descriptive word or phrase. Is each important scene, person, or action vividly described?

NO

- Brainstorm to discover more vivid details.
- Consider adding dialogue to bring people and events to life.

YES

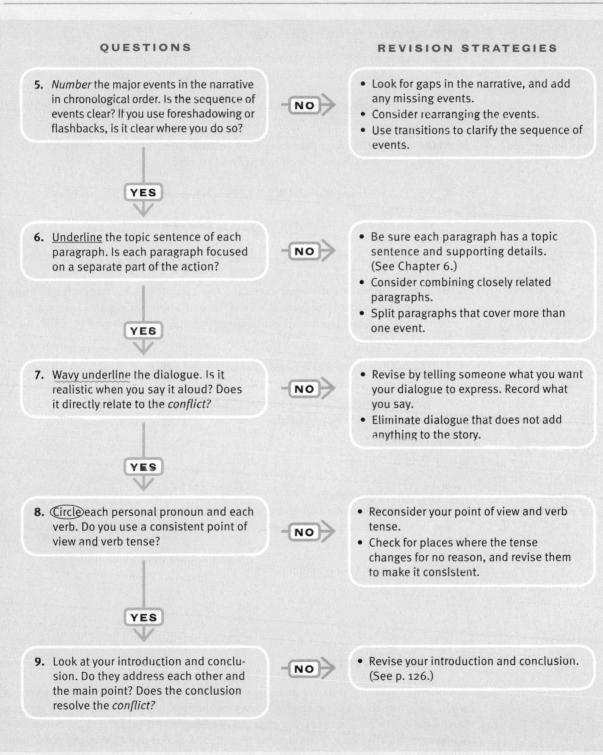

QUESTIONS

REVISION STRATEGIES

5. *Number* the major events in the narrative in chronological order. Is the sequence of events clear? If you use foreshadowing or flashbacks, is it clear where you do so?

NO

- Look for gaps in the narrative, and add any missing events.
- Consider rearranging the events.
- Use transitions to clarify the sequence of events.

YES

6. Underline the topic sentence of each paragraph. Is each paragraph focused on a separate part of the action?

NO

- Be sure each paragraph has a topic sentence and supporting details. (See Chapter 6.)
- Consider combining closely related paragraphs.
- Split paragraphs that cover more than one event.

YES

7. Wavy underline the dialogue. Is it realistic when you say it aloud? Does it directly relate to the *conflict?*

NO

- Revise by telling someone what you want your dialogue to express. Record what you say.
- Eliminate dialogue that does not add anything to the story.

YES

8. Circle each personal pronoun and each verb. Do you use a consistent point of view and verb tense?

NO

- Reconsider your point of view and verb tense.
- Check for places where the tense changes for no reason, and revise them to make it consistent.

YES

9. Look at your introduction and conclusion. Do they address each other and the main point? Does the conclusion resolve the *conflict?*

NO

- Revise your introduction and conclusion. (See p. 126.)

Editing and Proofreading

The last step is to check your revised narrative essay for errors in grammar, spelling, punctuation, and mechanics. Be sure to look for the types of errors that you tend to make. (Refer to your error log.)

For more on keeping an error log, see Chapter 9, p. 196.

For narrative essays, pay particular attention to the following kinds of sentence problems.

For more on varying sentence structure, see Chapter 9, p. 180.

1. **Make certain that your sentences vary in structure.** A string of sentences that are similar in length and structure is tedious to read.

   - The Ding Darling National Wildlife Preserve, ~~is~~ located on Sanibel Island,

     Florida, ~~It~~ was established in 1945 as the Sanibel Refuge. Its name

     was changed in 1967 to honor the man who helped found it.

2. **Be sure to punctuate dialogue correctly.** Use commas to separate each quotation from the phrase that introduces it, unless the quotation is integrated into your sentence. If your sentence ends with a quotation, the period should be inside the quotation marks.

   - The wildlife refuge guide noted, "American crocodiles are an endangered species and must be protected."
   - The wildlife refuge guide noted that, "American crocodiles are an endangered species and must be protected."

Essay in Progress 8

Edit and proofread your narrative essay, remembering to vary sentence patterns and punctuate dialogue correctly. Don't forget to look for the types of errors you tend to make.

Students Write

Aphonetip Vasavong, a native of Laos, was a nursing student at Niagara University when she wrote this essay in response to an assignment given by her first-year writing instructor to describe an event that changed her life. As you read the essay, notice how Vasavong's narrative creates conflict and tension and builds to a climax and resolution. Highlight the sections where you think the tension is particularly intense.

You Can Count on Miracles

Aphonetip Vasavong

Most of us have experienced unusual coincidences at least once in our lives--ones that are so unusual and meaningful that they could not have happened by chance alone. Many events that seem coincidental often have simple explanations; however, some of these incidents have no simple explanations. I had such an experience when I was eight years old and lost in the woods. Strange as it may seem, a rabbit led me to safety. I would not be here today if it were not for that rabbit.

Until I was eight, my family lived in Laos. In 1986, however, my family and I left Laos to prevent the Communists from capturing my father. He is an educated man, and at that time the Communist government wanted to imprison educated people. The government was placing such people in concentration camps, similar to those used in Germany and Eastern Europe during World War II, to prevent them from forming a party that might overthrow the Communists. To protect my father from being captured and imprisoned in Laos, my family decided to immigrate to America.

We had to leave Laos quickly and secretively. In order to prevent suspicion, we told our neighbors that we were taking a two-week family vacation to see our grandfather. Instead, we stayed with our grandmother for two days, until we were able to find someone willing to escort us across the river to Thailand. On the second night, we planned to board a boat that would take us to a small town where we could spend the night. I remember it was around 2 a.m. when my father woke us up. He divided the ten of us into two groups of five because it was too risky to walk to the river as a large group; people would be more likely to notice us and report us to the Communist soldiers. We were not allowed to speak or make any noise at all because we might have awakened people or disturbed their dogs. My father instructed us carefully: "Hold on to each other's jackets and stay in line. Move carefully and quietly, and we'll all be safe soon."

In a group with my brothers, my sister, and an escort lady, I was the last person in line. On the way to the river, everyone else was walking fast through a dark, wooded area, and I could not keep up with them. Somehow I accidentally let go of my sister's jacket and got left behind in the woods. I was alone in the middle of what seemed like nowhere. It was so dark I could not see anything or anyone. As I waited in terror for the escort lady to come back to look for me, I started to cry. I waited a while longer, and still no one came back for me.

Suddenly, something ran out of the bushes onto a nearby path. I could see that it was a rabbit. It was beautiful and bright, like a light. It came back toward me and stood in front of me. I reached out to pet it, but it ran toward the same path that it had come from a moment ago. I decided to follow the rabbit along the path. As I did, I was able to see my way through the woods because the rabbit and the path were bright, while the trees and the dense groundcover

Title: Vasavong foreshadows her thesis.

READING

Introduction: Vasavong establishes her point of view: she will be telling the story. In her thesis statement, she explains the significance and importance of her narrative.

Background information presents a conflict and creates tension.

Transitions help sequence events.

Exact details make the situation real and intense.

Vasavong uses dialogue to reveal her father's calm, supportive nature.

Tension begins to build.

remained dark. I continued to follow the rabbit along the path until it disappeared into the darkness. I looked around for the rabbit, and what I saw instead was my family getting into the canoes. I turned back once more to look for the rabbit, but it was gone. When I got on the canoe, I was relieved and overjoyed to see my family again. My father pulled me close to him and whispered, "We thought you were lost forever. How did you find us?"

Climax emphasized by dialogue

Conclusion: Vasavong returns to ideas presented in her introduction, emphasizing her belief that the rabbit did not appear by chance.

Unusual experiences such as mine occur to people everywhere, but most people do not take the time to think about their meaning. Some critics argue that these occurrences are merely coincidental. My experience leads me to believe otherwise. Being lost in the woods and having a brightly lit rabbit lead me safely to my family cannot be attributed to chance alone.

6

Analyzing the Writer's Technique

1. Evaluate the strength of Vasavong's thesis.
2. What ideas do you think should be expanded? That is, where did you find yourself wanting or needing more detail?
3. How effectively does Vasavong establish conflict and create tension?
4. Other than in the title, where does Vasavong use foreshadowing? Explain its effectiveness.
5. Evaluate the title, introduction, and conclusion of the essay.

Reacting to the Essay

1. Vasavong's family held a "trust no one" attitude. Why was that necessary? In what situation today, if any, would such an attitude be necessary?
2. Vasavong's father escaped Laos to avoid persecution because of his education. Where does persecution still exist today? Why does it occur?
3. Vasavong believes that the rabbit did not appear by chance. Do you agree? Why or why not?
4. Write a journal entry describing your interpretation of an unusual coincidence or a memorable event from your childhood.
5. Vasavong was hopelessly lost but eventually found her way. Write an essay about a situation you experienced in which the course of events took a sudden turn for better or worse.

READING A NARRATIVE

The following section provides advice for reading narratives. Two model essays illustrate the characteristics of narrative writing covered in this chapter and provide opportunities to examine, analyze, and react to the writer's ideas. The second essay uses a narrative to support an argument.

Working with Text: Reading Narratives

It is usually a good idea to read a narrative essay several times before you attempt to discuss or write about it. Preview the essay first to get an overview of its content and organization. Then read it through to familiarize yourself with the events and action, noting also who did what, when, where, and how. Finally, reread the narrative, this time concentrating on its meaning.

For more on previewing an essay and other reading strategies, see Chapter 3.

What to Look For, Highlight, and Annotate

1. Narrative elements. When reading a narrative, it is easy to become immersed in the story and to overlook its importance or significance. Therefore, as you read, look for the answers to the following questions. Highlight those sections of the essay that reveal or suggest the answers.

- What is the writer's thesis? Is it stated directly or implied?
- What is the role of each participant in the story?
- What does the dialogue reveal about or contribute to the main point?
- What is the conflict?
- How does the writer create tension?
- What is the climax?
- How is the conflict resolved?

2. Sequence of events. Especially for lengthy or complex narratives and for those that flash back and forward among events, it is helpful to draw a graphic organizer or number the sequence of events in the margins. Doing so will help you establish the sequence of key events.

3. Keys to meaning. The following questions will help you evaluate the reading and discover its main point.

- What is the author's purpose in writing this narrative?
- For what audience is it intended?
- What is the lasting value or merit of this essay? What does it tell me about life, people, jobs, or friendships, for example?
- What techniques does the writer use to try to achieve his or her purpose? Is the writer successful?

4. Reactions. As you read, write down your reactions to and feelings about the events, participants, and outcome of the narrative. Include both positive and negative reactions; do not hesitate to challenge participants, their actions, and their motives.

How to Find Ideas to Write About

Since you may be asked to write a response to a narrative, keep an eye out for ideas to write about *as you read*. Pay particular attention to the issue, struggle, or dilemma at hand. Try to discover what broader issue the essay is concerned with. For example, in a story about children who dislike eating vegetables, the larger issue

For more about discovering ideas for a response paper, see Chapter 3.

might be food preferences, nutrition, or parental control. Once you've identified the larger issue, you can develop your own ideas about it by relating it to your own experience.

Thinking Critically about Narration

A nonfiction narrative is often one writer's highly personal, subjective account of an event or a series of events. Unless you have reason to believe otherwise, assume that the writer is honest—that he or she does not lie or purposely distort the version of the experiences or incidents presented in the essay. You should also assume, however, that the writer chooses details selectively—to advance his or her narrative point. Use the following questions to think critically about the narratives you read.

Is the Writer Subjective?

Because a narrative is often highly personal, a critical reader must recognize that the information it contains is probably influenced by the author's values, beliefs, and attitudes. In "Right Place, Wrong Face," for example, the police officers are presented as uncaring and insensitive, but imagine how the police would describe the same incident. Two writers, then, may present two very different versions of a single incident.

What Is the Author's Tone?

Tone refers to how the author sounds to his or her readers or how he or she feels about the topic. Writers establish tone through word choice, sentence structure, and formality or informality. An author's tone can reflect many emotions—such as anger, joy, or fear. The tone of an essay narrating an event in the American war in Iraq might be serious, frightening, or alarming, whereas an essay narrating the activities of a procrastinating, well-meaning friend or relative might be light or humorous. The author's tone affects the reader's attitude toward the topic.

NARRATIVE ESSAY

As you read the following essay by Barbara Ehrenreich, consider how the writer uses the elements of narrative discussed in this chapter.

Selling in Minnesota
Barbara Ehrenreich

Barbara Ehrenreich is an award-winning political essayist, columnist, and social critic whose works have appeared in such publications as *Time*, the *Nation*, *Harper's*, and the *Atlantic*. She is the author of numerous books, including *Blood Rites: Origins and History of the Passions of War* (1997), *Bait and Switch: The (Futile) Pursuit of the American Dream* (2005), and *Dancing in the Streets: A History of Collective Joy* (2007). For *Nickel and Dimed: On (Not) Getting by in America* (2001), from which this selection is adapted, Ehrenreich spent a year doing minimum-wage work to discover the working conditions of low-paying jobs in the United States. As you read it, highlight or annotate each narrative element in the essay.

In my second week [of working at Wal-Mart], two things change. My shift changes from 1
10:00–6:00 to 2:00–11:00, the so-called closing shift, although the store remains open 24/7. No one tells me this; I find it out by studying the schedules that are posted, under glass, on the wall outside the break room. Now I have nine hours instead of eight, and my two fifteen-minute breaks, which seemed almost superfluous on the 10:00–6:00 shift, now become a matter of urgent calculation. Do I take both before dinner, which is usually about 7:30, leaving an unbroken two-and-a-half-hour stretch when I'm weariest, between 8:30 and 11:00? Or do I try to go two and a half hours without a break in the afternoon, followed by a nearly three-hour marathon before I can get away for dinner? Then there's the question of how to make the best use of a fifteen-minute break when you have three or more urgent, simultaneous needs—to pee, to drink something, to get outside the neon and into the natural light, and most of all, to sit down. I save about a minute by engaging in a little time theft and stopping at the rest room before I punch out for the break. From the time clock it's a seventy-five second walk to the store exit; if I stop at the Radio Grill, I could end up wasting a full four minutes waiting in line, not to mention the fifty-nine cents for a small-sized iced tea. So if I treat myself to an outing in the tiny fenced-off area beside the store, I get about nine minutes off my feet.

The other thing that happens is that the post–Memorial Day weekend lull definitely 2
comes to an end. Now there are always a dozen or more shoppers rooting around in ladies'. New tasks arise, such as bunching up the carts left behind by customers and steering them to their place in the front of the store every half hour or so. Now I am picking up not only dropped clothes but all the odd items customers carry off from foreign departments and decide to leave with us in ladies'—pillows, upholstery hooks, Pokémon cards, earrings, sunglasses, stuffed animals, even a package of cinnamon buns. And always there are the returns, augmented now by the huge volume of items that have been tossed on the floor or carried fecklessly to inappropriate sites. If I pick up misplaced items as quickly as I replace the returns, my cart never empties and things back up dangerously at the fitting room, where Rhoda or her nighttime replacement is likely to hiss: "You've got three carts waiting, Barb. What's the *problem*?"

Still, for the first half of my shift, I am the very picture of good-natured helpfulness. 3
Amazingly, I get praised by Isabelle, the thin little seventyish lady who seems to be Ellie's adjutant: I am doing "wonderfully," she tells me, and—even better—am "great to work with." But then, somewhere around 6:00 or 7:00, when the desire to sit down

becomes a serious craving, a Dr. Jekyll/Mr. Hyde transformation sets in. I cannot ignore the fact that it's the customers' sloppiness and idle whims that make me bend and crouch and run. They are the shoppers, I am the antishopper, whose goal is to make it look as if they'd never been in the store. At this point, "aggressive hospitality" gives way to aggressive hostility. Their carts bang into mine, their children run amok.

It's the clothes I relate to, not the customers. And now a funny thing happens to me   4 here on my new shift: I start thinking they're mine, not mine to take home and wear, because I have no such designs on them, just mine to organize and rule over. Same with ladies' wear as a whole. I patrol the perimeter with my cart, darting in to pick up misplaced and fallen items, making everything look spiffy from the outside. I don't fondle the clothes, the way customers do; I slap them into place, commanding them to hang straight, at attention, or lie subdued on the shelves in perfect order. In this frame of mind, the last thing I want to see is a customer riffling around, disturbing the place. In fact, I hate the idea of things being sold — uprooted from their natural homes, whisked off to some closet that's in God-knows-what state of disorder. I want ladies' wear sealed off in a plastic bubble and trucked away to some place of safety, some museum of retail history.

One night I come back bone-tired from my last break and am distressed to find a   5 new person folding T-shirts in the [turtlenecks] area, *my* [turtlenecks] area. It's already been a vexing evening. Earlier, when I'd returned from dinner, the evening fitting room lady upbraided me for being late — which I actually wasn't — and said that if Howard knew, he probably wouldn't yell at me this time because I'm still pretty new, but if it happened again. . . . And I'd snapped back that I could care less if Howard yelled at me. So I'm a little wary with this intruder in [turtlenecks], and, sure enough, after our minimal introductions, she turns on me.

"Did you put anything away here today?" she demands.   6

"Well, yes, sure." In fact I've put something away everywhere today, as I do on every   7 other day.

"Because this is not in the right place. See the fabric — it's different," and she   8 thrusts the errant item up toward my chest.

True, I can see that this olive-green shirt is slightly ribbed while the others are   9 smooth. "You've *got* to put them in their right places," she continues. "Are you check-ing the UPC numbers?"

Of course I am not checking the ten or more digit UPC numbers, which lie just under   10 the bar codes — nobody does. What does she think this is, the National Academy of Sciences? I'm not sure what kind of deference, if any, is due here: Is she my supervisor now? But I don't care, she's messing with my stuff. So I say, only without the numerals or the forbidden curse word, that (1) plenty of other people work here during the day, not to mention all the customers coming through, so why is she blaming me? (2) it's after 10:00 and I've got another cart full of returns to go, and wouldn't it make more sense if we both worked on the carts, instead of zoning the goddamn T-shirts?

To which she responds huffily, "I don't *do* returns. My job is to *fold*."   11

I leave that night shaken by my response to the intruder. If she's a supervisor, I could   12 be written up for what I said, but even worse is what I thought. Am I turning mean here, and is that a normal response to the end of a nine-hour shift? There was another out-break of mental wickedness that night. I'd gone back to the counter by the fitting room to pick up the next cart full of returns and found the guy who answers the phone at the counter at night, a pensive young fellow in a wheelchair, staring into space, looking even sadder than usual. And my uncensored thought was, At least you get to sit down.

This is not me, at least not any version of me I'd like to spend much time with. What   13 I have to face is that "Barb," the name on my ID tag, is not exactly the same person as Barbara. "Barb" is what I was called as a child, and still am by my siblings, and I sense that at some level I'm regressing. Take away the career and the higher education, and maybe what you're left with is this original Barb, the one who might have ended up working at Wal-Mart for real if her father hadn't managed to climb out of the mines. So it's interesting, and more than a little disturbing, to see how Barb turned out—that she's meaner and slyer than I am, more cherishing of grudges, and not quite as smart as I'd hoped.

Examining the Reading

1. Describe the working conditions at Wal-Mart as experienced by the author.
2. What sorts of tasks do the Wal-Mart employees perform? Provide details.
3. How and why does the author's attitude toward her job change as the essay progresses?
4. What details or sections of the essay identify Ehrenreich as a well-educated journalist rather than a low-wage worker?
5. Explain the meaning of each of the following words as it is used in the reading: *superfluous* (para. 1), *fecklessly* (2), *adjutant* (3), *errant* (8), and *regressing* (13). Refer to your dictionary as needed.

MAKING CONNECTIONS

Consumers and Workers

Both "Selling Civility" (pp. 209–10) and "Selling in Minnesota" (pp. 225–27) focus on employment and the services that workers provide to consumers. Each writer has a unique point to make about the relationship between consumers and workers.

Analyzing the Readings

1. Who is Ehrenreich's audience, and who is Scott's audience? What details do both authors use that would appeal to their respective audiences?
2. Ehrenreich conceals from her coworkers and employers that she intends to write about her experiences working in retail, and Scott conceals from the workers at the supermarket that they are being reviewed. What benefits does this concealment provide for each author? Do you agree with this approach to gathering information for an article? Why or why not?

Essay Idea

Write an essay about a particular experience that you had either as a worker or as a consumer that helped you better understand the relationship between consumers and workers. Cite both essays as examples.

Analyzing the Writer's Technique

1. Identify the writer's thesis. Is it implied or directly stated?
2. Describe the tone of Ehrenreich's essay. Highlight key phrases that reveal her attitude toward working at Wal-Mart.
3. The writer has to decide how to fit in her various breaks. Why does Ehrenreich include these details? What is she trying to convey about her job?
4. What other patterns of development does the author use? Provide examples of two, and explain how they contribute to the narrative.
5. Does Ehrenreich present an objective or a subjective view of a Wal-Mart worker? Explain your answer.

Visualizing the Reading

Use the chart below to record several particularly effective examples of each narrative characteristic used by Ehrenreich in "Selling in Minnesota." The first one is done for you.

Narrative Characteristic	Examples (Paragraph Number)
Uses dialogue	" 'You've got three carts waiting, Barb. What's the *problem*?' " (para. 2)
Includes sensory details	
Conveys action	
Suggests a sequence of events	
Builds tension	

Reacting to the Reading

1. Compare the author's portrayal of a retail store worker with your experiences as a shopper. Are her descriptions consistent with what you have experienced or observed?
2. Discuss whether this essay will affect the way you treat retail store employees. What adjustments might you make to your behavior in light of the conditions under which they work?
3. Ehrenreich makes a distinction between "Barb" and "Barbara," suggesting two different people, yet they merge as one. In what ways are you more than one person? Write a journal entry exploring this question.
4. Write an essay in which you narrate an on-the-job experience that reveals how you are treated by your employer or supervisor and suggests your attitude toward the workplace.

NARRATION COMBINED WITH OTHER PATTERNS

For more on reading and writing arguments, see Chapters 18 and 19.

In the following selection, Norma Molen uses narration within an essay that presents an argument.

Another Mother's Child:
A Letter to a Murdered Son

Norma Molen

Norma Molen read this letter on the steps of the Lincoln Memorial in Washington, D.C., during a Mother's Day rally against gun violence in 1992. The letter was published in *Catalyst*, a Salt Lake City alternative magazine, in 1993. Molen begins with the narrative, capturing her readers' attention and preparing them for her argument in favor of handgun restriction. As you read, notice how Molen integrates the narrative within her essay and makes it clear how the story illustrates her message.

Dear Steven,

We find it difficult to speak of your terrible tragedy, yet we feel we must. You told us 1
at Christmas break you were dating a beautiful graduate student, Susan Clements, who
lived in the women's wing of your dormitory. And just before you returned to school,
you casually mentioned that Susan had received threatening phone calls from an
ex-boyfriend, a graduate student at Stanford. You said there was nothing to worry
about, that he was all bluff, but that he was causing Susan a great deal of distress.
We were not too concerned because he was 3,000 miles away, yet we warned you not
to get involved. You insisted you could handle it.

On April 23, Andreas Drexler, the ex-boyfriend, appeared in the dormitory hall, just 2
as Susan was unlocking the door to her room. Drexler shot once and missed. You ran
to Susan's defense, and he shot you in the stomach, then ran down the hall and shot
Susan three times in the face. Susan died immediately, you lived five days on machines
before you were pronounced dead, and Drexler, despairing over his unspeakable
crime, shot himself with the same gun. An unimaginable nightmare.

Three talented students dead. And for what purpose? A moment of passion from 3
which there was no return.

We are sorry we brought you up in this violent land. Other advanced nations are ten 4
to fifty times safer from gun violence than the United States. You would still be alive if
you had been born in England, France, Germany, or Japan. We are a free people, but with
this freedom we kill a staggering number with handguns. We have learned to accept the
intolerable.

There is no legitimate need for a handgun in a civilized society, a technology 5
designed specifically for killing, a weapon for the coward. And we, like most Americans,
were lethargic about this grotesque carnage until you became a victim, not in a drug war,
but on the 14th floor of the graduate dormitory at Indiana University. The killing is everywhere: 25,000 last year. And more people arm themselves each day because we have
allowed the gun industry to promote a solution of complete madness.

Drexler, ironically a German, could never have committed this crime in his own 6
country because he couldn't have purchased a gun. In civilized countries people don't
buy handguns. The only exception in European countries is for members of target
shooting societies, but the gun is never taken from the target range.

The immense tragedy that can never change is that we lost you, our poet and writer, 7
our scholar. You disdained material things, always wore shorts and rode a bicycle,

even in winter. You even refused to have a driver's license. And every time we go to an outdoor restaurant, for a bike ride, or a walk up the canyon, there will be an empty place. You were cheated of a career already begun. You were a published writer at age 22 with a short story in a collection called *Flash Fiction*. Who knows what you might have contributed? Several literature professors said you were the brightest student they ever had. They also spoke of Susan in superlatives.

We think a wall like the Vietnam Memorial should be built in front of the Capitol building, except this time it should record the names of the victims killed in their own land because their senators and representatives did not have the integrity and common sense to establish laws that would protect the public. It would be a daily reminder that your blood, Susan's blood, and the blood of thousands of other victims stains the flag.   8

After you died, artist Randall Lake called to remind us of the portrait of you he'd begun to paint. We were thrilled to see it. He caught your intelligent eyes, firm chin, and high cheekbones, your full, thick hair, and he captured your stance. Yet it was not finished. An unfinished portrait is a perfect metaphor for your life. And Susan's. And all the others.   9

Examining the Reading

1. What main issue does Molen's essay address?
2. What is Molen's position on the issue? What reasons does she offer in support of her position?
3. Explain the meaning of each of the following words as it is used in the reading: *grotesque* (para. 5), *carnage* (5), *ironically* (6), *disdained* (7), and *superlatives* (7). Refer to your dictionary as needed.

Analyzing the Writer's Technique

1. What is Molen's thesis? (It is presented after the narrative.) Is its placement effective? Why or why not?
2. Describe the tone of Molen's essay. Give several examples of words and phrases that reveal her tone.
3. Explain how the narrative creates tension and builds to a climax.
4. Highlight several words or phrases that reveal Molen's subjective viewpoint.
5. Who is Molen's intended audience?

Reacting to the Reading

1. Do you think the letter format is effective? Why or why not?
2. Does Molen seriously advocate a wall similar to the Vietnam Memorial? What, if anything, do you think should be done to commemorate handgun victims?
3. Write a journal entry exploring or explaining your position on handgun ownership.
4. Molen states that her son was brought up in a violent land. Write an essay that describes a situation that would support this statement.

Applying Your Skills: Additional Essay Assignments

Write a narrative on one of the following topics, using the elements and techniques of narration you learned in this chapter. Depending on the topic you choose, you may need to do library or Internet research to gather enough support for your ideas.

For more on locating and documenting sources, see Part 5.

To Express Your Ideas

1. Write a narrative about an incident or experience from the past that you see differently now than you did then.
2. In "Right Place, Wrong Face," White says he always believed that the police "were supposed to serve and protect" him. Through the incident he describes in the essay, White learns otherwise. Write a narrative describing an incident involving police officers or law enforcement agents that you may have experienced, observed, or read about. Did the incident change your attitude about police or law enforcement or confirm opinions you already held?

To Inform Your Reader

3. Write an essay informing your reader about the characteristics of a strong (or weak) relationship, the habits of successful (or unsuccessful) students, or the ways of keeping (or losing) a job. Use a narrative to support one or more of your main points.

To Persuade Your Reader

4. "Selling Civility" is concerned with improving the quality of service that customers receive. Have you been treated very poorly or particularly well by a clerk? Do you think that store employees are civil and polite or uncivil? Or can little more be expected of them given the nature of the job and the pay? Are improvements or changes needed? Write an essay taking a position on this issue. Support your position using a narrative of your experience with clerks or employees.
5. "Another Mother's Child" is a persuasive essay that uses narration to support the writer's position on gun control. Write an essay persuading your reader to take a particular stand on an issue of your choosing. Use a narrative to support your position on the issue or tell how you arrived at it.

Cases Using Narration

6. Write a paper for a sociology course on the advantages of an urban, suburban, or rural lifestyle. Support some of your main points with events and examples from your own experiences.
7. Write a draft of the presentation you will give as the new personnel director of a nursing care facility in charge of training new employees. You plan to hold your first orientation session next week, and you want to emphasize the importance of teamwork and communication by telling related stories from your previous job experiences.

CHAPTER 11

Description: Portraying People, Places, and Things

Suppose you are volunteering at the Second Chance shelter for homeless cats. You are asked to write a description to accompany a photograph for the weekly "Available for Adoption" column in the community newspaper. The following description appeared for several weeks but received no response.

> This one-year-old gray and white female cat (neutered) needs a new home. The adoption fee is $75 and includes her first vet visit. Call 555-2298.

You decide a more appealing description is needed to interest readers and encourage them to consider adoption. Rewrite the advertisement, describing the cat in a way that will help convince readers to adopt her.

WRITING A DESCRIPTION

In rewriting the description, did you describe how the cat looks, feels, responds, or behaves? Did you choose details that emphasize its playfulness or willingness to interact with people? If so, you just wrote a successful description. In this chapter, you will learn how to write descriptions and how to use description to support and develop your ideas.

What Is Description?

Description presents information in a way that appeals to one or more of the five senses—sight, sound, smell, taste, and touch—usually creating an overall impression or feeling. You use description every day, to describe a pair of shoes you bought, a flavor of ice cream you tasted, or a concert you recently attended.

Description is an important and useful communication skill. If you were an eyewitness to a car theft, for example, the detective investigating the crime would ask you to describe what you saw. You will also use description in many situations in college and on the job, as the examples in the accompanying box show.

Writers rely on description to present detailed information about people, places, and things and to grasp and sustain their readers' interest. When you write vivid descriptions, you not only make your writing more lively and interesting but also indicate your attitude toward the subject through your choice of words and details.

In the following lively description of a sensory experience of taste, you will feel as if you, too, are eating chilli peppers.

SCENES FROM COLLEGE AND THE WORKPLACE

- For a *chemistry* lab report, you are asked to describe the odor and appearance of a substance made by combining two chemicals.

- In an *art history* class, your instructor asks you to visit a local gallery, choose a particular painting, and describe in a two-page paper the artist's use of line or color.

- As a *nurse* at a local burn treatment center, one of your responsibilities is to record on each patient's chart the overall appearance of and change in second- and third-degree burns.

Eating Chilli Peppers
Jeremy MacClancy

Jeremy MacClancy is an anthropologist and tutor at Oxford Brookes University in England who has written several scholarly works in the field of anthropology. This essay is taken from his book *Consuming Culture: Why You Eat What You Eat* (1993). As you read the selection, underline or highlight the descriptive words and phrases that convey what it's like to eat chilli peppers.

How come over half of the world's population have made a powerful chemical irritant the center of their gastronomic lives? How can so many millions stomach chillies?   1

Biting into a tabasco pepper is like aiming a flame-thrower at your parted lips.   2
There might be little reaction at first, but then the burn starts to grow. A few seconds later the chilli mush in your mouth reaches critical mass and your palate prepares for liftoff. The message spreads. The sweat glands open, your eyes stream, your nose runs, your stomach warms up, your heart accelerates, and your lungs breathe faster. All this is normal. But bite off more than your body can take, and you will be left coughing, sneezing, and spitting. Tears stripe your cheeks, and your mouth belches fire like a dragon celebrating its return to life. Eater beware!

As a general stimulant, chilli is similar to amphetamines — only quicker, cheaper,   3
non-addictive, and beneficial to boot. Employees at the tabasco plant in Louisiana rarely complain of coughs, hay fever, or sinusitis. (Recent evidence, however, suggests that too many chillies can bring on stomach cancer.) Over the centuries, people have used hot peppers as a folk medicine to treat sore throats or inflamed gums, to relieve respiratory distress, and to ease gastritis induced by alcoholism. For aching muscles and tendons, a chilli plaster is more effective than one of mustard, with the added advantage that it does not blister the skin. But people do not eat tabasco, jalapeno, or cayenne peppers because of their pharmacological side-effects. They eat them for the taste — different varieties have different flavors — and for the fire they give off. In other words, they go for the burn.

Eating chillies makes for exciting times: the thrill of anticipation, the extremity of the   4
flames, and then the slow descent back to normality. This is a benign form of masochism, like going to a horror movie, riding a roller coaster, or stepping into a cold bath after a sauna. The body flashes danger signals, but the brain knows the threat is not too great. Aficionados, self-absorbed in their burning passion, know exactly how to pace their whole chilli eating so that the flames are maintained at a steady maximum. Wrenched out of normal routines by the continuing assault on their mouths, they concentrate on the sensation and ignore almost everything else. They play with fire and just ride the burn, like experienced surfers cresting along a wave. For them, without hot peppers, food would lose its zest and their days would seem too dull. A cheap, legal thrill, chilli is the spice of their life.

In the rural areas of Mexico, men can turn their chilli habit into a contest of strength   5
by seeing who can stomach the most hot peppers in a set time. This gastronomic test, however, is not used as a way to prove one's machismo, for women can play the game as well. In this context, chillies are a non-sexist form of acquired love for those with strong hearts and fiery passions — a steady source of hot sauce for their lives.

The enjoyable sensations of a running nose, crying eyes, and dragon-like mouth   6
belching flames are clearly not for the timorous.

More tabasco, anyone?   7

Characteristics of Descriptive Writing

Successful descriptions offer readers more than just a list of sensory details or a catalog of characteristics. In a good description, the details work together to create a dominant effect or impression. Writers often use comparison to help readers experience what they are writing about.

Description Uses Sensory Details

Sensory details appeal to one or more of the five senses — sight, sound, smell, taste, and touch. For example, in the second paragraph of "Eating Chilli Peppers" (p. 235), MacClancy describes the physical sensations that chilli peppers create by using vivid language that appeals to the senses of sight and taste. By appealing to the senses in your writing, you too can help your readers experience the object, sensation, event, or person you aim to describe.

Sight. When you describe what something looks like, you help your reader create a mental picture of the subject. In the following excerpt, notice how Loren Eiseley uses visual detail to describe what he comes across in a field.

> One day as I cut across the field which at that time extended on one side of our suburban shopping center, I found a giant slug feeding from a funnel of pink ice cream in an abandoned Dixie cup. I could see his eyes telescope and protrude in a kind of dim, uncertain ecstasy as his dark body bunched and elongated in the curve of the cup.
>
> Loren Eiseley, "The Brown Wasps"

Eiseley describes shape ("funnel"), action ("bunched and elongated"), color ("pink," "dark"), and size ("giant") and includes specific details ("suburban shopping center," "Dixie cup") to help readers visualize the scene.

The description allows the reader to imagine the slug eating the ice cream in a way that a bare statement of the facts — "On my way to the mall, I saw a slug in a paper cup" — would not do.

Sound. Sound can also be a powerful descriptive tool. Can you "hear" the engines in the following description?

> They were one-cylinder and two-cylinder engines, and some were make-and-break and some were jump-spark, but they all made a sleepy sound across the lake. The one-lungers throbbed and fluttered, and the twin-cylinder ones purred and purred, and that was a quiet sound too. But now the campers all had outboards. In the daytime, in the hot mornings, these motors made a petulant, irritable sound; at night, in the still evening when the afterglow lit the water, they whined about one's ears like mosquitoes.
>
> E. B. White, "Once More to the Lake"

White conveys the sounds of the engines by using active verbs ("throbbed and fluttered," "purred and purred," "whined"), descriptive adjectives ("sleepy," "petulant," "irritable"), and a comparison ("like mosquitoes").

Writers of description also use *onomatopoeia,* words that approximate the sounds they describe. The words *hiss, whine, spurt,* and *sizzle* are common examples.

Smell. Smells are sometimes difficult to describe, partly because we do not have as many adjectives for smells as we do for sights and sounds. Smell can be an effective descriptive device, however, as shown here.

Driving through farm country at summer sunset provides a cavalcade of smells: manure, cut grass, honeysuckle, spearmint, wheat chaff, scallions, chicory, tar from the macadam road.

Diane Ackerman, A Natural History of the Senses

Notice how Ackerman lists nouns that evoke distinct odors and leaves it to the reader to imagine how they smell.

Taste. Words that evoke the sense of taste can make descriptions lively, as in "Eating Chilli Peppers." Consider also this restaurant critic's description of Vietnamese cuisine.

In addition to balancing the primary flavors—the sweet, sour, bitter, salty and peppery tastes whose sensations are, in the ancient Chinese system, directly related to physical and spiritual health—medicinal herbs were used in most dishes. . . . For instance, the orange-red annatto seed is used for its "cooling" effect as well as for the mildly tangy flavor it lends and the orange color it imparts.

Molly O'Neill, "Vietnam's Cuisine: Echoes of Empires"

Notice that O'Neill describes the variety of flavors ("sweet, sour, bitter, salty and peppery") in Vietnamese cuisine as well as the distinctive flavor ("mildly tangy") of annatto seeds.

Touch. Descriptions of texture, temperature, and weight allow a reader not only to visualize but almost to experience an object or a scene. In the excerpt that follows, Annie Dillard describes the experience of holding a Polyphemus moth cocoon.

We passed the cocoon around; it was heavy. As we held it in our hands, the creature within warmed and squirmed. We were delighted, and wrapped it tighter in our fists. The pupa began to jerk violently, in heart-stopping knocks. Who's there? I can still feel those thumps, urgent through a muffling of spun silk and leaf, urgent through the swaddling of many years, against the curve of my palm. We kept passing it around. When it came to me again it was hot as a bun; it jumped half out of my hand. The teacher intervened. She put it, still heaving and banging, in the ubiquitous Mason jar.

Annie Dillard, Pilgrim at Tinker Creek

Dillard describes the texture of the cocoon ("a muffling of spun silk and leaf"), its temperature ("warmed," "hot as a bun"), its weight ("heavy"), and its motion ("squirmed," "jerk violently, in heart-stopping knocks," "thumps," "jumped," "heaving and banging") to give readers an accurate sense of what it felt like to hold it.

Description Uses Active Verbs and Varied Sentences

Sensory details are often best presented through active, vivid verbs and varied sentences. Look, for instance, at the active verbs in this sentence from paragraph 2 of MacClancy's essay.

The sweat glands *open,* your eyes *stream,* your nose *runs,* your stomach *warms up,* your heart *accelerates,* and your lungs *breathe* faster.

In fact, active verbs are often more effective than adverbs in creating striking and lasting impressions, as the following example demonstrates.

ORIGINAL   The team captain *proudly* accepted the award.

REVISED   The team captain *marched* to the podium, *grasped* the trophy, and *gestured* toward his teammates.

Using varied sentences also contributes to the effective expression of sensory details. Be sure to use different types and patterns of sentences and to vary their lengths. Look again at the second paragraph in MacClancy's essay. Note how he varies his sentences to make the description interesting.

For more on varying sentence patterns and using active verbs, see Chapter 9, pp. 184 and 188.

Exercise 11.1

*Using **sensory details**, **active verbs**, and **varied sentences**, describe one of the common objects in the following list or one of your own choosing. Do not name the object in your description. Exchange papers with a classmate. Your reader should be able to guess the item you are describing from the details you provide.*

1. A piece of clothing
2. A food item
3. An appliance
4. A machine
5. A computer keyboard

Description Creates a Dominant Impression

An effective description leaves the reader with a **dominant impression**—an overall attitude, mood, or feeling about the subject. The impression may be awe, inspiration, anger, or distaste, for example.

For more on thesis statements, see Chapter 5, p. 101.

Let's suppose you are writing about an old storage box you found in your parents' attic, and the aspect of the box you want to emphasize (your slant) is *memories of childhood*. Given this slant, or angle, you might describe the box in several ways, each of which would convey a different dominant impression.

- "A box filled with treasures from my childhood brought back memories of long, sunny afternoons playing in our backyard."
- "Opening the box was like lifting the lid of a time machine, revealing toys and games from another era."
- "When I opened the box, I was eight years old again, fighting over my favorite doll with my twin sister, Erica."

Notice that each example provides a different impression of the contents of the storage box and would require a different type of support. That is, only selected objects from within the box would be relevant to each impression. Note, too, that in all of these examples, the dominant impression is stated directly rather than implied. Many times, however, writers rely on descriptive language to imply a dominant impression.

In "Eating Chilli Peppers," notice how all the details evoke the thrill of eating the peppers for those who love them; as MacClancy says, "they go for the burn." The first two sentences of the essay pose the questions that the remaining paragraphs answer. The answer is the dominant impression: Eating chilli peppers is thrilling. To write an effective description, you need to select details carefully, including only those that contribute to the dominant impression you are trying to create. Notice that MacClancy does not clutter his description by describing the size, shape, texture, or color of chilli peppers. Instead he focuses on their thrilling, fiery hotness and the side effects they cause.

Exercise 11.2

Read the following paragraph and cross out details that do not contribute to the dominant impression.

All morning I had had some vague sense that something untoward was about to happen. I suspected bad news was on its way. As I stepped outside, the heat of the summer sun, unusually oppressive for ten o'clock, seemed to sear right through me. In fact, now that I think about it, everything seemed slightly out of kilter that morning. The car, which had been newly painted the week before, had stalled several times. The flowers in the garden, planted for me by my husband, purchased from a nursery down the road, were drooping. It was as though they were wilting before they even had a chance to grow. Even my two cats, who look like furry puffballs, moved listlessly across the room, ignoring my invitation to play. It was then that I received the phone call from the emergency room telling me about my son's accident.

Description Uses Connotative Language Effectively

As noted in Chapter 9, most words have two levels of meaning—*denotative* and *connotative*. The denotation of a word is its precise dictionary meaning. For instance, the denotation of the word *flag* is "a piece of cloth used as a national emblem." Usually, however, feelings and attitudes are also associated with a word—emotional colorings or shades of meaning. These are the word's connotations. A common connotation of *flag* is patriotism—love and respect for one's country. As you write, be careful about the connotations of the words you choose. Select words that strengthen the dominant impression you are creating.

Description Uses Comparisons

When describing a person or an object, you can help your readers by comparing the person or object to something with which they are familiar. Several types of comparisons are used in descriptive writing—similes, metaphors, personification, and analogies. In a **simile** the comparison is direct and is introduced by *like* or *as*. MacClancy uses a number of telling similes in "Eating Chilli Peppers."

For more on similes, metaphors, and personification, see Chapter 9, p. 193.

- "Biting into a tabasco pepper is like aiming a flame-thrower at your parted lips."
- Eating chillies is "like going to a horror movie, riding a roller coaster, or stepping into a cold bath after a sauna."

A **metaphor** is indirect, implying the comparison by describing one thing as if it were another. Instead of the similes listed above, MacClancy could have used metaphors to describe the experience of eating chillies.

- Eating chilli peppers is a descent into a fiery hell.
- To eat chilli peppers is to ride the crest of a wave, waiting for the thrill.

Personification is a figure of speech in which an object is given human qualities or characteristics. "The television screen stared back at me" is an example. An **analogy** is an extended comparison in which one subject, often a more familiar one, is used to explain another. Like similes and metaphors, analogies add interest to your writing while making your ideas more real and accessible.

> ### Exercise 11.3
>
> *Write a paragraph describing a food you enjoy. Focus on one sense, as MacClancy does, or appeal to several senses. If possible, draw a comparison using a simile or a metaphor.*

Description Follows a Method of Organization

For more on these methods of organization, see Chapter 6, p. 118.

Effective descriptions must follow a clear method of organization. Three common methods of organization used in descriptive writing are spatial order, chronological order, and most-to-least or least-to-most order.

- When you use spatial order, you describe a subject in terms of the physical position of its parts—for example, from top to bottom, from left to right, or from near to far away. Or you may start from a central focal point and then describe the objects that surround it. For example, if you are describing a college campus, you might start by describing a building at the center of the campus—the library, perhaps. You would then describe the buildings that are near the library, and conclude by describing anything on the outskirts of the campus.

  In writing a description using spatial order, you can use either a fixed or a moving **vantage point**. With a *fixed vantage point*, you describe what you see from a particular position. With a *moving vantage point*, you describe your subject from different positions. A fixed vantage point is like a stationary camera trained on a subject from one direction. A moving vantage point is like a handheld camera that captures the subject from many directions.
- Chronological order works well when you need to describe events or changes that occur in objects or places over a period of time. You might use chronological order to describe the changes in a puppy's behavior as it grows or to relate changing patterns of light and shadow as the sun sets.
- You might use most-to-least or least-to-most order to describe the smells in a flower garden or the sounds of an orchestra tuning up for a concert.

Visualizing a Description: A Graphic Organizer

For more on graphic organizers, see Chapter 3, p. 55.

The graphic organizer shown in Figure 11.1 will help you visualize the elements of a description. When you write an essay in which your primary purpose is to describe something, you'll need to follow the standard essay format—title, introduction, body, and conclusion—with slight adaptations and adjustments. In a descriptive essay, the

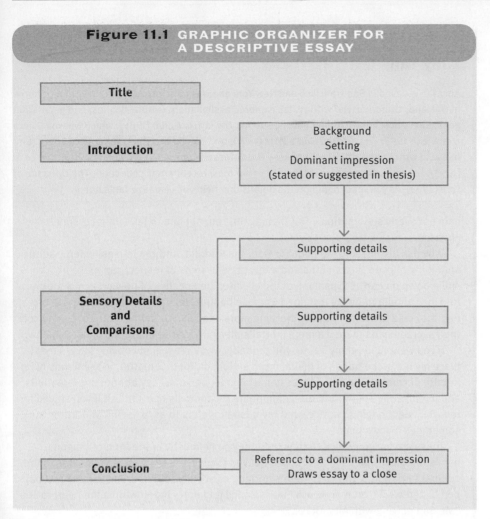

Figure 11.1 GRAPHIC ORGANIZER FOR A DESCRIPTIVE ESSAY

introduction provides a context for the description and presents the thesis statement, which states or suggests the dominant impression. The body of the essay presents sensory details that support the dominant impression. The conclusion draws the description to a close and makes a final reference to the dominant impression. It may offer a final detail or make a closing statement.

When you incorporate a description into an essay in which you also use other patterns of development, you will probably need to condense or eliminate one or more of the elements of a description essay.

The following essay, "Inferior Decorating," is a good example of description. Read the essay and then study the graphic organizer for it in Figure 11.2 (p. 244).

Inferior Decorating

Amy Tan

Amy Tan is based in San Francisco and New York and was born into a traditional Chinese home in Oakland, California. Her writing has explored assimilation, culture clashes, and generation gaps. She is best known for her novels, such as *The Joy Luck Club* (1989), which was made into a movie in 1993; *The Kitchen God's Wife* (1991); and *The Bonesetter's Daughter* (2000). She has also written two children's books — *The Chinese Siamese Cat* (1994) and *The Moon Lady* (1992). The following reading is taken from her most recent essay collection, *The Opposite of Fate* (2003). As you read, highlight the details that help you visualize Tan's home.

I am not overly superstitious. But then again, I am not one to take unnecessary 1
chances.

Why risk displeasing the gods (or God, the Buddha, and the muses) when a subtle 2
sprinkling of good-luck charms and a few tasteful signs of respect can make heaven
smile down on earth? (Speaking of the elevated perspective of holy ones: My mother
told me I should hang my inscribed Chinese banners *upside down* so that those on
high can read them more easily. Nothing more annoying to deities than to have to cock
their sacred heads to read a mere mortal's plea suspended hundreds of miles below.)

If you were to enter my home, you probably wouldn't see any obvious signs that I 3
place my life in the hands of divine intervention, or, for that matter, in the hands of an
interior decorator. The first impression is, I hope, one of a cozy abode: unpretentious
and intelligently appointed to accommodate the fur balls of a cat. But if you stayed for
tea, you might begin to notice what my husband refers to as "kitsch," or "clutter," or
sometimes "Amy's junk."

These are my good-luck charms, and they come mostly in the form of dragons, 4
fish, strategically placed mirrors, and heaven forgive me, New Age crystals. (As to the
cultural deviation of the last, there's nothing mystical about their inclusion. I just happen to agree with what my niece Melissa once told me — that it warms the heart to see
"Mr. Sun playing with Mrs. Glass.")

In the foyer at the top of the stairs is a rosewood chair, a bit of Chinese gothic whimsy 5
from the 1920s. The arch of the back and the hand rests are carved with dragons, their
piercing inlaid-ivory eyes guarding over its owner, me, another dragon. Next to the chair
is a bamboo-and-wire birdcage. This houses only lucky turquoise and copper Chinese
coins. Meanwhile, the birds (plastic and made in Taiwan), sit outside the cage and chirp
warnings whenever the cage of money is disturbed. On a carved stand opposite the birdcage sits a porcelain vase big enough for me to climb into. If you were to look inside the
vase, you'd see painted there a lionhead goldfish swimming about, which, along with an
electronic alarm system, is excellent for chasing off devilish spirits and thieves. Above
the vase is a mirror with a nineteenth-century dragon carving as its frame.

A word about mirrors: They can supposedly repel bad luck or attract good. I'm not 6
sure about which laws of physics apply. All I know is that I once had a neighbor whose
nightly hammering nearly drove my husband and me up the wall; after we aimed a
curved mirror in his direction — *total silence*. In my current home, the dragon mirror is
directed at a nice neighbor who has a surfeit of parking spaces in his garage. I have no
garage, but I'm usually lucky enough to find a space in front of my door.

My study is where I've applied most of my decorating skills. Scattered about are 7
chimes, banners with lucky sayings, and wooden fish — as well as a stuffed piranha for
fighting off heavy-duty distractions from writing.

And the location of my study is particularly auspicious, according to Chinese prin- 8
ciples of *feng shui* ("wind and water"). Its three bay windows overlook neighborhood
rooftops and face north toward water and mountains. In terms of San Francisco real
estate principles, it means I have a knockout view of the Presidio's eucalyptus forest,
the Golden Gate Bridge, San Francisco Bay, Angel Island, the Marin Headlands, and
Tiburon. But here's where the Chinese gods and literary muses come into conflict; the
muses have decreed that I hang shades in front of the view, the better to concentrate
on the computer screen, rather than on sailboats, mating pigeons, and cable TV repair
people shimmying across the slanted roofs.

While I'm on the subject of computer screens, some years ago, while writing my 9
first book, I stuck a Dymo-tape message across the top of my monitor that read: "Call
Your Guardian Angel." This was my reminder to think about my sources of inspiration. One day my mother saw the reminder, sat down at my desk, and proceeded to
have a "chat" with my computer, thinking that this was where her mother, whom she
considered my muse, now resided in motherboard sartorial splendor. Well, just in
case a hundred-year-old spirit really is my muse, I've placed three bamboo calligraphy
brushes below the monitor, as well as copper clappers from Tibet.

By far my best and favorite lucky charm sits in a corner of my office. It, or rather *she*, 10
is an exquisitely painted Chinese porcelain statue about twelve inches tall. I've grown
up seeing statues in Chinese restaurants and stores. They're usually kept in miniature
temples and given offerings of tea and oranges. Shopowners tend to pick a god or
goddess who corresponds to the kind of luck they wish to have flowing through their
doors, say the God of Money for a constantly ringing cash register, or the God of War
for aggressive business deals.

I chose an unnamed goddess while writing my then untitled second book. I didn't 11
think it was good manners to ask her for anything as crass as good reviews and placement on bestseller lists. And anyway, if she was anything like my mother, my goddess
had never even heard of the *New York Times*. In the end, I asked only that I be able to
write the best book I could, and that no matter what happened to it, I would have no
regrets, no sorrows. I called my statue Lady Sorrowfree and titled the last chapter after
her. I titled the book *The Kitchen God's Wife*, which was how she was known, as the
wronged spouse of a wandering husband. I gave her offerings of airline mini-bottles of
Jack Daniel's.

Do these things really work? All I know is this: I have been incredibly lucky these 12
past few years. What I may lack in terms of sense of style, I more than make up for by
giving myself a sense of luck.

And if my Chinese luck runs out, not to worry. I have the standard American charms 13 *To draw detailed graphic*
as well: insurance and lawyers.   *organizers using a computer,*
                                                                                         visit www.bedfordstmartins
                                                                                         .com/successfulwriting.

Exercise 11.4

*After examining each part of MacClancy's "Eating Chilli Peppers" (p. 235), draw a graphic
organizer that shows how this essay is constructed.*

Figure 11.2 GRAPHIC ORGANIZER FOR "INFERIOR DECORATING"

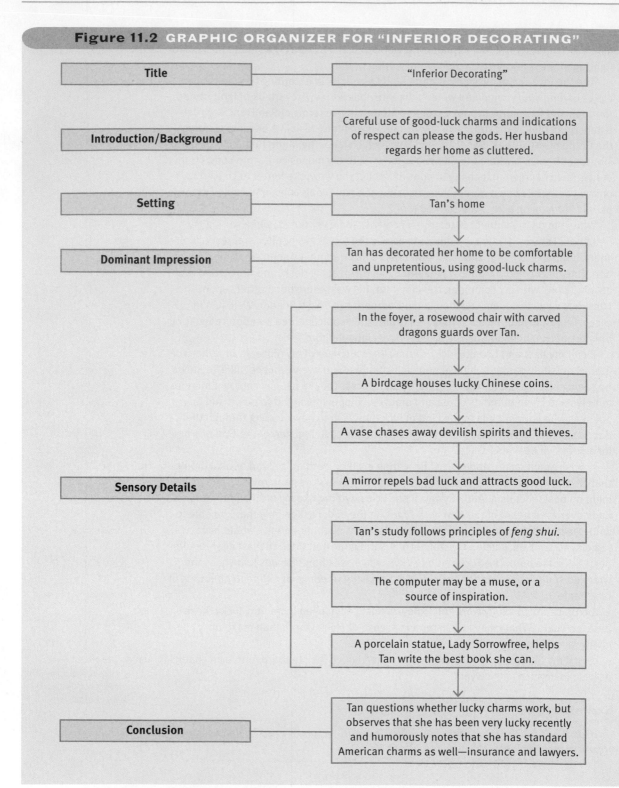

Title	"Inferior Decorating"
Introduction/Background	Careful use of good-luck charms and indications of respect can please the gods. Her husband regards her home as cluttered.
Setting	Tan's home
Dominant Impression	Tan has decorated her home to be comfortable and unpretentious, using good-luck charms.
Sensory Details	In the foyer, a rosewood chair with carved dragons guards over Tan.
	A birdcage houses lucky Chinese coins.
	A vase chases away devilish spirits and thieves.
	A mirror repels bad luck and attracts good luck.
	Tan's study follows principles of *feng shui*.
	The computer may be a muse, or a source of inspiration.
	A porcelain statue, Lady Sorrowfree, helps Tan write the best book she can.
Conclusion	Tan questions whether lucky charms work, but observes that she has been very lucky recently and humorously notes that she has standard American charms as well—insurance and lawyers.

Integrating Description into an Essay

Sometimes description alone fulfills the purpose of an essay. In most cases, however, you will use description in other types of essays. For instance, in a narrative essay, description plays an important role in helping readers experience events, reconstruct scenes, and visualize action. Similarly, you would use description to explain the causes or effects of a phenomenon, to compare or contrast animal species, and to provide examples of defensive behavior in children (illustration). Writers use description to keep their readers interested in the material. Description, then, is essential to many types of academic and business writing.

Use the following guidelines to build effective description into the essays you write.

1. **Include only relevant details.** Whether you describe an event, a person, or a scene, the sensory details you choose should enhance the reader's understanding of your subject.
2. **Keep the description focused.** Select enough details to make your essential points and dominant impression clear. Readers may become impatient if you include too many details.
3. **Make sure the description fits the essay's tone and point of view.** A personal description, for example, is not appropriate in an essay explaining a technical process.

In "Bloggers without Borders . . ." on page 262, the author incorporates description into a narrative essay.

A GUIDED WRITING ASSIGNMENT

The following guide will lead you through the process of writing an essay that uses description. You may choose to write a descriptive essay or to employ description within an essay that relies on another pattern of development. Depending on your learning style, you may choose to work through this Guided Writing Assignment in various ways. If you are an abstract learner, for example, you might begin by brainstorming about the general subject. If you are a concrete learner, you might prefer to begin by freewriting specific details. If you are a pragmatic learner, you might start by thinking about how to organize your description.

Learning Style Options

The Assignment

Write a descriptive essay using one of the following topics or one that you think of on your own. Your classmates are your audience.

1. An adult toy, such as a camera, a DVD player, a computer, golf clubs, or a cooking gadget
2. A hobby or sport that you enjoy either engaging in or observing others doing on campus, in your neighborhood, or on television
3. An annoying or obnoxious person or a pleasant, courteous one

For more on comparison and contrast, see Chapter 14. For more on narration, see Chapter 10.

As you develop your description, consider using other patterns of development. For example, you might compare and contrast an unfamiliar activity to one you engage in regularly, or you might narrate an incident that reveals a person's positive or negative qualities.

Generating Ideas and Details

Use the following steps to help you choose a topic and generate ideas.

Choosing a Topic

For more on conducting observations, see Chapter 21, p. 595.

To write an effective description, you must be familiar with the subject or have the opportunity to observe the subject directly. Never try to describe the campus computer lab without visiting it or the pizza served in the snack bar without tasting it.

Use the following suggestions to choose an appropriate topic.

For more on prewriting strategies, see Chapter 4.

1. Use freewriting, mapping, group brainstorming, or another prewriting technique to generate a list of specific objects, activities, or people that fit the assignment.
2. Look over your list of possible topics. Identify the one or two subjects that you find most interesting and that you can describe in detail.
3. Make sure your subject is one you are familiar with or one you can readily observe. You may need to observe the object, activity, or person several times as you work through your essay.

> **Essay in Progress 1**
> Using the preceding suggestions, choose a topic to write about for the assignment option you selected on page 245.

Considering Your Purpose, Audience, and Point of View

A descriptive essay may be objective, subjective, or both, depending on the writer's purpose. In an *objective* essay, the writer's purpose is to inform — to present information or communicate ideas without obvious bias or emotion. All writers convey their feelings to some extent, but in an objective essay the writer strives to focus on giving information. For example, a geologist's description of a rock formation written for a scientific journal would be largely objective; its purpose would be to inform readers of the height of the formation, the type of rock it contains, and other characteristics of the subject. Objective essays are generally written in the third person.

For more on purpose, audience, and point of view, see Chapter 4.

In a *subjective* essay, which is often written in the first person, the writer's purpose is to create an emotional response. Whereas an objective essay describes only what the writer observes or experiences, a subjective essay describes both the observation or experience *and* the writer's feelings about it. Therefore, a rock climber's description of a rock formation would focus on the writer's impressions of and reactions to the experience of climbing it, such as the feeling of the smooth rock on a hot day and the exhilaration of reaching the top. But the rock climber's description might also include objective details about the height and composition of the rock formation to help readers see and feel what it's like to climb one.

Once you've chosen a subject and considered your purpose and point of view, think about your audience. For this assignment, your audience is your classmates. How familiar are your classmates with your subject? If they are unfamiliar with the subject, you will need to provide a more thorough introduction and a greater amount of detail than if your audience has some knowledge of it.

Choosing an Aspect of Your Subject to Emphasize

Almost any subject you choose will be made up of many more details than you could possibly include in an essay. Start by selecting several possible slants, or angles on your subject that you would like to emphasize. If your subject is a person, you might focus on a particular character trait, such as compulsiveness or sense of humor, and then generate a list of descriptive details that illustrate the trait. To describe an object, you might emphasize its usefulness, value, or beauty. Choose the one slant that seems most promising and for which you generated plenty of sensory details.

For more on narrowing a topic, see Chapter 4, p. 80.

> **Essay in Progress 2**
> Using one or more prewriting techniques, come up with several possible slants on your subject and details to support them. Then choose the slant about which you can write the most effective description.

Collecting Details That Describe Your Subject

Once you've decided on a slant to emphasize, you're ready for the next step—collecting and recording additional sensory details. The following suggestions will help you generate details.

1. Brainstorm about your subject. Record any sensory details that support the slant you have chosen.
2. Try describing your subject to a friend, concentrating on the slant you have chosen. You may discover that details come quickly during conversation. Make notes on what you said and on your friend's response.
3. Draw a quick sketch of your subject and label the parts. You may find yourself recalling additional details as you draw.
4. Divide a piece of paper or a computer file into five sections. Label the sections *sight, sound, taste, touch,* and *smell.* Consider the following characteristics in developing sensory details.

Learning Style Options

For more on generating details, see Chapter 4, p. 86.

For more on prewriting strategies, see Chapter 4.

TABLE 11.1 Characteristics to Consider in Developing Sensory Details

Sight	Sound	Smell	Taste	Touch
Color	Volume	Agreeable/ disagreeable	Pleasant/ unpleasant	Texture
Pattern	Pitch	Strength	Salty, sweet, sour, bitter	Weight
Shape	Quality			Temperature
Size				

Finding Comparisons and Choosing a Vantage Point

Try to think of appropriate comparisons—similes, metaphors, or analogies—for as many details in your list as possible. Jot down your comparisons in the margin next to the relevant details in your list. Don't expect to find a comparison for each detail. Your goal is to discover one or two strong comparisons that you can use in your essay.

Next consider whether to use a fixed or moving vantage point. Ask yourself the following questions.

1. What vantage point(s) will provide the most useful information?
2. From which vantage point(s) can I provide the most revealing or striking details?

> **Essay in Progress 3**
> Use one or more of the preceding suggestions to develop details that support the aspect of your subject that you are emphasizing. Then find comparisons and decide on a vantage point.

Evaluating Your Details

Evaluate the details you have collected to determine which ones you can use in your essay. Begin by rereading all of your notes with a critical eye. Highlight vivid, concrete details that will create pictures in your reader's mind. Eliminate vague details as well as those that do not support your slant on the subject. If you are working on a computer, highlight usable ideas by making them bold or moving them to a separate page or document for easy access when drafting.

> **Trying Out Your Ideas on Others**
>
> Working in a group of two or three students, discuss your ideas and details for this chapter's assignment. Each writer should explain his or her slant on the subject and provide a list of the details collected for the subject. Then, as a group, evaluate the writer's details and suggest improvements.

> **Essay in Progress 4**
> Use your notes and the comments of your classmates to evaluate the details you have collected so far. Omit irrelevant and vague details, and add more vivid and concrete details if they are needed.

Creating a Dominant Impression

As noted earlier, think of the dominant impression as a thesis that conveys your main point and holds the rest of your essay together. The dominant impression also creates a mood or feeling about the subject, which all other details in your essay explain or support. The dominant impression you decide on should be the one about which you feel most knowledgeable and confident. It should also appeal to your audience, offer an unusual perspective, and provide new insights on your subject.

Essay in Progress 5
Using the preceding guidelines, select the dominant impression you want to convey about your subject, and do additional prewriting, if necessary, to gather enough details to support it.

Organizing and Drafting

Once you are satisfied with your dominant impression and your support for it, you are ready to organize your ideas and draft your essay.

For more on drafting an essay, see Chapter 6.

Choosing a Method of Organization

Select the method of organization that will best support your dominant impression. For example, if you have chosen to focus on a person's slovenly appearance, then a spatial (top to bottom, left to right) organization may be effective. If you are describing a scary visit to a wildlife preserve, then chronological order would be a useful method of organization. A most-to-least or least-to-most arrangement might work best for a description of the symptoms of pneumonia. Also consider organizing your details by the five senses. For instance, to describe a chocolate-chip cookie, you could give details about how it looks, how it smells, how it tastes, and how it feels in your mouth.

If you are working on a computer, use your word-processing program's cut-and-paste function to try different methods of organization.

Regardless of which method you choose for organizing your details, be sure to connect your ideas and guide your reader with transitional words and phrases.

For a list of transitions, see Chapter 7, p. 150.

Drafting the Description

As you draft your essay, remember that all of your details must support your dominant impression. Other details, no matter how interesting or important they may seem, should not be included. For example, if you are describing the way apes in a zoo imitate one another and humans, only details about how the apes mimic other apes and people should be included. Other details, such as the condition of the apes' environment and the types of animals nearby, do not belong in the essay. Be careful as well about the *number* of details you include. Too many details will tire your readers, but an insufficient number will leave your readers unconvinced of your main point. Select striking sensory details that make your point effectively; leave out details that tell the reader little or nothing.

For more on writing effective paragraphs, including introductions and conclusions, see Chapter 6.

Try also to include one or two telling metaphors or similes. If you cannot think of any, however, don't stretch to construct them. Effective comparisons usually come to mind as you examine your subject. Contrived comparisons will only lessen the impact of your essay.

As you write your description, remember that the sensory language you use should enable your readers to re-create the person, object, or scene in their minds. Keep the following three guidelines in mind as you write.

1. **Create images that appeal to the five senses.** As noted earlier, your descriptions should appeal to one or more of the senses. See pages 236–37 for examples of ways to engage each of the five senses.

2. **Avoid vague, general descriptions.** Use specific, not vague, language to describe your subject. Notice the differences between the following descriptions.

VAGUE	The pizza was cheaply prepared.
CONCRETE	The supposedly "large" pizza was miniature, with a nearly imperceptible layer of sauce, a light dusting of cheese, a few paper-thin slices of pepperoni, and one or two stray mushroom slices.

Vivid descriptions hold your readers' interest and give them a more complete picture of your subject. For example, notice how the list below becomes increasingly more concrete.

Animal → dog → golden retriever → male golden retriever → six-month-old male golden retriever puppy → Ivan, my six-month-old male golden retriever puppy

You can create a similar progression of descriptive words for any person, object, or place that you want to describe.

3. **Use figures of speech and analogies effectively.** Figures of speech (similes, metaphors) and analogies create memorable images that enliven your writing and capture your readers' attention. Here are some tips for using figurative language in your writing.

- Choose fresh, surprising images. Avoid overused clichés such as *cold as ice* and *it's a hop, skip, and a jump away.*
- Make sure the similarity between the two items being compared is apparent. If you write "Peter looked like an unpeeled tangerine," your reader will not be able to guess what characteristics Peter shares with the tangerine. "Peter's skin was as dimpled as a tangerine peel" gives the reader a clearer idea of what Peter looks like.
- Don't mix or combine figures of speech. Such expressions, called **mixed metaphors**, are confusing and often unintentionally humorous. For example, the following sentence mixes images of a hawk and a wolf.

The fighter jet was a hawk soaring into the clouds, growling as it sought its prey.

Essay in Progress 6

Draft your essay. Use the preceding suggestions to organize your details and support your dominant impression. Even if your essay is primarily descriptive, consider incorporating a narrative, an illustration, or a comparison (or another pattern of development) to strengthen the dominant impression.

Analyzing and Revising

If possible, set your draft aside for a day or two before rereading and revising it. As you reread, focus on overall effectiveness, not on grammar and mechanics. To analyze your draft, use one or more of the following strategies.

1. Reread your paper aloud, or ask a friend to do so as you listen. You may "hear" parts that seem contrived or skimpy, or notice descriptions that do not work.

2. Ask a classmate to read your draft and describe the dominant impression, comparing his or her version to the one you intended. Note ideas that your reader overlooked or misinterpreted.

3. Write an outline or draw a graphic organizer (using the format shown on p. 241), or update the outline or graphic organizer you prepared earlier. Look for ideas that do not seem to fit or that lack supporting details, and for places where your organization needs tightening.

Learning Style Options

Use Figure 11.3 to help you discover the strengths and weaknesses of your descriptive essay. You might also ask a classmate to review your essay using the questions in the flowchart. For each answer that refers you to the right column of the chart, ask your reviewer to explain why he or she answered in that way.

For more on the benefits of peer review, see Chapter 8, p. 162.

Figure 11.3 Flowchart for Revising a Descriptive Essay

QUESTIONS

1. Without looking at your essay, *write* a sentence that states the dominant impression the essay is to convey. Next, highlight the sentences in the essay that express the *dominant impression*. Do these sentences successfully convey the impression?

REVISION STRATEGIES

NO →
- Reread your essay. Make a list of the different impressions it conveys.
- Choose one impression that you have the most to say about, and brainstorm to develop additional details that support it.

YES ↓

2. Place a checkmark ✔ by each sensory detail. Does each detail support your *dominant impression?*

NO →
- Eliminate irrelevant sensory details.

YES ↓

3. Review the sensory details you have ✔ checkmarked. Have you included enough vivid language to help your reader visualize the topic? Are the connotations of your language appropriate?

NO →
- Brainstorm to discover additional sensory details.
- Replace passive verbs with active ones. Vary your sentences.
- For any words with inappropriate connotations, substitute words that better support your dominant impression.

YES ↓

(continued on next page)

(Figure 11.3 continued)

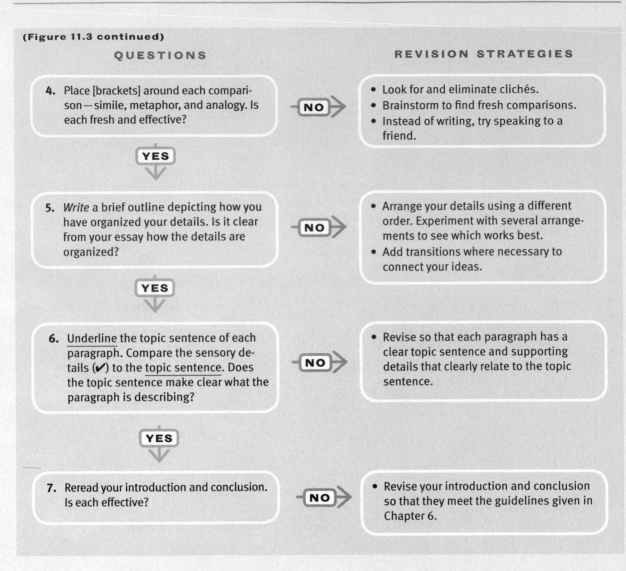

QUESTIONS   REVISION STRATEGIES

4. Place [brackets] around each comparison—simile, metaphor, and analogy. Is
each fresh and effective?

NO
- Look for and eliminate clichés.
- Brainstorm to find fresh comparisons.
- Instead of writing, try speaking to a friend.

YES

5. *Write* a brief outline depicting how you
have organized your details. Is it clear
from your essay how the details are
organized?

NO
- Arrange your details using a different order. Experiment with several arrangements to see which works best.
- Add transitions where necessary to connect your ideas.

YES

6. Underline the topic sentence of each
paragraph. Compare the sensory details (✔) to the topic sentence. Does
the topic sentence make clear what the
paragraph is describing?

NO
- Revise so that each paragraph has a clear topic sentence and supporting details that clearly relate to the topic sentence.

YES

7. Reread your introduction and conclusion.
Is each effective?

NO
- Revise your introduction and conclusion so that they meet the guidelines given in Chapter 6.

Essay in Progress 7
Using Figure 11.3 as a guide, as well as suggestions made by your classmate, revise
your essay.

Editing and Proofreading

For more on keeping an error log, see Chapter 9, p. 196.

The last step is to check your revised essay for errors in grammar, spelling, punctuation, and mechanics. Be sure to look for the types of errors you tend to make. (Refer
to your error log.)

For descriptive writing, pay particular attention to the punctuation of adjectives. Keep the following rules in mind.

1. Use a comma between coordinate adjectives that are not joined by *and*.

- Singh was a *confident, skilled* pianist.

Coordinate adjectives are a series of adjectives whose order can be changed (*skilled, confident pianist* or *confident, skilled pianist*).

2. Do not use commas between cumulative adjectives, whose order cannot be changed.

- *Two frightened brown* eyes peered at us from under the sofa.

You would not write *frightened two brown eyes*.

3. Use a hyphen to connect two words that work together as an adjective before a noun unless the first word is an adverb ending in *–ly*.

- *well-used* book
- *foil-wrapped* pizza
- *perfectly thrown* pass

Essay in Progress 8

Edit and proofread your essay, paying particular attention to the use and punctuation of adjectives and to the errors listed in your error log.

Students Write

Ted Sawchuck, a journalism student at the University of Maryland at College Park, wrote this essay in response to an assignment in one of his classes. He was asked to describe a workplace situation that he had experienced. As you read, study the annotations and pay particular attention to Sawchuck's use of sensory language that helps you see and feel what he has experienced.

Heatstroke with a Side of Burn Cream

Ted Sawchuck

I sprinkle the last layer of cheese on top of my nachos--no time to watch the cheddar melt--and turn sideways, nearly falling face-first on grimy, spongy rubber mats. Catching my fall and the plate, I whip a towel from my belt with my free hand, open the scalding-hot oven door, and slide in the chips to toast before slapping a palm on top of the now-light-brown quesadilla on the rack below and pulling it out onto a clean part of the towel for a 180 degree turn to the counter behind. A pizza cutter makes three smooth cuts; the quesadilla is plated

READING

1

Introduction: Sawchuck builds toward his dominant impression by describing a hectic evening in a restaurant kitchen.

with three small cups (guac, salsa, sour cream) and handed to the window. I slap the bell, bellow "Jamie! Nachos!", and spin back to my station too fast to see a gorgeous grad student scoop up the plate and scoot it out to her table.

Sawchuck identifies the topic of his description. Vivid, active verbs help readers visualize the setting.

Welcome to a restaurant kitchen during lunch or dinner rush, the time when the restaurant is packed with hungry people and the kitchen is maniacally cranking away at their orders. I'm thrashing appetizers, trying to keep up with college students' demands for fried goodies, nachos, and quesadillas. My friend A is working the grill, cooking fifteen burgers and a couple chicken breasts for sandwiches, and M, a mutual friend, is buzzing around prepping plates, flirting with waitresses, and handling salads and desserts, both of which require time away from the main preparation line.

In this paragraph and the next three, the topic sentences introduce different kinds of sensory details that help readers imagine the kitchen. Here, a comparison adds humor and realism to visual details.

The kitchen space I spend eight hours a day in is about the size of my one-room apartment, which is slightly larger than your average prison cell. Three people, and more on horribly busy days, work in that space, crammed in with four fryers, a massive grill, a griddle, an oven, a microwave, two refrigeration units with prep counters, bins of tortilla chips, a burning-hot steam table bigger than the grill, and vast tubs of bacon. If I put both arms out and rotated, I'd severely injure at least two people.

Sensory details describe the heat in the kitchen and Sawchuck's efforts to deal with it.

The most common problem for nonchefs is dealing with the heat. On one side of my work station are four fryers full of 350-degree oil. On the other, there is the steam table, so named because it boils water to keep things warm--especially deadly for forearms. Burns aren't the worst of it. You'll lose some skin, but you won't die. Overheating or dehydration can kill. When it's over 110 degrees in your workplace, fluid consumption is essential. I start gushing sweat the second I clock in and don't stop until about half an hour after clocking out. Even though we have huge buzzing exhaust fans to suck the greasy smoke away from our lungs and a warehouse-sized room fan to keep it at a low triple digits, I drink enough water to fill the steam table twice during busy times. My bandana frequently restrains ice cubes as well as rapidly tangling hair.

Sensory details describe the sounds in the kitchen.

The fans add to the noise, as do the chattering servers, the head chef yelling out orders, other cooks yelling out updates, and the music. Some kitchens run on music, others don't. I like to blare NPR when it is just me and A working, but on nights with a full staff, the rap music that gives rap music a bad name is trotted out--you know the kind I mean--the mainstream, with pre-choreographed dances, predictable couplets about the joys of 'caine and loose women, and frequently more bleeped words than heard. The volume at which such music is played means I have to scream everything and never hear orders. It's like playing tennis with a ball that randomly disappears.

Sensory details describe the physical dangers of the job. Notice how the sentences in this paragraph vary in length and structure.

There are uncountable ways to damage yourself in a restaurant kitchen. If you didn't touch anything--just stood there--you'd still be at risk for smoke inhalation, steam burns, knife cuts from other people, spills, splatters, and being bowled over--because no one stands

2

3

4

5

6

still in a professional kitchen. Even walking in a kitchen is dangerous. The only time the kitchen floor at the to-remain-nameless restaurant at which I cook is clean is immediately after washing, a process that results in innumerable gallons of grody gray water and the inadvertent freeing of at least one mouse from his glue trap. Moving in that kitchen is a constant struggle. Because the floor is slippery red tile, we put down thick rubber mats, which make standing for eight hours much easier on the knees. Unfortunately, these mats are coated, nay permeated, with everything we've ever spilled on them. Moving is like trying to skate across a frying pan with butter strapped to your feet. Sometimes you'll need to use a skating-like sliding motion to get through without falling face-first in the awfulness. Falling is worse, because if you grab to catch something your options are a fryer (bad), the grill (worse), or your head chef (worst of all).

Working in a restaurant during rush makes journalism on deadline look like elementary basket-weaving. While reporters are expected to get everything right in every story, they're only writing at most three stories a day. At one point during the worst dinner rush I can remember, I was cooking five nachos, eight quesadillas, four sampler plates, and three orders of wings at the same time. I had to get every component of those dishes right, from the plate they were served on to the garnish, serving size, cooking temperature, and appearance--and I needed to have done it fifteen minutes ago because the customers have been waiting. They don't care that we're so stacked up there's no more room in the oven for the nachos and quesadillas that are stacking up. Did I mention sampler plates have four items each, all with different cooking times and prep methods?

Working in a restaurant kitchen is like speaking a foreign language. Once you stop thinking about it and just do it, you can keep up, sometimes. Other times, the pressure builds up. Maybe half the restaurant fills up in five minutes, or it's game night in a college town. Maybe the servers screwed up and gave you all their tables' orders at once instead of as they came in. Either way, you've got to shift into the next gear. Sometimes it means throwing on ten orders of wings in fryers only meant to hold eight, then garnishing a stack of plates for the main course guys so they can focus on getting twenty burgers of different doneness levels cooked properly. For the appetizer guy, it usually means never being allowed to make a mistake, because any delay in appetizer futzes the flow of the meal. The main course is being cooked at the same time, so if my stuff comes in late, then the properly cooked main course will either be overdone or arrive cold because no one wants the main course five minutes after receiving an appetizer.

When you're late in the restaurant world, it's called being in the weeds. The origin of the name is unclear, but friends of mine note that you hide bodies where weeds grow because it's a sign of low foot traffic. Being in the weeds is not as bad as rendition to Egypt, but everyone, servers and management included, can see you're behind. In addition to

7   In the topic sentences of this paragraph and the next one, Sawchuck uses comparisons to try to convey the essence of restaurant kitchen work. Notice his organization for the essay: after several paragraphs presenting the concrete physical details of the job, he shifts to the more abstract issues of the mental complexity and time pressure involved.

8

Notice how the connotations of *futzes* support the dominant impression better than a more formal word such as *disrupts* would.

9   Sawchuck explains a term used in restaurant work that most readers will not know.

Conclusion: Sawchuck offers a final comment on restaurant kitchen work and makes a direct appeal to readers.

getting chewed out by the head chef (who would rather yell at you than help you), you lose any chance you had with that subtle, kittenish server. Not holding your own on the line means much less fun after work. When you're in the weeds (or "weeded"), you can ask for help or suck it up. Asking for help is frowned upon; your only route is taking a breath and pulling yourself out. I spend a lot of time in the weeds, unsurprising for a kid whose only chef-like experience was making breakfast on Sundays at home and the occasional grilled cheese sandwich.

Like print journalism and the armed forces, professional cooking requires a very specific   10 skill set. If you've got it, get a good knife and get to practicing. If not, be a little nicer next time the entree doesn't come exactly when you expect it.

Analyzing the Writer's Technique

1. Describe Sawchuck's dominant impression about working in a restaurant kitchen. Is it stated explicitly or implied?
2. Which examples of sensory language did you find particularly strong and engaging? What makes them effective? Which, if any, are weak, and how can they be improved?
3. The annotations point out some of the numerous comparisons Sawchuck uses to explain his topic. Identify several others. Which ones are particularly effective?
4. One of the annotations (para. 8) points out the connotations of a particular word Sawchuck uses. In paragraph 4, how are the connotations of "gushing sweat" different from those of other language he could have chosen, such as "sweating profusely" or "gushing perspiration"? Do you think he made the best choice, given the dominant impression he is trying to create? Why or why not?
5. In addition to description, what other patterns of development does the writer use? How do these patterns make the description more effective?

Reacting to the Essay

1. Sawchuck notes that falling behind on the job results in less fun after work. Have you found that job performance can affect off-the-job relationships with coworkers? If so, how?
2. Do you think Sawchuck is satisfied with his job despite the adverse working conditions? Discuss to what degree working conditions affect job performance and satisfaction.
3. Is it possible to be "in the weeds" academically? Write a journal entry exploring either reasons for being in the weeds or ways to get yourself out of the weeds.
4. Sawchuck describes the time pressures he experiences. Write an essay describing the time pressures you experience in either an academic or a workplace setting.

READING A DESCRIPTION

The following section provides advice for reading descriptive essays. Two model essays illustrate the characteristics of description covered in this chapter and provide opportunities to examine, analyze, and react to the writer's ideas. The second essay uses a description as part of a narrative essay.

Working with Text: Reading Descriptive Essays

When you read descriptive essays, you are more concerned with impressions and images than you are with the logical progression of ideas. To get the full benefit of descriptive writing, you need to connect what you are reading to your own senses of sight, sound, smell, touch, and taste. Here are some guidelines for reading descriptive essays.

For more on reading strategies, see Chapter 3.

What to Look For, Highlight, and Annotate

1. Plan on reading the essay more than once. Read it the first time to get a general sense of what's going on in the essay. Then reread it, this time paying attention to sensory details and highlighting particularly striking ones.
2. Be alert for the dominant impression as you read. If it is not directly stated, ask yourself this question: How does the author want me to feel about the subject?
3. Identify the author's method of organization.
4. Analyze each paragraph and decide how it contributes to the dominant impression. In a marginal annotation, summarize your analysis.
5. Observe how the author uses language to achieve his or her effect; notice especially the use of comparisons, sentence structure, and active verbs.
6. Study the introduction and conclusion. How does the introduction engage readers? How does the conclusion bring the essay to a satisfying close?
7. Evaluate the title. What meaning does it contribute to the essay?
8. Use marginal annotations or your journal to record the thoughts and feelings the essay evokes in you. Try to answer these questions: What did I feel as I read? How did I respond? What feelings was I left with after reading the essay?

How to Find Ideas to Write About

Since you may be asked to write a response to a descriptive essay, keep an eye out for ideas to write about as you read. Try to think of parallel situations that evoked similar images and feelings in you. For example, for an essay describing the peace and serenity the author experienced while sitting beside a remote lake in a forest, try to think of situations in which you felt peace and serenity or of how you felt when you visited a national park or wilderness area. Perhaps instead of pleasant feelings in this situation you had negative ones, such as anxiety about being in a remote spot. Such negative feelings may be worth exploring as well.

For more on discovering ideas for a response paper, see Chapter 3.

Thinking Critically about Description

The words a writer chooses to describe a subject can largely determine how readers view and respond to that subject. For example, suppose you want to describe a person's physical appearance. You can make the person seem attractive and appealing or ugly and repellent, depending on the details you choose and the words you select.

APPEALING   The stranger had an impish, childlike grin, a smooth complexion with high cheekbones, and strong yet gentle hands.

REPELLENT   The stranger had limp blond hair, cold vacant eyes, and teeth stained by tobacco.

Writers use details and word connotations to shape their essays and affect their readers' response. Use the following questions to think critically about the descriptions you read.

What Details Does the Writer Omit?

As you read an essay, ask yourself: What hasn't the writer told me? or What else would I like to know about the subject? As you have seen, writers often omit details because they are not relevant; they may also omit details that contradict the dominant impression they intend to convey.

To be sure you are getting a complete and fairly objective picture of a subject, consult more than one source of information. You have probably noticed that television news programs usually have slightly different slants on a news event, each offering different details or film footage. Once you view several versions of the same event, you eventually form your own impression of it by combining and synthesizing the various reports. Often, you must do the same thing when reading descriptions. Pull together information from several sources and form your own impression.

How Does the Writer Use Connotative Language?

The sensory details writers choose often reveal their feelings and attitudes toward the subject. If a writer describes a car as "fast and sleek," the wording suggests approval, whereas if the writer describes it as "bold and glitzy," the wording suggests a less favorable attitude. As you read, pay particular attention to connotations; they are often used intentionally to create a particular emotional response. Get in the habit of highlighting words with strong connotations or annotating them in the margin.

DESCRIPTIVE ESSAY

As you read the following essay by Cat Bohannon, consider how she uses the characteristics of description discussed in this chapter.

Shipwreck
Cat Bohannon

Cat Bohannon had completed her MFA in creative writing at the University of Arizona and was studying creative nonfiction at Columbia University when this essay, her first published piece, was included in the anthology *Best American Nonrequired Reading 2006*. As you read, highlight the descriptive phrases that have the strongest impact on you.

> And the Devil bubbled below the keel: "It's human, but is it Art?"
>
> — RUDYARD KIPLING

1   Katrin lies in front of me, face-down and covered in plastic. A Chinese man in his twenties moves back the film to expose her hand and carves a little slit down her thumb. Moving quickly, he peels the skin back with tweezers and a scalpel, and I can see the thick flesh at the heel of the palm. A thin layer of fat as yellow as the fruit of a mango sits on a membrane above the muscle, and with a quick cut and pull it cleaves cleanly away. He flicks the globule of fat into a little metal bowl. Within a few minutes, the hand is skinned enough that I can see a strip of ligament running from a fingertip to the wrist. She might have been a typist — the ligament is thick and developed, as if she relied on it. She might have been a writer. A journalist. A pianist.

2   Katrin is destined to be a part of Body Worlds — a set of exhibitions traveling through Europe and Asia, for which human corpses are made into mummies called "plastinates." Unlike the mummies of Egypt, however, these plastinates are perfectly preserved. Through a complicated process, the fluids in the body are replaced with a polymer. Thus a body can look much as it did upon death, hypothetically for thousands of years. Standing in the dissection hall in northeastern China, watching Katrin's hand being flayed, I notice the fingerprints peel off the pads of each finger in quick slips. Dr. Gunther von Hagens, a German anatomist, invented plastination in 1979 and immediately began taking volunteers — people willing to have their bodies plastinated after death. Katrin was one such volunteer. The worker holds up a fingerprint for me, transparent by the light of the window. Here in Dalian, Plastination City processes hundreds of bodies each year.

3   A few weeks ago, my brother e-mailed me from London with a picture of his new girlfriend and a hyperlink: www.bodyworlds.com. He was heading to China to write an article for *Science* magazine, and wondered if I wouldn't like to come along as a "poet in residence." (He's always concocting ways for me to tag along — if I weren't busy finishing grad school, in a few months I'd be on a ship in the Indian Ocean, trying to harpoon a sperm whale. Ya-hey, Ahab.) Having never been to Asia, and curious about China's frenzied pursuit of capitalism in the "new economic zone" of Dalian, I immediately agreed to go. I didn't check the link he'd sent me for another week. That's when I saw a child's head made entirely of plastinated veins.

4   They'd pumped resins through the circulatory system of the young body and then dipped the whole thing in acid — only the blood vessels were left. It looks like a faint red cloud of a child. A whisper and hush. I immediately checked out a copy of *Grey's Anatomy* and snagged a plane ticket on the cheap. When you go scuba diving, you fall into the water headfirst and backward. I think this was something like that.

A worker slides a scalpel under the lip of Katrin's thumbnail and pulls.   5

Body Worlds is "anatomical art," a tradition started in the Middle Ages when artists   6
such as Andreas Vesalius and Michelangelo explored the aesthetics of anatomy. Dead
bodies were depicted as partially flayed nudes, gracefully presenting their own organs.
This tradition has long since fallen out of fashion, and anatomy has been relegated to
anatomical museums, featuring jars of floating organs or virtual-reality tours of body
systems. Now, as if walking out of history, von Hagens has taken the Renaissance
nudes and brought them to life. But *his* nudes actually *are* nudes — every body on
display was once a living, breathing individual. This has shocked the people coming
to the London exhibition. Unlike the Renaissance audience, accustomed to plagues,
public hangings, and vivisections, we rarely encounter death in person.

Dr. von Hagens is away in South Korea, at a new exhibition in Seoul. So, armed with   7
a notepad, a translator, and Christine — the very press-shy manager of Plastination
City, a tall blond northern German with somewhat menacing teeth — I find myself here
in the dissection hallway around midmorning, and embark on a journey in which I will
see more dead bodies than I have ever seen in my life. My brother is off pursuing photos. I tuck my stomach into a tight little corner and order it to keep quiet.

The Body Worlds Web site keeps a running tally: before I left California, the wait to   8
get into the London exhibit (in a warehouse on the outskirts of town) was around two
hours. To date, more than 13.5 million people have gone through the doors. But why
are we coming? What do we want from Katrin? All she has to offer is muscle and teeth,
the white hair of nerves, the swollen sack of the heart — the shipwreck of her body. Yet
there's no lack of interest in her. Thousands of people have walked through row after
row of corpses in a peculiar hush, like a procession in a church. To try to find out why
we keep going to these exhibitions, I need to know just what kind of art this is. If these
were simple nudes, I wouldn't need to travel halfway across the planet. The nude is
familiar territory, with a pedigree going back thousands of years, written in stone and
patina. But these are not simulacra. Can a dead human body be a piece of art "about"
the human body?

I look down at death for answers. One worker begins stripping the skin from Katrin's   9
calf. Watching feels a little like staring down from a great precipice — a dizziness
and exhilaration and the simultaneous desire to jump and to run back to the car. As
the shin bone hovers behind fat and membranes, as a caterpillar shows through its
chrysalis, I scramble back to what I know about art. Artists have used parts of the body
in their work before — urine and blood, for instance. Spit. Artists have used animal
bones in their art, even. But no one's taken an entire *human* body and turned it into
raw material.

It's been said that every work of art has a subject. One might say that Picasso's   10
Guernica is about the horror of war, or that Monet's *Jardin de Giverny* is about the beauty
of peace. Even Duchamp's ubiquitous urinal had a subject — the piece was about art and
intent. Watching the skin gradually peeling off Katrin's extremities like the skin of a fruit,
I know that the subject of these pieces must have something to do with the body. But I'm
not sure that the subject of a sculpture can be itself. Michelangelo's *David* certainly isn't
"about" marble. So it seems unlikely that the subject of von Hagens's cadavers is the
nude. If these are indeed artworks, what is their subject? When asked, Dr. von Hagens
has answered mysteriously, "The body is the ship of the soul."

A man scrapes tissue off his gloved finger on the side of the metal table. The workers joke with one another in Chinese. I know they're joking because they're laughing. I don't speak a whiff of Chinese. I don't ask my translator because people should be allowed to go about their business without always explaining it to the American. This feels suspiciously like reading Pound's *Cantos*.   11

When asked about the aim of his exhibitions, Dr. von Hagens has said humans   12 "reveal their individuality not only through the visible exterior, but also through the interior of their bodies, as each one is distinctly different. Position, size, shape, and structure of skeleton, muscles, nerves, and organs determine our face within." But then, in these exhibitions, he purposefully changes the position and structure of these bodies to *reveal* something — we normally can't see organs through a wall of muscle, so he cuts a window in the muscle. There are buckets of spare organs across the room — is the "face within" still the same face without its nose or eyes? What if the face were rearranged like a Picasso? And what of this face belongs to the conscious individual that once resided in the body — the "ship" that carries us? His metaphors feel slippy. I've come to Dalian, a port town on the north rim of the Yellow Sea, to find out what happens when a human body becomes a work of art, and what that art could possibly be *about*.

While we stand around Katrin's corpse, Christine begins rattling off the four steps of   13 plastination. "First the bodies are dissected, to remove the skin and fatty layers." The metal bowls positioned around the table are filling with yellow fat. I notice one worker has a bowl perched in the hollow below Katrin's pubic bone. The fat wobbles with each addition. "After dissection, the bodies are further defatted in acetone. Once the body is done in defatting, it is impregnated with polymer." The bowl in Katrin's crotch leans worriedly to the left. "For the final step, the bodies are positioned in various gestures and given a gas cure to harden the polymer." The worker moves the bowl down between Katrin's knees. I look back up at Christine. "The tour will follow these steps, in order, so that you will see bodies at each stage of the process." She smiles, looking for recognition.

I tuck my notepad into my jacket. "Yes. That sounds lovely."   14

Examining the Reading

1. Explain the term *plastinates*.
2. Why are plastinates shocking to some people?
3. Explain the meaning of the title (see paras. 8, 10, and 12 for clues).
4. What issues does the author raise about the exhibit?
5. Explain the meaning of each of the following words as it is used in the reading: *hypothetically* (para. 2), *aesthetics* (6), *pedigree* (8), *chrysalis* (9), and *ubiquitous* (10). Refer to your dictionary as needed.

Analyzing the Writer's Technique

1. Express the essay's dominant impression in your own words.
2. Highlight examples of particularly effective sensory details. How do these contribute to the essay?

3. Identify several places in the essay where Bohannon makes comparisons to clarify her ideas.
4. Why does the author use the example of Katrin throughout the essay? What effect does it have?

Reacting to the Reading

1. Discuss the popularity of the Body World exhibit. Why do millions of people choose to see it?
2. Discuss why you would or would not consider being plastinated.
3. Write a journal entry exploring the definition of art. When is an object considered art? What do you value artistically? What are its characteristics?
4. The author seems to have mixed feelings about viewing the process of plastination. Write an essay describing a situation in which you had mixed feelings about something considered valuable or worthwhile by others.

DESCRIPTION COMBINED WITH OTHER PATTERNS

As you read the following essay, notice how the author uses description within an essay that traces a narrative.

READING

Bloggers without Borders . . .
Riverbend

This selection is an online post from the blog "Baghdad Burning," written by a woman calling herself Riverbend. She identified herself in her first blog post by writing, "I'm female, Iraqi and 24. I survived the war. That's all you need to know. It's all that matters these days anyway." Since August 2003, she has been posting about her personal experiences as well as providing political commentary on the situation in Iraq. As you read, notice how Riverbend creates and reinforces the dominant impression of the piece.

Syria is a beautiful country—at least I think it is. I say "I think" because while I perceive   1
it to be beautiful, I sometimes wonder if I mistake safety, security, and normalcy for 'beauty.' In so many ways, Damascus is like Baghdad before the war—bustling streets, occasional traffic jams, markets seemingly always full of shoppers . . . And in so many ways it's different. The buildings are higher, the streets are generally narrower and there's a mountain, Qasiyoun, that looms in the distance.

The mountain distracts me, as it does many Iraqis—especially those from Baghdad.   2
Northern Iraq is full of mountains, but the rest of Iraq is quite flat. At night, Qasiyoun blends into the black sky, and the only indication of its presence is a multitude of little, glimmering spots of light—houses and restaurants built right up there on the mountain. Every time I take a picture, I try to work Qasiyoun into it—I try to position the person so that Qasiyoun is in the background.

The first weeks here were something of a cultural shock. It has taken me these last   3
three months to work away certain habits I'd acquired in Iraq after the war. It's funny

how you learn to act a certain way and don't even know you're doing strange things—like avoiding people's eyes in the street or crazily murmuring prayers to yourself when stuck in traffic. It took me at least three weeks to teach myself to walk properly again—with head lifted, not constantly looking behind me.

It is estimated that there are at least 1.5 million Iraqis in Syria today. I believe it. 4 Walking down the streets of Damascus, you can hear the Iraqi accent everywhere. There are areas like Geramana and Qudsiya that are packed full of Iraqi refugees. Syrians are few and far between in these areas. Even the public schools in the areas are full of Iraqi children. A cousin of mine is now attending a school in Qudsiya and his class is composed of twenty-six Iraqi children and five Syrian children. It's beyond belief sometimes. Most of the families have nothing to live on beyond their savings, which are quickly being depleted with rent and the costs of living.

Within a month of our being here, we began hearing talk about Syria requiring visas 5 from Iraqis, like most other countries. Apparently, our esteemed puppets in power met with Syrian and Jordanian authorities and decided they wanted to take away the last two safe havens remaining for Iraqis—Damascus and Amman. The talk began in late August and was only talk until recently—early October. Iraqis entering Syria now need a visa from the Syrian consulate or embassy in the country they are currently in. In the case of Iraqis still in Iraq, it is said that an approval from the Ministry of Interior is also required (which kind of makes it difficult for people running away from militias OF the Ministry of Interior . . .). Today, there's talk of a possible fifty dollar visa at the border.

Iraqis who entered Syria before the visa was implemented were getting a one-month 6 visitation visa at the border. As soon as that month was over, you could take your passport and visit the local immigration bureau. If you were lucky, they would give you an additional month or two. When talk about visas from the Syrian embassy began, they stopped giving an extension on the initial border visa. We, as a family, had a brilliant idea. Before the commotion of visas began, and before we started needing a renewal, we decided to go to one of the border crossings, cross into Iraq, and come back into Syria—everyone was doing it. It would buy us some time—at least two months.

We chose a hot day in early September and drove the six hours to Kameshli, a bor- 7 der town in northern Syria. My aunt and her son came with us—they also needed an extension on their visa. There is a border crossing in Kameshli called Yaarubiya. It's one of the simpler crossings because the Iraqi and Syrian borders are only a matter of several meters. You walk out of Syrian territory and then walk into Iraqi territory—simple and safe.

When we got to the Yaarubiya border patrol, it hit us that thousands of Iraqis had 8 had our brilliant idea simultaneously—the lines to the border patrol office were endless. Hundreds of Iraqis stood in a long line waiting to have their passports stamped with an exit visa. We joined the line of people and waited. And waited. And waited . . .

It took four hours to leave the Syrian border, after which came the lines of the Iraqi 9 border post. Those were even longer. We joined one of the lines of weary, impatient Iraqis. "It's looking like a gasoline line . . ." my younger cousin joked. That was the beginning of another four hours of waiting under the sun, taking baby steps, moving forward ever so slowly. The line kept getting longer. At one point, we could see neither the beginning of the line, where passports were being stamped to enter Iraq, nor the end. Running up and down the line were little boys selling glasses of water, chewing gum and cigarettes. My aunt caught one of them by the arm as he zipped past us, "How many people are in front of us?" He whistled and took a few steps back to assess the situation, "A hundred! A thousand!" He was almost gleeful as he ran off to make business.

I had such mixed feelings standing in that line. I was caught between a feeling of   10
yearning, a certain homesickness that sometimes catches me at the oddest moments, and a heavy feeling of dread. What if they didn't agree to let us out again? It wasn't really possible, but what if it happened? What if this was the last time I'd see the Iraqi border? What if we were no longer allowed to enter Iraq for some reason? What if we were never allowed to leave?

We spent the four hours standing, crouching, sitting and leaning in the line. The   11
sun beat down on everyone equally—Sunnis, Shia and Kurds alike. E. tried to convince the aunt to faint so it would speed the process up for the family, but she just gave us a withering look and stood straighter. People just stood there, chatting, cursing or silent. It was yet another gathering of Iraqis—the perfect opportunity to swap sad stories and ask about distant relations or acquaintances.

We met two families we knew while waiting for our turn. We greeted each other like   12
long lost friends and exchanged phone numbers and addresses in Damascus, prom-ising to visit. I noticed the 23-year-old son, K., from one of the families was missing. I beat down my curiosity and refused to ask where he was. The mother was looking older than I remembered and the father looked constantly lost in thought, or maybe it was grief. I didn't want to know if K. was dead or alive. I'd just have to believe he was alive and thriving somewhere, not worrying about borders or visas. Ignorance really is bliss sometimes. . . .

Back at the Syrian border, we waited in a large group, tired and hungry, having   13
handed over our passports for a stamp. The Syrian immigration man, sifting through dozens of passports, called out names and looked at faces as he handed over the passports patiently, "Stand back please—stand back." There was a general cry toward the back of the crowded hall where we were standing as someone collapsed—as they lifted him I recognized an old man who was there with his family being chaperoned by his sons, leaning on a walking stick.

By the time we had reentered the Syrian border and were headed back to the cab   14
ready to take us into Kameshli, I had resigned myself to the fact that we were refugees. I read about refugees on the Internet daily . . . in the newspapers . . . hear about them on TV. I hear about the estimated 1.5 million plus Iraqi refugees in Syria and shake my head, never really considering myself or my family as one of them. After all, refugees are people who sleep in tents and have no potable water or plumbing, right? Refugees carry their belongings in bags instead of suitcases, and they don't have cell phones or Internet access, right? Grasping my passport in my hand like my life depended on it, with two extra months in Syria stamped inside, it hit me how wrong I was. We were all refugees. I was suddenly a number. No matter how wealthy or educated or comfort-able, a refugee is a refugee. A refugee is someone who isn't really welcome in any country—including their own . . . especially their own.

We live in an apartment building where two other Iraqis are renting. The people in   15
the floor above us are a Christian family from northern Iraq who got chased out of their village by Peshmerga, and the family on our floor is a Kurdish family who lost their home

in Baghdad to militias and were waiting for immigration to Sweden or Switzerland or some such European refugee haven.

The first evening we arrived, exhausted, dragging suitcases behind us, morale a little bit bruised, the Kurdish family sent over their representative — a nine-year-old boy missing two front teeth, holding a lopsided cake, "We're Abu Mohammed's house— across from you—mama says if you need anything, just ask—this is our number. Abu Dalia's family live upstairs, this is their number. We're all Iraqi too. . . . Welcome to the building."   16

I cried that night because for the first time in a long time, so far away from home, I felt the unity that had been stolen from us in 2003.   17

Examining the Reading

1. Why does Riverbend mention and describe the mountain? What is its significance?
2. Why does Riverbend object to the visa requirement?
3. What is Riverbend's attitude toward Iraqi authorities? How does she reveal it?
4. Explain Riverbend's statement "Ignorance really is bliss sometimes" (para. 12) in the context of this reading.
5. When and why does Riverbend finally feel the unity she has not experienced since 2003?
6. Explain the meaning of each of the following words or phrases as it is used in the reading: *normalcy* (para. 1), *cultural shock* (3), *esteemed* (5), *withering look* (11), and *morale* (16). Refer to a dictionary as needed.

(MAKING CONNECTIONS)

Journeys

Both Riverbend in "Bloggers without Borders" (p. 262) and Aphonotip Vasavong in "You Can Count on Miracles" (p. 221) describe a journey from one country to another. Riverbend describes a trip from Syria to Iraq and back to extend her visa; Vasavong describes her escape from Laos.

Analyzing the Readings

1. Compare how the two authors felt about their journeys. How does each author emphasize the importance of her journey?
2. What justification does each author offer for her decision to make the journey? How does each author explain her reasons to her readers?

Essay Idea

Write an essay describing a significant journey you have undertaken. It need not be to another country or even to a new physical place; it may be a mental road you have followed to gain a new perspective. Explain both why you made the journey and how it affected your life.

Analyzing the Writer's Technique

1. What dominant impression does Riverbend convey in this essay? Is it stated or implied? Explain your answers.
2. What is the significance of the essay's title?
3. Is the essay objective, subjective, or a mixture of both? Explain your answer.
4. What patterns other than description does Riverbend use in this essay? What purposes do they serve?

Visualizing the Reading

Riverbend conveys information about her journey and surroundings by using many of the characteristics of descriptive essays. Analyze her use of these characteristics by completing the following chart. Give several examples for each type of characteristic used, including the paragraph numbers for reference. The first one has been done for you.

Descriptive Characteristic	Examples
Active verbs	1. "as he zipped past us" (para. 9) 2. "I beat down my curiosity" (para. 12)
Sensory details (sound, smell, touch, sight, taste)	
Varied sentences	
Comparisons	
Connotative language	

Reacting to the Reading

1. Given the hardships of her refugee experience, how and why do you think Riverbend maintains a blog?
2. Discuss the factors that may have led to Riverbend's family's decision to leave Iraq.
3. Riverbend states that she "was suddenly a number" (para. 14). Discuss situations in which you or others have felt this way.
4. Write an essay in which you agree or disagree with Riverbend's statement that "ignorance really is bliss sometimes." Describe situations from your experience that either support or reject her view.

Applying Your Skills: Additional Essay Assignments

Write a descriptive essay on one of the following topics, using what you learned about description in this chapter. Depending on the topic you choose, you may need to conduct library or Internet research.

For more on locating and documenting sources, see Part 5.

To Express Your Ideas

1. Suppose a famous person, living or dead, visited your house for dinner. Write an essay describing the person and the evening and expressing your feelings about the occasion.
2. In "Eating Chilli Peppers," the author describes the love that some people have for eating peppers. Write an essay for your classmates describing a food that a family member or close friend enjoys but that you dislike.

To Inform Your Reader

3. Write an essay describing destruction or devastation you have observed as a result of a natural disaster (hurricane, flood), an accident, or a form of violence.
4. Write a report for your local newspaper on a local sporting event you recently observed or participated in.

To Persuade Your Reader

5. Write a letter to persuade your parents to loan you money. The loan may be to purchase a used car or to rent a more expensive apartment, for example. Include a description of your current car or apartment.
6. In "Shipwreck," the author describes her experiences touring the Plastination City dissection hall. Although she seemed to have mixed feelings about viewing the bodies being prepared for the Body Worlds exhibit, she learned a lot from the experience. Write a letter describing to a classmate an experience or activity that was difficult or that you had mixed feelings about, but that you found to be valuable. In your letter, try to persuade your reader to participate in difficult or challenging experiences.

Cases Using Description

7. Imagine that you are a product buyer for a cosmetics distributor, a food company, or a furniture dealership. Write a descriptive review of a product recommending to the board of directors whether or not to distribute it. Use something that you are familiar with or come up with your own product (such as an electronic gadget, an advice book on parenting, or a new cosmetic). Describe the product in a way that will help convince the company to accept your recommendation.
8. Write a brief description of your ideal internship. Then write an essay to accompany your application for your ideal summer internship. The sponsoring agency requires every applicant to submit an essay that describes the knowledge and experience the applicant can bring to the internship and the ways that the position would benefit the applicant personally and professionally.

CHAPTER 12

Illustration: Explaining with Examples

WRITING QUICK START

In a social problems class, the instructor projects the photograph shown on the opposite page onto a screen. The instructor makes the following statement: "Environmental pollution is a growing national problem." She asks the class to think of several examples of situations similar to the one shown in the photograph that confirm this view.

Using the instructor's statement as your topic sentence, write a paragraph that supports this statement with examples of different types of environmental pollution that you have either observed or read about.

WRITING AN ILLUSTRATION ESSAY

The sentences you have just written could be part of an illustration essay. Your essay might explain specific situations that illustrate your thesis about pollution and the environment. When writers use illustration, they support their points with clear, specific examples. This chapter will show you how to write an essay that uses illustration as the primary method of development, as well as how to use illustration in other types of essays.

What Is Illustration?

Illustration is a way of using examples to reveal the essential characteristics of a topic or to reinforce a thesis. By providing specific situations to make abstract ideas concrete, you can often connect them to situations within the reader's experience. Unfamiliar and complex ideas also can become clear once examples are provided. Most textbooks are filled with examples for this reason. Writers in academic and work situations commonly use illustration as well (see the accompanying box for examples).

In the following illustration essay, "Rambos of the Road," Martin Gottfried uses examples to support a thesis.

SCENES FROM COLLEGE AND THE WORKPLACE

- For a *literature class*, you are assigned to write an analysis of the poet Emily Dickinson's use of metaphor and simile. To explain your point about her use of animals in metaphors, you provide specific examples from several of her poems.

- You are studying sexual dimorphism—differences in appearance between the sexes—for a *biology* course. The following question appears on an exam: "Define sexual dimorphism, and illustrate its occurrence in several different species." In your answer, you give examples of peacocks, geese, and chickens, explaining how the males and females in each species differ in physical appearance.

- You are an *elementary school reading teacher* and have been asked by your principal to write a justification to the school board for the new computer software you have requested. You decide to give several examples of how the software will benefit particular types of students.

Rambos of the Road

READING

Martin Gottfried

Martin Gottfried has been a drama critic for such publications as the *New York Post*, the *Saturday Review*, and *New York*. He has also written several books, including *In Person: The Great Entertainers* (1985), *All His Jazz: The Life and Death of Bob Fosse* (1990), *George Burns and the Hundred-Year Dash* (1996), and *Balancing Act: The Authorized Biography of Angela Lansbury* (1998). This essay was first published in *Newsweek*, the weekly newsmagazine, in 1986. As you read the selection, notice where Gottfried employs compelling examples to support his thesis and highlight those you find particularly striking.

The car pulled up and its driver glared at us with such sullen intensity, such hatred, that I was truly afraid for our lives. Except for the Mohawk haircut he didn't have, he looked like Robert De Niro in *Taxi Driver*, the sort of young man who, delirious for notoriety, might kill a president. 1

He was glaring because we had passed him and for that affront he pursued us to the next stoplight so as to express his indignation and affirm his masculinity. I was with two women and, believe it, was afraid for all three of us. It was nearly midnight and we were in a small, sleeping town with no other cars on the road. 2

When the light turned green, I raced ahead, knowing it was foolish and that I was not in a movie. He didn't merely follow, he chased, and with his headlights turned off. No matter what sudden turn I took, he followed. My passengers were silent. I knew they were alarmed, and I prayed that I wouldn't be called upon to protect them. In that cheerful frame of mind, I turned off my own lights so I couldn't be followed. It was lunacy. I was responding to a crazy *as* a crazy. 3

"I'll just drive to the police station," I finally said, and as if those were the magic words, he disappeared. 4

It seems to me that there has recently been an epidemic of auto macho—a competition perceived and expressed in driving. People fight it out over parking spaces. They bully into line at the gas pump. A toll booth becomes a signal for elbowing fenders. And beetle-eyed drivers hunch over their steering wheels, squeezing the rims, glowering, preparing the excuse of not having seen you as they muscle you off the road. Approaching a highway on an entrance ramp recently, I was strong-armed by a trailer truck, so immense that its driver all but blew me away by blasting his horn. The behemoth was just inches from my hopelessly mismatched coupe when I fled for the safety of the shoulder. 5

And this is happening on city streets, too. A New York taxi driver told me that "intimidation is the name of the game. Drive as if you're deaf and blind. You don't hear the other guy's horn and you sure as hell don't see him." 6

The odd thing is that long before I was even able to drive, it seemed to me that people were at their finest and most civilized when in their cars. They seemed so orderly and considerate, so reasonable, staying in the right-hand lane unless passing, signaling all intentions. In those days you really eased into highway traffic, and the long, neat rows of cars seemed mobile testimony to the sanity of most people. 7

Perhaps memory fails, perhaps there were always testy drivers, perhaps — but everyone didn't give you the finger.

A most amazing example of driver rage occurred recently at the Manhattan end of the Lincoln Tunnel. We were four cars abreast, stopped at a traffic light. And there was no moving even when the light had changed. A bus had stopped in the cross traffic, blocking our paths: it was a normal-for-New-York-City gridlock. Perhaps impatient, perhaps late for important appointments, three of us nonetheless accepted what, after all, we could not alter. One, however, would not. He would not be helpless. He would go where he was going even if he couldn't get there. A Wall Street type in suit and tie, he got out of his car and strode toward the bus, rapping smartly on its doors. When they opened, he exchanged words with the driver. The doors folded shut. He then stepped in front of the bus, took hold of one of its large windshield wipers and broke it.

The bus doors reopened and the driver appeared, apparently giving the fellow a good piece of his mind. If so, the lecture was wasted, for the man started his car and proceeded to drive directly *into the bus*. He rammed it. Even though the point at which he struck the bus, the folding doors, was its most vulnerable point, ramming the side of a bus with your car has to rank very high on a futility index. My first thought was that it had to be a rental car.

To tell the truth, I could not believe my eyes. The bus driver opened his doors as much as they could be opened and he stepped directly onto the hood of the attacking car, jumping up and down with both his feet. He then retreated into the bus, closing the doors behind him. Obviously a man of action, the car driver backed up and rammed the bus again. How this exercise in absurdity would have been resolved none of us will ever know for at that point the traffic unclogged and the bus moved on. And the rest of us, we passives of the world, proceeded, our cars crossing a field of battle as if nothing untoward had happened.

It is tempting to blame such belligerent, uncivil and even neurotic behavior on the nuts of the world, but in our cars we all become a little crazy. How many of us speed up when a driver signals his intention of pulling in front of us? Are we resentful and anxious to pass him? How many of us try to squeeze in, or race along the shoulder of a lane merger? We may not jump on hoods, but driving the gantlet, we seethe, cursing not so silently in the safety of our steel bodies on wheels — fortresses for cowards.

What is it within us that gives birth to such antisocial behavior and why, all of a sudden, have so many drivers gone around the bend? My friend Joel Katz, a Manhattan psychiatrist, calls it "a Rambo pattern. People are running around thinking the American way is to take the law into your own hands when anyone does anything wrong. And what constitutes 'wrong'? Anything that cramps your style."

It seems to me that it is a new America we see on the road now. It has the mentality of a hoodlum and the backbone of a coward. The car is its weapon and hiding place, and it is still a symbol even in this. Road Rambos no longer bespeak a self-reliant, civil people tooling around in family cruisers. In fact, there aren't families in these machines that charge headlong with their brights on in broad daylight, demanding we get out of their way. Bullies are loners, and they have perverted our liberty of the open road into drivers' license. They represent an America that derides the values of decency and good manners, then roam the highways riding shotgun and shrieking freedom. By allowing this to happen, the rest of us approve.

Characteristics of Illustration Essays

Effective illustration essays support a generalization or explain or clarify something by providing specific, appropriate examples that maintain readers' interest and help fulfill the author's purpose. Because an illustration essay needs to be more than a list of examples, a well-thought-out organization is essential.

Illustration Can Be Used to Support Generalizations

Examples are an effective way to support a **generalization**—a broad statement about a topic. Often the thesis of an essay contains a generalization, and the body of the essay contains examples that support it. In "Rambos of the Road," Gottfried's thesis contains a generalization about "an epidemic of auto macho" behavior.

The following statements are generalizations because they make assertions about an entire group or category.

- Most college students are energetic, ambitious, and eager to get ahead in life.
- Gestures play an important role in nonverbal communication.
- Boys are more willing to participate in class discussions than are girls.

To explain and support any one of these generalizations, you would need to provide specific examples to show how or why the statement is accurate. For instance, you could support the first generalization by describing several college students who demonstrate energy and ambition. However, other types of support would need to accompany the examples of individual students. Relevant facts, statistics, expert opinions, personal observations, or descriptions could be used to show that the generalization applies to the majority of college students.

Exercise 12.1

Using one or more prewriting strategies for generating ideas, think of at least one example that supports each general statement.

1. Television offers some programs with educational or social value.
2. Today's parents are not strict enough with their children.
3. The favorite pastime of most men is watching sports on television.

Illustration Can Be Used to Explain or Clarify

Examples are also useful when you need to explain an unfamiliar topic, a difficult concept, or an abstract term.

Unfamiliar topics. When your audience has little or no knowledge of your topic, consider using examples to help your readers understand it. In "Rambos of the Road," Gottfried uses an extended example of real-life road rage to help his readers understand the topic.

Difficult concepts. Many concepts are difficult for readers to grasp by definition alone. For instance, a reader might guess that the term *urbanization*, a key concept in sociology, has something to do with cities. Defining the concept as, say, "the process by which an area becomes part of a city" would give the reader more to go on. But examples of formerly suburban areas that have become urban would make the concept immediately understandable.

Abstract terms. Abstract terms refer to ideas, rather than to concrete things you can see and touch. Terms such as *truth* and *justice* are abstract. Because abstractions are difficult to understand, examples help clarify them.

In many cases, however, abstract terms mean different things to different people. Here you give examples to clarify what *you* mean by an abstract term. Suppose you use the term *unfair* to describe your employer's treatment of employees. Readers might have different ideas of fairness. Providing examples of the employer's unfair treatment would make your meaning clear.

> ### Exercise 12.2
>
> *The following list contains a mix of unfamiliar topics, difficult concepts, and abstract terms. Choose three items from the list, and think of examples that illustrate their meanings.*
>
> 1. Phobia
> 2. Conformity
> 3. Gender role
> 4. Self-fulfilling prophecy
> 5. Sexual harassment

Illustration Takes Purpose and Audience into Account

A successful illustration essay uses either a series of related examples or one extended example to support its thesis. The number and type of examples to include will depend on your purpose and audience. In an essay arguing that one car is a better buy than another, you would need to give a series of examples to show the various models, years, and options available to potential car buyers. But in an essay written for an audience of high school students about the consequences of dropping out of school, a single poignant example might be appropriate.

Your audience also plays a role in deciding what types of examples to include in an essay. At times, technical examples may be appropriate; at other times, more personal or everyday ones are effective. For instance, suppose you want to persuade readers that the Food and Drug Administration should approve a new cancer drug. If your audience is composed of doctors, your examples would need to include statistical studies of the drug's effectiveness. But if your audience is the general public, you would include personal anecdotes about lives being saved and nontechnical examples of the drug's safety. In addition, try to choose examples that represent different aspects of or viewpoints on your topic. In writing about the new drug, for instance, you might include expert opinion from researchers as well as the views of doctors, patients, and a representative of the company that manufactures the drug.

Exercise 12.3

For one of the following topics, suggest examples that would suit the different audiences listed.

1. Your college's policy on academic dismissal
   a. First-year students attending a college orientation session
   b. Students facing academic dismissal
   c. Parents or spouses of students who have been dismissed for academic reasons
2. A proposal recommending that drivers over the age of sixty-five undergo periodic assessment of their ability to operate a motor vehicle safely
   a. Senior citizens
   b. State senators
   c. Adult children of elderly drivers

Illustration Uses Carefully Selected Examples

The examples you use to explain your thesis should be carefully chosen. Select examples that are relevant, representative, accurate, and striking. *Relevant* examples have a direct and clear relationship to your thesis. If your essay advocates publicly funded and operated preschool programs, support your case with examples of successful publicly funded programs, not privately operated ones.

An example is *representative* when it shows a typical or real-life situation, not a rare or unusual one. In many cases you will need to give several representative examples. For instance, in an essay arguing that preschool programs advance children's reading skills, one example of an all-day, year-round preschool would not be representative of all or most other programs.

Be sure the examples you include are *accurate* and *specific*. Report statistics objectively, and provide readers with enough information that they can evaluate the reliability of the data. Notice how the second example below provides better detail for the reader.

EXAMPLE LACKING DETAIL	Most students in preschool programs have better language skills than children who don't attend such programs.
DETAILED EXAMPLE	According to an independent evaluator, 73 percent of children who attended the Head Start program in Clearwater, after one year of attendance, had better language skills than students who did not attend the program.

For examples that are broad general categories, you will often find it helpful to include subexamples—specific examples that help explain the general examples. Suppose you are writing an essay about the problems that new immigrants to America face and include three examples—problems with the language, with the culture, and with technology. For the broad culture example, you might give subexamples of how some immigrants do not understand certain American holidays, ways of socializing, and methods of doing business.

Finally, choose examples that are *striking and dramatic* and that will make a strong, lasting impression on your readers. In "Rambos of the Road," we can visualize Gottfried's example of a bus driver leaping out of the bus and stamping on the hood of the car. Similarly, Gottfried's opening example of being followed by an angry driver creates tension; we want to keep reading to learn the outcome.

At times it may be necessary to conduct research to find examples outside of your knowledge and experience. For the essay on preschool programs, you would need to do library or Internet research to obtain statistical information. You might also interview a preschool administrator or teacher to gather firsthand anecdotes and opinions or visit a preschool classroom to observe the program in action.

Illustration Organizes Details Effectively

When you use examples to support a thesis, you need to decide how to organize both the examples and the details that accompany them. Often one of the methods of organization discussed in Chapter 6 will be useful—most-to-least, least-to-most, chronological, or spatial order. For example, in an essay explaining why people wear unconventional dress, the examples might be arranged spatially, starting with outlandish footwear and continuing upward to headgear. In other instances you may want to organize your examples according to another pattern of development, such as comparison and contrast or cause and effect. To support the thesis that a local department store needs to improve its customer services, you might begin by contrasting the department store with several computer stores that have better services and offering examples of the services provided by each.

Visualizing an Illustration Essay: A Graphic Organizer

For more on graphic organizers, see Chapter 3, p. 55.

The graphic organizer shown in Figure 12.1 will help you visualize the components of an illustration essay. As you can see, the structure is straightforward: The introduction contains background information and usually includes the thesis; the body paragraphs give one or more related examples; and the conclusion presents a final statement. For

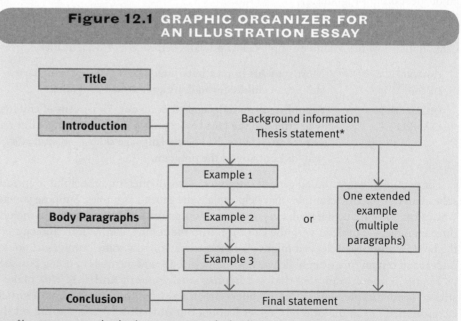

Figure 12.1 GRAPHIC ORGANIZER FOR AN ILLUSTRATION ESSAY

Title

Introduction — Background information / Thesis statement*

Body Paragraphs — Example 1 → Example 2 → Example 3   or   One extended example (multiple paragraphs)

Conclusion — Final statement

*In some essays, the thesis statement may be implied or may appear in a different position.

an essay using one extended example—such as a highly descriptive account of an auto accident intended to persuade readers to wear seat belts—the body of the essay would focus on the details of that one example.

The following essay, "Geeks in the Clubhouse," is an illustration essay. Read the essay, and then study the graphic organizer for it in Figure 12.2 (on p. 280).

Geeks in the Clubhouse

READING

Tim Gideon and Jeff Pearlman

Tim Gideon is the lead audio and video analyst for *PC Magazine*. Jeff Pearlman is a former senior writer for *Sports Illustrated*, and author of *The Bad Guys Won!* (2004) and *Love Me, Hate Me: Barry Bonds and the Making of an Antihero* (2007). The following article was first published in *PC Magazine* in 2006. It is written in journalistic style, with headings and subheadings, and does not have a separate conclusion—although the authors provide a sense of closure by beginning the last paragraph with *Finally* and ending it with a question to the reader. As you read, notice how the authors organize the examples they use to support their thesis.

Once upon a time, when football players were "gridiron warriors" and baseball play- 1 ers were required to house Ruben Studdard–size wads of tobacco in their cheeks at all times, athletes didn't demand an artificial edge (notwithstanding the occasional spitball or Vaseline ball). Sports were about honor—your strength against mine, your will against my will. It was Earl Campbell barreling into Mean Joe Greene; Bob Gibson pumping heat toward Hank Aaron; Dr. J dunking on Kareem.

Ah, memories. 2

In this era of enormous muscles and (even more) enormous contracts, any and all ad- 3 vantages will be utilized. Some (steroids, human growth hormones) have crippled the reputations of athletes worldwide. Thanks to modern technology, however, others are serving the sporting world incredibly well. It's not just the players who are enjoying the fruits of the new marriage between sports and technology, however: Fans are cashing in as well. Gone are the days of fumbling for exact change at the front of the concession line with a 32-ounce cold one in your hand. Just wave your cell phone and it's all taken care of. And fans don't have to worry about missing any of the action; now they can call up instant replays on their PDAs. All of this new sports tech isn't just confined to ballparks and stadiums; there is plenty of stuff you can take home as well. We took a look at it all. Check it out.

TECHNOLOGY ON THE FIELD

Back in the day, pro athletes wore Chuck Taylors and leather helmets; now they wear 4 Air Jordans and wield carbon-fiber clubs. Whereas today's sports equipment seems evolutionarily different from those old outfits, the future holds even more promise. Computers protect linebackers' skulls and refine swimmers' strokes—and tennis finally has instant replay.

Head games. If Major League Baseball is cursed by steroids, the National Football 5 League's current nemesis is concussions. From former New York Jets receivers Al Toon and Wayne Chrebet to Dallas Cowboys quarterback Troy Aikman, hundreds of football stars have been reduced to temporary invalids—and, in some cases, forced to retire—by repeated blows to the head. Now science is hitting back. Riddell, the nation's leading manufacturer of football helmets, has developed the Sideline Response System. A tiny encoder, placed within helmet padding, detects and rates the severity of any impact, then immediately reports the findings to a computer on the sideline. "Our goal is to recognize concussions when they happen so the player can immediately be treated," says Thad Ide, Riddell's vice president of research and development. "Multiple concussions . . . lead to bad medical spirals for our kids. This can end that." Thus far, six Division I universities—including perennial football powerhouses Oklahoma and Virginia Tech—have purchased the Sideline Response System, which costs $65,000 for 40 helmet units. The NFL should be next. "It's just a matter of time," says Tony Egues, equipment manager for the Miami Dolphins. "The league wants to see how it works in college and high school first. But I think we're looking at a potentially revolutionary object here." (www.riddell.com/srs/learnmore.html)

Aqua size. Few sports have been harder to modernize than competitive swimming.   6
Besides changing the fabric of a Speedo, what can one really do? Yet within the small office space of Swimming Technology Research in Tallahassee, Florida, a breakthrough has been made. Rod Havriluk, a former collegiate swimmer at Franklin & Marshall, has invented Aquanex, a sensor connected between a swimmer's middle and ring fingers that measures the force of both hands during each stroke. The data—synchronized with a video camera located within the pool—lets Havriluk break down a swimmer's strengths and weaknesses. "We watch the tape while reading the measurements, and it shows us exactly when he's utilizing energy well versus when he's wasting energy. It's invaluable." Several nationally ranked swimmers have bought into Aquanex, which costs $3,195 per system. (swimmingtechnology.com/avclinic.htm)

Guarding the line. For those who long for a return of John McEnroe-esque tantrums,   7
bad news: Tennis—the world's most tradition-rich (read: stubborn) sport—has gone modern. Beginning with this year's U.S. Open, several tournaments will debut instant replay. Through the Hawk-Eye electronic line-calling technology, players will be allowed to challenge up to three calls per set (if a player loses a challenge, he or she forfeits the remaining challenges for the set). When a player challenges a line call, an official replay will be provided to the television broadcast and in-stadium video boards. Hence, everyone will bear witness to the result. "It's a long time coming," says Justin Gimelstob, the ATP's 111th ranked singles player. "There's nothing worse than a sporting event being decided by a mistake." (www.hawkeyeinnovations.co.uk)

Now batting: iPod. If nothing is harder than hitting a baseball, then nothing is more te-   8
dious than watching someone hit a baseball—over and over and over again. Yet members of the Colorado Rockies are mastering both arts. Thanks to the Apple iPod with video, which can hold up to 150 hours of imagery, Rockies players can watch up to five seasons worth of at-bats—wherever, whenever. The idea was hatched this past spring training, when Brian Jones and Mike Hamilton, the team's video coordinators, tried downloading various baseball films onto players' iPods. It was such a resounding success that now each week Jones and Hamilton customize downloads for each player—featuring clips of recent hits and of past at-bats against upcoming opposing starting pitchers. Each player also has his own 2005 highlight reel included on his iPod, featuring background music. Check your head: Data from SRS helmets is relayed to a sideline laptop. After further review: Now that tennis balls travel over 100 mph, judges need the Hawk-Eye instant replay.

Technology for the fans. The plight of the modern-day sports fan: When you watch 9
the game at home, you get instant replay, commentary, and stats; you always know
what hole your favorite golfer's on; the beer is cold and cheap . . . and both it and the
bathroom are a short walk from your couch. Go to a game, and the thrill of being there
is often trumped by the exorbitant ticket prices, the long lines for the overpriced beer,
and the lack of replays and statistical information that the home fan takes for granted.
Not much can be done about the escalation of ticket prices, but these days, thanks
to the wonderful world of wireless, you can get a little more bang for your buck in the
other departments.

Instant replay, instant gratification. If you have a video-enabled mobile phone or 10
a PDA, there's a good chance you can receive instant replay of the game—while
you're watching from the stands—on any play you want. The best news? It's free
(for now at least). mReplay is a beta technology being developed by SIMS Research
at the University of California–Berkeley's School of Information Management &
Systems, and SkyBOX by Vivid is also on the way (though you can expect to pay
for SkyBOX). Both programs utilize the fan's PDA or cell phone (or SkyBOX's own
media player) to beam instant-replay footage of any play right to the fan, with unlimited replay options. While SkyBOX will target the in-stadium customer, mReplay
also lets fans outside of the stadium in on the fun. mReplay also allows users to
replay shots from several weeks or months prior, so you can watch that walk-off
homer as many times as you like. Check out www.mreplay.com and www.vividskyco
.com for more details.

Shots and stats. No sport asks more of its ticket-purchasing fans than golf, who suf- 11
fer from obstructed views, lots of hikes, and the inability to see more than one hole
simultaneously. The PGA recognized this problem and now installs kiosks equipped
with ShotLink technology all over each course. ShotLink (designed in partnership with
IBM) lets fans locate their favorite golfers on the course and provides real-time stats
of the event, including putt lengths, leader boards, and so on. PGA workers and volunteers are the source of the information, which they record with Palm devices and make
available to fans at the kiosks via a wireless system. To ensure the accuracy of ball
stats, the PGA uses over 36 "laser targeting devices" working over digital maps of each
course. Other sports are following suit—Wimbledon.org now allows fans access to Shot
Tracker, a visual representation of each volley and serve (again provided by targeting
lasers), along with searchable stats. For more about ShotLink, check out www.pgatour
.com/tourcast/more/about.

Wi-Food. Finally, stats and instant replay are great, but how about not standing in the 12
beer line for half an hour and missing the big play? Cingular has teamed up with the
Atlanta Hawks and Thrashers to test out NFC (near-field communication), which will
provide season ticket-holders at Philips Arena with a way to beat the lines. Sure, the
technology is limited right now (you need a specific Nokia phone and a Chase Visa
account), but it's being tested, and the idea is brilliant: Point your phone at a vending
booth, order your food, and pay for it on your phone; then all you have to do is pick it
up—no standing in line or fiddling with your wallet. Perhaps it's not as easy as walking to your fridge and grabbing a cold one, but it's a start—and your fridge isn't in the
tenth row midcourt, is it?

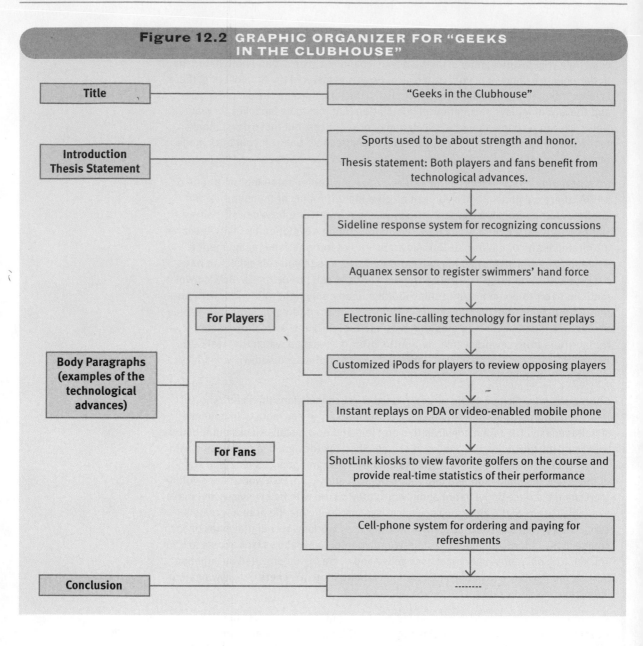

Figure 12.2 GRAPHIC ORGANIZER FOR "GEEKS IN THE CLUBHOUSE"

Title	"Geeks in the Clubhouse"
Introduction Thesis Statement	Sports used to be about strength and honor. Thesis statement: Both players and fans benefit from technological advances.

Body Paragraphs (examples of the technological advances)

For Players
- Sideline response system for recognizing concussions
- Aquanex sensor to register swimmers' hand force
- Electronic line-calling technology for instant replays
- Customized iPods for players to review opposing players

For Fans
- Instant replays on PDA or video-enabled mobile phone
- ShotLink kiosks to view favorite golfers on the course and provide real-time statistics of their performance
- Cell-phone system for ordering and paying for refreshments

Conclusion --------

Exercise 12.4

Draw a graphic organizer for "Rambos of the Road" (pp. 271–72).

Integrating Illustration into an Essay

Examples are an effective way to support a thesis that relies on one or more other patterns of development. You might, for instance, use examples in the following ways.

- To *define* a particular advertising ploy
- To *compare* two types of small businesses
- To *classify* types of movies
- To *show the effects* of aerobic exercise
- To *argue* that junk food is unhealthy because of its high fat and salt content

When using examples in an essay where illustration is not the main pattern of development, keep the following tips in mind.

1. **Be especially careful to choose examples that are relevant, representative, accurate, specific, and striking**, since in most cases you will include only one or two.
2. **Use clear transitions.** Be sure to use a clear transition to make it obvious that an example is to follow.
3. **Limit descriptive detail.** Provide enough details that your reader can understand how an example supports the point you want to make with it, but don't overwhelm your reader with too many details. Extended examples that are too detailed may distract your reader from the main point.

In "Words That Wound" (p. 296), Kathleen Vail uses illustration along with several other patterns of development (narration and description) to make a point about bullying.

A GUIDED WRITING ASSIGNMENT

The following guide will lead you through the process of writing an illustration essay. You will use examples to support your thesis, but you may need to use one or more of the other patterns of development to organize your examples or relate them to one another. Depending on your learning style, you may choose to work through this Guided Writing Assignment in different ways.

The Assignment

Write an illustration essay. Select one of the following topics or one that you think of on your own. Your audience consists of readers of your campus newspaper.

1. The connection between clothing and personality
2. The long-term benefits of a part-time job
3. The idea that you are what you eat
4. The problems of balancing school, job, and a family
5. Controlling or eliminating stress
6. Decision-making techniques
7. Effective (or ineffective) parenting
8. The popularity of a particular sport, television show, or hobby

As you develop your essay, consider using one or more of the other patterns of development. For example, you might use narration to present an extended example that illustrates the difficulties of balancing schoolwork with a job and family. You might

For more on narration, description, and comparison and contrast, see Chapters 10, 11, and 14.

compare decision-making techniques and give examples of each. Or you might describe your favorite television show and give examples from particular episodes.

Generating Ideas

Use the following guidelines to help you narrow a topic and generate ideas.

Narrowing Your Topic

For more on prewriting strategies, see Chapter 4.

Once you have chosen an assignment topic, be sure to use prewriting to narrow it so that it becomes a manageable topic. Be sure your narrowed topic can be supported by one or more examples.

Considering Your Purpose and Audience

Your purpose and audience will affect the type and number of examples you include. If you are writing a persuasive essay, you may need several examples to provide sufficient evidence. However, if you are writing an informative essay in which you explain how to select educational toys, one extended example may be sufficient.

For more on thesis statements, see Chapter 5, p. 101.

Consider your audience in deciding what kinds of examples to include. For this assignment, your audience is made up of readers of your campus newspaper. Think about whether this audience is interested in and familiar with your topic. If your audience is familiar with your topic, you may want to use complex examples. However, simple, straightforward examples would be appropriate for an audience unfamiliar with your topic.

Developing Your Thesis

Your next step is to develop a working thesis about your narrowed topic. The thesis in an illustration essay is the generalization that you will support with examples.

You can develop a thesis statement in several ways, depending on your learning style. For instance, a concrete learner writing about the effects of absent fathers on families may begin by listing the problems and behaviors that children in such families exhibit, and then develop a generalization from these examples. An abstract learner, in contrast, might write the thesis first and then generate examples that support the generalization.

As you brainstorm examples, you may think of situations that illustrate a different or more interesting thesis. Don't hesitate to revise or change your thesis as you discover more about your topic. Use the suggestions that follow to generate examples.

Learning Style Options

1. Jot down all of the instances or situations you can think of that illustrate your thesis.
2. Close your eyes and visualize situations that relate to your thesis.
3. Systematically review your life—year by year, place by place, or job by job—to recall situations that illustrate your thesis.
4. Discuss your thesis with a classmate. Try to match or better each other's examples.
5. Create two columns on a piece of paper or in a computer file. In the first column, list words describing how you feel about your narrowed topic. (For example, the topic *cheating on college exams* might generate such feelings as anger, surprise, and confusion.) In the second column, elaborate on these feelings by adding details about specific situations. (For example, you might write how surprised you were to discover your best friend had cheated on an exam.)

For more on library and Internet research, see Chapter 21.

6. Research your topic in the library or on the Internet to uncover examples outside your own experience.

Essay in Progress 1

Using the preceding guidelines, choose and narrow your topic. Then develop a working thesis statement and brainstorm examples that illustrate the thesis.

Choosing Your Examples

Once you have discovered a wealth of examples, your task is to select the ones that will best support your thesis and suit your audience and purpose. Use the following criteria in choosing examples.

1. **Choose relevant examples.** The examples you choose must clearly demonstrate the point or idea you want to illustrate. To support the thesis that high schools do not provide students with the instruction and training in physical education necessary to maintain a healthy lifestyle, you would not use as an example a student who is underweight because of a recent illness. Since lack of preparation in high school is not responsible for this student's problem, the case would be irrelevant to your thesis.

2. **Choose a variety of useful examples.** If you are using more than one example, choose examples that reveal different aspects of your topic. In writing about students who lack physical education skills, you would need to provide examples of students who lack different kinds of skills—strength, agility, and so forth. You can also add variety by using expert opinion, quotations, observations, or statistics to illustrate your thesis.

3. **Choose representative examples.** Choose typical cases, not rare or unusual ones. To continue with the thesis about physical education, a high school all-star football player who lacks adequate strength or muscular control would be an exceptional case. A recent graduate who did not learn to play a sport and failed to develop a habit of regular exercise would be a more representative example.

4. **Choose striking examples.** Include examples that capture your readers' attention and make a vivid impression.

5. **Choose accurate and specific examples.** Be sure the examples you include are as precise and specific as possible. They should be neither exaggerated nor understated.

6. **Choose examples that appeal to your audience.** Some examples will appeal to one type of audience more than to another type. If you want to illustrate high school graduates' lack of training in physical education for an audience of high school seniors, examples involving actual students may be most appealing, whereas for an audience of parents, expert opinion and statistics would be appropriate.

If you are working on a computer, highlight strong examples by making them bold or moving them to a separate page or document for easy access when drafting.

Trying Out Your Ideas on Others

Working in a group of two or three students, discuss your thesis and supporting examples for this chapter's assignment. Use the list of criteria above to guide the discussion and to make suggestions for improving each student's thesis and examples.

For more on drafting an essay,
see Chapter 6.

For more on chronological
organization, see Chapter 6.

For more on classification and
division, see Chapter 15.

For more on description, see
Chapter 11. For more on using
sufficient detail, see Chapter 7,
p. 147.

For more on transitions, see
Chapter 6, p. 124.

For more on writing effective
paragraphs, including
introductions and conclusions, see
Chapter 6.

> **Essay in Progress 2**
> Using the preceding suggestions and the feedback you received from classmates, evaluate your examples, and decide which ones you will include in your essay.

Organizing and Drafting

Once you are satisfied with your thesis and the examples you have chosen to illustrate it, you are ready to organize your ideas and write your draft essay.

Choosing a Method of Organization

Use the following guidelines to organize your essay.

1. **If you are using a single, extended example.** Relate events in the order in which they happened. However, if the example is not made up of events, you might use most-to-least, least-to-most, or spatial organization. For instance, if you want to use in-line skating as an example of the importance of protective athletic gear, you might arrange the details spatially, describing the skater's headgear first, then the elbow and wrist pads, and then the knee protection.
2. **If you are using several examples.** Many illustration essays order examples in terms of their importance, from most to least or from least to most important. However, other arrangements are possible. Examples of childhood memories, for instance, could follow chronological order.
3. **If you have many examples.** Consider grouping the examples in categories. For instance, in an essay about the use of slang words, you might classify examples according to how they are used by teenagers, by adults, and by other groups.

> **Essay in Progress 3**
> Using the preceding suggestions, choose a method for organizing your examples. Then draw a graphic organizer, or write an outline of your essay.

Drafting the Illustration Essay

Once you have decided on a method of organization, your next step is to write a first draft. Here are some tips for drafting an illustration essay.

1. **Use each paragraph to express one key idea; the example or examples in that paragraph should illustrate that key idea.** Develop your body paragraphs so that each one presents a single example or group of closely related examples.
2. **Use the topic sentence in each paragraph to make clear the particular idea that each example or set of examples illustrates.**
3. **Provide sufficient detail about each example.** Explain each one using vivid descriptive language. Your goal is to make your readers feel as if they are experiencing or observing the situation.
4. **Use transitions to move your readers from one example to another.** Without transitions such as *for example* and *in particular,* your essay will seem choppy and disconnected.
5. **Begin with an effective introduction.** In most illustration essays, the thesis is stated at the outset. Your introduction should also spark readers' interest and include background information about the topic.

6. **End with an effective conclusion.** Your essay should not end with your last example but should conclude with a final statement that pulls together your ideas and reminds readers of your thesis.

Essay in Progress 4
Using the preceding guidelines, write a first draft of your illustration essay.

Analyzing and Revising

If possible, set aside your draft for a day or two before rereading and revising it. As you reread, concentrate on organization, level of detail, and overall effectiveness, not on grammar or mechanics. To evaluate and revise your draft, use the following strategies.

Learning Style Options

1. Write an outline, draw a graphic organizer, or update the outline or organizer you created earlier. Look for weaknesses in how examples are organized.
2. Use Figure 12.3 to help you discover the strengths and weaknesses of your draft. You might also ask a classmate to review it using the questions in the flowchart. For each answer that refers you to the right column of the chart, ask your reviewer to explain why he or she answered in that way.

For more on the benefits of peer review, see Chapter 8, p. 162.

Essay in Progress 5
Revise your draft using Figure 12.3 and any comments you have received from peer reviewers.

Editing and Proofreading

The last step is to check your revised essay for errors in grammar, spelling, punctuation, and mechanics. Look for the types of errors you commonly make. (Refer to your error log.)

For more on keeping an error log, see Chapter 9, p. 196.

For illustration essays, pay particular attention to the following issues.

1. **Be consistent in the verb tense that you use in your extended examples.** When using an event from the past as an example, however, always use the past tense to describe it.

   ■ Special events *are* an important part of children's lives. Parent visitation day at school *was* an event my daughter *talked* about for an entire week. Children *are* also excited by . . .

2. **Be consistent in using first person (*I, me, we, us*), second person (*you*), or third person (*he, she, it, him, her, they, them*).**

   ■ I visited my daughter's first-grade classroom during parents' week last

   month. Each parent was invited to read a story to the class, and _{we} you were

   encouraged to ask the children questions afterward.

Figure 12.3 Flowchart for Revising an Illustration Essay

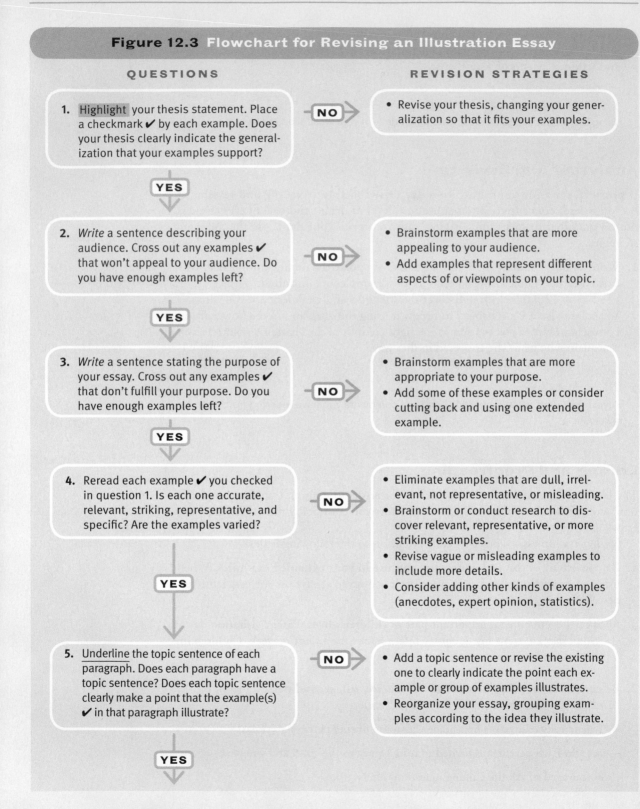

QUESTIONS

REVISION STRATEGIES

1. Highlight your thesis statement. Place a checkmark ✔ by each example. Does your thesis clearly indicate the generalization that your examples support?

— NO →
- Revise your thesis, changing your generalization so that it fits your examples.

YES

2. *Write* a sentence describing your audience. Cross out any examples ✔ that won't appeal to your audience. Do you have enough examples left?

— NO →
- Brainstorm examples that are more appealing to your audience.
- Add examples that represent different aspects of or viewpoints on your topic.

YES

3. *Write* a sentence stating the purpose of your essay. Cross out any examples ✔ that don't fulfill your purpose. Do you have enough examples left?

— NO →
- Brainstorm examples that are more appropriate to your purpose.
- Add some of these examples or consider cutting back and using one extended example.

YES

4. Reread each example ✔ you checked in question 1. Is each one accurate, relevant, striking, representative, and specific? Are the examples varied?

— NO →
- Eliminate examples that are dull, irrelevant, not representative, or misleading.
- Brainstorm or conduct research to discover relevant, representative, or more striking examples.
- Revise vague or misleading examples to include more details.
- Consider adding other kinds of examples (anecdotes, expert opinion, statistics).

YES

5. Underline the topic sentence of each paragraph. Does each paragraph have a topic sentence? Does each topic sentence clearly make a point that the example(s) ✔ in that paragraph illustrate?

— NO →
- Add a topic sentence or revise the existing one to clearly indicate the point each example or group of examples illustrates.
- Reorganize your essay, grouping examples according to the idea they illustrate.

YES

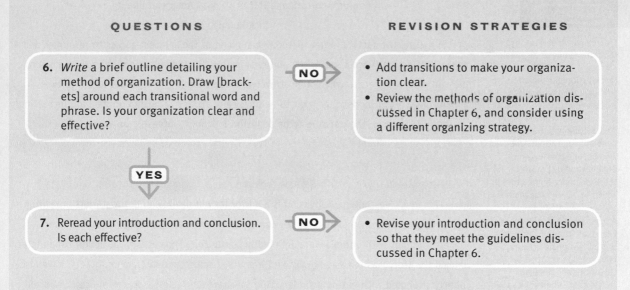

QUESTIONS

6. *Write* a brief outline detailing your method of organization. Draw [brackets] around each transitional word and phrase. Is your organization clear and effective?

NO →

YES ↓

7. Reread your introduction and conclusion. Is each effective?

NO →

REVISION STRATEGIES

- Add transitions to make your organization clear.
- Review the methods of organization discussed in Chapter 6, and consider using a different organizing strategy.

- Revise your introduction and conclusion so that they meet the guidelines discussed in Chapter 6.

---

3. Avoid sentence fragments when introducing examples. Each sentence must have both a subject and a verb.

- Technology has become part of teenagers' daily lives. ~~For example, high~~ *High*

    school students who carry iPhones~~,~~ *are one example.*

Essay in Progress 6
Edit and proofread your illustration essay, paying particular attention to consistent use of verb tense and point of view. Don't forget to look for the types of errors you tend to make.

Students Write

Nick Ruggia, a student at the University of Maryland at College Park, wrote this essay in response to an assignment in which he was asked to examine an American obsession. He chose to write about Americans' obsession with physical appearance. As you read his illustration essay, notice how he supports his thesis with a variety of examples.

READING

Conforming to Stand Out: A Look at American Beauty

Nick Ruggia

Title: Ruggia identifies his topic and suggests his thesis.

Introduction: Ruggia offers a biological basis for his thesis and explains why he is focusing on women. In his thesis statement, he makes a generalization about American women, and previews his organization by presenting his three examples in the order in which he will discuss them.

In nature, two factors largely determine survival of the species: access to resources and physical attraction (necessary for the ability to mate). Humans function under the same basic rules. In modern America, where almost everyone can acquire the basic resources to live, humans are striving harder than ever to be physically attractive. Although men are increasingly caught up in its grip, the pressure to be beautiful falls most intensely on women. The thin craze, the plastic surgery craze, and the body art craze represent some of the increasingly drastic lengths American women are being driven to in their quest for physical perfection.   1

A topic sentence introduces Example 1: the thin craze. In this paragraph and the next two, Ruggia uses specific celebrities and detailed statistics as subexamples to support his main examples (the three crazes). The statistics suggest that the celebrities are not unusual but representative of Americans in general. Ruggia cites the sources for his subexamples using MLA style.

Since Kate Moss's wafer-thin frame took the modeling industry by storm, skinny has driven America's aesthetics. Hollywood is a mirror for our desires, and our starlets are shrinking. Lindsay Lohan, once lauded for her curves, dropped to a disturbing weight, and her alleged struggles with bulimia were detailed in *Vanity Fair* (Thomas 2D), although Lohan later claimed the story was misleading. Nicole Ritchie and Angelina Jolie, among others, have also publicly struggled with eating disorders. And the stars aren't alone. According to the United States National Institutes of Mental Health, between 0.5 and 3.7 percent of American women will suffer from anorexia in their lifetimes, while another 1.1 to 4.2 percent will be bulimic and 2 to 5 percent will binge. These numbers exclude the disordered eaters who do not meet all the criteria necessary for diagnosis or do not accurately self-report. In a population of 300 million, these statistics represent millions of women struggling with food disorders. Men are not immune either, accounting for 5 to 15 percent of bulimia and anorexia diagnoses and 35 percent of binge-eating cases. The skinny obsession is spiraling out of control as more people risk death to be thin through diet pills and gastric bypass surgery.   2

A transitional sentence leads into the topic sentence for Example 2: the plastic surgery craze.

Ruggia cites striking subexamples.

But for every Kate Moss idolizer, there's a would-be Pamela Anderson. This ideal, fed by porn and Hollywood, is plastic perfection: instead of anorexically denying their curves, many women choose to enhance their features through surgery. The American Society of Plastic Surgeons (ASPS) reports that in 2006, there were nearly 11 million cosmetic surgeries in the United States and an additional 5.2 million reconstructive plastic surgeries ("11 Million"). While it must be remembered that the rule is not one surgery per person, so that the number of *patients* is lower than these figures, the scope of this practice is staggering nonetheless. Further evidence is provided by the surgically enhanced lips, stomachs, buttocks, and breasts that cover the pages of men's magazines all over the country. Strippers, porn stars like Jenna Jameson, and *Playboy* models like Anderson and the recently deceased Anna Nicole Smith flaunt enormous fake breasts. Clearly there is a disconnect between the sexless anorexic standard that so many women strive for and the bottle blonde bombshell that so many men favor. What everyone seems to agree on, though, is that plastic surgery is a response to the fear of aging. And in this way as well, men too are increasingly vulnerable to the superficial, with the ASPS reporting that they accounted for 12 percent of plastic surgeries in 2005 ("2005").   3

Body art, in the form of piercing and tattoos, also illustrates (literally) Americans' obses-   4
sion with physical appearance. The pierced and tattooed once jarred on public sensibilities,
but now these body modifications have gone mainstream. Even "alternative" piercings are now
accepted: Amy Winehouse, a heavily tattooed popular musician, has added to the popularity of
the "Monroe" piercing, located above the lip where Marilyn Monroe had a mole. Nearly half the
members of "Generation Next" have had a tattoo, piercing or "untraditional color" of hair (Pew
Research Center 21). Once largely limited to sailors, criminals, and punk rockers--and to men--
body art has become big business, drawing in more women as it spreads.

> A topic sentence
> introduces Example 3: the
> body art craze.

Maybe Americans have gone too far in basing their self-worth on physical appearance. Every   5
visible part of the human body has been marketed as a fixable flaw or an opportunity for more
adornment. Of course, Americans have always cared about their looks and made great efforts to improve them, but once most people kept the issue in perspective. Today, appearance rules. And men
increasingly are joining women in obedience to its commands. Both sexes, though, will find that
basing self-esteem on physical appearance, a fleeting commodity at best, is a recipe for misery.

> Conclusion: Ruggia
> acknowledges that attention
> to appearance is nothing
> new, but suggests that
> Americans today are placing
> too much emphasis on it.
> Ruggia lists his sources in
> MLA style, with the entries
> in alphabetical order.
> Notice the style for listing
> documents from Web sites
> sponsored by organizations
> and government agencies.

Works Cited

American Society of Plastic Surgeons. "2005 Gender Quick Facts." *Plastic Surgery.org*. ASPS,
22 Mar. 2007. Web. 10 Dec. 2007.

---. "11 Million Cosmetic Plastic Surgery Procedures in 2006--Up 7%." *Plastic Surgery.org*.
ASPS, 2006. Web. 10 Dec. 2007.

Pew Research Center for the People & the Press. *How Young People View Their Lives, Futures,
and Politics: A Portrait of "Generation Next."* Washington: Pew, 2007. *Pew Research Center
for the People & the Press.* Web. 11 Nov. 2007.

Thomas, Karen. "Year of Lows for Lohan: Actress Tells 'Vanity Fair' of Eating Disorders, Drug
Use." *USA Today* 5 Jan. 2006: 2D. Print.

United States. National Institutes of Mental Health. *The Numbers Count: Mental Disorders in
America*. NIMH, 7 Dec. 2007. Web. 10 Dec. 2007.

Analyzing the Writer's Technique

1. Evaluate the three main examples Ruggia provides. How well do they illustrate his
thesis? What other examples could he have used?
2. Ruggia used five sources in writing the essay. What kinds of sources are they? How
does his use of these sources strengthen his essay?
3. Ruggia uses celebrities and statistics as subexamples to support each of the topic
sentences about his three main examples. What other types of subexamples could
he have used?

Reacting to the Essay

1. Discuss the meaning and effectiveness of Ruggia's title.
2. To what extent do you agree that piercings and tattoos are widely accepted?
3. Ruggia asserts that people use body art to increase their physical attractiveness. Do you agree? What other reasons might people have for getting pierced or tattooed?
4. Are Americans obsessed with appearances in other ways? Write an essay explaining another American obsession. Use examples to support your thesis.

READING AN ILLUSTRATION ESSAY

The following section provides advice for reading illustration essays. Two exemplify the characteristics of illustration covered in this chapter and provide opportunities to examine, analyze, and react to the writer's ideas. The second essay uses illustration along with other methods of development.

Working with Text: Reading Illustration Essays

For more on reading strategies, see Chapter 3.

Examples are dramatic, real, and concrete, and it is easy to pay too much attention to them. Be sure to focus on the key points the examples illustrate. Here are some suggestions for reading illustration essays with a focused eye.

What to Look For, Highlight, and Annotate

1. Read the essay more than once. Read it first to grasp its basic ideas; reread it to analyze its structure and content.
2. Begin by identifying and highlighting the thesis statement. If the thesis is not directly stated, ask yourself this question: What one major point do all of the examples illustrate?
3. Study and highlight the examples. Note in the margin the characteristics or aspects of the thesis each example illustrates.
4. Record your response to each example, either by using annotations or by writing in a journal. Try to answer these questions: How well do the examples explain or clarify the thesis? Do I feel convinced of the writer's thesis after reading the essay? Would more or different examples have been more effective?
5. Notice how the examples are organized. Are they organized in order of importance, in chronological order, in spatial order, or by some other method?
6. Note how the examples fit with any other patterns of development used in the essay.

How to Find Ideas to Write About

When you are asked to write a response to an illustration essay, keep an eye out for ideas to write about as you read. Try to think of similar or related examples from your personal experience. While reading "Rambos of the Road," for instance, you might have thought about driving behaviors you have observed. You might have recalled other examples of drivers who exhibit road rage, who are oblivious to those around them, who are reckless, or who are careful and considerate. Each of these examples could lead you to a thesis and ideas for writing.

For more on discovering ideas for a response paper, see Chapter 3.

Thinking Critically about Illustration

When you read text that uses illustration to support generalizations, read with a critical eye. Study the examples and how they are used in the essay. Use the following questions to think critically about the examples you read.

1. What Is the Emotional Impact of the Examples?

A description of a tiger pacing in a small zoo enclosure, rubbing its body against a fence, and scratching an open sore would provide a vivid example of the behavior exhibited by some wild animals in captivity. Such an example can evoke feelings of pity, sympathy, or even outrage. Writers often choose examples to manipulate their readers' feelings, especially in persuasive writing. Although it is not necessarily wrong for a writer to use examples that evoke emotional responses, as a critical reader you should be aware of their use.

For more on emotional appeals, see Chapter 18, p. 500

When you encounter an example that evokes an emotional response, try to set your emotions aside and look at the example objectively. In the case of the essay about the tiger, for instance, you might ask, Why are animals held in captivity? What are the benefits of zoos?

2. How Well Do the Examples Support the Generalization?

Not all writers choose examples that convey a full picture of the subject. In the example about zoos, you might ask if the animals in all zoos are confined in small enclosures. Especially when you read persuasive writing, attempt to confirm through other sources that the writer's examples are fair and representative, and try to think of examples that might contradict the writer's point.

Also evaluate whether the writer provides enough good examples to support the generalization and lead you to accept the thesis. Study each example closely: Is it clear and fully explained? Is it relevant to the thesis? What other types of examples, such as statistics or expert opinion, might have strengthened the essay? In the essay about the tiger, for instance, the expert opinion of zoologists and statistics on the amount of space animals have in zoos and the number of species preserved in them would be relevant.

ILLUSTRATION ESSAY

As you read the following essay by Nell Bernstein, consider how the author uses the elements of illustration discussed in this chapter.

Goin' Gangsta, Choosin' Cholita: Claiming Identity
Nell Bernstein

Nell Bernstein is a San Francisco journalist and the author of *All Alone in the World: Children of the Incarcerated* (2005). The following excerpt from an essay originally appeared in 1994 in *West* magazine, the Sunday supplement to the *San Jose Mercury News*. It describes several California teenagers and their viewpoints on ethnic and racial identity. As you read the selection, highlight the statements and examples that reveal the teenagers' views.

Her lipstick is dark, the lip liner even darker, nearly black. In baggy pants, a blue plaid Pendleton, her bangs pulled back tight off her forehead, 15-year-old April is a perfect cholita, a Mexican gangsta girl.   1

But April Miller is Anglo. "And I don't like it!" she complains. "I'd rather be Mexican."   2

April's father wanders into the family room of their home in San Leandro, California, a suburb near Oakland. "Hey, cholita," he teases. "Go get a suntan. We'll put you in a barrio and see how much you like it."   3

A large, sandy-haired man with "April" tattooed on one arm and "Kelly" — the name of his older daughter — on the other, Miller spent 21 years working in a San Leandro glass factory that shut down and moved to Mexico a couple of years ago. He recently got a job in another factory, but he expects NAFTA* to swallow that one, too.   4

"Sooner or later we'll all get nailed," he says. "Just another stab in the back of the American middle class."   5

Later, April gets her revenge: "Hey, Mr. White Man's Last Stand," she teases. "Wait till you see how well I manage my welfare check. You'll be asking me for money."   6

A once almost exclusively white, now increasingly Latin and black working-class suburb, San Leandro borders on predominantly black East Oakland. For decades, the boundary was strictly policed and practically impermeable. In 1970 April Miller's hometown was 97 percent white. By 1990 San Leandro was 65 percent white, 6 percent black, 15 percent Hispanic, and 13 percent Asian or Pacific Islander. With minorities moving into suburbs in growing numbers and cities becoming ever more diverse, the boundary between city and suburb is dissolving, and suburban teenagers are changing with the times.   7

In April's bedroom, her past and present selves lie in layers, the pink walls of girlhood almost obscured, Guns N' Roses and Pearl Jam posters overlaid by rappers   8

---

*NAFTA (North American Free Trade Agreement): An agreement among Canada, the United States, and Mexico to ease restrictions on the exchange of goods and services. It had just gone into effect when this article was published.

Paris and Ice Cube. "I don't have a big enough attitude to be a black girl," says April, explaining her current choice of ethnic identification.

What matters is that she thinks the choice is hers. For April and her friends, identity   9
is not a matter of where you come from, what you were born into, what color your skin is. It's what you wear, the music you listen to, the words you use — everything to which you pledge allegiance, no matter how fleetingly.

The hybridization of American teens has become talk show fodder, with   10
"wiggers" — white kids who dress and talk "black" — appearing on TV in full gangsta regalia. In Indiana a group of white high school girls raised a national stir when they triggered an imitation race war at their virtually all white high school last fall simply by dressing "black."

In many parts of the country, it's television and radio, not neighbors, that   11
introduce teens to the allure of ethnic difference. But in California, which demographers predict will be the first state with no racial majority by the year 2000, the influences are more immediate. The California public schools are the most diverse in the country: 42 percent white, 36 percent Hispanic, 9 percent black, 8 percent Asian.

Sometimes young people fight over their differences. Students at virtually any   12
school in the Bay Area can recount the details of at least one "race riot" in which a conflict between individuals escalated into a battle between their clans. More often, though, teens would rather join than fight. Adolescence, after all, is the period when you're most inclined to mimic the power closest at hand, from stealing your older sister's clothes to copying the ruling clique at school.

White skaters and Mexican would-be gangbangers listen to gangsta rap and call   13
each other "nigga" as a term of endearment; white girls sometimes affect Spanish accents; blond cheerleaders claim Cherokee ancestors.

"Claiming" is the central concept here. A Vietnamese teen in Hayward, another   14
Oakland suburb, "claims" Oakland — and by implication blackness — because he lived there as a child. A law-abiding white kid "claims" a Mexican gang he says he hangs with. A brown-skinned girl with a Mexican father and a white mother "claims" her Mexican side, while her fair-skinned sister "claims" white. The word comes up over and over, as if identity were territory, the self a kind of turf.

Will Mosley says he and his friends listen to rap groups like Compton's Most   15
Wanted, NWA, and Above the Law because they "sing about life" . . . that is, what happens in Oakland, Los Angeles, anyplace but where Will is sitting today, an empty Round Table Pizza in a minimall.

"No matter what race you are," Will says, "if you live like we do, then that's the kind   16
of music you like."

And how do they live?   17

"We don't live bad or anything," Will admits. "We live in a pretty good neighbor-   18
hood, there's no violence or crime. I was just . . . we're just city people, I guess."

Will and his friend Adolfo Garcia, 16, say they've outgrown trying to be something   19
they're not. "When I was 11 or 12," Will says, "I thought I was becoming a big gangsta and stuff. Because I liked that music, and thought it was the coolest, I wanted to become that. I wore big clothes, like you wear in jail. But then I kind of woke up. I looked at myself and thought, 'Who am I trying to be?'"

They may have outgrown blatant mimicry, but Will and his friends remain con- 20
vinced that they can live in a suburban tract house with a well-kept lawn on a tree-
lined street in "not a bad neighborhood" and still call themselves "city" people
on the basis of musical tastes. "City" for these young people means crime, graffiti,
drugs. The kids are law-abiding, but these activities connote what Will admiringly
calls "action." With pride in his voice, Will predicts that "in a couple of years,
Hayward will be like Oakland. It's starting to get more known, because of crime
and things. I think it'll be bigger, more things happening, more crime, more graffiti,
stealing cars."

"That's good," chimes in 15-year-old Matt Jenkins, whose new beeper — an item that 21
once connoted gangsta chic but now means little more than an active social life — goes
off periodically. "More fun."

The three young men imagine with disdain life in a gangsta-free zone. "Too bland, 22
too boring," Adolfo says. "You have to have something going on. You can't just have
everyday life."

"Mowing your lawn," Matt sneers. 23

"Like Beaver Cleaver's house," Adolfo adds. "It's too clean out here." 24

Not only white kids believe that identity is a matter of choice or taste or that the 25
power of "claiming" can transcend ethnicity. The Manor Park Locos — a group of
mostly Mexican-Americans who hang out in San Leandro's Manor Park — say they
descend from the Manor Lords, tough white guys who ruled the neighborhood a generation ago.

Not every young Californian embraces the new racial hybridism. Andrea Jones, 26
20, an African-American who grew up in the Bay Area suburbs of Union City and
Hayward, is unimpressed by what she sees mainly as shallow mimicry. "It's full of
posers out here," she says. "When Boyz N the Hood came out on video, it was sold
out for weeks. The boys all wanna be black, the girls all wanna be Mexican. It's the
glamour."

Driving down the quiet, shaded streets of her old neighborhood in Union 27
City, Andrea spots two white preteen boys in Raiders jackets and hugely baggy
pants strutting erratically down the empty sidewalk. "Look at them," she says.
"Dislocated."

She knows why. "In a lot of these schools out here, it's hard being white," she says. 28
"I don't think these kids were prepared for the backlash that is going on, all the pride
now in people of color's ethnicity, and our boldness with it. They have nothing like
that, no identity, nothing they can say they're proud of.

"So they latch onto their great-grandmother who's a Cherokee, or they take on the 29
most stereotypical aspects of being black or Mexican. It's beautiful to appreciate different aspects of other people's culture — that's like the dream of what the 21st century
should be. But to garnish yourself with pop culture stereotypes just to blend — that's
really sad."

Those who dismiss the gangsta and cholo styles as affectations can point to the 30
fact that several companies market overpriced knockoffs of "ghetto wear" targeted
at teens.

But there's also something going on out here that transcends adolescent fad- 31
dishness and pop culture exoticism. When white kids call their parents "racist" for

nagging them about their baggy pants; when they learn Spanish to talk to their boy-friends; when Mexican-American boys feel themselves descended in spirit from white "uncles"; when children of mixed marriages insist that they are whatever race they say they are, all of them are more than just confused.

They're inching toward what Andrea Jones calls "the dream of what the 21st century 32 should be." In the ever more diverse communities of Northern California, they're also facing the complicated reality of what their 21st century will be.

Meanwhile, in the living room of the Miller family's San Leandro home, the argu- 33 ment continues unabated. "You don't know what you are," April's father has told her more than once. But she just keeps on telling him he doesn't know what time it is.

Examining the Reading

1. What does racial or ethnic identity mean to April Miller? According to Bernstein, by what standards does she define herself?
2. What does Bernstein mean by "the complicated reality" of the twenty-first century (para. 32)?
3. Explain the meaning of "claiming" (para. 14) as it is used in this essay.
4. What causes does Bernstein offer to explain why the California teenagers developed such attitudes about their racial and ethnic identity?
5. Explain the meaning of each of the following words as it is used in the reading: *impermeable* (para. 7), *hybridization* (10), *connoted* (21), and *affectations* (30). Refer to your dictionary as needed.

MAKING CONNECTIONS

Culture and Choosing Who You Are

Both "Goin' Gangsta, Choosin' Cholita: Claiming Identity" (pp. 292–95) and "Latin Lingo," which appears in Chapter 14 (pp. 419–21), describe how aspects of American culture — manner of dress and forms of language, for example—can be exchanged and combined into a new cultural fusion that people can identify with and participate in.

Analyzing the Readings

1. What do the readings express about how people identify themselves? What differences do you see in the points they make?
2. Write a journal entry illustrating how one or more cultures or subcultures influence your style, tastes, or interests. (*Subcultures* are groups that share parts of a dominant culture but have their own unique customs, lifestyle, or values. Vegetarians, jazz musicians, college football players, and medical doctors each form a subculture, for example.)

Essay Idea

Write an essay in which you explore how aspects of cultures or subcultures intersect and combine. How are you exposed to different cultures or subcultures?

Analyzing the Writer's Technique

1. What generalization does Bernstein make? How effectively is the generalization supported in this essay?
2. The writer uses the example involving April Miller in the introduction and conclusion. Do you find this strategy effective? Why or why not?
3. Evaluate Bernstein's use of illustration: Are the examples relevant and representative? Does Bernstein include enough examples? Explain your responses.
4. *Identity* is an abstract term. How does Bernstein make this term real and understandable?
5. What impact do Bernstein's examples have? How might various readers (white teenagers, members of the group being imitated, parents of teenagers) react to these examples?

Reacting to the Reading

1. Have you observed teenagers claiming an ethnic or a racial identity? How do they look and behave? What seems to motivate them?
2. What factors most contribute to your sense of identity? Write a journal entry describing who you are and how you define yourself. Include examples.
3. Write an essay discussing why you agree or disagree with this statement: Teenagers who establish their identities by copying members of racial or ethnic groups strengthen unwanted stereotypes.

ILLUSTRATION COMBINED WITH OTHER PATTERNS

As you read the following essay by Kathleen Vail, notice how she uses examples along with other patterns of development to support her main point.

(READING)

Words That Wound
Kathleen Vail

Kathleen Vail is managing editor of and a frequent contributor to the *American School Board Journal*, which covers school management, educational policy and law, school achievement, and research. The following selection appeared in the *American School Board Journal* in 1999. As you read the selection, look for and highlight the examples Vail uses to support her thesis.

Brian Head saw only one way out. On the final day of his life, during economics class, the 15-year-old stood up and pointed a semiautomatic handgun at himself. Before he pulled the trigger, he said his last words: "I can't take this anymore."   1

Brian's father, William Head, has no doubt why his only child chose to take his life   2
in front of a classroom full of students five years ago. Brian wanted everyone to know

the source of his pain, the suffering he could no longer endure. The Woodstock, Ga., teen, overweight with thick glasses, had been systematically abused by school bullies since elementary school. Death was the only relief he could imagine. "Children can't vote or organize, leave or run away," says Head. "They are trapped."

For many students, school is a torture chamber from which there is no escape. Every 3 day, 160,000 children stay home from school because they are afraid of being bullied, according to the National Association of School Psychologists. In a study of junior high and high school students from small Midwestern towns, nearly 77 percent of the students reported they'd been victims of bullies at school — 14 percent saying they'd experienced severe reactions to the abuse. "Bullying is a crime of violence," says June Arnette, associate director of the National School Safety Center. "It's an imbalance of power, sustained over a period of time."

Yet even in the face of this suffering, even after Brian Head's suicide five years ago, 4 even after it was revealed this past spring that a culture of bullying might have played a part in the Columbine High School shootings, bullying remains for the most part un-acknowledged, underreported, and minimized by schools. Adults are unaware of the extent and nature of the problem, says Nancy Mullin-Rindler, associate director of the Project on Teasing and Bullying in the Elementary Grades at Wellesley College Center for Research on Women. "They underestimate the import. They feel it's a normal part of growing up, that it's character-building."

After his son's death, William Head became a crusader against bullying, founding 5 an effort called Kids Hope to prevent others from suffering as Brian had. Unfortunately, bullying claimed another victim in the small town of Woodstock: 13-year-old Josh Belluardo. Last November, on the bus ride home from school, Josh's neighbor, 15-year-old Jonathan Miller, taunted him and threw wads of paper at him. He followed Josh off the school bus, hit the younger boy in the back of the head, and kicked him in the stomach. Josh spent the last two days of his life in a coma before dying of his injuries. Miller, it turns out, had been suspended nearly 20 times for offenses such as pushing and taunting other students and cursing at a teacher. He's now serving a life sentence for felony murder while his case is on appeal.

Bullying doesn't have to result in death to be harmful. Bullying and harassment 6 are major distractions from learning, according to the National School Safety Center. Victims' grades suffer, and fear can lead to chronic absenteeism, truancy, or dropping out. Bullies also affect children who aren't victimized: Bystanders feel guilty and help-less for not standing up to the bully. They feel unsafe, unable to take action. They also can be drawn into bullying behavior by peer pressure. "Any time there is a climate of fear, the learning process will be compromised," says Arnette.

A full 70 percent of children believe teachers handle episodes of bullying 7 "poorly," according to a study by John Hoover at the University of North Dakota at Grand Forks. It's no wonder kids are reluctant to tell adults about bullying incidents. "Children feel no one will take them seriously," says Robin Kowalski, professor of psychology at Western Carolina University, Cullowhee, N.C., who's done research on teasing behavior.

Martha Rizzo, who lives in a suburb of Cincinnati, calls bullying the "dirty little 8 secret" of her school district. Both her son and daughter were teased in school. Two boys in her son's sixth-grade class began taunting him because he wore sweatpants instead of jeans. They began to intimidate him during class. Once they knocked the pencil out of his hand during a spelling test when the teacher's back was turned. He failed the test. Rizzo made an appointment with the school counselor. The counselor told her he could do nothing about the behavior of the bullies and suggested she get counseling for her son instead. "Schools say they do something, but they don't, and it continues," says Rizzo. "We go in with the same problem over and over again."

Anna Billoit of Louisiana went to her son's middle school teachers when her son, who had asthma and was overweight, was being bullied by his classmates. Some of the teachers made the situation worse, she says. One male teacher suggested to her that the teasing would help her son mature. "His attitude was 'Suck it up, take it like a man,' " says Billoit.   9

Much bullying goes on in so-called transition areas where there is little or no adult supervision: hallways, locker rooms, restrooms, cafeterias, playgrounds, buses, and bus stops. When abuse happens away from adult eyes, it's hard to prove that the abuse occurred. Often, though, bullies harass their victims in the open, in full view of teachers and other adults. Some teachers will ignore the behavior, silently condoning it. But even when adults try to deal with the problem, they sometimes make things worse for the victim by not handling the situation properly. Confronting bullies in front of their peers only enhances the bullies' prestige and power. And bullies often step up the abuse after being disciplined. "People know it happens, but there's no structured way to deal with it," says Mullin-Rindler. "There's lots of confusion about what to do and what is the best approach."   10

Societal expectations play a part in adult reactions to childhood bullying. Many teachers and administrators buy into a widespread belief that bullying is a normal part of childhood and that children are better off working out such problems on their own. But this belief sends a dangerous message to children, says Head. Telling victims they must protect themselves from bullies shows children that adults can't and won't protect them. And, he points out, it's an attitude adults would never tolerate themselves. "If you go to work and get slapped on the back of the head, you wouldn't expect your supervisor to say, 'It's your problem — you need to learn to deal with it yourself,' " says Head. "It's a human-rights issue."   11

Ignoring bullying is only part of the problem. Some teachers go further by blaming the victims for their abuse by letting their own dislike for the victimized child show. "There's a lot of secret admiration for the strong kids," says Eileen Faucette of Augusta, Ga. Her daughter was teased so badly in the classroom that she was afraid to go to the blackboard or raise her hand to answer a question. The abuse happened in front of her teacher, who did nothing to stop it.   12

Head also encountered a blame-the-victim attitude toward his son. Brian would get into trouble for fighting at school, but when Head and his wife investigated what happened, they usually found that Brian had been attacked by other students. The school, Head said, wanted to punish Brian along with his attackers. "The school calls it fighting," Head says. "But it's actually assault and battery."   1

And changes are coming. This past April, five months after Josh Belluardo's death, **14** the Georgia State Legislature passed an anti-bullying law. The law defines bullying as "any willful attempt or threat to inflict injury on another person when accompanied by an apparent present ability to do so" or "any intentional display of force such as would give the victim reason to fear or expect immediate bodily harm." Schools are required to send students to an alternative school if they commit a third act of bullying in a school year. The law also requires school systems to adopt anti-bullying policies and to post the policies in middle and high schools.

Head was consulted by the state representatives who sponsored the bill, but he be- **15** lieves the measures don't go far enough. He urges schools to treat bullying behavior as a violation of the state criminal law against assault, stalking, and threatening, and to call the police when the law is broken.

He knows it's too late for Brian, too late for Josh, too late for the teens who died in **16** Littleton. But he continues to work, to educate and lobby on the devastating effects of bullying so that his son's death will not have been in vain.

"We should come clean and say what we've done in the past is wrong," says Head. **17** "Now we will guarantee we'll protect the rights of students."

Examining the Reading

1. How does Vail present bullying as both a general and a specific problem?
2. Why does bullying persist in school settings? Whom does the author blame?
3. How does bullying affect children who are not bullied?
4. Explain the statement that bullying is "an imbalance of power, sustained over a period of time" (para. 3).
5. Explain the meaning of each of the following words as it is used in the reading: *sustained* (para. 3), *crusader* (5), *compromised* (6), *condoning* (10), and *lobby* (16).

Analyzing the Writer's Technique

1. Does Vail provide a sufficient number of examples to support her thesis?
2. Examine the examples that are included in Vail's essay. What is the emotional impact of her examples?
3. Are the examples that Vail uses fair and representative of the situation in today's public schools?
4. What audience is Vail addressing? How do Vail's examples address her audience and purpose?

Visualizing the Reading

Analyze Vail's use of other patterns of development, in addition to illustration, by completing the chart on page 300. For each pattern, identify by paragraph number two places in the reading where each pattern in used.

Pattern of Development	Where Used in the Reading
Narration	
Cause and Effect	

Reacting to the Reading

1. Discuss whether bullying occurs among adults in more subtle ways.
2. What rules or policies could schools establish that would reduce bullying?
3. Write a journal entry exploring actions that would encourage more states to enact antibullying laws.
4. Write a letter to a school board or to a school district's superintendent urging that a policy on bullying be established. You might give examples that demonstrate why the policy is needed and suggest what regulations it might include.

Applying Your Skills: Additional Essay Assignments

For more on locating and documenting sources, see Part 5.

Write an illustration essay on one of the following topics, using what you learned about illustration in this chapter. Depending on the topic you choose, you may need to conduct library or Internet research.

To Express Your Ideas

1. In an article for the campus newspaper, explain what you consider to be the three most important qualities of a college instructor. Support your opinion with vivid examples from your experience.
2. Explain to a general audience the role played by grandparents within a family, citing examples from your family.

To Inform Your Reader

3. In "Rambos of the Road," Martin Gottfried explains the concept of "auto macho," also known as "road rage," using examples from his own experience. Explain the concept of *peer pressure,* using examples from your experience.

4. Describe to an audience of college students the qualities or achievements you think should be emphasized during job interviews. Give examples that show why the qualities or achievements you choose are important to potential employers.

To Persuade Your Reader

5. Argue for or against an increased emphasis on physical education in public schools. Your audience is your local school committee.
6. In a letter to the editor of a local newspaper, argue for or against the establishment of a neighborhood watch group.

Cases Using Illustration

7. Prepare the oral presentation you will give to your local town board to convince them to lower the speed limit on your street. Use examples as well as other types of evidence.
8. Write a letter to the parents of three-year-old children who will begin attending your day-care center this year, explaining how they can prepare their children for the day-care experience. Support your advice with brief but relevant examples.

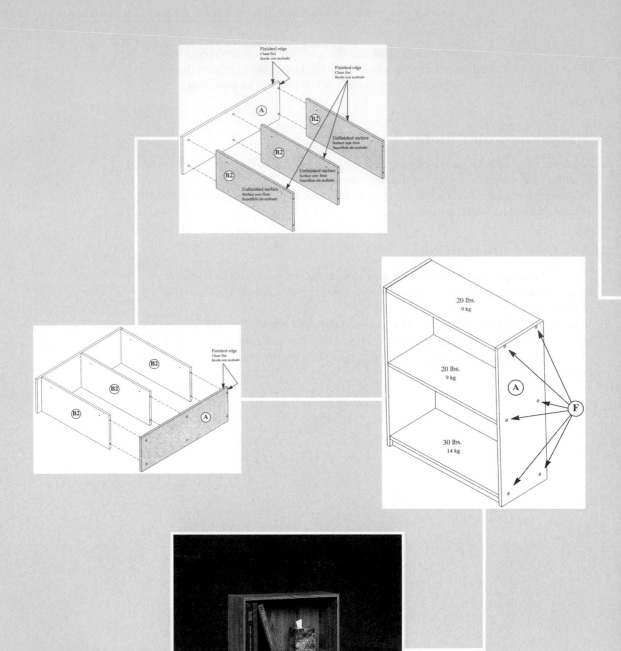

Finished edge
Chant fini
Borde con acabado

Finished edge
Chant fini
Borde con acabado

(A)

(B2)

(B2)

(B2)

Unfinished surface
Surface non-finie
Superficie sin acabado

Unfinished surface
Surface non-finie
Superficie sin acabado

Unfinished surface
Surface non-finie
Superficie sin acabado

Finished edge
Chant fini
Borde con acabado

(B2)

(B2)

(B2)

(A)

20 lbs.
9 kg

20 lbs.
9 kg

30 lbs.
14 kg

(A)

(F)

CHAPTER 13

Process Analysis: Explaining How Something Works or Is Done

WRITING QUICK START

Suppose you are a technical writer and have been asked to write the instructions that will accompany this diagram for assembling a bookshelf. Write a brief paragraph describing how to perform the steps shown in the diagram. Your audience consists of people who have bought the materials to assemble the bookshelf.

WRITING A PROCESS ANALYSIS

To describe the steps involved in assembling a bookshelf, you had to explain a process. You use process analysis whenever you explain how something is done or how it works—how to make lasagna, how to change a flat tire, or how a bill becomes law. This chapter will show you how to write a well-organized, easy-to-understand process analysis essay and how to incorporate process analysis into essays that use other patterns of development.

What Is Process Analysis?

A **process analysis** explains in step-by-step fashion how something works or how something is done or made. Process analyses provide people with practical information—directions for assembling equipment, instructions for registering for classes, an explanation of how a medication works. Whatever the purpose, the information in a process analysis must be accurate, clear, and easy to follow.

Process analysis is a common type of writing in college and on the job (see the accompanying box for a few examples). Two types of writing situations call for the use of process analysis.

- To explain *how to do something* to readers *who want or need to perform the process*
- To explain *how something works* to readers *who want to understand the process but not actually perform it*

The first type, a *how-to essay,* may explain how to teach a child the alphabet, for instance. Your primary purpose in writing a how-to essay is to present the steps in the process clearly and completely so that your readers can perform the task you describe. For the second type of process analysis, a *how-it-works essay,* you might explain how a popular radio talk show screens its callers. Your primary purpose in writing a how-it-works essay is to present the steps in the process clearly enough so that your readers

---

SCENES FROM COLLEGE AND THE WORKPLACE

- For a *child development* course, your assignment is to visit a day-care center, choose one confrontation between a child and a teacher, and explain how the teacher resolved the conflict.

- As part of a *chemistry* lab report, you are asked to summarize the procedure you followed in preparing a solution or conducting an experiment.

- While working as an *engineer* at a water treatment plant, you are asked by your supervisor to write a description of how the city's drinking water is tested and treated for contamination.

can fully understand it. At times, you may read or write essays that contain elements of both types of process analysis. In writing about how a car alarm system works, for example, you might find it necessary to explain how to activate and deactivate the system as well as how it works.

The following essay exemplifies a how-to process analysis essay.

How to Use Online Dating Sites
Ed Grabianowski

Ed Grabianowski is a freelance reporter and writer and a contributing writer for Howstuffworks.com, an online collection of articles explaining how specific processes work in a variety of fields, including business, entertainment, and science. The following article was posted in the "People" subsection of the site's "Culture" section. As you read, notice how Grabianowski both outlines the steps of the online dating process and offers the reader advice on how to date online successfully.

One of the basic human impulses is to develop a romantic relationship — and maybe even fall in love. But there are a lot of obstacles that might keep someone from meeting the love of his or her life in today's world. Maybe dating coworkers is against company policy. Perhaps you hate the bar scene. You might not be in the right mood to meet your soul mate while you're trekking through the grocery store. 1

People of all ages, lifestyles, and locations have been facing this problem for decades. In the last ten years or so, a new solution has arrived to help lonely hearts find their soul mates: online dating. In this article, we'll see what online dating is like, find out how (and if) it works, and get some helpful tips on making your online dating experience safe and successful. 2

GETTING STARTED

Online dating is simply a method of meeting people, and it has advantages and disadvantages. The variety of dating sites is constantly growing, with many sites focused on very specific groups or interests. There are sites for seniors, sites for Muslims, sites for fitness-oriented people, sites for people just looking for friends, and sites for people who are interested in more adult activities. In this article, we'll be focusing on the most basic type of dating site — one that works to bring two people together for a romantic relationship. While this article applies to the majority of popular dating sites, the rules and practices of any given individual site may differ. 3

When you first arrive at an online dating site, you can browse through profiles without entering any information about yourself. The amount of information you can see about each user depends on the site. Some sites allow users to restrict access to their profiles to paying members. Photos might not be displayed unless you have a paid membership. This helps preserve anonymity, since a coworker or family member can't accidentally stumble across your profile. They'd have to pay for a membership to see a picture of the person they're reading about. 4

Once you decide you're going to give it a shot, the first thing you need to do is create your profile. 5

CREATING A PROFILE

When it's time to make your own profile, you'll start with some basic information. Are   6
you a man or a woman? Are you looking to meet a man or a woman? What age range
are you interested in? Where do you live? (Some sites just ask for a zip code, while others may allow you to choose from a list of cities.) This is generally the same information
you provide to perform a simple search, or "browse."

When you first sign up, you fill out some basic Profile Information. Basic profile in-   7
formation may also include your birthdate and a valid email address. Site administrators will communicate with you through this address, and some sites allow messages
from users to be sent to your email anonymously. When they send you a message,
it is routed through the site's system and redirected to your email without the other
user ever seeing your address. Some sites use their own internal messaging system.
If you're especially concerned about privacy, it's easy enough to create a free email
account somewhere and use it solely for your online dating contacts.

Indicating your physical attributes is usually the next step. Height, weight, hair and   8
eye color, and body type are common pieces of data, while some sites ask about piercings and tattoos. At this point, the process becomes increasingly detailed. Interests and
activities, favorite sports, authors, music or movies, how you like to spend weekends —
these topics are all fair game. More personal questions might involve whether or not you
have children, whether or not you want children, your religious beliefs, and your political
views. Pets, occupation, income, and living situation are usually on the list as well.

Next you'll be asked to answer many of these same questions a second time, but   9
instead of indicating your own traits, you'll be describing your ideal date. The site will
then use this information and the information you provided about yourself to find suitable matches that you might want to contact. Most sites will also allow you to write
about yourself in a more freeform manner — a chance to get across more of your personality than a series of pull-down lists can offer.

Posting a photo of yourself is another important step. Most sites report a huge in-   10
crease in responses to ads that have photos posted. There will usually be guidelines
as to what sorts of photo you can post, and there might be an approval process before
it actually gets posted. In general, avoid posting revealing photos, don't post photos
with people other than yourself in them, and don't post glossy, "glam" photos. Although you want to look your best, try and make sure the photo is accurate to how you
currently look. If you're thirty-five, your high school yearbook photo isn't a good choice.
If you recently dyed your hair purple, try to get a photo that reflects that.

There's one last rule that needs to be mentioned, and it's an important one: Don't   11
put personal identification information in your profile. This includes your address,
phone number, social security number, full name, or place of employment. You might
meet people on the site that you'll want to share some of that information with down
the line, but it should never be public knowledge.

Now, let's go through some helpful tips on creating a profile that encourages people   12
to contact you.

CREATING A GOOD PROFILE

If you browse through a typical dating site, you will see hundreds of ads from people   13
who are "looking for Mr. Right." Nearly everyone "enjoys a night out on the town, but
also likes a quiet evening at home." It would be difficult to find someone who doesn't
like a good sense of humor in a date.

Begin with the subject. Inject some humor into your subject line or include one of 14
your interests. "Bogart fan seeking unusual suspects." "Come sail away with this boating enthusiast/Styx fan." This is the first thing people will see, and it needs to stand
out from the crowd.

When it comes to the profile itself, make sure you fill out the whole thing. Take your 15
time and put some thought into it. It may seem tedious or difficult to describe yourself,
but leaving sections blank or putting in short, generic answers makes it look like you
aren't really interested. Avoid phrases like, "I wouldn't normally use one of these dating
services, but my friends put me up to this." Remember, your target audience is other
people who are using this dating service. You don't want to start off by insulting them.

Think of specific aspects of your personality that you want to highlight. Then, don't 16
just state them — demonstrate them. Instead of "I enjoy Stanley Kubrick films," say,
"The other night I was watching *A Clockwork Orange*, and I found myself thinking it
would be a lot more fun to watch and discuss it with someone else." Humor is especially important. Not everyone shares the same sense of humor, so saying "I'm a funny
person" isn't sufficient. "I love quoting lines from Monty Python sketches and Simpsons
episodes" gives other users a better grasp of your personality.

Another key to success is knowing what you want and putting it in your profile. 17
You'll get more responses from people who are looking for the same thing you are,
whether you want to settle down with a long-term relationship or just want a date for
Friday night. "I think there is more of a mental connection first by online dating," said
one user, a teacher from New York. "Also, you know what you're looking for, not what
your friends think would be 'perfect' for you."

Last but not least, mind your grammar. Poor grammar and spelling doesn't lead to a 18
good first impression, so take the time to get it right.

MAKING CONTACT

If you've decided to become a paying member of a dating site, you can start contacting 19
other users if their profile appeals to you. These messages don't have to be very elaborate, since you've already put a lot of information into your profile. Something along
the lines of, "Hey, I saw your profile and it seems like we have some common interests.
Take a look at my profile, and if you're interested, send me a message," is probably
sufficient. You might send messages to several people at once, or you might contact
one at a time — it's up to each user.

From there, you simply wait. Some people will write back to let you know they're not 20
interested, while others will simply ignore your message. In some cases, the person you
wrote to might not be visiting the site anymore. But a few of your contacts will eventually respond, and other people will start contacting you after they see your profile. How
long it takes depends on the site and the individual user. Reports from dating-site users
range from one who cited a ratio of "about a million to one" contacts to actual dates to
another who had two dates almost immediately and is still dating one of them.

The amount of time between that first email and a first in-person date varies from 21
person to person. That's one of the benefits of online dating — you can take your time if
you want to and really get to know someone well before you ever meet. Or you can plan
a date right away and find out if there's any chemistry. Either way, it's important to keep
safety in mind, along with a few other things to make sure your first date goes smoothly.

It's important to talk to your date on the phone before you meet. Even if you've been 22
conversing via email for weeks, just one call can avoid a lot of problems. If the blonde,

twenty-four-year-old, female swimsuit model you've been writing to turns out to be a thirteen-year-old boy playing a joke, a phone call is a good way to find out.

Once it comes time to plan the actual date, choose a neutral, public setting and arrive   2
there independently. There are some dangerous people in the world, and even though they may be thankfully rare, it's still not a good idea to take a long hike into an isolated area with someone you don't know. Going to someone's house can be risky, too, for both men and women. In one case, a man went to meet a woman he met online, and when he arrived, she pulled a knife and took his wallet. Specific suggestions include a coffee shop, a busy restaurant, a college sports game, or a movie theater. The key is to make sure there will be plenty of other people around. Make sure you let someone know where you'll be going and what time you plan to return. A little caution never hurt anybody.

Of course the vast majority of dates will turn out to be perfectly normal, safe people.   2
However, quite a few of them can be boring, annoying, or just plain unattractive. For this reason, plan for a short first date. Dinner or a few cups of coffee won't take more than an hour or so, so even the worst date will be over soon enough. If all goes well, you can plan for more lengthy dates in the future.

Characteristics of Process Analysis Essays

A process analysis essay should include everything your reader needs to know to understand or perform the process. In addition to presenting an explicit thesis, the essay should provide a clear, step-by-step description of the process; define key terms; give any necessary background information; describe any equipment needed to perform the process; supply an adequate amount of detail; and, for a how-to essay, anticipate and offer help with potential problems.

Process Analysis Usually Includes an Explicit Thesis Statement

A process analysis usually contains a clear thesis that identifies the process to be discussed and suggests why the process is important or useful to the reader. In "How to Use Online Dating Sites," for instance, Grabianowski states, "In this article, we'll see what online dating is like, find out how (and if) it works, and get some helpful tips on making your online dating experience safe and successful" (para. 2).

Here are two examples of thesis statements for how-to process analyses.

Switching to a low-fat diet, a recent nutritional trend, can improve weight control dramatically.

By carefully preparing for a vacation in a foreign country, you can save time and prevent hassles.

Here are two examples of thesis statements for how-it-works essays.

Although understanding the grieving process will not lessen the grief that you experience after the death of a loved one, knowing that your experiences are normal does provide some comfort.

Advertisers often appeal to the emotions of the audience for whom a product is targeted; some of these appeals may be unethical.

Process Analysis Is Organized Chronologically

The steps or events in a process analysis are usually organized in chronological order—that is, the order in which the steps are normally completed. For essays that explain lengthy processes, the steps may be grouped into categories or divided into substeps to make the process easier to understand. Headings and transitional expressions and sentences are also often used to make the order of steps and substeps clear.

In "How to Use Online Dating Sites," Grabianowksi divides the process into two main steps ("Creating a Profile" and "Making Contact") and then each step into several substeps. To make his overall organization clear, he uses headings for these steps as well as for sections of background information ("Getting Started") and more specific advice about one of the main steps ("Creating a GOOD Profile"). To indicate his movement from one step or substep to the next, he also uses transitions such as *Next, Last, The first thing you need to do,* and *Once it comes time to plan the actual date.*

On occasion, the steps of a process may not have to occur in any particular order. For example, in an essay on how to resolve a dispute between two coworkers, the order of the recommended actions may depend on the nature of the dispute. In this situation, some logical progression of recommended actions should be used, such as starting with informal or simple steps and progressing to more formal or complex ones.

Exercise 13.1

Choose one of the following processes. It should be one you are familiar with and able to explain to others. Draft a working thesis statement and a chronological list of the steps or stages of the process.

1. How to use a computer program
2. How to study for an exam
3. How to perform a task at work
4. How to operate a machine
5. How to complete an application (such as for college, a job, or a credit card)

Process Analysis Provides Background Information Helpful to Readers

In some process analysis essays, readers may need background information to understand the process. For example, in an explanation of how CPR (cardiopulmonary resuscitation) works, general readers might need information on how the heart functions to understand how pressing down on a person's breastbone propels blood into the arteries.

In some cases your audience may not be familiar with the technical terms associated with the process you are describing. If so, be sure to define such terms. In describing how CPR works, you would need to explain the meanings of such terms as *airway, sternum,* and *cardiac compression.*

For more on defining terms, see Chapter 16, p. 415.

When special equipment is needed to perform the process, you should describe the equipment for readers. For example, in an essay explaining how to scuba dive to unfamiliar readers, you would need to describe equipment such as dive masks, buoyancy compensators, and dive gauges. If necessary, you should also explain where to obtain the equipment.

Exercise 13.2

Choose one of the following processes that you are familiar with and are able to explain to others. For the process you choose, list the technical terms and definitions that you need to use to explain the process.

1. How to perform a task at home or at work (such as changing the oil in a car or taking notes during a court hearing)
2. How a piece of equipment or a machine works (such as a treadmill or a lawn mower)
3. How to repair an object (such as restringing a tennis racket or a violin)

Exercise 13.3

For the process you selected in Exercise 13.2 (above), consider what background information and equipment are needed to understand and perform the process.

Process Analysis Provides an Appropriate Level of Detail

In deciding what to include in a process analysis essay, you should be careful not to overwhelm your readers with too many details. An explanation of how to perform CPR written by and for physicians could be highly technical, but it should be much less so if written for a friend who is considering whether to enroll in a CPR course. In "How to use Online Dating Sites," although Grabianowski is not writing about a technical topic, he is careful to provide details about how to build a good profile because he assumes that his audience is unfamiliar with how to do so.

Keep in mind that when you write essays explaining technical or scientific processes, you can use sensory details and figures of speech to make your writing lively and interesting. Rather than giving dry technical details, try using descriptive language.

For a process involving many complex steps or highly specialized equipment, consider using a drawing or diagram to help your readers visualize the steps they need to follow or understand. For example, in an essay explaining how to detect a wiring problem in an electric stove, you might include a diagram of the stove's circuitry.

Process Analysis Anticipates Trouble Spots and Offers Solutions

Especially in a how-to essay, you need to anticipate potential trouble spots or areas of confusion and offer advice to the reader on how to avoid or resolve them. In "How to Use Online Dating Sites," Grabianowski cautions readers about posting personal identification information in their profiles. A how-to essay should also warn readers of any difficult, complicated, or critical steps, encouraging them to pay special attention to a difficult step or to take extra care in performing a critical one. For instance, in a how-to essay on hanging wallpaper, you would warn readers about the difficulties of handling sheets of wallpaper and suggest folding the sheets to make them easier to work with.

Exercise 13.4

For one of the processes listed in Exercise 13.1 or Exercise 13.2, identify potential trouble spots in the process and describe how to avoid or resolve them.

Visualizing a Process Analysis Essay: A Graphic Organizer

The graphic organizer in Figure 13.1 shows the basic organization of a process analysis essay. When your main purpose is to explain a process, you should follow this standard format, including a title, an introduction, body paragraphs, and a conclusion. Your introduction should include any necessary background information and present your thesis statement. Your body paragraphs should explain the steps of the process in chronological order. Your conclusion should draw the essay to a satisfying close and refer to the thesis.

For more on graphic organizers, see Chapter 3, p. 55.

When you incorporate process analysis into an essay using one or more other patterns of development, briefly introduce the process and then move directly to the steps involved. If the process is complex, you may want to add a brief summary of it before the transition back to the main topic of the essay.

Read the following how-it-works essay, "How Internet Search Engines Work," and then study the graphic organizer for it in Figure 13.2 (on p. 315).

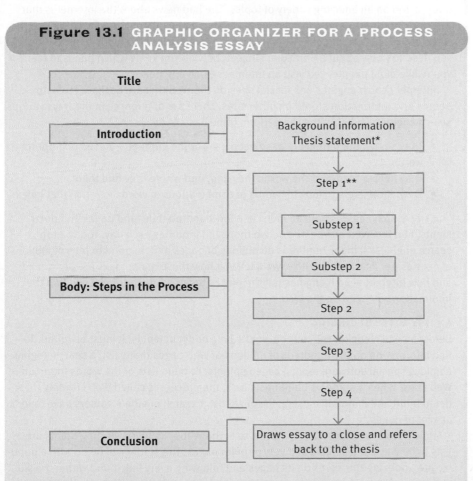

Figure 13.1 GRAPHIC ORGANIZER FOR A PROCESS ANALYSIS ESSAY

Title

Introduction — Background information / Thesis statement*

Step 1**
Substep 1
Substep 2
Step 2
Step 3
Step 4

Body: Steps in the Process

Conclusion — Draws essay to a close and refers back to the thesis

*In some essays, the thesis statement may be implied or may appear in a different position.
**In some essays, substeps may be included.

How Internet Search Engines Work
Curt Franklin

Curt Franklin has been writing about technologies and products in computing and networking since the early 1980s. His career has included senior and executive editorial positions
at *Byte*, ITWorld.com, and *Secure Enterprise*, and his articles have appeared in such publications as *Computerworld*, *InfoWorld*, and *Network World*. He has also produced, created,
or edited hundreds of podcasts and is the co-author, with George Colombo, of *The Absolute
Beginner's Guide to Podcasting* (2005). The following essay was written for Howstuffworks
.com. As you read, notice how Franklin explains potentially unfamiliar terms to help readers
understand the process he describes.

The good news about the Internet and its most visible component, the World Wide   1
Web, is that there are hundreds of millions of pages available, waiting to present
information on an amazing variety of topics. The bad news about the Internet is that
there are hundreds of millions of pages available, most of them titled according to the
whim of their author, almost all of them sitting on servers with cryptic names. When
you need to know about a particular subject, how do you know which pages to read? If
you're like most people, you visit an Internet search engine.

Internet search engines are special sites on the Web that are designed to help   2
people find information stored on other sites. There are differences in the ways various
search engines work, but they all perform three basic tasks:

- They search the Internet — or select pieces of the Internet — based on important
  words.
- They keep an index of the words they find, and where they find them.
- They allow users to look for words or combinations of words found in that index.

Early search engines held an index of a few hundred thousand pages and docu-   3
ments, and received maybe one or two thousand inquiries each day. Today a top
search engine will index hundreds of millions of pages and respond to tens of millions
of queries per day. In this article, we'll tell you how these major tasks are performed
and how Internet search engines put the pieces together in order to let you find the
information you need on the Web.

AN ITSY-BITSY BEGINNING

Before a search engine can tell you where a file or document is, it must be found. To   4
find information on the hundreds of millions of Web pages that exist, a search engine
employs special software robots, called spiders, to build lists of the words found on
Web sites. When a spider is building its lists, the process is called Web crawling. In order to build and maintain a useful list of words, a search engine's spiders have to look
at a lot of pages.

How does any spider start its travels over the Web? The usual starting points are   5
lists of heavily used servers and very popular pages. The spider will begin with a popular site, indexing the words on its pages and following every link found within the site.
In this way, the spidering system quickly begins to travel, spreading out across the
most widely used portions of the Web.

Google.com began as an academic search engine. In the paper that describes how   6
the system was built, Sergey Brin and Lawrence Page give an example of how quickly
their spiders can work. They built their initial system to use multiple spiders, usually
three at one time. Each spider could keep about 300 connections to Web pages open
at a time. At its peak performance, using four spiders, their system could crawl over
100 pages per second, generating around 600 kilobytes of data each second.

Keeping everything running quickly meant building a system to feed necessary in-   7
formation to the spiders. The early Google system had a server dedicated to providing
URLs to the spiders. Rather than depending on an Internet service provider for the do-
main name server (DNS) that translates a server's name into an address, Google had
its own DNS, in order to keep delays to a minimum.

When the Google spider looked at an HTML page, it took note of two things: 8

- The words within the page
- Where the words were found

Words occurring in the title, subtitles, meta tags and other positions of relative   9
importance were noted for special consideration during a subsequent user search.
The Google spider was built to index every significant word on a page, leaving out the
articles "a," "an," and "the." Other spiders take different approaches. These different
approaches usually attempt to make the spider operate faster, allow users to search
more efficiently, or both. For example, some spiders will keep track of the words in
the title, subheadings, and links, along with the hundred most frequently used words
on the page and each word in the first twenty lines of text. Lycos is said to use this
approach to spidering the Web. Other systems, such as AltaVista, go in the other direction, indexing every single word on a page, including "a," "an," "the," and other
"insignificant" words. The push to completeness in this approach is matched by other
systems in the attention given to the unseen portion of the Web page, the meta tags.

META TAGS

Meta tags allow the owner of a page to specify keywords and concepts under which the   10
page will be indexed. This can be helpful, especially in cases in which the words on the
page might have double or triple meanings — the meta tags can guide the search engine
in choosing which of the several possible meanings for these words is correct. There is,
however, a danger in overreliance on meta tags, because a careless or unscrupulous
page owner might add meta tags that fit very popular topics but have nothing to do with
the actual contents of the page. To protect against this, spiders will correlate meta tags
with page content, rejecting the meta tags that don't match the words on the page.

All of this assumes that the owner of a page actually wants it to be included in the   11
results of a search engine's activities. Many times the page's owner doesn't want it
showing up on a major search engine, or doesn't want the activity of a spider access-
ing the page. Consider, for example, a game that builds new, active pages each time
sections of the page are displayed or new links are followed. If a Web spider accesses
one of these pages and begins following all of the links for new pages, the game could
mistake the activity for a high-speed human player and spin out of control. To avoid
situations like this, the robot exclusion protocol was developed. This protocol, implemented in the meta-tag section at the beginning of a Web page, tells a spider to leave
the page alone — to neither index the words on the page nor try to follow its links.

BUILDING THE INDEX

Once the spiders have completed the task of finding information on Web pages (and   12
we should note that this is a task that is never actually completed—the constantly
changing nature of the Web means that the spiders are always crawling), the search
engine must store the information in a way that makes it useful. There are two key components involved in making the gathered data accessible to users:

- The information stored with the data
- The method by which the information is indexed

In the simplest case, a search engine could just store the word and the URL where it   13
was found. In reality, this would make for an engine of limited use, since there would
be no way of telling whether the word was used in an important or a trivial way on the
page, whether the word was used once or many times, or whether the page contained
links to other pages containing the word. In other words, there would be no way of
building the ranking list that tries to present the most useful pages at the top of the list
of search results.

To make for more useful results, most search engines store more than just the word   14
and URL. An engine might store the number of times that the word appears on a page.
The engine might assign a weight to each entry, with increasing values assigned to
words as they appear near the top of the document, in subheadings, in links, in the
meta tags, or in the title of the page. Each commercial search engine has a different
formula for assigning weight to the words in its index. This is one of the reasons that a
search for the same word on different search engines will produce different lists, with
the pages presented in different orders.

Regardless of the precise combination of additional pieces of information stored   15
by a search engine, the data will be encoded to save storage space. For example, the
original Google paper describes using 2 bytes, of 8 bits each, to store information on
weighting—whether the word was capitalized, its font size, position, and other information to help in ranking the hit. Each factor might take up 2 or 3 bits within the 2-byte
grouping (8 bits = 1 byte). As a result, a great deal of information can be stored in a
very compact form. After the information is compacted, it's ready for indexing.

An index has a single purpose: It allows information to be found as quickly as pos-   16
sible. There are quite a few ways for an index to be built, but one of the most effective
ways is to build a hash table. In hashing, a formula is applied to attach a numerical value
to each word. The formula is designed to evenly distribute the entries across a predeter-
mined number of divisions. This numerical distribution is different from the distribution
of words across the alphabet, and that is the key to a hash table's effectiveness.

In English, there are some letters that begin many words, while others begin fewer.   17
You'll find, for example, that the "M" section of the dictionary is much thicker than the
"X" section. This inequity means that finding a word beginning with a very "popular"
letter could take much longer than finding a word that begins with a less popular one.
Hashing evens out the difference, and reduces the average time it takes to find an
entry. It also separates the index from the actual entry. The hash table contains the
hashed number along with a pointer to the actual data, which can be sorted in whichever way allows it to be stored most efficiently. The combination of efficient indexing
and effective storage makes it possible to get results quickly, even when the user creates a complicated search.

Figure 13.2 GRAPHIC ORGANIZER FOR "HOW INTERNET SEARCH ENGINES WORK"

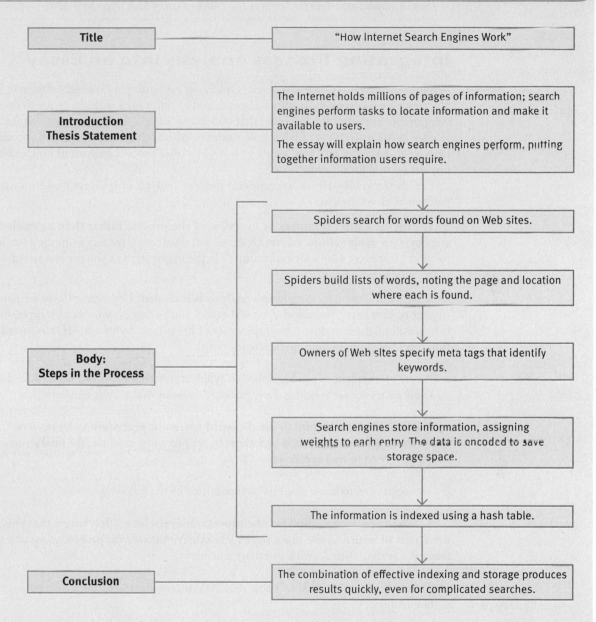

| Title | "How Internet Search Engines Work" |

Introduction Thesis Statement
- The Internet holds millions of pages of information; search engines perform tasks to locate information and make it available to users.
- The essay will explain how search engines perform, putting together information users require.

Body: Steps in the Process
- Spiders search for words found on Web sites.
- Spiders build lists of words, noting the page and location where each is found.
- Owners of Web sites specify meta tags that identify keywords.
- Search engines store information, assigning weights to each entry. The data is encoded to save storage space.
- The information is indexed using a hash table.

Conclusion
- The combination of effective indexing and storage produces results quickly, even for complicated searches.

To draw detailed graphic organizers using a computer, visit www.bedfordstmartins .com/successfulwriting.

Exercise 13.5

Draw a graphic organizer for "How to Use Online Dating Sites" (pp. 305–308).

Integrating Process Analysis into an Essay

While some essays you write will focus solely on explaining a process, others will incorporate a process analysis into a discussion that relies on a different pattern of development. Suppose, for instance, that you are writing a descriptive essay about an alcohol abuse program for high school students. Although description is your primary pattern of development, you decide to include a brief process analysis of how alcohol impairs mental funtioning.

Use the following tips to incorporate process analysis into essays based on other patterns of development.

1. Provide a brief summary or overview of the process rather than a detailed step-by-step explanation. Too much detail will divert your readers from the primary focus of your essay. Consider explaining only the major steps in the process rather than every step in detail.

2. Make it clear *why* the process analysis is included. Use a transitional sentence to alert readers that a process analysis will follow and to suggest why. For example, here is how you might introduce a brief summary of the process by which AIDS is spread through HIV (human immunodeficiency virus).

> Before you explain to teenagers *how* to avoid contracting HIV, you need to let them know *what* they are avoiding. Teenagers need to know that HIV is transmitted by . . .

3. It is sometimes helpful to use the word *process* or *procedure* to let readers know that a process analysis is to follow. In the preceding example, the final sentence might be revised to read as follows.

> Teenagers need to know that HIV is transmitted by the following process.

4. When you have completed the process analysis, let readers know that you are about to return to the main topic. You might conclude the process analysis of the way HIV is transmitted with a summary statement.

> Above all, teenagers need to know that HIV is transmitted through an exchange of bodily fluids.

In "Panacea" on page 333, Dorothy Allison uses process analysis along with other patterns of development to explain a memorable experience of cooking.

A GUIDED WRITING ASSIGNMENT

The following guide will help you write a process analysis essay. It may be either a how-to or a how-it-works essay. Although you will focus on process analysis, you may need to integrate one or more other patterns of development in your essay.

The Assignment

Write a process analysis essay on one of the following topics or one of your own choosing. Be sure the process you choose is one that you know enough about to explain to others or can learn about through observation or research. Your audience consists of readers who are unfamiliar with the process, including your classmates.

How-To Essay Topics

1. How to improve _____ (your study habits, your wardrobe, your batting average)
2. How to be a successful _____ (diver, parent, gardener)
3. How to make or buy _____ (an object for personal use or enjoyment)
4. How to prepare for _____ (a test, a job interview, an oral presentation)

How-It-Works Essay Topics

1. How your college _____ (spends tuition revenues, hires professors, raises money)
2. How _____ works (an answering machine, a generator, email, a cell phone)
3. How a decision is made to _____ (accept a student at a college, add or eliminate a local or state agency)
4. How _____ is put together (a quilt, a news broadcast, a football team, a Web site)

As you develop your process analysis essay, you will probably use narrative strategies, description (for example, to describe equipment or objects), or illustration (such as to show an example of part of the process).

For more on narration, description, and illustration, see Chapters 10–12.

Selecting a Process

The following guidelines will help you select a process to write about. You may want to use one of the prewriting techniques discussed in Chapter 14. Consider your learning style when you select a prewriting technique. You might try questioning, group brainstorming, or sketching a diagram of a process. Be sure to keep the following tips in mind.

- For a how-to essay, choose a process that you can visualize or perform as you write. Keep the equipment nearby for easy reference. In explaining how to scuba dive, for example, it may be helpful to have your scuba equipment in front of you.

- For a how-it-works essay, choose a topic about which you have background knowledge or for which you can find information. Unless you are experienced in woodworking, for example, do not try to explain how stains produce different effects on different kinds of wood.
- Choose a topic that is useful and interesting to your readers. Unless you can find a way to make an essay about how to do laundry interesting, do not write about it.

> **Essay in Progress 1**
> Using the preceding suggestions, choose a process to write about from the list of essay topics on page 317, or choose a topic of your own.

Considering Your Purpose, Audience, and Point of View

Your main aim in process analysis is to inform readers, but you may also want to persuade them that they should try the process (how-to) or that it is beneficial or should be changed (how-it-works). As you develop your essay, keep the following questions about your audience in mind.

For more on purpose, audience, and point of view, see Chapter 4, p. 82.

1. What background information does my audience need or want?
2. What terms should I define?
3. What equipment should I describe?
4. How much detail does my audience need or want?
5. What trouble spots require special attention and explanation?

Writers of how-to essays commonly use the second-person point of view, addressing the reader directly as *you*. The second person is informal and draws the reader in, as in "How to Use Online Dating Sites." For how-it-works essays, the third person (*he, she, it*) is commonly used, as in "How Internet Search Engines Work."

> **Essay in Progress 2**
> For the process you selected in Essay in Progress 1, use the preceding guidelines to consider your purpose, the needs of your audience, and your point of view.

Developing Your Thesis

For more on thesis statements, see Chapter 5.

The thesis of a process analysis essay tells readers *why* the process is important, beneficial, or relevant to them (see p. 308). Considering your audience is especially important in developing a thesis for a process analysis, since what may be of interest or importance to one audience may be of little interest to another audience.

> **Essay in Progress 3**
> Write a working thesis statement that tells readers why the process you have chosen for your essay is important, beneficial, or relevant to them.

Gathering Details

To gather appropriate and interesting details, you may need to do additional prewriting to generate details that will help you explain the process. Use the following suggestions.

1. List the steps in the process as they occur to you, keeping these questions in mind.

   - What separate actions are involved?
   - What steps are obvious to me but may not be obvious to someone unfamiliar with the process?
   - What steps, if omitted, will lead to problems or failure?

2. Discuss your process with classmates to see what kinds of details they need to know about your topic.

3. Once you have a list of steps, generate details through additional prewriting or by doing research in the library or on the Internet. You might include sensory details about the process. (Check the five questions on page 318 to make sure you have included sufficient detail.)

For more on prewriting strategies, see Chapter 4.

For more on library and Internet research, see Chapter 21.

Essay in Progress 4
Using the preceding guidelines, brainstorm a list of the steps involved in the process. Then add details that will help you explain the steps. If necessary, interview someone knowledgeable about the process, or do library or Internet research to gather more details.

Evaluating Your Ideas and Thesis

Is the process you have chosen meaningful and relevant to your audience? Start by re-reading everything you have written with a critical eye. Highlight usable details; cross out any that seem unnecessary or repetitious. As you review your work, add steps, details, definitions, and background information where they are needed.

Trying Out Your Ideas on Others

Working in a group of two or three students, discuss your ideas and thesis for this chapter's assignment. Each writer should state his or her topic and thesis and describe the steps in the process. Then, as a group, evaluate each writer's work. Group members should answer the following questions.

1. How familiar are you with the process the writer has chosen?

2. Is the writer's explanation of the process detailed and complete?

3. What additional information do you need to understand or perform the process?

4. What unanswered questions do you have about the process?

Essay in Progress 5
Using the preceding suggestions and the feedback you have received from classmates, evaluate your thesis and your steps and decide whether you need to add details.

Organizing and Drafting

For more on drafting an essay, see Chapter 6.

Once you have gathered enough details to explain the steps in the process, developed your thesis statement, and considered the advice of peer reviewers, you are ready to organize your ideas and draft your essay.

Organizing the Steps in the Process

For a process that involves fewer than ten steps, you can usually arrange the steps chronologically, devoting one paragraph to each step. However, for a more complex process, group the steps into three or four categories (or divide the process into three or four main steps and each step into substeps) to avoid overwhelming your reader.

Try experimenting with different orders and groupings. For an essay on how to run a garage sale, the steps might be grouped in the following way.

Group 1: Locating and collecting merchandise
Group 2: Advertising
Group 3: Pricing and setting up
Group 4: Conducting the sale

You may want to devote one paragraph to each group of steps. A topic sentence introduces the group, and the rest of the paragraph explains the individual steps involved.

> **Essay in Progress 6**
>
> Review the list of steps you generated in Essay in Progress 5. If your process involves ten or more steps, use the preceding guidelines to group the steps into related categories. Write an outline or draw a graphic organizer to ensure that your steps are in chronological order.

Drafting the Process Analysis Essay

Use the following guidelines to draft your essay.

1. Include reasons for the steps. Unless the reason is obvious, explain why each step or group of steps is important and necessary. For instance, if you mention that robberies often occur during garage sales, then readers will be more likely to take the precautions you suggest, such as locking the house and wearing a waist-wallet.

2. Consider using graphics and headings. A drawing or diagram is sometimes necessary to make your steps easier to understand. (Remember, however, that a graphic is not a substitute for a clearly written explanation.) When using a graphic, be sure to introduce it in your essay and refer to it by its title. If you are including more than one graphic, assign a number to each one (*Figure 1*, *Figure 2*) and include the number in your text reference.

When writing about a lengthy or complicated process, consider adding headings to divide the body of your essay. Headings also call attention to your main topics and signal changes in topic.

For more on transitions, see Chapter 6, p. 124.

3. Use transitions. To make the process easier to follow and avoid making your analysis sound monotonous, use transitions such as *before, removing the lid, next*, and *finally.*

4. Write an effective introduction. The introduction usually presents your thesis statement and includes necessary background information. It should also capture your readers' attention and interest. For a lengthy or complex process, consider including an overview of the steps or a brief list of them.

For more on writing effective paragraphs, including introductions and conclusions, see Chapter 6.

5. Use a tone appropriate to your audience and purpose. By the time your readers move from your introduction to the body of your essay, they should have a good idea of your tone. In some situations, a matter-of-fact tone is appropriate; other times, an emotional or humorous tone may be suitable.

For more on tone, see Chapter 9, p. 189

6. Write a satisfying conclusion. Especially in a how-it-works essay, simply ending with the final step in the process may sound incomplete to your readers. In your conclusion, you might emphasize the value or importance of the process, describe particular situations in which it is useful, or offer a final amusing or emphatic comment or anecdote.

> **Essay in Progress 7**
> Draft your process essay, using the organization you developed in Essay in Progress 6 and the preceding guidelines for drafting.

Analyzing and Revising

If possible, wait at least a day before rereading and revising your draft. As you reread, concentrate on organization and ideas, not on grammar or punctuation. Use one or more of the following suggestions to analyze your draft.

For more on the benefits of peer review, see Chapter 8, p. 162.

1. Read your essay aloud to one or two friends or classmates. Ask them to interrupt you if they have questions or if a step is unclear.

Learning Style Options

2. For a how-to essay, try visualizing the steps or following them exactly. Be careful to complete only the ones actually included in your essay. Following your directions to the letter will help you discover gaps and identify sections that are unclear.
3. Update the graphic organizer or outline you prepared earlier. Look to see if the steps are sequenced correctly and if each step is covered in enough detail.

Use Figure 13.3 to guide your analysis. You might also ask a classmate to review your draft essay using the questions in the flowchart.

> **Essay in Progress 8**
> Revise your draft using Figure 13.3 and any comments you received from peer reviewers.

For more on keeping an error log, see Chapter 9, p. 196.

Editing and Proofreading

The last step is to check your revised essay for errors in grammar, spelling, punctuation, and mechanics. As you edit and proofread your process analysis essay, watch out for two grammatical errors in particular — comma splices and shifts in verb mood.

1. Avoid comma splices. A comma splice occurs when two independent clauses are joined only by a comma. To correct a comma splice, add a coordinating conjunction

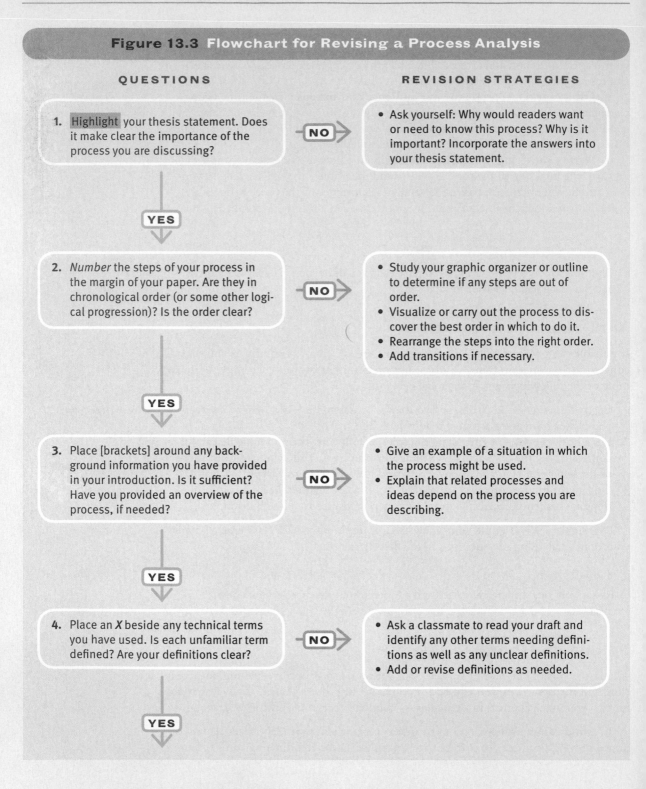

Figure 13.3 Flowchart for Revising a Process Analysis

QUESTIONS

REVISION STRATEGIES

1. Highlight your thesis statement. Does it make clear the importance of the process you are discussing?

—NO→

- Ask yourself: Why would readers want or need to know this process? Why is it important? Incorporate the answers into your thesis statement.

YES

2. *Number* the steps of your process in the margin of your paper. Are they in chronological order (or some other logical progression)? Is the order clear?

—NO→

- Study your graphic organizer or outline to determine if any steps are out of order.
- Visualize or carry out the process to discover the best order in which to do it.
- Rearrange the steps into the right order.
- Add transitions if necessary.

YES

3. Place [brackets] around any background information you have provided in your introduction. Is it sufficient? Have you provided an overview of the process, if needed?

—NO→

- Give an example of a situation in which the process might be used.
- Explain that related processes and ideas depend on the process you are describing.

YES

4. Place an *X* beside any technical terms you have used. Is each unfamiliar term defined? Are your definitions clear?

—NO→

- Ask a classmate to read your draft and identify any other terms needing definitions as well as any unclear definitions.
- Add or revise definitions as needed.

YES

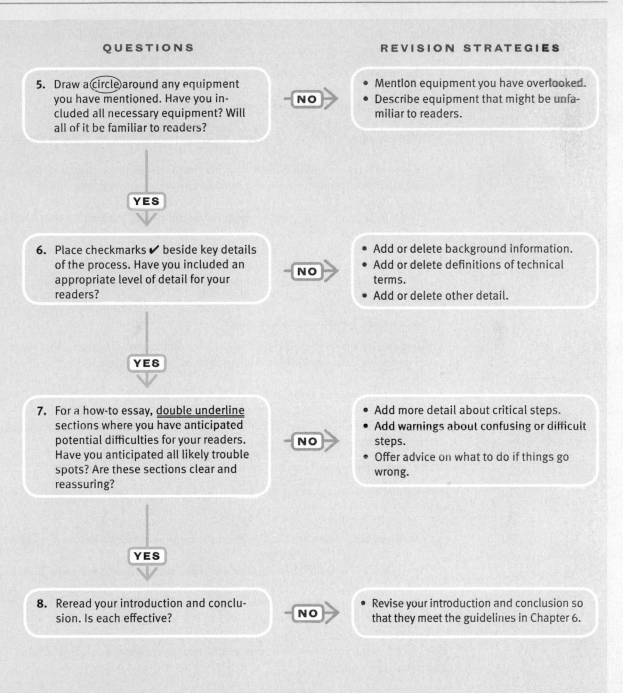

QUESTIONS		REVISION STRATEGIES
5. Draw a circle around any equipment you have mentioned. Have you included all necessary equipment? Will all of it be familiar to readers?	NO →	• Mention equipment you have overlooked. • Describe equipment that might be unfamiliar to readers.
↓ YES		
6. Place checkmarks ✔ beside key details of the process. Have you included an appropriate level of detail for your readers?	NO →	• Add or delete background information. • Add or delete definitions of technical terms. • Add or delete other detail.
↓ YES		
7. For a how-to essay, double underline sections where you have anticipated potential difficulties for your readers. Have you anticipated all likely trouble spots? Are these sections clear and reassuring?	NO →	• Add more detail about critical steps. • Add warnings about confusing or difficult steps. • Offer advice on what to do if things go wrong.
↓ YES		
8. Reread your introduction and conclusion. Is each effective?	NO →	• Revise your introduction and conclusion so that they meet the guidelines in Chapter 6.

(*and*, *but*, *for*, *nor*, *or*, *so*, or *yet*), change the comma to a semicolon, divide the sentence into two sentences, or subordinate one clause to the other.

- The first step in creating a flower arrangement is to choose an attractive

  container, the container should not be the focal point of the arrangement.

  [inserted: but]

- Following signs is one way to navigate a busy airport, looking for a map is another.

  [inserted: ;]

- To lower fat consumption in your diet, first learn to read food product labels, next eliminate those products that contain trans fats or unsaturated fats.

  [inserted: . Next]

- Place the pill on the cat's tongue, hold its mouth closed, rubbing its chin until it swallows the pill.

  [inserted: After you have placed]

2. Avoid shifts in verb mood. A verb can have three *moods* — indicative, imperative, and subjunctive. The **indicative mood** is used to express ordinary statements and to ask questions.

- The modem is built into the computer.

The **imperative mood** is used for giving orders, advice, and directions. The subject of a verb in the imperative mood is understood to be *you,* but it is not expressed.

- (You) Plant your feet firmly before swinging the club.

The **subjunctive mood** is used for making statements contrary to fact or for wishes and recommendations.

- I suggest that a new phone line be installed.

When writing a process analysis, be sure to use a consistent mood throughout your essay.

- The firefighters told the third-grade class the procedures to follow if a fire occurred in their school. They emphasized that children should leave the building quickly. Also, move at least 100 feet away from the building.

  [inserted: they should]

Essay in Progress 9

Edit and proofread your essay, paying particular attention to avoiding comma splices and shifts in verb mood.

Students Write

Eric Michalski wrote the following essay in response to an assignment that asked him to explain a process that he had mastered. As you read the essay, consider if the steps described in the essay clearly explain the process of making chili.

Feed Your Friends . . . and Their Friends . . . and Their Friends: Chili for Fifty

Eric Michalski

Cooking up chili for a large crowd is only a tad more difficult than whipping up a fractionally smaller batch. It's quite useful being the person who can feed a full hotel floor/campsite/election office/family reunion on a trip to the grocery store and a few hours' time. If this recipe is followed accurately, it'll result in a deeply flavorful mud-brown sludge that tastes much better than it looks.

When you're feeding a crowd, though, things do get complicated. The key is following a strict sequence. It's like learning a dance--you've got to follow the steps until you know it well enough to freestyle. All ingredients require some type of processing, which has to be done at a specific time to build the right flavor and texture while preserving the integrity of the individual components. Order is important, even though "precision" and "chili" don't share too many sentences.

To start off, you'll need a huge pot with a lid. Mine's a 32-quart monstrosity you could boil a cow's head in. (Don't ask how I know.) Cooking the chili in several smaller pots results in different kinds of chili--great, but not what we're looking for here. Beg, borrow, or rent a good large pot and lid for this one. Also essential are a knife, a cutting board, a cool drink (never cook without refreshment), and something for stirring the chili. A wooden spoon works great, as does a silicone spatula. Just don't use anything that'll melt in bubbling chili. A slotted spoon is stupid because you need to be able to taste; a regular spoon will get you a hand burn before you get a taste. If you plan on moving the chili pot, which you shouldn't, potholders are useful.

This recipe can be done on a hot plate if you have a gigantic one and a separate burner for sautéing, but I tested it on a four-burner gas stove. A slow cooker would work in a pinch, but as noted below, certain ingredients need to be browned in a pan separate from the main pot. You could even do it on a propane burner if you used a wok for the protein first.

Once you've assembled your tools, cover the bottom of your pot with extra virgin olive oil and put it on medium heat. Leave it uncovered while chopping four large white or yellow onions, one head of elephant garlic and two heads (*not cloves*) of regular garlic. By the time you're done with the alliums, your oil is ready for you. Toss in the onions and garlic, spread until more or less even, and then cover.

1

2

3

4

5

Title: Michalski identifies the process to be explained.

Introduction: Michalski explains the value of learning to make chili. His thesis statement reveals his attitude toward the topic.

As he often does throughout the essay, Michalski uses a transition to keep readers on track and a topic sentence to preview a paragraph's content. Here he also uses a figure of speech to warn that following the steps in order is crucial.

In paragraphs 3 and 4, Michalski describes the equipment necessary to carry out the process. He also warns *against* using certain equipment or moving the pot, and suggests alternatives for stirring and heating. Notice that throughout the rest of the essay, each paragraph is devoted to one step or to some other particular aspect of the process.

Another transitional phrase leads into the actual process. Michalski explains how two steps (heating oil and chopping onions and garlic) can be done simultaneously and clarifies to avoid misunderstanding.

A transitional sentence introduces the next step: cooking the sausage. Michalski uses sensory details and adds two cautionary notes at the end.

Time for the protein! Sausage is first, three pounds of whatever kind you like.   6
Kielbasa is great, maple breakfast sausage not so great, and Italian sausage entirely feasible. Cut the sausage into pieces of roughly equal size--dice size, like all the other protein in this recipe. Sauté the sausage in a separate pan until brown, then spread in a single layer on paper towels to drain. When cooked properly, the sausage will be brown and crisp on the outside and intensely sausagey on the inside. Unlike the chuck to be added next, this meat needs to be fully cooked before it goes in the chili pot. (But don't add any of the meat yet.)

Michalski offers detailed information about the next step (preparing and cooking the cubed chuck) and anticipates the one after that (cooking the ground beef).

Once the sausage is working and there's a little more oil in the pan, it's time to tend to   7
the other protein. Cut up three pounds of cubed chuck and trim the fat and gristle before coating in a 50–50 mix of fine yellow cornmeal and white flour and browning in the skillet. Open your pound and a half of ground beef (or one of the alternatives mentioned below) and thaw if necessary while your chuck is getting tasty. You want it cooked about halfway--brown inside but pink inside is fine. (This chili will cook for long enough to finish it.)

Michalski offers his readers alternatives for one of the ingredients.

Sauté the ground beef with cinnamon and black pepper until uniformly brown, then let   8
sit on paper towels. (As a substitute for this part of the protein mix, bison would work fine, but I like a fattier meat because you can always drain fat, but dry meat tastes awful. Venison and even ostrich are a little lean, but can be counterbalanced with sausage or bacon. Ground turkey is fine, and shredded leftover turkey can be your reason for giving thanks when facing a fridgeful of leftovers.)

Another transition leads to the next step: adding the vegetables and spices.

While the meat drains, add your veggies and spices to the mothership: one large (40.5-   9
ounce) can dark kidney beans, one large can light kidney beans, one small (15-ounce) can mixed diced tomatoes and jalapeños, a pound of diced tomatoes (if fresh, drain them on paper towels after dicing), and a bottle of your favorite Mexican chili-garlic sauce. Let the mixture come to a boil before adding the meat. If you've followed the recipe properly to this point, you'll have a pile of disgusting soaked paper towels in your trash can. Did you really want that stuff in your chili? (Didn't think so.)

Michalski emphasizes the importance of the next-to-last step: simmering.

The best chilis become that way through their final simmer, which brings all the fla-   10
vors together. Simmer for at least two hours. Skip or skimp on the simmering, and you might as well have just thrown random flavors into a pot for no reason. In fact, the truly hard-core chili cooks eschew the use of "artificial" thickeners and do the job with simmering alone. Those cooking on a more realistic time line, such as anyone making this recipe for the second time, will appreciate the way cornmeal- and flour-coated beef lends thickening mojo.

For the final step in the process, Michalski shares his special trick to enhance flavor.

Long-cooked chili can also benefit from a special trick only usable with massive batches.   11
When your chili tastes more or less how you want it to, crank the heat up on your stove and slowly stir the top of the chili only. Keep it moving, and occasionally check the bottom with

your spoon. Once you've got a decent crust on the bottom, scrape it up into your chili--done with a large enough batch, this will add dense smokiness and dark nuance to your nontraditional bowla'red.

I hate jalapeños, but if you insist on the most overdone flavor since cheddar you can slice them and serve them on the side. When you're making chili that's going to feed this many people, chances are that some of them are turned off by high levels of spice. Tell your capsaicin-addicted friends to bring their own hot sauce. Those looking to make fiery chili need only don rubber gloves and eye protection, chop ten habaneros, and add them at the very end.

12   Michalski offers a solution to the problem of level of spice.

Unless you're feeding enough people to make a serious dent in the contents of the pot right away, storage can be difficult due to the sheer volume of food involved. Work out a deal with the housemate/roommates/parents to use a section of the freezer for about twelve hours. Then ladle the gloppy yumminess into zipper-lock plastic bags. Fill each of the bags halfway and flatten so they freeze as flat squares--this makes reheating very easy. Most important, make sure to freeze what's left *immediately* after you're stuffed. Chili left out for even minutes can disappear in even the most upstanding homes/dorms.

13   Michalski offers practical advice on storage.

Chili's a full meal in a bowl--warm, comforting, and filling; it's like a nutritious hug. I make chili because my parents taught me, from as early as I can remember, to feed the hungry, clothe the naked, and nurse the sick. My closet is not overflowing with clothing and I have no medical training, so I cook for my friends and girlfriend and bask in their glow.

14   Conclusion: Michalski reiterates the value of making chili, using a figure of speech.

Analyzing the Writer's Technique

1. How successful is the introduction at providing a reason for learning the process?
2. Evaluate the essay's level of detail. Do you think you could make chili using Michalski's instructions? If not, where is additional detail needed?
3. What other problems, if any, might a beginning cook encounter in following Michalski's instructions?
4. Does Michalski's conclusion bring the essay to a satisfying close? Why or why not?

Reacting to the Essay

1. Discuss other processes in which following the steps in order is especially important.
2. Michalski regards chili as comfort food. Do you agree? What other foods fall into the same category?
3. Michalski cooks chili as an expression of friendship. Write an essay explaining something you do or have done for friends (or a particular friend) to solidify your friendship. Describe the process.

READING A PROCESS ANALYSIS

The following section provides advice for reading a process analysis. Two model essays illustrate the characteristics of process analysis covered in this chapter and provide opportunities to examine, analyze, and react to the writer's ideas. The second essay uses process analysis along with other methods of development.

Working with Text: Reading Process Analysis Essays

Process analysis is a common method of explaining; it is often used in textbooks, including this one, and in other forms of academic writing. To read a process analysis effectively, use the following suggestions.

What to Look For, Highlight, and Annotate

1. Look for and highlight the thesis statement. Try to discover why the writer believes the process is important or useful.
2. For a how-to essay, look for difficulties you might experience in the process or questions you may need to ask about it.
3. Highlight or underline each step or grouping of steps. Using a different colored highlighter or an asterisk (*), mark steps that the author warns are difficult or troublesome.

For more on reading strategies, see Chapter 3.

4. For a complex or especially important process (such as one you need to write about on an essay exam), outline or draw a graphic organizer of the steps. Try explaining each step in your own words without referring to the text.
5. For a how-to essay, imagine yourself carrying out the process as you read.
6. Highlight or use a symbol to mark new terms as they are introduced.
7. Annotate the sections that summarize complex steps.

How to Find Ideas to Write About

For more on discovering ideas for a response paper, see Chapter 3.

Look for ideas to write about *as you read*. Record your ideas and impressions as marginal annotations. Think about why *you* want or need to understand the process. Think of situations in which you can use or apply the information. Also try to think of processes similar to the one described in the essay. If you think of metaphors or analogies, make a note of them. Consider how other processes are the same as and different from the one in the essay.

Thinking Critically about Process Analysis

Although most process analyses are straightforward and informative, you should still consider the author's motives for writing and knowledge of the topic. Use the following questions to think critically about the process analyses you read.

What Are the Writer's Motives?

As you read, ask yourself, Why does the writer want me to understand or carry out this process? What is his or her motive? At times, an author may have a hidden motive for explaining a process. For example, a writer opposed to the death penalty may use graphic details about the process of executions to shock readers and persuade them to oppose the death penalty. Even a how-to article on a noncontroversial topic can have a hidden agenda, such as one entitled "How to Lose Ten Pounds" that was written by the owner of a weight-loss clinic.

Is the Writer Knowledgeable and Experienced?

When you read process analyses, always consider whether the writer has sufficient knowledge about or experience with the process. This step is especially important if you intend to perform the task. Following the advice of someone who is not qualified to give it can be a waste of time or even dangerous. For most writers, it is possible to check credentials and determine whether the writer is considered an expert in the field. In addition to checking the writer's credentials, consider whether he or she supports assertions with outside sources, expert opinion, and quotes from authorities.

PROCESS ANALYSIS ESSAY

As you read the following essay, notice how the author uses the elements of process analysis discussed in this chapter.

Remote Control: How to Raise a Media Skeptic
Susan Douglas

READING

Susan Douglas has been a media critic for the *Progressive* and senior editor of *In These Times*, another progressive magazine. She is the author of *Where the Girls Are: Growing Up Female with the Mass Media* (1994), *Listening In: Radio and the American Imagination* (1999), and *The Mommy Myth: The Idealization of Motherhood and How It Undermines Women* (with Meredith Michaels, 2004). Douglas has also written for such publications as the *Village Voice*, *Ms.*, the *Washington Post*, and the *Journal of American History*, and has lectured at colleges and universities around the country. The following selection—a how-to essay—is from a 1997 issue of the *Utne Reader*, a periodical that publishes articles from specialized magazines known as alternative media. As you read the selection, highlight the steps that Douglas outlines, and consider the order in which she presents them.

"Mommy, Mommy, come here now! Hurry, you're gonna miss it. It's Barbie's High-Steppin' Pony, and its legs really move! Hurreeeeey!"   1

"No!" I bark, as I'm wiping the dog barf up from the carpet, stirring the onions   2
again so they don't burn, and slamming the phone down on a caller from Citibank who

wants to know how I'm doin' today. It is 5:56 p.m., and I'm in no mood. "I don't come for commercials, and besides, the horse doesn't really move — they just make it look that way."

"Oh yeah?" demands my daughter, sounding like a federal prosecutor. "It can too. It's not like those old ones where you told me they faked it — this one really does move."

So now I have to go see, and indeed, the sucker takes batteries, and the stupid horse moves — sort of. "See, Mommy, the commercials don't always lie."

Moments like this prompt me to wonder whether I'm a weak-kneed, lazy slug or, dare I say it, a hypocrite. See, I teach media studies, and, even worse, I go around the country lecturing about the importance of media literacy. One of my talking points is how network children's programming is, ideologically, a toxic waste dump. Yet here I am, just like millions of parents during that portion of the day rightly known as hell hour — dinnertime — shoving my kid in front of Nickelodeon so my husband and I can get dinner on the table while we whisper sweet nothings like "It's your turn to take her to Brownies tomorrow" and "Oh, I forgot to tell you that your mother called three days ago with an urgent message."

We let her watch Nickelodeon, but I still pop in to ridicule Kool-Aid commercials or to ask her why Clarissa's parents (on *Clarissa Explains It All*) are so dopey. I am trying to have it both ways: to let television distract her, which I desperately need, and to help her see through its lies and banalities. I am very good at rationalizing this approach, but I also think it isn't a bad compromise for overworked parents who believe Barbie is the anti-Christ* yet still need to wash out grotty lunch boxes and zap leftovers at the end of the day.

It's best to be honest up front: My house is not media proofed. I am not one of those virtuous, haloed parents who has banished the box from the home. I actually believe that there are interesting, fun shows for my daughter to watch on TV. (And I'm not about to give up *ER*.)

But I'm also convinced that knowing about television, and growing up with it, provides my daughter with a form of cultural literacy that she will need, that will tie her to her friends and her generation and help her understand her place in the world. So instead of killing my TV, I've tried to show my daughter basic nonsense-detecting techniques. Don't think your choices are either no TV or a zombified kid. Studies show that the simple act of intervening — of talking to your child about what's on television and why it's on there — is one of the most important factors in helping children understand and distance themselves from some of the box's more repugnant imagery.

I recommend the quick surgical strike, between throwing the laundry in and picking up the Legos. Watch a few commercials with them and point out that commercials lie about the toys they show, making them look much better than they are in real life. Count how many male and female characters there are in a particular show or commercial and talk about what we see boys doing and what we see girls doing. Why, you might ask, do we always see girls playing with makeup kits and boys playing with little Johnny Exocet missiles? Real-life dads change diapers, push strollers, and feed kids,

---

Anti-Christ: In the Christian religion, the evil person who will appear in the days before Christ returns to earth.

but you never see boys doing this with dolls on commercials. Ask where the Asian and African American kids are. Point out how most of the parents in shows geared to kids are much more stupid than real-life parents. (By the way, children report that TV shows encourage them to talk back to their folks.) Tell them that all those cereals advertised with cartoon characters and rap music (like Cocoa Puffs and Trix) will put giant black holes in their teeth that only a dentist with a drill the size of the space shuttle can fix.

One of the best words to use when you're watching TV with your kids is *stupid*, as in   10
"Aren't Barbie's feet — the way she's always forced to walk on her tiptoes — really stupid?" or "Isn't it stupid that Lassie is smarter than the mom on this show?" (My favorite Barbie exercise: Put your kitchen timer on for a minute and make your daughter walk around on her tiptoes just like Barbie; she'll get the point real fast.) *Cool* — a word that never seems to go out of style — is also helpful, as in "Isn't it cool that on *Legends of the Hidden Temple* (a game show on Nickelodeon) the girls are as strong and as fast as the boys?" Pointing out what's good on TV is important too.

See, I think complete media-proofing is impossible, because the shallow, consum-   11
erist, anti-intellectual values of the mass media permeate our culture. And we parents shouldn't beat ourselves up for failing to quarantine our kids. But we can inoculate them — which means exposing them to the virus and showing them how to build up a few antibodies. So don't feel so guilty about letting them watch TV. Instead, have fun teaching them how to talk back to it rather than to you.

Examining the Reading

1. What is the author's view of children's television programming and of commercial advertisements? What, in particular, does she dislike?
2. What techniques does Douglas use to teach her daughter to be critical of what she views on television?
3. What benefits does Douglas claim that her daughter receives from television?
4. Explain the meaning of each of the following words as it is used in the reading: *hypocrite* (para. 5), *ideologically* (5), *banalities* (6), *rationalizing* (6), and *permeate* (11). Refer to your dictionary as needed.

Analyzing the Writer's Technique

1. Identify Douglas's thesis statement. What background information does she provide to support the thesis?
2. Discuss how Douglas's use of exaggeration supports her purpose in writing this essay.
3. Where does Douglas anticipate trouble spots in the process and offer solutions? In what places, if any, would more advice have been helpful to you?
4. Where does Douglas provide adequate detail? Identify those sections as well as any places where you think more detail is needed.
5. Does Douglas appear to be knowledgeable about her subject? Support your answer with evidence.

Visualizing the Reading

Douglas uses examples to explain the steps in the process of raising children to be skeptical about television. List the steps in the process and an example for each. The first one has been done for you. Add additional boxes, as necessary.

Step	Example
Ridicule commercials	Kool-Aid
Do expose children to media	
Point out gender stereotypes	
Express value judgments to the kids	

Reacting to the Reading

1. Explain why you agree or disagree with the writer's critical views of the "shallow, consumerist, anti-intellectual values of the mass media" (para. 11).
2. Look for misleading images or stereotypes in the television programs you watch. Then write a journal entry describing one such image or stereotype.
3. Douglas states that television provides her daughter with a form of cultural literacy. Select another aspect of contemporary life, and write an essay explaining how it contributes to cultural literacy.

(MAKING ◯ CONNECTIONS)

Preparing and Sharing Food

Both "Feed Your Friends" (pp. 325–27) and "Panacea" (pp. 333–35) discuss preparing and sharing food.

Analyzing the Readings

1. Both essays are written to explain the preparation of specific foods. How do the writer's purposes differ?
2. Evaluate the level of detail provided by each author.
3. Write a journal entry explaining the ways in which the authors are similar or different in their attitude toward cooking and sharing food.

Essay Idea

Both authors are home cooks. What benefits does home food preparation offer? Write an essay considering the importance of preparing food for others and eating meals together. You might explore ways in which preparing and sharing food is a social or cultural experience, for example.

PROCESS ANALYSIS COMBINED WITH OTHER PATTERNS

As you read the following essay by Dorothy Allison, notice how she combines process analysis with other patterns of development.

Panacea
Dorothy Allison

Dorothy Allison is the author of the novel *Bastard Out of Carolina* (1992), which was a finalist for a National Book Award, won several prizes for gay and lesbian literature, and was made into an award-winning movie. She has also published the novel *Cavedweller* (1998) as well as several books of poetry and short stories. In 2007 she received the Robert Penn Warren Award for Fiction from the Fellowship of Southern Writers. Much of her writing has focused on poverty in the South—especially its effect on women. In this essay, published in the *New York Times* food section in 2007, Allison describes two times in her life when making gravy had an effect on her. As you read, notice how she incorporates the steps of gravy making into her recounting of these two separate occasions.

Gravy is the simplest, tastiest, most memory-laden dish I know how to make: a little   1
flour, salt and pepper, crispy bits of whatever meat anchored the meal, a couple of
cups of water or milk and slow stirring to break up lumps. That's it. It smells of home,
the door locked against the night and a stillness made safe by the sound of a spoon
going round in a pan. It is anticipation, the last thing prepared before the meal comes
to the table, the bowl in Mama's hand closing the day out peacefully, no matter what
came before.

My mother's gravy was a savory country gravy, heavy on the black pepper. Best of all   2
was steak — cube steak. People call it country-fried steak, but Mama always called it
cube steak. She began with odd, indented slabs of cheap meat carried home from the
diner where she was on her feet all day. My sisters and I would pound the "steak" while
she rested. The little round mouth of the Coke bottle thudded into the meat over and
over until each piece was not only dimpled but flattened out half again as wide as it had
been. By the time Mama stopped us, the steaks would be tenderized almost to pieces.
Then she would shoo us out of the way, make up the biscuits and sift some of the flour
onto a plate. Dredged in flour, the steaks went into a hot cast-iron skillet with a good
covering of bacon fat. So long as we set the table and were useful, we were allowed to
watch Mama cook the steaks and then set them aside on a brown paper bag. Then she
took the plate of leftover flour and sprinkled it in the pan, stirring it as it browned and
the pan filled with little brown flour pebbles and charred bits of meat. A lot of water and
a little milk made steam rise up in a sweet cloud. Mama worked the gravy with a fork
until all was smooth and silky. She might pour the gravy over the steaks or she might
serve it in a bowl. It was not until I was grown that I understood that gravy poured over
the meat before it came to the table meant there was not much meat.

In one tract house or another, first in South Carolina and then Florida, where   3
we moved when I was a teenager, Mama made magic with cheap meat, flour and

determination — hiding from us how desperate things might be. She did such a good job of it that we came to believe cube steak a luxury, better than the rare T-bone our uncles might bring around as a surprise.

My son, Wolf, was born when I was past 40 and the author of a best-selling novel. That means he has grown up a middle-class child — one who sometimes asks me for stories of my childhood but knows nothing of what it means to grow up poor and afraid. I have worked to make sure of that. His favorite foods are all dishes I never even knew existed until I was a voting adult: spinach soufflés, steamed mussels and sautéed brussels sprouts. He has almost never eaten an egg yolk and never took an interest in gravy, not even on Thanksgiving turkey.

"No, thank you," he said, very politely.

My feelings were hurt. How could my child not like my gravy? Maybe it was the giblets I chopped and added? Next time I made a smooth, pristine gravy with no bits of anything. Wolf didn't touch it. This time I sighed. I had to face the truth. My gravy was nowhere near as good as my mother's had been, and my son was not me. He had never gone to bed hungry and had no idea how important a locked door could be. I could not be unhappy about that.

Then there was the duck.

It was three years ago, and I wanted to do something special for the holidays to celebrate our aunt Mary moving up from Arizona. At the grocery, there was a big sale sign — ducks and geese at discount. A duck, a goose, a British Christmas dinner. I had read the novels. I had a brand-new roasting pan. So just because I could, I bought one of each — the goose for Christmas and the duck for New Year's.

Christmas was wonderful, but the goose was not a success. It came out pretty but dry. I stripped the leftovers for the dogs and worried. What was I going to do with that duck? I thought about giving up and making a ham. But my pride got in my way. I could cook. I was my mother's daughter.

It was clear to me that what was going to be necessary was a gravy — a good gravy. I read up on ducks and followed directions. I hung the bird over the sink in the warm kitchen and watched the fat drip off. After a while the bird looked greasy but lean. I shooed everyone out and went back to basics. There was no bacon fat in my fridge, but there was bacon. I wrapped the duck in bacon, threw an obscuring layer of aluminum foil over the top and put it in the roasting pan.

You could smell the bacon in the steam coming out the top of the oven, but maybe I was the only one who noticed. It was New Year's after all, with family and friends and lots of dishes. There were greens and black-eyed peas and sweet potatoes with marshmallows. There were pies and loud music — lots of things to distract everyone away from the oven.

When the duck was done, I set it on a platter and disappeared the bacon slices. Then I poured off almost all the grease and took a spoon after the blackened bits in the bottom of the pan. Maybe the duck would be dry as the goose had been. But the bits in the bottom of the pan looked like great cracklings. I scraped and dredged and turned on the heat, then sprinkled flour and pepper across the oily surface. It cooked into the familiar brown pebbles. I squeezed a bite between my fingers and tasted salty, rich flavor. Uh-huh. A cup of skim milk brought up steam through which I stirred steadily. Another cup went after the first, then a cup of water. I used a fork to squash the lumps and kept stirring. Every now and then I would taste the gravy again and then go searching in my cupboard. Yes, more black pepper and a little bottled magic from K-Paul's Louisiana

Kitchen. At the last minute I reached over and spooned in some of the creamy liquid off the black-eyed peas. It made me laugh — but the gravy smelled wonderful.

Soon there were offers to help carry in the dishes. My son was standing by me at the stove. He was staring at the gravy I was still stirring. He leaned forward over the pan. 13

"Mmm." 14

I looked at him. His big green eyes were wide and hungry. I used a wooden spoon. Blew on the gravy to cool it, then let him lick a taste. 15

"Oh, that's wonderful!" he said. 16

After that everyone was quick to the table. The duck was perfect, everyone said so. I felt as if I had passed some ancient rite or earned some essential vindication. There was no gravy left when the meal was done. 17

Every now and then, I make duck again. But more often, I do what I know. I roast a chicken or pan-fry a steak and make pan gravy to go with it. Sometimes my boy comes to watch me cook. I watch him. He is getting so tall, now four inches taller than I and growing fast, while the world looms ever larger and more uncertain. I try not to worry. I try to make him feel he is home and safe and will always be so, no matter what comes to the door. 18

ROAST DUCK

1 4-to-6-pound duck

½ cup peeled and halved baby onions

½ cup chopped carrots

2 tablespoons butter, cut into cubes

½ teaspoon dried savory, sage or thyme

Salt and pepper

6 thick slices bacon

¼ cup flour

¾ cup whole milk

1. Preheat the oven to 350 degrees. Remove the duck giblets. If you choose, chop and sauté the giblets and set them aside to toss into the gravy later.

2. Prick the duck's skin with a fork. Rinse and pat dry with paper towels. Twist the wing tips under the back and place the duck, breast side up, on a rack set in a roasting pan. Stuff onions, carrots and butter into the cavity. Sprinkle the duck all over with the dried herbs and ½ teaspoon each of salt and pepper. Lay bacon slices crosswise over the breast. Roast duck in the oven until the internal temperature reaches 180 degrees, 1½ to 2 hours.

3. Place duck on a serving platter and tent with foil. Remove vegetables from cavity. (Check to see if the vegetables are edible. If still raw, microwave until tender and feed to the dogs.)

4. Prepare the gravy by pouring off all but 3 tablespoons of the fat from the pan. Place the pan over medium heat. Using a wooden spoon, scrape up the burned bits stuck to the bottom and then sprinkle with the flour. Cook, stirring, to toast the flour, about 3 minutes. Add the milk and ½ cup water. Bring to a boil, then reduce the heat and simmer. If too thick, loosen with water. Season with salt and pepper to taste. *Serves 4 to 6.*

Examining the Reading

1. What is Allison's purpose?
2. Explain the differences between Allison's childhood and that of her son.
3. The essay seems to have an underlying message, beyond the instructions on how to prepare gravy and roast a duck. What is that message?
4. Explain the meaning of each of the following words as it is used in the reading: *anchored* (para. 1), *anticipation* (1), *dredged* (2), *determination* (3), and *looms* (18).

Analyzing the Writer's Technique

1. Identify Allison's thesis.
2. Allison uses process analysis to explain how to prepare gravy and roast a duck. What other patterns of development does she use in the essay? Choose one pattern and explain how Allison uses it to develop her thesis.
3. What method of organization does this essay follow? Give examples from the essay to support your answer.
4. Explain the meaning of the title.

Reacting to the Reading

1. Allison includes the recipe for roast duck in her essay. Discuss whether following a recipe is always essential for well-prepared food, and if not, under what circumstances.
2. Allison's pride was injured when her son rejected her turkey gravy and when she cooked a goose unsuccessfully. Write a journal entry discussing situations in which failure can affect one's attitude or future performance.
3. Allison tries to make her son feel safe at home, and the essay suggests that her home cooking is part of the comfort. Write an essay describing a process that makes you feel comfortable or secure in your family home.

Applying Your Skills: Additional Essay Assignments

For more on locating and documenting sources, see Part 5.

Write a process analysis essay on one of the following topics. Depending on the topic you choose, you may need to conduct library or Internet research.

To Express Your Ideas

1. How children manage their parents
2. How to relax and do nothing
3. How to find enough time for your children

To Inform Your Reader

4. How to avoid or speed up red-tape procedures
5. How a particular type of sports equipment protects an athlete
6. How to remain calm while giving a speech

To Persuade Your Reader

7. How important it is to vote in a presidential election
8. How important it is to select the right courses in order to graduate on time
9. How important it is to exercise every day

Cases Using Process Analysis

10. In your communication course, you are studying friendship development and the strategies that people use to meet others. Write an essay describing the strategies people use to meet new people and develop friendships.
11. You are employed by a toy manufacturer and have been asked to write a brochure that encourages children to use toys safely. Prepare a brochure that describes at least three steps children can follow to avoid injury.

CHAPTER 14

Comparison and Contrast: Showing Similarities and Differences

The two photographs on the opposite page were taken at musical performances. Study the photographs and make two lists—a list of the ways the two scenes are similar and a list of the ways they are different. Include details that you notice about the performance, the audience, the setting, and so on.

   Write a paragraph about the photos that answers these questions: How are these two scenes the same, and how are they different?

WRITING A COMPARISON OR CONTRAST ESSAY

Your paragraph about the musical performances is an example of comparison and contrast writing. In it you probably wrote about similarities and differences in dress, behavior of the audience, and so forth. In addition, you probably organized your paragraph in one of two ways: (1) by writing about one performance and then the other or (2) by alternating back and forth between the two performances as you discussed each point of similarity or difference. This chapter will show you how to write effective comparison or contrast essays as well as how to incorporate comparison and contrast into essays using other patterns of development.

What Are Comparison and Contrast?

Using **comparison and contrast** involves looking at both similarities and differences. Analyzing similarities and differences is a useful decision-making skill that you use daily. You make comparisons when you shop for a pair of jeans, select a sandwich in the cafeteria, or choose a television program to watch. You also compare alternatives when you make important decisions about which college to attend, which field to major in, and which person to date.

You will find many occasions to use comparison and contrast in the writing you do in college and on the job (see the accompanying box for a few examples). In most essays of this type you will use one of two primary methods of organization, as the following two readings illustrate. The first essay, "Amusing Ourselves to Depth: Is *The Onion* Our Most Intelligent Newspaper?" by Greg Beato, uses a **point-by-point organization**. The writer moves back and forth between his two subjects (*The Onion* and traditional newspapers), comparing them on the basis of several key points or characteristics. The second essay, Ian Frazier's "Dearly Disconnected," uses a **subject-by-subject organization**. Here the author describes the key points or characteristics of one subject (pay phones) before moving on to those of his other subject (cell phones).

SCENES FROM COLLEGE AND THE WORKPLACE

- For a course in *criminal justice*, your instructor asks you to participate in a panel discussion comparing organized crime in three societies—Italy, Japan, and Russia.
- For a *journalism course*, you are assigned to interview two local television news reporters and write a paper contrasting their views on journalistic responsibility.
- As a *computer technician* for a pharmaceutical firm, you are asked to compare and contrast several models of notebook computers and recommend the one the company should purchase for its salespeople.

POINT-BY-POINT ORGANIZATION

Amusing Ourselves to Depth: Is *The Onion* Our Most Intelligent Newspaper?

READING

Greg Beato

Greg Beato is a San Francisco–based writer who has written for such publications as *Spin*, *Wired*, *Business 2.0*, and the *San Francisco Chronicle*. He created the webzine *Traffic* in 1995, and was a frequent contributor to the webzine *Suck.com* from 1996 to 2000. He also maintains a blog about media and culture, *Soundbitten*, which he started in 1997. This essay was published in *Reason*, a libertarian magazine, in 2007. As you read, notice how Beato uses comparison and contrast to make his case for the validity of "fake news."

In August 1988, college junior Tim Keck borrowed $7,000 from his mom, rented a Mac   1
Plus, and published a twelve-page newspaper. His ambition was hardly the stuff of future journalism symposiums: He wanted to create a compelling way to deliver advertising to his fellow students. Part of the first issue's front page was devoted to a story about a monster running amok at a local lake; the rest was reserved for beer and pizza coupons.

Almost twenty years later, *The Onion* stands as one of the newspaper industry's few   2
great success stories in the post-newspaper era. Currently, it prints 710,000 copies of each weekly edition, roughly 6,000 more than the *Denver Post*, the nation's ninth-largest daily. Its syndicated radio dispatches reach a weekly audience of one million, and it recently started producing video clips too. Roughly three thousand local advertisers keep *The Onion* afloat, and the paper plans to add 170 employees to its staff of 130 this year.

Online it attracts more than two million readers a week. Type *onion* into Google, and   3
The Onion pops up first. Type *the* into Google, and *The Onion* pops up first. But type "best practices for newspapers" into Google, and *The Onion* is nowhere to be found. Maybe it should be. At a time when traditional newspapers are frantic to divest themselves of their newsy, papery legacies, *The Onion* takes a surprisingly conservative approach to innovation. As much as it has used and benefited from the Web, it owes much of its success to low-tech attributes readily available to any paper but nonetheless in short supply: candor, irreverence, and a willingness to offend.

While other newspapers desperately add gardening sections, ask readers to share   4
their favorite bratwurst recipes, or throw their staffers to ravenous packs of bloggers for online question-and-answer sessions, *The Onion* has focused on reporting the news. The fake news, sure, but still the news. It doesn't ask readers to post their comments at the end of stories, allow them to rate stories on a scale of one to five, or encourage citizen-satire. It makes no effort to convince readers that it really does understand their needs and exists only to serve them. *The Onion*'s journalists concentrate on writing stories and then getting them out there in a variety of formats, and this relatively old-fashioned approach to newspapering has been tremendously successful.

Are there any other newspapers that can boast a 60 percent increase in their print   5
circulation during the last three years? Yet as traditional newspapers fail to draw

readers, only industry mavericks like the *New York Times*' Jayson Blair and *USA Today*'s Jack Kelley have looked to *The Onion* for inspiration.

One reason *The Onion* isn't taken more seriously is that it's actually fun to read. In   6
1985 the cultural critic Neil Postman published the influential *Amusing Ourselves to Death*, which warned of the fate that would befall us if public discourse were allowed to become substantially more entertaining than, say, a Neil Postman book. Today newspapers are eager to entertain—in their Travel, Food, and Style sections, that is. But even as scope creep has made the average big-city tree killer less portable than a ten-year-old laptop, hard news invariably comes in a single flavor: Double Objectivity Sludge.

Too many high priests of journalism still see humor as the enemy of seriousness: 7
If the news goes down too easily, it can't be very good for you. But do *The Onion* and its more fact-based acolytes, *The Daily Show* and *The Colbert Report*, monitor current events and the way the news media report on them any less rigorously than, say, the *Columbia Journalism Review* or *USA Today*?

During the last few years, multiple surveys by the Pew Research Center and the   8
Annenberg Public Policy Center have found that viewers of *The Daily Show* and *The Colbert Report* are among America's most informed citizens. Now, it may be that Jon Stewart isn't making anyone smarter; perhaps America's most informed citizens simply prefer comedy over the stentorian drivel the network anchormannequins dispense. But at the very least, such surveys suggest that news sharpened with satire doesn't cause the intellectual coronaries Postman predicted. Instead, it seems to correlate with engagement.

It's easy to see why readers connect with *The Onion*, and it's not just the jokes: De-   9
spite its "fake news" purview, it's an extremely honest publication. Most dailies, especially those in monopoly or near-monopoly markets, operate as if they're focused more on not offending readers (or advertisers) than on expressing a worldview of any kind. *The Onion* takes the opposite approach. It delights in crapping on pieties and regularly publishes stories guaranteed to upset someone: "Christ Kills Two, Injures Seven, in Abortion-Clinic Attack." "Heroic PETA Commandos Kill 49, Save Rabbit." "Gay Pride Parade Sets Mainstream Acceptance of Gays Back 50 Years." There's no predictable ideology running through those headlines, just a desire to express some rude, blunt truth about the world.

One common complaint about newspapers is that they're too negative, too focused   10
on bad news, too obsessed with the most unpleasant aspects of life. *The Onion* shows how wrong this characterization is, how gingerly most newspapers dance around the unrelenting awfulness of life and refuse to acknowledge the limits of our tolerance and compassion. The perfunctory coverage that traditional newspapers give disasters in countries cursed with relatability issues is reduced to its bare, dismal essence: "15,000 Brown People Dead Somewhere." Beggars aren't grist for Pulitzers, just punch lines: "Man Can't Decide Whether to Give Sandwich to Homeless or Ducks." Triumphs of the human spirit are as rare as vegans at an NRA barbecue: "Loved Ones Recall Local Man's Cowardly Battle with Cancer."

Such headlines come with a cost, of course. Outraged readers have convinced   11
advertisers to pull ads. Ginger Rogers and Denzel Washington, among other celebrities, have objected to stories featuring their names, and former *Onion* editor Robert

Siegel once told a lecture audience that the paper was "very nearly sued out of existence" after it ran a story with the headline "Dying Boy Gets Wish: To Pork Janet Jackson." But if this irreverence is sometimes economically inconvenient, it's also a major reason for the publication's popularity. It's a refreshing antidote to the he-said/ she-said balancing acts that leave so many dailies sounding mealy-mouthed. And while *The Onion* may not adhere to the facts too strictly, it would no doubt place high if the Pew Research Center ever included it in a survey ranking America's most trusted news sources.

During the last few years, big-city dailies have begun to introduce "commuter" pa- 12
pers that function as lite versions of their original fare. These publications share some of *The Onion*'s attributes: They're free, they're tabloids, and most of their stories are bite-sized. But while they may be less filling, they still taste bland. You have to wonder: Why stop at price and paper size? Why not adopt the brutal frankness, the willingness to pierce orthodoxies of all political and cultural stripes, and apply these attributes to a genuinely reported daily newspaper?

Today's publishers give comic strips less and less space. Editorial cartoonists and 13
folksy syndicated humorists have been nearly eradicated. Such changes have helped make newspapers more entertaining—or at least less dull—but they're just a start. Until today's front pages can amuse our staunchest defenders of journalistic integrity to severe dyspepsia, if not death, they're not trying hard enough.

SUBJECT-BY-SUBJECT ORGANIZATION

Dearly Disconnected

Ian Frazier

READING

Ian Frazier is an American writer and humorist, whose books include *Great Plains* (2001), *Family* (2002), and the humor collections *Dating Your Mom* (1986) and *Coyote v. Acme* (2002). His most recent book, *Gone to New York* (2005), is a collection of columns he wrote for the *New Yorker* magazine both as a staff writer and independently. He is also a contributing editor for *Outside* magazine. The following essay was adapted from a column that appeared in *Mother Jones* magazine in 2000. As you read, highlight the key points Frazier makes about pay phones and cell phones and his attitude toward each.

Before I got married I was living by myself in an A-frame cabin in northwestern Montana. 1
The cabin's interior was a single high-ceilinged room, and at the center of the room, mounted on the rough-hewn log that held up the ceiling beam, was a telephone. The woman I would marry was living in Sarasota, Florida, and the distance between us suggests how well we were getting along at the time. We had not been in touch for several months; she had no phone. One day she decided to call me from a pay phone. We talked for a while, and after her coins ran out I jotted the number on the wood beside my phone and called her back. A day or two later, thinking about the call, I wanted to talk to her again. The only number I had for her was the pay phone number I'd written down.

The pay phone was on the street some blocks from the apartment where she 2
stayed. As it happened, though, she had just stepped out to do some errands a few

minutes before I called, and she was passing by on the sidewalk when the phone rang. She had no reason to think that a public phone ringing on a busy street would be for her. She stopped, listened to it ring again, and picked up the receiver. Love is pure luck; somehow I had known she would answer, and she had known it would be me.

Long afterwards, on a trip to Disney World in Orlando with our two kids, then aged six and two, we made a special detour to Sarasota to show them the pay phone. It didn't impress them much. It's just a nondescript Bell Atlantic pay phone on the cement wall of a building, by the vestibule. But its ordinariness and even boringness only make me like it more; ordinary places where extraordinary events have occurred are my favorite kind. On my mental map of Florida that pay phone is a landmark looming above the city it occupies, and a notable, if private, historic site.

I'm interested in pay phones in general these days, especially when I get the feeling that they are about to go away. Technology, in the form of sleek little phones in our pockets, has swept on by them and made them begin to seem antique. My lifelong entanglement with pay phones dates me; when I was young they were just there, a given, often as stubborn and uncongenial as the curbstone underfoot. They were instruments of torture sometimes. You had to feed them fistfuls of change in those pre-phone-card days, and the operator was a real person who stood maddeningly between you and whomever you were trying to call. And when the call went wrong, as communication often does, the pay phone gave you a focus for your rage. Pay phones were always getting smashed up, the receivers shattered to bits against the booth, the coin slots jammed with chewing gum, the cords yanked out and unraveled to the floor.

There was always a touch of seediness and sadness to pay phones, and a sense of transience. Drug dealers made calls from them, and shady types who did not want their whereabouts known, and otherwise respectable people planning assignations, and people too poor to have phones of their own. In the movies, any character who used a pay phone was either in trouble or contemplating a crime. Mostly, pay phones evoked the mundane: "Honey, I'm just leaving. I'll be there soon." But you could tell that a lot of undifferentiated humanity had flowed through these places, and that in the muteness of each pay phone's little space, wild emotion had howled.

The phone on the wall of the concession stand at Redwood Pool, where I used to stand dripping and call my mom to come and pick me up; the sweaty phones used almost only by men in the hallway outside the maternity ward at Lenox Hill Hospital in New York; the phone in the old wood-paneled phone booth with leaded glass windows in the drugstore in my Ohio hometown — each one is as specific as a birthmark, a point on earth unlike any other. Recently I went back to New York City after a long absence and tried to find a working pay phone. I picked up one receiver after the next without success. Meanwhile, as I scanned down the long block, I counted half a dozen or more pedestrians talking on their cell phones.

It's the cell phone, of course, that's putting the pay phone out of business. The pay phone is to the cell phone as the troubled and difficult older sibling is to the cherished newborn. You sometimes hear people yelling on their cell phones, but almost never yelling at them. Cell phones are toylike, nearly magic, and we get a huge kick out of them, as often happens with technological advances until the new wears off. When I see a cellphone user gently push the little antenna and fit the phone back into its brushed-vinyl carrying case and tuck the case inside his jacket beside his heart, I feel sorry for the beat-up pay phone standing in the rain.

People almost always talk on cell phones while in motion—driving, walking down the street, riding on a commuter train. The cell phone took the transience the pay phone implied and turned it into VIP-style mobility and speed. Even sitting in a restaurant, the person on a cell phone seems importantly busy and on the move. Cell-phone conversations seem to be unlimited by ordinary constraints of place and time, as if they represent an almost-perfect form of communication, whose perfect state would be telepathy. 8

And yet no matter how we factor the world away, it remains. I think this is what drives me so nuts when a person sitting next to me on a bus makes a call from her cell phone. Yes, this busy and important caller is at no fixed point in space, but nevertheless I happen to be beside her. The job of providing physical context falls on me; I become her call's surroundings, as if I'm the phone booth wall. For me to lean over and comment on her cell-phone conversation would be as unseemly and unexpected as if I were in fact a wall; and yet I have no choice, as a sentient person, but to hear what my chatty fellow traveler has to say. 9

I don't think that pay phones will completely disappear. Probably they will survive for a long while as clumsy old technology still of some use to those lagging behind, and as a backup if ever the superior systems should temporarily fail. Before pay phones became endangered I never thought of them as public spaces, which of course they are. They suggested a human average; they belonged to anybody who had a couple of coins. Now I see that, like public schools and public transportation, pay phones belong to a former commonality our culture is no longer quite so sure it needs. 10

I have a weakness for places—for old battlefields, car-crash sites, houses where famous authors lived. Bygone passions should always have an address, it seems to me. Ideally, the world would be covered with plaques and markers listing the notable events that occurred at each particular spot. A sign on every pay phone would describe how a woman broke up with her fiancé here, how a young ballplayer learned that he had made the team. Unfortunately, the world itself is fluid, and changes out from under us. Eventually pay phones will become relics of an almost-vanished landscape, and of a time when there were fewer of us and our stories were on an earlier page. Romantics like me will have to reimagine our passions as they are—unmoored to earth, like an infinitude of cell-phone messages flying through the atmosphere. 11

Characteristics of Comparison or Contrast Essays

When writers use comparison and contrast, they consider subjects with characteristics in common, examining similarities, differences, or both. Whether used as the primary pattern of development or alongside another pattern, comparison and contrast can be used for various purposes to make a point about a subject.

Comparison or Contrast Has a Clear Purpose

A comparison and contrast essay usually has one of three purposes: *to express ideas, to inform,* or *to persuade.* In an essay about the two musical performances shown in the chapter-opening photographs, the purpose could be to express your ideas about rock concerts and orchestral concerts, based on your experiences attending the two kinds of performances. Alternatively, the purpose could be to inform readers about how both kinds of performances follow certain established rituals and standards in the behavior of the performers and the audience. Finally, the purpose could be to persuade readers that orchestral concerts should abandon outdated standards of formality in order to attract younger audiences. Whatever the purpose of a comparison and contrast essay, it should be made clear to readers. In "Amusing Ourselves to Depth" (p. 341), for example, it's clear that the author intends to compare and contrast *The Onion* with traditional newspapers.

Comparison or Contrast Considers Shared Characteristics

You cannot compare two things unless they have something in common. When making a comparison, then, a writer needs to choose a **basis of comparison**—a fairly broad common characteristic on which to base the essay. For an essay comparing baseball and football, for example, a basis of comparison might be the athletic skills required or the rules and logistics of each sport. To develop the essay, the writer examines the two subjects using **points of comparison**—specific characteristics relating to the basis of comparison. In an essay using athletic skills as a basis of comparison, for example, points of comparison might be height and weight requirements, running skills, and hand-eye coordination. In an essay based on rules and logistics, points of comparison might include scoring, equipment, and playing fields.

Exercise 14.1

For three items in the following list, identify two possible bases of comparison you could use to compare each pair of topics.

1. Two means of travel or transportation
2. Two means of communication (emails, telephone calls, postal letters, telephone text messages)
3. Two pieces of equipment
4. Two magazines or books
5. Two types of television programming

A Comparison or Contrast Essay Fairly Examines Similarities, Differences, or Both

Depending on their purpose, writers using comparison and contrast may focus on similarities, differences, or both. In an essay intended to *persuade* readers that performers Beyoncé Knowles and Jennifer Lopez have much in common in terms of talent and cultural influence, the writer would focus on similarities—hit records, millions of fans, and parts in movies. However, an essay intended to *inform* readers about the singers would probably cover both similarities and differences, discussing the singers' different childhoods or singing styles.

An essay focusing on similarities often mentions a few differences, usually in the introduction, to let readers know the writer is aware of the differences. Conversely, an essay that focuses on differences might mention a few similarities.

Whether you cover similarities, differences, or both in an essay, you should strive to treat your subjects fairly. Relevant information should not be purposely omitted to show one subject in a more favorable light. In an essay about Knowles and Lopez, for instance, you should not leave out information about Lopez's charity work in an effort to make Knowles appear to be a nicer person. In "Dearly Disconnected," Frazier regrets the demise of the pay phone but admits that cell phones are "toylike, nearly magic."

Comparison or Contrast Makes a Point

Whatever the purpose of a comparison or contrast essay, its main point about its subjects should spark readers' interest rather than bore them with a mechanical listing of similarities or differences. This main point can serve as the thesis for the essay, or the thesis can be implied in the writer's choice of details. In "Amusing Ourselves to Depth," for example, the thesis statement is implied in paragraphs 3 and 13: In comparison to the brutal honesty of *The Onion*, traditional newspapers seem timid and dull.

An explicit thesis has three functions.

1. It identifies the *subjects* being compared or contrasted.
2. It suggests whether the focus is on *similarities, differences,* or *both.*
3. It states the *main point* of the comparison or contrast.

Notice how the following three sample theses meet the above criteria. Note, too, that each thesis suggests why the comparison or contrast is meaningful and worth reading about.

- [———similarities———] [———subjects———]
  Similar appeals in commercials for three popular breakfast cereals reveal
  [———main point———]
  America's obsession with fitness and health.

- [———difference———] [———subjects———] [———similarities———]
  Although different in purpose, weddings and funerals each draw families
  [———main point———]
  together and confirm family values.

- [———subjects———]
  The two cities Niagara Falls, Ontario, and Niagara Falls, New York, demonstrate
  [———differences———] [———main point———]
  two different approaches to appreciating nature and preserving the environment.

> ### Exercise 14.2
>
> *For one of the topic pairs you worked on in Exercise 14.1 (p. 346), select the basis of comparison that seems most promising. Then write a thesis statement that identifies the subjects, the focus (similarities, differences, or both), and the main point.*

Comparison or Contrast Considers a Sufficient Number of Significant Characteristics and Details

A comparison or contrast essay considers characteristics that are significant as well as relevant to the essay's purpose and thesis. In "Amusing Ourselves to Depth," for example, Beato considers such significant characteristics as circulation, type of information presented, degree of seriousness, and honesty.

Although the number of details can vary by topic, usually at least three or four significant characteristics are needed to support a thesis. Each characteristic should be fully described or explained so that readers can grasp the main point of the comparison or contrast. A writer may use sensory details, dialogue, examples, expert testimony, and other kinds of detail in a comparison or contrast essay. In "Dearly Disconnected," Frazier supports his points by using anecdotes and vivid descriptions.

Visualizing a Comparison or Contrast Essay: Two Graphic Organizers

For more on graphic organizers, see Chapter 3, p. 55.

Suppose you want to compare two houses (house A and house B) built by the same architect for the purpose of evaluating how the architect's style has changed over time. After brainstorming ideas, you decide to base your essay on these points of comparison— layout, size, building materials, and landscaping. You could organize your essay in one of two ways—point by point or subject by subject.

Point-by-Point Organization

In a *point-by-point organization,* you would go back and forth between the two houses, noting similarities and differences between them on each of the four points of comparison, as shown in the graphic organizer in Figure 14.1.

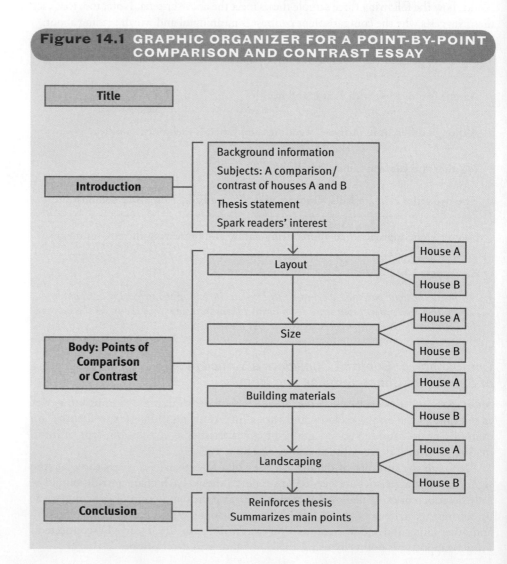

Figure 14.1 GRAPHIC ORGANIZER FOR A POINT-BY-POINT COMPARISON AND CONTRAST ESSAY

Title

Introduction
Background information
Subjects: A comparison/ contrast of houses A and B
Thesis statement
Spark readers' interest

Body: Points of Comparison or Contrast

Layout — House A, House B

Size — House A, House B

Building materials — House A, House B

Landscaping — House A, House B

Conclusion
Reinforces thesis
Summarizes main points

Subject-by-Subject Organization

In a *subject-by-subject organization,* you would first discuss all points about house A—its layout, size, building materials, and landscaping. Then you would do the same for house B. This pattern is shown in the graphic organizer in Figure 14.2.

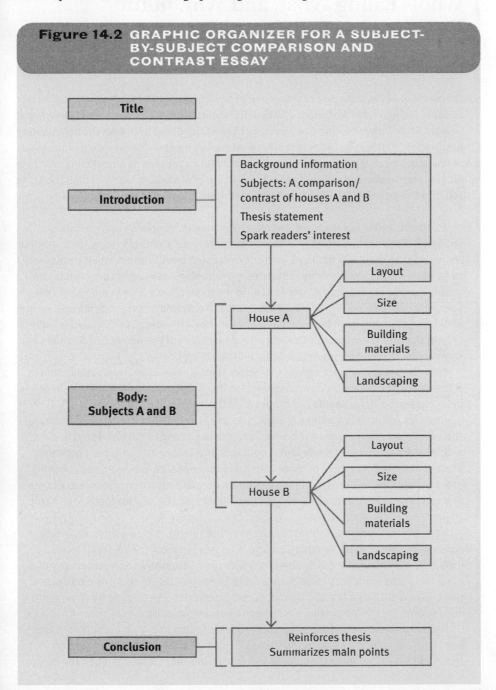

Figure 14.2 GRAPHIC ORGANIZER FOR A SUBJECT-BY-SUBJECT COMPARISON AND CONTRAST ESSAY

Title

Introduction
- Background information
- Subjects: A comparison/contrast of houses A and B
- Thesis statement
- Spark readers' interest

Body: Subjects A and B

House A
- Layout
- Size
- Building materials
- Landscaping

House B
- Layout
- Size
- Building materials
- Landscaping

Conclusion
- Reinforces thesis
- Summarizes main points

The following essay uses a point-by-point organization. Read the essay, and then study the graphic organizer for it in Figure 14.3 on page 352.

Who's Eating What, and Why, in the United States and Europe?

Thomas Kinnear, Kenneth Bernhardt, and Kathleen Krentler

Thomas Kinnear is professor of marketing at the University of Michigan. He is a former editor of the *Journal of Marketing*. Kenneth Bernhardt is regents professor of marketing at Georgia State University and has served as chair of the Board of the American Marketing Association. Kathleen Krentler is professor of marketing and vice president of programs at the Academy of Marketing Science. This essay first appeared as a marketing profile in Kinnear and Bernhardt's college textbook, *Principles of Marketing*, fourth edition (1995). As you read the selection, highlight the thesis statement and the points of comparison.

Do European and U.S. consumers eat alike? Yes and no. People's eating habits are strongly influenced by a number of factors besides taste. Cultural values, demographic characteristics, personal finances, and concern about the environment all help determine what you eat. Furthermore, advances in technology, laws, and competition are factors in what foods are available to you. To the extent that U.S. and European consumers are influenced similarly by these factors, you would expect and, indeed, would find their eating habits to be remarkably similar. However, because the relative influence of many of these variables differs on the two sides of the Atlantic, U.S. diners and Europeans often find themselves eating different things.

Perhaps one of the most significant factors that appears to account for differences is the variation in social values. Consumers in the United States, for example, have been interested in the health and fitness aspects of their food for some time. This interest has resulted in a deluge of diet and other types of "lite" food on U.S. grocery shelves. European consumers, however, are just beginning to get interested in diet and "lite" foods. A recent study found both U.S. and European consumers primarily interested in the fat content of foods. After this commonality, however, the concerns of the two groups diverged. Europeans want (in descending order) freshness, vitamin and mineral content, and nutritional value while Americans look for foods low in salt, cholesterol, and sugar.

Ironically, as European interest in diet and "lite" goods is increasing, many U.S. consumers appear to be switching back to what has been called real food. Increasingly, healthy eating in the U.S. alternates with the consumption of heartier fare. Like other food producers, McDonald's appears to be responding to this move by downplaying its reduced-fat McLean Deluxe Burger (dubbed the McFlopper by some cynics) and introducing the Mega Mac, a half-pound hamburger patty.

Recent statistics reveal a demographic difference that may also account for variation in eating habits. A study found that 44 percent of Western European women reported being homemakers and only 33 percent said they worked outside the home.

This is approximately the reverse of U.S. statistics on these same factors. Marketers realize that the presence of a full-time homemaker in a home is likely to account for different shopping, cooking, and eating habits for the entire family.

Economic and ecological factors can also help shape our eating habits. Consumers in the United States have traditionally been concerned with price. In the last few years, European consumers have become increasingly cost-conscious as well, due in large part to a recessionary economy throughout the early 1990s. Consumers with less money to spend and less optimism about the economy are likely to eat differently. Consumers on both sides of the Atlantic are also increasingly concerned about the environment. Marketers have found themselves having to respond to demands for reductions in excessive packaging, for example.   5

Advances in technology mean changes in what consumers eat. The introduction of the microwave oven, for example, has affected what's for dinner in U.S. households for the last twenty years. Microwavable food is a relatively new phenomenon in Europe, however.   6

Traditionally, European consumers have claimed that having a wide variety is much less important to them than it is to residents of the United States. However, increased competition from popular private-label products is pushing producers in industries like breakfast cereals to introduce more products into the European market. Time will tell whether European consumers will become more like U.S. consumers and respond to broader product offerings or whether they reject the strategy.   7

The changes in the European market brought on by economic, competitive, and social upheaval [are] providing opportunities for marketers who respond appropriately. Pepsico Corporation, for example, entered the Polish market in 1993 with "3-in-1" outlets combining Pizza Hut, Taco Bell, and KFC. The outlets have been very successful.   8

Smart marketers should be less concerned with whether U.S. and European consumers are alike and more concerned with monitoring the variety of factors that account for potential similarities and differences. Attention to the dynamic nature of those factors will produce opportunities for the alert marketer.   9

Exercise 14.3

Draw a graphic organizer for "Amusing Ourselves to Depth" (p. 341) or "Dearly Disconnected" (p. 343).

To draw detailed graphic organizers using a computer, visit www.bedfordstmartins.com/successfulwriting.

Integrating Comparison and Contrast into an Essay

Although you will write some essays using comparison and contrast as the primary pattern of development, in most cases you will integrate comparisons or contrasts into essays that rely on other patterns, such as description, process analysis, or argument. Comparisons or contrasts can be particularly effective in persuasive essays.

A special type of comparison that you may have occasion to use is an **analogy**, which helps readers understand something unfamiliar by comparing it to something

Figure 14.3 GRAPHIC ORGANIZER FOR "WHO'S EATING WHAT, AND WHY, IN THE UNITED STATES AND EUROPE?"

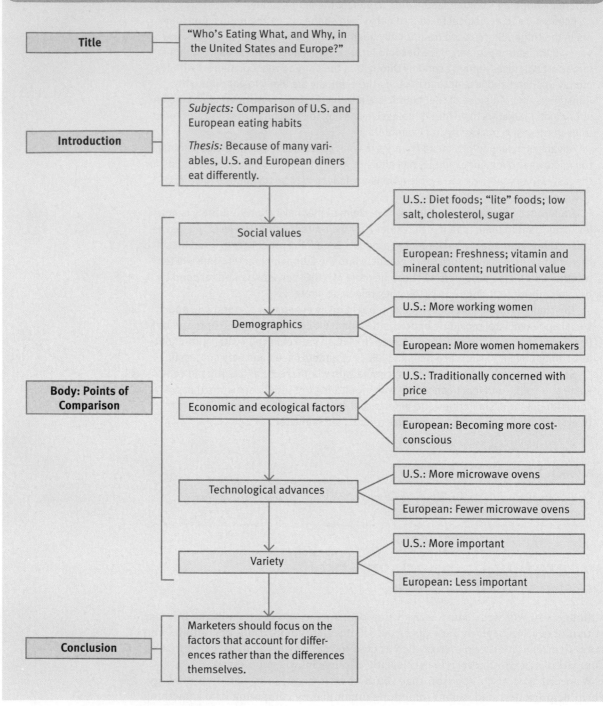

familiar. For example, a writer could explain the evolution of the universe by comparing it to the stages of human life.

Use the following tips to incorporate comparison or contrast into essays based on other patterns of development.

1. **Determine the purpose of the comparison or contrast.** What will it contribute to your essay?
2. **Introduce the comparison or contrast clearly.** Tell your readers how it supports the main point of the essay. Do not leave it to them to figure out why the comparison is included.
3. **Keep the comparison or contrast short and to the point.** An extended comparison will distract readers from the overall point of your essay.
4. **Organize the points of the comparison or contrast.** Even though it is part of a larger essay, the comparison or contrast should follow a point-by-point or subject-by-subject organization.
5. **Use transitions.** Transitional words and expressions are especially important in easing the flow into the comparison or contrast and then back to the essay's primary pattern of development.

In "Defining a Doctor, with a Tear, a Shrug, and a Schedule" on page 370, Abigail Zuger uses comparison and contrast along with other patterns of development.

A GUIDED WRITING ASSIGNMENT

The following guide will lead you through the process of writing a comparison or contrast essay. Although you will focus on comparing or contrasting your subjects, you may need to integrate one or more other patterns of development in your essay.

The Assignment

Write a comparison or contrast essay on one of the following topic pairs or one of your own choosing. Depending on the topic pair you choose, you may need to use Internet or library sources to develop and support your ideas about the subjects. Your audience is your classmates.

1. Two public figures
2. Two forms of entertainment (movies, concerts, radio, music videos) or one form of entertainment as it is used today and as it was used ten or more years ago
3. Two styles of communication, dress, or teaching
4. The right and wrong ways of doing something
5. Your views versus your parents' or grandparents' views on an issue
6. Two different cultures' approaches to a rite of passage, such as birth, puberty, marriage, or death

7. Two different cultures' views on the roles that should be played by men and women in society
8. Two products from two different eras

For more on process analysis, see Chapter 13. For more on cause and effect, see Chapter 17.

As you develop your comparison or contrast essay, consider using one or more other patterns of development. For example, you might use process analysis to explain the right and wrong ways of doing something or cause and effect to show the results of two teaching styles on learners.

Generating Ideas

Generating ideas involves first choosing subjects to compare and then prewriting to discover similarities, differences, and other details about the subjects.

Choosing Subjects to Compare

For more on prewriting strategies, see Chapter 4.

Learning Style Options

Take your time selecting the assignment option and identifying specific subjects for it. Use the following guidelines to get started.

1. Some of the options listed on page 353 are concrete (comparing two public figures); others are more abstract (comparing communication styles or views on an issue). Consider your learning style and choose the option with which you are most comfortable.
2. If you are a social learner, choose subjects that your classmates are familiar with so that you can discuss your subjects with them. Try group brainstorming about various possible subjects.
3. Choose subjects with which you have some firsthand experience or that you are willing to research. You might try questioning or writing assertions to help you generate ideas.
4. Choose subjects that interest you. You will have more fun writing about them, and your enthusiasm will enliven your essay. Try mapping or sketching to come up with interesting subjects.

> **Essay in Progress 1**
> Using the preceding suggestions, choose an assignment option from the list on page 353 or an option you think of on your own. Then do some prewriting to help you select two specific subjects for your comparison or contrast essay.

Choosing a Basis of Comparison and a Purpose

Suppose you want to compare or contrast two well-known football players—a quarterback and a linebacker. If you merely present the various similarities and differences between the two players, your essay will lack direction. To avoid this problem, you need to choose a basis of comparison and a purpose for writing. You could compare the players on the basis of the positions they play, using the height, weight, skills, and training needed for each position as points of comparison. Your purpose would be to *inform* readers about the two positions. Alternatively, you could base your comparison on their performances on the field; in this case, your purpose might be to *persuade* readers to accept your evaluation of both players. Other bases of comparison might be the players' media images, contributions to their teams, or service to the community.

Once you have a basis of comparison and a purpose in mind, try to state them clearly in a few sentences. Refer to these sentences as you work to keep your essay on track.

Essay in Progress 2

For the assignment option and subjects you selected in Essay in Progress 1, decide on a basis of comparison and a purpose for your essay. Describe both clearly in a few sentences. Keep in mind that you may revise your basis of comparison and purpose as your essay develops.

Considering Your Audience and Point of View

As you develop your comparison or contrast essay, keep your audience in mind. Choose points of comparison that will interest your readers. For this chapter's assignment, your audience is made up of your classmates. You also need to think about point of view, or how you should address your readers. Most comparison or contrast essays are written in the third person. However, the first person may be appropriate when you use comparison and contrast to express personal thoughts or feelings.

For more on audience and point of view, see Chapter 4, p. 83.

Discovering Similarities and Differences and Generating Details

Your next step is to discover how your two subjects are similar, how they are different, or both. Depending on your learning style, you can approach this task in a number of different ways.

Learning Style Options

1. **On paper or on your computer, create a two-column list of similarities and differences.** Jot down ideas in the appropriate column.
2. **Ask a classmate to help you brainstorm aloud by mentioning only similarities; then counter each similarity with a difference.** Write notes on the brainstorming.
3. **For concrete subjects, try visualizing them.** Take notes on what you see, or draw a sketch of your subjects.
4. **Create a scenario in which your subjects interact.** For example, if your topic is automobiles of today and seventy-five years ago, imagine taking your great-grandfather, who owned a Model T Ford, for a drive in a 2009 luxury car. How would he react? What would he say?
5. **Do research on your two subjects at the library or on the Internet.**

Keep in mind that your readers will need plenty of details to grasp the similarities and differences between your subjects. Description, examples, and facts will make your subjects seem real to your readers.

For more on description, see Chapter 11.

Try to maintain an even balance between your two subjects; gather roughly the same amount of detail for each. This guideline is especially important if your purpose is to demonstrate that subject A is preferable to or better than subject B. Your readers will become suspicious if you provide plenty of detail for subject A and only sketchy information for subject B.

For more on library and Internet research, see Chapter 21.

Essay in Progress 3

Use the preceding suggestions and one or more prewriting strategies to discover similarities and differences and to generate details about your two subjects.

Developing Your Thesis

For more on thesis statements, see Chapter 5, p. 101.

The thesis statement for a comparison or contrast essay needs to fulfill the three criteria noted earlier: It should identify the subjects; suggest whether you will focus on similarities, differences, or both; and state your main point. In addition, your thesis should tell readers why your comparison or contrast of the two subjects is important or useful to them. Look at the following sample thesis statements.

WEAK   The books by Robert B. Parker and Sue Grafton are similar.

REVISED   The novels of Robert B. Parker and Sue Grafton are popular
                because readers are fascinated by the intrigues of witty, inde-
                pendent private detectives.

The first thesis is weak because it does not place the comparison within a context or give the reader a reason to care about it. The second thesis is more detailed and specific. It provides a basis for comparison and indicates why the similarity is worth reading about.

> ### Essay in Progress 4
>
> Using the preceding suggestions, write a thesis statement for this chapter's essay as-signment. The thesis should identify the two subjects of your comparison; tell whether you will focus on similarities, differences, or both; and convey your main point to readers.

Evaluating Your Ideas and Thesis

With your thesis in mind, review your prewriting by underlining or highlighting ideas that pertain to your thesis and eliminating those that do not. If you are working on a computer, highlight these key ideas in bold type or move them to a separate file. Try to identify the points or characteristics by which you can best compare your subjects. For example, if your thesis is about evaluating the performance of two football players, you would probably select various facts and details about their training, the plays they make, and their records. Think of points of comparison as the main similarities or differences that support your thesis.

Take a few minutes to evaluate your ideas and thesis. Make sure you have enough points of comparison to support your thesis and enough details to develop those points. If necessary, do additional prewriting to generate sufficient support for your thesis.

> ### Essay in Progress 5
>
> Using the preceding suggestions and comments from your classmates, list the points of comparison you plan to use in your essay and evaluate your ideas and thesis. Refer to the list of characteristics on pages 345–47 to help you with your evaluation.

> ### Trying Out Your Ideas on Others
>
> Working in a group of two or three students, discuss your ideas and thesis for this chapter's assignment. Each writer should state his or her topic, thesis, and points of comparison. Then, as a group, evaluate each writer's work.

Organizing and Drafting

Once you have evaluated your thesis, points of comparison, and details, you are ready to organize your ideas and draft your essay.

For more on drafting an essay, see Chapter 6.

Choosing a Method of Organization

Before you begin writing, decide whether you will use a point-by-point or a subject-by-subject organization (review Figures 14.1 and 14.2). To select a method of organization, consider the complexity of your subjects and the length of your essay. You may also need to experiment with the two approaches to see which works better. It is a good idea to make an outline or draw a graphic organizer at this stage.

Here are a few other guidelines to consider.

1. **The subject-by-subject method tends to emphasize the larger picture, whereas the point-by-point method emphasizes details and specifics.**
2. **The point-by-point method often works better for lengthy essays because it keeps both subjects current in your reader's mind.**
3. **The point-by-point method is often preferable for complicated or technical subjects.** For example, if you compare two computer systems, it would be easier to explain the function of a memory card once and then describe the memory cards in each of the two systems.

> **Essay in Progress 6**
>
> Choose a method of organization—point by point or subject by subject—and organize the points of comparison you generated in Essay in Progress 5.

Drafting the Essay

Use the following guidelines when writing your first draft.

1. If you are using point-by-point organization, keep the following suggestions in mind.

- Work back and forth between your two subjects, generally discussing the subjects in the same order for each point. If both subjects share a particular characteristic, then you may want to mention them together.
- Use a separate paragraph for each point of comparison, in most cases.
- Arrange your points of comparison carefully. You might, for example, start with the clearest, simplest points and then move on to more complex ones.

2. If you are using a subject-by-subject organization, keep the following suggestions in mind.

- Be sure to cover the same points for both subjects.
- Cover the points of comparison in the same order in both halves of your essay.
- Write a clear statement of transition wherever you switch from one subject to the other.

3. Use transitions. Transitions are especially important in helping readers follow the points you make in a comparison or contrast essay. Transitions alert readers to shifts between subjects or to new points of comparison. An essay that lacks transitions sounds choppy and unconnected. Use transitional words and phrases such as *similarly, in contrast, on the one hand, on the other hand,* and *not only . . . but also.*

For more on transitions, see Chapter 6, p. 124.

For more on writing effective paragraphs, including introductions and conclusions, see Chapter 6.

4. Write an effective introduction. The introduction should spark your readers' interest, present your subjects, state your thesis, and include any background information your readers may need.

5. Write a satisfying conclusion. Your conclusion should offer a final comment on your comparison or contrast, reminding readers of your thesis. For a lengthy or complex essay, you might want to summarize your main points as well.

> ### Essay in Progress 7
> Using the organization you developed in Essay in Progress 6 and the preceding guidelines for drafting, write a first draft of your comparison or contrast essay.

Analyzing and Revising

If possible, set your draft aside for a day or two before rereading and revising it. As you reread, concentrate on ideas and not on grammar or punctutation. Use one or more of the following suggestions to analyze your draft.

Learning Style Options

1. Reread your essay aloud, or ask a friend or classmate to do so as you listen.
2. Draw a graphic organizer, make an outline, or update the organizer or outline you prepared earlier. A graphic organizer or outline will indicate whether your organization contains inconsistencies or gaps.
3. Read each paragraph with this question in mind: So what? If any paragraph does not answer that question, revise or delete it.

For more on the benefits of peer review, see Chapter 8, p. 162.

Use Figure 14.4 to guide your analysis of the strengths and weaknesses in your draft essay. You might also ask a classmate to review your draft essay using the questions in the flowchart. Your reviewer should consider each question listed in the flowchart, explaining each "No" answer.

> ### Essay in Progress 8
> Revise your draft using Figure 14.4 and any comments you received from peer reviewers.

Editing and Proofreading

The last step is to check your revised essay for errors in grammar, spelling, punctutation, and mechanics. Be sure to check your error log for the types of errors you tend to make.

As you edit and proofread your comparison or contrast essay, watch out for the following types of errors.

For more on keeping an error log, see Chapter 9, p. 196.

1. Make sure to use the right forms of adjectives and adverbs when comparing two items (comparative) and three or more items (superlative). The following examples show how adjectives and adverbs change forms.

	Adjectives	Adverbs
Positive	sharp	early
Comparative	sharper	earlier
Superlative	sharpest	earliest

Figure 14.4 Flowchart for Revising a Comparison or Contrast Essay

QUESTIONS

REVISION STRATEGIES

1. Highlight your thesis statement. Does it identify the subjects being compared and state your main point? Does it or do nearby sentences express a clear purpose (to express ideas, inform, or persuade)?

 NO

- Revise your thesis using the suggestions on p. 356.
- Brainstorm a list of reasons for making the comparison. Make the most promising reason your purpose.

YES

2. *Write* the basis of comparison at the top of your paper. Is your basis of comparison clear? Does it clearly relate to your thesis?

NO

- Ask a friend or classmate to help you think of a clear or new basis for comparison.

YES

3. *List* your points of comparison. Place a checkmark ✔ next to the sentences that focus on similarities between the subjects. Mark an *X* next to the sentences that focus on differences. Have you included all significant points of comparison? Do you fairly examine similarities and differences? Is each similarity or difference significant, and does each support your thesis?

NO

- Delete any discussion of similarities or differences that are not significant or that do not support your thesis.
- Review your prewriting to see if you overlooked any significant points of comparison. If so, revise to add them.
- If you have trouble thinking of points of comparison, conduct research or ask a classmate to suggest ideas.

YES

4. Underline the topic sentence of each paragraph. Does each paragraph have a clear topic sentence? If you are using point-by-point comparison, is each paragraph focused on a separate point or shared characteristic?

NO

- Follow the guidelines for writing clear topic sentences (p. 141).
- Consider splitting paragraphs that focus on more than one point or characteristic and combining paragraphs that focus on the same one.

YES

(continued on next page)

(Figure 14.4 continued)

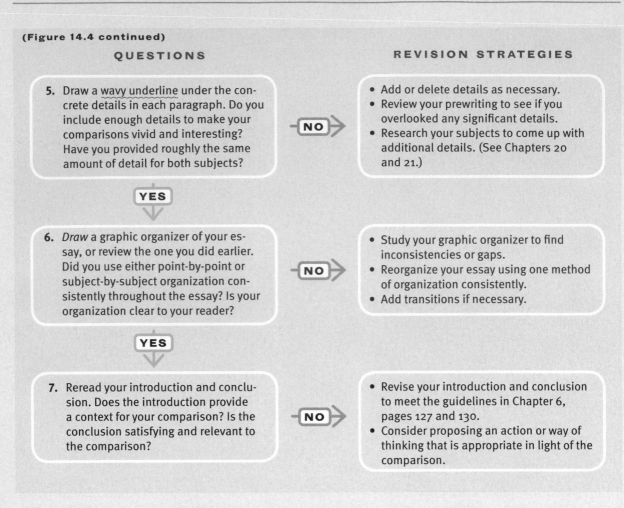

QUESTIONS

REVISION STRATEGIES

5. Draw a wavy underline under the concrete details in each paragraph. Do you include enough details to make your comparisons vivid and interesting? Have you provided roughly the same amount of detail for both subjects?

NO →

- Add or delete details as necessary.
- Review your prewriting to see if you overlooked any significant details.
- Research your subjects to come up with additional details. (See Chapters 20 and 21.)

YES

6. *Draw* a graphic organizer of your essay, or review the one you did earlier. Did you use either point-by-point or subject-by-subject organization consistently throughout the essay? Is your organization clear to your reader?

NO →

- Study your graphic organizer to find inconsistencies or gaps.
- Reorganize your essay using one method of organization consistently.
- Add transitions if necessary.

YES

7. Reread your introduction and conclusion. Does the introduction provide a context for your comparison? Is the conclusion satisfying and relevant to the comparison?

NO →

- Revise your introduction and conclusion to meet the guidelines in Chapter 6, pages 127 and 130.
- Consider proposing an action or way of thinking that is appropriate in light of the comparison.

■ Both *No Country for Old Men* and *Michael Clayton* were suspenseful, but I liked

Michael Clayton ~~best.~~ better.

■ George, Casey, and Bob are all bad at basketball, but Bob's game is ~~worse.~~ worst.

2. Make sure that items in a pair linked by correlative conjunctions (*either . . . or, neither . . . nor, not only . . . but also*) are in the same grammatical form.

■ The Grand Canyon is not only a spectacular tourist attraction but also

~~scientists consider it~~ a useful geological record./ for scientists.

Essay in Progress 9
Edit and proofread your essay, paying particular attention both to adjectives and adverbs used to compare and to items linked by correlative conjunctions.

Students Write

Heather Gianakos was a first-year student when she wrote the following comparison and contrast essay for her composition course. Although she has always enjoyed both styles of cooking that she discusses, she needed to do some research in the library and on the Internet to learn more about their history. As you read the essay, consider the writer's thesis and points of comparison.

Border Bites

Heather Gianakos

Chili peppers, tortillas, tacos: All these foods belong to the styles of cooking known as Mexican, Tex-Mex, and southwestern. These internationally popular styles often overlap; sometimes it can be hard to tell which style a particular dish belongs to. Two particular traditions of cooking, however, play an especially important role in the kitchens of Mexico and the American Southwest: native-derived Mexican cooking ("Mexican"), and Anglo-influenced southwestern cooking, particularly from Texas ("southwestern"). The different traditions and geographic locations of the inhabitants of Mexico and of the Anglo American settlers in the Southwest have resulted in subtle, flavorful differences between the foods featured in Mexican and southwestern cuisine.

Many of the traditions of southwestern cooking grew out of difficult situations--cowboys and ranchers cooking over open fires, for example. Chili, which can contain beans, beef, tomatoes, corn, and many other ingredients, was a good dish to cook over a campfire because everything could be combined in one pot. Dry foods, such as beef jerky, were a convenient way to solve food storage problems and could be easily tucked into saddlebags. In Mexico, by contrast, fresh fruits and vegetables such as avocados and tomatoes were widely available and did not need to be dried or stored. They could be made into spicy salsa and guacamole. Mexicans living in coastal areas could also enjoy fish and lobster dishes (Jamison and Jamison 5).

Corn has been a staple in the American Southwest and Mexico since the time of the Aztecs, who made tortillas (flat, unleavened bread, originally made from stone-ground corn and water) similar to the ones served in Mexico today (Jamison and Jamison 5). Southwesterners, often of European descent, adopted the tortilla but often prepared it with wheat flour, which was easily available to them. Wheat-flour tortillas can now be found in both Mexican and southwestern cooking, but corn is usually the primary grain in dishes with precolonial origins. Tamales (whose name derives from a word in Nahuatl, the Aztec group of languages) are a delicious example: A hunk of cornmeal dough, sometimes combined with ground meat, is wrapped in corn husks and steamed. In southwestern cooking, corn is often used for leavened corn bread, which is made with corn flour rather than cornmeal and can be flavored with jalapeños or back bacon.

1   Introduction indicates Gianakos will examine both similarities and differences but will focus on differences. Her thesis statement gives a basis of comparison of her two subjects, Mexican and southwestern cooking: the traditions and geographic locations of the people who developed them. It also makes a point: that these differences have led to the differences in the food.

2   Subject A: southwestern
Subject B: Mexican
Point of comparison #1: the physical conditions in which the two styles developed. Notice that Gianakos uses point-by-point comparison, discussing both subjects in each paragraph and often using transitions between them. She also cites sources for her information.

3   **Point of comparison #2:** the use of corn and wheat

Point of comparison #3: the
use of chicken

Subject A: southwestern

Subject B: Mexican

Meat of various kinds is often the centerpiece of both Mexican and southwestern tables.   4
However, although chicken, beef, and pork are staples in both traditions, they are often prepared quite differently. Fried chicken rolled in flour and dunked into sizzling oil or fat is a
popular dish throughout the American Southwest. In traditional Mexican cooking, however,
chicken is often cooked more slowly, in stews or baked dishes, with a variety of seasonings,
including ancho chiles, garlic, and onions.

Point of comparison #4: the
use of beef

Subject A: southwestern

Subject B: Mexican

Ever since cattle farming began in Texas with the early Spanish missions, beef has been   5
eaten both north and south of the border. In southwestern cooking, steak--flank, rib eye, or
sirloin--grilled quickly and served rare is often a chef's crowning glory. In Mexican cooking,
beef may be combined with vegetables and spices and rolled into a fajita or served ground in a
taco. For a Mexican food purist, in fact, the only true fajita is made from skirt steak, although
Mexican food as it is served in the United States often features chicken fajitas.

Point of comparison #5: the
use of pork

Subject A: southwestern

Subject B: Mexican

In Texas and the Southwest United States, barbecued pork ribs are often prepared in bar-   6
becue cook-offs, similar to chili-cooking competitions. Such competitions have strict rules for
the preparation and presentation of the food and for sanitation (Central Texas). However, while
the BBQ is seen as a southwestern specialty, barbecue ribs as they are served in southwestern-
themed restaurants today actually come from a Hispanic and Southwest Mexican tradition dating from the days before refrigeration: Since pork fat, unlike beef fat, has a tendency to become
rancid, pork ribs were often marinated in vinegar and spices and then hung to dry. Later the
ribs were basted with the same sauce and grilled (Campa 278). The resulting dish has become a
favorite both north and south of the border, although in Mexican cooking, where beef is somewhat less important than in southwestern cooking, pork is equally popular in many other forms,
such as chorizo sausage.

Conclusion: Gianakos
returns to the idea of overlap
mentioned in the introduction
and makes clear her purpose—
to inform readers about the
differences between the two
cuisines.

Cooks in San Antonio or Albuquerque would probably tell you that the food they cook is as   7
much Mexican as it is southwestern. Regional cuisines in such areas of the Southwest as New
Mexico, Southern California, and Arizona feature elements of both traditions; chimichangas--
deep-fried burritos--actually originated in Arizona (Jamison and Jamison 11). Food lovers who
sample regional specialties, however, will note--and savor--the contrast between the spicy, fried
or grilled, beef-heavy style of southwestern food and the richly seasoned, corn- and tomato-
heavy style of Mexican food.

Gianakos lists her sources at
the end of her paper, following
MLA style.

Works Cited

Campa, Arthur L. *Hispanic Culture in the Southwest*. Norman: U of Oklahoma P, 1979. Print.
Central Texas Barbecue Association. "CTBA Rules." *Central Texas Barbecue Association*. CTBA,
    16 Aug. 2004. Web. 6 May 2005.
Jamison, Cheryl Alters, and Bill Jamison. *The Border Cookbook*. Boston: Harvard Common,
    1995. Print.

Analyzing the Writer's Technique

1. Evaluate Gianakos's title and introduction. Do they provide the reader with enough background on her topic?
2. Using a point-by-point organization, Gianakos presents her two subjects in the same order—first southwestern cuisine, then Mexican cuisine—for each point of comparison except in paragraph 3. Why do you think she discusses the two cuisines together in this paragraph?
3. How does Gianakos's use of sources contribute to her essay?

Reacting to the Essay

1. What other regional cuisines might make effective topics for a comparison and contrast essay?
2. Gianakos compares the cuisines of the American Southwest and Mexico using the traditions and geographic locations of the people who lived there as the basis of comparison. In your journal, explore several other possible bases of comparison that could be used to compare these cuisines.
3. Write an essay comparing foods of two other regional cuisines.

READING COMPARISON AND CONTRAST

The following section provides advice for reading comparison and contrast essays. Two model essays illustrate the characteristics of comparison and contrast covered in this chapter and provide opportunities to examine, analyze, and react to the writer's ideas. The second essay uses comparison and contrast along with other methods of development.

Working with Text: Reading Comparison or Contrast Essays

Reading a comparison and contrast essay is somewhat different from reading other kinds of essays. First, the essay contains two or more subjects instead of just one. Second, the subjects are being compared, contrasted, or both, so you must follow the author's points of comparison between or among them. Use the following guidelines to read comparison and contrast essays effectively.

For more on reading strategies, see Chapter 3.

What to Look For, Highlight, and Annotate

1. As you preview the essay, determine whether it uses the point-by-point or subject-by-subject organization. Knowing the method of organization will help you move through the essay more easily.
2. Identify and highlight the thesis statement, if it is stated explicitly. What does it tell you about the essay's purpose, direction, and organization?

For more on previewing, see Chapter 3, p. 47.

3. Read the essay once to get an overall sense of how it develops. As you read, highlight each point of comparison the writer makes.
4. Review the essay by drawing a graphic organizer (see Figures 14.1 and 14.2). Doing so will help you learn and recall the key points of the essay.

How to Find Ideas to Write About

For more on discovering ideas for a response paper, see Chapter 3.

To respond to or write about a comparison and contrast essay, consider the following strategies.

- Compare the subjects using a different basis of comparison. If, for example, an essay compares or contrasts athletes in various sports on the basis of salary, you could compare them according to the training required for each sport.
- For an essay that emphasizes differences, consider writing about similarities, and vice versa.
- To write an essay that looks at one point of comparison in more depth, you might do research or interview an expert on the topic.

Thinking Critically about Comparison and Contrast

Comparison and contrast writing can be quite straightforward when the writer's purpose is only to inform. However, when the writer's purpose is also to persuade, you need to ask the following critical questions.

Does the Author Treat Each Subject Fairly?

Examine whether the author gives equal and objective coverage to each subject. If one of the subjects seems to be favored or given special consideration (or if one seems not to be treated fairly, fully, or adequately), the author might be *biased*—that is, introducing his or her own values or attitudes into the comparison. The lack of balance may not be intentional, and even a biased piece of writing is not necessarily unreliable, but you should be aware that other points of view may not have been presented.

How Does the Organization Affect Meaning?

In thinking about the question of fairness, notice especially whether and how the author uses a point-by-point or subject-by-subject organization. These two organizations provide different emphases. Point by point tends to maintain a steady balance, keeping the reader focused on both subjects simultaneously, while subject by subject tends to allow in-depth consideration of each subject separately. If a writer wants to present one subject more favorably than the other, he or she may present that subject and all its characteristics first, thereby shaping the reader's attitude toward it in a positive way before the reader encounters the second subject. Alternatively, a writer may present all the faults of the less favored subject first and then leave the reader with a final impression of the more favored subject. Even in point-by-point organization, the order in which the subjects are discussed for each point may suggest the writer's preference for one or the other. As you consider the method of organization, ask yourself how the essay would be different if the other method had been used or if the order of the two subjects had been reversed.

COMPARISON AND CONTRAST ESSAY

As you read the following essay by psychologist Daniel Goleman, notice how the writer uses the elements of comparison and contrast discussed in this chapter.

His Marriage and Hers: Childhood Roots
Daniel Goleman

Daniel Goleman holds a Ph.D. in behavioral and brain sciences and has published a number of books on psychology, including *Vital Lies, Simple Truths* (1985), *Working with Emotional Intelligence* (1998), *Destructive Emotions: A Scientific Dialogue with the Dalai Lama* (2003), and *Social Intelligence: The New Science of Human Relationships* (2006). Goleman reported on the brain and behavioral sciences for the *New York Times* for many years, and was elected a fellow of the American Association for the Advancement of Science for his efforts to bring psychology to the public. In his book *Emotional Intelligence* (1995), from which the following selection was taken, Goleman describes the emotional skills required for daily living, and explains how to develop those skills. As you read the selection, notice how the writer uses comparison and contrast to explore his subject—differences between the sexes—and highlight his key points of comparison.

As I was entering a restaurant on a recent evening, a young man stalked out the door, his face set in an expression both stony and sullen. Close on his heels a young woman came running, her fists desperately pummeling his back while she yelled, "Goddamn you! Come back here and be nice to me!" That poignant, impossibly self-contradictory plea aimed at a retreating back epitomizes the pattern most commonly seen in couples whose relationship is distressed: She seeks to engage, he withdraws. Marital therapists have long noted that by the time a couple finds their way to the therapy office, they are in this pattern of engage-withdraw, with his complaint about her "unreasonable" demands and outbursts, and her lamenting his indifference to what she is saying.

This marital endgame reflects the fact that there are, in effect, two emotional realities in a couple, his and hers. The roots of these emotional differences, while they may be partly biological, also can be traced back to childhood and to the separate emotional worlds boys and girls inhabit while growing up. There is a vast amount

of research on these separate worlds, their barriers reinforced not just by the different games boys and girls prefer but by young children's fear of being teased for
having a "girlfriend" or "boyfriend."[1] One study of children's friendships found that
three-year-olds say about half their friends are of the opposite sex; for five-year-olds
it's about 20 percent, and by age seven almost no boys or girls say they have a best
friend of the opposite sex.[2] These separate social universes intersect little until teenagers start dating.

Meanwhile, boys and girls are taught very different lessons about handling emo-   3
tions. Parents, in general, discuss emotions—with the exception of anger—more
with their daughters than their sons.[3] Girls are exposed to more information about
emotions than are boys: when parents make up stories to tell their preschool children,
they use more emotion words when talking to daughters than to sons; when mothers
play with their infants, they display a wider range of emotions to daughters than to
sons; when mothers talk to daughters about feelings, they discuss in more detail the
emotional state itself than they do with their sons—though with the sons they go into
more detail about the causes and consequences of emotions like anger (probably as a
cautionary tale).

Leslie Brody and Judith Hall, who have summarized the research on differences   4
in emotions between the sexes, propose that because girls develop facility with
language more quickly than do boys, this leads them to be more experienced at articulating their feelings and more skilled than boys at using words to explore and substitute for emotional reactions such as physical fights; in contrast, they note, "boys, for
whom the verbalization of affects is de-emphasized, may become largely unconscious
of their emotional states, both in themselves and others."[4]

At age ten, roughly the same percent of girls as boys are overtly aggressive, given   5
to open confrontation when angered. But by age thirteen, a telling difference between
the sexes emerges: Girls become more adept than boys at artful aggressive tactics like
ostracism, vicious gossip, and indirect vendettas. Boys, by and large, simply continue
being confrontational when angered, oblivious to these more covert strategies.[5] This
is just one of many ways that boys—and later, men—are less sophisticated than the
opposite sex in the byways of emotional life.

When girls play together, they do so in small, intimate groups, with an emphasis   6
on minimizing hostility and maximizing cooperation, while boys' games are in larger
groups, with an emphasis on competition. One key difference can be seen in what
happens when games boys or girls are playing get disrupted by someone getting hurt.
If a boy who has gotten hurt gets upset, he is expected to get out of the way and stop
crying so the game can go on. If the same happens among a group of girls who are
playing, the game stops while everyone gathers around to help the girl who is crying. This difference between boys and girls at play epitomizes what Harvard's Carol
Gilligan points to as a key disparity between the sexes: boys take pride in a lone,
tough-minded independence and autonomy, while girls see themselves as part of a
web of connectedness. Thus boys are threatened by anything that might challenge
their independence, while girls are more threatened by a rupture in their relationships. And, as Deborah Tannen has pointed out in her book *You Just Don't Understand,*
these differing perspectives mean that men and women want and expect very different

things out of a conversation, with men content to talk about "things," while women seek emotional connection.

In short, these contrasts in schooling in the emotions foster very different skills,   7
with girls becoming "adept at reading both verbal and nonverbal emotional signals, at expressing and communicating their feelings," and boys becoming adept at "minimizing emotions having to do with vulnerability, guilt, fear, and hurt."[6] Evidence for these different stances is very strong in the scientific literature. Hundreds of studies have found, for example, that on average women are more empathic than men, at least as measured by the ability to read someone else's unstated feelings from facial expression, tone of voice, and other nonverbal cues. Likewise, it is generally easier to read feelings from a woman's face than a man's; while there is no difference in facial expressiveness among very young boys and girls, as they go through the elementary-school grades boys become less expressive, girls more so. This may partly reflect another key difference: women, on average, experience the entire range of emotions with greater intensity and more volatility than men—in this sense, women are more "emotional" than men.[7]

All of this means that, in general, women come into a marriage groomed for the   8
role of emotional manager, while men arrive with much less appreciation of the importance of this task for helping a relationship survive. Indeed, the most important element for women—but not for men—in satisfaction with their relationship reported in a study of 264 couples was the sense that the couple has "good communication."[8] Ted Huston, a psychologist at the University of Texas who has studied couples in depth, observes, "For the wives, intimacy means talking things over, especially talking about the relationship itself. The men, by and large, don't understand what the wives want from them. They say, 'I want to do things with her, and all she wants to do is talk.' " During courtship, Huston found, men were much more willing to spend time talking in ways that suited the wish for intimacy of their wives-to-be. But once married, as time went on the men—especially in more traditional couples—spent less and less time talking in this way with their wives, finding a sense of closeness simply in doing things like gardening together rather than talking things over.

This growing silence on the part of husbands may be partly due to the fact that,   9
if anything, men are a bit Pollyannaish about the state of their marriage, while their wives are attuned to the trouble spots: in one study of marriages, men had a rosier view than their wives of just about everything in their relationship—lovemaking, finances, ties with in-laws, how well they listened to each other, how much their flaws mattered.[9] Wives, in general, are more vocal about their complaints than are their husbands, particularly among unhappy couples. Combine men's rosy view of marriage with their aversion to emotional confrontations, and it is clear why wives so often complain that their husbands try to wiggle out of discussing the troubling things about their relationship. (Of course this gender difference is a generalization and is not true in every case; a psychiatrist friend complained that in his marriage his wife is reluctant to discuss emotional matters between them and he is the one who is left to bring them up.)

The slowness of men to bring up problems in a relationship is no doubt compounded   10
by their relative lack of skill when it comes to reading facial expressions of emotions.

Women, for example, are more sensitive to a sad expression on a man's face than are men in detecting sadness from a woman's expression.[10] Thus a woman has to be all the sadder for a man to notice her feelings in the first place, let alone for him to raise the question of what is making her so sad.

Consider the implications of this emotional gender gap for how couples handle the grievances and disagreements that any intimate relationship inevitably spawns. In fact, specific issues such as how often a couple has sex, how to discipline the children, or how much debt and savings a couple feels comfortable with are not what make or break a marriage. Rather, it is how a couple discusses such sore points that matters more for the fate of their marriage. Simply having reached an agreement about how to disagree is key to marital survival; men and women have to overcome the innate gender differences in approaching rocky emotions. Failing this, couples are vulnerable to emotional rifts that eventually can tear their relationship apart. . . . [T]hese rifts are far more likely to develop if one or both partners have certain deficits in emotional intelligence.

NOTES

1. The separate worlds of boys and girls: Eleanor Maccoby and C. N. Jacklin, "Gender Segregation in Childhood," in H. Reese, ed., *Advances in Child Development and Behavior* (New York: Academic Press, 1987).
2. Same-sex playmates: John Gottman, "Same and Cross Sex Friendship in Young Children," in J. Gottman and J. Parker, eds., *Conversation of Friends* (New York: Cambridge University Press, 1986).
3. This and the following summary of sex differences in socialization of emotions are based on the excellent review in Leslie R. Brody and Judith A. Hall, "Gender and Emotion," in Michael Lewis and Jeannette Haviland, eds., *Handbook of Emotions* (New York: Guilford Press, 1993).
4. Brody and Hall, "Gender and Emotion," 456.
5. Girls and the arts of aggression: Robert B. Cairns and Beverley D. Cairns, *Lifelines and Risks* (New York: Cambridge University Press, 1994).
6. Brody and Hall, "Gender and Emotion," 454.
7. The findings about gender differences in emotion are reviewed in Brody and Hall, "Gender and Emotion."
8. The importance of good communication for women was reported in Mark H. Davis and H. Alan Oathout, "Maintenance of Satisfaction in Romantic Relationships: Empathy and Relational Competence," *Journal of Personality and Social Psychology* 53, no. 2 (1987): 397–410.
9. The study of husbands' and wives' complaints: Robert J. Sternberg, "Triangulating Love," in Robert Sternberg and Michael Barnes, eds., *The Psychology of Love* (New Haven: Yale University Press, 1988).
10. Reading sad faces: The research is by Dr. Ruben C. Gur at the University of Pennsylvania School of Medicine.

Examining the Reading

1. Summarize the differences that Goleman claims exist between men's and women's ways of expressing emotion.
2. According to Goleman, what are the root causes of the differences between how men and women express emotion?
3. How can the emotional differences between spouses cause marital difficulties, according to the writer?

4. Explain how boys and girls play differently, according to Goleman.
5. Explain the meaning of each of the following words as it is used in the reading: *epitomizes* (para. 1), *articulating* (4), *ostracism* (5), *vendettas* (5), *disparity* (6), and *empathic* (7). Refer to your dictionary as needed.

Analyzing the Writer's Technique

1. What is Goleman's thesis?
2. Identify the purpose of the essay, and list the points of comparison.
3. For each point of comparison, evaluate the evidence Goleman offers to substantiate his findings. Do you find the evidence sufficient and convincing? Why or why not? What other information might the writer have included?
4. What types of details does Goleman provide to explain each point of comparison?
5. Do you think Goleman maintains an objective stance on the issue, despite his gender? Explain your answer.

Reacting to the Reading

1. Do you think any of Goleman's generalizations about men and women are inaccurate and, if so which one(s)? Discuss the evidence, if any, that would prove Goleman wrong.
2. In your journal, describe a situation from your experience that either confirms or contradicts one of Goleman's generalizations.
3. Make a list of the emotional differences and resulting behavioral conflicts between men and women that you have observed. Decide which differences are explained by Goleman. Write an essay reporting your findings.
4. Write an essay contrasting the emotional behaviors of a couple you know.

(MAKING) (CONNECTIONS)

Attitudes toward Work

Both "Selling in Minnesota" (Chapter 10, pp. 225–27) and "Defining a Doctor, with a Tear, a Shrug, and a Schedule" (pp. 370–71) explore attitudes toward work.

Analyzing the Readings

1. What different attitudes toward work do the readings present?
2. Watch a television program, and then write a journal entry analyzing the attitudes toward work that the characters exhibit. How closely do the characters' attitudes match the attitudes presented in either reading?

Essay Idea

Write an essay explaining your attitude toward work and comparing or contrasting it to the attitude presented in either of the readings.

COMPARISON AND CONTRAST COMBINED
WITH OTHER PATTERNS

In the following reading, notice how Abigail Zuger uses comparison and contrast to explain a change that is occurring in the training of doctors and in expectations for medical students' behavior.

Defining a Doctor, with a Tear, a Shrug, and a Schedule
Abigail Zuger

Abigail Zuger is associate clinical professor of medicine at Albert Einstein College of Medicine and an attending physician at St. Luke's-Roosevelt Hospital Center, both in New York City. She has been caring for HIV-infected patients in the New York area since 1981, and her experiences working in the early years of the AIDS epidemic led her to write *Strong Shadows: Scenes from an Inner City AIDS Clinic* (1995). Zuger is an associate editor of *Journal Watch*, an online medical digest, and frequently writes on medical subjects for a variety of publications. This essay was published in the *New York Times* in 2004.

I had two interns to supervise that month, and the minute they sat down for our first meeting, I sensed how the month would unfold.   1

The man's white coat was immaculate, its pockets empty save for a sleek Palm Pilot   2
that contained his list of patients. The woman used a large loose-leaf notebook instead, every dog-eared page full of lists of things to do and check, consultants to call, questions to ask. Her pockets were stuffed, and whenever she sat down, little handbooks of drug doses, wadded phone messages, pens, highlighters, and tourniquets spilled onto the floor.

The man worked the hours legally mandated by the state, not a minute more, and   3
sometimes considerably less. He was seldom in the hospital before 8 in the morning and left by 5 unless he was on call. He ate a leisurely lunch every day and was never late for rounds. The woman got to the hospital around dawn and was on the move for the rest of the day. Sometimes she went home when she was supposed to, but sometimes, if one of her patients was particularly sick, she would sign out to the covering intern and keep working, often talking to patients' relatives long into the night. "I am now breaking the law," she would announce cheerfully to no one in particular, then trot off to do just a few final chores.

The man had a strict definition of what it meant to be a doctor. He did not, for instance,   4
"do nurses' work" (his phrase). When one of his patients needed a specimen sent to the lab and the nurse didn't get around to it, neither did he. No matter how important the job was, no matter how hard I pressed him, he never gave in. If I spoke sternly to him, he would turn around and speak just as sternly to the nurse. The woman did everyone's work. She would weigh her patients if necessary (nurses' work), feed them (aides' work), find salt-free pickles for them (dietitians' work), and wheel them to X-ray (transporters' work).

The man was cheerful, serene, and well rested. The woman was overtired, hyper-   5
emotional, and constantly late. The man was interested in his patients, but they never

kept him up at night. The woman occasionally called the hospital from home to check on hers. The man played tennis on his days off. The woman read medical articles. At least, she read the beginnings; she tended to fall asleep halfway through.

I felt as if I was in a medieval morality play[1] that month, living with two costumed symbols of opposing philosophies in medical education. The woman was working the way interns used to: total immersion seasoned with exhaustion and adrenaline. As far as she was concerned, her patients were her exclusive responsibility. The man was an intern of the new millennium. His hours and duties were delimited; he saw himself as part of a health-care team, and his patients' welfare as a shared responsibility.

6

This new model of medical internship got some important validation in the *New England Journal of Medicine* last week, when Harvard researchers reported the effects of reducing interns' work hours to 60 per week from 80 (now the mandated national maximum). The shorter workweek required a larger staff of interns to spell one another at more frequent intervals. With shorter hours, the interns got more sleep at home, dozed off less at work, and made considerably fewer bad mistakes in patient care.

7

Why should such an obvious finding need an elaborate controlled study to establish? Why should it generate not only two long articles in the world's most prestigious medical journal but also three long, passionate editorials? Because the issue here is bigger than just scheduling and manpower.

8

The progressive shortening of residents' work hours spells nothing less than a change in the ethos of medicine itself. It means the end of Dr. Kildare, Superstar—that lone, heroic healer, omniscient, omnipotent, and ever-present. It means a revolution in the complex medical hierarchy that sustained him. Willy-nilly, medicine is becoming democratized, a team sport.

9

We can only hope the revolution will be bloodless. Everything will have to change. Doctors will have to learn to work well with others. They will have to learn to write and speak with enough clarity and precision so that the patient's story remains accurate as care passes from hand to hand. They will have to stop saying "my patient" and begin to say "our patient" instead.

10

It may be, when the dust settles, that the system will be more functional, less error-prone. It may be that we will simply have substituted one set of problems for another. We may even find that nothing much has changed. Even in the Harvard data, there was an impressive range in the hours that the interns under study worked. Some logged in over 90 hours in their 80-hour workweek. Some put in 75 instead. Medicine has always attracted a wide spectrum of individuals, from the lazy and disaffected to the deeply committed. Even draconian scheduling policies may not change basic personality traits or the kind of doctors that interns grow up to be.

11

My month with the intern of the past and the intern of the future certainly argues for the power of the individual work ethic. Try as I might, it was not within my power to modify the way either of them functioned. The woman cared too much. The man cared too little. She worked too hard, and he could not be prodded into working hard enough. They both made careless mistakes. When patients died, the man shrugged and the woman cried. If for no other reason than that one, let us hope that the medicine of the future still has room for people like her.

12

---

[1]*morality play:* a play performed in the Middle Ages in which characters represent abstractions (love, death, peace, and so on); its purpose is to teach a lesson about right and wrong.

Examining the Reading

1. How do the two interns differ in their approach to medicine?
2. What different philosophies of medicine do the two interns represent?
3. Describe the working conditions of interns.
4. What do we learn about the author and her philosophy of medical practice?
5. Explain the meaning of each of the following words as it is used in the reading: *delimited* (para. 6), *ethos* (9), *omniscient* (9), *omnipotent* (9), and *draconian* (11). Refer to your dictionary as needed.

Analyzing the Writer's Technique

1. Highlight Zuger's thesis and evaluate its placement.
2. Identify the points of comparison on which the essay is based.
3. What other patterns of development does the author use? Give one example and explain how it contributes to the essay.
4. Evaluate the effectiveness of the point-by-point organization. How would the essay differ if it had been written using a subject-by-subject organization?
5. Evaluate the essay's conclusion. How does it reflect the thesis and organization of the essay?

Visualizing the Reading

Analyze Zuger's use of point-by-point organization by first identifying the different points of comparison in her essay. The first one has been done for you. Add additional rows to the box as needed.

Points of Comparison	The Man	The Woman
Organizational styles	Efficient (Palm Pilot)	Disorganized (overstuffed pockets and notebook)

Reacting to the Reading

1. Discuss an experience of visiting a doctor or hospital. Within which philosophy of medical care did your treatment fall?
2. Discuss the training and education you will need for a career you are interested in pursuing. What knowledge and skills will you need to succeed in the field, and how will the training provide them?

3. Write a journal entry exploring whether medical care has become depersonalized. Give examples from your experience.
4. Write an essay comparing or contrasting males and females in another profession (teachers, police officers, nurses).

Applying Your Skills: Additional Essay Assignments

Write a comparison or contrast essay on one of the following topics, using what you have learned in this chapter. Depending on the topic you choose, you may need to conduct library or Internet research.

For more on locating and documenting sources, see Part 5.

To Express Your Ideas

1. Compare two families that you know or are part of. Include points of comparison that reveal what is valuable and important in family life.
2. Compare your values and priorities today to those you held when you were in high school.
3. Compare your lifestyle today to the lifestyle you intend to follow after you graduate from college.

To Inform Your Reader

4. Compare library resources to those available on the Internet.
5. Compare two sources of information or communication as Beato does in "Amusing Ourselves to Depth" (p. 341).

To Persuade Your Reader

6. Choose a technological change that has occurred in recent years, as Frazier does in "Dearly Disconnected" (p. 343), and argue either that it is beneficial or that its drawbacks outweigh its usefulness compared with the old technology.
7. Compare two views on a controversial issue, arguing in favor of one of them.
8. Compare two methods of doing something (such as disciplining a child or training a pet), arguing that one method is more effective than the other.

Cases Using Comparison and Contrast

9. You are taking a course in photography and have been asked to write a paper comparing and contrasting the advantages and uses of black-and-white versus color film. Your instructor is your audience.
10. You are working in the advertising department of a company that manufactures in-line skates. Your manager has asked you to evaluate two periodicals and recommend which one the company should use to run its advertisements.

CHAPTER 15

Classification and Division: Explaining Categories and Parts

The cartoon on the opposite page humorously suggests a way books in a bookstore might be classified. Take a few minutes to think of other ways books in a bookstore could be classified for convenient reference, or brainstorm other humorous ways books might be classified.

Write a paragraph describing your system. Come up with a title for each section and describe what books would belong in each section. Include the characteristics of each bookstore section.

WRITING A CLASSIFICATION OR DIVISION ESSAY

In categorizing the types of books in the bookstore, the cartoonist used a process called *classification;* grouping things into categories based on specific characteristics. This chapter will show you how to write effective classification and division essays as well as how to incorporate classification and division into essays using other patterns of development.

What Are Classification and Division?

You use classification to organize things and ideas daily. Your dresser drawers are probably organized by categories, with socks and sweatshirts in different drawers. Grocery stores, phone directories, libraries, and even restaurant menus arrange items in groups according to similar characteristics.

Classification, then, is a process of sorting people, things, or ideas into groups or categories to help make them more understandable. For example, your college catalog classifies its course offerings by school, division, and department.

Division, similar to classification, begins with *one* item and breaks it down into parts. Thus, for example, the humanities department at your college may be divided into English, modern languages, and philosophy, and the modern language courses might be further divided into Spanish, French, Chinese, and Russian. Division is closely related to process analysis, which is covered in Chapter 13.

A classification or division essay explains a topic by describing types or parts. For example, a classification essay might explore types of advertising—direct mail, radio, television, newspaper, and so forth. A division essay might describe the parts of an art museum—exhibit areas, museum store, visitor services desk, and the like.

You will find many occasions to use classification and division in the writing you do in college and the workplace (see the accompanying box for a few examples). In the following essay, Jerry Newman classifies the kinds of managers he found in fast-food restaurants. An example of a division essay, "A Brush with Reality: Surprises in the Tube" by David Bodanis, appears on page 383.

SCENES FROM COLLEGE AND THE WORKPLACE

- For a course in *anatomy and physiology*, you are asked to study the structure and parts of the human ear by identifying the function of each part.

- As part of a *business management* report, you need to consider how debt liability differs for three types of businesses—a single proprietorship, a partnership, and a corporation.

- While working as a *facilities planner*, you are asked to conduct a feasibility study of several new sites. You begin by sorting the sites into three categories: within state, out of state, and out of country.

My Secret Life on the McJob:
Fast Food Managers

Jerry Newman

Jerry Newman is a professor of management at the State University of New York–Buffalo and coauthor of the textbook *Compensation*, ninth edition (2007). He has also worked as a business consultant at AT&T, Hewlett-Packard, RJR Nabisco, and McDonald's. This selection is from *My Secret Life on the McJob: Lessons in Leadership Guaranteed to Supersize Any Management Style* (2007), which Newman wrote after working at various fast-food restaurants to learn about their operation and management. As you read, highlight each category of manager that Newman establishes.

I thought all my fast food stores would be pretty similar. They weren't. Some stores   1
made employees wear name tags, going as far as sending people home if they
repeatedly didn't wear their name tags, while other stores didn't seem to care. In
some stores crews socialized after work, but in others they barely talked to each
other, even during work. Even though every chain had strict rules about every facet
of food production and customer interaction, how employees were treated was part
of an individual store culture, and this varied from store to store. These differences
could often be traced to the managers' values and practices and how consistently
they were applied both by the managers and by their *sensei*,[1] much more so than
any edicts from headquarters. The best-run store I worked at was [a] Burger King;
the worst-run store was also a Burger King. If corporate rules had a controlling
impact, shouldn't stores have been much more similar? At one McDonald's the
employees were extremely friendly; at another the tension between groups was
palpable. The differences, I think, can be traced to the managers. The following
is a sampler of the types of managers I encountered. Only the last group, performance managers, was good at finding a *sensei* and developing consistent people
practices.

THE TOXIC MANAGER

Most new employees learn through feedback. When you're first learning a job, there's   2
relatively little ego involvement in feedback; good managers seem to know this and
in early days of employment are quick to point out better ways of doing a task. [Toxic]
managers, though, use sarcasm or disrespectful comments to indicate when they are
unhappy with your work. One of the worst offenders I ran into was the store manager at
Arby's, who admitted that the main reason he was hiring me was to change the store
culture. He said he was tired of employees who were vulgar and disrespectful, but it
didn't take long for me to realize that the role model for their behavior was actually
the manager himself—Don. His attitude and style set the tone for everyone else in his
store. Almost as bad, the key individual with the necessary attributes to be a *sensei*
shared Don's disregard for the feelings of others. Don, in particular, didn't confine

---

[1]*Sensei:* A Japanese word for "teacher" or "master." Newman uses it to mean an employee who is not a manager but who is both highly skilled at his or her job and socially influential among fellow employees.

his wrath to "bad" employees. Bill, a diligent long-timer, messed up a coupon order. A customer had an entertainment book coupon for one Value Meal free with the purchase of another. There was a labyrinth of steps to complete some of the discounts correctly. When Bill made the error, it was right before the end of Don's shift, and Don tore into him, saying loudly enough for everyone to hear, "Well, I'm leaving before Bill can make my life any more miserable." It didn't take long to infect others with this lack of respect for employees.

THE MECHANICAL MANAGER

The most common type of manager I encountered was the Mechanical Manager, who   3
was for the most part either an assistant manager or a shift manager, not a full store manager. You could spot the Mechanical Managers from across the room—they did their jobs, day after day, as if fast food was slow death. They didn't want to be there, and they were just going through the motions. They typically had gotten their jobs because they were reliable crew members and had put in enough time that some reward was needed to keep them working. A promotion has a certain finality, though—it makes you confront reality: Is this what I want out of life? Most say "No," and that's probably why I didn't see very many store managers who were mechanical. Before most store managers had reached that level (one store manager told me it was a ten-year journey), those who weren't interested in fast food as a lifetime career had moved on to other career pursuits. While looking for other opportunities, though, they did what was necessary to get by. Luis at McDonald's was the perfect example.

In my first McDonald's experience I made myself a grid showing all of the sand-   4
wiches and their ingredients. After a day of having instructions blasted at me, I needed a visual training aid to finally put things together. I shared this grid with Luis on my third day, expecting he might already have training materials like this (as was the case at Wendy's) or that he could use it to train other visual learners. As I handed Luis the Excel spreadsheet, I watched his face and saw no reaction. None. He told me he'd leave it for Kris, the store manager. Clearly he saw the value in it—he didn't toss it, after all—but a reinforcing response for my initiative required a level of involvement he didn't or couldn't muster.

THE RELATIONSHIP MANAGER

The Relationship Manager was a relatively rare breed in my experience. James was   5
the prototype. He led by building relationships and demonstrating that he cared about our destinies—hard to do when it seemed like every week someone was leaving and another person was coming on board. From the first day, James was very different from what I was used to. When I first met him for my job interview, he was fifteen minutes late because he was out picking up an employee whose car had broken down. I never saw any other manager pick up or take home a crew member who had transportation problems. In fact, at one store I watched Mary, an older worker teetering on the edge of poverty, sit in a booth out front for two hours waiting for her husband to pick her up after his shift at a Sam's Club. As I came to learn, this kindness wasn't unusual for James. And in being kind, James created a culture that was much more friendly and supportive than that in many of the other fast food places I had experienced. Even the

way James responded to my quitting was refreshing. With my back problems becoming increasingly worse, I called James to tell him that I was quitting and dreaded leaving him in the lurch. But he was amazingly kind, telling me to take care of myself and forcefully telling me to pick up my check.

THE PERFORMANCE MANAGER

It's easy to spot the Performance Manager. Here relationships are still important, but now they serve as a means to ensure performance. Through word or deed she very quickly lets you know what is expected. I like this. No ambiguity, no doubt about what it takes to make the grade. The best at this was Kris, who, it seemed to me, watched for slackers much more closely than did the managers at other fast food places. She told me during the interview that I would be watching DVDs my first day. She also mentioned that one of the new people had taken three to four bathroom breaks while watching the videos, which was an excessive number, she thought. She also commented that she might be losing some people because she thought they were slower than they should be. I got the message: She would be watching my work and looking to see if I was going to goof off. My experience in other places was that you got fired for only two things: not showing up and insubordinate behavior. Clearly she was adding a third reason—poor performance. Good for her! 6

Kris's watchful eye extended beyond bathroom breaks. I found out the hard way that taking breaks, even unpaid ones, wasn't allowed unless legally required. Apparently in New York State, you're not entitled to a break until after five hours of work. So when I asked Kris for a break before the appointed time, she answered with an emphatic "No." Kris's message was clearly that we do our jobs by the book, no exceptions. 7

Over time at this Burger King I began to notice that Kris wasn't a taskmaster all the time. Sure, during busy times she was prone to exhort the staff to work faster. And she didn't tolerate leaning (remember, "If you've got time to lean, you've got time to clean"). But this attitude relaxed a bit during slower times, and it especially relaxed for the better workers like Daniel, Eric, and Craig, three of the fastest guns on the sandwich assembly board. 8

Characteristics of Classification and Division Essays

A successful classification or division essay is meaningful to its audience. The writer uses one principle of classification or division, with exclusive categories or parts that are broad enough to include all of the members of the group.

Classification Groups and Division Divides Ideas According to One Principle

To sort items into groups, a writer needs to decide on what basis to do so. For example, birds could be classified in terms of their size, habitat, or diet. For a division essay, the writer must decide into what parts to divide the topic. A journalist writing about a new aquarium could divide the topic according to type of fish displayed, suitability for children of different ages, or quality of the exhibits.

To develop an effective set of categories or parts, a writer needs to choose one principle of classification or division and use it consistently throughout the essay or other piece of writing. In "My Secret Life on the McJob: Fast Food Managers," Newman classifies managers according to their management style.

Once a writer chooses a principle of classification or division, the next step is to identify a manageable number of categories or parts. An essay classifying birds according to diet, for example, might use five or six types of diet, not twenty.

Classification or Division Follows a Principle Determined by the Writer's Purpose and Audience

Because several different principles can be used to categorize any group, the writer's purpose and audience should determine the principle of classification. The personnel director of a college might classify professors by age in preparing a financial report for trustees that projects upcoming retirements, whereas a student writing a humor column for the campus newspaper might categorize professors by teaching style.

To develop a meaningful classification, therefore, choose a principle that will both interest your readers and fulfill your purpose. If, for instance, you want to inform parents about the types of day-care facilities in your town, you could classify day-care centers according to the services they offer because your readers would be looking for that information. A journalist writing to persuade readers of his newspaper that a new aquarium is designed for children might divide the exhibits according to their suitability for children of different ages.

Exercise 15.1

Brainstorm three different principles of classification or division you could use for each of the following topics.

1. Sports teams
2. Fast-food restaurants
3. Convenience stores
4. Academic subjects
5. Novels

Classification Uses Categories and Division Uses Parts That Are Exclusive and Comprehensive

The categories or parts you choose should not overlap. In other words, a particular item should fit in no more than one category. A familiar example is age: The categories *25 to 30* and *30 to 35* are not mutually exclusive since someone who is thirty would fit into both. In an essay about the nutritional value of pizza, you could divide your topic into carbohydrates, proteins, and fats, but you should not add a separate category for saturated fat, since saturated fat is already contained in the fats category.

The categories or parts you choose should also be comprehensive. In a division essay, all the major parts of an item should be included. In a classification essay, each member of the group should fit into one category or another. For example, an essay categorizing fast-food restaurants according to the type of food they serve would have to include a category for pizza.

Exercise 15.2

Choose a principle of classification or division for two of the topics listed in Exercise 15.1. Then make a list of the categories in which each item could be included or parts into which each item could be divided.

Classification or Division Fully Explains Each Category or Part

A classification or division essay contains adequate detail so that each category or part can be understood by readers. In "My Secret Life on the McJob: Fast Food Managers," Newman clearly presents the four types of managers, using personal experience, examples, and description. Details such as these enable readers to "see" the writer's categories or parts in a classification or division essay.

Classification or Division Develops a Thesis

The thesis statement in a classification or division essay identifies the topic and may reveal the principle used to classify or divide the topic. In most cases it also suggests why the classification or division is relevant or important.

Here are a few examples of thesis statements.

Most people consider videos a form of entertainment; however, videos can also serve educational, commercial, and political functions.

The Grand Canyon is divided into two distinct geographical areas—the North Rim and the South Rim—each of which offers different views, facilities, and climatic conditions.

Visualizing a Classification or Division Essay: A Graphic Organizer

The graphic organizer shown in Figure 15.1 outlines the basic organization of a classification or division essay. The introduction announces the topic, gives background information, and states the thesis. The body paragraphs explain the categories or parts and their characteristics. The conclusion brings the essay to a satisfying close by reinforcing the thesis and offering a new insight on the topic.

For more on graphic organizers, see Chapter 3, p. 55.

Read the division essay on page 383 and then study the graphic organizer for it in Figure 15.2 (on p. 385).

Figure 15.1 GRAPHIC ORGANIZER FOR A CLASSIFICATION OR DIVISION ESSAY

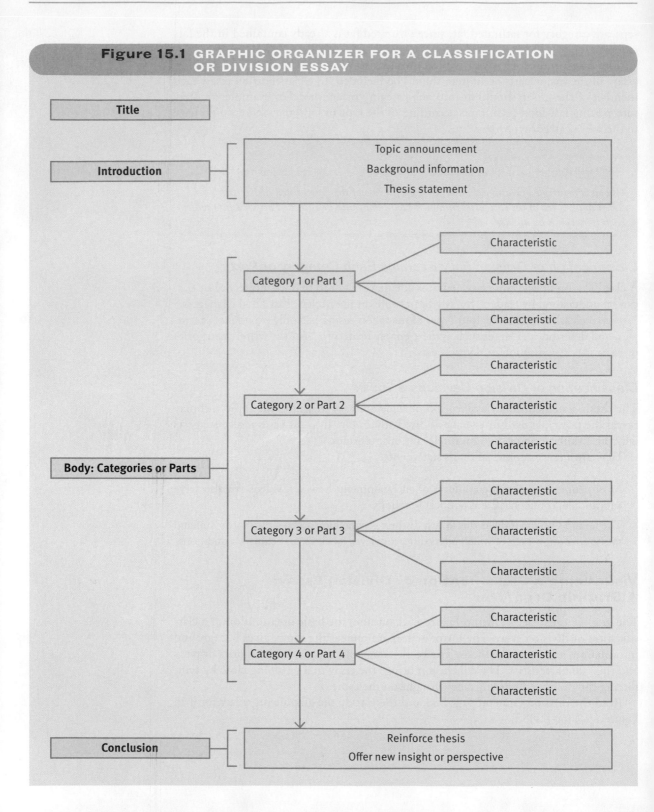

A Brush with Reality: Surprises in the Tube

David Bodanis

David Bodanis is a journalist and the author of several books, including *The Body Book* (1984), *The Secret Garden* (1992), *The Secret Family* (1997), *Electric Universe: The Shocking True Story of Electricity* (2005), and *Passionate Minds: The Great Love Affair of the Enlightenment* (2006). The following essay is from *The Secret House* (1986), a book that traces a family of five through a day, analyzing foods they eat and products they use. As you read the selection, highlight the writer's thesis and the sections where he divides his topic into parts.

Into the bathroom goes our male resident, and after the most pressing need is satisfied, it's time to brush the teeth. The tube of toothpaste is squeezed, its pinched metal seams are splayed, pressure waves are generated inside, and the paste begins to flow. But what's in this toothpaste, so carefully being extruded out? 1

Water mostly, 30 to 45 percent in most brands: ordinary, everyday simple tap water. 2 It's there because people like to have a big gob of toothpaste to spread on the brush, and water is the cheapest stuff there is when it comes to making big gobs. Dripping a bit from the tap onto your brush would cost virtually nothing; whipped in with the rest of the toothpaste, the manufacturers can sell it at a neat and accountant-pleasing $2 per pound equivalent. Toothpaste manufacture is a very lucrative occupation.

Second to water in quantity is chalk: exactly the same material that schoolteachers 3 use to write on blackboards. It is collected from the crushed remains of long-dead ocean creatures. In the Cretaceous seas chalk particles served as part of the wickedly sharp outer skeleton that these creatures had to wrap around themselves to keep from getting chomped by all the slightly larger other ocean creatures they met. Their massed graves are our present chalk deposits.

The individual chalk particles—the size of the smallest mud particles in your 4 garden—have kept their toughness over the aeons, and now on the toothbrush they'll need it. The enamel outer coating of the tooth they'll have to face is the hardest substance in the body—tougher than skull, or bone, or nail. Only the chalk particles in toothpaste can successfully grind into the teeth during brushing, ripping off the surface layers like an abrading wheel grinding down a boulder in a quarry.

The craters, slashes, and channels that the chalk tears into the teeth will also 5 remove a certain amount of built-up yellow in the carnage, and it is for that polishing function that it's there. A certain amount of unduly enlarged extra-abrasive chalk fragments tear such cavernous pits into the teeth that future decay bacteria will be able to bunker down there and thrive; the quality control people find it almost impossible to screen out these errant super-chalk pieces, and government regulations allow them to stay in.

In case even the gouging doesn't get all the yellow off, another substance is worked 6 into the toothpaste cream. This is titanium dioxide. It comes in tiny spheres, and it's the stuff bobbing around in white wall paint to make it come out white. Splashed around onto your teeth during the brushing it coats much of the yellow that remains. Being water soluble it leaks off in the next few hours and is swallowed, but at least for the quick glance up in the mirror after finishing it will make the user think his teeth are truly white. Some manufacturers add optical whitening dyes—the stuff more commonly found in washing machine bleach—to make extra sure that that glance in the mirror shows reassuring white.

These ingredients alone would not make a very attractive concoction. They would stick in the tube like a sloppy white plastic lump, hard to squeeze out as well as revolting to the touch. Few consumers would savor rubbing in a mixture of water, ground-up blackboard chalk, and the whitener from latex paint first thing in the morning. To get around that finicky distaste the manufacturers have mixed in a host of other goodies.

To keep the glop from drying out, a mixture including glycerine glycol—related to the most common car antifreeze ingredient—is whipped in with the chalk and water, and to give that concoction a bit of substance (all we really have so far is wet colored chalk), a large helping is added of gummy molecules from the seaweed *Chondrus crispus*. This seaweed ooze spreads in among the chalk, paint, and antifreeze, then stretches itself in all directions to hold the whole mass together. A bit of paraffin oil (the fuel that flickers in camping lamps) is pumped in with it to help the moss ooze keep the whole substance smooth.

With the glycol, ooze, and paraffin we're almost there. Only two major chemicals are left to make the refreshing, cleansing substance we know as toothpaste. The ingredients so far are fine for cleaning, but they wouldn't make much of the satisfying foam we have come to expect in the morning brushing.

To remedy that, every toothpaste on the market has a big dollop of detergent added too. You've seen the suds detergent will make in a washing machine. The same substance added here will duplicate that inside the mouth. It's not particularly necessary, but it sells.

The only problem is that by itself this ingredient tastes, well, too like detergent. It's horribly bitter and harsh. The chalk put in toothpaste is pretty foul-tasting too, for that matter. It's to get around that gustatory discomfort that the manufacturers put in the ingredient they tout perhaps the most of all. This is the flavoring, and it has to be strong. Double rectified peppermint oil is used—a flavorer so powerful that chemists know better than to sniff it in the raw state in the laboratory. Menthol crystals and saccharin or other sugar simulators are added to complete the camouflage operation.

Is that it? Chalk, water, paint, seaweed, antifreeze, paraffin oil, detergent, and peppermint? Not quite. A mix like that would be irresistible to the hundreds of thousands of individual bacteria lying on the surface of even an immaculately cleaned bathroom sink. They would get in, float in the water bubbles, ingest the ooze and paraffin, maybe even spray out enzymes to break down the chalk. The result would be an uninviting mess. The way manufacturers avoid that final obstacle is by putting something in to kill the bacteria. Something good and strong is needed, something that will zap any accidentally intrudant bacteria into oblivion. And that something is formaldehyde—the disinfectant used in anatomy labs.

So it's chalk, water, paint, seaweed, antifreeze, paraffin oil, detergent, peppermint, formaldehyde, and fluoride (which can go some way towards preserving children's teeth)—that's the usual mixture raised to the mouth on the toothbrush for a fresh morning's clean. If it sounds too unfortunate, take heart. Studies show that thorough brushing with just plain water will often do as good a job.

Figure 15.2 GRAPHIC ORGANIZER FOR "A BRUSH WITH REALITY: SURPRISES IN THE TUBE"

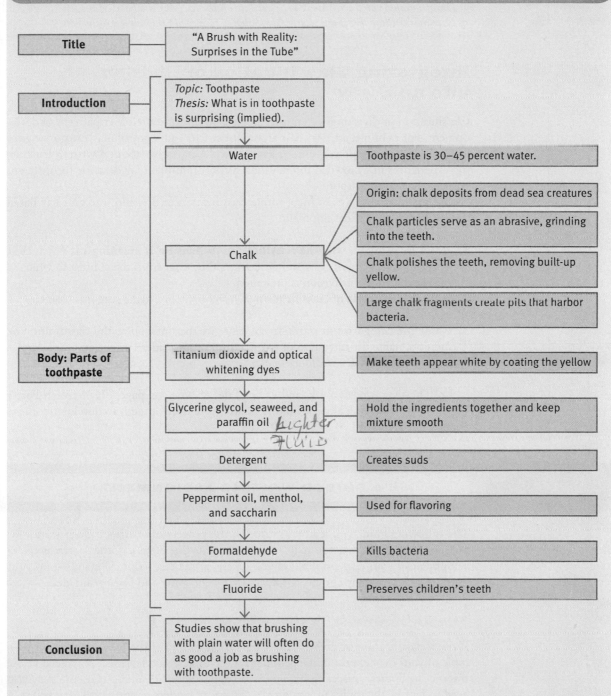

To draw detailed graphic
organizers using a computer,
visit www.bedfordstmartins
.com/successfulwriting.

Exercise 15.3

Draw a graphic organizer for "My Secret Life on the McJob: Fast Food Managers" (p. 377). Note that because this is an excerpt from a book, it does not include a conclusion.

Integrating Classification or Division into an Essay

Classification or division is often used along with one or more other patterns of development. For example, an essay that argues for stricter gun control may categorize guns in terms of their firepower, use, or availability. A narrative about a writer's frustrating experiences in a crowded international airport terminal may describe the different parts or areas of the airport.

Use the following tips to incorporate classification or division into an essay based on another pattern of development.

1. **Avoid focusing on why the classification or division is meaningful.** When used as a secondary pattern, its significance should be clear from the context in which the classification or division is presented.
2. **State the principle of classification.** Do so briefly but make sure it is clear to your readers.
3. **Name the categories or parts.** In the sentence that introduces the classification or division, name the categories or parts to focus your readers' attention on the explanation that follows.

In "The Dog Ate My Disk, and Other Tales of Woe" on page 403, Carolyn Foster Segal uses classification along with other patterns of development to develop her thesis about student excuses.

A GUIDED WRITING ASSIGNMENT

The following guide will lead you through the process of writing a classification or division essay. Note that you may need to integrate one or more other patterns of development in your essay to develop your thesis or make a point. Depending on your learning style, you may choose various ways of generating and organizing ideas.

The Assignment

Write a classification or division essay on a topic in one of the following lists or on a topic of your own choosing. Depending on the topic you select, you may need to use Internet or library sources to develop and support your ideas about it. You may also need to narrow the topic. Your audience consists of readers of your local newspaper.

Classification

1. Types of pets
2. Types of sports fans
3. Types of movies
4. Types of classmates
5. Types of shoppers
6. Types of television dramas

Division

1. Your family
2. A machine or a piece of equipment
3. An organization
4. A sports team or an extracurricular club
5. A public place (building, stadium, department store, or theme park)
6. Your college

As you develop your classification or division essay, consider using one or more other patterns of development. For example, in a classification essay, you might compare and contrast types of sports fans or give examples of types of movies. In a division essay, you might describe the parts of a theme park or another public place.

For more on description, illustration, and comparison and contrast, see Chapters 11, 12, and 14.

Generating Ideas

There are two primary methods for generating ideas and for classifying or dividing those ideas. With method 1, you first generate details and then group the details into categories or parts. With method 2, you first generate categories or parts and then generate details that support them. Here is how both methods apply to classification essays and division essays:

Classification

Method 1: First think of details that describe the group. Then use the details to categorize group members.

Method 2: First identify categories. Then think of details that describe each category.

Division

Method 1: Brainstorm details about your topic and then group the details into parts or sections.

Method 2: Think about how your topic can be divided into easy-to-understand parts. Then think of details that describe each part.

Method 1 is effective when you approach the classification or division from part to whole—identifying details and then grouping the details. Depending on your learning style and your topic, it may be easier to start by creating categories or parts and then filling in details about each one. In this case, use method 2.

For more on purpose, audience, and point of view, see Chapter 4, p. 82.

Considering Your Purpose, Audience, and Point of View

Your principle of classification or division, your categories or parts, and your details must all fit your purpose and audience. If your purpose is to inform novice computer users about the components of a personal computer (PC), your parts and details must be straightforward and nontechnical. However, if your purpose is to persuade computer technicians to purchase a particular kind of PC, your parts and details would be more technical. For this Guided Writing Assignment, your audience consists of readers of your local newspaper.

As you work on your classification or division essay, ask yourself the following questions.

- Is my principle of classification or division appropriate for my purpose and audience?
- Do my categories or parts and my details advance the purpose of the essay?
- Will my readers understand the categories or parts?
- What point of view will best suit my purpose and audience—first, second, or third person? The first person (*I, we*) or second person (*you*) may be appropriate in informal writing if you or your audience have personal knowledge of or experience with the topic you are classifying or dividing. The third person (*he, she, it, they*) is appropriate in more formal writing or for topics less familiar to you or your audience.

Generating Details and Grouping Them into Categories or Parts

For more on prewriting strategies, see Chapter 4.

For more on observation, see Chapter 21, p. 595.

Work through the following tasks in whatever order suits your topic and your learning style, using either method 1 or method 2 (p. 387).

Learning Style Options

Generating details. For each category or part, you need to supply specific details that will make it clear and understandable to your readers. As you work on your essay, then, write down examples, situations, or sensory details that illustrate each category or part. Use one or more of the following strategies.

1. Visit a place where you can observe your topic or the people associated with it. For example, to generate details about pets, visit a pet store or an animal shelter. Make notes on what you see and hear. Record conversations, physical characteristics, behaviors, and so forth.
2. Discuss your topic with a classmate or friend. Focus your talk on the qualities and characteristics of your topic.
3. Brainstorm a list of all the features or characteristics of your topic that come to mind.
4. Draw a map or diagram that illustrates your topic's features and characteristics.
5. Conduct library or Internet research to discover facts, examples, and other details about your topic.

For more on library and Internet research, see Chapter 21.

Choosing a principle of classification or division. Look for shared features or characteristics. Your principle of classification or division should be interesting, meaningful, and worthwhile to your audience. Experiment with several principles of classification or division until you find one that fits your purpose and audience.

Choosing categories or parts. Use the following suggestions to determine your categories or parts.

1. *In a classification essay*, make sure most or all members of the group fit into one of your categories. For example, in an essay about unsafe driving habits, you would include the most common bad habits. *In a division essay*, no essential parts should be left out. For example, in an essay about parts of a baseball stadium, you would not exclude the infield or bleachers.
2. *In a classification essay*, be sure the categories are exclusive; each group member should fit into one category only. In the essay about unsafe driving habits, the categories of reckless drivers and aggressive drivers would overlap, so exclusive categories should be used instead. *In a division essay*, make sure the parts do not overlap. In the essay about the parts of a baseball stadium, the parts "playing field" and "infield" would overlap, so it would be better to use three distinct parts of the field—infield, outfield, and foul-ball area.
3. Create specific categories or parts that will engage your readers. *In a classification essay*, categorizing drivers by their annoying driving habits would be more interesting than simply distinguishing between "good" and "bad" drivers. *A division essay* on players' facilities in a baseball stadium—dugout, locker room, and bullpen—might be more interesting to sports fans than an essay describing different seating sections of the stadium.
4. Choose descriptive names that emphasize the distinguishing feature of the category or part. *In a classification essay*, you might categorize highway drivers as "I-own-the-road" drivers, "I'm-in-no-hurry" drivers, and "I'm-daydreaming" drivers. *In a division essay* about the parts of a baseball stadium, you might use "home-run heaven" to name one part.

Do not hesitate to create, combine, or eliminate categories or parts, as needed.

> **Essay in Progress 1**
> Choose a topic for your classification or division essay from the list of assignment options on page 387, or choose one on your own. Then use the preceding guidelines for method 1 *or* method 2 to generate details about your topic, choose a principle of classification or division, and devise a set of categories or parts. Whatever method you use, list the examples, situations, or other details that you will use to describe each category or part. You might try drawing a graphic organizer.

Developing Your Thesis

Once you choose categories or parts and are satisfied with your details, you are ready to develop a thesis for your essay. Remember that your thesis statement should identify your topic and reveal your principle of division or classification. In most cases, it should also suggest why your classification or division is useful or important. Notice how the following weak theses have been strengthened by showing both what the categories are and why they are important.

For more on thesis statements, see Chapter 5, p. 101.

WEAK	There are four types of insurance that most people can purchase.
REVISED	If you understand the four common types of insurance, you will be able to make sure that you, your family members, and your property are protected.
WEAK	Conventional stores are only one type of retailing; other types are becoming more popular.
REVISED	Although conventional stores are still where most people purchase products, three new types of shopping are becoming increasingly popular—face-to-face sales conducted in a home, sales via telephone or computer, and sales from automatic vending machines.

Draft your thesis and then check your prewriting to make sure you have enough details to support the thesis. If necessary, do some additional prewriting.

Essay in Progress 2

Using the preceding guidelines, develop a thesis for your classification or division essay.

Evaluating Your Ideas and Thesis

Take a few minutes to evaluate your ideas and thesis. Start by rereading everything you have written with a critical eye. Highlight the most useful details and delete those that are repetitious or irrelevant. If you are working on a computer, highlight useful details in bold type or move them to a separate file. As you review your work, add useful ideas that come to mind.

Trying Out Your Ideas on Others

Working in a group of two or three students, discuss your ideas and thesis for this chapter's assignment. Each writer should describe to the group his or her topic, principle of classification or division, and categories or parts. Then, as a group, evaluate each writer's work and suggest recommendations for improvement.

Essay in Progress 3

Using the preceding suggestions and comments from your classmates, evaluate your thesis, your categories or parts, and the details you plan to use in your essay. Refer to the list of characteristics on pages 379–81 to help you with your evaluation.

Organizing and Drafting

For more on drafting an essay, see Chapter 6.

Once you have evaluated your categories or parts, reviewed your thesis, and considered the advice of your classmates, you are ready to organize your ideas and draft your essay.

Choosing a Method of Organization

Choose the method of organization that best suits your purpose. One method that works well in classification essays is the least-to-most or most-to-least arrangement. You might arrange your categories in increasing order of importance or from most to least common, difficult, or frequent. Other possible sequences include chronological order (when one category occurs or is observable before another) or spatial order (when you classify physical objects).

For more on methods of organization, see Chapter 6, p. 118.

Spatial order often works well in division essays, as does order of importance. In describing the parts of a baseball stadium, you might move from stands to playing field (spatial order). In writing about the parts of a hospital, you might describe the most important areas first (operating rooms and emergency department) and then move to less important facilities (waiting rooms and visitor cafeteria).

To experiment with different methods of organization, create a new computer file for each possible method and try each one.

Drafting the Classification or Division Essay

Once you decide how to organize your categories or parts, your next step is to write a first draft. Use the following guidelines to draft your essay.

1. **Explain each category or part.** Begin by defining each one, taking into account the complexity of your topic and the background knowledge of your audience. Define any unfamiliar terms. Then provide details that describe each category or part, and show how each is distinct from the others. Include a wide range of details—sensory details, personal experiences, examples, and comparisons and contrasts.

2. **Provide roughly the same amount and kind of detail and description for each of your categories or parts.** For instance, if you give an example of one type of mental disorder, you should give an example for every other type discussed in the essay. Generally, allow one or more paragraphs for each category or part.

For more on transitions, see Chapter 6, p. 124.

3. **Consider using headings or lists.** Presenting the parts or categories within a numbered list or in sections with headings can help make them clear and distinct. Headings or lists can be especially useful when you have a large number of categories or parts.

4. **Use transitions.** You need transitions to keep your reader on track as you move from one category or part to another. In addition, transitions help distinguish key features between and within categories or parts.

5. **Consider using a visual.** Diagrams, charts, or other visuals can make your system of classification or division clearer for your readers.

6. **Write an effective introduction.** Your introduction usually includes your thesis statement and suggests why the classification or division is useful. It also should provide background information and explain further, if needed, your principle of classification or division.

For more on writing effective paragraphs, including introductions and conclusions, see Chapter 6.

7. **Write a satisfying conclusion.** Your conclusion should bring your essay to a satisfying close, reemphasizing your thesis or offering a new insight or perspective on the topic.

If you have trouble finding an appropriate way to conclude your essay, return to your statement about why the classification or division is useful and important, and try to extend or elaborate on that statement.

Essay in Progress 4
Draft your classification or division essay, using an appropriate method of organization and the preceding guidelines for drafting.

Analyzing and Revising

As you review your draft, remember that your goal is to revise your classification or division essay to make it clearer and more effective. Focus on content and ideas and not on grammar, punctuation, or mechanics. Use one or more of the following strategies to analyze your draft.

1. **Reread your essay aloud.** You may "hear" parts that need revision.
2. **Ask a friend or classmate to read your draft** and to give you his or her impression of your categories of classification or division. Compare your reader's impressions with what you intend to convey, and revise your draft accordingly.
3. **Draw a graphic organizer, make an outline, or update the organizer or outline you drew or made earlier.** In particular, look for any categories or parts that lack sufficient details, and revise to include them.

For more on the benefits of peer review, see Chapter 8, p. 162.

Use Figure 15.3 to guide your analysis of the strengths and weaknesses in your draft essay. You might also ask a classmate to review your draft using the questions in the flowchart. For each "No" response, ask your reviewer to explain his or her answer.

Essay in Progress 5
Revise your draft using Figure 15.3 and any comments you received from peer reviewers.

Editing and Proofreading

The last step is to check your revised essay for errors in grammar, spelling, punctuation, and mechanics. Watch for the types of errors you tend to make (refer to your error log).

For more on keeping an error log, see Chapter 9, p. 196.

When editing a classification or division essay, pay specific attention to two particular kinds of grammatical error—choppy sentences and omitted commas following introductory elements.

For more on combining sentences and varying sentence patterns, see Chapter 9.

1. **Avoid short, choppy sentences, which can make a classification or division essay sound dull and mechanical.** Try combining a series of short sentences and varying sentence patterns and lengths.

- *, such as German shepherds and sheepherding dogs,*
  Working dogs are another one of the American Kennel Club's breed

  categories. ~~These include German shepherds and sheepherding dogs.~~

- *The fountain pen, one*
  ~~One~~ standard type of writing instrument, ~~is the fountain pen. It is~~ some-

  times messy and inconvenient to use.

Figure 15.3 Flowchart for Revising a Classification and Division Essay

QUESTIONS

REVISION STRATEGIES

1. Highlight your thesis statement. Do it and the rest of your introduction explain your principle of classification or division and suggest why it is important?

 NO

- Revise your thesis to make your justification stronger or more apparent.
- Add explanatory information to your introduction.

YES

2. *Write* the principle of classification you used at the top of your paper. Do you use this principle consistently throughout the essay? Does it fit your audience and purpose? Does it clearly relate to your thesis?

 NO

- Review or brainstorm other possible principles of classification of your topic, and decide if one of them better fits your audience and purpose.
- Revise your categories and parts to fit either your existing principle or a new one.
- Rewrite your thesis to reflect your principle of classification.

YES

3. Underline the categories or parts. Do they cover all or most members of the group or all major parts of the topic? Are your categories or parts exclusive (not overlapping)?

 NO

- Brainstorm or do research to add categories or parts.
- Revise your categories or parts so that each item fits into one group only.

YES

4. Place checkmarks ✔ beside the details that explain each category or part. Does your essay fully explain each one? (If it reads like a list, answer "No.")

 NO

- Brainstorm or do research to discover more details.
- Add examples, definitions, facts, and expert testimony to improve your explanations.

YES

(continued on next page)

(Figure 15.3 continued)

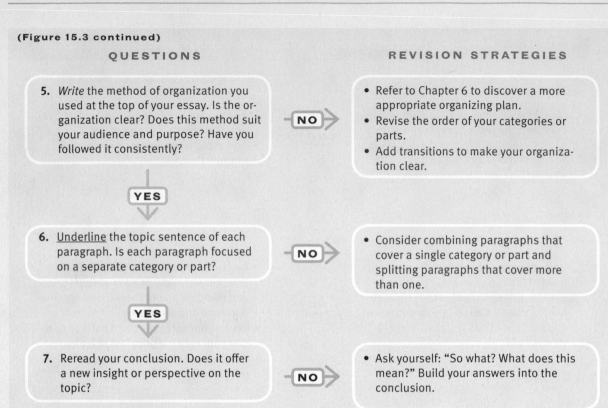

QUESTIONS   REVISION STRATEGIES

5. *Write* the method of organization you used at the top of your essay. Is the organization clear? Does this method suit your audience and purpose? Have you followed it consistently?

—NO→
- Refer to Chapter 6 to discover a more appropriate organizing plan.
- Revise the order of your categories or parts.
- Add transitions to make your organization clear.

YES↓

6. Underline the topic sentence of each paragraph. Is each paragraph focused on a separate category or part?

—NO→
- Consider combining paragraphs that cover a single category or part and splitting paragraphs that cover more than one.

YES↓

7. Reread your conclusion. Does it offer a new insight or perspective on the topic?

—NO→
- Ask yourself: "So what? What does this mean?" Build your answers into the conclusion.

2. **Add a comma after opening phrases or clauses that are longer than four words.**

- When describing types of college students, be sure to consider variations in age.

- Although there are many types of cameras, most are easy to operate.

Essay in Progress 6
Edit and proofread your essay, paying particular attention to sentence variety and length as well as comma usage.

Students Write

Sunny Desai was a student at the University of Maryland at College Park when he wrote the following essay in response to an assignment for his writing course, in which he was asked to address the national debate about immigration. As you read the essay, notice how Desai uses classification as his primary method of organization.

Immigration: Legal and Illegal

Sunny Desai

The immigration debate in the United States has raged on for a number of years without much movement toward an agreement on how to deal with the issue. Some Americans believe immigration needs to be curtailed; they argue that immigrants are draining our economy and social services, and take jobs that citizens could hold. Others believe that immigration is beneficial and maintains America's identity as a melting pot of cultures. Reflecting the views of the public, lawmakers and political candidates are also sharply divided on the immigration issue. From the standpoint of legal status, there are many types and subtypes of people who are currently in the United States but not American citizens. Understanding these distinctions is the key to good policy decisions and to informed choices by voters. Most people understand that noncitizens can be classified into two major categories, legal and illegal; within each category, however, are subdivisions that are less well known.

For the millions of citizens of other countries who are in the United States legally, the most common method of entry is through a visa--a document that demonstrates a person's eligibility to enter, but with particular constraints, including purpose of visit and length of stay. The Web site of the Department of State points out that when the holder of a visa arrives at a checkpoint for entry into the United States, an immigration officer will determine whether he or she is actually allowed in. There are many types of visas; in fact, according to the Department of Homeland Security (DHS), there are over seventy types altogether (*Immigration Classifications*). The overwhelming majority of visa holders, however, fall into four main groups. The most common one is the tourist visa, which allows a person to remain in the country only temporarily, for a variable length of time. Applicants must pass a security clearance and show that they have enough money to cover their visit.

Another major type of visa is the H1B visa, for those seeking temporary residence for work-related reasons. The visa is mostly used by outsourcing firms and technology companies. In 2007, Microsoft and Intel were among the ten highest receivers of H1B visas; the rest of the top ten were outsourcing companies, mostly based in India (Herbst 63). However, many doctors and nurses also arrive in the United States in this way. As explained on the Web site of the U.S. Citizenship and Immigration Services, a DHS agency, the H1B visa is used mostly by professional workers, since a bachelor's degree or its equivalent is often an eligibility requirement. Even where this is not the case, unskilled laborers are often excluded because of the

1 Title: Desai identifies the subject and its two primary classifications.

Introduction: Desai describes the controversy over immigration, identifies legality as his principle of classification, and explains the importance of classifying noncitizens. In his thesis statement, he identifies the two major categories he will discuss.

2 Desai introduces the first category of noncitizens—people who are in the country legally, most commonly through holding visas. He cites sources for his information, as he continues to do throughout the essay.

Desai indicates that his classification is comprehensive, including all major categories, and introduces the first subcategory of the legal category: people on tourist visas.

3 The second subcategory: those on H1B visas. Notice that at the beginning of this paragraph and the next four, Desai uses a transition to signal the next category or subcategory.

Desai provides details to fully explain this type of visa.

limited number of visas available. For those who are eligible, the H1B visa is a desirable path to naturalization--the process that leads to U.S. citizenship. Typically, it is issued for three years, with the option to renew it once. However, the employer can decide to apply for fewer years (*Employment Authorization*).

The third and fourth subcategories: holders of student and business visas.

Apart from tourists and H1B workers, the other two major categories of noncitizens with temporary legal status in the United States are holders of student visas and business visas. Temporary entrance is allowed for those seeking to study in the country or having some sort of business to conduct, whether they are employees of a multinational corporation or foreign entertainers touring America. The duration of these visas varies greatly, ranging from months to years. The rules of entry also differ: Some visas allow for multiple entries whereas others only allow one entry.

The fifth subcategory: permanent legal residents.

Besides these groups who are allowed to visit the United States temporarily, some people maintain permanent legal residency here but remain citizens of other nations. Permanent legal residents have identification cards generally called "green cards," also known as permanent resident cards. Most people who get green cards already live in the United States and had some sort of family relationship that helped them obtain it. According to the DHS's Office of Immigration Statistics, other factors that may enhance a person's ability to become a permanent legal resident are employment-based skills, birth in a country with a low rate of immigration to the United States, and status as a refugee or seeker of political asylum. For many, holding a green card is the first step toward becoming a citizen. Unlike a visa, it allows someone to travel abroad for up to a year without losing permanent residency status. The card is valid for ten years, after which it can be renewed (Office of Immigration Statistics).

The second category of noncitizens, those whose presence is illegal, and the first subcategory of this group, those who entered illegally.

In addition to those with green cards and valid visas, there are a large number of noncitizens living illegally in the United States. By one estimate, up to twelve million illegal immigrants were in the country as of 2006, the vast majority from Latin America ("Estimates" 2). All of these people are committing a crime under the Immigration and Nationality Act. The phrase "illegal immigrants" may conjure up images of people secretly crossing the U.S.-Mexico border, and certainly many do enter by hiding in trucks, walking through the desert, or swimming across a border river. According to the Pew Hispanic Center, more than half of illegal immigrants enter the country without a visa. Many enter for seasonal employment opportunities and return back home; however, such immigration is also deemed illegal.

The second subcategory of illegal residents: visa overstays.

But people who entered the country illegally are not the only ones whose presence here is illegal. The other type of illegal "immigrants" is the visa overstays. Members of this group entered the country legally, using a visa, but have stayed beyond its expiration date. When they stay past their allotted time, they, like those who have entered without a visa, are subject to deportation.

Many immigrants, legal or illegal, are in the country because they want to work here. The temporary-work visa program is now fairly limited and restrictive, but since we already have such a program in place, it would not be too difficult to add new categories to cover other kinds of "guest workers." Currently, illegal immigrants are doing mostly jobs Americans do not want to do. But if we make them leave, the economy would suffer. Therefore, creating a program that allows laborers to find seasonal work and then return home is a plausible solution to the immigration debate.

8 Conclusion: Desai proposes a solution to the immigration debate.

Works Cited

"Estimates of the Unauthorized Migrant Population for States Based on the March 2005 CPS."
    Pew Hispanic Center. Pew Research Center, 2006. Web. 12 Nov. 2007.

Herbst, Moira. "Guess Who's Getting the Most Work Visas." *Business Week* 6 Mar. 2008: 62-64.
    Print.

United States. Dept. of Homeland Security. Office of Immigration Statistics. *U.S. Legal
    Permanent Residents: 2006*. By Kelly Jeffreys. 2007. *Homeland Security*. Web. 16 Mar. 2008.

---.---. U.S. Citizenship and Immigration Services. *Employment Authorization*. 2008. *U.S. Citizen-
    ship and Immigration Services*. Web. 16 Mar. 2008.

---.---.---. *Immigration Classifications and Visa Categories*. 2008. *U.S. Citizenship and Immigra-
    tion Services*. Web. 12 Nov. 2007.

---. Dept. of State. *What Is a Visa?* 2008. *Travel.State.Gov*. Web. 16 Mar. 2008.

Analyzing the Writer's Technique

1. According to Desai, why is it important to understand the classification of immigrants?
2. What types of evidence does Desai use to develop his essay?
3. Consider Desai's tone. What kind of audience does he address?

Reacting to the Reading

1. What other reasons could Desai have used to establish the importance of his classification?
2. Discuss other principles of classification that might be used to classify noncitizens.
3. Write a journal entry describing Desai's attitude toward noncitizens.

READING A CLASSIFICATION OR DIVISION ESSAY

The following section provides advice for reading a classification or division essay as well as two model essays. The first essay illustrates the characteristics of classification covered in this chapter. The second essay uses classification along with other methods of development. Both essays provide opportunities to examine, analyze, and react to the writers' ideas.

Working with Text: Reading a Classification or Division Essay

For more on reading strategies, see Chapter 3.

A classification or division essay is usually tightly organized and relatively easy to follow. Use the following suggestions to read classification essays, division essays, or any writing that uses classification or division.

What to Look For, Highlight, and Annotate

1. Highlight the thesis statement, the principle of classification, and the name or title of each category or part.
2. Use a different color highlighter (or another marking method, such as asterisks or numbers) to identify the key details of each category.
3. Mark important definitions and vivid examples for later reference.
4. Add annotations indicating where you find a category or part confusing or where you think more detail is needed.

How to Find Ideas to Write About

For more on discovering ideas for a response paper, see Chapter 3.

To gain a different perspective on the reading, think of other ways of classifying or dividing the topic. For example, consider an essay that classifies types of exercise programs at health clubs according to the benefits they offer for cardiovascular health. Such exercise programs could also be classified according to their cost, degree of strenuousness, type of exercise, and so forth.

Thinking Critically about Classification and Division

When reading classification or division, particularly if its purpose is to persuade, focus on both the comprehensiveness and the level of detail by asking the following questions.

Does the Classification or Division Cover All Significant Categories or Parts?

To be fair and honest, a writer should discuss all the significant categories or parts into which a subject can be classified or divided. It would be misleading, for example, for a writer to classify unemployed workers into only two groups—those who have been laid off or downsized, and those who lack skills for employment—because many people are unemployed for other reasons. This classification fails to consider those who are unable to work due to illness; those who were fired for personal reasons, such as incompetence; and those who choose not to work while they raise children or pursue an education.

Does the Writer Provide Sufficient Detail about Each Category?

An objective and fair classification or division analysis requires that each category be treated with the same level of detail. To provide many details for some categories and just a few for others suggests a bias. For example, if a writer classifying how high school students spend their time goes into great detail about leisure activities and offers little detail on part-time jobs or volunteer work, the writer may create a false impression that students care only about having fun and make few meaningful contributions to society.

CLASSIFICATION ESSAY

As you read the following selection by Joseph A. DeVito, consider how the writer employs the elements of classification or division discussed in this chapter.

Territoriality
Joseph A. DeVito

READING

Joseph A. DeVito holds a Ph.D. from the University of Illinois and is a professor of communication at Hunter College. He is also the author of numerous college textbooks, including *The Interpersonal Communication Book*, eleventh edition (2007), *Essentials of Human Communication*, sixth edition (2008), and *Human Communication*, ninth edition (2003), from which this excerpt is taken. As you read the selection, highlight the categories the writer uses to explain the territoriality of human behavior.

One of the most interesting concepts in ethology (the study of animals in their natural surroundings) is territoriality. For example, male animals will stake out a particular territory and consider it their own. They will allow prospective mates to enter but will defend it against entrance by others, especially other males of the same species. Among deer, the size of the territory signifies the power of the buck, which in turn determines how many females he will mate with. Less powerful bucks will be able to control only small parcels of land and so will mate with only one or two females. This is a particularly adaptive measure, since it ensures that the stronger members will produce most

1

of the offspring. When the "landowner" takes possession of an area—either because it is vacant or because he gains it through battle—he marks it, for example, by urinating around the boundaries. The size of the animal's territory indicates the status of the animal within the herd.

The size and location of human territory also say something about status (Mehrabian, 1976; Sommer, 1969). An apartment or office in midtown Manhattan or downtown Tokyo, for example, indicates extremely high status. The cost of the territory restricts it to those who have lots of money.   2

Status is also signaled by the unwritten law granting the right of invasion. Higher-status individuals have more of a right to invade the territory of others than vice versa. The boss of a large company, for example, can invade the territory of a junior executive by barging into her or his office, but the reverse would be unthinkable.   3

Some researchers claim that territoriality is innate and demonstrates the innate aggressiveness of humans. Others claim that territoriality is learned behavior and is culturally based. Most, however, agree that a great deal of human behavior can be understood and described as territorial, regardless of its origin.   4

Types of Territories

Primary territory. Primary territories are your exclusive preserve: your desk, room, house, or backyard, for example. In these areas you are in control. It's similar to the home field advantage that a sports team has when playing in its own ballpark. When you are in these primary areas, you generally have greater influence over others than you would in someone else's territory. For example, when in their own home or office people take on a kind of leadership role; they initiate conversations, fill in silences, assume relaxed and comfortable postures, and maintain their positions with greater conviction. Because the territorial owner is dominant, you stand a better chance of getting your raise, your point accepted, and the contract resolved in your favor if you are in your own primary territory (Marsh, 1988).   5

Secondary territory. Secondary territories, although they do not belong to you, are associated with you perhaps because you have occupied them for a long period of time or they have been assigned to you. For example, your desk in a classroom may be a secondary territory if it was assigned to you or if you have regularly occupied it and others treat it as yours. Your neighborhood turf, a cafeteria table that you regularly occupy, or a favorite corner of a local coffee shop may be secondary territories. You feel a certain "ownership-like" attachment to the place although it is really not yours in any legal sense.   6

Public territory. Public territories are those areas that are open to all people: a park, movie house, restaurant, or beach, for example. The European café, the food court in a suburban mall, and the public spaces in large city office buildings are public spaces that, although established for eating, also serve to bring people together and to stimulate communication. The electronic revolution, however, may well change the role of public space in stimulating communication (Drucker & Gumpert, 1991; Gumpert & Drucker, 1995). For example, home shopping clubs make it less necessary for people to go shopping "downtown" or to the mall, and consequently they have less opportunity to run into other people and to talk and to exchange news. Similarly, electronic mail permits communication without talking and without even going out of one's home to mail a letter. Perhaps the greatest change is telecommuting (Giordano, 1989), which   7 allows people to work without even leaving their homes. The face-to-face communication that normally takes place in an office is replaced by communication via computer.

TERRITORIAL ENCROACHMENT

Look around your home. You probably see certain territories that different people have staked out and where invasions are cause for at least mildly defensive action. This is perhaps seen most clearly with siblings who each have (or "own") a specific chair, room, radio, and so on. Father has his chair and Mother has her chair.   8

In classrooms where seats are not assigned, territoriality can also be observed. When a student sits in a seat that has normally been occupied by another student, the regular occupant will often become disturbed and resentful.   9

Following Lyman and Scott (1967; DeVito & Hecht, 1990), Table 1 identifies the three major types of territorial encroachment: violation, invasion, and contamination.   10

You can react to encroachment in several ways (Lyman & Scott, 1967; DeVito & Hecht, 1990). The most extreme form is *turf defense.* When you cannot tolerate the intruders, you may choose to defend the territory against them and try to expel them. This is the method of gangs that defend "their" streets and neighborhoods by fighting off members of rival gangs (intruders) who enter the territory.   11

A less extreme defense is *insulation,* a tactic in which you erect some sort of barrier between yourself and the invaders. Some people do this by wearing sunglasses to avoid eye contact. Others erect fences to let others know that they do not welcome interpersonal interaction.   12

Linguistic collusion, another method of separating yourself from unwanted invaders, involves speaking in a language unknown to these outsiders. Or you might use professional jargon to which they are not privy. Linguistic collusion groups together those who speak that language and excludes those who do not know the linguistic code. Still another type of response is *withdrawal*; you leave the territory altogether.   13

MARKERS

Much as animals mark their territory, humans mark theirs with three types of markers: central, boundary, and earmarkers (Hickson & Stacks, 1993). *Central markers* are items you place in a territory to reserve it. For example, you place a drink at the bar, books on your desk, and a sweater over the chair to let others know that this territory belongs to you.   14

Boundary markers set boundaries that divide your territory from "theirs." In the supermarket checkout line, the bar placed between your groceries and those of the   15

TABLE 1 Three Types of Territorial Encroachment

Name	Definition	Example
Violation	Unwarranted use of another's territory and thereby changing the meaning of that territory	Entering another's office or home without permission
Invasion	Entering the territory of another and thereby changing the meaning of that territory	Parents entering a teen's social group
Contamination	Rendering a territory impure	Smoking a cigar in a kitchen

person behind you is a boundary marker. Similarly, the armrests separating seats in movie theaters and the rises on each side of the molded plastic seats on a bus or train are boundary markers.

Earmarkers—a term taken from the practice of branding animals on their ears—are those identifying marks that indicate your possession of a territory or object. Trademarks, nameplates, and initials on a shirt or attaché case are all examples of earmarkers.

16

REFERENCES

DeVito, J. A., & Hecht, M. L. (Eds.). (1990). *The nonverbal communication reader*. Prospect Heights, IL: Waveland.

Drucker, S. J., & Gumpert, G. (1991). Public space and communication: The zoning of public interaction. *Communication Theory, 1* (November), 294–310.

Giordano, J. (1989). *Telecommuting and organizational culture: A study of corporate consciousness and identification*. Unpublished doctoral dissertation, University of Massachusetts, Amherst, MA.

Gumpert, G., & Drucker, S. J. (1995). Place as medium: Exegesis of the café drinking coffee, the art of watching others, civil conversation—with excursions into the effects of architecture and interior design. *The Speech Communication Annual, 9* (Spring), 7–32.

Hickson, M. L., & Stacks, D. W. (1993). *NVC: Nonverbal communication: Studies and applications,* 3rd ed. Dubuque, IA: Wm. C. Brown.

Lyman, S. M., & Scott, M. B. (1967). Territoriality: A neglected sociological dimension. *Social Problems, 15,* 236–249.

Marsh, P. (1988). *Eye to eye: How people interact*. Topsfield, MA: Salem House.

Mehrabian, A. (1976). *Public places and private spaces*. New York: Basic Books.

Sommer, R. (1969). *Personal space: The behavioral basis of design*. Upper Saddle River, NJ: Prentice-Hall/Spectrum.

Examining the Reading

1. Describe the three types of territories that DeVito identifies in his classification.
2. According to the writer, in what ways do humans react to territorial encroachment?
3. Describe the three types of territorial markers that DeVito discusses and classifies.
4. Explain the meaning of each of the following words as it is used in the reading: *innate* (para. 4), *dominant* (5), *encroachment* (10), *expel* (11), and *collusion* (13). Refer to your dictionary as needed.

Analyzing the Writer's Technique

1. What is DeVito's thesis?
2. What principle of classification does the writer use to establish the three types of territories? Does he employ the same principle or a different one in his classifications of encroachment and markers?
3. What other patterns of development does DeVito use to explain his classification of territoriality, encroachment, and markers?
4. Evaluate the introduction. What methods are employed to spark readers' interest in the topic of territoriality?

Reacting to the Reading

1. Discuss examples of secondary territoriality that you have observed or experienced.
2. Discuss other possible principles of classification that might be used to classify human territories.

3. Write a journal entry describing how you dealt with a situation involving territorial encroachment.

4. Write a classification essay explaining how college students use markers to identify their territory.

CLASSIFICATION COMBINED WITH OTHER PATTERNS

In the following essay, Carolyn Foster Segal combines classification with other patterns of development to support a thesis about student excuses.

The Dog Ate My Disk, and Other Tales of Woe

Carolyn Foster Segal

Carolyn Foster Segal is an associate professor of English at Cedar Crest College in Allentown, Pennsylvania, where she specializes in American literature, poetry, creative writing, and women's film. She has published poems in *Buffalo Spree* magazine; *Phoebe: A Journal of Feminist Scholarship, Theory, and Aesthetics*; and the *Bucks County Writer*, as well as many essays in the *Chronicle of Higher Education*, a weekly newspaper for college faculty and administrators. The following essay appeared in the *Chronicle* in 2000. As you read, notice how Segal's classification essay also uses description and illustration to fully explain each category she identifies.

Taped to the door of my office is a cartoon that features a cat explaining to his feline teacher, "The dog ate my homework." It is intended as a gently humorous reminder to my students that I will not accept excuses for late work, and it, like the lengthy warning on my syllabus, has had absolutely no effect. With a show of energy and creativity that would be admirable if applied to the (missing) assignments in question, my students persist, week after week, semester after semester, year after year, in offering excuses about why their work is not ready. Those reasons fall into several broad categories: the family, the best friend, the evils of dorm life, the evils of technology, and the totally bizarre.

The Family. The death of the grandfather/grandmother is, of course, the grandmother of all excuses. What heartless teacher would dare to question a student's grief or veracity? What heartless student would lie, wishing death on a revered family member, just to avoid a deadline? Creative students may win extra extensions (and days off) with a little careful planning and fuller plot development, as in the sequence of "My grandfather/grandmother is sick"; "Now my grandfather/grandmother is in the hospital"; and finally, "We could all see it coming—my grandfather/grandmother is dead."

Another favorite excuse is "the family emergency," which (always) goes like this: "There was an emergency at home, and I had to help my family." It's a lovely sentiment, one that conjures up images of Louisa May Alcott's little women rushing off with baskets of food and copies of *Pilgrim's Progress,* but I do not understand why anyone would turn to my most irresponsible students in times of trouble.

The Best Friend. This heartwarming concern for others extends beyond the family to friends, as in, "My best friend was up all night and I had to (a) stay up with her in the

1

2

3

4

dorm, (b) drive her to the hospital, or (c) drive to her college because (1) her boyfriend broke up with her, (2) she was throwing up blood [no one catches a cold anymore; everyone throws up blood], or (3) her grandfather/grandmother died."

At one private university where I worked as an adjunct,[1] I heard an interesting spin that incorporated the motifs of both best friend and dead relative: "My best friend's mother killed herself." One has to admire the cleverness here: A mysterious woman in the prime of her life has allegedly committed suicide, and no professor can prove otherwise! And I admit I was moved, until finally I had to point out to my students that it was amazing how the simple act of my assigning a topic for a paper seemed to drive large numbers of otherwise happy and healthy middle-aged women to their deaths. I was careful to make that point during an off week, during which no deaths were reported.

The Evils of Dorm Life. These stories are usually fairly predictable; almost always feature the evil roommate or hallmate, with my student in the role of the innocent victim; and can be summed up as follows: My roommate, who is a horrible person, likes to party, and I, who am a good person, cannot concentrate on my work when he or she is partying. Variations include stories about the two people next door who were running around and crying loudly last night because (a) one of them had boyfriend/girlfriend problems; (b) one of them was throwing up blood; or (c) someone, somewhere, died. A friend of mine in graduate school had a student who claimed that his roommate attacked him with a hammer. That, in fact, was a true story; it came out in court when the bad roommate was tried for killing his grandfather.

The Evils of Technology. The computer age has revolutionized the student story, inspiring almost as many new excuses as it has Internet businesses. Here are just a few electronically enhanced explanations:

- The computer wouldn't let me save my work.
- The printer wouldn't print.
- The printer wouldn't print this disk.
- The printer wouldn't give me time to proofread.
- The printer made a black line run through all my words, and I know you can't read this, but do you still want it, or wait, here, take my disk. File name? I don't know what you mean.
- I swear I attached it.
- It's my roommate's computer, and she usually helps me, but she had to go to the hospital because she was throwing up blood.
- I did write to the newsgroup, but all my messages came back to me.
- I just found out that all my other newsgroup messages came up under a diferent name. I just want you to know that its really me who wrote all those messages, you can tel which ones our mine because I didnt use the spelcheck! But it was yours truely :) Anyway, just in case you missed those messages or don't belief its my writting, I'll repeat what I sad: I thought the last movie we watched in clas was borring.

The Totally Bizarre. I call the first story "The Pennsylvania Chain Saw Episode." A commuter student called to explain why she had missed my morning class. She had gotten

---

[1]*adjunct:* part-time instructor

up early so that she would be wide awake for class. Having a bit of extra time, she walked outside to see her neighbor, who was cutting some wood. She called out to him, and he waved back to her with the saw. Wouldn't you know it, the safety catch wasn't on or was broken, and the blade flew right out of the saw and across his lawn and over her fence and across her yard and severed a tendon in her right hand. So she was calling me from the hospital, where she was waiting for surgery. Luckily, she reassured me, she had remembered to bring her paper and a stamped envelope (in a plastic bag, to avoid bloodstains) along with her in the ambulance, and a nurse was mailing everything to me even as we spoke.

That wasn't her first absence. In fact, this student had missed most of the class meetings, and I had already recommended that she withdraw from the course. Now I suggested again that it might be best if she dropped the class. I didn't harp on the absences (what if even some of this story were true?). I did mention that she would need time to recuperate and that making up so much missed work might be difficult. "Oh, no," she said, "I can't drop this course. I had been planning to go on to medical school and become a surgeon, but since I won't be able to operate because of my accident, I'll have to major in English, and this course is more important than ever to me." She did come to the next class, wearing—as evidence of her recent trauma—a bedraggled Ace bandage on her left hand. 9

You may be thinking that nothing could top that excuse, but in fact I have one more story, provided by the same student, who sent me a letter to explain why her final assignment would be late. While recuperating from her surgery, she had begun corresponding on the Internet with a man who lived in Germany. After a one-week, whirlwind Web romance, they had agreed to meet in Rome, to *rendezvous* (her phrase) at the papal Easter Mass. Regrettably, the time of her flight made it impossible for her to attend class, but she trusted that I—just this once—would accept late work if the pope wrote a note. 10

Examining the Reading

1. Identify the categories of student excuses that Segal identifies.
2. Do some student excuses turn out to be legitimate? Give an example from the reading.
3. What obvious mistake did the student who offered the chain-saw excuse make?
4. Explain the meaning of each of the following words as it is used in the reading: *bizarre* (para. 1), *veracity* (2), *conjures* (3), *motifs* (5), and *harp* (9). Refer to your dictionary as needed.

Analyzing the Writer's Technique

1. Is it helpful or unnecessary for Segal to list her five categories in her thesis?
2. What is the function of the essay's title?
3. Who is Segal's audience?
4. Describe the tone of the essay. What does it reveal about Segal's attitude toward students?
5. What other patterns of development does Segal use in the essay?

Visualizing the Reading

What types of supporting information does Segal supply to make her categories seem real and believable? Review the reading and complete the following chart by filling in at least one type of support for each category. The first one has been done for you.

Category	Types of Support
1. The Family	Examples (death of grandmother/grandfather) Quotations
2. The Best Friend	
3. The Evils of Dorm Life	
4. The Evils of Technology	
5. The Totally Bizarre	

Reacting to the Reading

1. As a student, how do you react to the essay? Have you observed these excuses being made (or perhaps even made them yourself)? Do you agree that they are overused? Or did you find the essay inaccurate, unfair, or even upsetting?
2. Write a journal entry exploring how you think instructors should handle students who make false excuses.
3. Write an essay classifying the excuses you have seen coworkers or supervisors make in the workplace to cover up or justify their poor performance, tardiness, or irresponsibility.

(MAKING (CONNECTIONS)

The Workplace

Both "My Secret Life on the McJob: Fast Food Managers" (pp. 377–79) and "Selling in Minnesota" (pp. 225–27) deal with employment in low-level service jobs. As you answer the following questions, keep in mind that both authors are professionals who were working under the guise of learning the habits, characteristics, and problems that everyday workers face in such jobs.

Analyzing the Readings

1. What workplace problems did both Ehrenreich and Newman observe?
2. Write a journal entry exploring the differences and/or similarities that exist between working at Wal-Mart and working at fast-food restaurants.

Essay Idea

Write an essay in which you explore attitudes toward and expectations about work. You might consider its value, besides a weekly paycheck, or you might examine what type of work is rewarding.

Applying Your Skills: Additional Essay Assignments

Write a classification or division essay on one of the following topics, using what you learned about classification and division in this chapter. Depending on the topic you choose, you may need to conduct library or Internet research.

For more on locating and documenting sources, see Part 5.

To Express Your Ideas

1. Explain whether you are proud of or frustrated with your ability to budget money. For example, you might classify budget categories that are easy to master versus those that cause problems.
2. Explain why you chose your career or major. Categorize the job opportunities or benefits of your chosen field, and indicate why they are important to you.
3. Divide a store—such as a media shop, clothing store, or grocery store—into departments. Describe where you are most and least tempted to overspend.

To Inform Your Reader

4. Write an essay for the readers of your college newspaper classifying college instructors' teaching styles.
5. Explain the parts of a ceremony or an event you have attended or participated in.
6. Divide a familiar substance into its components, as Bodanis does in "A Brush with Reality: Surprises in the Tube" (p. 383).

To Persuade Your Reader

7. Categorize types of television violence to develop the argument that violence on television is either harmful to children or not harmful to children.
8. In an essay that categorizes types of parenting skills and demonstrates how they are learned, develop the argument that effective parenting skills can be acquired through practice, training, or observation.
9. Brainstorm a list of situations in which college students are in close contact, such as in a classroom, dorm room, shared apartment, or cafeteria. Choose one situation and, using DeVito's essay "Territoriality" for reference, write an essay classifying the types of behaviors students use there to mark their territory and prevent territorial encroachment. Develop an argument that these behaviors are necessary for maintaining harmony and well-being among those involved.

Cases Using Classification or Division

10. Write an essay for an introductory education class identifying a problem you have experienced or observed in the public education system. Divide public education into parts to better explain your problem.
11. You oversee the development of the annual catalog for a large community college, including the section describing the services offered to students. Decide how that section of the catalog should be organized, and then list the categories it should include. Finally, write a description of the services in one category.

CHAPTER 16

Definition: Explaining What You Mean

The photograph on the opposite page depicts an all-too-common scene following a natural disaster. Suppose your psychology instructor shows this photograph to the class and asks, "What human behavior is being exhibited here?" What would be your response? You might say the volunteer relief workers are demonstrating altruism, or generosity, or compassion, for example.

Write a paragraph defining the behavior of the Salvation Army workers. First, decide upon a term that describes their behavior. Write a brief definition of the term you chose and then explain the qualities or characteristics of the behavior.

WRITING A DEFINITION

In your paragraph, you named and described the behavior illustrated in the photo, perhaps including one or more characteristics that distinguish it from other behaviors. In other words, you have just written a definition. This chapter will show you how to write effective definitions, how to explore and explain a topic using an extended definition, and how to incorporate definition into essays using other patterns of development.

What Is a Definition?

A **definition** is a way of explaining what a term means or which meaning is intended when a word has a number of different meanings. You use definitions every day in a variety of situations. If you call a friend a *nonconformist,* she might ask you exactly what you mean, or you and a friend might disagree over what constitutes *feminism.*

Often a definition is intended for someone who is unfamiliar with the thing or idea being defined. You might define *slicing* to someone unfamiliar with golf or explain the term *koi* to a person unfamiliar with tropical fish. Many academic and work situations require that you write or learn definitions, as the examples in the box below indicate.

The essay that follows is an example of a definition of freegans.

SCENES FROM COLLEGE AND THE WORKPLACE

- On an exam for a *health and fitness course,* the following short-answer question appears: "Define the term *wellness.*"

- Your *philosophy* instructor asks you to write a paper exploring the ethics of mercy killing; as part of the essay, you need to define the concepts *terminal illness* and *chronic condition.*

- As a *chemical engineer* responsible for your department's compliance with the company's standards for *safety* and *work efficiency,* you write a brief memo to your staff defining each term.

Freegans at Work
Sarah Dowdey

READING

Sarah Dowdey is an editor at Howstuffworks.com, a Web site that provides articles explaining the ways specific processes and concepts work in a variety of fields. As you read the following essay, highlight the different aspects of the freegan lifestyle, which Dowdey describes in order to define the term.

For most people, consumerism is an ingrained and unavoidable way of life. We work, we spend, we trash, and we buy again. It's a cycle that seems all but inescapable in an industrialized society. But a group of people that call themselves freegans think they've found a way out—a way to exit the consumer cycle and live off the grid. They scavenge instead of buy, volunteer instead of work, and squat instead of rent. But there's a catch—to live off the grid, they have to eat out of the trash.

1

One man's trash is another man's treasure. A group of freegans forages through bags outside a store in New York City.

That's right. Freegans are Dumpster divers who rescue furniture, clothes, household items, and even food cast off by others. Freegans aren't homeless; in fact, most could easily afford to buy their own food. They've instead chosen to live what they believe is an ethical, unadulterated lifestyle and disassociate themselves from capitalism and consumerism.

2

The word *freegan* is a combination of "free"—as in it's free because you found it in a Dumpster—and "vegan," a vegetarian who abstains from all animal products. Not all freegans are strict vegetarians, however. Some would rather eat found meat, dairy, and eggs than let food go to waste. Many freegans extend their beliefs beyond the food they eat. In addition to Dumpster diving, some freegans squat on abandoned property

3

or grow gardens on empty lots. Some choose not to hold jobs and instead volunteer or teach repair workshops for other freegans.

Because the movement is so ideologically centered, critics accuse freegans of being   4
hypocritical. After all, avoiding purchases in a developed nation is essentially impossible. If you're still buying gas and electricity to cook scavenged food, you're still very much on the grid. Freegans, however, maintain that every little bit counts; each scavenged item helps minimize the cycle of consumption. And with Americans wasting 96 billion pounds of food a year—a quarter of the nation's supply [source: EPA]—do freegans have a point? Is society really so wasteful that people can subsist safely and happily on trash alone?

FREEGAN PHILOSOPHY

While the thrill of a good find is motivation enough for some Dumpster divers, freegans   5
are usually driven by their anti-consumerist beliefs. Although freeganism is not an offi-cial organization, a Web site, freegan.info, serves as the movement's hub. Many freegans use it to meet other scavengers and learn how to forage. The site advertises classes and scavenging sites, and briefs newcomers on the philosophy behind freeganism.

Freegans believe that consumerism destroys the environment and degrades society.   6
They believe that deforestation, factory farming, and unfair labor practices are a natu-ral result of a profit-centered culture. Most importantly, they think that working and buying give implicit approval to capitalism and its sometimes unpleasant side effects. So freegans choose not to buy. They resist electronics upgrades and changing fash-ions. They repair what they already own. They trade among themselves. They scavenge for what they need. And because most industrialized societies produce a lot of waste, freegans can usually get by quite comfortably with only the occasional purchase.

Of course when you scavenge all of your food; avoid buying clothes, furniture, and   7
gadgets; and maybe even squat on abandoned property, you have fewer expenses. With reduced financial dependence, freegans are able to choose jobs that harmonize with freegan ecological and social beliefs. They often find that they can work less and sometimes not at all. Freegans, however, are quick to point out that they're not lazy. Many use their spare time to volunteer, campaign for pet issues, teach repair work-shops, and, of course, scavenge.

Freegans also believe that society relies too much on oil. Some freegans convert   8
their cars to run on biodiesel. Others walk or bike when possible. Freegan.info even suggests hitchhiking and train hopping, two unconventional alternatives to the stan-dard green transportation solutions of hybrid cars and carbon offsets.

Freegans imagine a future of small, localized economies, where people work less   9
and spend more time together. Some even hope for a return to a pre-agricultural state, believing that gatherer cultures are the epitome of civilization.

FREEGANISM IN PRACTICE

Most freegans live in cities where trash is high quality and plentiful. New York City, with   10
its density and wealth, is practically the capital of freeganism. Because freegans tend to concentrate in urban areas, most practice urban foraging. Freegans look for furniture or bags of clothing on curbsides, electronics in office Dumpsters, and food behind gro-cery stores and restaurants.

Dedicated freegans usually establish a routine—a set of Dumpsters they visit   11
weekly or even daily. Many learn when trash goes out and when Dumpsters are

unattended. Although it's always illegal to venture behind a fenced-off area marked "no trespassing," laws on Dumpster diving vary considerably. Oddly enough, a 1988 ruling by the Supreme Court, California v. Greenwood, gave tacit approval to Dumpster divers. Although the ruling originally justified the police's search of a suspected narcotics trafficker's trash, freegans use it as an excuse to scavenge food and other cast-off items. Cities with anti-scavenging laws, however, can still fine Dumpster divers.

Many stores also discourage freegans. They're usually afraid of lawsuits from divers who get sick from discarded food. Stores that donate their excess food claim they leave nothing palatable in the trash. Freegans disagree. Stores throw out large amounts of aesthetically damaged goods like bruised fruit or crushed boxes. They also discard products that have reached their sell-by date. Although sell-by dates provide a general idea of when food will go bad, they are not safety dates. Trash from grocery stores and restaurants is also different from that of the average residential "herbie curbie." Stores usually bag discarded food separately from other trash.   12

Some freegans engage in wild foraging to collect edible plants in woods or parks. Freegan.info hosts guided foraging trips to identify plants that are safe to eat. Freegans also grow their own food. Some create plots on their own property; others practice guerrilla gardening and convert abandoned lots into community gardens. And since freegans understandably do not like to throw things out, many engage in free sharing—trading at markets where no money changes hands.   13

GLEANING AND FOOD RECOVERY

Freegans might seem like a fairly radical bunch, but the idea of scavenging for food is really nothing new. Gleaning (collecting abandoned food from fields or other sources) has been around since ancient times. It's even mentioned in the Bible as a form of charity: Farmers would harvest their crops and allow the poor to collect the leftovers. Most modern field gleaners collect food passed over by mechanical harvesting equipment or food that is not marketable because of minor imperfections. Large gleaning organizations like the Society of St. Andrew donate millions of pounds of food to the poor and homeless and attract tens of thousands of volunteers.   14

The United States Department of Agriculture promotes food recovery as a way to get fresh, healthy food to America's hungry. In addition to field gleaning, organizations salvage perishable food from wholesale and retail stores, nonperishable items from food drives, and prepared food from restaurants and dining halls. Less wasted food also means less money spent on disposal: Trashing excess food costs the nation $1 billion per year [source: EPA]. If someone gets sick from donated food and it's not a case of gross negligence, the Bill Emerson Good Samaritan Food Donation Act protects charitable individuals and businesses.   15

Although freeganism likely has roots in the hobo subculture of the Great Depression, it's also a product of the antiglobalization movements that began in the 1960s. One charitable antiglobalization and antiwar movement, Food Not Bombs, began recovering food in 1980 to provide free vegetarian meals for the hungry. It's not too surprising that people would eventually make the leap from charitable gleaning to foraging as a way of personal subsistence. Freeganism has spread around the world—Dumpster divers forage in England, Sweden, Brazil, and South Korea. Most freegans, however, try to retain some semblance of charity and generosity. They   16 usually forage in groups but resist the urge to hoard every attractive find. They some-times eat community dinners—potlucks made from scavenged food. As long as there is edible food and usable products in the trash, people will be there to pick up the waste.

SOURCES

"Bacteria and Foodborne Illness." National Digestive Diseases Information Clearinghouse. http://digestive.niddk.nih.gov/ddiseases/pubs/bacteria/index.htm

"California v. Greenwood." Fight Identity Theft. http://www.fightidentitytheft.com/shred_supreme_court.html

"A Citizen's Guide to Food Recovery." United States Department of Agriculture. http://www.usda.gov/news/pubs/gleaning/content.htm

Douglas, Julie. "What Is Freedom?" *Sunday Paper*. July 1–7, 2007. http://wetlandspreserve.org/uploadedPictures/SundayPaper.pdf

"Food Labeling." United States Department of Agriculture. http://www.fsis.usda.gov/Fact_Sheets/Food_Product_Dating/index.asp

"Food Not Bombs." http://www.foodnotbombs.net/firstindex.html

Freegan.info. http://freegan.info/

"Freegans." BBC News. http://www.bbc.co.uk/london/content/articies/2006/01 /06/insldeout_freegans_feature.shtml

Greenwall, Megan. "Diving for Dinner." *Washington Post*. August 16, 2006. http://www.washingtonpost.com/wp-dyn/content/artlcle/2006/08/15/AR2006081501248.html

Kurutz, Steven. "Not Buying It." *New York Times*. June 21, 2007. http://www.nytimes.com/2007/06/21/garden/21freegan.html?ex=1340164800&en=0f4b14f33c3f52da&ei=5124&partner

Relph, Daniela. "No Such Thing as a Free Lunch?" BBC News. http://news.bbc.co.uk/2/hi/uk_news/magazine/6933744.stm

Society of St. Andrew. http://www.endhunger.org/lndex.htm

"Waste Not/Want Not." Environmental Protection Agency. http://www.epa.gov/epaoswer/nonhw/reduce/wastenot.htm

Characteristics of Extended Definitions

If you were asked to define the term *happiness,* you would probably have trouble com-ing up with a brief definition because the emotion is experienced in a variety of situa-tions. However, you could explore the term in an essay and explain all that it means to you. Such a lengthy, detailed definition is called an **extended definition**.

Extended definitions are particularly useful in exploring a topic—in examining its various meanings and applications. In some instances, an extended definition may be-gin with a brief standard definition that anchors the essay's thesis statement. At other times, an extended definition may begin by introducing a new way of thinking about the term. Whatever approach is used, the remainder of the definition then clarifies the term by using one or more other patterns of development.

An Extended Definition Is Focused and Detailed

An extended definition focuses on a specific term and discusses it in detail. In "Freegans at Work," Dowdey concentrates on a specific lifestyle choice. She explains the origin of the word *freegans*, describes the freegan philosophy, explains how and where freegans forage for food, and discusses the similarities to gleaning.

An Extended Definition Often Includes a Brief Explanation of the Term

In an essay that provides an extended definition of a **term**, readers often find it useful to have a brief definition to help them begin to grasp the concept. A brief or standard definition is the kind found in a dictionary and consists of three parts:

- The *term* itself
- The *class* to which the term belongs
- The *characteristics or details* that distinguish the term from all others in its class

For example, a wedding band is a piece of jewelry. "Jewelry" is the **class** or group of objects that includes wedding bands. To show how a wedding band differs from other members of that class, you would need to provide its **distinguishing characteristics**—the details that make it different from other types of jewelry: it is a ring, often made of gold, that the groom gives to the bride or the bride gives to the groom during a marriage ceremony.

Here are a few more examples of this three-part structure.

Term	Class	Distinguishing Characteristics
fork	utensil	Two or more prongs
		Used for eating or serving food
Dalmatian	breed of dog	Originated in Dalmatia
		Has short, smooth coat with black or dark brown spots

To write a standard definition, use the following guidelines.

1. **Describe the class as specifically as possible.** This will make it easier for your reader to understand the term you define. In the preceding example, notice that for *Dalmatian* the class is not *animal* or *mammal*, but *breed of dog*.
2. **Do not use the term (or forms of the term) as part of your definition.** Do not write, "*Mastery* means that one has *mastered* a skill." In place of *mastered*, you could use *learned*, for example.
3. **Include enough distinguishing characteristics so that your readers will not mistake the term for something similar within the class.** If you define *answering machine* as "a machine that records phone messages," your definition would be incomplete because cell phones also record phone messages. To make the definition complete, you would need to add "land-line" before "phone messages."
4. **Do not limit the definition so much that it becomes inaccurate.** Defining *bacon* as "a smoked, salted meat from the side of a pig that is served at breakfast" would be too limited because bacon is also served at other meals. To make the definition accurate, you could either delete "that is served at breakfast" or add a qualifying expression like "usually" or "most often" before "served."

Look at the following definition of the term *bully*, taken from a magazine article on the topic. As you read it, study the highlighting and marginal notes.

Term

Three characteristics

Distinguishes this term from similar terms

The term *bully* does not have a standard definition, but Dan Olweus, professor of psychology at the University of Bergen, has honed the definition to three core elements — bullying involves a pattern of *repeated aggressive behavior* with *negative intent* directed from one child to another where there is a *power difference*. Either a larger child or several children pick on one child, or one child is clearly more dominant than the others. Bullying is not the same as garden-variety aggression; although aggression may involve similar acts, it happens between two people of equal status. By definition, the bully's target has difficulty defending him- or herself, and the bully's aggressive behavior is intended to cause distress.

Example of power difference

Hara Estroff Marano, "Big. Bad. Bully."

Exercise 16.1

Write a standard definition for two of the following terms.

1. hero

4. ATM

2. giraffe

5. friendship

3. science fiction

Exercise 16.2

For one of the terms listed in Exercise 16.1, list the distinguishing characteristics that you might use in building an extended definition.

An Extended Definition Makes a Point

The thesis of an extended definition essay tells why the term is worth reading about. In "Freegans at Work," Dowdey says in her first paragraph that the cycle of consumerism "seems all but inescapable" but tells readers that freegans believe they have found "a way to exit the consumer cycle and live off the grid."

The following thesis statements include a brief definition and make a point about the term.

> Produced by the body, hormones are chemicals that are important to physical as well as emotional development.

> Euthanasia, the act of ending the life of someone suffering from a terminal illness, is an issue that should not be legislated; rather, it should be a matter of personal choice.

An Extended Definition Uses Other Patterns of Development

To explain the meaning of a term, writers usually integrate one or more other patterns of development. Suppose you want to define the term *lurking* as it is used in the context of the Internet, where it usually means reading postings or comments on an online forum without directly participating in the ongoing discussion. You could develop the essay by using one or more other patterns, as noted in the following list.

Pattern of Development	*Defining the Term* Lurking
Narration (Chapter 10)	Relate a story about learning something important by lurking.
Description (Chapter 11)	Describe the experience of lurking.
Illustration (Chapter 12)	Give examples of typical situations involving lurking.
Process analysis (Chapter 13)	Explain how to lurk in an Internet chatroom.
Comparison and contrast (Chapter 14)	Compare and contrast lurking to other forms of observation.
Classification and division (Chapter 15)	Classify the reasons people lurk—for information, entertainment, and so on.
Cause and effect (Chapter 17)	Explain the benefits or outcomes of lurking.
Argument (Chapters 18 and 19)	Argue that lurking is an ethical or unethical practice.

In "Freegans at Work," Dowdey relies on several patterns of development. She uses *process analysis* to describe how freegans find food and other consumer goods; she uses *comparison and contrast* to compare freegans to gleaners; and she uses *cause and effect* to explain why freegans have chosen their lifestyle.

Exercise 16.3

For one of the terms listed in Exercise 16.1 (p. 416), describe how you might use two or three patterns of development in an extended definition of the term.

An Extended Definition May Use Negation and Address Misconceptions

A writer may use **negation**—explaining what a term *is not* as well as what *it is*—to show how the term is different from the other terms in the same class. For example, in an essay defining *rollerblading,* you might clarify how it is unlike *roller skating,* which uses a different type of wheeled boot that allows different kinds of motions. In "Freegans at Work," Dowdey explains that freegans are not homeless or too poor to buy food (para. 2), not all strict vegetarians (3), not organized into an official group (5), and not lazy (7).

You can also use negation to clarify personal meanings. In defining what you mean by *relaxing vacation,* you might include examples of what is not relaxing—the pressure to see something new every day, long lines, crowded scenic areas, and many hours in a car each day.

In addition, an extended definition may need to address popular misconceptions about the term being defined. In an essay defining *plagiarism,* for instance, you might correct the mistaken idea that plagiarism is only passing off an entire paper written by someone else as your own, explaining that it actually also includes using excerpts from other writers' work and not giving them credit.

Exercise 16.4

For two of the following broad topics, select a narrowed term and develop a standard defini-tion of it. Then, for each term, consider how you could address misconceptions and use nega-tion in an extended definition of the term.

1. A type of dance
2. A play, call, or player position in a sport
3. A piece of clothing (hat, jacket, or jeans)
4. A term related to a course you are taking
5. A type of business

Visualizing an Extended Definition Essay: A Graphic Organizer

For more on graphic organizers, see Chapter 3, p. 55.

The graphic organizer in Figure 16.1 shows the basic organization of an extended definition essay. The introduction announces the term, provides background information,

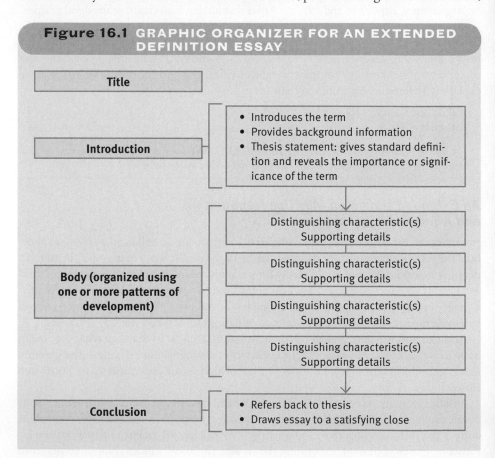

Figure 16.1 GRAPHIC ORGANIZER FOR AN EXTENDED DEFINITION ESSAY

Title

Introduction
- Introduces the term
- Provides background information
- Thesis statement: gives standard defini-tion and reveals the importance or signif-icance of the term

Body (organized using one or more patterns of development)

Distinguishing characteristic(s)
Supporting details

Distinguishing characteristic(s)
Supporting details

Distinguishing characteristic(s)
Supporting details

Distinguishing characteristic(s)
Supporting details

Conclusion
- Refers back to thesis
- Draws essay to a satisfying close

and usually includes the thesis statement (which briefly defines the term and indicates its significance to readers). The body paragraphs, which are organized using one or more patterns of development, present the term's distinguishing characteristics along with supporting details. The conclusion refers back to the thesis and brings the essay to a satisfying close.

As you read the following essay, "Latin Lingo," look for the elements illustrated in the basic graphic organizer for an extended definition. Then study the graphic organizer for the essay in Figure 16.2.

Latin Lingo
Ilan Stavans

READING

Ilan Stavans is a Mexican American essayist, translator, and commentator known for his insights into American, Hispanic, and Jewish cultures. He is the author of many books, including *The Hispanic Condition* (1995); *Dictionary Days: A Defining Passion* (2005); and his autobiography, *On Borrowed Words: A Memoir of Language* (2001). He was the host of the PBS show *Conversations with Ilan Stavans*, which ran from 2001 to 2006. Stavans has received a Guggenheim Fellowship, the Latino Literature Prize, and Chile's Presidential Medal. As you read this essay, which was originally published in the Boston *Globe* in 2003, notice how he uses comparison and negation to define Spanglish.

Quick: What's the word Cuban Americans use in Miami for *traitor*? *Kennedito*. And what do Mexicans in East LA call an Uncle Tom? *Burrito*.   1

As any lexicographer will tell you, neither of these words, at least in the above   2
senses, appears in a standard Spanish lexicon. And they are nowhere to be found in the *Oxford English Dictionary,* either. Instead, they demonstrate the rapidly growing vocabulary of Spanglish, a jazzy hybrid language, part English and part Spanish, that is audible almost everywhere in the United States today.

But is Spanglish really a language? After all, a true language ought to be capable   3
of expressing complex emotions and being understood by a wide range of speakers. And like Spanish or English, it has its academies and its concordances and other reference tools. Or does it? In defining Yiddish, the linguist Max Weinreich famously said that the difference between a language and a dialect is that the former has an army and a navy behind it. On this account, Yiddish was never a language: It inspired no national anthem, and no president or prime minister ever spoke it at official functions. And yet Yiddish masterpieces are enjoyed worldwide, and at one point in the not-too-distant past, four-fifths of the globe's Jewish population spoke Yiddish.

Not only does Spanglish lack an army and a dignitary, it has not acquired the level   4
of standardization that Yiddish achieved by the end of the nineteenth century. But its status is only likely to increase. Linguists distinguish between a "pidgin," a simplified combination of languages used for communication between groups speaking different

tongues, and a "creolized" language—which boasts a more fully developed syntax and vocabulary than a pidgin because it has become a community's native tongue. For years Spanglish was essentially a pidgin, but there are fascinating signs that more formal rules are being developed.

If nothing else, countless Hispanics north of the Rio Grande have become trilingual: 5 They speak Spanish and English—and they also speak Spanglish. This is especially so for members of the younger urban generation.

To its detractors, Spanglish represents an unacceptable middle ground—a trap, 6 really. Witness the limited English-language fluency of scores of Latinos: Clearly, the detractors say, bilingual education hasn't done its work. But this view is not entirely fair. Given the circumstances of rapid and ongoing migration, the acquisition of English in the Latino community is fast and solid and comparable to the language learning of previous immigrant groups. And yet Spanglish isn't going away as English proficiency grows. Instead, it's gaining momentum.

How to explain this phenomenon? First, it is necessary to remember that 7 Spanglish isn't only a hot Latino property. Stop at your local music store to browse through the rap and hip-hop sections. You'll be surprised by the number of non-Hispanic groups that use Spanglish. Or think of Arnold Schwarzenegger's "Hasta la vista, baby," not to mention the talking Chihuahua in the commercial announcing, "Yo quiero Taco Bell." Then watch "The Brothers Garcia" on Nickelodeon and "George Lopez" on ABC, both of which have large non-Hispanic followings. Or better, ask permission to enter the kitchen of a Chinese restaurant or the backroom of a flower shop. The moment you hear expressions like "Washea los dishes, por favor," uttered by one staffperson, a Korean, to another, a Salvadoran, you'll know something is afoot. Meanwhile, thanks to the spread of American films, fashion, and sports, Spanglish is present across the hemisphere, from Buenos Aires to Medellín.

Of course, linguistic puritans hate it, especially those sitting in the pristine 8 chambers of the Royal Academy of the Spanish Language in Madrid. For them, the *jerga loca,* as people call it, has a stink to it. Spaniards have never been entirely happy with the way Latin Americans treat their language. And now that Hispanics in the United States have become a political and economic force, the problem is compounded. How often have I been asked by a *purista*: "Well, if any Spanish lexicon records the word *techo* to describe a roof, why on earth should Latinos use *roofa*?" The purists believe that Spanglish is the result of *pereza*: laziness. But they forget that the majority of Latino homes in Gringolandia don't have a dictionary. And in any case, it's not dictionaries that tell people how to speak. Rather, it's the other way around.

Of course, the purists are right about one thing: There isn't one standardized 9 Spanglish, but many. A type of Dominicanish is spoken by Dominican Americans in Washington Heights, and it's different from the Pachuco spoken by Mexicans in El Paso and the Cubonics used by Cubans in Union City. And don't forget the ubiquitous cyber-Spanglish, used primarily by Webones on the Internet.

And yet, each of these Spanglishes shows its own inclination toward standard-ization. Thanks to radio, TV, newspapers, and particularly the Internet—nothing travels faster than Spanglish *en la Web*—certain words are understood from coast to coast and beyond our borders. This has prompted corporations and advertising firms to attempt to profit from the linguistic jumble. Not long ago, Hallmark inaugurated a new line of greeting cards: "Feeling sick? No te sientes bien?" asks one that I bought in Boston. "Watch un poco de televisión / Drink your *té* con miel y limón / Habla on the telephone / Before you know it, y de repente / you'll be feeling ¡excelente!" In my office I have a sepia poster designed to recruit Latinos to the U.S. Army. It shows a mestizo mother and cadet son and reads, "Yo soy el Army!" . . .   **10**

While most of these quotations are of fairly recent vintage, Spanglish is nothing new. It has been around in some form for more than 150 years, ever since the Treaty of Guadalupe Hidalgo in 1848 transferred two-thirds of Mexico's territory—what is nowa-days the Southwest—to the Anglos. Inevitably, the inhabitants of California, Arizona, New Mexico, Colorado, and elsewhere adapted their customs and language to novel conditions.   **11**

Spanglish can also claim a literacy legacy. For decades, Dominican and Puerto Rican authors in particular have carried out a linguistic revolution. The poetry of Miguel Algarín and Tato Laviera and the prose of Junot Díaz, Piri Thomas, Luis Rafael Sánchez, and Giannina Braschi—especially her novel "Yo-Yo Boing!"—testify to it, as does the polemical short story "Pollito Chicken" by Ana Lydia Vega, in which the au-thor dissects the Nuyorican vernacular. Her protagonist is a hilarious Puerto Rican in New York, who views her relatives in San Juan as decidedly inferior. I'm often asked: But does a regular Spanish or English reader understand these poems and stories? The answer is: Maybe. Partial knowledge of one or the other language might allow one to capture the author's overall meaning—or it might not. Last year, out of curios-ity and playfulness, I rendered the first chapter of "Don Quixote of La Mancha" into Spanglish. My translation began: "In un placete de La Mancha of which nombre no quiero remembrearme, vivía, not so long ago, uno de esos gentlemen who always tienen una lanza in the rack, una buckler antigua, a skinny caballo, y un grayhound para el chase."   **12**

The results of my experiment were published in newspapers in Spain and throughout the Americas. I found the experience of rewriting Cervantes liberating. The explanation is straightforward: For many Latinos, myself included, Spanglish is more than a tongue and a marketing tool—it's a political stand and an ID card. "English is broken here!" used to be the stigma attached to our neighborhoods. We've finally realized that, paraphrasing one of Richard Nixon's cabinet members, if it ain't broken, no lo fixées!   **13**

So—is Spanglish a language or a dialect? A creole or a pidgin? It depends on the dictionary at your disposal and the people you surround yourself with. And what kind of future will it have? It is difficult to say. What matters, though, is the present: In that realm, it is firmly *rooteado*.   **14**

Figure 16.2 GRAPHIC ORGANIZER FOR "LATIN LINGO"

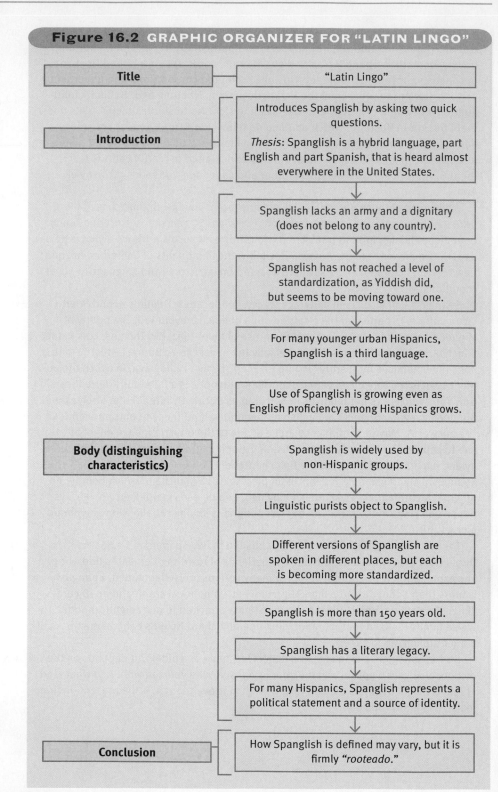

Title	"Latin Lingo"
Introduction	Introduces Spanglish by asking two quick questions. *Thesis*: Spanglish is a hybrid language, part English and part Spanish, that is heard almost everywhere in the United States.
Body (distinguishing characteristics)	Spanglish lacks an army and a dignitary (does not belong to any country).
	Spanglish has not reached a level of standardization, as Yiddish did, but seems to be moving toward one.
	For many younger urban Hispanics, Spanglish is a third language.
	Use of Spanglish is growing even as English proficiency among Hispanics grows.
	Spanglish is widely used by non-Hispanic groups.
	Linguistic purists object to Spanglish.
	Different versions of Spanglish are spoken in different places, but each is becoming more standardized.
	Spanglish is more than 150 years old.
	Spanglish has a literary legacy.
	For many Hispanics, Spanglish represents a political statement and a source of identity.
Conclusion	How Spanglish is defined may vary, but it is firmly *"rooteado."*

Exercise 16.5

Draw a graphic organizer for "Freegans at Work" on page 411.

To draw detailed graphic
organizers using a computer,
visit www.bedfordstmartins
.com/successfulwriting.

Integrating Definitions into an Essay

You will often need to include either standard or extended definitions in writing that is based on other patterns of development. For example, on college exams, you may need to write a definition as part of a response to an essay question. Definitions are also useful for explaining unfamiliar terms in any type of essay. Whatever the type of essay, the following kinds of terms usually require definition.

- **Define judgmental terms.** Judgmental terms mean different things to different people. If you describe a policy as "fiscally unsound," you would need to define your use of *fiscally unsound.*
- **Define technical terms**. Technical terms are used in a particular field or discipline. In the field of law, for example, such terms as *writ, deposition, hearing,* and *plea* have very specific meanings. Especially when writing for an audience that is unfamiliar with your topic, be sure to define technical terms.
- **Define abstract terms**. Abstract terms refer to ideas or concepts rather than physical objects. Examples are *happiness, heroism,* and *conformity.* Because abstract terms can seem vague or, like judgmental terms, mean different things to different people, they often need explanation and definition.
- **Define controversial terms**. The definitions of terms that evoke strong emotions— such as *politically correct, affirmative action,* and *chemical warfare*—are often the subject of controversy. When writing about controversial subjects, define exactly how you use each related term in an essay.

  In general, if you are not sure whether a term needs a definition, you should include one. At times you may want to provide your definition in a separate sentence or section. At other times a brief definition or synonym can be incorporated into a sentence. In this case, you use commas, dashes, or parentheses to set off the definition.

  Implicit memory, or the nonconscious retention of information about prior experiences, is important in eyewitness accounts of crimes.

  Empathy—a shared feeling of joy for people who are happy or distress for people who are in pain—explains the success of many popular films.

  In "The Animal Kingdom Storms Reality TV and the Documentary Industry" (p. 438), Alicia Rebensdorf uses definition within an essay that mixes several other methods of development.

A GUIDED WRITING ASSIGNMENT

The following guide will lead you through the process of writing an extended definition essay. Although you will focus on definition, you will need to integrate one or more other patterns of development to develop your essay.

The Assignment

Write an extended definition essay on one of the following topics or one that you choose on your own. You will need to narrow one of these general topics to a more specific term for your essay. Your audience is made up of your classmates.

1. A type of music (rock, jazz, classical)
2. Inappropriate behavior
3. A type of television show
4. Social problems
5. Leisure time
6. Athletics

For more on using examples or comparison and contrast, see Chapters 12 and 14.

As you develop your extended definition essay, consider how you can use one or more other patterns of development. For example, you might include several examples of the inappropriate behavior you choose to write about, or you might explain R & B music by comparing it to and contrasting it with rock music. For more on patterns of development, see page 416–17.

Generating Ideas

The following guidelines will help you narrow your general topic and identify distinguishing characteristics.

Narrowing the General Topic to a Specific Term

For more on narrowing a topic, see Chapter 4, p. 80.

For more on prewriting strategies, see Chapter 4.

Your first step is to narrow the broad topic you have selected to a more specific term. For example, *celebrity* is probably too broad a topic for a brief essay, but the topic can be narrowed to a particular type of celebrity, such as a *sports celebrity, Hollywood celebrity, local celebrity,* or *political celebrity.* You might then focus your definition on sports celebrities, using Eli Manning and Serena Williams as examples to illustrate the characteristics of the term.

For more on classification and division, see Chapter 15.

Use the following suggestions for finding a suitable narrowed term for your definition essay.

Learning Style Options

1. Use a branching diagram or clustering to classify the general topic into specific categories. Choose the category that you are especially interested in or familiar with.
2. Think of someone who might serve as an example of the general topic and consider focusing your definition essay on that person.
3. Discuss your general topic with a classmate to come up with specific terms related to it.

Essay in Progress 1

For the assignment option you chose on page 424 or on your own, narrow your general term into several specific categories of terms. Then choose one narrowed term for your extended definition essay.

Considering Your Purpose, Audience, and Point of View

Carefully consider your purpose and audience before you develop details for your essay. The purpose of a definition essay can be expressive, informative, or persuasive. You might, for example, write an essay that defines *search engines* and that expresses your frustration or success with using them to locate information on the Internet. Or you might write an informative essay on search engines in which you discuss the most popular ones. Finally, you might write a persuasive essay in which you argue that one search engine is superior to all others.

For more on purpose, audience, and point of view, see Chapter 4, p. 82.

When your audience is unfamiliar with a term, you will need to present detailed background information and define all specialized terms that you use. Your audience for this Guided Writing Assignment is your classmates. As you develop your essay, keep the following questions in mind.

1. What, if anything, can I assume my audience already knows?
2. What does my audience need to know to understand or accept my definition?

In addition, consider which point of view will be most effective for your essay. Most definition essays are written in the third person, while the first and second person are used occasionally, as in "Freegans at Work" and "Latin Lingo."

Identifying Distinguishing Characteristics and Supporting Details

The following suggestions will help you identify distinguishing characteristics and supporting details for the specific term you intend to define in your essay.

1. Discuss the term with a classmate, making notes as you talk.
2. Brainstorm a list of (a) words that describe your term, (b) people and things that might serve as examples of the term, and (c) everything a person would need to know to understand the term.
3. Observe a person who is associated with the term or who performs some aspect of it. Take notes on your observations.
4. Look up the term's *etymology,* or origin, in the *Oxford English Dictionary, A Dictionary of American English,* or *A Dictionary of Americanisms,* all of which are available in the reference section of your library. Take notes; the word's etymology will give you some of its characteristics and details, and might give you ideas on how to organize your essay.
5. Think of incidents or situations that reveal the meaning of the term.
6. Think of similar and different terms with which your reader is likely to be more familiar.
7. Do a search on the Internet for the term. Visit three or four Web sites and take notes on or print out what you discover at each site.

Learning Style Options

For more on observation, see Chapter 21, p. 595.

For more on Internet research, see Chapter 21, p. 581.

For more on thesis statements, see Chapter 5, p. 101.

Essay in Progress 2

For the narrowed term you selected in Essay in Progress 1, use the preceding suggestions to generate a list of distinguishing characteristics and supporting details.

Developing Your Thesis

Once you have gathered the distinguishing characteristics and supporting details for your term, you are ready to develop your thesis. It is a good idea to include a brief standard definition of the term within your thesis and an explanation of why your extended definition might be useful, interesting, or important to readers.

Notice how the following weak thesis statement can be revised to reveal the writer's main point.

WEAK   Wireless cable is a means of transmitting television signals through the air by microwave.

REVISED   The future of wireless cable, a method of transmitting television signals through the air using microwaves, is uncertain.

Essay in Progress 3

Write a working thesis statement that briefly defines your term and tells readers why understanding it might be useful or important to them.

Evaluating Your Ideas and Thesis

Take a few minutes to evaluate your ideas and thesis. Highlight details that best help your readers distinguish your term from other similar terms. If you are writing on a computer, highlight key information in bold type or move it to a separate file. Also check your prewriting to see if you have enough details—examples, facts, descriptions, expert testimony, and so forth. If you find that your characteristics or details are skimpy, choose a different method from the list on page 425 to generate additional material. If you find you still need more details, research the term in the library or on the Internet.

Trying Out Your Ideas on Others

Working in a group of two or three students, discuss your ideas and thesis for this chapter's assignment. Each writer should state his or her term, thesis, distinguishing characteristics, and supporting details. Then, as a group, evaluate each writer's work and offer suggestions for improvement.

Essay in Progress 4

Using the preceding suggestions and comments from your classmates, evaluate your thesis, distinguishing characteristics, and details. Refer to the list of characteristics on pages 414–17 to help you with your evaluation.

Organizing and Drafting

Once you have evaluated your distinguishing characteristics, supporting details, and thesis, and considered the advice of your classmates, you are ready to organize your ideas and draft your essay.

For more on drafting an essay, see Chapter 6

Choosing Other Patterns of Development

To a considerable extent, the organization of an extended definition essay depends on the other pattern or patterns of development you decide to use. Try to choose the pattern(s) before you begin drafting your essay, using Table 4.2 on p. 92 to help you. Use patterns that suit your audience and purpose as well as the term. For instance, narrating a story about lurking in online forums might capture the interest of an audience unfamiliar with such forums and thus help persuade them to explore them, whereas classifying different types of people who lurk might be of interest to an audience of forum sponsors whom you are trying to inform about ways they might encourage lurkers to participate.

With your pattern(s) firmly in mind, think about how to organize your characteristics and details. An essay incorporating several patterns of development might use a number of arrangements. At this stage, it is a good idea to make an outline or draw a graphic organizer.

For more on organizing an essay, see Chapter 6.

> **Essay in Progress 5**
>
> For the thesis you wrote in Essay in Progress 3, decide which pattern(s) of development you will use to develop your characteristics and details. Draw a graphic organizer or write an outline to help you see how each pattern will work.

Drafting an Extended Definition Essay

Use the following guidelines to draft your essay.

1. **Include enough details.** Be sure you include sufficient information to enable your reader to understand each characteristic.
2. **Consider including the history or etymology of the term.** You might include a brief history of your term in the introduction or in some other part of your essay to capture your readers' interest.
3. **Use transitions.** As you move from characteristic to characteristic, be sure to use a transitional word or phrase to signal each change and guide your readers along. The transitions *another, also,* and *in addition* are especially useful in extended definitions.

For more on transitions, see Chapter 6, p. 124.

4. **Write an effective introduction and a satisfying conclusion.** Your introduction should introduce the term, provide any needed background information, and state your thesis (which often includes a standard definition as well as your main point). When introducing your term, it may be helpful to use negation, explaining what the term is and what it is not, as Dowdey does in the second and third paragraphs of "Freegans at Work." You might also use your introduction to justify the importance of your topic, as Dowdey does in the first paragraph.

For more on writing effective paragraphs, including introductions and conclusions, see Chapter 6.

Your conclusion should reinforce your thesis and draw the essay to a satisfying close, as Stavans's conclusion does in "Latin Lingo."

Essay in Progress 6

Draft your extended definition essay, using the pattern(s) of development you selected in Essay in Progress 5 and the preceding guidelines for drafting.

Analyzing and Revising

If possible, set your draft aside for a day or two before rereading and revising it. As you review your draft, concentrate on your ideas and organization, not on grammar or mechanics. Use one or more of the following suggestions to analyze your draft.

Learning Style Options

1. Delete or make unreadable the title and all mentions of the term, and then ask a classmate to read your essay. Alternatively, you could read your essay aloud, substituting "Term X" each time the term occurs. Then ask your classmate to identify the term you are defining. If your reader or listener cannot come up with the term or a synonym for it, you probably need to make your distinguishing characteristics more specific or add details.

2. Test your definition by trying to think of exceptions to it as well as other terms that might be defined in the same way.

   - *Exceptions.* Try to identify exceptions to your distinguishing characteristics. Suppose, for example, you define *sports stars* as people who exemplify sportsmanlike behavior. Since most people can name current sports stars who indulge in unsportsmanlike behavior, this distinguishing characteristic needs to be modified or deleted.

   - *Other terms that fit all of your characteristics.* For example, in defining the term *bulletproof vest*, you would explain that it is a piece of clothing worn by law-enforcement officers, among others, to protect them from bullets and other life-threatening blows. Another kind of protective clothing—a helmet—would also fit your description, however. You would need to add information about *where* on the body a bulletproof vest is worn.

3. To see if your essay follows the organization you intend, draw a graphic organizer or make an outline (or update the organizer or outline you made earlier).

For more on the benefits of peer review, see Chapter 8, p. 162.

Use Figure 16.3 to guide your analysis. You might also ask a classmate to review your draft using the questions in the flowchart. For each "No" answer, ask your reviewer to explain his or her answer. In addition, ask your reviewer to describe his or her impressions of your main point and distinguishing characteristics. Your reviewer's comments will help you identify the parts of your essay that need revision.

Essay in Progress 7

Revise your draft using Figure 16.3 and any comments you received from peer reviewers.

Figure 16.3 Flowchart for Revising an Extended Definition Essay

QUESTIONS

REVISION STRATEGIES

1. Highlight your thesis statement. Does it include a brief definition of the term? Does it indicate why your extended definition is useful, interesting, or important?

 NO

- Use the guidelines on pages 414–17 to identify the class and distinguishing characteristics of your term, and incorporate a standard definition into your thesis.
- Ask yourself, Why is this definition worth reading about? Add your answer to your thesis.

YES

2. Place checkmarks ✔ beside the distinguishing characteristics of your definition. Do they make your term distinct from similar terms? Is each characteristic true in all cases?

 NO

- Do additional research or prewriting to discover more characteristics and details you can add to the definition.
- Eliminate characteristics and details that limit the definition too much.

YES

3. *Write* the name of the pattern(s) of development you used in your essay. Does each clearly connect your details and help explain the distinguishing characteristics of your term?

 NO

- Review the list of patterns on pages 416–17 and consider substituting or adding one or more of them to enhance your definition.

YES

4. Draw [brackets] around sections where you use negation or address misconceptions. Does each section eliminate possible misunderstandings? Are there other places where you need to do so?

 NO

- Revise your explanation of what your term is not.
- Add facts or expert opinion to correct readers' mistaken notions about the term.

 YES

(continued on next page)

(Figure 16.3 continued)

QUESTIONS		REVISION STRATEGIES

5. <u>Underline</u> the topic sentence of each paragraph. Does each paragraph have a clear topic sentence and focus on a particular characteristic? Is each paragraph well developed?

 NO →

- Consider combining paragraphs that cover the same characteristic or splitting paragraphs that cover more than one.
- Add or revise topic sentences and supporting details (see Chapter 6).

↓ **YES**

6. Reread your introduction and conclusion. Does the introduction provide necessary background information? Does your conclusion bring the essay to a satisfying close?

NO →

- Add background information that sets a context for the term you are defining.
- Revise your introduction and conclusion so that they meet the guidelines presented in Chapter 6 (pp. 126–31).

Editing and Proofreading

For more on keeping an error log, see Chapter 9, p. 196

The final step is to check your revised essay for errors in grammar, spelling, punctuation, and mechanics. Be sure to check your error log for the types of errors you commonly make.

As you edit and proofread your extended definition essay, watch out for the following types of errors commonly found in this type of writing.

1. Avoid the awkward expressions *is when* or *is where* in defining your term. Instead, name the class to which the term belongs.

- Early bird specials ~~is when~~ restaurants ~~offer reduced-price dinners~~ *are reduced-priced dinners offered in* late in the afternoon and early in the evening.

- A rollover is ~~where~~ *a transaction in which* an employee transfers money from one retirement account to another.

2. Make sure subjects and verbs agree in number. When two subjects are joined by *and*, the verb should be plural.

- Taken together, the military and Medicare ~~costs~~ *cost* U.S. taxpayers an enormous amount of money.

When two nouns are joined by *or,* the verb should agree with the noun closest to it.

- For most birds, the markings or wing span ~~are~~ ^{is} easily observed with a pair of good binoculars.

When the subject and verb are separated by a prepositional phrase, the verb should agree with the subject of the sentence, not with the noun in the phrase.

- The features of a hot-air balloon ^{are} ~~is~~ best learned by studying the attached diagram.

Essay in Progress 8

Edit and proofread your essay, paying particular attention to avoiding *is when* or *is where* expressions and correcting errors in subject-verb agreement.

Students Write

David Harris was a student at the State University of New York at Geneseo when he wrote the following essay. The assignment was to write an extended definition of a specialized term related to one of his areas of interest. Being a sports fan, Harris chose the salary cap that was instituted in the National Football League in the 1990s. As you read, note how Harris uses other patterns of development—such as narration, comparison and contrast, and cause and effect—to define the salary cap as an innovation that has been beneficial to the league.

READING

Title: Harris identifies his subject and suggests its importance.

Leveling the Playing Field: The NFL Salary Cap

David Harris

In the 1990s, professional sports salaries, including those for football players, increased at record-breaking rates. Previously, players had been "owned" by a specific team, and when their contracts ran out, they needed permission to negotiate with other teams. With the arrival of free agency in the 1970s and 1980s, players became free to negotiate with any team after a contract expired. This freedom caused bidding wars, which eventually raised salaries dramatically. To control the expense of these rising salaries, the National Football League (NFL) instituted a salary cap in 1994. A salary cap in professional sports is a limit on the amount of money a team can spend on player salaries, either per player or as a total limit for the team's roster--or both ("Salary Cap"). The NFL salary cap is a total team limit that changes from year to year, is strictly enforced without exceptions; and has given every team, regardless of revenue, a chance to compete for the league championship.

1

Introduction: Harris provides background information on events that led up to the NFL salary cap. Before introducing his specific topic, Harris defines salary caps in general. He cites a source for this definition, as he does for other information throughout the essay.

In his thesis statement, he focuses on a specific term—the NFL salary cap— and offers a brief definition of it that makes a point about its importance for maintaining competition between teams.

Harris provides additional background information on how caps originated.

The National Football League owners had searched for ways to increase profitability by limiting ballooning player salaries. As a result of collective bargaining with the NFL players' union during 1993, a salary cap was arrived at as a way of controlling salaries and of leveling the competitive playing field across the league. The players' association was granted a form of free agency that would allow players to market themselves to other teams after a certain number of years of service. In exchange for this limited free agency, the owners were granted the salary cap.

2

Harris presents his first distinguishing characteristic—that the NFL cap is a team limit—and provides details about the consequences of this characteristic. Notice that the first sentence in this paragraph is a topic sentence supported by the rest of the paragraph—a pattern followed in each of the next three paragraphs.

As noted earlier, the NFL salary cap is a team rather than a per-player limit. In 2007 the cap was $109 million ("Salary Cap FAQ"); each NFL team had to bring down its total of salaries paid to this $109 million mark. However, a player's salary is not always the same as his value according to the salary cap. A player's value under the cap equals his salary for a given year plus the portion of the signing bonus he receives that year. Signing bonuses can be distributed over the length of a contract unevenly if the team chooses to do so. As a result, many teams run into huge salary cap problems because of back-loaded contracts. A team that wins the Super Bowl one year could have to cut many of its star players to remain under the salary cap the next year. A rookie's contract is typically much smaller than that of a proven player. So replacing a high-priced veteran, who may have a heavily back-loaded contract, with a low-cost rookie is an excellent way to manage a cap and translates into more money for players at other positions. Therefore, continued success in the NFL is a product of good management and good scouting, which can help teams stay under their caps.

3

The second distinguishing characteristic: changes from year to year.

The NFL salary cap changes from year to year. In 2005 the cap was $85.5 million, but it increased by 19.3 percent to $102 million in 2006 and by 6.8 percent to $109 million in 2007 ("Salary Cap FAQ"). The salary cap is not randomly set but is derived from league revenues. It is a calculation of a percentage of the combined revenue of all teams divided by the thirty-two teams in the NFL.

4

The third distinguishing characteristic: no exceptions, with penalties for violations. Harris provides details and examples of these policies.

The cap is a "hard" limit; no team can exceed it without penalty for any reason. It is in effect for the whole season. If a team exceeds the salary cap at any point in the season, the NFL has the right to cut any player, starting from the lowest salary, until the team is below the set cap. Cutting a player from a team eliminates him from the team's payroll, but any other team can acquire him at his current contracted rate. This provides a huge incentive for teams to carefully manage their cap numbers throughout the season. Furthermore, teams that violate this cap may be made to forfeit upcoming draft picks or can be fined up to $1 million per day for each day they remain in violation. In 2000, both the Pittsburgh Steelers and the San Francisco 49ers were penalized draft picks, and the 49ers were fined as well for violation of this policy.

5

The fourth distinguishing characteristic: preserving competition.

The salary cap has the added benefit of keeping smaller-city teams, such as the Buffalo Bills, in contention with the larger-city teams. Since the NFL salary cap was instituted in 1994, no team has won more than three Super Bowls. Only the 1998 and 1999 Denver Broncos and the 2004 and 2005 New England Patriots won consecutive Super Bowls, and since 1994 the most appearances in the Super Bowl by one team has been five, by the Patriots ("Super Bowl History").

6

Sports without salary caps have had more trouble keeping the level of competition equal. In Major League Baseball, for example, the largest baseball markets dominate, and teams in smaller cities cannot compete. The New York Yankees' team salary has been the highest in the league since 1996, and since then they have made a total of six appearances in the World Series, have won four times, and have finished first in their division every year except 1997 and 2007 ("World Series History"). Due to the salary cap, since 1994 no team has come close to this kind of dominance in the NFL.

> 7   Harris uses a comparison with Major League Baseball, which lacks a salary cap, as evidence for the competitive effect of the NFL cap.

The NFL and the players have benefited greatly from the addition of the salary cap. Under the salary cap, fan interest has grown to record levels, and professional football has become the most financially successful of American sports leagues. And this wealth has been shared: As the teams' revenues have increased, so have the athletes' salaries. The salary cap has had a tremendous impact on the game of football, the fans of football, and the owners of football teams. The cap keeps all teams in contention. For that, the fans are grateful.

> 8   Conclusion: Harris comments on the effects of the NFL salary cap and reiterates its benefits.

Works Cited

"Regular Season Standings." *MLB.com*. MLB Advanced Media, 2007. Web. 27 Sept. 2007.

"Salary Cap." *Word IQ.com*. WordIQ.com, 2004. Web. 25 Apr. 2007.

"Salary Cap FAQ." *Askthecommish.com*. Ask the Commish.com LLC, 2007. Web. 3 Mar. 2007.

"Super Bowl History." *NFL.com*. NFL Enterprises, 2007. Web. 27 Sept. 2007.

"World Series History." *Baseball-Almanac.com*. Baseball Almanac, 2007. Web. 3 Mar. 2007.

Analyzing the Writer's Technique

1. Evaluate the background information Harris provides. Is it sufficient for readers who are unfamiliar with the topic?
2. What patterns of development does Harris use to define the NFL salary cap?
3. Evaluate the effectiveness of his title, introduction, and conclusion.

Reacting to the Essay

1. Discuss whether the salaries of professional football players are commensurate or out of proportion with the risk and skill involved in the game.
2. Discuss whether salary caps should be instituted for other professional teams.
3. Write a journal entry exploring the impact of professional football (or another professional sport you are familiar with) on our society.

READING DEFINITIONS

The following section provides advice for reading definitions as well as two model essays. The first essay illustrates the characteristics of an extended definition covered in this chapter. The second essay uses definition along with other methods of development. Both essays provide opportunities to examine, analyze, and react to the writers' ideas.

Working with Text: Reading Definitions

For more on reading strategies, see Chapter 3.

As you encounter new fields of study throughout college, you will be asked to learn sets of terms that are specific to academic disciplines. Articles in academic journals, as well as most textbooks, contain many new terms.

If you need to learn a large number of specialized terms, try the index-card system. Using three- by five-inch cards, write a word on the front of each card, and on its back write the word's meaning, pronunciation, and any details or examples that will help you remember it. Be sure to write the definition in your own words; don't copy the author's definition. To study, test yourself by reading the front of the cards and trying to recall the definition on the back of the cards. Then reverse the process. Shuffle the pack of cards to avoid learning terms in a particular order.

What to Look For, Highlight, and Annotate

1. As you read a definition, identify the class and highlight or underline the distinguishing characteristics. Mark any that are unclear or for which you need further information.

2. Make sure you understand how the term differs from similar terms, especially those presented in the same article or chapter. If a textbook or article does not sufficiently explain how two or more terms differ, check a standard dictionary. Each academic field of study also has its own dictionaries that list terms specific to the discipline. Examples include *Music Index, Taber's Cyclopedic Medical Dictionary,* and *A Dictionary of Economics.*

3. Highlight definitions using a special color of pen or highlighter, or designate them using annotations. You might use *V* for vocabulary, *Def.* for definition, or some other annotation.

How to Find Ideas to Write About

For more on discovering ideas for a response paper, see Chapter 3.

As you read an extended definition or an article containing brief definitions, jot down any additional characteristics or examples that come to mind. When you respond to the article, you might write about how the definition could be expanded to include these. You might also try the following strategies.

- Think of other terms in the same class that you might write about.
- Try to relate the definitions to your own experience. Where or when have you observed the characteristics described? Your personal experiences might be used in an essay in which you agree with or challenge the writer's definitions.

- If the writer has not already done so, you might use negation to expand the meaning of the term, or you might explore the word's etymology.

Thinking Critically about Definition

Some definitions are more straightforward and factual than others. Standard definitions of terms such as *calendar, automobile,* or *taxes* are not likely to be disputed by most readers. At other times, however, definitions can reflect bias, hide unpleasantness, and evoke conflicting reactions and emotions in readers. Use the following questions to think critically about the definitions you read.

Are the Writer's Definitions Objective?

Especially in persuasive essays, definitions are sometimes expressed in subjective, emotional language that is intended to influence the reader. For example, a writer who defines a *liberal* as "someone who wants to allow criminals to run free on the streets while sacrificing the rights of innocent victims" reveals a negative bias toward liberals and intends to make the reader dislike them. When reading definitions, think critically. Ask yourself the following questions.

1. Do I agree with the writer's definition of this term?
2. Do I think these characteristics apply to all members of this group?
3. Is the writer's language meant to inflame my emotions?

Are the Writer's Definitions Evasive?

A **euphemism** is a word or phrase that is used in place of an unpleasant or objectionable word. For example, *irregularity* is often used in commercials as a euphemism for *constipation,* while *passed away* is often used instead of *died.* At times, a writer may offer a euphemism as a synonym. For example, in describing a military action in which innocent civilians were killed, a writer may characterize the killings as "collateral damage." Be alert to the use of euphemisms. Like persuasive definitions, they are intended to shape your thinking.

EXTENDED DEFINITION ESSAY

Dude, Do You Know What You Just Said?
Mike Crissey

READING

Mike Crissey is a staff writer for the Associated Press. The following article, which appeared in the *Pittsburgh Post-Gazette* on December 8, 2004, is based on research done by Scott Kiesling, a professor of linguistics at the University of Pittsburgh. Kiesling's work focuses on the relationship between language and identity, particularly in the contexts of gender, ethnicity, and class. As you read, notice how the writer uses a combination of expert testimony, anecdotal evidence, and personal observations to support his main point.

Dude, you've got to read this. A University of Pittsburgh linguist has published a schol-   1
arly paper deconstructing and deciphering *dude,* the bane of parents and teachers,
which has become as universal as *like* and another vulgar four-letter favorite. In his paper in the fall edition of the journal *American Speech,* Scott Kiesling says *dude* is much
more than a greeting or catchall for lazy, inarticulate, and inexpressive (and mostly
male) surfers, skaters, slackers, druggies, or teenagers. "Without context there is no
single meaning that dude encodes and it can be used, it seems, in almost any kind of
situation. But we should not confuse flexibility with meaninglessness,"
Kiesling said.

Originally meaning "old rags," a "dudesman" was a scarecrow. In the late 1800s,   2
a "dude" was akin to a dandy, a meticulously dressed man, especially in the western
United States. *Dude* became a slang term in the 1930s and 1940s among black zoot
suiters and Mexican American pachucos. The term began its rise in the teenage lexicon
with the 1982 movie *Fast Times at Ridgemont High.* Around the same time, it became
an exclamation as well as a noun. Pronunciation purists say it should sound like
"duhd"; "dood" is an alternative, but it is considered "uncool" or old.

To decode *dude,* Kiesling listened to conversations with fraternity members he   3
taped in 1993 and had undergraduate students in sociolinguistics classes in 2001 and
2002 write down the first twenty times they heard *dude* and who said it during a three-
day period. He's also a lapsed *dude*-user who during his college years tried to talk like
Jeff Spicoli, the slacker surfer "dude" from *Fast Times at Ridgemont High.*

According to Kiesling, *dude* has many uses: an exclamation ("Dude!" and "Whoa,   4
Dude!"); to one-up someone ("That's so lame, dude"); to disarm confrontation ("Dude,
this is so boring"), or simply to agree ("Dude"). It's inclusive or exclusive, ironic or
sincere.

Kiesling says *dude* derives its power from something he calls cool solidarity: an   5
effortless or seemingly lazy kinship that's not too intimate; close, dude, but not that
close. *Dude* "carries . . . both solidarity (camaraderie) and distance (non-intimacy)
and can be deployed to create both of these kinds of stance, separately or together,"
Kiesling wrote. Kiesling, whose research focuses on language and masculinity, said
that cool solidarity is especially important to young men — anecdotally the predomi-
nant *dude*-users — who are under social pressure to be close with other young men but
not enough to be suspected as gay. "It's like *man* or *buddy.* There is often this male-
male addressed term that says, 'I'm your friend but not much more than your friend,'"
Kiesling said. Aside from its duality, *dude* also taps into nonconformity, despite everyone using it, and a new American image of leisurely success, he said.

The nonchalant attitude of *dude* also means that women sometimes call each other   6
dudes. And less frequently, men will call women *dudes* and vice versa, Kiesling said.
But that comes with some rules, according to self-reporting from students in a 2002
language and gender class at the University of Pittsburgh included in his paper. "Men
report that they use *dude* with women with whom they are close friends, but not with
women with whom they are intimate," according to his study.

His students also reported that they were least likely to use the word with parents,   7
bosses, and professors. "It is not who they are but what your relationship is with them.
With your parents, you likely have a close relationship, but unless you're Bart Simpson,
you're not going to call your parent *dude,*" Kiesling said. "There are a couple of young

professors here in their thirties and every once in a while we use *dude*. Professors are dudes, but most of the time they are not."

And *dude* shows no signs of disappearing. "More and more our culture is becoming youth centered. In southern California, youth is valued to the point that even active seniors are dressing young and talking youth," said Mary Bucholtz, an associate professor of linguistics at the University of California, Santa Barbara. "I have seen middle-aged men using *dude* with each other."

So what's the point, dude? Kiesling and linguists argue that language and how we use it is important. "These things that seem frivolous are serious because we are always doing it. We need to understand language because it is what makes us human. That's my defense of studying *dude*," Kiesling said.

Examining the Reading

1. What are some of the uses of the word *dude*?
2. Who uses the word *dude* and when?
3. What is the history of the word *dude*?
4. Explain what is meant by "cool solidarity."
5. Explain the meaning of each of the following words as it is used in the reading: *catchall* (para. 1), *meticulously* (2), *lexicon* (2), and *sociolinguistics* (3). Refer to your dictionary as needed.

Analyzing the Writer's Technique

1. Identify the thesis statement of this essay and evaluate its effectiveness.
2. Why does the author include what the word does not mean and mention to whom people do not say it?
3. What are the distinguishing characteristics of the term *dude*?
4. Evaluate the introduction. How does it capture readers' interest?
5. Could the term *dude* be considered a euphemism? If so, what words or phrases does it replace?

Visualizing the Reading

To define a term, authors frequently make use of other methods of development in addition to definition. Analyze how Crissey uses other methods by completing the following chart. The first one has been done for you.

Method of Development	Example
Narration	Crissey describes the origin of the term in time sequence (para. 2).
Classification	
Literary Analysis	
Division	

> ### MAKING CONNECTIONS
>
> #### Language
>
> Both "Latin Lingo" (pp. 419–21) and "Dude, Do You Know What You Just Said?" (pp. 435–37) discuss language change and evolution.
>
> **Analyzing the Readings**
>
> 1. In what way does each essay make a point about language change and evolution?
> 2. Write a journal entry exploring this question: Why do various groups or cultures use words and phrases that are unique to that particular group or culture?
>
> **Essay Idea**
>
> Write an essay in which you explore language change and evolution among college students. Give examples of new words and phrases that have recently entered your speaking vocabulary.

Reacting to the Reading

1. Linguist Kiesling is a "lapsed *dude*-user" (para. 3). Do you think this fact affects his ability to study and research its use?
2. Write a journal entry discussing the uses and users of the word *dude* that you have observed. Do your observations conform with those identified in the essay?
3. Choose a slang or informal word or phrase that is used on your campus or among your friends. Write an essay defining the term and explaining its uses.

DEFINITION COMBINED WITH OTHER PATTERNS

In the following selection, Alicia Rebensdorf uses an extended definition as well as other patterns to discuss animal documentary television shows.

READING

The Animal Kingdom Storms Reality TV and the Documentary Industry
Alicia Rebensdorf

Alicia Rebensdorf is the author of *Chick Flick Road Kill: A Behind the Scenes Odyssey into Movie-Made America* (2007), and her articles have been published in *Salon* and the *Los Angeles Times*. She has also been an assistant editor at *Trips* magazine and at AlterNet, a progressive news and opinion Web site where she headed the MediaCulture department. She works for the National Public Radio show *On the Media*. As you read the following essay, published on AlterNet in 2008, notice how Rebensdorf describes specific examples of animal documentary to define the type of program she is writing about.

Earlier this month, black-and-white billboard portraits of the family don were erected throughout New York City. They advertised a popular mob drama known for its sex, murder, and conflicted loyalties. The caption: *Tony's Out. Flowers' In*. The third season of Animal Planet's *Meerkat Manor* was officially here.

But Flowers isn't the only furry film star that's in. Lapping at the success of movies *March of the Penguins* and *Winged Migration*, a wave of feature-length nature documentaries is coming soon to a theater near you. August saw the release of *Arctic Tale*, a touching story of a baby walrus's and polar bear's first year. It will be followed by *The Elephants of the Okavango*, the touching story of an eight-week-old elephant calf's journey through the desert. And there's also *Turtle's Song*, a touching story of a loggerhead turtle's journey from egg to ocean, and *Earth*, which follows four migrating animals and their broods.

The upright, big-eyed meerkats will have a big year. Following the success of *Meerkat Manor*, both the BBC and the Discovery Network have feature-length meerkat films in production. The cinematographer of *Winged Migration* is also at work on *Les Animaux Amoureux*. The subtle anthropomorphism of the French title is a bludgeon in its English translation: *Animals in Love*. The cuddliness of these protagonists has inspired Desson Thomson of the *Washington Post* to name the trend the rise of the "fuzzumentary."

The name is equally descriptive, however, of the genre's blurring of traditional documentaries with Hollywoodized narratives. *Arctic Tale* used composite animals to create a fictional story of a polar cub it named Nanu and a walrus pup Seela. *The Elephants of the Okavango* publicity promotes the emotional range of its infant star, Jani; and *Queen of the Kalahari*, which is structured as a prequel to the *Meerkat Manor* series, is sure to follow the show's soap format with named cast members and telenova narration: "Finally, young Daisy tries to join the group unnoticed, but it's not going to work. She reeks of Carlos's aftershave. Despite her attempts to apologize, the group is confused and angry."

Though more overt than the TV documentaries from the Mutual of Omaha–sponsored *Wild Kingdom* series on Animal Planet, this is not an entirely new phenomenon. As *Watching Wildlife* author Cynthia Chris points out, while we tend to think of nature programming as unmediated, historically "wildlife film narration has ascribed to a fairly conservative set of ideological values." They portray the nuclear family as a firm social unit and cast those outside this unit as antagonists. Their girl-meets-boy narratives suggest universality on uniquely human social constructions. They also tend to favor species whose looks we can relate to and whose behavior can seem to match our own.

But this new genre, critics say, pushes that sort of moralizing even further. As Thomson writes, "Nature does not exist purely to entertain children. And these bears and walruses—which would devour us if given half a chance—are not fuzzy toys softshoe shuffling across a rapidly melting snow stage." Also, as exhibited in the fuss around *March of the Penguins*, when some on the right lauded the bird's conservative values and progressives shot back with evidence of their one-season matrimony, these quasidocumentaries can manipulate animals' inherently apolitical behavior into powerful political agendas.

I was recently watching an episode of *Meerkat Manor* in which one of the females (they called her Tosca) had given birth to a litter of pups. The narrator, Sean Astin, who played one of the hobbits in the *Lord of the Rings* trilogy, called her "the wayward daughter," and said the baby-daddy was likely from a rival meerkat gang. According to his script, Tosca was kicked out of the den for reproducing without "her mother's permission." Never mind the question of just how a meerkat green-lights a pregnancy, it seemed he stopped just short of calling her a slut. It might have been a little hypo-critical to accuse others of anthropomorphism while I talked back to the TV, telling a certain hobbit he was a condescending prude. Still, I cared to remind: She's a meerkat. Getting knocked up is her primary purpose in life.

The difference this go around, however, is that the conservatives who often benefit from these documentaries are no longer on the winning side of the story line. Direc-tors following the classic nature narrative—a year in the life of a particular animal—are increasingly including commentary on how those seasons have been affected by climate change. The *New York Post*'s Kyle Smith wrote of *Arctic Tale*: "The film warns that the animals are at dire risk because of the shrinking ice cap, but the message is stamped in with editorializing: When a polar bear tries to find a hunk of ice to stand on, Latifah says, 'This is not like any winter mother bear has seen before.' (Really? In what inter-view did she tell you that?)"   8

One can argue that a creature needn't be cognizant of a narrative for it to be true. Climate change is affecting many habitats, whether or not we recognize it. Heck, other animals should be so lucky to be anthropomorphized. Coral reefs are in dire shape—if only they had eyes. Plankton levels are dropping, threatening the ocean's entire ecosystem. I don't see them being a part of a Happy Meal tie-in anytime soon.   9

But even if the science of global warming is irrefutable, Smith still has a point. As far as we've come in studying animal behavior, we still have little idea of an animal's emotional cognizance. When it comes to media representation, animals—maddeningly inarticulate as they are—are entirely at our whim. By adding a couple baby animals, a dramatic soundtrack, and a few key close-ups, directors structure emotional motivations where there is little proof such feelings even exist. "In the scene where a mother polar bear has to cast off the baby because she can't fend for the both of them anymore, it's got sort of that tough-love feel. But you see that emotion in the footage," Adam Ravetch, one of the filmmakers of *Arctic Tale,* told the *New York Times*. But try fitting the infanticide that figures in many animal colonies to a jazzy soundtrack. Critics on both sides are right to be wary of the sort of cherry-picked scenes and narrative leaps that dominate these fuzzumentaries.   10

After reality television got big, some producers made an active push to rename the genre. Their alternatives—docusoap or unscripted drama—never gained much ground, but their resistance to the "reality" moniker was effective in dampening accusations against them. Over time, we've come to accept the manipulations they make for dra-matic effect: the out-of-context eye rolling, the reductive good vs. evil story arcs. Just because it is made from sugar, it doesn't taste like sugar. Most viewers are well aware of the splendafication of reality television and consume it accordingly.   11

Nature filmmakers are now responding similarly. They suggest their films aren't so overreaching as our expectations are staid. Adam Leipzig, president of National   12

Geographic Films, has tried to do the same with this genre: "I don't call it a documentary. I call it a 'wildlife adventure,' because this is a movie you go to because it's
fun and entertaining, not because it's good for you." Animal Planet's website pitches
Meerkat Manor as "*All My Children* meets *Mutual of Omaha's Wild Kingdom.*"

But for as much as *Meerkat Manor* sounds like *Laguna Beach* and *Arctic Tale*   13
looks like *Survivor,* such wordplay might not be enough. Roger Scruton, a research
professor at the Institute for the Psychological Sciences who writes widely on
animal rights issues, suggests we need a new framework for our animal-human
relationships. He argues that "negotiation, compromise and agreement" are the
foundation of all human communities and that, rather than assigning animals rights
based on a moral framework, we should give them rights based on how we use
them: as pets, food, or scientific study. It only seems fair that, as movie stars, they
deserve the same.

Examining the Reading

1. Explain how Desson Thomson (para. 3) coined the term *fuzzumentary*. In what
   ways is it descriptive of the shows it describes?
2. In what ways do fuzzumentaries convey moral values?
3. Explain why critics object to fuzzumentaries.
4. What current human issues are being built into fuzzumentaries?
5. In what ways are fuzzumentaries similar to or a part of reality TV?
6. Explain the meaning of each of the following words as it is used in the reading:
   anthropomorphism (para. 3), *unmediated* (5), *antagonists* (5), *editorializing* (8),
   cognizant (9) and *splendafication* (11). Refer to your dictionary as needed.

Analyzing the Writer's Technique

1. Identify and evaluate Rebensdorf's thesis statement.
2. What characteristics of fuzzumentaries does Robensdorf identify in the essay?
3. What patterns of development, other than definition, does Robensdorf employ?
4. What technique does the author use in the introduction to capture reader's interest? Does the conclusion bring the essay to a satisfactory close?

Reacting to the Reading

1. Discuss fuzzumentaries you have seen. How do they exhibit (or not exhibit) the
   characteristics described in this essay?
2. Write a journal entry exploring the nature of reality TV. Should animals be part of
   this genre?
3. Write an essay agreeing or disagreeing with Roger Scruton's (para. 13) position
   that animal rights should be assigned to them based on their use by humans.

For more on locating and documenting sources, see Chapters 21 and 22.

Applying Your Skills: Additional Essay Assignments

Write an extended definition essay on one of the following topics, using what you learned about definition in this chapter. Depending on the topic you choose, you may need to conduct library or Internet research.

To Express Your Ideas

Choose a specific audience and write an essay defining and expressing your views on one of the following terms.

1. Parenting
2. Assertiveness
3. Sexual harassment

To Inform Your Reader

4. Write an essay defining a term from a sport, hobby, or form of entertainment. Your audience is a classmate who is unfamiliar with the sport, hobby, or pastime.
5. Write an essay defining the characteristics of the "perfect job" you hope to hold after graduation. Your audience is your instructor.
6. Write an essay defining an important concept in a field of study, perhaps from one of your other courses. Your audience consists of students not enrolled in the course.

To Persuade Your Reader

"Freegans at Work" (p. 411) addresses the issue of consumer waste and excess. Write an essay defining a term and demonstrating that the issue is either increasing or decreasing in your community. Your audience consists of readers of your local newspaper. Choose a term from the following list.

7. Racism or ethnic stereotyping
8. Sexual discrimination
9. Age discrimination

Cases Using Definition

10. You are a fifth-grade teacher and are working on a lesson plan entitled "What Is American Democracy?" How will you limit the term *American democracy*

to define it for your audience? What characteristics and details will you include?

11. Write a press release for a new menu item as part of your job as public relations manager for a restaurant chain. First choose the new menu item, and then define the item and describe its characteristics using sensory details.

CHAPTER 17

Cause and Effect: Using Reasons and Results to Explain

Assume you are a journalist for your local newspaper reporting on a natural disaster that has occurred in a nearby town. Your immediate task is to write a story to accompany the photograph shown on the opposite page.

Write a paragraph telling your readers why the disaster occurred and what happened as a result of it. For the purpose of this activity, you should make up a plausible account of the event you see in the photograph.

WRITING A CAUSE-AND-EFFECT ESSAY

Your paragraph is an example of cause-and-effect writing. By describing why the protest happened, you explained *causes.* By explaining what happened as a result of the protest, you explained *effects.* This chapter will show you how to write strong causal analyses as well as how to incorporate cause and effect into essays using other patterns of development.

What Are Causes and Effects?

A **cause-and-effect essay**, also called a *causal analysis,* analyzes (1) *causes* (why an event or phenomenon happens), (2) *effects* (what happens because of the event or phenomenon), or (3) both causes and effects.

Almost everything you do has a cause and produces an effect. If you skip lunch because you need to study for a test, you feel hungry. If you drop a glass because it is slippery, it breaks. Young children attempting to discover and make sense of the world around them continually ask "Why?" Adults also think about and govern their lives in terms of causes and effects: "What would happen if I turned a paper in late?" or "Why does the wind pick up before a storm?" Many academic disciplines also focus on *why* questions: Psychologists are concerned with *why* people behave as they do; biologists study *why* the human body functions and reacts as it does; historians consider *why* historical events occurred.

Many everyday occasions require you to use causal analyses. If your child is hurt in an accident, the doctor may ask you to describe the accident and its effects on your child. You will also find many occasions to use causal analysis in the writing you do in college and on the job (see the accompanying box for examples).

In the following essay, Jurriaan Kamp examines the effects of diet on behavior.

SCENES FROM COLLEGE AND THE WORKPLACE

- For an essay exam in your *twentieth-century history* course, you are required to discuss the causes of U.S. involvement in the Korean conflict.

- For a *health and nutrition* course, you decide to write a paper on the relationship between diet and heart disease.

- For your job as an *investment analyst*, you need to explain why a certain company is going to be profitable in the next year.

Can Diet Help Stop Depression and Violence?
Jurriaan Kamp

Jurriaan Kamp is the author of *Because People Matter: Building an Economy That Works for Everyone* (2000) and *Small Change: How Fifty Dollars Can Change the World* (2006). He has worked on the staff of the European Parliament; as a freelance newspaper correspondent in India; and as chief economics editor of the *NRC Handelsblad*, a leading Dutch newspaper. In 1994, Kamp and Hélène de Puy, his wife, started the progressive monthly magazine *Ode*. As you read the following essay, published on AlterNet in 2007, highlight the results of each scientific study that Kamp uses to support the cause-and-effect relationship he proposes.

The best way to curb aggression in prisons? Longer jail terms, maybe, or stricter security 1 measures? How about more sports and exercise? Try fish oil. How can children enhance their learning abilities at school? A well-balanced diet and safe, stimulating classrooms are essential, but fish oil can provide an important extra boost. Is there a simple, natural way to improve mood and ward off depression? Yoga and meditation are great, but—you guessed it—fish oil can also help do the trick. A diet rich in vitamins, minerals, and fatty acids like omega-3 is the basis for physical well-being. Everybody knows that. But research increasingly suggests that these same ingredients are crucial to psychological health too. And that's a fact a lot of people seem to find hard to swallow.

The relationship between nutrition and aggression is a case in point. In 2002, 2 Bernard Gesch, a physiologist at Oxford University, investigated the effects of nutritional supplements on inmates in British prisons. Working with 231 detainees for four months, Gesch gave half the group of men, ages eighteen to twenty-one, multivitamin, mineral, and fatty-acid supplements with meals. The other half received placebos. During the study, Gesch observed that minor infractions of prison rules fell by 26 percent among men given the supplements, while rule-breaking behavior in the placebo group barely budged. The research showed more dramatic results for aggressive behavior. Incidents of violence among the group taking supplements dropped 37 percent, while the behavior of the other prisoners did not change.

Gesch's findings were recently replicated in the Netherlands, where researchers 3 at Radboud University in Nijmegen conducted a similar study for the Dutch National Agency of Correctional Institutions. Of the 221 inmates, ages eighteen to twenty-five, who participated in the Dutch study, 116 were given daily supplements containing vitamins, minerals, and omega-3 for one to three months. The other 105 received placebos. Reports of violence and aggression declined by 34 percent among the group given supplements; at the same time, such reports among the placebo group rose 13 percent.

Gesch is quick to emphasize that nutritional supplements are not magic bullets 4 against aggression, and that these studies are just "promising evidence" of the link between nutrition and behavior. "It is not suggested that nutrition is the only explanation of antisocial behavior," he says, "only that it might form a significant part." But Gesch is just as quick to emphasize that there is no down side to better nutrition, and in prisons in particular, the cost of an improved diet would be a fraction of the cost of other ways of addressing the problem of violence among inmates. Still, the menu in

British prisons hasn't changed in the five years since Gesch published his results, even though the former chief inspector of prisons in the United Kingdom, Lord Ramsbotham, told the British newspaper the *Guardian* last year that he is now "absolutely convinced that there is a direct link between diet and antisocial behavior, both that bad diet causes bad behavior and that good diet prevents it."

Yet the effect of nutrition on psychological health and behavior is still controversial, at least in part because it is so hard to study. Our moods, emotions, and actions are influenced by so many factors: everything from our genes to our communities to our personal relationships. How can the role of diet be isolated among all these competing influences? That's exactly why Gesch conducted his study in prisons. In a prison, there are far fewer variables, since all detainees have the same routine. Do the results of the inmate trials reach beyond the prison walls? Gesch thinks so: "If it works in prisons, it should work in the community and the society at large. If it works in the United Kingdom and in the Netherlands, it should work in the rest of the world."

Another place improved nutrition seems to be working is in the city of Durham in northeastern England. There, Alex Richardson, a physiologist at Oxford University, conducted a study at twelve local primary schools. The research examined 117 children ages five to twelve, all of whom were of average ability but were underachieving. Instructors suspected dyspraxia, a condition that interferes with coordination and motor skills and is thought to affect at least 5 percent of British children. Possible signs of dyspraxia *may* include having trouble tying shoelaces or maintaining balance. The condition frequently overlaps with dyslexia and attention deficit hyperactive disorder (ADHD), and is part of a range of conditions that include autistic-spectrum disorders.

Half the group of children in Richardson's study was given an omega-3 supplement for three months; the other half received an olive oil placebo. The results: Children given the omega-3 supplements did substantially better at school than those in the control group. When it came to spelling, for example, the omega-3 group performed twice as well as expected, whereas the control group continued to fall behind.

Richardson came to the study of nutrition through neurology. Her interest was sparked by the rapid rise of conditions like ADHD, autism, dyslexia, and dyspraxia. The incidence of these disorders has increased fourfold in the past fifteen to twenty years. "These disorders overlap considerably," she says, "but a real solution is rarely offered. A dyslexic child is assigned a special teacher. A kid with dyspraxia is sent to a physical therapist. One with ADHD is prescribed Ritalin. And you've got to learn to live with autism." But as Richardson writers in *They Are What You Feed Them*: "There is always something that can be done. Don't ever believe it if anyone tells you otherwise." One of the things that can be done, according to Richardson, is to boost your child's intake of omega-3.

Of course, omega-3 is not the only answer to ADHD, autism, dyslexia, dyspraxia, or other psychological or behavioral disorders, which also include Alzheimer's disease. Studies like Richardson's suggest, however, that it may play an important role in stimulating the brain, keeping it healthy, and helping it ward off debilitating conditions.

And it looks like we need all the help we can get. Behavioral dysfunctions like ADHD are currently the fastest-growing type of disorder worldwide. Twenty years ago, no one had even heard of ADHD. Today, everyone knows a kid who is taking Ritalin. The World Health Organization (WHO) estimates that the number of people with psychological disorders will double by 2020—and that around that time, depression will surpass heart and vascular disease as the No. 1 most preventable cause of death. The WHO adds that psychological disorders account for four of the ten most common causes of disability and that a quarter of the general population will be affected by them at some point in their lives.

So what's a consumer to do? Eat fish. Working with the U.S. National Institutes of Health (NIH), American physician and psychiatrist Joseph Hibbeln compared data on fish consumption with figures on depression and murder in a large number of countries around the world. Fish are a rich and ready source of omega-3. In countries in which fish consumption is low, Hibbeln found that the likelihood of suffering from depression was up to fifty times greater than in countries where it is high. 11

Some 6.5 percent of New Zealanders suffer from severe depression; these citizens also eat very little fish. In Japan, where fish consumption is high, 0.1 percent of the population suffers from depression. Manic depression (bipolar disorder) is rare in Iceland, which has the highest per capita fish consumption in the world, but is quite common in Brazil and Germany, where people don't eat as much fish. Hibbeln also found that, on average, the risk of being murdered is thirty times greater in countries where fish consumption is low compared to countries where it is high. 12

Cultural and other factors certainly influence these statistics, but the comparisons are nevertheless illustrative. Overall, in subsequent trials, Hibbeln found that depressive and aggressive feelings diminished by about 50 percent after taking fish-oil capsules for two to four weeks. Based on this and other research, the WHO concluded in a report last year: "Certain dietary choices, including fish consumption, balanced intake of micronutrients, and a good nutritional status overall, also have been associated with reduced rates of violent behavior." 13

It almost sounds too good to be true, but research is beginning to confirm that vitamins, minerals, and fatty acids can reduce aggression and improve psychological well-being. That could be a simple recipe for a more peaceful world. 14

Characteristics of Cause-and-Effect Essays

As you can see from Kamp's essay on the relation between diet and behavior, a causal analysis explains causes or effects or both. In addition, a cause-and-effect essay includes a thesis, follows a logical organizational plan, develops each cause or effect fully, and may recognize or dispel readers' assumptions about the topic.

Causal Analysis May Focus on Causes, Effects, or Both

In deciding whether to consider causes, effects, or both, it is important to distinguish the causes from the effects. Some are relatively easy to identify.

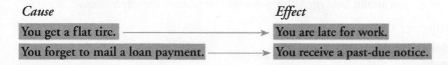

Cause	*Effect*
You get a flat tire.	You are late for work.
You forget to mail a loan payment.	You receive a past-due notice.

In complex situations, however, the causes and effects are less clear, and causes may not always be clearly separable from effects. For example, some people have an obsession with dieting (*effect*) because they have a poor body image (*cause*). Yet an obsession with dieting (*cause*) can lead to a poor body image (*effect*).

To identify causes and effects, think of causes as the *reasons that something happened* and effects as the *results of the thing that happened.*

Cause   *Effect*

X happened because . . . ⟵——— EVENT X ———⟶ The result of X was . . .

Exercise 17.1

Working either alone or with a classmate, list one or more possible causes for each of the following events or phenomena.

1. You observe a peacock strutting down a city street.
2. You are notified by the airline that the flight you had planned to take tonight has been canceled.
3. Your phone frequently rings once and then stops ringing.
4. Your town decides to fund a new public park.
5. Your best friend keeps saying, "I'm too busy to get together with you."

Exercise 17.2

Working either alone or with a classmate, list one or more possible effects for each of the following events.

1. You leave your backpack containing your wallet on the bus.
2. You decide to change your major.
3. Your spouse is offered a job in a city five hundred miles away from where you live now.
4. You volunteer as a Big Brother or Big Sister.
5. A close relative becomes very ill.

Multiple causes and effects. Causal analysis can be complex when it deals with an event or phenomenon that has multiple causes, effects, or both.

1. Several causes may produce a single effect. For example, you probably chose the college you attend (*one effect*) for a number of reasons (*multiple causes*).

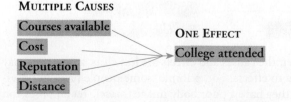

MULTIPLE CAUSES

Courses available
Cost
Reputation
Distance

ONE EFFECT
College attended

2. One cause may have several effects. For instance, your decision to quit your part-time job (*one cause*) will have several results (*multiple effects*).

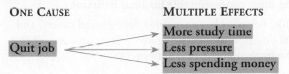

ONE CAUSE   MULTIPLE EFFECTS

Quit job → More study time
→ Less pressure
→ Less spending money

3. Related events or phenomena may have both multiple causes and multiple effects. For instance, in urban areas an increase in the number of police patrolling the street along with the formation of citizen watch groups (*multiple causes*) will result in less street crime and more small businesses (*multiple effects*).

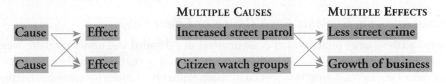

         MULTIPLE CAUSES   MULTIPLE EFFECTS

Cause → Effect   Increased street patrol → Less street crime

Cause → Effect   Citizen watch groups → Growth of business

Chains of events. In some cases a series of events forms a chain in which each event is both the effect of what happened before it and the cause of the next event. In other words, a simple event can produce a chain of consequences.

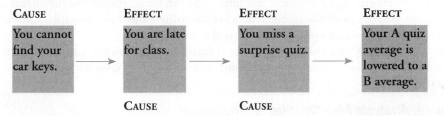

CAUSE   EFFECT   EFFECT   EFFECT

| You cannot find your car keys. | → | You are late for class. | → | You miss a surprise quiz. | → | Your A quiz average is lowered to a B average. |

         CAUSE   CAUSE

Once you clearly separate causes and effects, you can decide whether to focus on causes, effects, or both.

Causal Analysis Includes a Clear Thesis Statement

Most cause-and-effect essays have a clear thesis statement that identifies the topic, makes an assertion about that topic, and suggests whether the essay focuses on causes, effects, or both. In "Can Diet Help Stop Depression and Violence?" Kamp makes it clear that his topic is diet and makes an assertion about it: A diet rich in vitamins, minerals, and fatty acids may contribute to psychological health by reducing depression and violence.

The following sample thesis statements show two other ways of approaching an essay about unsportsmanlike conduct. One emphasizes causes, the other emphasizes causes and effects, and both make assertions about the topic.

CAUSES   The root causes of unsportsmanlike behavior lie in how society
                  regards athletes, elevating them to positions of fame and heroism and
                  thereby making them unaccountable for their behavior.

CAUSES AND   Unsportsmanlike behavior has numerous deep-rooted causes, and
EFFECTS   regardless of its origin, it produces negative effects on fans, other
                  players, and the institutions they represent.

Causal Analysis Follows a Logical Organization

A cause-and-effect essay is organized logically and systematically. It may present causes
or effects in chronological order—the order in which they happened. Alternatively,
a most-to-least or least-to-most order may be used to sequence the causes or effects
according to their importance. An essay about increased immigration to the United
States might begin with the most important causes and progress to lesser ones.

Causal Analysis Explains Each Cause or Effect Fully

A causal analysis essay presents each cause or effect in a detailed and understandable way.
Examples, facts, descriptions, comparisons, statistics, and quotations may be used to explain causes or effects. Kamp uses several of these elements to make his essay interesting
and understandable. He uses statistics to report the results of various research studies
and includes quotations by researchers to emphasize and interpret their findings.

For most cause-and-effect essays, you will need to research your topic to locate evidence that supports your thesis. In an essay about the effects on children of viewing
violence on television, for instance, you might need to locate research or statistics that
document changes in children's behavior after watching violent programs. In addition
to statistical data, expert opinion is often used as evidence.

For example, Kamp includes the expert opinion of physician and psychiatrist
Joseph Hibbeln to emphasize the role of fish consumption in eliminating depression
(para. 13).

Causal Analysis May Confirm or Challenge Readers' Assumptions

Some cause-and-effect essays affirm or question popular ideas that readers may assume
to be true. An essay on the effects of capital punishment might attempt to dispel the
notion that it is a deterrent to crime. Similarly, in "Can Diet Help Stop Depression
and Violence?" Kamp dispels the notion that longer jail terms or stricter security measures is the best way to control aggressive behavior in prisons. Dealing with the causes
or effects that readers assume to be primary is an effective strategy because it creates a
sense of completeness—or the impression that nothing has been overlooked and that
other viewpoints have been recognized.

Visualizing Cause-and-Effect Essays: Three Graphic Organizers

For more on graphic organizers,
see Chapter 3, p. 55.

The graphic organizers in Figures 17.1 through 17.3 show the basic organization of
three types of causal-analysis essays. Figure 17.1 shows the organization of an essay
that examines either causes *or* effects. Figure 17.2 shows the organization of an essay

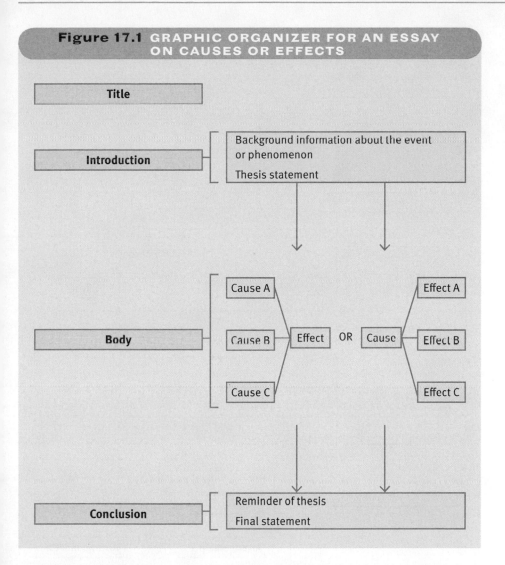

Figure 17.1 GRAPHIC ORGANIZER FOR AN ESSAY ON CAUSES OR EFFECTS

Title

Introduction — Background information about the event or phenomenon / Thesis statement

Body — Cause A, Cause B, Cause C → Effect OR Cause → Effect A, Effect B, Effect C

Conclusion — Reminder of thesis / Final statement

that examines a chain of causes and effects, while Figure 17.3 shows two possible arrangements for an essay that focuses on multiple causes and effects. All three types of causal analyses include an introduction (which identifies the event, provides background information, and states a thesis) as well as a conclusion. Notice in Figures 17.2 and 17.3 that causes are presented before effects. Although this is the typical arrangement, writers sometimes reverse it by discussing effects first and then causes to create a sense of drama or surprise.

When you incorporate causes, effects, or both into an essay that is not primarily a causal analysis, you can adapt one of these organizational plans to suit your purpose.

The essay on page 455 — "Sprawl Is Harmful to Wildlife" — is an example of a causal analysis. Read the essay and then study the graphic organizer for it in Figure 17.4 on page 457.

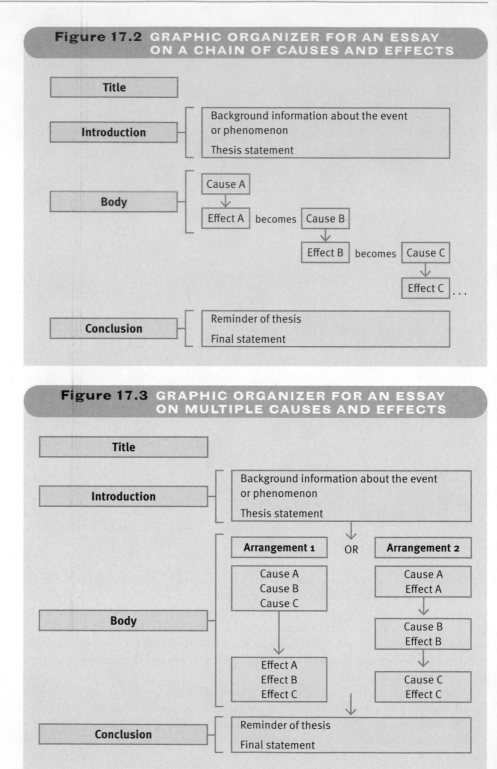

Figure 17.2 GRAPHIC ORGANIZER FOR AN ESSAY ON A CHAIN OF CAUSES AND EFFECTS

Title

Introduction — Background information about the event or phenomenon

Thesis statement

Body — Cause A → Effect A becomes Cause B → Effect B becomes Cause C → Effect C . . .

Conclusion — Reminder of thesis

Final statement

Figure 17.3 GRAPHIC ORGANIZER FOR AN ESSAY ON MULTIPLE CAUSES AND EFFECTS

Title

Introduction — Background information about the event or phenomenon

Thesis statement

Body

Arrangement 1   OR   Arrangement 2

Cause A   Cause A
Cause B   Effect A
Cause C

Cause B
Effect B

Effect A
Effect B   Cause C
Effect C   Effect C

Conclusion — Reminder of thesis

Final statement

Sprawl Is Harmful to Wildlife
Jutka Terris

READING

Jutka Terris is the coauthor of *Solving Sprawl: Models of Smart Growth in Communities across America* (2001). She has worked on smart growth and transportation policy for the Natural Resources Defense Council and was previously the national field director for 20/20 Vision, a grassroots environmental and peace advocacy organization. Terris also worked on urban environmental issues during service with AmeriCorps/Neighborhood Green Corps. As you read, highlight the effects that Terris names as resulting from the cause of urban sprawl.

1 First there were tents, then huts, then farmhouses and fields, then towns and cities. Ever since humans set foot on this continent, permanent human settlements have been built and expanded on landscapes that were previously home to wildlife. While loss of habitat to human settlement is not new, the last few decades have seen a dramatic increase in its pace. Nearly one-sixth of the total base of land developed in our country's long history was claimed for development in just ten years, from 1982 to 1992. But this expansion was not due to an unprecedented population boom in the 1980s. Instead, urban sprawl was rapidly outpacing population growth. From 1960 to 1990, the amount of developed land in all U.S. metropolitan areas more than doubled—while population grew by less than 50 percent. Today, this rapid growth continues. Moreover, some of the fastest growth is occurring far beyond our urban areas, in still-rural communities sixty to seventy miles from metropolitan beltways. Such exurbs already account for sixty million people and one-quarter of the recent population growth of the lower forty-eight states. In the exurbs, developments are often far away from each other, connected only by a system of highways and roads. Such "leapfrog developments" exacerbate the fragmentation of wildlife habitats.

2 Roads and sprawling neighborhoods are replacing pristine wildlife habitats at an alarming pace, putting the survival and reproduction of plants and animals at risk. In just the last few decades, rapidly growing human settlements have consumed large amounts of land in our country, while wildlife habitats have shrunk, fragmented, or disappeared altogether. If the current land use pattern—expansion of built areas at rates much faster than population growth—continues, sprawl could become the problem for U.S. wildlife in the twenty-first century.

3 There is wildlife in all these fast-growing areas, metropolitan and rural, and species do not fare well when the natural landscapes are paved over and built on. What kind of wildlife is most at risk? Since sprawl is claiming open lands nationwide across a varied landscape, the species affected by it are also varied. One victim of sprawl, the Florida panther, is among the most endangered large mammals in the world. It is now reduced to a single population of an estimated thirty to fifty adults.

4 In the Southwest, where especially rapid growth is taking place, plant and animal species of the fragile desert ecosystem are at risk. For example, the silent victims of Tucson's rapid expansion into the Sonoran Desert in Arizona include the ancient ironwood, the creosote bush, and the graceful saguaro cactus. Disappearing with them are animal species such as the endangered pygmy owl—a beautiful, hand-sized, brown-and-white flecked raptor—and the Sonoran pronghorn—a graceful creature that looks like an antelope but is, in fact, the sole survivor of a distinct ancient family dating back twenty million years.

In Southern California, another booming area, the coastal sage ecosystem is   5
unraveling. Sprawling development has wiped out over 90 percent of this landscape,
identified by the U.S. Fish and Wildlife Service as "one of the most depleted habitat
types in the United States." What is left is badly fragmented, and as a result, the region
has experienced a dramatic loss of native species of birds and small mammals. Other
species in trouble include the redleg frog and the Pacific pond turtle in Sonoma Valley,
California; the piping plover, a tiny bird living and nesting on the Atlantic coast; the
dusky salamander in New York state's streams; the hawksbill sea turtle in the Gulf of
Mexico; the desert tortoise in the Mojave and Colorado deserts; and the nocturnal lynx,
with its trademark bobbed tail, in parts of the Northwest and New York State.

HABITATS ARE BEING DESTROYED

Before we can talk about change, it is important to understand the many ways that our cur-   6
rent patterns of growth hurt wildlife. Habitat loss is one of the most familiar. This concept is
perhaps easiest to grasp when a complete transformation of the natural landscape occurs.
Almost no on-site wildlife can survive the transition from a meadow to a large new factory,
or to an office complex or a "big-box" retail outlet surrounded by a vast concrete parking
lot. But can wildlife survive when the new use is a residential suburb with some grass and
trees? Or an office campus, where buildings are surrounded by green landscaping?

While a few species can adapt to such human-shaped environments, many can-   7
not. And since our suburbs and office campuses are remarkably similar all around the
country (and are thus often completely oblivious to their natural surroundings), we are
essentially cultivating the few species that do well with irrigated lawns and Norway
maples and have learned to eat from our garbage cans and bird feeders. All this is at
the expense of the many species that depend on more fragile local habitats.

This trend is called generalization of habitat, and results in the survival of hardy   8
species such as pigeons, squirrels, and raccoons. While the overall biomass may not
decline—the generalists take over where more sensitive species are disappearing—the
total number of species plummets. Standing in a suburban backyard, one may still
hear birds singing, but the choir is not nearly as diverse as it was before the subdivisions came and the mature trees were chopped down.

Another serious problem is habitat fragmentation. When roads, houses, and malls   9
break up ecosystems, large populations that were once genetically diverse are broken
up into small groups. With amphibians, for example, even a single road across their
habitat may be enough to create genetically divergent groups. A result may be a lack
of enough genetic variety within each subgroup, resulting in degenerative inbreeding.
This has been a significant factor in the decline of the Florida panther, as fragmentation of wetland and forest habitats has resulted in new generations suffering serious,
sometimes fatal, genetic flaws.

Fragmentation of habitat may also separate a species from its feeding or breed-   10
ing grounds. In some cases, not even the first generation survives. Or, a species may
survive only until the first environmental stress, such as a drought, occurs, when it is
trapped in a small and isolated area. Prior to habitat fragmentation, the thirsty wildlife
could find relief at a nearby river during droughts. After development, that river may
now be on the other side of a five-lane highway or a strip mall, impossible to reach.
The more fragmented, the more vulnerable to any stress an ecosystem is.

Figure 17.4 GRAPHIC ORGANIZER FOR "SPRAWL IS HARMFUL TO WILDLIFE"

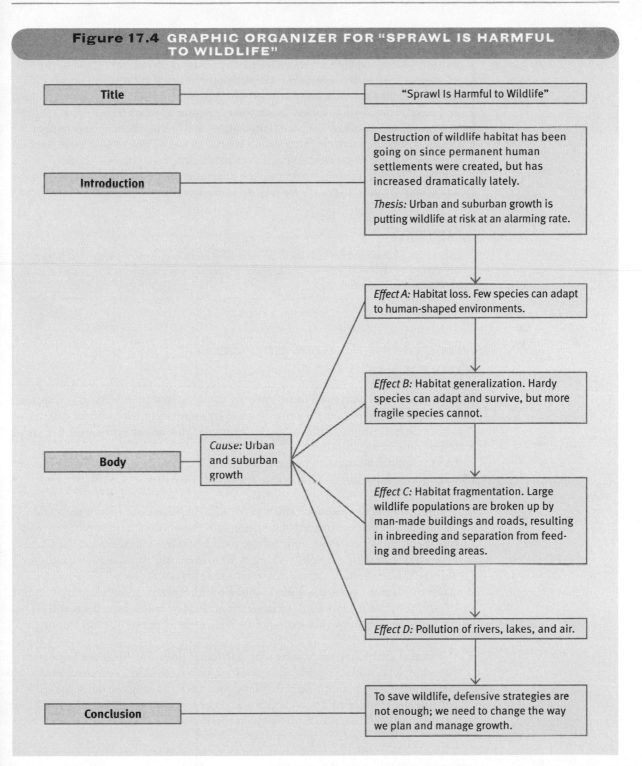

Title — "Sprawl Is Harmful to Wildlife"

Introduction —

Destruction of wildlife habitat has been going on since permanent human settlements were created, but has increased dramatically lately.

Thesis: Urban and suburban growth is putting wildlife at risk at an alarming rate.

Body — *Cause:* Urban and suburban growth

Effect A: Habitat loss. Few species can adapt to human-shaped environments.

Effect B: Habitat generalization. Hardy species can adapt and survive, but more fragile species cannot.

Effect C: Habitat fragmentation. Large wildlife populations are broken up by man-made buildings and roads, resulting in inbreeding and separation from feeding and breeding areas.

Effect D: Pollution of rivers, lakes, and air.

Conclusion —

To save wildlife, defensive strategies are not enough; we need to change the way we plan and manage growth.

FURTHER EFFECTS OF SPRAWL

Habitat loss, generalization, and fragmentation are sprawl's three most damaging impacts on wildlife. But sprawl does more: it also pollutes our rivers, lakes, and air, further threatening species. It is easy to see why Michael Klemens of the Wildlife Conservation Society described sprawl as an "extremely severe problem for wildlife," and why ecologist Joseph McAuliffe calls sprawl "an environmental abomination."

However, not all is lost—yet. The United States still has an abundance of natural areas where wildlife thrives. The question is what we can do now to save them from the rising tide of development. Ultimately, purely defensive strategies—setting aside wildlife reserves, attempting to prevent the diminution of endangered species—are insufficient. We need to change the way we plan and manage our growth.

Exercise 17.3

Draw a graphic organizer for "Can Diet Help Stop Depression and Violence?" on page 447. Use Figure 17.3, Arrangement 2, as a model, listing various research studies as causes and then outcomes as effects.

To draw detailed graphic organizers using a computer, visit www.befrodstmartins .com/successfulwriting.

Integrating Cause and Effect into an Essay

While some of your essays will focus solely on causal analysis, other essays will include cause and effect with other patterns. In an essay comparing two popular magazines that have different journalistic styles, for example, you might explain the effects of each style on readers' attitudes.

Use the following tips to integrate causal analyses into essays that rely on other patterns of development.

1. **Use transitions to announce shifts to a causal explanation.** If your readers do not expect a causal explanation, launching into one without a transition may confuse them. In writing about your college president's decision to expand the Career Planning Center, for example, you might introduce your discussion of causes by writing "Three primary factors were responsible for her decision."
2. **Keep the causal explanation direct and simple.** Since your overall purpose is not to explore causal relationships, an in-depth analysis of causes and effects will distract your readers from your main point. Therefore, focus on the most important causes and effects.
3. **Use causal analysis to emphasize why particular points or ideas are important.** For example, if you are writing an explanation of how to hold a successful yard sale, your readers are more likely to follow your advice to keep the house locked and valuables concealed if you include anecdotes and statistics that demonstrate the effect of not doing so, such as those about thefts during such sales.

To read an essay that integrates causal analysis with several other patterns of development, see "Hitting the 'Granite Wall'" by Gary M. Stern on page 476.

A GUIDED WRITING ASSIGNMENT

The following guide will lead you through the process of writing a cause-and-effect essay. Although you will focus primarily on causal analysis, you will probably need to integrate one or more other patterns of development into your essay. Depending on your learning style, you may work through this assignment in different ways. This Guided Writing Assignment will provide you with alternatives.

The Assignment

Write a cause-and-effect essay on one of the following topics or one that you choose on your own. Your essay may consider causes, effects, or both. Keep the length of your essay in mind as you think about this issue. It would be unrealistic, for example, to try to discuss both the causes and effects of child abuse in a five-page paper. Your audience consists of your classmates or members of the community in which you live.

1. The popularity (or lack of popularity) of a public figure
2. Cheating on college exams
3. Rising college costs
4. A current trend or fad
5. A major change or decision in your life
6. A problem on campus or in the community
7. A major national or international event

As you develop your causal-analysis essay, consider how you can use one or more other patterns of development. For example, you might use narration to help explain the effects of a particular community problem. In an essay about the causes of a current fad, you might compare the fad to one that is obsolete. Or you might classify rising college costs in an essay covering the causes and effects of that phenomenon.

For more on narration, see Chapter 10. For more on comparison and contrast, see Chapter 14. For more on classification, see Chapter 15.

Generating Ideas

When selecting an event or phenomenon to write about, be sure to choose one with which you are familiar or about which you can find information in the library or on the Internet.

Considering Your Purpose, Audience, and Point of View

Once you choose a topic, your next step is to decide on your purpose. A cause-and-effect essay may be expressive, but more often it is informative, persuasive, or both. In an essay about the effects of the death of a close relative, for example, you would express your feelings about the person by showing how the loss affected you. An essay may examine the causes of academic cheating (informative) and propose policies that could help alleviate the problem (persuasive).

For more on purpose, audience, and point of view, see Chapter 4, p. 82.

As you generate ideas, keep your audience in mind as well. For this Guided Writing Assignment, your audience consists of your classmates or members of your community.

If they are unfamiliar with the topic you are writing about or if your topic is complex, consider limiting your essay to primary causes or effects (those that are obvious and easily understood). If your audience is generally familiar with your topic, then you can deal with secondary causes or effects.

The level of technical detail you include should also be determined by your audience. Suppose you are writing to explain the climatic conditions that cause hurricanes and your audience is your classmates. For this audience, you would provide far fewer technical details than you would for an audience of environmental science majors.

The point of view you choose should suit your audience and purpose. Although academic writing usually uses the third person, the first person may be used to relate relevant personal experiences.

Discovering Causes and Effects

For more on prewriting strategies, see Chapter 4.

After considering your purpose, audience, and point of view, use the following suggestions to help you discover causes, effects, or both.

Learning Style Options

1. Write your topic in the middle of the page or at the top of your computer screen. Brainstorm all possible causes and effects, writing causes on the left and effects on the right.
2. Replay the event in your mind. Ask yourself, Why did the event happen? and What happened as a result of it? Make notes on the answers.
3. Try asking questions and writing assertions about the problem or phenomenon. Did a chain of events cause the phenomenon? What effects are not obvious?
4. Discuss your topic with a classmate or friend. Ask his or her opinion on the topic's causes, effects, or both.

For more on library and Internet research, see Chapter 21.

5. Research your topic in the library or on the Internet. You might begin by entering a keyword about the topic into an Internet search engine. Make notes on possible causes and effects or print out copies of the relevant Web pages you discover.

6. Ask a friend or classmate to interview you about your topic. Try to explain causes, effects, or both as clearly as possible.

> **Essay in Progress 1**
> For the assignment option you chose on page 459 or on your own, use the preceding suggestions to generate a list of causes, effects, or both for your topic.

Identifying Primary Causes and Effects

Once you have a list of causes or effects (or both), your next task is to sort through them and decide which causes or effects are *primary*, or most important. For example, if your topic is the possible effects of television violence on young viewers, two primary effects might be an increase in aggressive behavior and a willingness to accept violence as normal. Less important, or *secondary*, effects might include learning inappropriate or offensive words. In essays about controversial issues, primary causes or effects may differ depending on the writer.

Use the following questions to help you decide which causes and effects are most important.

Causes

What are the most obvious and immediate causes?
What cause(s), if eliminated, would drastically change the event, problem, or phenomenon?

Effects

What are the obvious effects of the event, problem, or phenomenon?
Which effects have the most serious consequences? For whom?

Essay in Progress 2
Review the list you prepared in Essay in Progress 1. Separate primary causes and primary effects from secondary ones.

Checking for Hidden Causes, Effects, and Errors in Reasoning

Once you identify primary and secondary causes and effects, examine them to be sure you have not overlooked any causes and effects and have avoided common reasoning errors.

Hidden causes and effects. Be on the alert for the hidden causes or effects that may underlie a causal relationship. For example, if a child often reports to the nurse's office complaining of a stomachache, a parent may reason that the child has digestive problems. However, a closer study of the behavior may reveal that the stomachaches are the result of stress and anxiety. To avoid overlooking hidden causes or effects, be sure to examine a causal relationship closely. Do not assume the most obvious or simplest explanation is the only one.

Mistaking chronology for causation. Avoid the *post hoc, ergo propter hoc* ("after this, therefore because of this") fallacy—the assumption that because event B followed event A in time, A caused B to occur. For example, suppose you decide against having a cup of coffee one morning, and later the same day you score higher than ever before on a political science exam. Although one event followed the other in time, you cannot assume that reducing your coffee intake caused the high grade.

To avoid the *post hoc* fallacy, look for evidence that one event did indeed cause the other. Plausible evidence might include testimony from others who experienced the same sequence of events or documentation proving a causal relationship between the events.

Mistaking correlation for causation. Just because two events occur at about the same time does not mean they are causally related. For example, suppose sales of snow shovels in a city increased at the same time sales of gloves and mittens increased. The fact that the two events occurred simultaneously does not mean that snow shoveling causes people to buy more mittens and gloves. Most likely, a period of cold, snowy weather caused the increased sales of these items. Again, remember that evidence is needed to verify that the two events are related and that a causal relationship exists.

For more on errors in reasoning, see Chapter 18, p. 501.

Misidentifying causal relationships. In some situations it is not clear whether one thing causes another or whether the causal relationship actually works the other way around. For example, consider the relationship between failure in school and personal problems. Does failure in school cause personal problems, or do personal problems cause failure in school? In some cases the first possibility may be true, and in others the second possibility. In still other situations a third factor, such as an inappropriate classroom environment, may be the cause of both the failure and the problems. Be sure you have evidence that a causal relationship not only exists but also works in the direction you think it does.

Gathering Evidence

A convincing cause-and-effect essay must give a complete explanation of each primary cause or effect that you include. To explain your causes and effects, you'll probably use one or more other patterns of development. For example, you may need to narrate events, present descriptive details, define important terms, explain processes unfamiliar to the reader, include examples that illustrate a cause or an effect, or make comparisons to explain unfamiliar concepts.

At this point, it is a good idea to do some additional prewriting to gather evidence to support your causes, effects, or both. You may also want to search on the Web to obtain more specific information, or pay a visit to your college library. Whatever approach you take, try to discover several types of evidence, including facts, expert opinion, personal observation, quotations, and statistics.

Developing Your Thesis

Once you are satisfied with your causes and effects and the evidence you have generated to support them, your next step is to develop a working thesis. As noted earlier, the thesis for a causal analysis identifies the topic, makes an assertion about the topic, and tells whether the essay focuses on causes, effects, or both.

For more on thesis statements, see Chapter 5, p. 101.

Use the following tips to write a clear thesis statement.

1. **State the cause-and-effect relationship.** Do not leave it to your reader to figure out the causal relationship. In the following example, note that the original thesis is weak and vague, whereas the revision clearly states the causal relationship.

                                                                       for people

- Breathing paint fumes in a closed environment can be dangerous. ~~People~~

                                              because their lungs are especially sensitive to irritants.

    suffering from asthma and emphysema ~~are particularly vulnerable.~~

The revised thesis makes the cause-and-effect connection explicit by using the word *because* and by including necessary information about the problem.

2. **Avoid overly broad or absolute assertions.**

                        a major

- Drugs are ~~the root~~ cause of inner-city crime.

The revised thesis acknowledges drugs as one cause of crime but does not claim that drugs are the only cause.

3. Use qualifying words.

may be
- Overemphasizing competitive sports ~~is~~ harmful to the psychological development of young children.

Changing the verb from *is* to *may be* qualifies the statement, allowing room for doubt.

4. Avoid an overly assertive or a dogmatic tone.

Substantial evidence suggests
- ~~There is no question~~ that American youths have changed in response to the culture in which they live.

The phrase *Substantial evidence suggests* creates a less dogmatic tone than *There is no question.*

> **Essay in Progress 3**
> Using the preceding guidelines, study your list of causes, effects, or both; gather evidence; and develop a working thesis for your essay.

Evaluating Your Ideas and Thesis

Start by rereading everything you have written with a critical eye. Highlight causes, effects, and evidence that seem usable; cross out items that are unnecessary or repetitious or that don't support your thesis. If you are working on a computer, highlight useful material in bold type or move it to a separate file. If your evidence is skimpy, do additional research or prewriting to generate more information. Also think about how you can use other patterns of development (such as comparison or illustration) to further support your thesis.

> **Trying Out Your Ideas on Others**
> Working in a group of two or three students, discuss your ideas and thesis for this chapter's assignment. Each writer should describe his or her topic (the event, problem, or phenomenon), thesis, causes or effects (or both), and supporting evidence. Then, as a group, evaluate each writer's work and causal analysis, pointing out any errors in reasoning and suggesting additional causes, effects, or evidence.

> **Essay in Progress 4**
> Using the preceding suggestions and your classmates' comments, evaluate your thesis and the evidence you have gathered to support it. Refer to the characteristics of cause-and-effect essays discussed on pages 449–52 to help you with this step.

Organizing and Drafting

For more on drafting an essay, see Chapter 6.

Once you have evaluated your cause-and-effect relationship and thesis and considered the advice of your classmates, you are ready to organize your ideas and draft your essay.

Choosing a Method of Organization

Review Figures 17.1, 17.2, and 17.3 to find the graphic organizer that is closest to your essay's basic structure. Then choose a method of organization that will help you present your ideas effectively. Chronological order works well when there is a clear sequence of events. In explaining why an entrepreneur was successful in opening a small business, for example, you might trace the causes in the order they occurred. However, if a particular event was crucial to the entrepreneur's success (such as the decision to advertise on a local television station), you might decide to save that cause for last and lead up to it to create suspense. In this case, the causes would be arranged from least to most important. Use a word-processing program to experiment with different methods of organizing your ideas.

Drafting the Cause-and-Effect Essay

After deciding how to organize the essay, your next step is to write a first draft. Use the following guidelines to draft your essay.

1. **Provide well-developed explanations.** Be sure that you provide sufficient evidence that the causal relationship exists. Choose a variety of types of evidence (examples, statistics, expert opinion, and so on), and try to develop each cause or effect into a detailed paragraph with a clear topic sentence.

For more on transitions, see Chapter 6, p. 124.

2. **Use strong transitions.** Use a transition each time you move from an explanation of one cause or effect to an explanation of another. When you move from discussing causes to discussing effects (or vice versa) or when you shift to a different pattern of development, use strong transitional sentences to alert your reader to the shift. Transitional words and phrases that are useful in cause-and-effect essays include *in addition, furthermore, more important,* and *finally.*

3. **Avoid overstating causal relationships.** Words and phrases such as *it is obvious, without doubt, always,* and *never* suggest that a causal relationship is beyond question and without exception. Instead, use words and phrases that qualify, such as *it is possible, it is likely,* and *most likely.*

For more on writing effective paragraphs, including introductions and conclusions, see Chapter 6.

4. **Write an effective introduction.** Your introduction should identify the topic and causal relationship as well as draw your reader into the essay.

5. **Write a satisfying conclusion.** Your conclusion may remind readers of your thesis and should draw your essay to a satisfying close.

> **Essay in Progress 5**
> Draft your cause-and-effect essay, using an appropriate method of organization and the preceding guidelines for drafting.

Analyzing and Revising

As you review your draft, concentrate on how you organize and present your ideas, not on grammar, punctuation, or mechanics. Use one or more of the following suggestions to analyze your draft.

1. Reread your essay aloud or ask a friend to do so as you listen. You may "hear" sections that are unclear or that require more evidence.
2. Draw a graphic organizer or update the one you drew earlier, using Figure 17.1, 17.2, or 17.3 as a model. Then study the visual organization of your ideas. Do they proceed logically? Do you see a way to organize your ideas more effectively for your readers? As an alternative, outline your essay or update an outline you made earlier to analyze your essay's structure.

Learning Style Options

Regardless of the technique you use, look for unsupported assumptions, errors in reasoning, and primary or secondary causes or effects you may have overlooked.

Use Figure 17.5 to guide your analysis of the strengths and weaknesses of your draft. You might also ask a classmate to read your paper and then summarize the primary causes, effects, or both that your paper discusses. If he or she misses or misinterprets any causes or effects, focus your revision on strengthening your explanation of the material that confused your reader. Also ask your classmate to use Figure 17.5 to react to and critique your essay. Your reviewer should consider each question listed in the flowchart and, for each "No" response, try to explain his or her answer.

For more on the benefits of peer review, see Chapter 8, p. 162.

Essay in Progress 6

Revise your draft using Figure 17.5 and any comments you received from peer reviewers.

Editing and Proofreading

The final step is to check your revised essay for errors in grammar, spelling, punctuation, and mechanics. Be sure to check your error log for the types of errors you commonly make.

For more on keeping an error log, see Chapter 9, p. 196.

As you edit and proofread your causal-analysis essay, watch out for two types of errors commonly found in this type of writing—wordy sentences and mixed constructions.

1. **Revise wordy sentences.** When explaining causal relationships, writers often use complex and compound-complex sentences. These sentences can sometimes become wordy and confusing. Look for ways to eliminate empty phrases and simplify your wording.

   - As you are already well aware, viruses of certain types in a computer file often create errors that you cannot explain in documents and may eventually result in lost data.

Figure 17.5 Flowchart for Revising a Cause-and-Effect Essay

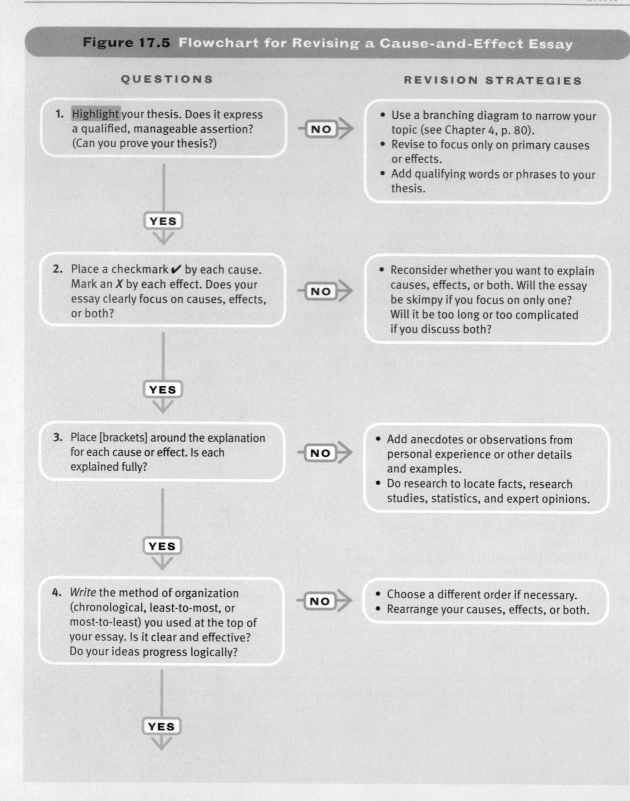

QUESTIONS

REVISION STRATEGIES

1. Highlight your thesis. Does it express a qualified, manageable assertion? (Can you prove your thesis?)

NO →
- Use a branching diagram to narrow your topic (see Chapter 4, p. 80).
- Revise to focus only on primary causes or effects.
- Add qualifying words or phrases to your thesis.

YES ↓

2. Place a checkmark ✔ by each cause. Mark an *X* by each effect. Does your essay clearly focus on causes, effects, or both?

NO →
- Reconsider whether you want to explain causes, effects, or both. Will the essay be skimpy if you focus on only one? Will it be too long or too complicated if you discuss both?

YES ↓

3. Place [brackets] around the explanation for each cause or effect. Is each explained fully?

NO →
- Add anecdotes or observations from personal experience or other details and examples.
- Do research to locate facts, research studies, statistics, and expert opinions.

YES ↓

4. *Write* the method of organization (chronological, least-to-most, or most-to-least) you used at the top of your essay. Is it clear and effective? Do your ideas progress logically?

NO →
- Choose a different order if necessary.
- Rearrange your causes, effects, or both.

YES ↓

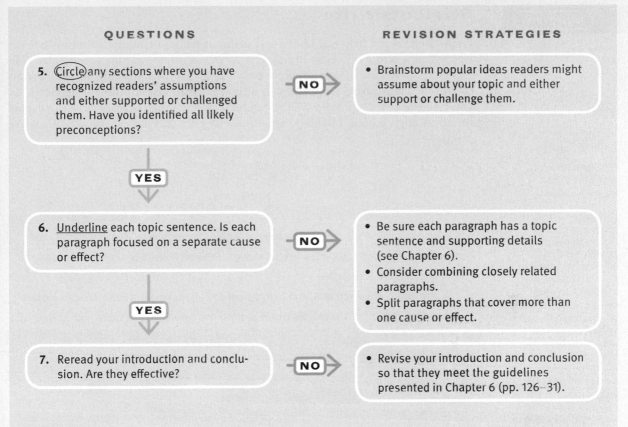

QUESTIONS

REVISION STRATEGIES

5. (Circle) any sections where you have recognized readers' assumptions and either supported or challenged them. Have you identified all likely preconceptions?

NO →

• Brainstorm popular ideas readers might assume about your topic and either support or challenge them.

YES

6. Underline each topic sentence. Is each paragraph focused on a separate cause or effect?

NO →

• Be sure each paragraph has a topic sentence and supporting details (see Chapter 6).
• Consider combining closely related paragraphs.
• Split paragraphs that cover more than one cause or effect.

YES

7. Reread your introduction and conclusion. Are they effective?

NO →

• Revise your introduction and conclusion so that they meet the guidelines presented in Chapter 6 (pp. 126–31).

2. **Revise to eliminate mixed constructions.** A mixed construction happens when a writer connects phrases, clauses, or both that do not fit together in a sentence.

Although   *Samantha*
■ ~~Samantha,~~ although she was late for work, ~~but~~ was not reprimanded by her boss.

Using both *although* and *but* makes this a mixed sentence. To avoid mixed constructions, check words that join your phrases and clauses. Pay attention to prepositions and conjunctions. Also, check to be sure that the subjects of your sentences can perform the actions described by the verbs. If not, revise the sentence to supply the appropriate verb.

encourages   *to*
■ The college ~~hopes~~ all students ~~will~~ take a freshman seminar.

Essay in Progress 7
Edit and proofread your essay, paying particular attention to eliminating wordiness and mixed constructions.

READING

Students Write

Harley Tong was a first-year liberal arts major at Niagara County Community College when he wrote this essay in response to an assignment for his writing class. He was asked to write a cause-and-effect essay explaining why and how he took action to correct a frustrating or unpleasant situation or resolve a problem he faced. As you read the essay, notice how Tong carefully presents the causes of his early departure from high school. Highlight the causes he cites and indicate which causes are primary.

Title: Tong uses a descriptive title to suggest his subject.

Introduction: Tong begins with general statements about his topic and then moves into his specific personal situation. In his thesis statement, he indicates that he will focus on a chain of causes and effects and gives an overview of the specific causes and effects and the order in which he will present them.

Tong presents cause #1: lack of challenging coursework. Notice that in this paragraph and the next four, he uses a transitional word or phrase in introducing each cause and provides a full explanation of each one.

Cause #2: problems with classmates.

Cause #3: dissatisfaction with faculty.

An Early Start

Harley Tong

For many students, high school is a place to enjoy the company of friends while getting an education. For some, it's a challenge to keep up with coursework while participating in clubs, organizations, and sports. For a few others, though, it seems a waste of time and a struggle to remain interested in schoolwork. [1]

A year ago, I was a sophomore in high school and an honor roll student with an average in the nineties, but all of the courses I took seemed uninteresting. I felt that high school was not the place for me. The combination of the unchallenging coursework, hostile fellow students, mediocre faculty, and unfair school policies led me to make the decision to go directly to college after my sophomore year, a decision that in turn resulted in vocational and extracurricular benefits as well as academic and social ones. [2]

First of all, the courses I was taking in high school presented no challenge for me. Many of them were at the Regents level rather than at the higher levels like honors or advanced placement. Even though I had been moved ahead in my science and language classes, I was never placed into honors-level classes. I wanted to stay ahead and be challenged by my coursework, but there wasn't much work to do. I became bored because the classes moved so slowly and became repetitive in certain areas. [3]

The way I was treated by other students also played an important part in my decision. In high school, I never seemed to fit in with anyone. A lot of students belonged to their own groups of friends. These groups discriminated against anyone who didn't fit in. They often made me feel out of place. Many students verbally assaulted me in the halls and during homeroom. Some students also started fights with me, and as a result, I was suspended frequently. [4]

In addition, I wanted to leave high school because I felt that many of my teachers and counselors were uninspiring and unsupportive. Many teachers were incapable of doing their jobs or just did them poorly. Most teachers taught by having us copy notes from the overhead projector or chalkboard, or they simply handed us our notes. I received little support from my counselor or any of the other faculty members in my attempt to leave [5] high school early. My counselor thought that I wasn't mature enough to handle the college workload or the atmosphere. My global studies teacher, who had talked to my counselor and learned that I wanted to leave school early, told me how she felt about the idea in front of the entire class. She also told me that our principal would never approve of "such a stupid idea."

School policies were another major factor in my decision to leave high school. The administration's views on students' rights and how they should be interpreted were very unfair. Free speech was almost totally banned, and other basic rights were denied to students. Students were not allowed to voice opinions about teachers and their teaching styles or actions in class. There were no teacher evaluation forms for students to fill out. Policies concerning fighting, harassment, and skipping class could be lightly or heavily enforced depending on whether or not you were a favorite of the teachers. My suspensions resulted from the school's policy regarding fighting: Even though I was attacked and did not do anything to defend myself, I was still punished for being involved. These suspension policies, which were allegedly designed by administrators to protect students, actually prevented students from keeping up with class work and maintaining good grades.

6 · Cause #4: unfair school policies.

During my sophomore year, I came up with a plan that would allow me to attend the local community college instead of taking my junior and senior years at the high school. I would take equivalent course material at the college and transfer the grades and credits back to the high school. While I took the courses required for high school graduation, I would also be completing requirements for my graduation from college. As the year drew to a close, I arranged for a meeting between the principal and my father. My father gave his permission, and the school finally agreed to my plan.

7 · Tong begins explaining the primary effect—his decision to leave high school for college—that resulted from the causes he has outlined. In paragraph 8, he details how this effect led to other practical effects.

All of the things that made high school so miserable for me that year finally seemed unimportant because I was on my way to a better education. Over the summer, I held three jobs to earn money for tuition and then started to work for a local construction company, which I still work for. During my first semester, I took the maximum of eighteen credit hours and worked full time to raise money for the spring semester. I also worked at the college radio station and was given my own show for the spring semester. I worked hard over the semester and got good grades as a result.

8

My experiences since I left high school have been great. I have made many new friends, enjoyed all of my professors, and joined a few clubs. Everyone at college thinks my leaving high school early was an incredible opportunity, and they are all very supportive. This was probably one of the best things I have ever done, and I hope I can keep on being successful not only in school but also in other aspects of life. I have no regrets about leaving high school and hope that what I did will make it easier for students in similar situations to realize that they can live up to their potential.

9 · Conclusion: Tong presents both the positive social and emotional effects of his decision to leave high school for college and the practical effects resulting from that decision. He ends by both dispelling an assumption readers may have had, noting that his decision did *not* cause regret, and expressing his hope that his story will have an inspiring effect on others.

Analyzing the Writer's Technique

1. Describe Tong's audience and purpose.
2. What patterns of development does the writer use to support his thesis and maintain readers' interest?
3. Evaluate the introduction and conclusion.

Reacting to the Essay

1. How does your high school experience compare to Tong's? Did you experience or observe any similar problems? Were there benefits to your high school experience that were missing from Tong's?
2. Tong mentions several grievances he had with his high school. Evaluate your high school experience. How would you grade your counselors, teachers, and peers? Be sure to support your grades with specific examples.
3. Tong devised an unconventional plan to solve a problem. Write a journal entry describing an unconventional step you either took or considered taking to solve a problem you faced.

READING CAUSE-AND-EFFECT ESSAYS

The following section provides advice for reading causal analyses. Two model essays illustrate the characteristics of causal analysis covered in this chapter and provide opportunities to examine, analyze, and react to the writer's ideas. The second essay uses causal analysis with other patterns of development.

Working with Text: Reading Causal Analyses

For more on reading strategies, see Chapter 3.

Reading cause-and-effect essays requires critical thinking and analysis as well as close attention to detail. The overall questions to keep in mind are these: What is the relationship between the events or phenomena the writer is describing and the proposed causes or effects? Has the writer perceived this relationship accurately and completely?
    Use the following suggestions when reading text that deals with causes and effects.

What to Look For, Highlight, and Annotate

1. Identify the author's thesis. Look for evidence that suggests a causal relationship actually exists.
2. Make a specific effort to distinguish between causes and effects. Mark or highlight causes in one color and effects in another.
3. Annotate causes or effects that are unclear or that are not supported by sufficient evidence.

4. Distinguish between primary and secondary causes or effects, especially in a lengthy or complex essay. Mark primary causes *PC* and secondary causes *SC.*
5. Be alert for key words that signal a causal relationship. A writer may not always use obvious transitional words and phrases. Notice how each of the following examples suggests a cause or effect connection.

CAUSES

One *source* of confusion on the issue of gun control is . . .
A court's decision *is motivated by* . . .

EFFECTS

One *impact* of the Supreme Court decision was . . .
One *result* of a change in favored-nation status may be . . .

6. As you read, fill in a graphic organizer to map a complex causal relationship, sorting causes from effects (see Figures 17.1, 17.2, and 17.3).
7. Establish the sequence of events for an essay that is not organized chronologically. Some authors may discuss effects before presenting causes. Other authors may not mention the key events in a complex series of events in the order they occurred. Use your computer to draw a time line or write a list of the events in chronological order.

How to Find Ideas to Write About

To respond to or write about a cause-and-effect essay, consider the following strategies.

For more on discovering ideas for a response paper, see Chapter 3.

- If the essay discusses the causes of an event, a phenomenon, or a problem, consider writing about the effects or vice versa.
- Think of and write about secondary or other possible causes or effects the writer does not mention.
- For a chain-of-events essay, write about what might have happened if the chain had been broken at some point.
- Write about a cause-and-effect relationship from your own life that is similar to one in the essay.

Thinking Critically about Cause and Effect

Reading and evaluating causal relationships involves close analysis and may require that you do research to verify a writer's assertions. Use the following questions to think critically about the causal analyses you read.

What Is the Writer's Purpose?

Consider how the writer is describing certain causes or effects and how this description advances his or her purpose, such as to persuade readers to accept a particular position on an issue. A graphic description of the physical effects of an experimental drug on laboratory animals, for example, may strengthen a writer's argument against the use of animals in medical research.

Does the Writer Cover All Major Causes or Effects?

Consider whether the writer presents a fair description of all major causes or effects. For example, a writer arguing in favor of using animals for medical research might fail to mention the painful effects of testing on laboratory animals. Conversely, a writer who opposes using animals for medical research might fail to mention that several human diseases are now controllable as a result of tests performed on animals. In either case, the writer does not offer a complete, objective account.

Does the Writer Provide Sufficient Evidence for the Causal Relationship?

Look for whether the writer provides *sufficient* supporting evidence to prove the existence of a causal relationship between the events or phenomena. For example, suppose a writer makes this assertion: "Medical doctors waste the resources of health insurance companies by ordering unnecessary medical tests." For support the writer relies on one example involving a grandparent who was required to undergo twenty-two tests and procedures before being approved for minor outpatient surgery. This anecdote is relevant to the writer's assertion, but one person's experience is not enough to prove a causal relationship. Consider whether the writer might have provided the additional support (such as statistics and expert opinion) or whether adequate support could not be found for the assertion.

CAUSAL-ANALYSIS ESSAY

The following essay by Laurence Steinberg reports the results of his research into the causal relationship between students' part-time employment and diminished achievement in school.

READING

Part-Time Employment Undermines Students' Commitment to School
Laurence Steinberg

Laurence Steinberg is professor of psychology at Temple University. His books include *Adolescence* (eighth edition, 2007); *When Teenagers Work* (1986); *Beyond the Classroom: Why School Reform Has Failed and What Parents Need to Do* (1996), from which this essay is taken; and *The Ten Basic Principles of Good Parenting* (2004). Steinberg reports the results of research he and his colleagues conducted on high school students. As you read the selection, highlight the causes and effects Steinberg discusses.

There are a variety of barometers by which one can measure the impact of employment on student achievement, and we used several in our research. We compared the grades of students who work a great deal with those who work in limited amounts or not at all. We also contrasted workers with nonworkers, and those who work a lot with

1

those who work a little, on different indicators of their commitment to education, such as how much time they spend on homework, how often they cut classes, or how far they want to go in school. And finally, we looked at the impact of employment on various measures of student engagement, such as how hard students try and how steadily they pay attention in class.

All in all, our research shows that heavy commitment to a part-time job during the school year — say, working twenty hours per week or more — significantly interferes with youngsters' school achievement and scholastic commitment. Students who work a lot perform worse in school, are less committed to their education, and are less engaged in class than their classmates who work less or not at all. For example, in our study, students who were working more than twenty hours weekly were earning lower grades, spending less time on homework, cutting class more often, and cheating more frequently, and they reported lower levels of commitment to school and more modest educational aspirations.

It has become clear from our research, as well as a host of other studies, that the key issue is not whether a student works but how much time he or she devotes to a job. Working for more than twenty hours per week is likely to be harmful, but working for less than ten hours per week does not seem to take a consistent toll on school performance. Most probably, the effects of working for between ten and twenty hours weekly vary from student to student — some can handle it, while others can't. We should keep in mind, however, that half of all employed seniors, about one-third of all juniors, and about one-fifth of all sophomores work above the twenty-hour threshold — indicating that large numbers of students are at risk of compromising their school careers by their part-time jobs. These findings suggest that one reason for widespread student disengagement is the fact that so many students are working at part-time jobs.

In our study, we were able to examine whether working long hours lessens youngsters' commitment to school or, alternatively, whether disengagement from school leads students to work. We did this by following students over time, as they increased or decreased their work hours, and studying how different patterns of employment affected school performance and engagement. When students increase their work hours, does their commitment to school decline as a result? When students cut back on their employment, does their school performance improve?

The answer to both of these questions is yes. While it is true that the more disengaged students are more likely to work long hours to begin with, it appears that working makes a bad situation worse. In other words, over time, the more students work, the less committed to school they become, even if they begin work with a more negative attitude toward school. (Working long hours also adversely affects students who enter the workplace with positive attitudes toward school.) When students withdraw from the labor force, however, or cut back on their work hours, their interest in school rises. The good news, then, is that the negative effects of working on schooling are reversible.

There are several explanations for the negative effects of working on students' engagement in school. First, when students work many hours each week, they have less time to devote to school assignments. According to our studies, one common response to this time pressure is for working students to cut corners by taking easier classes, copying assignments from other students, cutting class, or refusing to do work that is assigned by their teachers. Over time, as these become established practices, students' commitment to school is eroded bit by bit. About one-third of the students in our study said they take easier classes because of their jobs.

Second, in order to work twenty or more hours each week, many students must   7
work on weekday evenings. Evening work may interfere not only with doing homework but with both sleep and diet — studies show that working teenagers get less rest and eat less healthy meals than nonworking teenagers — and burning the midnight oil may make working teenagers more tired in school. Teachers frequently complain about working students falling asleep in class. Nearly a third of the students in our study said they were frequently too tired from work to do their homework.

Third, it appears that the excitement of earning large amounts of spending   8
money may itself make school seem less rewarding and interesting. Although mind-wandering during school is considered a hallmark of adolescence, working students report significantly more of it than nonworkers. Indeed, the "rush" from earning and spending money may be so strong that students who have a history of prolonged intensive employment — those who, for example, have been working long hours since their sophomore year — are actually at greater risk than their classmates of dropping out before graduating.

Finally, working long hours is associated with increased alcohol and drug use.   9
Students who work long hours use drugs and alcohol about 33 percent more often than students who do not work. Alcohol and drug use, in turn, are linked to disengagement from school, so any activity that leads adolescents to drink or experiment with drugs is likely to depress their school performance. Interestingly enough, our longitudinal studies show that working long hours leads to increased alcohol and marijuana use. Teenagers with between $200 and $300 of discretionary income per month have a lot more money to spend on drugs and alcohol than their peers, and this is one of the things they spend their earnings on.

Given the widespread belief that employment during adolescence is supposed to   10
be character-building, it no doubt will come as a surprise to many readers to hear that working at a part-time job diminishes students' engagement in school and increases their drug and alcohol use. But studies of how student workers actually spend their time on the job suggest that the real surprise is that we've held on to the myth of the benefits of adolescent work experience for as long as we have.

Examining the Reading

1. What measures does Steinberg use to assess the effects of employment on students' academic performance?
2. Does Steinberg's study conclude that working long hours is a cause of students' disinterest in school, an effect of their disinterest, or both?
3. According to Steinberg's study, what happens when students stop working twenty or more hours per week?
4. Explain the meaning of each of the following words as it is used in the reading: *barometers* (para. 1), *engaged* (2), *toll* (3), *eroded* (6), and *longitudinal* (9). Refer to your dictionary as needed.

Analyzing the Writer's Technique

1. Identify Steinberg's thesis.
2. What is the writer's purpose?
3. Does the essay focus on causes, effects, or both? What type of evidence does Steinberg use? Is it sufficient?
4. Describe the overall organization of the essay. Can you identify a chain of events anywhere in the essay? If so, draw a graphic organizer of it.
5. Highlight the transitional words and phrases Steinberg uses to guide readers through the essay
6. Evaluate the conclusion. How does Steinberg draw the essay to a close?

Visualizing the Reading

Steinberg identifies several possible explanations for the negative effects of working on student performance. Use the diagram below to summarize these effects. The first one has been done for you.

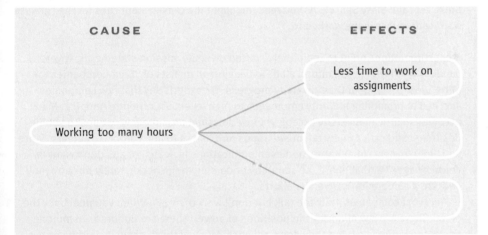

CAUSE

EFFECTS

Working too many hours

Less time to work on assignments

Reacting to the Reading

1. Steinberg seems to overlook the fact that some high school students must work because their families need the money. Do you think Steinberg is unfair to students who must work?
2. Steinberg cites four negative effects of employment on the academic performance of high school students. Write a journal entry explaining which effect you find most (or least) compelling. Can you think of additional effects? Use your experiences with work and school to support your answer.
3. Steinberg's research study involved high school students. Would you expect similar findings in a study of the effects of employment on the academic performance of college students? Write an essay examining the effects of excessive work hours on college students.

PATTERNS COMBINED

In the following essay, Gary M. Stern uses cause and effect as well as other patterns to support his assertion about hidden obstacles to Latinos' career advancement in U.S. workplaces.

READING

Hitting the "Granite Wall"
Gary M. Stern

Gary M. Stern is a New York–based freelance author who has written for the *Wall Street Journal*, Reuters, *Investor's Business Daily*, *Vanity Fair*, *Woman's World*, *American Way*, and *USA Weekend*. He served as ghostwriter for *Garden of Dreams*, a 2004 book about the history of Madison Square Garden; is coauthor of *Minority Rules*: *Turn Your Ethnicity into a Competitive Edge* (2006); and has written nonfiction children's books, including a biography of Andre Agassi and a book on Congress. He has profiled Eddie Murphy, Rob Reiner, Spike Lee, and Sissy Spacek. As you read, highlight the causes Stern cites for the "granite wall" Latinos face in the workplace.

Most corporations point to their finely crafted diversity mission statements, diversity   1
councils filled with multicultural staff, and inclusion on lists of "Best Companies for
Minorities" as proof of their diversity progress. Yet experts say that few companies
succeed at promoting minority employees to high levels of Corporate America. Many
accomplish little in diversity except window dressing, promote few Latinos to senior
positions, and cause many talented Latinos and blacks to flee corporate careers. Since
most employees, consultants, and even publications in search of ads don't want to
"burn bridges" and alienate the company endorsing their checks, rarely does anyone
criticize a corporation's diversity efforts.

Yet most companies "talk the talk but don't walk the walk. When you peel back the   2
onion, there are few minorities in positions of power. There are hundreds of minorities at the junior level, but they don't advance. Many of these diversity initiatives are
marketing campaigns to get consumer dollars," says Kenneth Arroyo Roldan, the CEO
of Wesley, Brown, Bartle & Roldan, one of the country's largest minority executive recruiting firms, based in New York. Out of frustration with observing diversity obstacles,
Roldan has decided to speak out.

Many companies have done an effective job of recruiting and hiring talented minori-   3
ties and adding to their minority suppliers, he acknowledges. But many minority employees in the fifth to seventh year stagnate in their job and become frustrated, watching
their white non-Hispanic colleagues advance in the corporation. "Most minorities find
the glass ceiling and hit a granite wall," he says. Stuck in their jobs, "many minorities
leave the corporation out of frustration and become entrepreneurial," says Roldan.

But Roldan also faults Latinos themselves for not understanding "how the dance is   4
played." Too many Latinos gravitate toward non-revenue-producing specialties such
as public relations and ethnic marketing and fail to get on the fast track. "It's not your
dad's Chevrolet. Many Hispanics have cultural inhibitions to jumping jobs," he says.

Moreover, Latinos tend to network with each other in Hispanic organizations, which leads to "talking with each other" but not advancing their careers, he says.

Companies aren't explicitly discriminating or trying to inhibit Latino advancement. 5 "It's not intentional; it's educational. Most companies don't have the skills to advance talented minorities. They may not have the architecture in place to have certain programs or mentors," Roldan says. Corporations offer sensitivity training and minority internship programs, but until corporations open the executive suites and corporate boards to Latinos and African Americans, real progress won't happen, he says.

A study by Donna María Blancero and Robert G. Del Campo for *Hispanic MBA Maga-* 6 *zine* affirms Roldan's point that Latinos have been kept out of the corporate power structure. Though Latinos account for 10 percent of the workforce, they number 4.5 percent of managers. Since serving as a CEO or senior officer is often a prerequisite for being named to a company's influential board of directors, Hispanics are rarely named to a board. Only 1.7 percent of board members are Hispanics.

Why do so few talented and educated Latinos advance beyond a certain plateau? 7 Blancero, an associate professor of business administration at Touro University International in Cypress, California, attributes it to a combination of factors including an inability to identify a mentor. "Mentors only select people they think will be successful and often that's not a racial or ethnic minority. If you're a Hispanic woman in an organization, how many senior Hispanic women can you find who will mentor you?" she asks rhetorically. Furthermore, "most Latinos are the first ones in their family with a college degree. We haven't learned how to play golf at a country club. We have networks that look like ourselves," she says.

But the corporate culture often discourages Latino advancement. "Corporate culture 8 is [still] dominated by white male America," says Alfonso Martínez, the president of the Hispanic Association on Corporate Responsibility (HACR), a Washington, D.C.–based nonprofit that advocates for Hispanic inclusion in Corporate America and has signed partnership agreements with twenty-seven *Fortune* 500 companies. "The formal and informal networks established by the dominant culture have not been sufficiently flexible. People who don't fit the dominant culture are seen as different and therefore included at lesser rates," he adds. What can companies specifically do to create actual change and promote Latino advancement? Blancero would like to see managers held accountable for promoting talented minorities and for their ability to create a level playing field. Training managers to prevent them from excluding people from promotion based on stereotypes and preconceived notions would also help. Creating a mentoring system that gives Latinos access to people in power that can groom them for future positions is critical.

The few Latinos who manage to surmount the obstacles must do more to change the 9 dominant culture, adds Martínez. He points to Jim Padilla, chief operating officer at Ford Motor Company, who in 2003 spearheaded a Multicultural Alliance, which brings together ten divisions at Ford to collaborate on multicultural efforts. Suggestions from the Multicultural Alliance contributed to Ford's naming Latina Kim Casiano as a member of its board of directors, creating a Multicultural Affairs public affairs officer, and "making everyone at Ford aware that recruiting and developing minorities is a priority," explains Blanca Fauble, director of its Multicultural Alliance, based in Dearborn, Michigan.

Some companies are using their board of directors to make a real difference in di- 10 versity, Martínez says. For example, MGM Mirage in 2002 established a board diversity committee, chaired by Alexis M. Herman, the former U.S. Secretary of Labor and board member, which has the same status as the compensation and audit committees. This sends the message that "diversity at MGM Mirage is a critical business priority," notes Punam Mathur, its senior vice president in charge of Corporate Diversity and Community Affairs, based in Las Vegas, Nevada. Since 53 percent of its forty two thousand employees at its ten hotel and casinos are minorities, the company is committed to establishing a level playing field. Though 9.4 percent of its managerial staff is Latino, the committee is trying to increase that number to reflect its 25 percent Latino staff. Accomplishments of the diversity committee include establishing a $500,000 recruitment/ scholarship at the University of Nevada–Las Vegas Hotel School to attract more minorities to the school (students are 9 percent Latino and 2 percent African American) and provide paid summer internships at MGM Mirage and mentors at the hotel.

For one longtime corporate worker, finding the right mentor and taking risks were   11 keys to his success. Carlos Linares, who was born in Cuba and immigrated to the United States at age four, started as an AT&T account executive, selling long-distance services to small businesses in San Francisco in 1984. Over an eighteen-year career, he made several job changes including a stint in human resources but then, guided by a mentor, became a sales manager for Latin America for AT&T Network Systems in Miami in 1993. He ultimately managed a staff of six thousand people, overseeing sales in the Caribbean and parts of South America.

How was Linares able to surmount the hurdles that thwart so many other Latinos?   12 Art Medieros, a senior manager, mentored Linares at Lucent Technologies (a spinoff of AT&T) and "taught me a lot about being an executive and running a large, complex operation," he says. Medieros promoted Linares twice and upon his retirement recommended Linares for regional president, which helped secure the position. As regional president, Linares helped grow Lucent's business in Latin America from $185 million to $1 billion from 1997 through 1999. "I advanced because of my work ethic, results, the fact that I could lead people and work effectively in the corporation across several organizations," says Linares, who is based in Davie, Florida. In 2002, he left Lucent (which slashed two-thirds of its staff) and is now seeking a CEO position. His advice: avoid dead-end staff jobs and get involved in profit-and-loss responsibilities, where producing profits leads to promotions.

What will it take for Latinos to gain access to actual power at *Fortune* 500 companies?   13 Roldan replies, "We need to develop future leaders. There's no feeder pool. Hispanics are an increasingly larger group with more buying power, but too often diversity means African Americans." Blancero adds, "There has to be an accountable culture that does not discriminate. Organizations are filled with micro-inequities. Accountable managers must be rewarded."

HACR's Martínez encourages Latinos to take control of their own careers, without   14 blaming corporate culture. Hispanics have to rid themselves of feeling victimized and must "gain advanced degrees, find their own individual advocacy voice, and know that with success comes responsibility," he says.

Examining the Reading

1. According to Stern, why are Latinos failing to move up the corporate ladder?
2. How does the corporate culture discourage Latino advancement?
3. According to Stern, how can Latinos move forward in the business world?

4. What can companies do to promote the advancement of Latinos?
5. Explain the meaning of each of the following words as it is used in the reading: *stagnate* (para. 3), *entrepreneurial* (3), *prerequisite* (6), *surmount* (9), and *micro-inequities* (13). Refer to your dictionary as needed.

Analyzing the Writer's Technique

1. Identify Stern's thesis statement.
2. What does Stern hope to accomplish by writing this essay?
3. Why does the author include the personal story of Carlos Linares? What causes and effects of Linares's life are relevant to the essay?
4. Evaluate Stern's comparisons of Latinos to African Americans. Why does he include these?
5. Evaluate the evidence that Stern provides to support the reasons he offers for Latinos' lack of advancement. What other kinds of evidence would strengthen the essay?

Reacting to the Reading

1. Discuss the issue of discrimination in the workplace. How widespread is it, and where do you see it?
2. Write a journal entry exploring what factors, other than those addressed by Stern, might contribute to Latinos' "hitting the granite wall."
3. Write an essay exploring the value of a mentor. What opportunities, insights, or advantages does mentorship offer?

(MAKING (CONNECTIONS)

Racial Discrimination

Both "Hitting the 'Granite Wall'" (pp. 476–78) and "Right Place, Wrong Face" (pp. 203–204) deal with the effects of racial discrimination.

Analyzing the Readings

1. While both authors address racial discrimination, they use two very different approaches (one describes many incidents; the other focuses on a single incident). They also use two different points of view. Explain the advantages and disadvantages of each approach and point of view. To what type(s) of audience does each appeal?
2. Write a journal entry exploring whether you feel the incidents of discrimination in these two essays are typical and representative of racial discrimination in U.S. society.

Essay Idea

Write an essay in which you describe the effects of discrimination on a particular person or group with which you are familiar. Define what discrimination the group faces and propose solutions. (You need not limit yourself to racial discrimination; you might discuss age, sex, weight, or workplace discrimination, for example.)

Applying Your Skills: Additional Essay Assignments

For more on locating and documenting sources, see Part 5.

Write a cause-and-effect essay on one of the following topics, using what you learned about causal analysis in this chapter. Depending on the topic you choose, you may need to conduct library or Internet research.

To Express Your Ideas

1. Write an essay explaining the causes of a "bad day" you recently experienced.
2. Suppose you or a friend or a relative won a large cash prize in a national contest. Write an essay about the effects of winning the prize.

To Inform Your Reader

3. Young children frequently ask the question *why*. Choose a *why* question you have been asked by a child or think of a *why* question you have always wondered about (Examples: Why is the sky blue? Why are sunsets red? Why do parrots learn to talk?). Write an essay answering your question. Your audience is young children.
4. Write an essay explaining how you coped with a stressful situation.
5. Write a memo to your supervisor at work explaining the causes and effects of requiring employees to work overtime.

To Persuade Your Reader

6. Write a letter to the dean of academic affairs about a problem at your school. Discuss causes, effects, or both and propose a solution to the problem.
7. Write a letter to the editor of your local newspaper explaining the possible effects of a proposed change in your community and urging citizens to take action for or against it.
8. Write a letter to the sports editor of your city's newspaper. You are a fan of a professional sports team, and you just learned that the team was sold to new owners who may move the team to a different city. In your letter, explain the effects on the city and the fans if the team moves away.

Cases Using Cause and Effect

9. Your psychology professor invites you to participate in a panel discussion on the psychology of humor. You are required to research this question: What makes a joke funny? Conduct research on the topic, and write a paper summarizing your findings for the panel discussion.
10. A controversy has arisen concerning the use of campus email. Students use the college computer system to send personal email as well as to complete course-related tasks, and some students have complained that campus email is being used to post messages on social networking sites that defame other students' character. In a letter to the student newspaper, either defend the students' right to use campus email to post such messages or call for a policy that limits such use. Be sure to give reasons in support of your position.

PART 4

Reading and Writing Arguments

CHAPTER 18

Reading Arguments

Study the photograph on the opposite page. What current issue does the photograph address? What stance or position do the demonstrators take on the issue? What reasons might the demonstrators offer to support their position?

Write a paragraph that answers these questions. Your first sentence should identify the issue and state a position about it. The remaining sentences should give reasons why the position should be accepted.

The paragraph you have just written is an example of a brief argument. An **argument** makes a claim and offers reasons and evidence in support of the claim. You evaluate arguments at home, work, and school every day. A friend may try to convince you to share an apartment, or your parents may urge you to save more money. Many arguments, including print advertisements and television commercials, require you to analyze visual as well as verbal messages. In your college courses and at work, you often need to judge the claims and weigh the evidence of arguments (see the accompanying box for a few examples).

In this chapter, you will learn how to read, analyze, and evaluate arguments. In Chapter 19, you will learn strategies for writing effective argument essays.

The Basic Parts of an Argument

In everyday conversation, an argument can be a heated exchange of ideas between two people. College roommates might argue over who should clean the sink or who left the door unlocked the previous night. Colleagues in a company might argue over policies or procedures. An effective argument is a logical, well-thought-out presentation of ideas that makes a claim about an issue and supports that claim with evidence. An ineffective argument may be an irrational, emotional release of feelings and frustrations. Many sound arguments, however, combine emotion with logic. A casual conversation can also take the form of a reasoned argument, as in the following sample dialogue.

SCENES FROM COLLEGE AND THE WORKPLACE

- To prepare for a class discussion in a *sociology* course, you are asked to read and evaluate an essay proposing a solution to the decline of city centers in large urban areas.

- In a *mass communication* class, your instructor assigns three articles that take different positions on the issue of whether journalists should provide graphic coverage of accidents and other human tragedies. You are asked to articulate your own opinion on this issue.

- While working as a *purchasing agent* for a carpet manufacturer, you are listening to a sales pitch by a sales representative trying to convince you to purchase a new type of plastic wrapping used for shipping carpets.

DAMON: I've been called for jury duty. I don't want to go. They treat jurors so badly!

MARIA: Why? Everybody is supposed to do it.

DAMON: Have you ever done it? I have. First of all, they force us to serve, whether we want to or not. And then they treat us like criminals. Two years ago I had to sit all day in a hot, crowded room with other jurors while the TV was blaring. I couldn't read, study, or even think! No wonder people will do anything to get out of it.

Damon argues that jurors are treated badly. He offers two reasons to support his claim, and uses his personal experiences to support the second reason (that jurors are treated "like criminals"), which also serves as an emotional appeal.

An effective argument must clearly state an *issue,* a *claim,* and *support.* In the preceding exchange between Damon and Maria, for instance, "fairness of jury duty" is the issue, "jury duty is unfair" is the claim, and Damon's two reasons are the support. In many cases an argument also recognizes or argues against opposing viewpoints, in which case it includes a *refutation.* Although this example does not include a refutation, consider how Damon might refute the opposing claim that jury duty gives citizens the privilege of participating in the justice system. Like most types of essays, an argument should end with a *conclusion* that sums up the main points and provides a memorable closing statement or idea.

As you read the following argument essay, note the issue, the writer's claim, and the support she offers. In addition, look for places where the writer recognizes or refutes opposing views.

When Volunteerism Isn't Noble
Lynn Steirer

Lynn Steirer was a student at Northampton County Area Community College when she wrote the following essay, which was published in the *New York Times* in 1997. It appeared on the op-ed page, a forum for discussing current issues that appears opposite the editorial page.

Engraved in stone over the front entrance to my old high school is the statement, "No Man Is Free Who Is Not Master of Himself." No surprise for a school named Liberty.   1

Some time ago, the Bethlehem school board turned its back on the principle for which my school was named when it began requiring students to perform community service or other volunteer work. Students would have to show that they had done sixty hours of such service, or they would not receive their high school diploma.   2

That forced me to make a decision. Would I submit to the program even though I thought it was involuntary servitude, or would I stand against it on principle? I chose principle and was denied a diploma.   3

Bethlehem is not alone in requiring students to do volunteer work to graduate. Other school districts around the country have adopted such policies, and in the state of Maryland, students must do volunteer work to graduate.   4

Volunteerism is a national preoccupation these days. It all began when retired   5
general Colin Powell, at President Clinton's request, led a three-day gathering in
Philadelphia of political and business leaders and many others. General Powell called
for more people to volunteer. That was a noble thought.

But what President Clinton had in mind goes far beyond volunteering. He called for   6
high schools across the country to make community service mandatory for graduation.
In other words, he wanted to *force* young people to do something that should be, by its
very definition, voluntary.

That would destroy, not elevate, the American spirit of volunteerism. I saw firsthand   7
how many of my classmates treated their required service as a joke, claiming credit for
work they didn't do or exaggerating the time it actually took.

Volunteering has always been important to me. As a Meals on Wheels aide and a   8
Girl Scout, I chose to give hundreds of hours to my community, at my own initiative.

While my family and I fought the school's mandatory service requirement, I contin-   9
ued my volunteering, but I would not submit my hours for credit. Two of my classmates
joined me in this act of civil disobedience. At the same time, with the assistance of the
Institute for Justice, a Washington legal-policy group, we sued the school board.

As graduation neared, a school official pulled me aside and said it was not too late   10
to change my mind. That day, I really thought about giving in. Then he asked the question that settled it for me. "After all," he said, "what is more important, your values or
your diploma?"

I chose to give up my diploma, eventually obtaining a graduate equivalency degree   11
instead. The courts decided against us and, unfortunately, the Supreme Court declined
to hear our case. The school has continued the program.

Volunteering is important. But in a country that values its liberty, we should make   12
sure that student "service" is truly voluntary.

The Issue

An argument is concerned with an **issue**—a controversy, a problem, or an idea about
which people hold different points of view. In "When Volunteerism Isn't Noble," the
issue is mandatory community service for high school graduation.

✓ The Claim

The **claim** is the point the writer tries to prove, usually the writer's view on the
issue. Consider, for example, whether you think the death penalty is right or
wrong. You could take one of three stands — or make one of three claims — on
this issue.

The death penalty is never right.
The death penalty is always right.
The death penalty is the right choice under certain circumstances.

The claim often appears as part of the thesis statement in an argument essay. In
Steirer's argument about volunteerism, the claim is that forcing students to volunteer

will "destroy, not elevate, the American spirit of volunteerism" (para. 7). In some essays, however, the claim is implied rather than stated directly.

There are three types of claims: *claims of fact, claims of value,* and *claims of policy.* A **claim of fact** can be proved or verified. A writer employing a claim of fact bases the claim on verifiable facts or data, as in the following example.

Global warming has already taken a serious toll on the environment.

A **claim of value** focuses on showing how one thing or idea is better or more desirable than other things or ideas. Issues involving questions of right versus wrong or acceptable versus unacceptable often lead to claims of value. Such claims are subjective opinions or judgments that cannot be proved. In "When Volunteerism Isn't Noble," for instance, Steirer claims that community service should be "truly voluntary" (para. 12). Here is an example of a claim of value.

Doctor-assisted suicide is a violation of the Hippocratic oath and therefore should not be legalized.

A **claim of policy** offers one or more solutions to a problem. Often the verbs *should, must,* or *ought* appear in the statement of the claim.

The motion picture industry must accept greater responsibility for the consequences of violent films.

Exercise 18.1

Either on your own or with one or two classmates, choose two of the following issues and write two claims for each. Use different types of claims—for example, if one statement is a claim of value, the other should be a claim of policy or a claim of fact.

1. Legalization of drugs
2. Stem cell research claim of fact
3. Music and the Internet
4. Protection for endangered species
5. Global warming —claim of fact.

The Support

The support consists of the ideas and information intended to convince readers that the claim is sound or believable. Three common types of support are *reasons, evidence,* and *emotional appeals.*

Reasons

When writers make claims about issues, they have reasons for doing so. In "When Volunteerism Isn't Noble," for example, Steirer's claim—that community service should not be mandatory for high school graduation—is supported by several reasons,

For more on reasons as support in an argument, see Chapter 19, p. 519.

including her observation that students treat the mandatory community service "as a joke" (para. 7). A **reason**, then, is a general statement that backs up a claim. It explains why the writer's view on an issue is reasonable or correct. However, reasons alone are not sufficient support for an argument. Each reason must be supported by evidence and often by emotional appeals.

Evidence

In an argument, **evidence** usually consists of facts, statistics, and expert opinion. Examples and observations from personal experience can also serve as evidence. The following examples show how different types of evidence may be used to support a claim about the value of reading to children.

CLAIM	Reading aloud to preschool and kindergarten children improves their chances of success in school.
FACTS	First-grade children who were read to as preschoolers learned to read earlier than children who were not read to.
STATISTICS	A 1998 study by Robbins and Ehri demonstrated that reading aloud to children produced a 16 percent improvement in the children's ability to recognize words used in a story.
EXPERT OPINION	Dr. Maria Morealle, a child psychologist, urges parents to read two or three books to their children daily (Pearson 52).
EXAMPLES	Stories about unfamiliar places or activities increase a child's vocabulary. For example, reading a story about a farm to a child who lives in a city apartment will acquaint the child with such new terms as *barn*, *silo*, and *tractor*.
PERSONAL EXPERIENCE	When I read to my three-year-old son, I notice that he points to and tries to repeat words.

In "When Volunteerism Isn't Noble," Steirer offers several examples of how high school students treat mandatory community service "as a joke": they claim credit unfairly and exaggerate their time spent doing volunteer work. The writer also uses her personal experience at Liberty High School to support her claim.

Emotional Appeals

Emotional appeals evoke the needs or values that readers care deeply about. For instance, a writer might appeal to readers' need for safety and security when urging them to install deadbolts on their apartment doors. You would appeal to the value that a sick friend places on your friendship if you urge him to visit a medical clinic by saying, "If you won't go for your own good, then do it for me."

Appealing to needs. People have various **needs**, including physiological needs (food and drink, health, shelter, safety, sex) and psychological needs (a sense of belonging or accomplishment, self-esteem, recognition by others, self-realization). Appeals to needs are used by your friends and family, by people who write letters to the editor, and by personnel directors who write job listings. Advertisements often appeal directly or indirectly to one or more various needs.

Appealing to values. A **value** is a principle or quality that is judged to be important, worthwhile, or desirable, such as freedom, justice, loyalty, friendship, patriotism, duty, and equality. Values are difficult to define because not everyone considers the same principles or qualities important. Even when people agree on the importance of a value, they may not agree about what that value means. For example, although most people value honesty, some would say that white lies intended to protect a person's feelings are dishonest, while others would maintain that white lies are justified. Arguments often appeal to values that the writer assumes most readers will share. Steirer, in her essay on volunteerism, appeals to two widely held values—that it is worthy to stand up for one's own principles (para. 3) and that "No Man Is Free Who Is Not Master of Himself" (para. 1).

Exercise 18.2

As the director of a day-care center, you need to create a budget report for next year. The report will itemize purchases and expenses as well as justify the need for each purchase or expenditure. Choose two of the following items and write a justification (reasons) for their purchase, explaining why each item would be beneficial to the children (evidence).

1. DVD player
2. Tropical fish tank
3. Microwave
4. Read-along books with tapes
5. Set of Dr. Seuss books

The Refutation

The **refutation**, also called the *rebuttal*, recognizes and argues against opposing viewpoints. Suppose you want to argue that you deserve a raise at work (your claim). As support for your claim, you will remind your supervisor of the contributions and improvements you have made while you have been employed by the company, your length of employment, your conscientiousness, and your promptness. But you suspect that your supervisor may still turn you down, not because you don't deserve the raise but because other employees might demand a similar raise. By anticipating this potential objection, you can build into your argument the reasons that the objection is not valid. You may have more time invested with the company and more responsibilities than the other employees, for example. In doing so, you would be offering a refutation.

Basically, refutation involves finding a weakness in the opponent's argument, either by casting doubt on the opponent's reasons or by questioning the accuracy, relevancy, and sufficiency of the opponent's evidence.

Sometimes writers are unable to refute an opposing view or may choose not to, perhaps because the opposing view is weak. However, most writers of arguments

For more on refutation, acknowledgment, and accommodation, see Chapter 19, p. 522.

acknowledge or accommodate the opposing viewpoint in some way if they cannot refute it. They **acknowledge** an opposing view by simply stating it. By **accommodating** an opposing view, they note that the view has merit and find a way of addressing it. In an argument opposing hunting, for example, a writer might simply *acknowledge* the view that hunting bans would cause a population explosion among wild animals. The writer might *accommodate* this opposing view by stating that if a population explosion were to occur, the problem could be solved by reintroducing natural predators into the area.

General Strategies for Reading Arguments

To understand the complex relationships among the ideas presented in an argument, you'll need to read it at least two times. Read it once to get an overview of the issue, claim, and support. Then reread it both to identify the structure and to evaluate the ideas and the relationships among them.

For more on reading strategies, see Chapter 3.

Because argument essays can be complex, you will find it helpful to annotate and summarize them. You may want to photocopy the essay before you begin reading, so that you can mark it up in the various ways suggested in this section. The following strategies, which you should use before and while reading, will help focus your attention on what is important and make the task of writing about what you have read easier.

Before You Read

1. **Think about the title.** The title may suggest the focus of the essay in a direct statement or in a synopsis of the claim. Here are a few examples of titles.

    "In Defense of Voluntary Euthanasia"
    "The Case for Medicalizing Heroin"
    "Voting: Why Not Make It Mandatory?"

    You can tell from the titles that the first essay argues for euthanasia, the second supports the use of heroin for medical purposes, and the third argues for mandatory voting laws.

(**Exercise 18.3**)

For each of the following essay titles, predict the issue and the claim you would expect the author to make.

1. "The Drugs I Take Are None of Your Business"
2. "Watch That Leer and Stifle That Joke at the Water Cooler"
3. "Crazy in the Streets: A Call for Treatment of Street People"
4. "Penalize the Unwed Dad? Fat Chance"
5. "A Former Smoker Applauds New Laws"

---

2. **Check the author's name and credentials.** If you recognize the author's name, you may have some sense of what to expect or what not to expect in the essay. For example, an essay written by syndicated columnist Dave Barry, known for his humorous articles, would likely make a point through humor or sarcasm, whereas an essay by Al Gore would take an earnest, serious approach. You also want to determine whether the author is qualified to write on the issue at hand. Essays in newspapers, magazines, and academic journals often include a brief review of the author's credentials and experience related to the issue. Books include biographical notes about the author. When an article lacks an author's name, which often happens in newspapers, you need to evaluate the reliability of the publication in which the article appears.

For more on evaluating sources, see Chapter 20, p. 561.

3. **Check the original source of publication.** If the essay does not appear in its original source, use the headnote, footnotes, or citations to determine where the essay was originally published. Some publications have a particular viewpoint. *Ms.* magazine, for instance, has a feminist slant. *Wired* generally favors advances in technology. If you are aware of the viewpoint that a publication advocates, you can sometimes predict the stand an essay will take on a particular issue. The publication's intended audience can also provide clues.

4. **Check the date of publication.** The date of publication provides a context for the essay and helps you evaluate it. The more recent an article is, the more likely it is to reflect current research or debate on an issue. For instance, an essay on the existence of life on other planets written in the 1980s would lack recent scientific findings that might confirm or discredit the supporting evidence. When obtaining information from the World Wide Web, you should be especially careful to check the date the article was posted or last updated.

5. **Preview the essay.** Read the opening paragraph, any headings, the first sentence of one or two paragraphs per page, and the last paragraph. Previewing may also help you determine the author's claim.

6. **Think about the issue before you read.** When you think about the subject of the argument before reading, you may be less influenced by the writer's appeals and more likely to maintain an objective, critical viewpoint. Write the issue at the top of a sheet of paper, in your journal, or in a word-processing document. Then create two columns for reasons and evidence supporting the two opposing positions on the issue, listing as many ideas as you can in each column.

While You Read

1. **Read first for an initial impression.** During your first reading, do not concentrate on specifics. Instead, read to get an overall impression of the argument and to identify the issue and the author's claim. Also try to get a general feel for the essay, the author, and the approach the author takes toward the topic. Do not judge or criticize; focus on what the author has to say.

2. **Read a second time with a pen in hand.** As you reread the essay, mark or highlight the claim, reasons, and key supporting evidence. Write annotations, noting appeals to needs and values. Jot down ideas, questions, or challenges to the writer's argument as they come to mind. Summarize reasons and key supporting evidence

as you encounter them. In an argument, one idea is often linked to the next. Consequently, readers often find it useful and necessary to reread earlier sections before moving ahead.

3. **Underline key terms or unfamiliar words.** Because an argument can depend on defining terms in a specific way, it is especially important to understand how the writer defines key terms and concepts. In arguments, precise definitions are crucial. If the author does not define terms precisely, look up their meanings in a dictionary. Jot down the definitions in the margins.

Ted Koerth was a first-year student at the University of Virginia when he wrote the following editorial for the campus newspaper, the *Cavalier Daily.*

Economic Affirmative Action

Ted Koerth

Title: Koerth clearly identifies the issue.

Two words probably do not exist that can stir up more of a conversational frenzy than *affirmative action*. The debate surrounding such policies presents itself daily in the media, a seemingly never-ending saga destined to go back and forth forever. [1]

Introduction: Koerth gives an overview of both sides of the issue of affirmative action.

Proponents of such policies argue that they not only give an advantage to underrepresented minority groups but also help to settle some cosmic score that went askew during the first two hundred years of American history. People who oppose affirmative action measures argue that they encourage acceptance of underqualified applicants, and that sufficient reparation time has elapsed. A growing majority of those opponents think that minorities do not deserve the push they get--hence the rise in complaints of reverse discrimination. [2]

Koerth refers to the claim he will make but does not say at this point exactly what it is. He leads up to his thesis gradually, first giving reasons and evidence and only stating his specific claim near the end of the essay, in paragraph 8.

Despite the deeply felt emotions both sides of the debate harbor, a fair way to reform affirmative action's current state does exist. Many of the qualms some have with affirmative action have to do with the fact that it is based solely on race, for race is natural and unintentional. None of us chooses our race. So to treat someone differently because of his or her race demonstrates a glaring ignorance on the part of the prejudiced. We must consider, however, the opposite side of the coin, which often does not receive as much thought. [3]

Reason #1: Race should not be used as the basis for a "helping hand" from one group to another.

If we cannot judge people poorly because of their race, we cannot judge them superior for the same reason, nor should we use race to decide that a certain class of individuals needs a helping hand from any other. [4]

Reason #2: Race-based affirmative action denies the ability of minority groups to achieve without it.

Here the affirmative action argument comes into play. The problem starts when race becomes the basis for giving out advantages, such as college admissions. Choosing minority groups for special treatment in admissions implies that those groups lack the ability to achieve those things on their own, a bigoted assumption totally without founding. Granted, simple demographics demonstrate that certain ethnic groups are more highly represented in certain classes, but we cannot consider that an exclusive phenomenon, given that no group of people has all the same characteristics. Therefore, a generalization implying that any certain number of racial groups needs help lacks reason. For that reason, we need to fix affirmative action. [5]

Koerth recognizes and refutes an opposing view: that affirmative action is needed because

If two students have had the exact same opportunities during their lives but one is an American Indian and the other a Caucasian, the American Indian will receive acceptance priority if her academic achievements are similar, simply because she belongs to an underrepresented group. That implies that an American Indian who achieves is out of the ordinary--a foolish assumption.

Take another example: Two students, one white and one Asian American, score the same on standardized tests and are equally qualified for a job. The white student, however, comes from a lower class, single-parent family, and the Asian student comes from the family of an affluent judge. If those two have equal academic achievements, affirmative action as it now exists would likely give a boost to the Asian student, though he has lived an easier life. The extra efforts the Caucasian student made go unnoticed, and he receives no boost.

For those reasons, America needs an affirmative action system that gives a boost not to members of groups that unfortunately suffered from past discrimination, because the days of rampant discrimination in the United States have passed for the most part. Continuing to pay back groups who previously had to deal with prejudice unfairly punishes other racial majorities for the sins of their ancestors. Instead, we need a system that gives a boost to those who have had to overcome considerable financial, physical, or other obstacles to achieve what they have achieved. Such a policy would not shut any ethnic group out of the process; it would only include anyone who has succeeded without financial assistance. If it occurs that a majority of those who benefit from that system still come from minority groups, that is fine. At least they have benefited from a system that recognizes their situation, not just their skin color.

The affirmative action debate roars on in the United States, with animosity on both sides building constantly. Our current system supposes a certain inherent inferiority of minority groups who in the past have experienced discrimination--an inferiority that simply does not exist. If the government were to institute an equal opportunity system that tries to help those who have had to deal with financial and physical obstacles, we could ease tensions and deal more fairly with admissions policies. Until we can respect the abilities of all ethnic groups, our country will divide its people along racial lines as the tension rises to a fever pitch.

6 members of minority groups are more likely to have low incomes and social status.

Evidence: Koerth uses two hypothetical examples. Note that in the second example he implies a third reason for his claim—the idea that college applicants should get a "boost" if they have had to make "extra efforts" to overcome difficult conditions.

7

8

In his thesis statement, Koerth makes a claim of policy.

Koerth recognizes and accommodates another opposing view: that since most of those who would benefit from his proposed system would be the same people who benefit from the current one, why change it?

Conclusion: Koerth explains the value of his claim.

9

Strategies for Following the Structure of an Argument

In some ways an argument resembles a building. The writer lays a foundation and then builds on that foundation. Reasons and evidence presented early in the essay often support ideas introduced later on, as the lower floors in a building support the higher ones. Once you recognize an argument's plan or overall structure, you are in a better position to understand it and evaluate its strengths and weaknesses. This section offers strategies for following the structure of an argument—including identifying key elements in a graphic organizer and writing a summary—which can help you analyze and evaluate an essay.

co-operate

Using a Graphic Organizer

The graphic organizer shown in Figure 18.1 outlines the basic relationships among ideas in an argument essay. However, unlike the graphic organizers in Part 3 of this

Figure 18.1 GRAPHIC ORGANIZER FOR AN ARGUMENT ESSAY

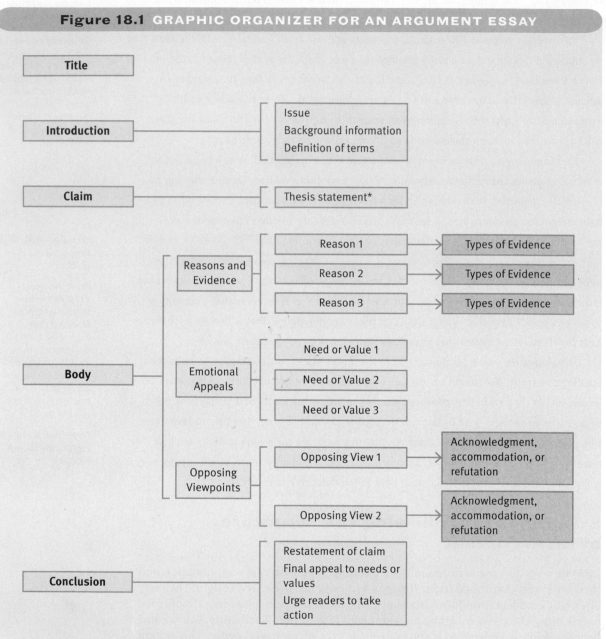

*The thesis statement may appear anywhere within the argument.

text, this organizer does not necessarily reflect the order in which the ideas are presented in an argument essay. Instead, Figure 18.1 provides a way for you, as a reader, to organize those ideas. That is, an argument does not necessarily state (or imply) the issue in the first paragraph; however; the issue is the first thing you need to identify to follow the structure of an argument. Similarly, the claim may not appear in the first paragraph (though it is often stated early in the essay), and the evidence may be presented at various places within the essay. Regardless of the order a writer follows, his or her ideas can be shown in a graphic organizer like the one in Figure 18.1. To construct such an organizer, use the following suggestions.

1. **Read and highlight the essay before drawing a graphic organizer.** Visual learners, however, may prefer to fill in the organizer as they read.
2. **Record ideas in your own words,** not in the author's words.
3. **Reread difficult or confusing parts of the essay before filling in those sections of the organizer.**
4. **Try working through the organizer with a classmate.**

Study the graphic organizer for "Economic Affirmative Action" in Figure 18.2.

Learning Style Options

See Chapter 21, p. 589, for suggestions on paraphrasing. For more on reading difficult material, see Chapter 3, p. 55.

To draw detailed graphic organizers using a computer, visit www.bedfordstmartins .com/successfulwriting.

> ### Exercise 18.4
>
> *Draw a graphic organizer for "When Volunteerism Isn't Noble" on page 485.*

Writing a Summary

Writing a summary of an argument is another useful way to study the structure of ideas in an essay. A summary eliminates detail; only the major supporting ideas remain. You can write a summary after you draw a graphic organizer or use a summary to uncover an argument's structure.

The following guidelines will lead you through the process of writing a summary. (When you draw a graphic organizer first, start with summary step 4.)

For more on summarizing, see Chapter 3, p. 63.

1. **Read the essay two or more times before you attempt to summarize it.**
2. **Divide the argument into sections or parts, noting the function of each section in the margin.** You might write "offers examples" or "provides statistical backup," for instance. Label the issue, the claim, sections offering reasons and evidence, opposing viewpoints, and the conclusion.
3. **Write brief marginal notes stating the main point of each paragraph or each related group of paragraphs.** It may be helpful to use one margin for a content summary and the other to indicate function. Study the accompanying sample annotated portion of "When Volunteerism Isn't Noble."

Figure 18.2 GRAPHIC ORGANIZER FOR "ECONOMIC AFFIRMATIVE ACTION"

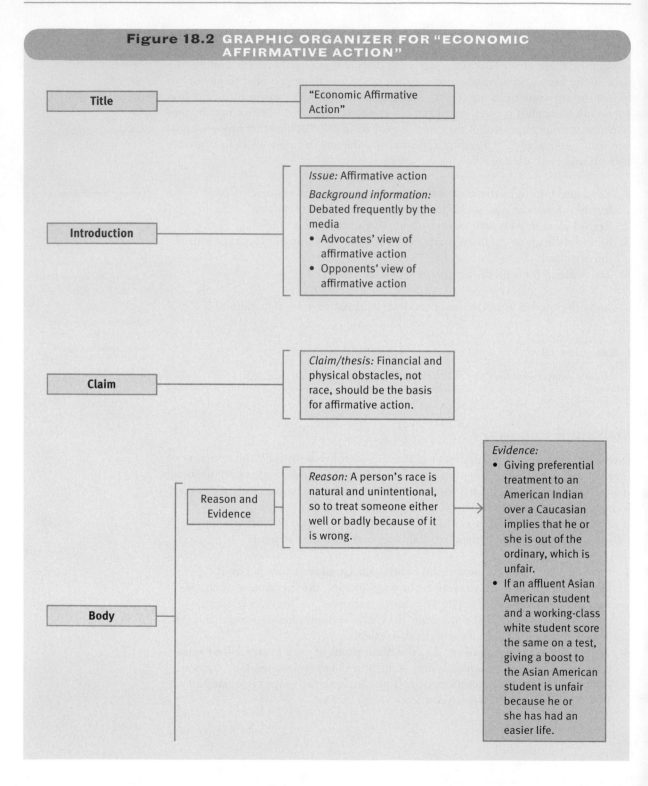

Figure 18.2 *(continued)*

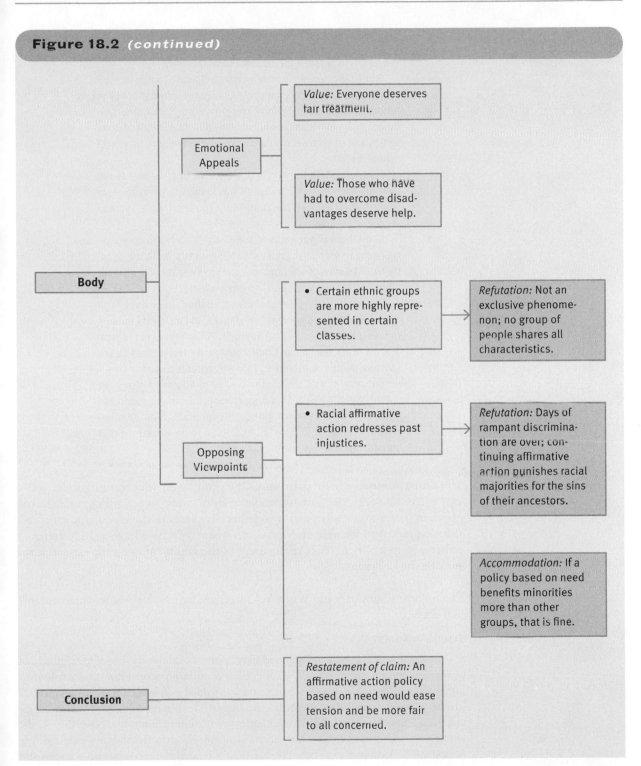

Engraved in stone over the front entrance to my old high school is the statement, "No Man Is Free Who Is Not Master of Himself." No surprise for a school named Liberty.

background   Some time ago, the Bethlehem school board turned its back on the principle for which my school was named when it began requiring students to perform community service or other vol- *mandatory policy* unteer work. Students would have to show that they had done sixty hours of such service, or they would not receive their high school diploma.

That forced me to make a decision. Would I submit to the *writer's dilemma* program even though I thought it was involuntary servitude, or would I stand against it on principle? I chose principle and was denied a diploma.

Bethlehem is not alone in requiring students to do volun- *other schools have similar policy* teer work to graduate. Other school districts around the country have adopted such policies, and in the state of Maryland, students must do volunteer work to graduate.

Volunteerism is a national preoccupation these days. It all began when retired general Colin Powell, at President Clinton's request, led a three-day gathering in Philadelphia of political *opposing viewpoint* and business leaders and many others. General Powell called *Powell & Clinton support* for more people to volunteer. That was a noble thought.

But what President Clinton had in mind goes far beyond volunteering. He called for high schools across the country to make community service mandatory for graduation. In other words, he wanted to *force* young people to do something that *forcing isn't voluntary* should be, by its very definition, voluntary.

Learning Style Options   **4. Develop a summary from your notes.** Depending on your learning style, you may prefer to work from parts to whole or from whole to parts. Pragmatic learners often prefer to start by putting together the pieces of the argument (individual paragraphs) to see what they produce, whereas creative learners may prefer to begin with a one-sentence restatement of the argument and then expand it to include the key points.

The following summary of "When Volunteerism Isn't Noble" shows an acceptable level of detail.

SAMPLE SUMMARY

The Bethlehem school board required sixty hours of community service for high school graduation, but the writer refused to submit her community service hours (as a volunteer for Meals on Wheels and as a Girl Scout) and was denied a diploma. Other school districts in other states have similar requirements. In addition, General Powell favored volunteerism, and President Clinton called for a mandatory graduation requirement. Nevertheless, the writer maintains that making volunteerism mandatory destroys it. She cites the following personal observation as evidence: Her classmates treated the requirement as a joke and cheated in reporting their hours. The writer feels strongly that in a free society, community service should be voluntary. She gave up her diploma because of this conviction, though she eventually received a high school equivalency degree. She also sued the school board, but the U.S. Supreme Court refused to consider the case.

Exercise 18.5

Write a summary for "Economic Affirmative Action" on page 492.

Strategies for Analyzing and Evaluating an Argument

The graphic organizer shown in Figure 18.1 provides you with an easy way to lay out the ideas in an argument essay. Once you are familiar with an essay's content and organization, the next step is to analyze and evaluate the argument, including the writer's claim and support for the claim.

Review the list of reasons and evidence you wrote before reading "Economic Affirmative Action" (see p. 492), noting the points covered as well as those not covered. Consider the ideas raised in the argument, and write about them in your journal. Explore your overall reaction; raise questions; talk back to the author. Compare your ideas on the issue with those of the author. You will then be ready to analyze the argument more systematically. (For a checklist covering all of these elements, see Table 18.2 on p. 502.)

For more on raising questions about an essay, see Chapter 3.

Analyzing the Elements of and Reasoning in an Argument

To analyze an argument, you need to study closely the writer's purpose, audience, definitions of key terms in the claim, credibility, and support (reasons and evidence). You also need to evaluate his or her emotional appeals, treatment of opposing viewpoints, possibly faulty reasoning, and conclusion.

The Basic Components

As you read an argument, consider the following aspects of any persuasive writing.

- **The writer's purpose** Try to discover the writer's motive for writing. Ask yourself: Why does the writer want to convince me of this? What does he or she stand to gain, if anything? If a writer stands to profit personally from the acceptance of an argument, be especially careful to ask critical questions.
- **The intended audience** Writers often reveal the intended audience by the language they use and the familiarity or formality of their tone. Also look at the reasons and types of evidence offered, the emotional appeals and examples, and the comparisons the writer makes.
- **Definitions of key terms** Underline any terms in the statement of the claim that can have more than one meaning. Then read through the essay to see if these terms are clearly defined and used consistently.

- **The writer's credibility** As you read an argument, judge the writer's knowledge and trustworthiness. Ask yourself if the writer seems to have a thorough understanding of the issue, acknowledges opposing views and addresses them respectfully, and establishes common ground with the reader.

For more on evaluating evidence, see Chapter 5, p. 104.

- **Support: reasons and evidence** Does the writer supply sufficient reasons and evidence that are relevant to the claim and accurate? Facts offered as evidence should be accurate, complete, and taken from reputable sources. In particular, statistical evidence should be current and from reliable sources. The evidence should be typical, and any authorities cited should be experts in their field.

Emotional Appeals

As noted earlier in the chapter, writers of arguments appeal to or engage readers' emotions. Such appeals are a legitimate part of an argument. However, a writer should not attempt to manipulate readers' emotions to distract them from the issue and the evidence. Table 18.1 presents some common unfair emotional appeals.

Opposing Viewpoints

If an argument essay takes into account opposing viewpoints, you must evaluate these viewpoints and the way the writer deals with them. Ask yourself the following questions.

- **Does the author state the opposing viewpoint clearly?** Can you tell from the essay what the opposition says?
- **Does the author present the opposing viewpoint fairly and completely?** That is, does the author recognize the opposing viewpoint and treat it with respect, or does

TABLE 18.1 Common Unfair Emotional Appeals

Emotional Appeal	Example
Name-calling: using an emotionally loaded term to create a negative response	"That reporter is an *egotistical bully*."
Ad hominem: attacking the opponent rather than his or her position on the issue	"How could anyone who didn't fight in a war criticize the president's foreign policy?"
False authority: quoting the opinions of celebrities or public figures about topics on which they are not experts	"According to singer Jennifer Hope, welfare reform is America's most urgent social problem."
Plain folks: urging readers to accept an idea or take an action because it is suggested by someone who is just like they are	"Vote for me. I'm just a regular guy."
Appeal to pity: arousing sympathy by telling hard-luck or excessively sentimental stories	"Latchkey children come home to an empty house or apartment, a can of soup, and a note on the refrigerator."
Bandwagon: appealing to readers' desire to conform ("Everyone's doing it, so it must be right")	"It must be okay to exceed the speed limit, since so many people speed."

he or she attempt to discredit or demean those holding the opposing view? Does the author present all the major parts of the opposing viewpoint or only those parts that he or she is able to refute?

- **Does the author clearly show why the opposing viewpoint is considered wrong or inappropriate?** Does the author apply sound logic? Are reasons and evidence provided?
- **Does the author acknowledge or accommodate points that cannot be refuted?**

As you read, jot down clues or answers to these questions in the margins of the essay.

Faulty Reasoning

In an argument essay, a writer may inadvertently or deliberately introduce **fallacies**, or errors in reasoning or thinking. Several types of fallacies can weaken an argument; undermine a writer's claim; and call into question the relevancy, believability, or consistency of supporting evidence. Following is a brief review of the most common types of faulty reasoning.

For more on reasoning, see Chapter 19, p. 520.

Circular reasoning. Also called **begging the question**, *circular reasoning* occurs when a writer uses the claim (or part of it) as evidence by simply repeating the claim in different words. The statement "*Cruel* and unusual experimentation on helpless animals is *inhumane*" is an example.

Hasty generalization. A *hasty generalization* occurs when the writer draws a conclusion based on insufficient evidence or isolated examples. If you taste three chocolate cakes and conclude on the basis of that small sample that all chocolate cakes are overly sweet, you would be making a hasty generalization.

Sweeping generalization. When a writer claims that something applies to all situations and instances without exception, the claim is called a *sweeping generalization.* To claim that all computers are easy to use is a sweeping generalization because the writer is probably referring only to the models with which he or she is familiar.

False analogy. When a writer compares two situations that are not sufficiently parallel or similar, the result is a *false analogy.* Just because two items or events are alike in some ways does not mean they are alike in all ways. If you wrote, "A human body needs rest after strenuous work, and a car needs rest after a long trip," you would falsely compare the human body with an automobile engine.

Non sequitur. A *non sequitur*—which means "it does not follow"—occurs when no logical relationship exists between two or more ideas. For example, the comment "Because my sister is financially independent, she will make a good parent" is a non sequitur, as no logical relationship exists between financial independence and good parenting.

Red herring. With a *red herring,* a writer attempts to distract readers from the main issue by raising an irrelevant point. For example, suppose you are arguing that television commercials for alcoholic beverages should be banned. To mention that some parents give sips of alcohol to their children distracts readers from the issue of television commercials.

For more on the post hoc *fallacy, see Chapter 17, p. 461.*

Post hoc fallacy. The *post hoc, ergo propter hoc* ("after this, therefore because of this") fallacy, or *post hoc* fallacy, occurs when a writer assumes that event A caused event B simply because B followed A. For example, the claim "Student enrollment fell dramatically this semester because of the recent appointment of the new college president" is a post hoc fallacy because other factors may have contributed to the decline in enrollment.

Either-or fallacy. An *either-or* fallacy argues that there are only two sides to an issue and that only one of them is correct. For instance, on the issue of legalizing drugs, a writer may argue that all drugs must be *either* legalized *or* banned, ignoring other positions (such as legalizing marijuana use for cancer patients undergoing chemotherapy).

Exercise 18.6

Locate at least one brief argument essay or article and bring it to class. Working in a group of two or three students, analyze each argument using the preceding guidelines and the checklist in Table 18.2.

TABLE 18.2 **Checklist for Analyzing an Argument Essay**

Element	Questions
1. The issue	• What is in dispute?
2. The claim	• Is the claim stated or implied? • Is it a claim of fact, value, or policy? • Does the author give reasons for making the claim?
3. The support	• What facts, statistics, expert opinions, examples, and personal experiences are presented? • Are appeals made to needs, values, or both?
4. The writer's purpose	• Why does the author want to convince readers to accept the claim? • What if anything does the author stand to gain if the claim is accepted?
5. The intended audience	• Where is the essay published? • To whom do the reasons, evidence, emotional appeals, examples, and comparisons seem targeted?
6. Definitions of key terms	• Are key terms in the claim clearly defined, especially terms that have ambiguous meanings?
7. The writer's credibility	• Is the author qualified, fair, and knowledgeable? • Does the author establish common ground with readers?
8. The strength of the argument: reasons and evidence	• Does the author supply several reasons to back up the claim? • Is the evidence relevant, accurate, current, and typical? • Are the authorities cited reliable experts? • Are fallacies or unfair emotional appeals used?
9. Opposing viewpoints	• Does the author address opposing viewpoints clearly and completely, without using fallacies? • Does the author acknowledge, accommodate, or refute opposing viewpoints with logic and relevant evidence?

Thinking Critically about Argument

Synthesizing Your Reading

In many academic situations, you will need to read and compare two or more sources on a given topic. This skill, called *synthesis,* involves drawing together two or more sets of ideas to discover similarities and differences and create new ideas and insights. You will synthesize sources—including books, articles and essays, textbook materials, and lecture notes—in writing research papers, preparing for class discussions, and studying for tests. Synthesis is especially important when you read two or more argument essays on one issue. Because each author is trying to show that his or her point of view is the correct one, you need to consider all sides of the issue carefully to develop your own position, especially if you intend to write your own argument about the topic. Use the following questions to guide your synthesis of arguments or any other sources.

- On what points do the sources agree?
- On what points do the sources disagree?
- How do the sources differ in viewpoint, approach, purpose, and type of support?
- What did I learn about this topic from the sources?
- What can I conclude about this topic based on what I read?
- With which sources do I agree?
- How can I support my views on this topic?

The pair of essays on organ donation in this chapter and the pair on sport utility vehicles in Chapter 19 provide you with two opportunities to practice your synthesizing skills.

Applying Your Skills: Additional Readings

The following essays take differing views on the issue of the sale of human organs. Use the checklist in Table 18.2 and the strategies for reading arguments presented in this chapter to analyze and evaluate each essay.

How Much Is That Kidney in the Window?
Bruce Gottlieb

READING

Bruce Gottlieb has worked as a staff writer and editor for *Slate* and contributed numerous pieces to other publications, such as the *New York Times Magazine*. After being a writer for several years, he went to law school and currently serves as a legal adviser on wireless and international issues for the Federal Communications Commission. This essay appeared in the *New Republic* in 2000. As you read the selection, underline or highlight Gottlieb's claim and the reasons he gives to support it.

Eight years ago, an article appeared in an obscure Israeli medical journal, *Medicine and Law,* arguing that American citizens should be permitted to sell their kidneys. This would require changing federal law, which since 1984 has made selling any organ, even one's own, a felony punishable by up to five years in jail. The author of the article was a Michigan pathologist named Jack Kevorkian.

Kevorkian's argument was that the current system of accepting kidneys only from dead patients and Good Samaritan donors provides too few kidneys. While this was true even then, the situation is worse today. As of April 30, there were 44,989 people on the waiting list for a kidney transplant. About 2,300 of them will die this year while waiting. If kidney sales were permitted, Kevorkian argued, these lives would almost certainly be saved.

He may be right. In recent years, economists and economically minded lawyers at the University of Chicago and Yale Law School have made similar arguments. The idea was endorsed two years ago in the pages of *The Lancet* by a group of prominent transplant surgeons from Harvard Medical School and hospitals in Canada and England. Of course, legalizing kidney sales remains a fringe view, both within the medical profession and outside it. But that needs to change.

There are several familiar arguments against legalizing kidney sales, beginning with the idea that giving up a kidney is too dangerous for the donor. But, popular though this argument is, the statistics don't bear it out—at least relative to other risks people are legally permitted to assume. In terms of effect on life expectancy, donating one of your two kidneys is more or less equivalent to driving an additional sixteen miles to work each day. No one objects to the fact that ordinary jobs—like construction or driving a delivery van—carry roughly similar risks.

Another common objection is that government ought to encourage altruism, not profit seeking. But from the perspective that matters—the recipient's—this distinction is irrelevant, so long as the donated kidney works. It's not as if the point of kidney transplants were to improve the donor's karma. Moreover, kidneys from cadavers function for eight years, on average, whereas those from live donors last seventeen years. (The reason is that kidneys can be "harvested" from live donors in circumstances less hectic than death and that donors and recipients can be better matched.)

This brings us to the most powerful objection to the sale of kidneys—that, in practice, it would result in the poor selling parts of their bodies to the rich. But in today's healthcare economy, that probably wouldn't be the case. For several decades, Congress has mandated that Medicare pay the medical bills of any patient—of any age—who requires dialysis. Transplant surgery and postsurgical drug treatment are expensive, yes, but they're nothing compared to dialysis, which costs about $40,000 per year. That's a savings of $40,000 per year for the seventeen years or so during which a transplanted kidney will function. In other words, insurers and the federal government would probably be happy to buy a kidney for anyone who needs one. They'd even be willing to pay donors considerable sums—$50,000, $100,000, or more. (Indeed, according to one estimate, if kidneys could be found for all the patients now on dialysis, Medicare would break even after just two years.)

At these prices, there would be no shortage of sellers. The government could 7
enforce price floors to keep competitive sellers from bidding down the going
rate for kidneys. And given the amount of money involved, it seems downright
contradictory to argue that the poor should be prevented from taking the deal on
the grounds that poverty is unfair. The solution to poverty is anyone's guess, but
restricting poor people's economic opportunities definitely isn't the answer. Nor
is it enough to say that there are better and more humane ways of leveling the distribution of wealth than allowing kidney sales. To argue against kidney selling, one
must provide a better practical way of helping the disadvantaged. It does a poor
person who wishes to sell his kidney no favors to tell him instead to lobby Congress for an increase in the minimum wage or a more egalitarian tax code. Besides,
the kidney waiting list contains a disproportionate share of minorities. Thirty-five
percent of the people on the waiting list are black; 12 percent are Hispanic. If the
point of the current law is to temper the effects of income inequality, asking racial
minorities to shoulder an unequal share of the burden is surely a step in the wrong
direction.

Sure, critics will say that allowing kidney sales is the beginning of a slippery slope 8
towards selling other, more essential organs. This, of course, would be a moral disaster, since it would mean legalizing serious maiming (selling eyes) or even murder
(selling hearts or lungs). But the very outrageousness of this will keep it from happening. A slippery-slope argument is convincing only when it shows that the slipping
would be either inevitable (for example, that legalizing abortion when a condom
breaks means people would be less careful about birth control, thereby increasing
abortions) or unconscious (outlawing child porn would lead to outlawing *Lolita,* since
bureaucrats can't tell the difference). But it's easy for legislators to draft a law that
clearly allows kidney selling but forbids other forms of organ selling. (Kidneys are
fairly unique in that, while everybody has two, somebody with just one can lead an almost entirely normal life.) And it seems implausible that a member of Congress would
mistake public approval of kidney sales for approval of economic transactions that
leave sellers dead or partially blind.

Nicholas L. Tilney, a Harvard Medical School professor and transplant surgeon, wrote 9
a paper in 1989 against kidney selling. He says this is still the view of "100 out of 100
transplant surgeons." But in 1998—as the kidney shortage became more acute—he co-
authored, along with other surgeons, lawyers, and philosophers, the provocative *Lancet*
paper that argued for legalizing kidney sales. "We debated this question for about two
years before writing that piece," says Tilney. "All of us transplanters, and I'm sure the
public, have this tremendous gut reaction against it. That was sort of our initial reaction.
And then, when we all got around and really thought about this and talked about it, our
thinking began to change."

The prospect of someone going under the knife to earn a down payment on a 10
new house or to pay for college is far from pleasant. But neither is the reality of
someone dying because a suitable kidney can't be found. The free market may
be the worst way to allocate kidneys. The worst, that is, except for all the other
alternatives.

Examining the Reading

1. Why does Gottlieb favor organ sales?
2. Summarize the opposing viewpoints to organ sales that Gottlieb refutes.
3. Why does Gottlieb feel that allowing the poor to sell their organs is justifiable?
4. Explain the meaning of each of the following words as it is used in the reading: *fringe* (para. 3), *altruism* (5), *egalitarian* (7), *disproportionate* (7), and *provocative* (9). Refer to your dictionary as needed.

Analyzing the Writer's Technique

1. What is Gottlieb's claim? Is it a claim of fact, value, or policy? Explain how you know.
2. In what order does Gottlieb arrange the opposing viewpoints he discusses?
3. How does Gottlieb use expert opinion in this essay?
4. Most of the essay is devoted to refuting opposing viewpoints, while very few reasons in support of organ sales are given directly. Is this an effective argument, despite the lack of reasons?
5. What types of emotional appeals does Gottlieb make? Explain each.

Reacting to the Reading

1. Explain the meaning of the essay's title. How does it relate to the essay's claim?
2. Does mention of Dr. Kevorkian help or hinder Gottlieb's argument? Explain the reasons behind your answer.
3. Write a journal entry in which you explore reasons in support of organ donation.
4. Suppose you were offered $10,000 for one of your kidneys, which would be removed in a foreign country to avoid any legal problems in the United States. Write an essay explaining your response to the offer.

(READING)

"Strip-Mining" the Dead: When Human Organs Are for Sale
Gilbert Meilaender

Gilbert Meilaender is professor of Christian ethics at Valparaiso University. An associate editor of the *Journal of Religious Ethics*, Meilaender specializes in religious ethics and bio-ethics, and has served as a member of President George W. Bush's Council on Bioethics. His books include *Faith and Faithfulness: Basic Themes in Christian Ethics* (1994), *Working: Its Meaning and Its Limits* (2000), and *Bioethics: A Primer for Christians* (2005). This essay originally appeared in the *National Review* in 1999. As you read, highlight Meilaender's claim and the reason he gives to support it.

Eliminate suffering and expand the range of human choice. That sentence expresses   1
the moral wisdom toward which our society is moving, and it is very minimal wisdom

indeed. We can observe this minimalism at work especially well in the realm of bio-ethics, where we seem unable to find any guidance other than (1) relieve suffering and (2) promote self-determination. In accordance with such wisdom, we have forged ahead in the use of new technologies at the beginning of life and—with constantly increasing pressure for assisted suicide—at the end of it.

Less noticed—and perhaps not quite as significant—is the continuing pressure 2 to increase the supply of organs for transplant. For the past quarter-century, transplantation technology has made rapid progress, though the "success rates" given for transplants may often conceal an enormous amount of suffering and frustration endured by those who accept a transplant as the price of possible survival. During this time, there has been continuing debate about what policies ought to govern the procurement of organs from the dead for transplant. Should we simply wait to see whether the dying person, or, after death, his family, decides to offer usable organs? Should we require, as some states now do, that medical caregivers request donation? Should we presume that organs for transplant may be salvaged from a corpse unless the deceased had explicitly rejected the possibility or the family rejects it later? Should we "buy" organs, using financial incentives to encourage people to sell what they had not thought or wanted to give? And if we did use financial inducements, could one also sell organs such as kidneys even before death?

What we think about such questions depends on why we think some people might 3 hesitate to give organs for transplant. If their refusal is a thoughtless act, perhaps we simply need greater public education and awareness to encourage more people to give. If their refusal is not just thoughtless but wrong, perhaps we should authorize medical professionals routinely to salvage cadaver organs for transplant. If their refusal is selfish or, at least, self-regarding, perhaps we should appeal to their self-regarding impulses with an offer of financial compensation.

Moreover, if it is, as we are so often told, a "tragedy" or a "catastrophe" that many 4 die while waiting for an organ transplant, perhaps we need to be more daring in our public policy. That is the view of many who are in the transplant business and many who ponder transplantation as a public-policy issue. While these issues have been debated over the last several decades, our society has steadfastly refused to consider any form of payment for organs. "Giving" rather than "selling" has been the moral category governing organ procurement. Indeed, the National Organ Transplant Act of 1984 forbids "any person to knowingly acquire, receive, or otherwise transfer any human organ for valuable consideration for use in human transplantation, if the transfer affects interstate commerce."

It's not hard to understand our national reluctance to permit the buying and 5 selling of human organs for transplant, for it expresses a repugnance that is deeply rooted in important moral sentiments. In part, the very idea of organ transplantation—which is, after all, in Leon Kass's striking phrase, "a noble form of cannibalism"—is unsettling. If we cannot always articulate clearly the reasons that it troubles us, the sentiment is nonetheless powerful. To view the body—even the newly or nearly dead body—as simply a useful collection of organs requires that we stifle within ourselves a fundamental human response. "We do not," C. S. Lewis once wrote, "look at trees either as Dryads or as beautiful objects while we cut them into beams; the first man who did so may have felt the price keenly, and the bleeding trees in Virgil and Spenser may be far-off echos of that primeval sense of impiety." Far more powerful impulses must be overcome if we are to view the human form simply as a natural object available for our use. Perhaps we are right to view it as such when transplantation is truly lifesaving, but doing so exacts a cost. By insisting that organs must be given freely rather than bought and sold, we have tried to find a way to live with the cost. The "donated" organ—even separated from the body, objectified, and used—remains, in a sense, connected with the one who freely gave it, whose person we continue to respect. By contrast, buying and selling—even if it would provide more organs needed for transplant—would make of the body simply a natural object, at our disposal if the price is right.

Our repugnance is rooted also in the sense that some things are simply not for sale. As a medium of exchange, money makes possible advanced civilization, which depends on countless exchanges in which our interdependence is expressed. But if we allow ourselves to suppose that it is a universal medium of exchange, we are bound to lose our moral bearings. Although there is nothing degrading about buying and selling, since exchange binds us together and allows us to delight in the diversity of goods, commerce enhances human life only when that life itself is not also turned into a commodity. Hence, our society has over time had to make clear that certain things— ecclesiastical and public offices, criminal justice, human beings themselves—may not be bought and sold.   6

Discussing the limits to money as a medium of exchange, Michael Walzer recounts an instructive story from our own history. In 1863, during the Civil War, the Union enacted an Enrollment and Conscription Act, which was the first military draft at the national level in our history. But the act contained a provision that allowed any man whose name was drawn in the lottery to purchase an exemption by paying $300 for a substitute (which, in effect, also offered an incentive for others who wanted or needed $300, even at the risk of death). Anti-draft riots broke out in July 1863 after the first drawing of lots, and we have never since—at least in such overt, crass form—allowed citizens to buy their way out of military service. It is one of those things that should not be for sale, one instance in which money should not be allowed to serve as a medium of exchange, and so we block that exchange.   7

Similarly, we have decided to block exchanges for human organs, even though they do take place in some other countries. That decision has been under attack for some time. It has even been criticized by Thomas Peters, for example, as—behold here the degradation of our public moral discourse—"imposing" the value of altruistic dona- tion on those who do not appreciate such a value, or "coercing" families "to accept concepts foreign to them at a time of great personal loss." But the first real crack in the public-policy dike appeared in May of 1999, when the state of Pennsylvania an- nounced its intention to begin paying relatives of organ donors $300 toward funeral expenses of their deceased relative. (Clearly, $300 doesn't buy as much as it did in 1863.)   8

Pennsylvania's decision has been characterized by Charles Krauthammer as "strip- mining" the dead—and this in an essay defending the decision. It would, Krauthammer asserts, violate human dignity to permit the living to sell organs, but the newly dead   9 body may be treated as a commodity if doing so promises "to alleviate the catastrophic shortage of donated organs." (Note, again, the language of catastrophe. Just as many workers might not have known their labor was "alienated" until Marxists told them, so we might not have thought it "catastrophic" that we die rather than strip-mine the human body in order to stay alive until transplant technology began to tell us it was.) Indeed, Krauthammer quite reasonably claims that the Pennsylvania program is, if anything, far too timid. If the idea is to get more organs for transplant, he suggests that not $300 but $3,000—paid directly to relatives rather than to funeral homes—might be more the ticket.

To the degree that he persuades us, however, we might well judge that 10
Krauthammer himself has been too timid. Pennsylvania's plan for compensation continues to operate within the organ-donation system currently in place. It aims simply to provide a somewhat greater incentive for people to donate organs. What it will not affect is the reluctance—based in sound moral sentiment—of medical caregivers to ask dying people or their families to consider organ donation. If we really face a tragedy of catastrophic proportions, we might do better to allow organ-procurement firms seeking a profit to be the middleman. (After all, a human kidney was recently offered for sale on the Internet auction site eBay—and the bidding reached $5.7 million before the company stopped it.) With profit to be made, firms would find ways to overcome our natural reluctance to ask others to strip-mine the dead body. We could deal not only with our reluctance to give organs but also with our reluctance to ask for them by letting the market do what it does best. That Krauthammer does not suggest this—even for organs from the dead—suggests to me that he finds more "dignity" than he thinks not only in still-living human beings but also in the newly dead body.

Or, again, if it is a catastrophe that we face, we might simply abandon the claim 11
that it is always necessary to wait for death before procuring organs for transplant. For example, as Robert Arnold and Stuart Youngner have noted, a ventilator-dependent patient could request that life support be removed and that, eight or so hours before, he be taken to the operating room and anesthetized, to have his kidneys, liver, and pancreas taken out. Bleeding vessels could be tied off, and the patient's heart would stop only after the ventilator was removed later that day, well before the patient could die of renal, hepatic, or pancreatic failure. And, of course, if our moral wisdom is confined to relieving suffering and respecting autonomy, we may find ourselves very hard pressed to explain why this should not be done—especially in the face of a "catastrophic shortage" of organs.

One might ask, If my death is an evil, why not at least try to get some good for others out of it? If my corpse is no longer my person, as it surely is not, why not treat it as a 12
commodity if doing so helps the living? Ah, but that corpse is my mortal remains. There is no way to think of my person apart from it and no way to gaze upon it without thinking of my person—which person is a whole web of human relations, not a thing or a commodity. A corpse is uncanny precisely because we cannot, without doing violence to our humanity, divorce it fully from the person. To treat those mortal remains with respect, to refuse to see them as merely in service of other goods, is our last chance to honor the "extraterritoriality" of each human life and to affirm that the human person

is not simply a "part" of a human community. Perhaps, if we do so honor even the corpse, I or some others will not live as long as we might, but we will have taken at least a small step toward preserving the kind of society in which anyone might wish to live.

More than a quarter century ago, writing about "Attitudes toward the newly dead," William F. May called attention to one of the Grimm Brothers tales about a young man who is incapable of horror. He does not shrink back from a hanged man, and he attempts to play with a corpse. His behavior might seem childish, but it is in fact inhuman. And his father sends him away "to learn how to shudder"—that is, to become human. In our society—where we devote enormous energy and money to keeping human beings alive—perhaps we too, in the face of proposals to strip-mine the dead, should consider learning once again how to shudder.

Examining the Reading

1. Summarize Meilaender's reasons for opposing human organ sales.
2. Explain the meaning of the quotation that transplantation is "a noble form of cannibalism" (para. 5).
3. Why does Meilaender oppose organ sales but seem to approve of organ donation?
4. Explain the meaning of each of the following words as it is used in the reading: *bioethics* (para. 1), *catastrophe* (4), *ecclesiastical* (6), *uncanny* (12), and *extraterritoriality* (12). Refer to your dictionary as needed.

Analyzing the Writer's Technique

1. What is Meilaender's claim?
2. To what needs and values does Meilaender appeal?
3. Explain the analogy that Meilaender draws between the Civil War draft exemption and organ donation. Is this an effective analogy? Why?
4. What opposing viewpoints does Meilaender recognize? Does he refute them? If so, how?
5. The last paragraph includes a reference to a Grimm Brothers tale. Is this reference effective in concluding the essay?

Reacting to the Reading

1. Strip-mining usually refers to the practice of stripping away soil and land, usually to sell products. Discuss whether organ sales can be compared to strip-mining. What similarities or differences exist?
2. Do you agree or disagree that a still-living human and a newly dead body should be treated with the same degree of respect and dignity?
3. Write a journal entry suggesting guidelines—in addition to the two suggested in paragraph 1—for the field of bioethics.
4. Meilaender suggests that part of being human is knowing how to shudder. Write an essay explaining whether you think the ability to shudder is a distinct and necessary human characteristic.

Integrating the Readings

1. Which writer's argument did you find more convincing? Why?
2. Compare how each writer introduces the issue. In what context does each writer frame the issue?
3. How do you think Gottlieb might respond to Meilaender's claim?
4. If you could seek further information from each author, what questions would you ask?

Don't Trash Your Cell Phone -- Recycle It!

Help keep toxic metals out of the environment with the Recycle My Cell Phone campaign.

Host a cell phone collection in your community

Cell phones contain toxic metals that can pollute the environment and threaten human health. When recycled responsibly, the metals can be put back into circulation, decreasing the need for new metal mining.

Help us make a difference by setting up a responsible **cell phone recycling program in your community or workplace**. It's free, easy and helps keeps phones out of the waste stream.

Make Earth Day every day! You can **recycle your old cell phone** for free from the comfort of your own home today.

RECYCLE MY PHONE   **BECOME A PARTNER**   **WHY RECYCLE**   **ABOUT US**

CHAPTER 19

Writing Arguments

Suppose you are doing research and you locate the Web site shown on the opposite page. Its home page presents a brief argument: It identifies an issue (disposal of cell phones), makes a claim (cell phones should be recycled), and invites readers to enter the site to find out how they can start a cell phone recycling program in their communities (take action).

Working alone or with one or two classmates, rewrite the Web page as a brief argument of one to three paragraphs. The claim is your thesis. Add support of your own to strengthen the argument: evidence, emotional appeals, and so on. Also consider why some readers might disagree with the claim and offer reasons to refute this view. Conclude your brief argument with a convincing statement.

WRITING AN ARGUMENT

By following the steps in the Writing Quick Start, you successfully started to build an argument. You made a claim, supported it with evidence, and refuted opposing views. This chapter will show you how to write clear, effective arguments.

✓ What Is an Argument?

You encounter arguments daily in casual conversations, in newspapers, in classrooms, and on the job. Of the many arguments we hear and read, however, relatively few are convincing. A **sound argument** makes a claim and offers reasons and evidence in support of that claim. A sound argument also anticipates opposing viewpoints and acknowledges, accommodates, and/or refutes them.

The ability to construct and write sound arguments is an important skill in many aspects of life. Many political, social, and economic issues, for instance, are resolved through public and private debate. Knowing how to construct a sound argument is also essential to success in college and on the job (see the accompanying box for a few examples).

The following essay argues in favor of abolishing the U.S. penny.

SCENES FROM COLLEGE AND THE WORKPLACE

- For a *health science* course, you are part of a group working on an argument essay claiming that the results of genetic testing, which can predict a person's likelihood of contracting serious diseases, should be kept confidential.

- As a student member of the *Affirmative Action Committee* on campus, you are asked to write a letter to the editor of the campus newspaper defending the committee's recently drafted affirmative action plan for minorities and women.

- As a *lawyer* representing a client whose hand was seriously injured on the job, you must argue to a jury that your client deserves compensation for the work-related injury.

Abolish the Penny
William Safire

[handwritten: statement should the penny be abolish?]

William Safire, a former speechwriter for Richard Nixon and Spiro Agnew, was a longtime op-ed columnist for the *New York Times*. He is best known for "On Language," his column on grammar, usage, and etymology in the weekly *New York Times Magazine*, and he has published many books, including *Lend Me Your Ears: Great Speeches in History* (1997), *The Right Word in the Right Place at the Right Time: Wit and Wisdom from the Popular "On Language" Column in the* New York Times Magazine (2004), and *Before the Fall: An Inside View of the Pre-Watergate White House* (2005). He won the Pulitzer Prize for commentary in 1978. As you read the following June 2, 2004, essay, notice how Safire gives his own reasons for abolishing the penny and anticipates possible counterarguments.

[handwritten right margin: claim]

Because my staunch support of the war in Iraq has generated such overwhelming reader enthusiasm, it's time to reestablish my contrarian credentials. (Besides, I need a break.) Here's a crusade sure to infuriate the vast majority of penny-pinching traditionalists: The time has come to abolish the outdated, almost worthless, bothersome, and wasteful penny. Even President Lincoln, who distrusted the notion of paper money because he thought he would have to sign each greenback, would be ashamed to have his face on this specious specie.   1

[handwritten right margin: Reason. for Abolish the penny Paragraph 1, 2, 3.]

That's because you can't buy anything with a penny any more. Penny candy? Not for sale at the five-and-dime (which is now a "dollar store"). Penny-ante poker? Pass the buck. Any vending machine? Put a penny in and it will sound an alarm. There is no escaping economic history: it takes nearly a dime today to buy what a penny bought back in 1950. Despite this, the U.S. Mint keeps churning out a billion pennies a month.   2

Where do they go? Two-thirds of them immediately drop out of circulation, into piggy banks or—as the *Times*'s John Tierney noted five years ago—behind chair cushions or at the back of sock drawers next to your old tin-foil ball. Quarters and dimes circulate; pennies disappear because they are literally more trouble than they are worth. The remaining 300 million or so—that's 10 million shiny new useless items punched out every day by government workers who could be more usefully employed tracking counterfeiters—go toward driving retailers crazy. They cost more in employee-hours—to wait for buyers to fish them out, then to count, pack up, and take them to the bank—than it would cost to toss them out. That's why you see "penny cups" next to every cash register; they save the seller time and the buyer the inconvenience of lugging around loose change that tears holes in pockets and now sets off alarms at every frisking place.   3

Why is the U.S. among the last of the industrialized nations to abolish the peskiest little bits of coinage? At the G-8 summit next week, the Brits and the French—even the French!—who dumped their low-denomination coins thirty years ago, will be laughing at our senseless jingling. The penny-pinching horde argues: those $9.98 price tags save the consumer 2 cents because if the penny was abolished, merchants would "round up" to the nearest dollar. That's pound-foolish: the idea behind the 98-cent (and I can't even find a cent symbol on my keyboard any more) price is to fool you into thinking that "it's less than 10 bucks." In truth, merchants would round down to $9.95, saving the consumer billions of paper dollars over the next century.   4

Why people hang on to the penny.

What's really behind America's clinging to the pesky penny? Nostalgia cannot be 5
the answer; if we can give up the barbershop shave with its steam towels, we can give
up anything. The answer, I think, has to do with zinc, which is what pennies are mostly
made of; light copper plating turns them into red cents. The powerful, outsourcing zinc
lobby—financed by Canadian mines as well as Alaskan—entices front groups to whip
up a frenzy of save-the-penny mail to Congress when coin reform is proposed.

But when the penny is abolished, the nickel will boom. And what is a nickel made 6
of? No, not the metallic element nickel; our 5-cent coin is mainly composed of copper. And where is most of America's copper mined? Arizona. If Senator John McCain
would get off President Bush's back long enough to serve the economic interests of his
Arizona constituents, we'd get some long-overdue coin reform.

emotional appeal

What about Lincoln, who has had a century-long run on the penny? He's still hon- 7
ored on the $5 bill, and will be as long as the dollar sign remains above the 4 on key-
boards. If this threatens coin reformers with the loss of Illinois votes, put Abe on the
dime and bump F.D.R.[1]

conclusion

What frazzled pollsters, surly op-ed[2] pages, snarling cable talkfests, and issue- 8
starved candidates for office need is a fresh source of hot-eyed national polarization.
Coin reform can close the controversy gap and fill the vitriol void. Get out those bumper stickers: Abolish the penny!

[1] *F.D.R.:* Franklin Delano Roosevelt, U.S. president from 1933 to 1945.

[2] *op-ed:* the opinion section of the newspaper that is opposite the editorial page.

Characteristics of Argument Essays

All arguments are concerned with issues. In developing an argument essay, you need to
narrow or limit the issue, make a clear and specific claim about the issue, analyze your
audience, and give reasons and evidence to support the claim. In addition, you should
follow a logical line of reasoning; use emotional appeals appropriately; and acknowledge, accommodate, and/or refute opposing views.

An Argument Focuses on an Arguable, Clearly Defined, and Narrowed Issue

An **issue** is a controversy, problem, or idea about which people disagree. In choosing
an issue, therefore, be sure it is arguable—one that people have differing opinions on.
For example, arguing that education is important in today's job market is pointless
because people generally agree on that issue.

Depending on the issue you choose and the audience you write for, a clear definition of the issue may be required. Well-known issues need little definition, but for less
familiar issues, readers may need background information. In an argument about the
awarding of organ transplants, for example, you would give readers information about
the scarcity of organ donors versus the number of people who need transplants. Notice
how Safire announces and defines the issue in "Abolish the Penny," paragraph 1.

In addition, the issue you choose should be narrow enough to deal with adequately
in an essay-length argument. For an essay on organ transplants, for instance, you could
limit your argument to transplants of a particular organ or to one aspect of the issue,

such as who does and does not receive them. When you narrow your issue, your thesis will be more precise and your evidence more specific. You can also provide more effective arguments against an opposing viewpoint.

Exercise 19.1

Working alone or in a group of two or three students, choose two of the following issues. For each issue, consider ways to limit the topic, and list the background information readers might need to understand the issue.

1. Moral implications of state-operated lotteries
2. Computer networks and the right to privacy
3. Speech codes on campus
4. Religious symbols on public property 5/8. Religious symbols
5. Mandatory drug testing

An Argument States a Specific Claim in a Thesis

To build a convincing argument, you need to make a clear and specific **claim**, one that tells readers your position on the issue. If writing arguments is new to you, it is usually best to state your claim in a strong thesis early in the essay. Doing so will help you keep your argument on track. As you gain experience in writing arguments, you can experiment with placing your thesis later in the essay. In "Abolish the Penny," Safire makes a clear, specific claim in his opening paragraph: "The time has come to abolish the outdated, almost worthless, bothersome, and wasteful penny."

For more on types of claims, see Chapter 18, p. 486.

Here are a few examples of how general claims can be narrowed into clear and specific thesis statements.

GENERAL	More standards are needed to protect children in day care centers
SPECIFIC	Statewide standards are needed to regulate the child-to-caregiver ratio and the qualifications of workers in day-care centers.
GENERAL	The use of animals in testing should be prohibited.
SPECIFIC	The testing of cosmetics and skin-care products on animals should be prohibited.

While all arguments make and support a claim, some also call for specific action to be taken. An essay opposing human cloning, for example, might argue for a ban on that practice as well as urge readers to voice their opinions in letters to congressional representatives. Claims of policy often include a call for action.

For more on claims of policy, see Chapter 18, p. 487.

Regardless of the argument, you need to be careful about the way you state your claim. Avoid a general or absolute statement; your claim will be more convincing if you qualify or limit it. For example, if a writer arguing in favor of single-sex education makes the claim "Single-sex educational institutions are *always* more beneficial to girls than are coeducational schools," then opponents could easily cite exceptions to the claim and thereby show weaknesses in the argument. However, if the claim is qualified—as in "Single-sex educational institutions are *often* more beneficial to girls than are coeducational schools"—then an exception would not necessarily weaken the argument.

Exercise 19.2

Choose two of the following issues. Then, for each issue, write two thesis statements—one that makes a claim and contains a qualifying term, and another that makes a claim and calls for action.

1. Controlling pornography on the Internet
2. Limiting immigration
3. Limiting political campaign spending
4. Restricting testing of beauty products on animals
5. Promoting competitive sports for young children

An Argument Depends on Careful Audience Analysis

To build a convincing argument, you need to know your audience. Because an argument is intended to influence readers' thinking, begin by anticipating your readers' views. First determine how familiar your audience is with the issue. Then decide whether your audience agrees with your claim, is neutral about or wavering on the claim, or disagrees with the claim.

Agreeing audiences. When you write for an audience that agrees with your claim, the focus is usually on urging readers to take a specific action. Agreeing audiences are the easiest to write for because they already accept your claim. Instead of presenting large amounts of facts and statistics as evidence, you can concentrate on reinforcing your shared viewpoint and building emotional ties with your audience. By doing so, you encourage readers to act on their beliefs. *emotional appeal*

For more on emotional appeals, see Chapter 18, p. 488.

Neutral or wavering audiences. Audiences are neutral or wavering when they have not made up their minds about or given much thought to an issue. Although they may be somewhat familiar with the issue, they may have questions about, misunderstandings about, or no interest in it. When writing for a neutral or wavering audience, emphasize the importance of the issue, and clear up misunderstandings readers may have about it. Your goals are to make readers care about the issue, establish yourself as a knowledgeable and trustworthy writer, and present solid evidence in support of your claim.

Logic. Structuring

Disagreeing audiences. The most challenging type of audience is the disagreeing audience—one that holds viewpoints in opposition to yours. Such an audience may have strong feelings about the issue and may distrust you because you don't share their views on something they care deeply about.

In writing for a disagreeing audience, your goal is to persuade readers not necessarily to accept but at least to consider your views on the issue. Be sure to follow a logical line of reasoning. Rather than stating your claim early in the essay, it may be more effective to build slowly to your thesis. First establish a **common ground**—a basis of trust and goodwill—with your readers by mentioning shared interests, concerns, experiences, and points in your argument. Then when you state your claim, the audience may be more open to considering it.

In "Abolish the Penny," Safire writes for a disagreeing audience. In the opening paragraph, he recognizes that he is likely to infuriate "penny-pinching traditionalists." Safire openly acknowledges the opposing viewpoint in paragraph 4, where he summarizes the argument of the "penny-pinching horde." He establishes a common ground with his readers by mentioning shared concerns (about productivity of government workers and political lobbyists) and referring to well-respected historical figures such as Abraham Lincoln and Franklin Delano Roosevelt.

Exercise 19.3

Choose one of the following claims, and discuss how you would argue in support of it for an agreeing audience, a neutral or wavering audience, and a disagreeing audience.

1. Public school sex education classes should be mandatory because they help students make important decisions about their lives.

2. Portraying the effects of violent crime realistically on television may help reduce the crime rate.

3. Children who spend too much time interacting with a computer may fail to learn how to interact with people.

An Argument Presents Reasons Supported by Convincing Evidence

In developing an argument, you need to have reasons for making a claim. A **reason** is a general statement that backs up a claim; it answers the question, Why do I have this opinion about the issue? You also need to support each reason with evidence. Suppose you want to argue that high school uniforms should be mandatory for three reasons: The uniforms (1) reduce clothing costs for parents; (2) help eliminate distractions in the classroom; and (3) reduce peer pressure. Each of your reasons would need to be supported by evidence, facts, statistics, examples, personal experience, or expert testimony. Carefully linking your evidence to reasons helps readers see how the evidence supports your claim.

Be sure to choose reasons and evidence that will appeal to your audience. In the argument about mandatory school uniforms, high school students would probably not be impressed by your first reason—reduced clothing costs for parents—but they might consider your second and third reasons if you cite evidence that appeals to them, such as personal anecdotes from students. For an audience of parents, facts and statistics about reduced clothing costs and improved academic performance would be appealing types of evidence. In "Abolish the Penny," Safire offers several reasons for his claim, and supports them with examples. For instance, pennies drop out of circulation, fall behind chair cushions, or hide at the back of sock drawers.

An Argument Follows a Logical Line of Reasoning

The reasons and evidence in an argument should follow a logical line of reasoning. The most common types of reasoning are induction and deduction (see the diagrams below). Whereas **inductive reasoning** begins with evidence and moves to a conclusion, **deductive reasoning** begins with a commonly accepted statement or premise and shows how a conclusion follows from it. You can use one or both types of reasoning to keep your argument on a logical path.

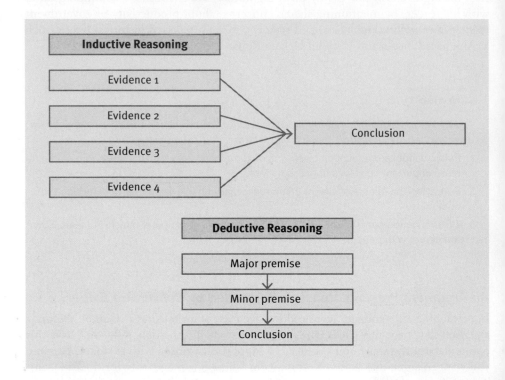

Inductive reasoning. Inductive reasoning starts with specific evidence and moves to a generalization or conclusion. For example, suppose you go shopping for a new pair of sneakers. You try on one style of Nikes. It doesn't fit, so you try a different style. It doesn't fit either. You try two more styles, neither of which fits. Finally, because of your experience, you draw the conclusion that either you need to remeasure your feet or Nike does not make a sneaker that fits your feet. Think of inductive reasoning as a process of coming to a conclusion after observing a number of examples.

When you use inductive reasoning, you make an *inference,* or guess, about the cases that you have not experienced. In doing so, you run the risk of being wrong. Perhaps some other style of Nikes would have fit.

When building an inductive argument, be sure to consider all possible explanations for the cases you observe. In the shoe store, for example, perhaps the salesperson brought you the wrong size sneakers. You also need to be sure that you have *sufficient* and *typical* evidence on which to base your conclusion. Suppose you observe one food-stamp recipient selling food stamps for cash and another using them to buy candy bars. From these observations you conclude that the food-stamp program should be abolished. Your reasoning is faulty, however, because these two cases are not typical of food-stamp recipients and not sufficient for drawing a conclusion. You must scrutinize your evidence and make sure that you have enough typical evidence to support your conclusion.

When you use inductive reasoning in an argument essay, the conclusion becomes the claim, and the specific pieces of evidence support your reasons for making the claim. For example, suppose you make a claim that Pat's Used Cars is unreliable. As support you might offer the following reasons and evidence.

REASON	Pat's Used Cars does not provide accurate information about its products.
EVIDENCE	My sister's car had its odometer reading tampered with. My best friend bought a car whose chassis had been damaged, yet the salesperson claimed the car had never been in an accident.
REASON	Pat's Used Cars doesn't honor its commitments to customers.
EVIDENCE	The dealership refused to honor the ninety-day guarantee for a car I purchased there. A local newspaper recently featured Pat's in a report on businesses that fail to honor guarantees.

Deductive reasoning. Deductive reasoning begins with **premises**, statements that are generally accepted as true. Once the premises are accepted as true, then the conclusion must also be true. The most familiar deductive argument consists of two premises and a conclusion. The first statement, called a **major premise**, is a general statement about a group. The second statement, called a **minor premise**, is a statement about an individual belonging to that group. You have probably used this three-step reasoning, called a **syllogism**, without realizing it. For example, suppose you know that any food containing dairy products makes you ill. Because frozen yogurt contains dairy products, you conclude that frozen yogurt will make you ill.

When you use deductive reasoning, putting your argument in the form of a syllogism will help you write your claim and organize and evaluate your reasons and evidence. Suppose you want to support the claim that state funding for Kids First, an early childhood program, should remain intact. You might use the following syllogism to build your argument.

MAJOR PREMISE	State-funded early childhood programs have increased the readiness of at-risk children to attend school.
MINOR PREMISE	Kids First is a popular early childhood program in our state.
CONCLUSION	Kids First is likely to increase the readiness of at-risk children to attend school.

Your thesis statement would be "Because early childhood programs are likely to increase the readiness of at-risk children to attend school, state funding for Kids First should be continued." Your evidence would be the popularity and effectiveness of Kids First.

For more on fallacies, see Chapter 18, p. 501.

As you develop a logical argument, you also need to avoid introducing **fallacies**, or errors in reasoning.

An Argument Appeals to Readers' Needs and Values

For more on emotional appeals, see Chapter 18, p. 488.

Although an effective argument relies mainly on credible evidence and logical reasoning, emotional appeals can help support and enhance a sound argument. **Emotional appeals** are directed toward readers' needs and values. **Needs** can be biological or psychological (food and drink, sex, a sense of belonging, esteem). **Values** are principles or qualities that readers consider important, worthwhile, or desirable. Examples include honesty, loyalty, privacy, and patriotism. In "Abolish the Penny," Safire appeals to the human need for efficiency to convince his readers to abolish outdated and worthless goods. Safire is also aware of the value of patriotism, as he assures readers that presidential figures will remain on currency.

An Argument Recognizes Opposing Views

Recognizing or countering opposing arguments forces you to think hard about your own claims. When you listen to readers' objections, you may find reasons to adjust your own reasoning and develop a stronger argument. In addition, readers will be more willing to consider your claim if you take their point of view into account.

There are three methods of recognizing opposing views in an argument essay: *acknowledgment, accommodation,* and *refutation.*

1. When you **acknowledge** an opposing viewpoint, you admit that it exists and show that you have considered it. For example, readers opposed to mandatory high school uniforms may argue that a uniform requirement will not eliminate peer pressure because students will use other objects to gain status — such as backpacks, iPods, hairstyles, and cell phones. You could acknowledge this viewpoint by admitting that there is no way to stop teenagers from finding ways to compete for status.

2. When you **accommodate** an opposing viewpoint, you acknowledge readers' concerns, accept some of them, and incorporate them into your own argument. In arguing for mandatory high school uniforms, you might accommodate readers' view that uniforms will not eliminate peer pressure by arguing that the uniforms will eliminate one major and expensive means of competing for status.

3. When you **refute** an opposing viewpoint, you demonstrate the weakness of the opponent's argument. Safire refutes opposing views in his essay on abolishing the penny. He acknowledges that some people fear that abolishing the penny would encourage merchants to "round up" their prices to the next dollar. He refutes this fear by reassuring readers that merchants would more likely "round down" to a lower price.

> ### Exercise 19.4
>
> *For the three claims listed in Exercise 19.3, identify opposing viewpoints and consider how you could acknowledge, accommodate, or refute them.*

Visualizing an Argument Essay: A Graphic Organizer

The graphic organizer shown in Figure 19.1 will help you analyze arguments as well as plan those that you write. Unlike the graphic organizers in Part 3, this organizer does not necessarily show the order in which an argument may be presented. Some arguments, for example, may begin with a claim, whereas others may start with evidence or opposing viewpoints. Whatever your argument's sequence, you can adapt this organizer to fit your essay. Note, however, that not every element will appear in every argument.

Read the following essay by Rachel Jones, and then study the graphic organizer for it in Figure 19.2 on page 526.

Not White, Just Right
Rachel Jones

READING

Rachel Jones is a journalist, currently reporting on education, social policy, and welfare reform issues for NPR. She has worked as a reporter for the *St. Petersburg Times*, the *Detroit Free Press*, and the *Chicago Reporter*, as well as a national correspondent for Knight-Ridder newspapers. She is a former president of the Journalism and Women Symposium. This essay first appeared in *Newsweek,* a weekly newsmagazine, in 1997. As you read the selection, highlight Jones's claim, supporting evidence, and counterarguments.

In December of 1982, *Newsweek* published a My Turn column that launched my professional writing career and changed the course of my life. In that essay, entitled "What's Wrong with Black English," I argued that black youngsters need to become proficient in standard English. While the dialect known as black English is a valid part of our cultural history, I wrote, success in America requires a mastery of communications skills.   1

Fourteen years later, watching the increasingly heated debate over the use of black English in struggling minority urban school districts, I can't help but offer my own experience as proof that the premise is greatly flawed. My skill with standard English propelled me from a life of poverty and dead ends to a future I could have scarcely imagined. It has opened doors for me that might never have budged an inch for a poor black girl from Cairo, Illinois. It has empowered me in ways I can't begin to explain.   2

That empowerment still amazes me. The column, one that Ralph Waldo Emerson might have described as "a frank and hearty expression of what force and meaning is in me," has assumed an identity of its own, far beyond what I envisioned. It has been reprinted in at least fifty college English texts, anthologies, and writing course books. I still have a scrapbook of some of the letters that poured in from around the country, from blacks and whites, overwhelmingly applauding my opinion. An editor in Detroit said he recognized my name on a job-application letter because he'd clipped the column and used it in a class he'd taught.   3

Recently, a professor from Brigham Young University requested permission to record the material on a tape used for blind students. But perhaps the most humbling experience of all occurred in 1991, when I was on fellowship in Chicago and received a phone call from a twenty-year-old college student. He had just read the essay in one of his textbooks and, on impulse, dialed directory assistance, seeking my name. Because the column was written in 1982, when I'd been a student in Carbondale—and Chicago wasn't my hometown—there was no reason for him to have found me; I could have been anywhere in the world.   4

Figure 19.1 GRAPHIC ORGANIZER FOR AN ARGUMENT ESSAY

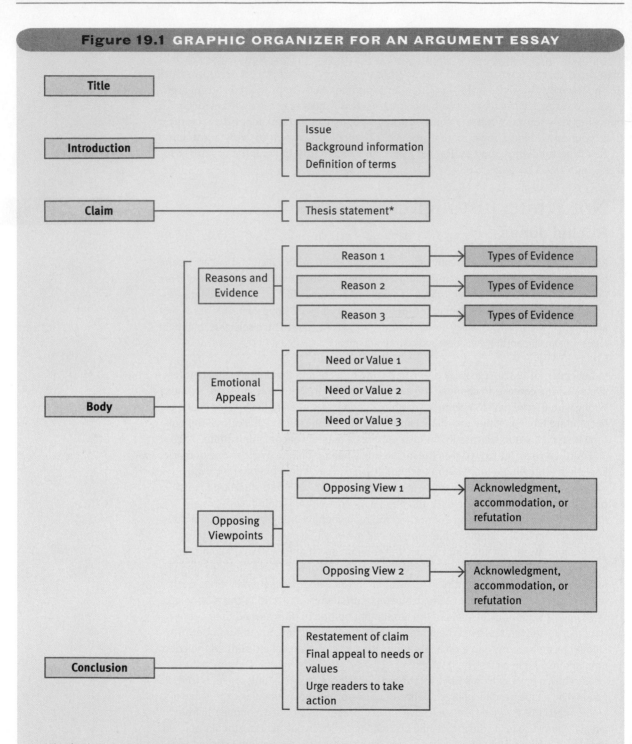

*The thesis statement may appear anywhere within the argument.

We talked for about an hour that night. He thanked me profusely for writing that   5
column. He was biracial and said that all his life his peers had teased him for "talking
proper, for wishing [he] was *all* white." He said he was frustrated that so many black
kids believed that speaking articulately was a white characteristic.

He thanked me so often it was almost unnerving. I hung up the phone in a sort of daze.   6
Something I had written, communicated from my heart, had touched him so deeply he
had to reach out to me. It brings tears to my eyes remembering it; I related to him so well.

I, too, had been ridiculed as a youth for my proper speech. But I had lots of support   7
at home, and many poor urban black youths today may not share my advantages. Every
afternoon my eight older brothers and sisters left their schoolbooks piled on every
available surface, so I was poking through *The Canterbury Tales*[1] by age eight. My sister
Julie corrected me every time I used "ain't" or "nope." My brother Peter was a star on
the high-school debate team. And my mother, Eloise, has one of the clearest, most
resonant speaking voices I've ever known. Though she was a poor housekeeper when I
was growing up, she was articulate and plain-spoken.

Knowing the price that was paid for me to develop my abilities, it's infuriating to   8
hear that some young blacks still perceive clear speech as a Caucasian trait. Whether
they know it or not, they're succumbing to a dangerous form of self-abnegation that
rejects success as a "white thing." In an age of backlash against affirmative action,
that's a truly frightening thought.

To me, this "whitewashing" is the crux of the problem. Don't tell me that calling   9
Ebonics[2] a "bridge" or an "attempt to reach children where they are" will not deepen this
perception in the minds of disadvantaged young blacks. And though Oakland, California,
school administrators[3] have amended their original position on Ebonics, it still feels like
a very pointed political statement to me, one rooted in the ongoing discussions about
socioeconomic justice and educational equity for blacks. As much as I respect the cultural foundations of Ebonics, I think Oakland trivializes these discussions and stokes the
fires of racial misunderstanding. Senator Lauch Faircloth may have been too hasty in calling the Oakland school board's plan to introduce Ebonics "political correctness gone out
of control," but he's hardly to be condemned for raising the flag of concern.

When immigrants worldwide fight to come to the United States, many seeking to gain   10
even the most basic English skills, claiming a subset of language for black Americans is a
damning commentary on our history of inequity and lack of access to equal educational
opportunities in this country. Frankly, I'm still longing for a day when more young blacks
born in poverty will subscribe to my personal philosophy. After a lifetime of hard work
to achieve my goal of being a writer, of battling racism and forging my own path, I've decided that I really don't care if people like me or not. But I demand that they *understand*
me, clearly, on my own terms. My mastery of standard English gave me a power that no
one can take away from me, and it is important for any group of people hoping to succeed in America. As a great-granddaughter of slaves, I believe success is my birthright.

As I said back in December of 1982, I don't think I "talk white; I think I talk right."   11
That's not quite grammatically correct, but it's a blessing to know the difference.

---

[1] The Canterbury Tales: A collection of poems written by English author Geoffrey Chaucer (1340?–1400).

[2] *Ebonics:* The study of black English as a language.

[3] *Oakland School District:* The school board originally voted to treat African American students as bilingual; the
board modified this plan to focus on teaching proficiency in standard English.

Figure 19.2 GRAPHIC ORGANIZER FOR "NOT WHITE, JUST RIGHT"

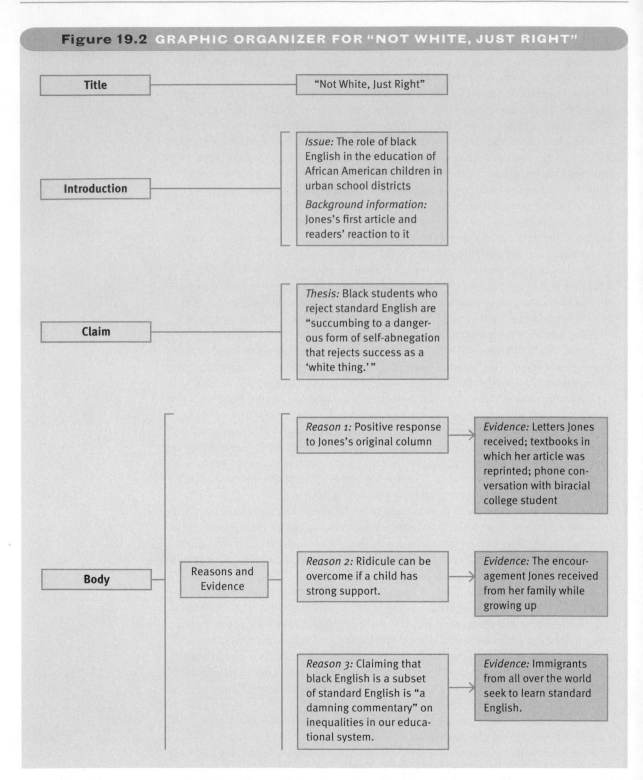

Figure 19.2 *(continued)*

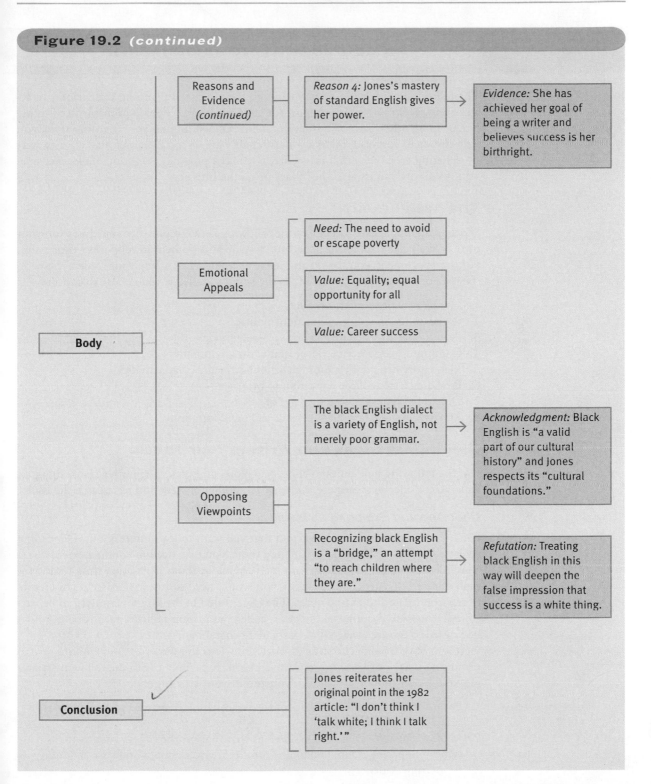

For more on the patterns of development, see Chapters 10–17.

A GUIDED WRITING ASSIGNMENT

The following guide will lead you through the process of planning and writing an argument essay. In presenting support for your argument, you will probably need to use one or more other patterns of development. Depending on your learning style, you may choose to approach the essay in different ways. A social learner may want to start by debating an issue with a classmate, whereas a pragmatic or concrete learner may want to research an issue in the library or on the Internet.

The Assignment

Write an argument essay on one of the following issues or one that you choose on your own. Make a claim about the issue, and develop an argument in support of your claim. For this assignment, you should also select an audience. Analyze your readers' views on the issue and target your argument to the specific audience you choose to address.

1. Buying American-made products
2. Racial quotas in college admissions policies
3. Professional athletes and celebrities as role models
4. Community service as a college graduation requirement
5. Mandatory drug testing for high school extracurricular activities
6. Providing a free college education to prisoners
7. Donating kidneys to save the lives of others
8. An environmental problem or issue in your community

Generating Ideas and Writing Your Thesis

Use the following guidelines to choose, explore, and make a tentative claim about an issue; to consider your purpose, audience, and point of view; and to research the issue.

Choosing and Exploring an Issue

Choose an issue that interests you and that you want to learn more about. Depending on how much you already know about a topic, you may need to conduct extensive research. For instance, to write an informed argument about mandatory drug testing for high school extracurricular activities, you would need to research existing laws, types of tests, and state and local policies. The issues listed in the assignment need to be narrowed. The issue about racial quotas in college admission policies, for instance, might be limited to private colleges in a particular geographic region.

For more on prewriting strategies, see Chapter 4.

If you have trouble choosing an issue, move to the next step and explore several promising issues until you can make a decision. Experiment with the following strategies to discover those that work for you and fit your learning style.

Learning Style Options

1. Brainstorm about different sides of the issue. Think of reasons and evidence that support various viewpoints.
2. Make a tentative claim, and list reasons that support the claim. Then switch sides, state an opposing claim, and brainstorm to discover reasons and corresponding supporting evidence.

3. Draw a map of the issue, connecting ideas as they come to mind. Then narrow your issue: Start with one or two key ideas you generated and draw another map.

4. Conduct a mock argument with a classmate. Choose opposing views on the issue and defend your positions. Take notes on the argument. Notice the reasons and evidence you and your opponent use to support your positions.

5. Write the issue at the top of a piece of paper or in a computer file. Then divide the list into two columns, listing pros in one column and cons in the other.

6. Examine the issue by answering these key questions.

- What is the issue? How can I best define it?
- Is it an arguable issue?
- What are some related issues?
- How can I narrow the issue for an essay-length argument?
- What are my views on the issue? How can I state my claim?
- What evidence supports my claim?
- Does my argument include a call for action? What do I want readers to do, if anything, about the issue?
- Does the issue have a compromise position?

7. Talk with others who have experience with the issue or are experts. For example, if you argue for stricter laws to prevent child abuse, a case worker for a child welfare agency may be able to help you narrow the issue, gather evidence, and address opposing viewpoints. A friend who experienced abuse as a child could provide another perspective. Keep in mind that sensitive topics should be approached tactfully, and requests for confidentiality should be respected.

For more on conducting an interview, see Chapter 21, p. 593.

8. Use the Internet. Use a search engine to locate discussion forums on your topic as well as Web sites that deal with the issue.

For more on Internet research, see Chapter 21, p. 581.

> **Essay in Progress 1**
> Use the preceding suggestions to choose an issue to write about (one from the list of assignments on page 528 or one you think of on your own) and to explore and narrow the issue.

Considering Your Purpose, Audience, and Point of View

Once you choose an issue and begin to explore it, carefully consider your purpose, audience, and point of view. Think about what you want to happen as a result of your argument: Do you want your readers to change their minds? Do you want them to feel more certain of their existing beliefs? Or would you have them take some specific action?

An effective argument is tailored to its audience. The reasons and the types of evidence you offer, the needs and values to which you appeal, and the common ground you establish all depend on your audience. Remember that for this Guided Writing Assignment, you select the audience for your essay. Use the following questions to analyze your audience.

1. What do my readers already know about the issue? What do they need to know?

2. How familiar are my readers with the issue? Do they have firsthand experience with it, or is their knowledge limited to what they've heard in the media and from other people?

3. **Do my readers care about the issue?** Why or why not?
4. **Is my audience an agreeing, neutral or wavering, or disagreeing audience?** How do their beliefs or values affect their views?
5. **What shared views or concerns can I use to establish a common ground with my readers?**

For more on purpose, audience, and point of view, see Chapter 4, p. 82.

In an argument essay, you can use the first-, second-, or third-person point of view, depending on the issue, your purpose for writing about it, and the reasons you offer in support of your claim. If it is important that your readers feel close to you and accept you or your experiences as part of your argument, the first person will help you achieve this closeness. In "Not White, Just Right," Jones uses the first person because she is offering her personal experiences as evidence. If you want to establish a familiarity with your audience, the second person may be most effective. The third person creates the most distance between you and your readers and works well when you want to establish an objective, impersonal tone.

Researching the Issue

Research is often an essential part of developing an argument. Reading or hearing what others have to say about an issue helps you gather background information, reliable evidence, and alternative viewpoints. Use the following guidelines to gather information on your topic.

For more on library and Internet research, see Chapter 21.

For more on note-taking and on avoiding plagiarism, see Chapter 21, pp. 586 and 591. For more on documenting sources, see Chapter 22.

1. **Skim through library sources,** such as books, magazine and newspaper articles, encyclopedia entries, and textbooks.
2. **Watch television news programs, documentaries, or talk shows on your topic.**
3. **Research the issue on the World Wide Web.**
4. **Take notes as you read your sources.** Also add ideas to your brainstormed lists, notes, or maps. As you jot down notes, take steps to avoid plagiarizing the words and ideas of other writers. Enclose direct quotations from sources in quotation marks, summarize and paraphrase information from sources carefully, and record all of the publication details you will need to cite your sources (author, title, publisher and site, publication date, page numbers, and so on).

> **Essay in Progress 2**
> Using the preceding suggestions, consider your purpose, audience, and point of view. Be sure to answer the questions listed on pages 529–30; your responses will help you tailor your argument—including your evidence and emotional appeals—to your intended audience.

Developing Your Thesis and Making a Claim

For more on thesis statements, see Chapter 5, p. 101.

After doing research and reading what others have to say about the issue, your views on it may have softened, hardened, or changed in some other way. Before you develop a thesis and make a claim about the issue, consider your views on it in light of your research.

As you draft your thesis, be careful to avoid statements that are unarguable, too general, or too absolute. Note the difference between the following examples.

UNARGUABLE FACT	In recent years, U.S. consumers have experienced an increase in credit card fraud.
TOO GENERAL	Many problems that U.S. consumers complain about are mostly their own fault.
TOO ABSOLUTE	U.S. consumers have no one but themselves to blame for the recent increase in credit card fraud.
ARGUABLE/SPECIFIC/LIMITED	Although the carelessness of merchants and electronic tampering contribute to the problem, U.S. consumers are largely to blame for the recent increase in credit card fraud.

Essay in Progress 3

Using the preceding suggestions, write a working thesis that clearly expresses your claim about the issue.

Evaluating Your Ideas, Evidence, and Claim

Once you are satisfied with your working thesis, take a few minutes to evaluate the reasons and evidence you will use to support your claim. Begin by rereading everything you have written with a critical eye. Look for ways to organize your reasons (such as in order of their strength or importance), and group your evidence for each reason. Draw a graphic organizer of your reasons and evidence, using Figure 19.1 as a model.

To draw detailed graphic organizers using a computer, visit www.bedfordstmartins .com/successfulwriting.

> **Trying Out Your Ideas on Others**
>
> Working in a group of two or three students, discuss your claim, reasons, and evidence. Each writer should state his or her issue, claim, reasons, and evidence for this chapter's assignment. Then, as a group, evaluate each writer's work.

Essay in Progress 4

Using the list of the characteristics of argument essays on pages 516–22 and comments from your classmates, evaluate your claim and the reasons and evidence you have gathered to support it. (You might also use the questions in Table 18.2, page 502, to help you evaluate your claim, reasons, and evidence.)

Considering Opposing Viewpoints

Once you evaluate the key elements in your argument, you are ready to consider opposing viewpoints and plan how to acknowledge, accommodate, or refute them. Your argument will be weak if you fail to at least acknowledge opposing viewpoints. Your readers may assume you did not think the issue through or that you dismissed alternative views without seriously considering them.

Create a list of reasons for and against your position, or review the one you made earlier. Then try to group the objections to form two or more points of opposition.

To acknowledge an opposing viewpoint without refuting it, you can mention the opposition in your claim, as shown in this claim about enforcing speed limits.

- **Although speed-limit laws are intended to save lives, the conditions that apply to specific highways should be taken into account when enforcing them.**

The opposing viewpoint appears in a dependent clause attached to an independent clause that states the claim. By including the opposing viewpoint in this way, you show that you take it seriously but that you think it is outweighed by your claims.

To accommodate an opposing viewpoint, find a portion of the opposing argument that you can build into your argument. One common way to accommodate objections is to suggest alternative causes for a particular situation. For example, suppose your argument defends the competency of most high school teachers. You suspect, however, that some readers think the quality of most high school instruction is poor and attribute it to teachers' laziness or lack of skill. You can accommodate this opposing view-point by suggesting that the poor instruction some schools provide may be due to large class size rather than teachers' incompetence.

If you choose to argue that an opposing viewpoint is simply wrong, you must refute it by pointing out problems or flaws in your opponent's reasoning or evidence. To refute an opponent's reasoning, check to see if your opponent uses faulty reasoning or fallacies. To refute an opponent's evidence, use one or more of the following guidelines.

For more on fallacies, see Chapter 18, p. 501.

1. **Give a counterexample** (one that is an exception to the opposing view). For instance, if the opponent argues that dogs are useful for protection, give an example of a situation in which a dog did not protect its owner.
2. **Question the opponent's facts.** If an opponent claims that few professors give essay exams, present statistics demonstrating that a significant percentage of professors do give essay exams.
3. **Demonstrate that an example is not representative.** If an opponent argues that professional athletes are overpaid and cites the salaries of two famous quarterbacks, cite statistics that show that these salaries are not representative of professional athletes in general.
4. **Demonstrate that the examples are insufficient.** If an opponent argues that horseback riding is a dangerous sport and offers two examples of riders who were seriously injured, point out that two examples are not sufficient proof.
5. **Question the credibility of an authority.** If an opponent quotes a television personality on welfare reform, point out that the person has not studied the issue the way a sociologist or public-policy expert has.
6. **Question outdated examples, facts, or statistics.** If your opponent presents evidence that is not recent on the need for more campus parking, you can argue that the situation has changed (enrollment has declined, bus service has increased).
7. **Present the full context of a quotation or group of statistical evidence.** If an opponent quotes an authority selectively or cites incomplete statistics from a research study on ozone depletion and its effects on skin cancer, the full context may show that your opponent has "edited" the evidence to suit his or her claim.

Essay in Progress 5

Write your claim on a piece of paper or in a computer file. Below it, list all possible opposing viewpoints. Then describe one or more strategies for acknowledging, accommodating, or refuting each opposing view.

Trying Out Your Ideas on Others

Working in a group of two or three students, present your strategies for acknowledging, accommodating, or refuting opposing views. Critique each other's strategies, and suggest others that each writer might use.

Organizing and Drafting

You are now ready to organize your ideas and draft your essay. You need to decide on a line of reasoning, choose a method of organization, and develop your essay accordingly.

Choosing a Line of Reasoning and a Method of Organization

To develop a method of organizing an argument, you might use *induction, deduction,* or both. Inductive reasoning begins with specific evidence and moves to a general conclusion. Deductive reasoning starts with an observation that most people accept and shows how a certain conclusion follows from it. Whether you choose to use one or both lines of reasoning, this decision will influence how you organize your essay.

Here are four common ways to organize an argument.

Method I	Method II	Method III	Method IV
Claim/thesis	Claim/thesis	Reasons/evidence	Opposing viewpoints
Reasons/evidence	Opposing viewpoints	Opposing viewpoints	Reasons/evidence
Opposing viewpoints	Reasons/evidence	Claim/thesis	Claim/thesis

The method you choose depends on your audience and your issue. You also need to decide the order in which you will discuss the reasons and evidence and the opposing viewpoints. Will you arrange them from strongest to weakest? Most to least obvious? Most to least familiar? In planning your organization, try drawing a graphic organizer or making an outline. Try different ways of organizing your essay on the computer, creating a document file for each alternative.

Drafting the Argument Essay

Once you have chosen a method of organization for your argument, you are ready to write your first draft. Use the following guidelines to draft your essay.

For more on drafting an essay, see Chapter 6.

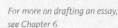

For more on writing effective paragraphs, including introductions and conclusions, see Chapter 6.

1. **Write an effective introduction.** Your introduction should accomplish several things. It should *identify the issue* and *offer needed background information* based on your assessment of your audience's knowledge and experience. In addition, it should *define the terms* to be used in the argument. Most argument essays also include a thesis in the introduction, where you make your *claim.* Finally, the introduction should *engage readers* and *create goodwill* toward you and your argument. Several strategies can help you engage your readers right away.

   - Open by relating a personal experience, ideally one with which your readers can identify. (See "When Volunteerism Isn't Noble" by Lynn Steirer, p. 485.)
   - Open with an attention-getting remark. (See "Not White, Just Right" by Rachel Jones, p. 523.)
   - Open by recognizing a counterargument.

2. **Establish an appropriate tone.** The tone you adopt should depend on the issue and the type of claim you make as well as the audience to whom you write. For an argument on a serious issue such as the death penalty, you would probably use a serious, even somber tone. For a call-to-action argument, you might use an energetic, enthusiastic tone. For a disagreeing audience, you might use a friendly, nonthreatening tone. Be sure to avoid statements that allow no room for opposing viewpoints (such as "It is obvious that . . ."). Also avoid language that may insult or alienate your reader ("Anybody who thinks differently just does not understand the issue").

3. **State your reasons clearly, and provide evidence for each one.** In an essay about mandatory high school uniforms, for example, you might use a reason (such as "Requiring high school uniforms will reduce clothing costs for parents") as a topic sentence for a paragraph. The rest of the paragraph would then consist of evidence supporting that particular reason.

For more on documenting sources, see Chapter 22.

4. **Cite the sources of your research.** As you present your evidence, be sure to include a citation for each quotation, summary, or paraphrase of ideas or information you borrow from sources. Even when you do not use an author's exact wording, you need to cite the original source.

For more on transitions, see Chapter 6, p. 124.

5. **Use strong transitions.** Make sure you use transitions to move clearly from reason to reason in your argument, as in "*Also relevant* to the issue . . ." and "*Furthermore,* it is important to consider . . ." Also be certain that you have distinguished your reasons and evidence from those of the opposition. Use a transitional sentence such as "Those opposed to the death penalty claim . . ." to indicate that you are about to introduce an opposing viewpoint. A transition such as "Contrary to what those in favor of the death penalty maintain . . ." can be used to signal a refutation.

6. **Write a satisfying conclusion.** You can end an argument essay in a number of ways. Choose the strategy that will have the strongest impact on your audience.

   - Restate your thesis. (See "Not White, Just Right" by Rachel Jones, p. 523.)
   - Make a final appeal to values. (See "When Volunteerism Isn't Noble" by Lynn Steirer, p. 485.)

- Project into the future. (See "Economic Affirmative Action" by Ted Koerth, p. 492.)
- Urge readers to take a specific action.
- Call for further study and research.

Essay in Progress 6

Using the preceding suggestions for organizing and drafting, choose the line of reasoning your argument will follow and a method of organization; then write your first draft.

Analyzing and Revising

If possible, set your draft aside for a day or two before rereading and revising it. Then, as you review your draft, focus on discovering weak areas and strengthening your overall argument, not on grammar or mechanics. Use one or more of the following suggestions to analyze your draft.

1. Read your draft essay, put it aside, and write one sentence that summarizes your argument. Compare your summary sentence and thesis (statement of claim) to see if they agree or disagree. If they do not agree, your argument needs a stronger focus.
2. Read your essay aloud or ask a friend to do so as you listen. You may "hear" parts of your argument that do not seem to follow.
3. Make an outline or draw a graphic organizer or update one you did earlier. Look to see if the outline or graphic organizer reveals any weaknesses in your argument (for example, you don't have enough reasons to support your claim).

Learning Style Options

Use Figure 19.3 to guide your analysis. You might also ask a classmate to review your draft essay using the questions in the flowchart. For each "No" response, ask your reviewer to explain why he or she responded in that way.

For more on the benefits of peer review, see Chapter 8, p. 162.

Essay in Progress 7

Revise your draft using Figure 19.3 and any comments you received from peer reviewers.

Editing and Proofreading

The last step is to check your revised essay for errors in grammar, spelling, punctuation, and mechanics. Be sure to check your error log for the types of errors you tend to make. Look for the following two grammatical errors in particular.

For more on keeping an error log, see Chapter 9, p. 196.

1. **Make sure that you use the subjunctive mood correctly.** In an argument, you often write about what would or might happen in the future. When you use the verb *be* to speculate about future conditions, use *were* in place of *was*.

   - If all animal research ~~was~~ *were* outlawed, progress in the control of human diseases would be slowed dramatically.

Figure 19.3 Flowchart for Revising an Argument Essay

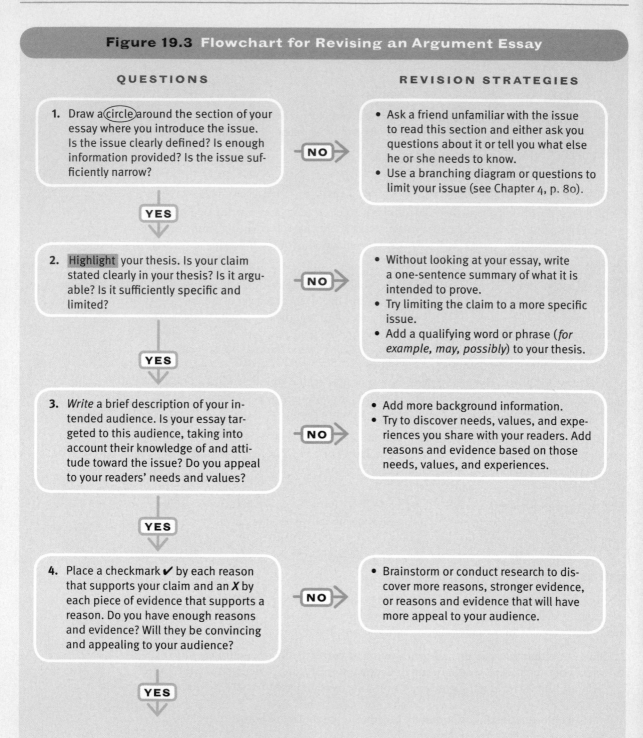

QUESTIONS

REVISION STRATEGIES

1. Draw a (circle) around the section of your essay where you introduce the issue. Is the issue clearly defined? Is enough information provided? Is the issue sufficiently narrow?

NO →

- Ask a friend unfamiliar with the issue to read this section and either ask you questions about it or tell you what else he or she needs to know.
- Use a branching diagram or questions to limit your issue (see Chapter 4, p. 80).

YES ↓

2. Highlight your thesis. Is your claim stated clearly in your thesis? Is it arguable? Is it sufficiently specific and limited?

NO →

- Without looking at your essay, write a one-sentence summary of what it is intended to prove.
- Try limiting the claim to a more specific issue.
- Add a qualifying word or phrase (*for example, may, possibly*) to your thesis.

YES ↓

3. *Write* a brief description of your intended audience. Is your essay targeted to this audience, taking into account their knowledge of and attitude toward the issue? Do you appeal to your readers' needs and values?

NO →

- Add more background information.
- Try to discover needs, values, and experiences you share with your readers. Add reasons and evidence based on those needs, values, and experiences.

YES ↓

4. Place a checkmark ✔ by each reason that supports your claim and an *X* by each piece of evidence that supports a reason. Do you have enough reasons and evidence? Will they be convincing and appealing to your audience?

NO →

- Brainstorm or conduct research to discover more reasons, stronger evidence, or reasons and evidence that will have more appeal to your audience.

YES ↓

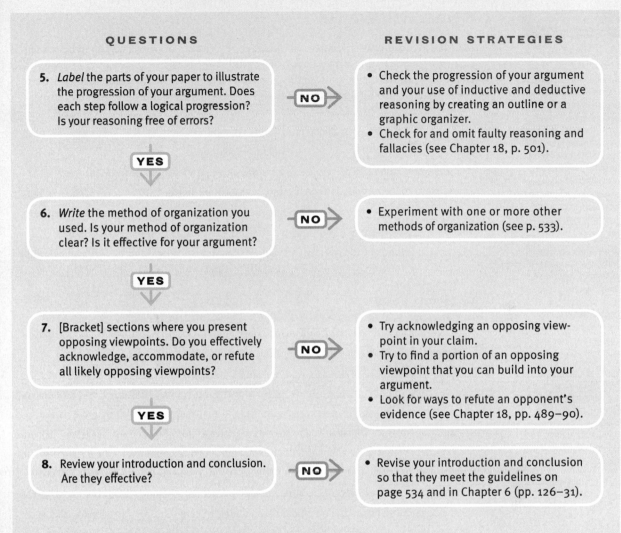

QUESTIONS | REVISION STRATEGIES

5. *Label* the parts of your paper to illustrate the progression of your argument. Does each step follow a logical progression? Is your reasoning free of errors?

NO →

- Check the progression of your argument and your use of inductive and deductive reasoning by creating an outline or a graphic organizer.
- Check for and omit faulty reasoning and fallacies (see Chapter 18, p. 501).

YES ↓

6. *Write* the method of organization you used. Is your method of organization clear? Is it effective for your argument?

NO →

- Experiment with one or more other methods of organization (see p. 533).

YES ↓

7. [Bracket] sections where you present opposing viewpoints. Do you effectively acknowledge, accommodate, or refute all likely opposing viewpoints?

NO →

- Try acknowledging an opposing viewpoint in your claim.
- Try to find a portion of an opposing viewpoint that you can build into your argument.
- Look for ways to refute an opponent's evidence (see Chapter 18, pp. 489–90).

YES ↓

8. Review your introduction and conclusion. Are they effective?

NO →

- Revise your introduction and conclusion so that they meet the guidelines on page 534 and in Chapter 6 (pp. 126–31).

2. Look for and correct ambiguous pronouns. A pronoun must refer to another noun or pronoun, called its *antecedent*. The pronoun's antecedent should be clearly named — not just implied.

- Children of divorced parents are often shuttled between two homes, and

  this lack of stability
  ‸that can be confusing and disturbing to them.

Essay in Progress 8

Edit and proofread your essay, paying particular attention both to your use of the verb *be* in sentences that speculate about the future and to pronoun reference. Don't forget to look for errors you often make.

READING

Students Write

Stanford DeWinter was a first-year student at Seattle Pacific University when he wrote the following essay arguing why today's college students should be concerned about the AIDS crisis. As you read the essay, note the patterns of development DeWinter uses to structure his argument. Also highlight the thesis and the reasons DeWinter gives to support it.

Introduction: DeWinter identifies the issue and gives statistical background information on it. Throughout the essay, he provides source citations for his information. He names his audience—college students—and assumes they are perhaps not well informed about the issue.

In his thesis statement, DeWinter makes a claim of policy that he limits by emphasizing its importance for certain fields of study. He tries to establish common ground with his audience.

DeWinter presents his first reason and supports it with facts and statistical evidence. Note that he uses a serious, informative tone throughout.

DeWinter offers statistical evidence to support his second reason.

AIDS and You: A World Crisis and Its Local Effects

Stanford DeWinter

The world HIV/AIDS crisis poses one of the greatest health problems of all time. According to the World Health Organization, across the planet in 2007, a total of 33.2 million people were living with HIV, over 2 million died in that year, and there were 2.5 million new infections (United Nations). Many college students may not understand how directly this crisis affects them. However, today's students will be tomorrow's leaders, and the AIDS crisis will be even worse then. Therefore, all college students--and especially those planning to go into the fields of health care, politics and public policy, business and finance, and education--should learn about the impact that AIDS is having so that they can face the challenges ahead. No matter what their field of study, students can apply their knowledge to action now that will give them preparation and experience for future careers and involvement.   1

Anyone interested in health care will have to address the HIV/AIDS issue in multiple ways. Doctors and nurses are on the front lines of the war against HIV/AIDS, both at home and abroad. Although great advances have been made in the treatment of HIV-positive patients, the disease remains a threat in the United States, where thousands of new cases are diagnosed each year. In addition, many countries currently have a shortage of qualified medical personnel. For example, in China, where about one million people are infected, only two hundred doctors are trained to deal with HIV/AIDS; although the United States cannot fill all the gaps, we can make a huge difference in the quality and availability of care (Chase). Furthermore, this issue will affect biology and chemistry students intending to go into research. The race to find medications to treat, cure, and vaccinate for HIV/AIDS involves many huge biotech companies, pharmaceutical companies, and other types of research institutions.   2

Much of this research into the causes of AIDS and potential treatments is funded by the U.S. government and privately run foundations, so college students considering a career in politics or the not-for-profit sector will need to be informed about the disease. For example, the National Institutes of Health--a government institution--requested almost $3 billion for AIDS research in its fiscal year 2008 budget request (United States). In many cases, politicians must be knowledgeable enough to make decisions about such uses of tax dollars and explain them to constituents. Other funds come from private foundations and not-for-profit organizations. The Gates Foundation alone has given almost $2 billion in support of its HIV/AIDS and   3

Tuberculosis Global Health Program since 1994 ("Recent Global Health Grants"). Students in-terested in fund-raising, fund management, and development may find that proposals dealing with HIV/AIDS research, education, and treatment will come their way in large numbers.

Not only is the human cost in lives outrageous, but the financial cost of HIV/AIDS is ris-ing as local economies fail. When local economies are unstable, the world economy becomes more unstable. As explained in a recent *Fortune* magazine article, as the rates of infection in Russia, China, and India rise, the damage to the world economy increases (Gunther). One reason for this is the huge amount of work American companies outsource to these parts of the world. A study headed by Sydney Rosen and published in the *Harvard Business Review* states that "the epidemic both adds to companies' labor costs and slows growth rates in many developing economies." This study explains in detail how expensive AIDS is for companies since they end up spending extra money on AIDS-related issues to conduct business both at home and abroad. The researchers claim that businesses should join the fight to prevent and cure AIDS to maintain financial health. Therefore, any student who is interested in business, finance, or economics will be dealing with this issue as a professional.

Teachers will have to present a great deal of information to their students as the epidemic becomes more and more serious. The HIV/AIDS issue will affect almost every subject area taught. One organization, the Association for Childhood Education International (ACEI), has already anticipated this need and has created an extensive list of resources for educators. This group states that "Children and young adolescents must have access to accurate medical infor-mation and services necessary to develop life skills, as they are the group most affected by the prevalence of HIV/AIDS." Second, the ACEI recognizes that because many parents and teach-ers are dying from HIV/AIDS, children need a larger support system of schools, organizations, and individuals to raise them. Third, the group stresses that HIV/AIDS is a global problem and therefore deserves the attention of all people, "not just those that fail to bring the disease under control" ("World AIDS Day 2003"). This is a call to everyone, and perhaps especially to college students, who have the opportunity to explore a variety of approaches and solutions.

Some might say that we should focus only on our own nation and not get involved in the problems of other countries. However, HIV/AIDS is a problem that cuts across all lines: regional, social, economic, gender, sexual orientation, religion, and ethnicity. Because of the huge number of people worldwide who are affected and the severity of the disease, we must look beyond our own borders to help all those in need. College students are progressing through an educational stage during which they become less focused on themselves and more focused on the world and their place in it. Part of this discovery will be the realization that the HIV/AIDS epidemic is a crucial point of awareness. As a result, students, no matter what their job plans, should be prepared to work for employers that are becoming more globally aware and requiring that their employees become involved in service projects.

4 In paragraph 4, DeWinter leads up to his third reason at the end of the paragraph by making a logical appeal involving economic stability.

5 DeWinter uses expert opinions as evidence to support his fourth reason.

6 DeWinter recognizes and refutes the opposing viewpoints that Americans should focus only on HIV/AIDS in their own country and that only students with certain career plans need to be concerned with the issue.

Conclusion: DeWinter makes a call for action—campus and community involvement. He makes emotional appeals based on orphaned children, human rights, and "the future of the human race."

Students should thoroughly educate themselves on this issue and become involved in some way, not only to prepare themselves for their careers but also to make a difference in the future of the human race. What could be a better cause than one that affects so many people at home and abroad? This disease has ripped apart the fabric of many societies. Children are being orphaned in staggering numbers. It is a basic human right that people should not live in disease-ravaged communities. In fact, it is amoral to ignore or avoid the HIV/AIDS epidemic. We must be involved in changing the course of this devastating disease. Start now by investigating campus programs and other opportunities in your community. Go further into the international scene by searching on the Internet for ways to unite with people around the world joined in this fight to save and improve lives.

7

Works Cited

Chase, M. "Lack of AIDS Doctors in Poor Countries Stalls Treatment." *Wall Street Journal* 13 July 2004: B1. Print.

Gunther, Marc. "A Crisis Business Can't Ignore." *Fortune* 23 Aug. 2004: 72. Print.

"Recent Global Health Grants." *Bill & Melinda Gates Foundation*. Bill & Melinda Gates Foundation, July 2007. Web. 18 Oct. 2007.

Rosen, Sydney, et al. "AIDS Is Your Business." *Harvard Business Review* 81 (2003): 80. Print.

United Nations. UN Programme on HIV/AIDS and World Health Organization. *2007 World AIDS Epidemic Update*. Geneva: United Nations, 2007. Print.

United States. National Institutes of Health. Office of AIDS Research. *Fiscal Year 2008 Trans-NIH Plan for HIV-Related Research*. Sept. 2007. *NIH Office of AIDS Reasearch*. Web. 15 Oct. 2007.

"World AIDS Day 2003: Stigma and Discrimination." *Association for Childhood Education International*. Assn. for Childhood Educ. Intl., Nov. 2002. Web. 12 Oct. 2007.

Analyzing the Writer's Technique

1. Evaluate DeWinter's thesis statement. How does it suggest the organization of the essay? How is it reinforced in the essay's conclusion?
2. What additional types of evidence could DeWinter have used to support his reasons?

Reacting to the Reading

1. Discuss how the HIV/AIDS crisis has affected your life or the lives of others you know.
2. In what ways is the HIV/AIDS crisis recognized on your campus or in your community? Does more need to be done to build awareness of the crisis?
3. Write a journal entry analyzing how your chosen career (or a career that you are considering) relates to and may be affected by the HIV/AIDS crisis.

READING AN ARGUMENT

The following section provides advice for reading an argument as well as two essays that take opposing views on a current issue—the recent popularity of sport utility vehicles (SUVs). Each essay illustrates the characteristics of argument covered in this chapter and provides opportunities to examine, analyze, and react to the writer's ideas. For additional information on reading arguments critically, see Chapter 18, "Reading Arguments."

For more on reading arguments, see Chapter 18, especially the discussions of types of claims (pp. 486–87) and types of evidence (p. 488).

Working with Text: Responding to Arguments

How to Find Ideas to Write About

Since you may be asked to write a response to an argument, keep an eye out for ideas to write about as you read.

For more on discovering ideas for a response paper, see Chapter 3.

1. **Additional supporting evidence.** Use annotations to record additional examples, personal experiences, or other evidence that comes to mind in support of the author's claim. These ideas may be helpful in writing your own essay in support of this writer's claim. They might also provide a start for a paper on one aspect of the writer's argument.
2. **Opposing viewpoints and evidence.** Note any opposing views that come to mind as you read. Record events or phenomena that do not support the claim or that contradict one of the author's reasons. Keep the following question in mind: When would this not be true? The ideas you generate may be useful in writing an essay in which you support an opposing claim.
3. **Related issues.** Think of issues that are similar to the one under discussion in the essay. You may notice, for example, that the line of reasoning applied to the issue of "riding the bus rather than driving" may in part be applicable to the issue of "walking rather than riding."

Keep these guidelines in mind as you read the following pair of essays by Andrew Simms and John Merline on the issue of SUVs.

Would You Buy a Car That Looked Like This?
Andrew Simms

READING

Andrew Simms is policy director and head of the Climate Change Programme for the New Economics Foundation in England. Simms's writing has appeared in the *Guardian* and *Resurgence;* he is also the author of *An Environmental War Economy* (2001) and *The Health of the Planet and the Wealth of Nations: A Story of Ecological Debt* (2005). As you read, evaluate the evidence Simms uses to support his argument against SUVs.

They clog the streets and litter the pages of weekend colour* supplements. Sport   1
utility vehicles or SUVs, otherwise known as 4x4s, four-wheel drives, and all-terrain
wagons, have become badges of middle-class aspiration. They are also dangerous,
fabulously polluting, and, as part of a general transport problem, set to become, according to the World Health Organisation, one of the world's most common causes of
death and disability—ahead of TB, HIV, and war. . . .

With the Kyoto Protocol about to kick in and a major conference on global warming   2
starting in Buenos Aires in two weeks, it is time for some fresh thinking on SUVs. . . .
The gap between image and reality with SUVs is reminiscent of that in tobacco industry
advertising. After all, the scientific consensus over the causes and consequences of
climate change closely mirrors that about smoking and cancer. And in the same way as
the tobacco advertisers, car advertisers have tried to associate their product with masculinity, health, and the outdoor life. So shouldn't SUVs now be labelled in the same
way as cigarette packets, with messages such as . . . "Climate change can seriously
damage your health"? This might not entirely stop people driving SUVs, but it would
force them to accept the consequences. The case for regulation of this sort is growing
like a giant cloud of vehicle exhaust.

According to a 2004 World Health Organisation (WHO) report, 1.2 million people   3
across the world are killed in road crashes each year and 50 million injured. If
nothing changes, the numbers are projected to rise by 65 percent in twenty years.
In Britain alone, there were 290,607 reported road casualties in 2003, including
3,508 deaths.

The WHO compares the global burden of diseases by looking at the years of poten-   4
tial life lost as a result of premature death and the years of productive life lost due to
disability. In 1990, road traffic accidents ranked ninth on these criteria. By 2020, they
will be third. And this does not include the contribution of vehicle emissions to respiratory disease and deaths or to the injuries caused by climate change.

SUVs, by almost any measurements, are more dangerous than other passenger   5
cars. The Ford Explorer, America's biggest-selling SUV, is sixteen times more likely than
the typical family car to kill the occupants of another car in a crash. Pedestrians, too,
are more at risk. You're twice as likely to be killed if you get hit by a 4x4. Even the widespread belief that, come the crunch, so to speak, the SUV owner is better off is a myth.
New US federal traffic data reported in the *New York Times* shows that "people driving
or riding in a sport utility vehicle in 2003 were nearly 11 percent more likely to die in an
accident than people in cars." One of the SUV's key selling points, its height, which
is meant to make you feel safer, makes these cars twice as likely to be caught in fatal
"rollover" accidents as ordinary cars. The US Consumers Union also reports that SUVs
suffer from greater rear-view blind spots — which may account for the rise of more than
50 percent (to 91) last year in the number of US parents who killed their children by
reversing over them.

As the [British] Health Secretary, John Reid, put it the other day: "In a free society,   6
men and women ultimately have the right within the law to choose their own lifestyle,

---

*This article was published in England; therefore, you will see variations in spelling that are used and accepted
in England.

even when it may damage their own health." But, he added, "people do not have the right to damage the health of others, or to impose an intolerable degree of nuisance on others." And when it comes to choosing cars, it seems that neither industry nor the self-absorbed consumer can be trusted to do the right thing.

In the US, by the end of the twentieth century, overall vehicle economy had dropped 7 to its lowest level in twenty years. According to the Union of Concerned Scientists, "two decades of fuel-saving technologies, that could have helped curb carbon dioxide emissions, have instead gone into increasing vehicle weight and performance." The figures bear them out. In 1985, SUVs accounted for only one in fifty vehicles sold in the US. Now they make up one in four. . . .

In the US, people don't drive them just because they like them. Amazingly, the 8 US government waves them on with tax breaks. Even the most costly SUVs—owned by lawyers, real estate agents, plastic surgeons, film stars, and so on—get breaks that can be worth up to $35,000. This is because SUVs are modelled on the frames of commercial vehicles. In other words, as far as the US taxman is concerned, they're really trucks. A sales tax credit designed for light trucks of more than 6,000 lb ended up being applied to the full range of big cars. This encourages manufacturers to build larger, weightier, and more polluting vehicles. Adding transport insult to climate injury, such vehicles are also exempted from emissions limits imposed on US manufacturers.

None of this is a problem if you listen to the industry. "CO_2 is not a pollutant. 9 Repeat, not a pollutant," says the SUV Owners of America, an industry front group run by a PR firm that has worked for General Motors, DaimlerChrysler, and Ford. "It is a naturally occurring part of the air we breathe." Carbon dioxide is "not" a pollutant only in the way that arsenic is "not" a poison. It's all a question of dosage. And that's the problem with SUVs.

So would fuel taxes change behaviour? Yes, in part. But fuel duties have been po- 10 litically out of favour since the country was held to ransom during the fuel blockades. And to change behaviour significantly, the taxes have to be very high. The Society of Motor Manufacturers says that "environmental factors are very low on people's list of priorities when it comes to buying a car." So the New Economics Foundation is looking at the model of tobacco labelling as a way to help people kick the SUV habit. Canadian government research, backed by World Bank findings, shows that there is a direct relationship between the size of warnings and the effect on personal behaviour. "The larger the health warning message," reports Health Canada, "the more effective it is at encouraging smokers to stop smoking."

Where cigarette smoke contains benzene, nitrosamines, formaldehyde, and hydro- 11 gen cyanide, as the warnings tell us, car exhaust has benzene, particulates, nitrogen oxides, and carbon monoxide. Smoking kills, but so do SUVs, their exhaust, and the global warming to which they disproportionately contribute.

Opinion is already turning against the vehicles. It is not only London's [mayor] Ken 12 Livingstone who wants to restrict them. The Paris city council has declared that SUVs are "totally unacceptable." In Rome, the city government has proposed to treble the permit rate for SUV owners to enter the city centre. So labelling is the logical next step. The only issue would be classifying the guilty parties. The urban off-roader, crossover

SUV, Chelsea tractor, four-wheel drive, or 4x4 is instantly recognisable with or without the bullbars. The group encompasses vehicles with similar size and style that are marketed as sport utility vehicles but which may not incorporate substantial off-road features. Styling aside, a threshold could be set to trigger the labelling, such as having a certain number of typical features, on the basis that "if it walks like a duck and talks like a duck . . ."

Fuel efficiency, already used as a basis for assessing vehicle excise duty, could also   13
be key, with the labelling kicking in when efficiency drops below a certain threshold. Like those for cigarettes, the warnings could cover 30–50 percent of the vehicles' surface area. People could still drive them, but when they did, they would publicly accept the consequences of their actions and help the education drive on traffic safety and global warming.

At the least, cigarette-style car labelling would help the industry move out of denial.   14
A recent advert for the Chrysler Crossfire invited the reader to "kiss the sky" with the car. But in an age of global warming, a more honest slogan for a 23 mpg vehicle would have been "rip it apart." Label up, and let's go.

Examining the Reading

1. Why does Simms believe that SUVs should have warning labels?
2. What emotional appeals does Simms make?
3. According to the author, why do people drive SUVs?
4. In what ways does Simms believe our lives would be better without SUVs?
5. Explain the meaning of each of the following words as it is used in the reading: *aspiration* (para. 1), *reminiscent* (2), *consensus* (2), *disproportionately* (11), and *treble* (12). Refer to your dictionary as needed.

Analyzing the Writer's Technique

1. Highlight Simms's claim and evaluate its placement in the essay.
2. What types of evidence does Simms use to support his argument? Which of these do you find most compelling? Explain your answer.
3. What arrangement of details does the author use to present the argument? What other arrangement could have been used?
4. Identify the opposing viewpoints that Simms refutes. How does he refute them? How effective are his refutations?
5. Explain the author's conclusion.

Reacting to the Reading

1. What solutions—other than warning labels—might encourage people not to buy SUVs?
2. Write a journal entry about the labeling of dangerous products. Is it appropriate for automobiles?
3. Write an essay taking a position on citizens' right to choose habits and behaviors that might harm or injure them. Is this an essential part of a free society?

Why Consumers Have Been Choosing SUVs
John Merline

John Merline is the senior director of editorial services at AOL. He has also served as the Washington, D.C., bureau chief of *Investors Business Daily*; editor of *Consumers' Research* magazine; and an editorial writer for *USA Today*. This article was published in *Consumers' Research*. As you read, notice how Merline anticipates and refutes opposing evidence as he argues in favor of SUVs.

In recent months, a variety of consumer groups and environmentalists have launched   1
a ferocious campaign aimed at disarming American drivers of sport utility vehicles (SUVs). One group, the Detroit Project, went so far as to charge that SUV drivers were supporting terrorism every time they filled up their gas tanks. A Christian group complained that driving SUVs was not in keeping with the teachings of Jesus Christ. Consumer activist Joan Claybrook, head of Public Citizen, charged that SUVs are "a bad bargain for society and a nightmare for American roads." They are, she said, "the dangerous offspring of a heady mix of profit-driven special interest politics and corporate deception."

According to these critics, SUVs are: 2

- *Road hazards:* They are prone to deadly rollovers and crush cars unlucky enough to crash into them.
- *Gas hogs:* Their relatively low mileage increases the nation's dependence on foreign oil.
- *Pollution machines:* They emit more pollutants than smaller cars, thereby increasing global warming and smog.

The only problem with all these pointed barbs is that few of them withstand close   3
scrutiny. SUVs are not nearly as dangerous as critics allege, and they are getting safer both for their own occupants and those in other cars colliding with them in accidents. Forcing SUVs to be more fuel efficient, or pushing buyers to buy allegedly more sensible smaller cars, would have little meaningful impact on the nation's dependence on foreign oil. SUVs aren't increasing air pollution in cities, and their effect on global warming, if any, is negligible.

Road hazards? According to Public Citizen's Claybrook, SUVs "are no safer for their   4
drivers than midsize and large cars, and are extremely dangerous for others on the road." Claybrook claims that fatality rates for SUVs are actually higher than for regular cars, despite the fact that they are generally larger and heavier than such cars. Claybrook and others argue that one safety weakness of SUVs is their higher rollover risk. Because they are taller than ordinary cars, SUVs have a higher center of gravity, making them more likely to roll over in extreme driving conditions. And, she and others say, because SUVs' bumpers are higher than those on cars, they can impose severe crash penalties on car drivers. The higher bumpers can ride over car bumpers and safety bars in doors, imposing more deadly crash forces on car passengers.

A close look at the data reveals a different picture. According to the Insurance   5
Institute for Highway Safety, drivers are less likely to die in SUVs than in passenger
cars. In 2001, there were 73 driver deaths per million 1- to 3-year-old SUVs, the study
found, compared with 83 deaths per million cars of the same vintage. So, whatever
the propensity to roll over, SUVs apparently make up for it by being safer in other
areas.

The second concern is that SUVs have a tendency to overpower smaller cars in   6
crashes. They might protect their own occupants, but make the highways less safe for
others. This compatibility problem is a reasonable concern, to some extent. In 1990,
for example, the average weight difference between cars and light trucks—a category
that includes minivans and pickups as well as SUVs—was 830 pounds. According to
the National Highway Traffic Safety Administration, this difference had increased to
1,130 pounds by 2001. All other things being equal, heavier cars have an advantage in
a crash over lighter cars. And because the bumpers don't always match up, an SUV can
ride over a car's crumple zone.

But those who argue that SUVs must change to fix this problem overlook the   7
other possible solution: making smaller cars heavier and more crash resistant. That
would arguably protect drivers and passengers in these cars not only when they col-
lide with an SUV, but in the many other crashes that involve trucks, buses, or fixed
objects.

Finally, the overall fatality rate on the highways has dropped 27.4 percent since   8
1990, a time that saw sales of SUVs explode. If SUVs were the incredible safety men-
ace that Joan Claybrook alleges, one would expect to have seen the opposite trend in
fatalities.

Gas hogs? Because SUVs get less mileage than do cars, critics charge that they con-   9
tribute to the nation's dependence on foreign oil. Indeed, in the past ten years, the
nation's dependence on imports has climbed from 42 percent to 54 percent of oil consumption. Syndicated columnist and book author Arianna Huffington mounted an ad
campaign complaining that because SUVs consume more gasoline than cars, drivers
were guilty of supporting the oil-producing regimes in the Persian Gulf—some of which
have been accused of providing financial support to terrorists. "What is your SUV doing
to our national security?" asked one ad sponsored by Huffington's group, the Detroit
Project. At the very least, SUV critics insist that these cars be mandated by the federal
government to be more fuel efficient.

The connection seems to make sense until the data are more closely examined.   10
First, while SUVs generally consume more gasoline than do cars, they are not the rapacious gas hogs critics suggest. True, the largest SUVs get, on average, just 17 miles per
gallon. But relatively few of these vehicles sell each year. Indeed, the most popular
SUVs are midsize ones, which get an average 20.7 mpg, according to the Oak Ridge
National Laboratory. That's just 5 mpg less than a large car, and just 3 mpg less than
an average minivan.

What's more, despite the surge in sales of SUVs over the past ten years, over-   11
all fuel economy on the road has actually improved. Consider: In this decade,
SUVs went from 5 percent of all registered cars on the road to 11 percent. Yet fuel

economy of all cars on the road climbed nearly 7 percent between 1990 and 2000, according to the Oak Ridge National Laboratory. It appears, then, that many new car buyers, even those buying SUVs, are trading in less fuel-efficient cars for more fuel-efficient ones.

Pollution machines? Environmentalists argue that dirtier SUVs are creating an intense   12
new air-pollution burden on cities, and contributing to global warming because they emit more carbon dioxide than do more fuel-efficient vehicles. As one environmentalist group puts it: "Sport utility vehicles can spew 30 percent more carbon monoxide and hydrocarbons and 75 percent more nitrogen oxides than passenger cars." These are pollutants that combine with sun and heat to form smog. The critics note that several popular SUVs get among the lowest rankings for air pollution put out by the Environmental Protection Agency.

Yet even as SUVs have come to dominate new car sales, air quality has improved.   13
According to the Environmental Protection Agency, the amount of nitrogen oxide in the air dropped 11 percent between 1992 and 2001. Ozone dropped 3 percent. Carbon monoxide was down 38 percent. Those gains came not only as the car market shifted over toward more SUVs, minivans, and light trucks, but as cars overall were driven more. Miles traveled over the past ten years climbed 30 percent. The reason may be similar to the reason for the improvements seen over the past decade in overall fuel economy. A driver who trades in a dirty old car for a slightly less polluting new SUV has helped improve the environment, even if the SUV isn't the cleanest new car coming off the assembly line.

The claim that SUVs are contributing meaningfully to global warming is also a   14
stretch. Gasoline consumption in the United States is but one source of so-called greenhouse gases in this country, which themselves are just one source of global greenhouse gas emissions. Assuming that greenhouse gases are warming the planet in a way that will be harmful to humans, a claim that is still subject to much dispute, even eliminating all SUVs would do nothing measurable to warming trends over the next hundred years. All cars on the road account for only about half of oil consumption in this country, and SUVs account for a fraction of that. According to the United Nations, even if all countries in the world cut their emissions of greenhouse gases back to 1990 levels—which would take a far more radical and widespread effort to reduce energy consumption than just making SUVs more efficient—the result would push back eventual temperature increases by roughly ten years.

The role of consumers. Overlooked in such attacks on SUVs is the important role con-   15
sumers play, not just in the shape of the car market but in overall highway safety. Over the past decade, sales of SUVs climbed an eye-popping 312 percent. Sales of cars—a category that excludes SUVs, minivans, and light trucks —actually dropped 10 percent. Joan Claybrook and other SUV critics attribute this to clever marketing on the part of carmakers, who allegedly make fat profits on SUV sales. But no amount of slick advertising can convince families living on a budget to buy an expensive SUV if more modestly priced vehicles are available to meet their needs. More likely, SUVs, along with minivans, are popular because they do, in fact, serve so many families' needs.

Those with children who want to travel or carry sporting equipment or tow things have few reasonable choices aside from these large vehicles.

Driver behavior is also completely overlooked by SUV critics. Almost all roll- 16 over fatalities could be prevented, for example, if drivers and passengers of SUVs simply buckled up. As Runge of the National Highway Traffic Safety Administration, puts it: "We can reduce the effects of the rollover problem overnight if all occupants would simply buckle their safety belts. They are 80 percent effective in preventing deaths in rollovers involving light trucks." Yet, Runge notes, "72 percent of the occupants of these vehicles who die in rollover crashes are not wearing safety belts."

In the end, SUVs may not be perfect. And they may not be the sort of car some con- 17 sumers would choose to buy. But that's the beauty of the free market. Consumers get to decide what cars and what toasters and what homes and what computers best serve their needs. Despite what SUV critics might think, it appears that consumers are making reasonable choices with their hard-earned money.

Examining the Reading

1. According to Merline, why do people buy SUVs?
2. Identify the three opposing viewpoints that the author refutes.
3. Merline refutes SUV critics. What direct reasons of his own does he give in support of SUVs?
4. According to the author, how can manufacturers improve the outcome of accidents between SUVs and smaller cars?
5. Explain the meaning of each of the following words as it is used in the reading: *barbs* (para. 3), *syndicated* (9), *mandated* (9), and *rapacious* (10). Refer to your dictionary as needed.

Analyzing the Writer's Technique

1. Evaluate the expert opinion that the author provides. Are these sources you know and respect?
2. What types of evidence does Merline offer to refute the opposing viewpoints?
3. What types of emotional appeal does Merline use? How do they contribute to the article?
4. Merline briefly identifies the opposing viewpoints and then addresses each in detail. Why does he do this, and is it effective?
5. What is the author's conclusion? Is it an appropriate ending? How does it establish common ground with his audience?

Visualizing the Reading

Evaluate the types of evidence that Merline uses to support his claim by completing the following chart. For each type of evidence listed, provide at least one example from the reading. The first one has been done for you.

Type of Evidence	Example from Essay
Example	"A driver who trades in a dirty old car for a slightly less polluting new SUV" (para. 13)
Statistics	
Expert Opinion	
Fact	

Reacting to the Reading

1. What factors, other than increased sale of SUVs, might account for the decrease in the overall highway fatality rate since 1990?
2. Write a journal entry exploring whether the rollover threat is sufficient to prevent you from purchasing or riding in an SUV.
3. Write an argumentative essay about environmental hazards. Choose one hazard, and argue for policies or actions to control that hazard.

Integrating the Readings

1. Which essay did you find more convincing? Why?
2. Compare the ways in which the authors present and support their arguments.
3. How do you think the two authors would respond to each other on issues of safety, pollution, and fuel economy?
4. What further information would you need to clarify the issues examined in these essays?

Applying Your Skills: Additional Essay Assignments

To Persuade Your Reader

Write an argument essay on one of the following topics. Narrow the topic to focus on an issue that can be debated, such as a problem that could be solved by reforms or legislation. Depending on the topic you choose, you may need to do library or Internet research. Your audience is made up of your classmates and instructor.

For more on locating and documenting sources, see Part 5.

1. Professional sports
2. College policies
3. Cell phones
4. Movie ratings
5. Presidential campaigns

Cases Using Argument

1. Write an essay for a sociology course, arguing your position on the following statement: The race of a child and that of the prospective parents should be taken into consideration in making adoption decisions.

2. You have a job as a copy editor at a city newspaper. Write a proposal that explains and justifies your request to work at home one day per week. Incorporate into your argument the fact that you could use your home computer, which is connected to the newspaper's computer network.

PART 5

Writing with Sources

CHAPTER 20

Planning a Paper with Sources

WRITING QUICK START

Suppose you are enrolled in a public speaking class. Your instructor gives the class a number of photographs of significant national monuments and directs each student to choose one photograph and prepare a speech on what the history of the monument is and what it is intended to represent. You've chosen the picture of the Vietnam Veterans' Memorial Wall in Washington, D.C., shown on the opposite page.

Write a brief statement summarizing what you already know about the Vietnam Veterans' Memorial Wall and indicating what further information you would need to speak or write in detail about this monument.

Before planning a speech about the monument shown in the photograph, you would probably need to consult several sources to learn more about it. What further information would you need to support your ideas? How would you be sure the information contained in your sources is relevant and reliable? How would you detect a writer's bias? This chapter will answer these and other questions about choosing and evaluating useful sources. It will also lead you through the process of planning a paper with sources.

Sources of information come in many forms. They include all print materials (books, newspapers, magazines, brochures, scholarly journals), media sources (DVDs, television, radio), and electronic sources (CD-ROMs, blogs and podcasts, email). Interviews, personal observations, and surveys are also sources of information. The various kinds of sources are discussed in more detail in Chapter 21.

You can use sources in a variety of ways. For instance, you may plan a paper that is based primarily on your own experiences but discover aspects of the topic that need additional support from outside sources. At other times you may start a paper by checking several sources to narrow your topic or become more familiar with it. Finally, you may be asked to write a research paper, which requires the most extensive use of sources. See the accompanying box for a few other examples of situations that would require using sources.

When Should You Use Sources?

You should use sources whenever your topic demands more factual information than you can provide from your own personal knowledge and experience. Sources are classified as *primary* or *secondary*. **Primary sources** include historical documents (letters, diaries, speeches); literary works; autobiographies; original research reports; eyewitness accounts; and your own interviews, observations, or correspondence. For example, a report on a study of heart disease written by the researcher who conducted the study is a primary source, as is a novel by William Faulkner. In addition, what *you* say or write can be a primary source. Your own interview with a heart-attack survivor for a paper on heart disease is a primary source. **Secondary sources** report or comment on

---

SCENES FROM COLLEGE AND THE WORKPLACE

- For an *astronomy* course, you are asked to write a two-page report on black holes. Your textbook contains basic information on the subject, but you need to consult other sources to complete the assignment.

- For a *contemporary American history* assignment, you need to write a five-page research paper on a current issue (such as national health insurance), explaining the issue and reporting on current developments.

- You are a *journalist* and will interview your state governor. You need background information on the governor's position on several issues of local concern.

primary sources. A journal article that reviews several previously published research reports on heart disease is a secondary source. A book written about Faulkner by a literary critic or biographer is a secondary source.

Using Sources to Add Details to an Essay

The following suggestions will help you use sources to add details to a paper and thus provide stronger support for your thesis.

- **Make general comments more specific.** For example, instead of saying that "the crime rate in New York City has decreased over the past few years," use statistics indicating the exact percentage of the decrease.
- **Give specific examples that illustrate your main points.** If you are writing about why some companies refuse to accept orders online, for instance, locate a business that has such a policy and give details about its rationale.
- **Supply technical information.** If you are writing about a drug that lowers high blood pressure, gather information from sources about its manufacture, ingredients, effectiveness, cost, and side effects so that you can make informed, accurate comments.
- **Support opinions with evidence.** If you state that more federal assistance is needed for public education, you might provide statistics, facts, expert opinion, or other evidence to back up your statement.
- **Provide historical information.** If you are writing about space stations, for example, find out when the first one was established, what country launched it, and so forth to add background information to your paper.
- **Locate information about similar events or ideas.** For example, if you are writing about a president's intervention in a labor strike, find out if other presidents have intervened in similar strikes. You can then point out similarities and differences. You can also compare different writers' ideas on an issue. For example, in a paper about the consequences of divorce, you could use a source that deals with negative consequences and one that deals with benefits.

Using Sources to Write a Research Paper

A research paper requires you to collect and analyze information on a topic from a variety of sources. Depending on your topic, you may use primary sources, secondary sources, or both. For a research paper comparing the speeches of Abraham Lincoln to those of Franklin D. Roosevelt, you would probably read and analyze the speeches (primary sources). You might also create your own primary source by interviewing a local historian. But for a research paper comparing Lincoln's and Roosevelt's domestic policies, you would probably rely on several histories or biographies (secondary sources). Many research papers incorporate both primary and secondary sources. While researching Lincoln's and Roosevelt's domestic policies, for instance, you might consult some original documents (primary sources).

Regardless of the sources you use, your task is to organize and present your findings in a meaningful way. When you write a research paper, you don't simply "glue together" the facts, statistics, information, and quotations you find in sources. Like any other essay-length writing, a research paper has a thesis, and the thesis is supported throughout the paper. Although the information from outside sources is not your own, the interpretation you give it should be your own.

In a research paper or in any paper with sources, it is essential to acknowledge your sources fairly and correctly. To do so, include parenthetical, or in-text, citations in the body of the paper and a corresponding list of works cited or references at the end of the paper.

For more on systems for documenting sources, see Chapter 22, pp. 618 (MLA) and 634 (APA).

Whether you use sources to add details to an essay or to write a research paper, it is helpful to approach the process of locating, evaluating, and using sources in a systematic way. Figure 20.1 presents an overview of this process. The following sections of this chapter will help you plan a paper with sources and learn how to evaluate source material.

Planning Your Paper

Although starting your research in the library or on the Internet may seem like a good idea, usually the best place to begin is at your desk. There you can think about the assignment and devise a plan for completing it. This section describes several tasks that you should accomplish before you begin your research, as shown in Figure 20.2.

FIGURE 20.1 Locating and Using Sources: An Overview

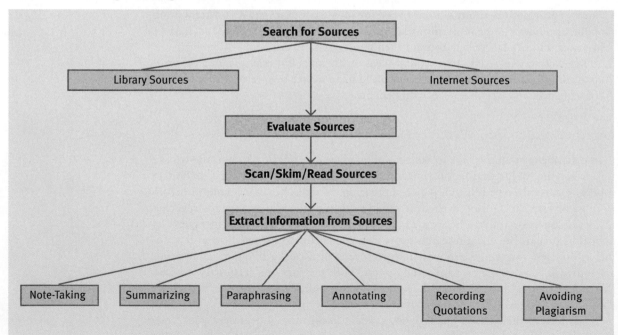

FIGURE 20.2 Writing a Paper Using Sources

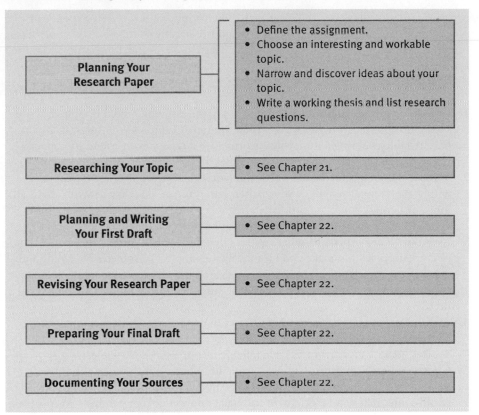

Defining the Assignment

Not all assignments have the same purpose. Many are informative, asking you to explain (for example, "Explain the treatment options for breast cancer") or to explore an issue (for example, "Examine the pros and cons of legalizing casino gambling"). Still others are persuasive, asking you to take and support a particular position (for example, "Defend or argue against your college's proposal to eliminate athletic scholarships").

Before you begin researching an assigned topic, be sure you understand what your instructor expects. If your instructor announces the assignment in class, write down what he or she says, including any examples. When you are ready to begin the research paper days or weeks later, you may find it helpful to review exactly what your instructor told you. In addition, make sure you understand any limits on the topic, any minimum or maximum length requirements, the due date (and late penalties), and any requirements about the number and kinds of sources you need to consult. Finally, be sure you know which documentation style you are expected to use.

Choosing an Interesting and Workable Topic

Most instructors allow you to choose your own topic for a research paper. You will save time in the long run if you spend enough time at the outset choosing one that is interesting and workable. Too many students waste hours researching a topic that they finally realize is too difficult, broad, or ordinary. The following tips will help you avoid such pitfalls.

1. **Choose an interesting topic.** You will enjoy the assignment and be able to write more enthusiastically if you work with a topic that captures your interest. If you have trouble choosing a topic, brainstorm with a classmate or friend. A conversation will often help you discover new angles on ordinary topics.
2. **Choose a manageable topic.** Make sure you can adequately cover the topic within the assigned length of your paper. For example, don't try to write about all kinds of family counseling programs in a five- to ten-page paper. Instead, limit your topic to one type, such as programs for adolescents.
3. **Avoid ordinary topics.** Familiar subjects that have been thoroughly explained in many sources seldom make good topics. For example, the subjects of "childhood obesity" or "the dieting craze" have been thoroughly discussed in many newspapers and magazines. If you use such a topic, be sure to come up with a different slant on it.
4. **Avoid topics that are too current.** Topics that are currently in the news or for which a new breakthrough has just been reported do not typically make good choices because in many cases little reliable information is available.
5. **Choose a practical topic.** Choose a topic for which sources are readily available—on the Internet, at your college library, or through interlibrary loan. Avoid topics that require extensive technical knowledge that you lack. Most of us, for example, should not write a paper comparing the mechanical performance of two hybrid engines or the chemical makeup of two drugs.

Narrowing and Discovering Ideas about Your Topic

The following techniques will help you narrow your topic and discover ideas about it.

Do Some Preliminary Reading

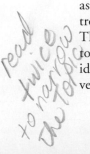

For more on library and Internet sources, see Chapter 21.

It is often a good idea to do some preliminary reading to discover the scope, depth, and breadth of your topic. Either at your library or online, you might glance through part of a general encyclopedia, such as *Encyclopaedia Britannica,* to gain a brief overview of your topic.

Be sure to consider other kinds of sources as well. A specialized encyclopedia, such as *The McGraw-Hill Encyclopedia of Science and Technology,* and your library's electronic catalog can help you identify the subtopics into which a topic can be broken. The weekly *CQ Researcher,* whose database contains thousands of articles on current topics, is another useful reference to consult for background information and to get ideas for topics. Or consider scanning a current magazine index for coverage of controversial issues. You can also ask a reference librarian for assistance.

Try Prewriting

To uncover interesting topics or to narrow a broad topic, use one or more prewriting techniques. Prewriting may also reveal an interesting idea that may eventually become your thesis. A branching diagram may be particularly helpful in narrowing a topic.

For more on prewriting, see Chapter 4.

View Your Topic from Different Perspectives

Another technique, questioning, can help you view your topic in different ways. Try asking questions about your topic from a variety of perspectives—psychological, sociological, scientific or technical, historical, political, and economic. Add other perspectives that apply to your topic. Here is how one student used questioning to analyze different perspectives on television advertising.

TOPIC: TELEVISION ADVERTISING

Perspective	*Questions*
Psychological	• How does advertising affect people? • Does it affect everyone the same way? • What emotional appeals are used? • How do emotional appeals work?
Sociological	• How do different groups of people respond differently to ads? • Is advertising targeted toward specific racial and ethnic groups?
Scientific or technical	• How are ads produced? • Who writes them? • Are the ads tested before they are broadcast?
Historical	• What is the history of advertising? • When and where did it begin?
Political	• What is the history of political advertising? • Why are negative political advertisements effective?
Economic	• How much does a television ad cost? • Is the cost of advertising added on to the price of the product?

This list of questions yielded a wide range of interesting subtopics about advertising, including emotional appeals, targeting ads to particular racial or ethnic groups, and negative political advertising. You might try this technique with a friend or classmate, working together to devise questions.

Exercise 20.1

Working with one or two classmates, narrow each of the following topics until you reach a topic that would be manageable for a five- to ten-page research paper.

1. Job interviews
2. U.S. prison system
3. Video games
4. Terrorism
5. Extinction of animal species

Research Paper in Progress 1

Choose a broad topic for your research paper. In your paper you will state a thesis and provide evidence for your thesis. Your audience consists of your classmates. Begin by using one or more prewriting techniques to narrow and generate ideas about your topic. Then reread your work and highlight useful ideas. Choose one of the following broad topics, or come up with one on your own. Refer to Table 4.2 on page 92 for other general topic suggestions.

1. Extreme sports
2. Cross-racial child adoptions
3. Sexual harassment: what it is and is not
4. How credit card use can lead to violations of privacy
5. Campus security and safety

If you are uncertain about the topic you have chosen, be sure to check with your instructor. Most instructors don't mind if you clear your topic with them; in fact, some encourage or even require this step. Your instructor may also suggest a way to narrow your topic, recommend a useful source, or offer to review your outline at a later stage.

Writing a Working Thesis and Listing Research Questions

Once you choose and narrow a topic, try to determine, as specifically as possible, the kinds of information you need to know about it. Begin by writing a working thesis for your paper and listing the research questions you need to answer.

One student working on the general topic of child abuse, for example, used prewriting and preliminary reading to narrow his focus to physical abuse and its causes. Since he already had a few ideas about possible causes, he used those ideas to write a working thesis. He then used his thesis to generate a list of research questions. Notice how the student's questions follow from his working thesis.

WORKING THESIS	**The physical abuse of children often stems from parents' emotional instability and a family history of child abuse.**
RESEARCH QUESTIONS	**If a person was physically abused as a child, how likely is that person to become an abusive parent?**
	What kinds of emotional problems seem to trigger the physical abuse of children?
	Which cause is more significant—a family history of abuse or emotional problems?
	Is there more physical abuse of children now than there was in the past, or is more abuse being reported?

A working thesis and a list of research questions will enable you to approach your research in a focused way. Instead of running helter-skelter from one aspect of your topic to another, you will be able to zero in on the specific information you need from sources.

Exercise 20.2

For one of the following topics, write a working thesis and four or more research questions.

1. Methods of controlling pornography on the Internet
2. The possibility that some form of life has existed on other planets
3. Reasons for the extinction of dinosaurs
4. Benefits of tracing your family's genealogy (family tree)
5. Ways that elderly family members affect family life

Research Paper in Progress 2

Review the list of ideas you generated in Research Paper in Progress 1. Underline the ideas for which you need further details or supporting evidence, and list the information you need. Then, using the preceding guidelines, write a working thesis and a list of research questions.

Choosing and Evaluating Useful Sources

Once you have a working thesis and a list of research questions, stop for a moment before you charge off to the library or your computer. Many students make the mistake of photocopying many articles, printing out dozens of Web pages, and lugging home numerous books only to find that the sources are not useful or that several contain identical information. Save yourself time by taking a few minutes to think about print and electronic sources and about which sources will be most relevant and reliable. Consider as well how to distinguish between facts and opinions, how to identify bias, and how to recognize generalizations or assumptions.

Using Online and Print Sources

Deciding when to use the Internet and when to use traditional library print sources can be complicated. In terms of convenience, it may be easier to access sources online from your dorm room or home rather than visiting the library. You may also be able to use your home computer to access many of the library's resources, including its catalog of books, indexes, and electronic databases. But even though some students find the use of print sources too cumbersome and time-consuming, online sources also have their drawbacks. First, although the Internet is a vast network of information, that information is unorganized. There is no central source that organizes or catalogs it the way a library does for print materials. Second, Internet sources are not stable—that is, a source you find one day may disappear the next, or the content may change. Finally, because almost anyone can publish on the Internet with no "screening" by publishers, editors, librarians, or experts in the subject area, you cannot be as confident as you can with print sources that a particular online source is credible and authoritative. These concerns are especially important for sources you find on your own, such as through a

Google search, rather than in an electronic database to which your library subscribes. (Use the guidelines on p. 563–65 to evaluate Internet sources.)

Some sources are available both online and in print, including many periodicals and certain reference books, such as the *Oxford Encyclopedia of Food and Drink in America*. Some are only online, including blogs, video and audio material, and some magazines and journals. However, there are many sources that are available only in print form, including most books. Following are a few specific situations in which using a print source is often preferable to using an online source.

- **To find specific facts.** It may be easier to find a single fact, such as the date of a president's inauguration, by looking in a reference book rather than doing research on the Web.
- **To do historical or in-depth research on a topic.** Books may be essential to some types of research because they represent years of study by authorities on the subject. Some historical information and data are not available on the Internet.

Choosing Relevant Sources

A *relevant* source contains information that helps you answer one or more of your research questions. Answering the following questions will help you determine whether a source is relevant.

For more on audience, see Chapter 4, p. 83.

1. **Is the source too general or too specialized for your intended audience?** Some sources may not contain the detailed information your audience requires; others may be too technical and require background knowledge that your audience does not have. For example, suppose you are researching the environmental effects of recycling cans and bottles. If your audience consists of science majors, an article in *Reader's Digest* might be too general. Conversely, an article in *Environmental Science and Technology* would be written for scientists and may be a bit too technical for your purposes.
2. **Is the source recent enough for your purposes?** In rapidly changing fields of study, outdated sources are not useful unless you need to give a historical perspective. For example, a ten-year-old article on using air bags to improve car safety will not include information on recent discoveries about the dangers that air bags pose to children riding in the front passenger seat.

Choosing Reliable Sources

A *reliable* source is honest, accurate, and credible. Answering the following questions will help you determine whether a source is reliable. (To check the reliability of an Internet source, consult pp. 563–65 as well.)

1. **Is the source scholarly?** Although scholars often disagree with each other, they make a serious attempt to present accurate information. In addition, an article that appears in a scholarly journal or textbook has been reviewed by a panel of professionals in the field prior to publication. Therefore, scholarly sources tend

to be trustworthy. For more on the differences between scholarly and popular sources, refer to Table 21.1 on page 579.

2. **Does the source have a solid reputation?** Some magazines, such as *Time* and *Newsweek,* are known for responsible reporting, whereas other periodicals have a reputation for sensationalism and should be avoided or approached skeptically. Web sites, too, may or may not be reputable.

3. **Is the author an expert in the field?** Check the author's credentials. Information about authors may be given in a headnote; at the end of an article; on a home page in a link; or in the preface, on the dust jacket, or at the beginning or end of a book. You might also check a reference book such as *Contemporary Authors* to verify an author's credentials.

4. **Does the author approach the topic fairly and objectively?** A writer who states a strong opinion is not necessarily biased. However, a writer who ignores opposing views, distorts facts, or ignores information that does not fit his or her opinion is presenting a biased and incomplete view of a topic. Although you can use a biased source to understand a particular viewpoint, you must also seek out other sources that present alternative views. For more on bias and viewpoint, see pp. 567–68.

Exercise 20.3

Working in a small group, discuss why the sources listed for each topic below would or would not be considered relevant and reliable. Assume that the classmates in your writing course are your audience.

1. Topic: Caring for family members with Alzheimer's disease
   a. Introductory health and nutrition textbook
   b. Article in *Women's Day* titled "Mother, Where Are You?"
   c. Article from a gerontology journal on caring for aging family members
2. Topic: Analyzing the effects of heroin use on teenagers
   a. Newspaper article written by a former heroin user
   b. Article from the *Journal of Neurology* on the biochemical effects of heroin on the brain
   c. Pamphlet on teenage drug use published by the National Institutes of Health
3. Topic: Implementing training programs to reduce sexual harassment in the workplace
   a. Article from the *Christian Science Monitor* titled "Removing Barriers for Working Women"
   b. Personal Web site relating an incident of harassment on the job
   c. Training manual for employees of General Motors

Evaluating Internet Sources

The Internet offers many excellent and reputable sources. Not all sites are accurate and unbiased, however, and misinformation often appears on the Web. Use the following

For more practice evaluating Web sites, visit www.bedfordstmartins .com/successfulwriting/tutorials.

> **TABLE 20.1 Evaluating Internet Sources**
>
> | *Purpose* | • Who sponsors or publishes the site—an organization, a corporation, a government agency, or an individual?
• What are the sponsor's goals—to present information or news, opinions, products to sell, or fun? |
> |---|---|
> | *Author* | • Who wrote the information on the site?
• Is the information clearly presented and well written? |
> | *Accuracy* | • Are ideas supported by credible evidence? Is there a works-cited list or bibliography?
• Is the information presented verifiable?
• Are opinions clearly identified as such? |
> | *Timeliness* | • When was the site first created? What is the date of the last revision?
• Does the specific document you are using have a date?
• Are the links up-to-date? |

questions to evaluate the reliability of Internet sources. (Table 20.1 summarizes these questions.)

What Is the Site's Purpose?

Web sites have many different purposes. They may provide information or news, advocate a particular point of view, or try to sell a product. Many sites have more than one purpose. A pharmaceutical company's site, for instance, may offer health advice in addition to advertising its own drugs. Understanding the purposes of an Internet source will help you deal with its potential biases.

For more about bias, see pp. 567–68.

To determine the purpose of any site, start by identifying the sponsor of the site—the organization or person who paid to place it on the Web. The copyright usually reveals the owner of a site, and often a link labeled "About Us," "About Me," or "Mission Statement" will take you to a description of the sponsor.

What Are the Author's Credentials?

It helps to know who wrote the specific Web page you are looking at. The sponsors of many Web sites have professionals write their content. When this is the case, the writer's name and credentials are usually listed, and his or her email address may be provided. This kind of information can help you determine whether the Web page is a reliable resource. If information about an author is not available on the site or is sketchy, you might conduct a search for the author's name on the Web.

Regardless of who the author of the site is, the information should be well written and organized. If it is carelessly put together, you should be wary of it. In short, if the sponsor did not spend time presenting information correctly and clearly, the information itself may not be very accurate.

Is the Site's Information Accurate?

In addition to paying attention to how a site's material is written and organized, ask yourself the following questions.

- **Is a bibliography or a list of works cited provided?** If sources are not included, you should question the accuracy of the site.
- **Can the accuracy of the information be checked elsewhere?** In most instances you should be able to verify Internet information by checking another source, often simply by clicking on links in the original source.
- **Is the document in complete form?** If you're looking at a summary, use the site to try to find the original source. If you can't locate the original, be skeptical of the source that contains the summary. Original information generally has fewer errors and is often preferred in academic papers.

If Internet information is available in print form, it is usually a good idea to try to obtain the print version. There are several reasons for doing so. First, when an article goes on the Web, errors may creep in. In addition, since Web sites often change addresses or content, a reader of your paper may not be able to find the site or content that you used. Finally, page numbers in print sources are easier to cite than those in electronic ones (which may not include standard page numbering).

Is the Site Up-to-Date?

Even though the Web has a reputation for providing current information, not all Web sites are up-to-date. You can check the timeliness of a site by asking yourself the following questions about dates.

- **When was the site first established?**
- **If the site has been revised, what is the date of the last revision?**
- **When was the document you are looking at posted to the site?** Has it been updated?

This kind of information generally appears at the bottom of a site's home page or at the end of a particular document. If no dates are given, check some of the links. If the links are outdated and nonfunctioning, the information at the site is probably outdated as well.

Analyzing and Thinking Critically about Sources

Whether you search a library for sources—such as relevant books or journal articles—or find them on the Internet, you should first make sure that your sources are relevant and reliable. In addition, when you use sources in your paper, you will need to analyze them and think critically. As a critical reader, you need to recognize that multiple viewpoints exist and find the sources that express them. If you can sort through each writer's ideas and watch for opinions, bias, generalizations, and assumptions, you will be well on your way to locating useful research.

Separating Facts from Opinions

It is important to understand the difference between facts and opinions. **Facts** are statements that can be proven to be either true or false; evidence exists to verify facts. **Opinions**, on the other hand, are statements that reveal beliefs or feelings and are neither true nor false. For example, "The Boston Red Sox won the 2007 World Series" is a fact, whereas "The Boston Red Sox are the best team in baseball" is an opinion. For more examples of facts and opinions, see the box below on this page.

Facts are considered reliable if they are taken from a reputable source or can be verified. For example, the date of President John F. Kennedy's assassination—November 22, 1963—is a fact that can be found in many reputable sources. Opinions, however, are not always based on facts and should be evaluated carefully. Before accepting someone's opinion, try to find evidence that supports it. Several opinions exist, for instance, concerning why and how President Kennedy was shot. Some of these opinions may be more reliable than others.

When authors present an opinion, they often alert their readers by using certain words and phrases, such as the following:

as I see it	possibly
in my opinion	some experts believe
in my view	supposedly
it is probable	this seems to indicate

A special type of opinion is **expert opinion**—the attitudes or beliefs expressed by authorities on the topic. Like other writers, experts often use qualifying words and phrases when they offer an opinion. An expert on government finance may write, for example, "*It seems likely* that Social Security payments will decline for future generations of Americans."

DON'T CONFUSE FACTS AND OPINIONS

FACT	The planet Earth has six times the volume of Mars.
OPINION	Humans will probably destroy the planet Earth if they don't stop polluting it.
FACT	After inventing the telephone in 1876, Alexander Graham Bell worked on dozens of other inventions, many of which aided the deaf.
OPINION	Alexander Graham Bell's invention of the telephone is considered the most important technological innovation of the nineteenth century.
FACT	Many vitamin-fortified foods are now available in supermarkets.
OPINION	Supermarkets need to carry a wider variety of organic foods.

Opinions of people who are not experts on the topic may be useful to read and consider as a means of shaping your own opinions, but they do not belong in a source-based paper. Expert opinion, however, is definitely usable. When you quote or paraphrase it, be sure to give appropriate credit to your source.

For more on documenting sources, see Chapter 22.

Exercise 20.4

Label each of the following statements as fact (F), opinion (O), or expert opinion (EO).

1. According to child psychologists Gerber and Gerber, children who watch prime-time television shows that depict crime consider the world more dangerous than those who do not watch crime shows. *EO*

2. The best symphonies are shorter than twenty minutes. *O*

3. Most medical experts recommend that women age forty and older have a mammogram once every one to two years. *EO*

4. About half the population of Uruguay lives in Montevideo. *O*

5. More women earned doctoral degrees in engineering in 2007 than in 1984. *O*

6. Private companies should not be allowed to sell concessions inside our national parks. *O*

7. The mountains of Northern Idaho contain the most scenic landscapes in the country. *F*

8. Many business leaders agree that it is important to hire people who love their work. *O*

Identifying Bias or Viewpoint

Many relevant and reliable sources may provide only a portion of the information you need for your essay. For example, if you are writing an essay on problems in the nursing profession, the *American Journal of Nursing* might be a reliable source, but it would probably not contain articles that are critical of nurses.

Many writers have a particular point of view and interpret information in their own way. For example, suppose you are writing an essay on home schooling for an introductory education class. You find a book titled *The Home Schooling Movement: What Children Are Missing* that was written by someone who taught high school for thirty years. While the book may offer valuable information, its title suggests that the author would probably support classroom instruction and perhaps discuss the shortcomings of home schooling in detail but downplay its advantages. This one-sided view of home schooling, then, would be biased. **Bias** refers to a publisher's or writer's own views or particular interest in a topic. A biased source is not necessarily unreliable, but you need to notice the bias and find additional sources that present other opinions.

To find bias in someone's writing, first consider the author's background. For example, the viewpoint of a father who has written a book about home schooling his five children is likely to be very different from that of a long-term high school teacher. Then look carefully at the author's descriptive and connotative language. In the father's book, for instance, does he tend to use many words with negative connotations when he is talking about traditional classroom education? Finally, consider the author's

For more information on descriptive language, connotative language, and tone, see pp. 189–92 and 236.

overall tone. Can you tell how the father feels about home schooling? Does he sound enthusiastic and positive?

> **Exercise 20.5**
>
> *Examine each of the following sources and their annotations. Discuss whether the source is likely to be objective (O), somewhat biased (SB), or heavily biased (HB).*

O

1. Roleff, Tamara L., ed. *Gun Control: Opposing Viewpoints.* Farmington Hills, MI: Greenhaven Press, 2007. Print.
   This book contains several articles that present the pros and cons of different issues relating to gun control. The articles are written by experts and give bibliographic references.

O

2. Malcolm X. *The Autobiography of Malcolm X.* New York: Ballantine, 1965. Print.
   Malcolm X tells his life story in this autobiography, which was published just before his death.

HB

3. Green, Amy. "Missions Boot Camp." *Christianity Today* 52 (2008): 60. Print.
   This article describes a summer camp for young people heading off on mission trips.

SB

4. Fink, George, ed. *Encyclopedia of Stress.* San Diego: Academic Press, 2007. Print.
   Four volumes of in-depth coverage related to the psychology and physiology of stress.

Recognizing Generalizations

A **generalization** is a statement about a large group of items based on experience with or observation of only a limited part of that group. If, for example, you often saw high school students in your town hanging out on the streets and creating disturbances, you might make the following generalization: "The high school students in this town are not well behaved." You could not be sure about your generalization, however, unless you observed every high school student in town, and doing so might well cause you to change your generalization. Look at the following generalizations. You probably won't agree with all of them.

- U.S. colleges and universities give more funding to their athletic programs than to their libraries.
- Home-schooled children do not interact socially with other children their own age.
- Banks in this country no longer provide basic customer services.
- Big companies are laying off great portions of their workforces.
- Circus animals are abused.

A writer's generalization is his or her interpretation of a particular set of facts. If generalizations are backed up by experience or sufficient evidence, they are probably trustworthy. An expert on heart disease, for example, would probably make reliable generalizations about the risks of high cholesterol. If a writer is not an expert, however, and does not provide solid support for generalizations, you would be wise to consult different sources.

Exercise 20.6

Label each of the following statements either fact (F) or generalization (G). Indicate what support or documentation would be necessary for you to evaluate its accuracy.

G 1. Many women want to become pilots. G

F 2. Elephants can vocalize at frequencies below the range of human hearing.

F 3. In certain parts of the Red Sea, the temperature of the water can reach 138 degrees Fahrenheit.

G 4. Most people who live in San Diego are associated with the U.S. Navy.

G 5. People all over the world donated money to help the survivors of the 2004 tsunamis.

Identifying Assumptions

As you may recall from Chapter 18, assumptions are ideas or generalizations that people accept as true without questioning their validity. Writers often use an assumption at the beginning of an essay and then base the rest of the essay on that assumption. If the assumption is false or cannot be proven, however, then the ideas that flow from it may also be incorrect. For instance, the following excerpt begins with an assumption (highlighted) that the writer makes no attempt to prove or justify.

for some women

Childbirth is a painful experience, intolerable even with appropriate medications. In response to this pain, modern women should accept the painkillers offered to them by their doctors. Why be a martyr? You have to suffer sleepless nights because of your child for the rest of your life; bring them into this world on your terms—pain free. Women should not be embarrassed or reluctant to request anesthesia during labor.

The author assumes that all women find childbirth intolerably painful and then argues that women should request anesthesia during labor. But if the writer's initial assumption is false, much of the argument that follows should be questioned.

As you read, be aware of assumptions, especially those at the start of an essay. Ask yourself how the essay would be affected if the initial assumption were untrue. If you disagree with some of the assumptions in a source, check other sources to obtain different viewpoints.

Exercise 20.7

Each of the following statements contains one or more assumptions. Identify the assumption(s) made in each statement.

1. Computer users expect Web sites to entertain them with graphics, sound, and video.

2. In response to the problem of ozone depletion, the U.S. Environmental Protection Agency has designed various programs to reduce harmful emissions. The EPA wants to stop the production of certain substances so that the ozone can repair itself over the next fifty years.

3. Only the routine vaccination of all children can eliminate the threat of serious disease and ensure optimum public health. These shots should be administered without hesitation. Parents must have full confidence in their doctors on this matter.

4. Since so many athletes and coaches approve of the use of performance-enhancing drugs, these substances should be allowed without regulation.

5. Because they recognize that meat consumption is environmentally damaging, environmentalists are often vegetarians.

Working with Text: Reading Sources

Reading sources involves some special skills. Unlike textbook reading, in which your purpose is to learn and recall the material, you usually read sources to extract the information you need about a topic. Therefore, you can often read sources selectively, reading only the relevant parts and skipping over the rest. Use the following strategies for reading sources: scan, skim, and then read closely.

Scanning a Source

Scanning means "looking for" the information you seek without actually reading a source from beginning to end. Just as you scan a phone directory to locate a phone number, you scan a source to extract needed information.

Use the following guidelines to scan sources effectively.

1. **Determine how the source is organized.** Is it organized chronologically or by topic? It could also be organized by chapter, subject, or author.
2. **For journal articles, check the abstract or summary; for books, scan the index and table of contents.** You can quickly determine whether the source contains the information you need and, if so, approximately where to find it.
3. **Keep key words or phrases in mind as you scan.** For example, if you are searching for information on welfare reform, key phrases might include *welfare system, entitlement programs, benefits,* and *welfare spending.*
4. **Scan systematically.** Don't scan a source randomly, hoping to see what you need. Instead, follow a pattern as you sweep your eyes across the material. For charts, tables, and indexes, use a downward sweep. For prose material, use a zigzag or Z-pattern, sweeping across several lines of print at a time.

Skimming a Source

Skimming (also called *previewing*) is a quick way to find out whether a source suits your purposes without taking the time to read it completely. Skimming also allows you to determine whether any sections deserve close reading. As you skim a source, mark or jot down sections that might be worth returning to later.

For more on previewing, see Chapter 3, p. 47.

Use the guidelines on pp. 47–48 to skim a source effectively; adapt them to fit each particular source.

Reading a Source Closely

Once you identify the sections within a source that contain the information you need—by scanning, skimming, or both—*read* those sections closely and carefully. To be sure you do not take information out of context, also read the paragraphs before and after the material you have chosen.

For more on strategies for close reading, see Chapter 3, pp. 50–57.

Improving Your Reading of Electronic Sources

When you read material on the Internet, you often need some different reading strategies. The following advice should help you read Web sites more productively.

For more practice reading Web sites, visit www.bedfordstmartins .com/successfulwriting/tutorials.

- **When you reach a new site, explore it quickly to discover how it is organized and what information is available.** Remember that the first screen may grab your attention but rarely contains substantive information. Find out if there is a search option or a guide to the site (a site map). Doing an initial exploration is especially important on large and complex sites, where you may have a number of different choices for locating information.
- **Keep in mind that text on Web sites does not usually follow the traditional text pattern.** Instead of containing paragraphs, a Web page may show a list of topic sentences that you have to click on to get details. In addition, electronic pages are often designed to stand alone: They are brief and do not depend on other pages for meaning. In many instances, background information is not supplied.
- **Follow your own learning style in making decisions about what paths to follow.** Because Web sites have menus and links, readers create their own texts by following or ignoring different paths. This is quite different from print text, which offers readers far fewer choices. Some readers may prefer to begin with "the big picture" and then move to the details; others may prefer to do the opposite. A pragmatic learner may move through a site systematically, either clicking on or ignoring links as they appear on the screen. A spatial learner, in contrast, would probably look at the graphics first. All readers should make sure that they don't skip over important content.

Learning Style Options

- **Focus on your purpose.** Regardless of your learning style, keep in mind the information you are looking for. If you don't focus on your purpose, you may wander aimlessly through the site and waste valuable research time.

CHAPTER 21

Finding Sources and Taking Notes

Suppose you are enrolled in a seminar on the environment. Your instructor gives the class a number of photographs and directs each student to choose one and write a paper about the environmental issues it reflects. You've chosen the photograph shown on the opposite page.

Write a brief statement describing the environmental issue the photograph represents. Consider where you might go to learn more about this issue, and make a list of the sources you would consult.

What issue did you write about? What sources of information did you list? Did you include both print and Internet sources? Do you need to conduct a personal interview or do a survey? Once you find information that is useful for your paper, what procedures should you use to record information for later use? This chapter will answer these and other questions about how to locate sources and take accurate notes.

Regardless of the kind of research you are doing, it is helpful to approach the process of locating and using sources in a systematic way, as shown in Figure 21.1. If you already have a narrowed topic for a research paper, be sure to write a working thesis and research questions before you start looking for specific sources. If you have a general topic and need help narrowing it, several kinds of library or online sources—such as encyclopedias and subject directories—may be helpful. In either case, it is a good idea to consult the advice in Chapter 20 about planning a paper and evaluating sources.

You will have many opportunities to use sources in the writing you do in college and at work (see the accompanying box for a few examples).

An Overview of Library Sources

Your college library is an immense collection of print, media, and online sources on a wide variety of topics. Learning to use this library will help you locate sources effectively.

Learning Your Way around the Library

It is a good idea to become familiar with your college library *before* you need to use it. Following are a few ways to do so.

1. **Take a formal tour of the library.** Many colleges offer library tours during the first few weeks of the term. On a tour, you'll learn where everything is located and discover how to use important services, such as interlibrary loans and online database searches.

For guided practice touring the library, visit www.bedfordstmartins .com/successfulwriting/tutorials.

2. **Take your own tour.** Obtain a map or floor plan from the circulation desk and use it to tour the library. Inspect the popular magazine collection; see what electronic resources are available. Try to become comfortable with the library so that the first

---

SCENES FROM COLLEGE AND THE WORKPLACE

- For an *anthropology* course, you are asked to analyze the differences between the religious practices of two cultures.

- For an *art history* course, you are asked to write a biography of a famous Renaissance artist.

- As *supervisor* of a health-care facility, you decide to conduct a survey of the staff to determine employees' interest in flexible working hours.

FIGURE 21.1 Writing a Research Paper Using Sources

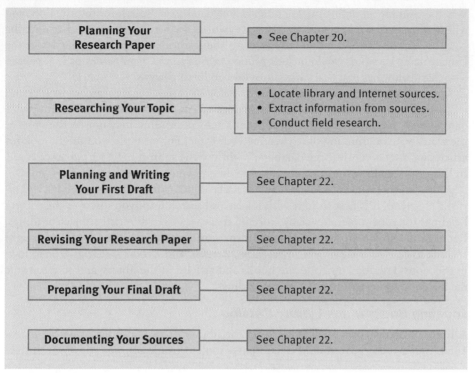

time you need to use it, you can get to work easily. Keep the floor plan in your bag or notebook for future reference.

3. **Consult reference librarians.** Librarians are usually available at the reference desk to advise you about what sources to use and where to locate them. Reference librarians can often save you time, so don't hesitate to ask them for help.

4. **Check the library's Web site.** Most libraries have a Web site created by librarians to present all the resources that are available to you. Look for a link to the library's catalog, including a way to check your library account. The online databases for journal articles will be listed on the Web site along with access instructions. Your librarians may also have posted lists of helpful Web sites that they have used with students over many semesters. Finally, library hours, services, policies, maps, and ways to contact the library staff should also appear on the site.

Locating Useful Library Sources

The sources you need will often be stored in electronic databases available through your college library or an online service. Learning how to use keyword searches and subject headings will help you locate relevant materials.

Searching Using Keywords

Whether you use an online catalog or an online database to search for information, you will need to perform keyword searches. **Keywords** are words or phrases that describe your topic. For example, if you are writing about alternative political parties in the United States, keywords would include *politics, political parties, third parties,* or *U.S. politics.* The chart below has practical suggestions for conducting keyword searches.

Once you enter a keyword, the online catalog or search engine searches its files and returns a list of pertinent sources. Most catalogs and databases also search by using standard **subject headings**. Keep in mind that a subject heading may not be the same as the words you are thinking of to describe your topic. For example, you might look for articles on *drug abuse,* but the database might use the subject heading *substance abuse.* In this case, searching for *substance abuse* could give you more relevant search results.

Most databases publish a list of the subject headings (sometimes they call it a *thesaurus*). In general, it is best to start with a keyword search until you discover the subject headings for your topic, especially since all databases have different subject headings. For example, if you are searching for information on *welfare reform,* keywords might include *welfare system, entitlement programs, benefits,* and *welfare spending.* The following sections describe how to locate books and articles in the library and in electronic databases using keywords and subject headings.

Locating Books in the Library Catalog

A library's catalog lists books owned by the library. It may also list available magazines, newspapers, government documents, and electronic sources. However, it does

> **SUGGESTIONS FOR CONDUCTING KEYWORD SEARCHES**
>
> - Place quotation marks around a phrase to limit your search. For example, **"single motherhood"** will give you topics related to *single motherhood.* Without quotation marks, a keyword search would provide all the sources that use the word *single* as well as all the sources that use the word *motherhood.*
>
> - Use *AND* to join words that must appear in a document. For example, **psychology AND history** would provide sources that mention both *psychology* and *history.* For some searches, you may need to use a plus (+) sign instead of *AND.*
>
> - Use *OR* to indicate synonyms when only one needs to appear in the document. For example, **job OR career** would provide more options than just *job* or just *career.*
>
> - Place *NOT* before words that should not appear in the document. For example, **camels NOT cigarettes** would provide sources only on the animal. In some searches, you may need to use a minus (–) sign instead of *NOT.*
>
> - Use parentheses to group together keywords and combine the group with another set of keywords. For example, **(timepiece OR watch OR clock) AND production** would provide sources on the production of any of these three items.
>
> - Use an asterisk (*) to indicate letters that may vary in spelling or words that may have variant endings. For example, a search for **"social psycholog*"** will find sources with the words *psychology, psychologist, psychologists,* and so forth.

not list individual articles included in magazines and newspapers. Before the widespread use of computers, a library's catalog was made up of three- by five-inch index cards. Now, though, almost all libraries have a computerized catalog, which allows you to search online for sources—by keyword title, author, or subject—from terminals in the library. Directions usually appear on or near the screen, and most libraries also allow access to their catalogs from outside computers—at home or in a computer lab on campus. Figure 21.2 shows a typical search page of an online library catalog.

When searching the library catalog for books on a specific topic, you may need to view two or three screens before you find information about a specific book. First you will get a list of relevant titles, then you will need to select the title that interests you. On the next screen you will get more about that item. The call number, location, and availability may be on this screen, or you might have to click once more to find specific information on obtaining that item. Figure 21.3 shows the results of an online search by subject for the topic *human-animal relationships*. Online catalogs offer many conveniences. The screen often indicates whether the book is on the shelves, whether it has been checked out, and when it is due back. Some systems allow you to reserve the book by entering your request on the computer.

For more practice using your library's catalog, visit www.bedfordstmartins .com/successfulwriting/ tutorials.

FIGURE 21.2 Library Catalog Search Page

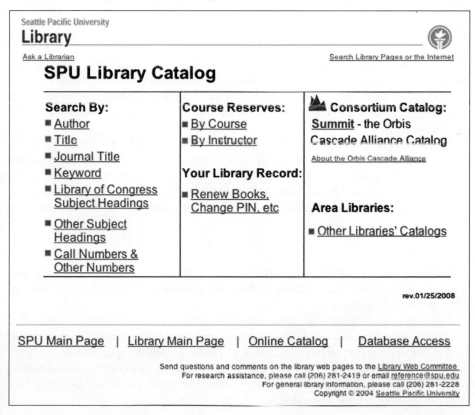

Seattle Pacific University
Library

Ask a Librarian — Search Library Pages or the Internet

SPU Library Catalog

Search By:	**Course Reserves:**	**⛰ Consortium Catalog:**
▪ Author	▪ By Course	**Summit** - the Orbis
▪ Title	▪ By Instructor	**Cascade Alliance Catalog**
▪ Journal Title		About the Orbis Cascade Alliance
▪ Keyword	**Your Library Record:**	
▪ Library of Congress Subject Headings	▪ Renew Books, Change PIN, etc	**Area Libraries:**
▪ Other Subject Headings		▪ Other Libraries' Catalogs
▪ Call Numbers & Other Numbers		

rev.01/25/2008

SPU Main Page | Library Main Page | Online Catalog | Database Access

Send questions and comments on the library web pages to the Library Web Committee
For research assistance, please call (206) 281-2419 or email reference@spu.edu
For general library information, please call (206) 281-2228
Copyright © 2004 Seattle Pacific University

FIGURE 21.3 Library Catalog Search Results

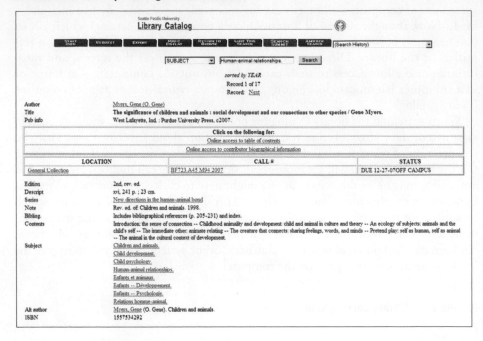

For older or special collections, some libraries still maintain card catalogs that index all the items in that particular collection. A traditional card catalog includes three types of cards: title, author, and subject. Arranged alphabetically, the three types of cards may be filed together, or there may be a separate catalog for the subject cards.

The catalog provides call numbers that tell you where to locate books on the library's shelves. Once you have a specific call number, use your library floor plan and the call-number guides posted on shelves to locate the appropriate section of the library and the book you need. Be sure to scan the surrounding books, which are usually on related topics. You may discover other useful sources that you overlooked in the catalog.

Bibliographies

A **bibliography** lists sources on a particular subject, including books, articles, and government publications. Some bibliographies also provide brief summaries or descriptions of the sources they list.

To locate a bibliography on your subject, combine the word *bibliography* with a relevant keyword for your topic. For example, you could search your library's online catalog for *human-animal communication* and *bibliography*. Also, some libraries publish their own bibliographies or pathfinders to guide students to important sources on certain topics. Look for these on the library's Web site, or ask the librarians if they have any such guides available as handouts.

Locating Articles Using Periodical Indexes

Periodicals include newspapers, popular magazines, and scholarly journals. Periodicals differ by content and frequency of publication. Table 21.1 summarizes the differences between popular magazines (such as *People*) and scholarly journals (such as the *American Journal of Psychology*). For academic essays, it is best not to rely solely on information from popular magazines.

Because periodicals are published daily, weekly, or monthly, they often contain up-to-date information about a subject. A library's catalog does not list specific articles from magazines or journals. However, it does list the periodicals, indexes, and abstracts to which the library subscribes. **Indexes** list articles by title, author, and subject. **Abstracts** list articles and also provide a brief summary of each one. Most indexes and abstracts are available as computer databases as well as in print form.

More and more of the periodical databases provided by libraries give users access to full-text articles. Since most libraries subscribe to more than one database provider, it may be necessary to check for the full text in a database other than the one in which

---

TABLE 21.1 A Comparison of Scholarly Journals and Popular Magazines

	Scholarly Journal	Popular Magazine
Who reads it?	Researchers, professionals, students	General public
Who writes it?	Researchers, professionals	Reporters, journalists, freelance writers
Who decides what to publish in it?	Other researchers (peer review)	Editors, publishers
What does it look like?	Mostly text, some charts and graphs, little or no advertising	Many photos, many advertisements, eye-catching layout
What kind of information does it contain?	Results of research studies and experiments, statistics and analysis, in-depth evaluations of specialized topics, overviews of all the research on a subject (literature review), bibliographies and references	Articles of general interest, easy-to-understand language, news items, interviews, opinion pieces, no bibliographies (sources cited informally within the article)
Where is it available?	Sometimes by subscription only, large bookstores, large public library branches, college/university libraries, online	Newsstands, most bookstores, most public library branches, online
How often is it published?	Monthly to quarterly	Weekly to monthly
What are some examples?	*Journal of Bioethics, American Journal of Family Law, Film Quarterly*	*Newsweek, Popular Science, Psychology Today*

you found the citation or abstract. Look for an article linker that checks your library's other databases for you with one click.

Finally, when you are searching, look for options that allow you to refine your search. Many databases allow users to limit by date and publication type. Look for a place to choose "peer reviewed" or "newspapers and magazines" if you need to locate an article from a particular kind of source. Once you locate a relevant article, find out what your options are for emailing, printing, and saving it. Also, check with the librarian for inter-library loan options if you cannot locate the full text or hard copy of an article you want.

General periodical indexes. General indexes list articles on a wide range of subjects that have been published in popular magazines. One commonly used online index is EBSCO, whose extensive databases list articles published in thousands of magazines, journals, and newspapers. Some entries include only abstracts, but depending on the type of agreement your library has, you may have access to full-text articles as well. One EBSCO database is Academic Search Premier, which provides access to the full text of articles for almost five thousand journals, magazines, and newspapers, as well as abstracts for another eight thousand periodicals (check with your library about getting the full text when only an abstract is provided). Academic Search Premier covers almost all subject areas and is especially geared toward college students. In fact, about 3,500 of the full-text journals are peer-reviewed.

You can search Academic Search Premier by keyword using terms that you have brainstormed for your topic. Once you find a relevant article, take a look at the subject terms that Academic Search Premier has listed for that article—they may or may not match the keywords you have been using. For example, you might search for "eating habits" and discover that the database uses the term "food habits" to describe this topic. You can then click on the "food habits" link to find more articles on the topic. You can also start out by looking at a list of the database's subject terms. Click on the subject terms link on the search page and browse for applicable terms. The list of subject terms for "animal communication" follows.

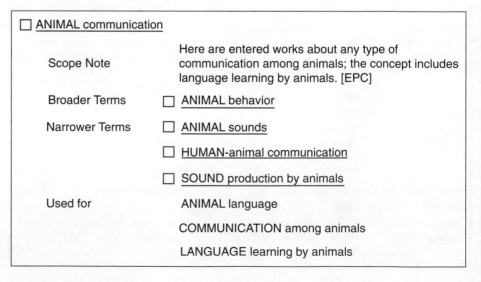

☐ ANIMAL communication	
Scope Note	Here are entered works about any type of communication among animals; the concept includes language learning by animals. [EPC]
Broader Terms	☐ ANIMAL behavior
Narrower Terms	☐ ANIMAL sounds
	☐ HUMAN-animal communication
	☐ SOUND production by animals
Used for	ANIMAL language
	COMMUNICATION among animals
	LANGUAGE learning by animals

Specialized periodical indexes and abstracts. Specialized indexes and abstracts reference either scholarly and technical articles within a specific academic field of study or materials of a particular type, such as book reviews, abstracts of doctoral dissertations, and articles and essays published in books, rather than periodicals. A list of common specialized indexes follows. Check with your library for coverage dates and access instructions.

Applied Science and Technology Index
Art Index
Biological and Agricultural Index
Book Review Digest
Business Index
Dissertation Abstracts
Education Index
Engineering Index
Essay and General Literature Index
Historical Abstracts
Humanities Index

MLA International Bibliography of
    Books and Articles in the Modern
    Languages and Literature
Monthly Catalog of U.S. Government
    Publications
Music Index
Physics Abstracts
Psychological Abstracts
Science Index
Sociological Abstracts

Here is a sample entry on the topic of *mammals* from the *Art Index*.

SAMPLE ENTRY FROM THE *ART INDEX*

Mammals

1. Haynes, G. The catastrophic extinction of North American mammoths and mastodonts. *World Archaeology* v. 33 no. 3 (February 2002) p. 391–416
2. Powell, E. A. Curtains for overkill? [extinction of mammoths]. *Archaeology* v. 55 no. 1 (January/February 2002) p. 16–17

Doing Research on the World Wide Web

The Web contains millions of Web sites, most of which are not grouped together in any organized way. Therefore, you will need to use a subject directory or search engine to locate the information you need.

Subject directories. A **subject directory** uses various categories and subcategories to classify Web resources. Some subject directories also include reviews or evaluations of sites. A subject directory can be especially helpful when you have decided on a general topic for an essay but need to narrow it further. Some subject directories are part of a search engine, whereas others are stand-alone sites.

Search engines. A **search engine** is an application that can help you find information on a particular topic by typing a keyword, phrase, or question into a search box. Eight commonly used search engines and their URLs follow.

USEFUL SEARCH ENGINES

Search Engine	*URL*
AltaVista	www.altavista.com
Go.com	www.go.com
Google	www.google.com
Google Scholar	http://scholar.google.com
HotBot	www.hotbot.com
Kartoo	www.kartoo.com
Lycos	www.lycos.com
Yahoo!	www.yahoo.com

For more practice selecting and evaluating a search engine, visit www.bedfordstmartins .com/successfulwriting/ tutorials.

If a keyword or phrase is too general, a search could turn up hundreds or perhaps thousands of sites, most of which will not be helpful to you. Your searches will be more productive if you use the guidelines for keyword searches on page 576.

Since different search engines usually generate different results, it is a good idea to use more than one search engine when you are researching a given topic. For a general search, you might start with a search engine such as Google. Once you've narrowed your topic, however, you might want to use a more specialized search engine, such as one that is geared to a particular discipline or specialty. For example, if your topic involves the Democratic Party, Google might point you to a site named Political Science Resources on the Web, which has its own search engine.

Locating Useful Internet Sources

As noted earlier, although the Internet offers vast amounts of information, it does have one major drawback: Its information is often less reliable than information in print sources because anyone can post on the Internet. To be certain that your information from online sources is reliable, you will want to evaluate it, and you might want to maintain a list of reliable Web sites that provide accurate and thorough information.

For more on evaluating Internet sources, see Chapter 20, pp. 563–65.

Once you identify usable sources, be sure to keep track of their URLs so that you can find the sites again easily and cite them in your paper. You can save Web addresses on your own computer as bookmarks or favorites (depending on the Web browser you use), which allows you to return to a site by clicking on its name. You can also organize your bookmarks or favorites into folders—such as *career, library information,* or *news sites*—so that you can easily find your sources.

Following are some generally useful and reliable Web sites that you should remember.

News sites. Newspapers, television networks, and popular magazines have companion Web sites that provide current information and late-breaking news stories. Useful sites include

- BBC   www.bbc.co.uk
- *The New York Times*   www.nytimes.com
- CNN Interactive   www.cnn.com
- *The Washington Post*   www.washingtonpost.com
- MSNBC   www.msnbc.com

General reference sites. The following sites offer reliable general reference information:

- Altapedia Online   www.altapedia.com
- Britannica Online   www.eb.com
- Encyclopedia Smithsonian www.si.edu/resource/faq

Table 21.2 lists some good places to begin research in academic disciplines.

TABLE 21.2 Web Sources for Academic Research

Academic Discipline	Site Title and Affiliation	Site URL
Humanities	Voice of the Shuttle (University of California, Santa Barbara)	http://vos.ucsb.edu
	Edsitement (National Endowment for the Humanities)	http://edsitement.neh.gov/websites_all.asp
	Humbul Humanities Hub (Resource Discovery Network)	http://www.humbul.ac.uk/help/subjects.html
Literature	LitLinks (Bedford/St. Martin's)	http://www.bedfordstmartins.com/litlinks/
	Representative Poetry Online (University of Toronto)	http://rpo.library.utoronto.ca/display/index.cfm
	Literary Resources on the Net (Jack Lynch, Rutgers University)	http://andromeda.rutgers.edu/~jlynch/Lit/
History	History@Bedford/St. Martin's	http://www.bedfordstmartins.com/history/
	Librarians' Index to the Internet history links	http://lii.org/search/file/history
	History Internet Resources (James Madison University Libraries)	http://www.lib.jmu.edu/history/internet.aspx
Social Sciences	Social Sciences Information Gateway (Resource Discovery Network)	http://sosig.esrc.bris.ac.uk
	Social Science Libraries and Information Services (Yale University Library)	http://www.library.yale.edu/socsci/subjguides/
Science	Eurekalert (American Association for the Advancement of Science)	http://www.eurekalert.org/
	Nature.com (Nature Publishing Group)	http://www.nature.com/index.html
	SciCentral	http://www.scicentral.com/
Medicine	Health Information (National Institutes of Health)	http://health.nih.gov/
	WebMD	http://www.webmd.com/
	PubMed Central (National Institutes of Health)	http://www.pubmedcentral.nih.gov
Business	Hoover's Online	http://www.hoovers.com/free/
	Bureau of Labor Statistics	http://stats.bls.gov/
	SEC Filings & Forms (EDGAR)	http://www.sec.gov/edgar.shtml

Listservs and Newsgroups

The Internet's listservs and newsgroups are discussion forums where people interested in a particular topic or field of research can communicate and share information about it. A listserv is an email discussion group; messages are sent automatically to subscribers' email accounts. Some listservs allow anyone to subscribe, whereas others require a moderator's permission. A newsgroup, in contrast, does not require membership, and messages are posted to a news server for anyone to read and respond to. A central network called *Usenet* provides access to thousands of newsgroups.

Consult the frequently asked questions (FAQs) for a listserv or newsgroup to determine if it suits your needs and, for a listserv, to see how to subscribe. Keep in mind that messages posted to listservs and newsgroups are not usually checked for accuracy and are not always reliable sources of information (though in general, listserv discussions tend to be more serious and focused than newsgroup discussions). You can use electronic discussion forums to become familiar with a topic; obtain background information; discover new issues, facets, or approaches; identify print sources of information; and build your interest in a topic. To locate discussion groups, use a Web search engine to search for the term *discussion groups* or *Usenet*.

Email

Many authors, researchers, and corporations are willing to respond to email requests for specific information, but you should first make sure the information you need is not already available through more traditional sources. To locate email addresses, consult an online directory such as Bigfoot (bigfoot.com) or Internet Address Finder (www.iaf.net). (Any directory may include obsolete entries.) Email search directories are also available through Yahoo! and elsewhere. While not complete, they do contain a great deal of information.

When you send an email message to someone you don't know, be sure to introduce yourself and briefly describe the purpose of your inquiry. Provide complete information about yourself, including the name of your school and how to contact you, and politely request the information you need.

Extracting Information from Sources

As you read sources, you will need to take notes to use later. The following section discusses systems for note-taking and explains how to write various types of notes—for summaries, paraphrases, and quotations. It also offers advice for avoiding plagiarism.

Gathering Necessary Citation Information

For more on works-cited lists, see Chapter 22, pp. 622 (MLA) and 638 (APA).

As you work with print sources, be sure to record complete information for each source, using a form like the one shown in Figure 21.4. Filling out an information

FIGURE 21.4 Bibliographic Information Worksheet for Print Sources

Author(s) _____

Title _____

Beginning Page _____ _____   Ending Page _____ _____

Title of Journal _____

Volume Number _____   Issue Number _____

Date of Issue _____ ____   _____

Call Number _____

Publisher _____

Place of Publication _____ _____

Copyright Date _____ _____

worksheet will help you locate the source again—in case you need to verify something or find additional information.

When using electronic sources, be sure to print out all the information you will need to cite the source. For Web sources, this includes the author and title of the document; the title of the site; the sponsoring organization; the date of publication or of the last update; the number of pages, paragraphs, sections, or screens, if they are numbered in the document; the access date; and the URL. For an online periodical article, be sure your printouts also include the periodical name, any volume and issue numbers, and the print publication information (periodical name, publisher, date, and so on) if the article was originally published in print.

Constructing an Annotated Bibliography

Another approach, which some instructors require, is to prepare an **annotated bibliography**—a list of all the sources you *consulted* in researching your topic and a brief summary of each source's content and focus. You will find that it is easier to write the annotations as you do your research—while each source is fresh in your mind. Although preparing an annotated bibliography is time-consuming, it can be very helpful during the drafting or revising stage. If you realize, for instance, that you need more information on a particular subtopic, your annotations can often direct you to the most useful source.

If you are putting together an annotated bibliography intended only for your own use, you might simply write your annotations at the bottom of each information worksheet. For an annotated bibliography that will be submitted to your instructor, you would need to alphabetize it and use correct bibliographic format. Here is a sample annotated bibliography for researching the benefits of cooperative learning in the classroom.

SAMPLE ANNOTATED BIBLIOGRAPHY

Hill, Jane, and Kathleen Flynn. *Classroom Instruction That Works with English Language Learners.*
Alexandria, VA: Association for Supervision and Curriculum Development, 2006. Print.
Contains one chapter on cooperative learning as related to teaching ESL, giving
research and teaching strategies.

Huss, John A. "Gifted Education and Cooperative Learning: A Miss or a Match?" *Gifted Child
Today* Fall (2006): 19. Print.
Article from a trade journal aimed at teachers. Gives a thorough overview of the
important studies on cooperative learning and also its relationship to teaching
gifted students.

Johnson, Roger T., and David W. Johnson. *The Cooperative Learning Center of the University of
Minnesota.* The University of Minnesota, 17 Apr. 2002. Web. 23 Apr. 2005.
Huge Web site maintained by top authorities on the subject; provides dozens of
research articles on many issues.

Littleton, Karen, Dorothy Miell, and Dorothy Faulkner, eds. *Learning to Collaborate, Collaborat-
ing to Learn.* New York: Nova Science, 2004. Print.
Collection of essays written by experts in the field of group learning. Applies
the concept of collaborative learning to a variety of subject areas and student
populations.

*For more on bibliographic format,
see Chapter 22, pp. 622 (MLA) and
638 (APA).*

Vermette, Paul, Laurie Harper, and Shelley DiMillo. "Cooperative and Collaborative Learning
with Four- to Eight-Year-Olds: How Does Research Support Teachers' Practice?" *Journal of
Instructional Psychology* June (2004): 130. Print.
Scholarly article reporting on several studies that deal with cooperative learning.
Relates these studies to actual classroom practices. Includes references.

Systems of Note-Taking

When you take research notes, you'll probably need to copy quotes, write paraphrases, and make summary notes. There are three ways to record your research: on note cards, on your computer, or on copies of source material.

Regardless of the system you use, be sure to designate a place to record your own ideas, such as different-colored index cards, a notepad, or a computer folder. Be careful as well not to simply record (or highlight) quotations. Writing summary notes or paraphrases helps you think about the ideas in your source, how they fit with other ideas, and how they might work in your research paper.

Note Cards

Some researchers use four- by six-inch or five- by eight-inch index cards for note-taking. If you use this system, put information from only one source or about only one subtopic on each card. At the top of the card, indicate the author of the source

FIGURE 21.5 Sample Note Card

Schmoke & Roques, 17-25

Medicalization

> *Medicalization is a system in which the government would control the release of narcotics to drug addicts.*
> *— would work like a prescription does now — only gov't official would write prescription*
> > *— addicts would be required to get counseling and health services*
> > *— would take drug control out of hands of drug traffickers (paraphrase, 18)*

and the subtopic that the note covers. Be sure to include page numbers in case you need to go back and reread the article or passage. If you copy an author's exact words, place the information in quotation marks and include the term *direct quotation* and the page number in parentheses. If you write a summary note (see p. 588) or paraphrase (see p. 589), write *paraphrase* or *summary* on the card and the page number of the source. When you use this system, you can rearrange your cards and experiment with different ways of organizing as you plan your paper. Figure 21.5 shows a sample note card.

Computerized Note-Taking

Another option is to type your notes into computer files and organize your files by subtopic. To do so, use a computer notebook to create small "note cards," or use a hypertext card program. As with note cards, keep track of sources by including the author's name and the page numbers for each source, and make a back-up copy of your notes. If you have access to a computer in the library, you can type in summaries, paraphrases, and direct quotations while you are doing the research, eliminating the need to type or recopy them later.

Annotated Copies of Sources

This approach is most appropriate for very short papers that do not involve numerous sources or extensive research. To use this system, photocopy or print the source material; underline or highlight useful information; and write your reactions, paraphrases, and summary notes in the margins or on attachments to the appropriate page. Annotating source material often saves time because you don't need to copy quotations or write lengthy notes. The disadvantage, in addition to the expense of photocopying, is that this system does not allow you to sort and rearrange notes by subtopic.

For more on highlighting and annotating, see Chapter 3, p. 53.

When you highlight and annotate a source, be selective about what you mark or comment on, keeping the purpose of your research in mind. One student who was researching anthropomorphism annotated the following excerpt from *When Elephants*

Weep: The Emotional Lives of Animals by Jeffrey Masson and Susan McCarthy. Note how this student underlined key points related to his research. Notice also how his annotations comment on, summarize key points of, and question the text.

SAMPLE ANNOTATIONS AND UNDERLINING

*def

The greatest obstacle in science to investigating the emotions of other animals has been an inordinate desire to avoid anthropomorphism. Anthropomorphism* means the ascription of human characteristics—thought, feelings, consciousness, and motivation—to the nonhuman. When people claim that the elements are conspiring to ruin their picnic or that a tree is their friend, they are anthropomorphizing. Few believe that the weather is plotting against them, but anthropomorphic ideas about animals are held more widely. Outside scientific circles, it is common to speak of the thoughts and feelings of pets and wild and captive animals. Yet many scientists regard the notion that animals feel pain as the grossest sort of anthropomorphic error.

!
Wrong! If so, then why do vets use anesthesia?

Cats and dogs are prime targets of anthropomorphism, both wrongly and rightly. Ascribing unlikely thoughts and feelings to pets is common: "She understands every word you say." "He sings his little heart out to show how grateful he is." Some people deck reluctant pets in clothing, give them presents in which they have no interest, or assign their own opinions to the animals. Some dogs are even taught to attack people of races different from their owners'. Many dog lovers seem to enjoy believing that cats are selfish, unfeeling creatures who heartlessly use their deluded owners, compared with loving, loyal, and naive dogs. More often, however, people have quite realistic views about their pets' abilities and attributes. The experience of living with an animal often provides a strong sense of its abilities and limitations—although even here, as for people living intimately with people, preconceptions can be more persuasive than lived experience, and can create their own reality.

dog lovers vs. cat lovers why?

People have preconceived notions of certain breeds of dogs as vicious.

Jeffrey Masson and Susan McCarthy,
When Elephants Weep: The Emotional Lives of Animals

Writing Summary Notes

For more on writing summaries, see Chapter 3, p. 63.

Much of your note-taking will be in the form of summary notes, which condense information from sources. Take summary notes when you want to record the gist of an author's ideas but do not need the exact wording or a paraphrase. Use the following guidelines to write effective summary notes. Remember that everything you put in summary notes must be in your own words.

1. **Record only information that relates to your topic and purpose.** Do not include irrelevant information.
2. **Write notes that condense the author's ideas into your own words.** Include key terms and concepts or principles. Do not include specific examples, quotations, or anything that is not essential to the main point. Do not include your opinion, even a positive one. (You can include any comments in a separate note, as suggested earlier.)

3. **Record the ideas in the order in which they appear in the original source.**
   Reordering ideas might affect the meaning.
4. **Reread your summary to determine whether it contains sufficient information.**
   Would it be understandable to someone who has not read the original source? If
   not, revise the summary to include additional information.
5. **Jot down the publication information for the sources you summarize.** Unless
   you summarize an entire book or poem, you will need page references when you
   write your paper and prepare a works-cited list.

A sample summary is shown below. It summarizes the first four paragraphs of the
essay "Dude, Do You Know What You Just Said?" by Mike Crissey, which appears in
Chapter 16 (pp. 435–37). Read or reread the essay, and then study the summary.

SAMPLE SUMMARY

Scott Kiesling, a linguist, has studied the uses and meanings of the popularly used
word *dude*. Historically, *dude* was first used to refer to a dandy and then became a
slang term used by various social groups. For his study, Kiesling listened to tapes of
fraternity members and asked undergraduate students to record uses of the term. He
determined that it is used for a variety of purposes, including to show enthusiasm
or excitement, to one-up someone, to avoid confrontation, and to demonstrate
agreement.

Writing Paraphrases

When you paraphrase, you restate the author's ideas in your own words. You do not
condense ideas or eliminate details as you do in a summary. Instead, you use different
sentence patterns and vocabulary but keep the author's intended meaning. In most
cases, a paraphrase is approximately the same length as the original material. Compose
a paraphrase when you want to record the author's ideas and details but do not want to
use a direct quotation. Remember to paraphrase only the ideas or details you intend to
use—not an entire article.

When paraphrasing, be especially careful not to *plagiarize*—to use an author's
words or sentence structure as if they were your own (see p. 591). Read the following
excerpt from a source; then compare it to the acceptable paraphrase that follows and to
the example that includes plagiarism.

EXCERPT FROM ORIGINAL

Learning some items may interfere with retrieving others, especially when the
items are similar. If someone gives you a phone number to remember, you may be
able to recall it later. But if two more people give you their numbers, each successive
number will be more difficult to recall. Such proactive interference occurs when
something you learned earlier disrupts recall of something you experienced later. As
you collect more and more information, your mental attic never fills, but it certainly
gets cluttered.

David G. Myers, *Psychology*

ACCEPTABLE PARAPHRASE

When proactive interference happens, things you have already learned prevent you from remembering things you learn later. In other words, details you learn first may make it harder to recall closely related details you learn subsequently. You can think of your memory as an attic. You can always add more junk to it. However, it will become messy and disorganized. For example, you can remember one new phone number, but if you have two or more new numbers to remember, the task becomes harder.

UNACCEPTABLE PARAPHRASE — INCLUDES PLAGIARISM

When you learn some things, it may interfere with your ability to remember others. This happens when the things are similar. Suppose a person gives you a phone number to remember. You probably will be able to remember it later. Now, suppose two persons give you numbers. Each successive number will be harder to remember. Proactive interference happens when something you already learned prevents you from recalling something you experience later. As you learn more and more information, your mental attic never gets full, but it will get cluttered.

Although the preceding paraphrase does substitute some synonyms—*remember* for *retrieving,* for example—it is still an example of plagiarism. The underlined words are copied directly from the original. The shaded words show substitution of synonyms. Notice, too, that the structure of the last two sentences of the unacceptable paraphrase is nearly identical to the structure of the last two sentences of the original.

Writing paraphrases can be tricky, because simply rewording an author's ideas is not acceptable, and letting an author's language "creep in" is easy. There are also many ways to write an acceptable paraphrase of a particular passage. The following guidelines should help you write effective paraphrases.

1. **Read first; then write.** You may find it helpful to read material more than once before you try paraphrasing.
2. **If you must use any of the author's wording, enclose it in quotation marks.** If you do not use quotation marks, you may inadvertently use the same wording in your paper, which would result in plagiarism.
3. **Work sentence by sentence, restating each in your own words.** To avoid copying an author's words, read a sentence, cover it up, and then write. Be sure your version is accurate but not too similar to the original. As a rule of thumb, no more than two or three consecutive words should be the same as in the original.
4. **Choose synonyms that do not change the author's meaning or intent.** Consult a dictionary, if necessary.
5. **Use your own sentence structure.** Using an author's sentence structure can be considered plagiarism. If the original uses lengthy sentences, for example, your paraphrase of it should use shorter sentences.

Be sure to record the publication information (including page numbers) for the sources you paraphrase. You will need this information to document the sources in your paper.

Exercise 21.1

Write a paraphrase of the following excerpt from a source on animal communication.

Another vigorously debated issue is whether language is uniquely human. Animals obviously communicate. Bees, for example, communicate the location of food through an intricate dance. And several teams of psychologists have taught various species of apes, including a number of chimpanzees, to communicate with humans by signing or by pushing buttons wired to a computer. Apes have developed considerable vocabularies. They string words together to express meaning and to make and follow requests. Skeptics point out important differences between apes' and humans' facilities with language, especially in their respective abilities to order words using proper syntax. Nevertheless, these studies reveal that apes have considerable cognitive ability.

David G. Myers, *Psychology*

Recording Quotations

Sometimes it is advisable, and even necessary, to use a direct quotation—a writer's words exactly as they appear in the original source. Use quotations to record wording that is unusual or striking or to report the exact words of an expert on your topic. Such quotations, when used sparingly, can be effective in a paper. When using a direct quotation, be sure to record it precisely as it appears in the source. The author's spelling, punctuation, and capitalization must be recorded exactly. Also write down the page number on which the material being quoted appears in the original source. Be sure to indicate that you are copying a direct quotation by including the term *direct quotation* and the page number in parentheses.

You may delete a word, phrase, or sentence from a quotation as long as you do not change the meaning of the quotation. Use an ellipsis mark (three spaced periods)— . . . —to indicate that you have made a deletion.

Avoiding Plagiarism

Plagiarism is the use of someone else's ideas, wording, or organization without any acknowledgment of the source. If you take information from a source on uses of eye contact in communication and do not indicate where you got the information, you have plagiarized. If you copy the six-word phrase "Eye contact, particularly essential in negotiations" from a source without enclosing it in quotation marks, you have plagiarized.

Plagiarism is intellectually dishonest and is considered a form of cheating because you are submitting someone else's work as your own. Harsh academic penalties are applied to students found guilty of plagiarism; these often include receiving a failing grade on the paper, failing the entire course, or even being dismissed from the institution.

What Counts as Plagiarism

There are two types of plagiarism—intentional (deliberate) and unintentional (done by accident). Both are equally serious and both carry the same academic penalties. Below is a quick reference guide to determining if you have plagiarized.

For more on documentation, see Chapter 22.

To avoid plagiarism, be especially careful when taking notes from a source. Place anything you copy directly in quotation marks and record the source. Record the source for any information you paraphrase or summarize. Be sure to separate your own ideas from ideas expressed in the sources you are using. One way to do this is to use two different colors of ink or two different print sizes (if using a computer). Another way is to use different sections of a notebook or different computer files to distinguish your own ideas from those of others.

Cyberplagiarism

For more on citing Internet sources, see Chapter 22.

The term *cyberplagiarism* refers to borrowing information from the Internet without giving credit to the source posting the information. It also refers to "cut-and-paste plagiarism"—the practice of copying text directly from an Internet source and pasting it into your own essay without giving credit. Purchasing a student paper for sale on the Internet and submitting it as your own work is a third form of cyberplagiarism. Use the following suggestions to avoid unintentional plagiarism.

- Never copy and paste directly from an Internet source into your paper. Instead, cut and paste information you want to save into a separate file. Enclose the material you pasted in quotation marks to remind yourself that it is someone else's wording.
- Be sure to record all the source's information, including the name of the site, the URL, the date of access, and so on.
- When you make notes on ideas, opinions, or theories you encounter on the Internet, be sure to include complete source information for each item.

YOU HAVE PLAGIARIZED IF YOU HAVE . . .

- Directly copied information word for word without using quotation marks, whether or not you acknowledged the source.
- Reworded and reorganized (paraphrased) information from a source without acknowledging the source.
- Borrowed someone else's organization or sequence of ideas without acknowledging the source.
- Reused someone else's visual material (graphs, tables, charts, maps, diagrams) without acknowledging the source.
- Submitted another student's work as your own.

Exercise 21.2

The following piece of student writing is a paraphrase of a source on the history of advertising. Working with another student, evaluate the paraphrase and discuss whether it would be considered an example of plagiarism. If you decide the paraphrase is plagiarized, rewrite it so it is not.

ORIGINAL SOURCE

Everyone knows that advertising lies. That has been an article of faith since the Middle Ages – and a legal doctrine, too. Sixteenth-century English courts began the Age of Caveat Emptor by ruling that commercial claims – fraudulent or not – should be sorted out by the buyer, not the legal system. ("If he be tame and have ben rydden upon, then caveat emptor.") In a 1615 case, a certain Baily agreed to transport Merrell's load of wood, which Merrell claimed weighed 800 pounds. When Baily's two horses collapsed and died, he discovered that Merrell's wood actually weighed 2,000 pounds. The court ruled the problem was Baily's for not checking the weight himself; Merrell bore no blame.

Cynthia Crossen, *Tainted Truth*

PARAPHRASE

It is a well-known fact that advertising lies. This has been known ever since the Middle Ages. It is an article of faith as well as a legal doctrine. English courts in the sixteenth century started the Age of Caveat Emptor by finding that claims by businesses, whether legitimate or not, were the responsibility of the consumer, not the courts. For example, there was a case in which one person (Baily) used his horses to haul wood for a person named Merrell. Merrell told Baily that the wood weighed 800 pounds, but it actually weighed 2,000 pounds. Baily discovered this after his horses died. The court did not hold Merrell responsible; it stated that Baily should have weighed the wood himself instead of accepting Merrell's word.

Conducting Field Research

Depending on your research topic, you may need—or want—to do field research to collect original information. Check with your instructor before doing so. This section discusses three common types of field research—interviews, surveys, and observation—all of which generate primary source material.

Interviewing

An interview lets you obtain firsthand information from a person who is knowledgeable about your topic. For example, if the topic of your research paper is *treatment of teenage alcoholism,* it might be a good idea to interview an experienced substance abuse counselor who works with teenagers. Use the following suggestions to conduct effective interviews.

1. **Choose interview subjects carefully.** Be sure your subjects work in the field you are researching or are experts on your topic. Also try to choose subjects that may provide you with different points of view. If you are researching a corporation, for

example, try to interview someone from upper management as well as white- and blue-collar workers.

2. **Arrange your interview by letter, phone, or email well in advance.** Describe your project and purpose, explaining that you are a student working on an assignment. Indicate the amount of time you think you'll need, but don't be disappointed if the person shortens the time or denies your request altogether. You should also be some-what flexible about whom you interview. For example, a busy vice president may refer you to an assistant or to another manager.

3. **Plan the interview.** Come to the interview with a list of questions you want to ask; your subject will appreciate the fact that you are prepared and not wasting his or her time. Try to ask open rather than closed questions, which can be answered in a word or two. "Do you think your company has a promising future?" could be answered yes or no, whereas "How do you account for your company's turnaround last year?" might spark a detailed response. Open questions usually encourage people to open up and reveal attitudes as well as facts.

4. **Take notes during the interview.** Take a notebook to write in, since you probably will not be seated at a table or desk. Write the subject's responses in note form and find out whether you may quote him or her directly. If you want to tape-record the interview, be sure to ask the subject's permission.

5. **Evaluate the interview.** As soon as possible after the interview, reread your notes and fill in information you did not have time to record. Also write down your reactions while they are still fresh in your mind. Record these in the margin or in a different color ink so that they are distinguishable from the interview notes. Try to write down your overall impression and an answer to this question: What did I learn from this interview?

Using a Survey

A survey is a set of questions designed to get information quickly from a large number of people. Surveys can be conducted face-to-face, by phone, by email, or by regular mail. Surveys are often used to assess people's attitudes or intended actions. For example, we frequently read the results of surveys that measure the popularity of political figures.

Use the following suggestions to prepare effective surveys.

1. **Clarify the purpose of the survey.** Write a detailed list of what you want to learn from the survey.

2. **Design your questions.** A survey can include closed or open questions or both, but most use closed questions in either a multiple-choice or a ranking-scale format (see box). Closed questions usually work better in surveys because their short, direct answers are easy to tally and interpret. An open question such as "What do you think of the food served in the cafeteria?" would elicit a variety of responses that would be difficult to summarize in your paper.

3. **Test your survey questions.** Try out your questions on a few classmates, family members, or friends to be sure they are clear and that they will provide the infor-mation you need.

> **EXAMPLES OF CLOSED QUESTIONS**
>
> **Multiple Choice**
> How often do you purchase lunch in the campus cafeteria?
>
> a. 1–2 days per week
> b. 3–4 days per week
> c. 5–6 days per week
> d. Every day of the week
>
> **Ranking**
> On a scale of 1 to 5 (1 — poor and 5 = excellent), rate the quality of food in the campus cafeteria.
>
> *Poor*   *Excellent*
> 1   2   3   4   5

4. **Select your respondents.** Your respondents—the people who provide answers to your survey—must be *representative* of the group you are studying and must be *chosen at random*. For example, if you are planning a survey to learn what students on your campus think about mandatory drug testing for athletes, you should choose a group of respondents—or a sample—that is similar to your school's student population. For most campuses, then, your group of respondents would contain both men and women, be racially and ethnically diverse, and represent the various ages and socioeconomic groups of students. Your sample should also be random; respondents should be unknown to you and not chosen for a specific reason. One way to draw a random sample is to give the survey to every fifth or tenth name on a list or every fifteenth person who walks by.

5. **Summarize and report your results.** Tally the results and look for patterns in the data. If the sample is fairly large, use a computer spreadsheet to tabulate results. In your paper, discuss your overall findings, not individual respondents' answers. Explain the purpose of the survey as well as how you designed it, selected a sample, and administered the survey to respondents. You may also want to include a copy of the survey and tabulations in an appendix.

Conducting Observations

The results obtained from observation—the inspection of an event, a scene, or an activity—can be an important primary source in a research paper. For instance, you might observe and report on a demonstration at a government agency or a field trial at a dog show. Firsthand observation can give you valuable insights on the job as well. You might, for example, need to observe and report on the condition of hospital patients or on the job performance of your employees.

Use the following tips to conduct observations effectively.

1. **Arrange your visit in advance.** Unless you are doing an observation in a public place, obtain permission from the company or organization in advance, and make the purpose of your visit clear when arranging your appointment.
2. **Take detailed notes on what you observe.** Write down the details you will need to describe the scene vividly in your paper. For instance, if you visit a mental health clinic, note details about patient care, security, hygiene, and the like. You might sketch the scene, especially if you are a spatial learner, or use a tape recorder or video camera if you have permission to do so. Try to gather enough information to reconstruct your visit when you draft your paper.
3. **Approach the visit with an open mind.** A closed-minded approach can defeat the purpose of observation. For example, if you observe a dog show with the preconceived notion that the dogs' owners are only interested in winning, your closed-minded view might keep you from discovering that dog shows serve other purposes (such as promoting friendship between owners).
4. **Create a dominant impression.** As soon as possible after your visit, evaluate your observations. Ask yourself about what you saw and heard. Then describe your dominant impression of what you observed and the details that support it. Details from the dog show, for example, might include the attitude and attire of owners and judges and the way the dogs were groomed.

Finding Sources for Your Own Topic

Before you begin to locate sources for your topic, you should review the information in Chapter 20, which describes how to plan a paper with sources and how to choose and evaluate useful sources, whether in the library or online. Here are a few pointers that will help you conduct your own research.

1. **Begin with a narrowed topic, a working thesis, and some research questions** (see pp. 558–61).
2. **Decide what kinds of sources will best answer your research questions**— recent journal articles, historical works, personal interviews, and so forth (see pp. 561–65).
3. **Remember to consider whether each source will be truly useful.** Is it relevant and reliable (see pp. 562–63)? Is it biased in some way (see pp. 567–68)?
4. **Keep track of citation information for each source while you do your research** (see pp. 584–85).
5. **Decide what system of note-taking you will use**—note cards, computer files, or annotated copies (see pp. 586–88).
6. **As you take notes, paraphrase or summarize information appropriately, and copy quotations word for word** (see pp. 588–91).

Research Paper in Progress 3

For the topic you worked on in Research Papers in Progress 1 and 2, locate a minimum of six sources that answer one or more of your research questions. Your sources should include at least one book, one magazine article, one scholarly journal article, one Internet source, and two other sources of any type. On a scale of 1 to 5 (where 1 is low, 5 is high), rank the relevancy and reliability of each source you located using the guidelines provided in Chapter 20, pages 562–63. Use the following chart to structure your responses.

Source	Relevancy Rating	Reliability Rating
1.		
2.		
3.		
4.		
5.		
6.		

Research Paper in Progress 4

For the three most relevant and reliable sources you identified in Research Paper in Progress 3, use the suggestions on pages 586–91 to take notes on your sources. Your goal is to provide information and support for the ideas you developed earlier. Choose a system of note-taking, writing summary notes and paraphrases and recording quotations as needed. As you work, try to answer your research questions and keep your working thesis in mind.

CHAPTER 22

Writing a Paper Using Sources

WRITING QUICK START

Suppose you have been assigned to write a research paper for a mass communication course on a topic related to human communication involving more than two people. You struggle with choosing a topic for nearly a week, when suddenly, as you walk down a busy street, you notice several bumper stickers on a parked car. You decide to write about bumper stickers and begin to think about how to categorize them into types.

Make a list of the bumper-sticker slogans in the photograph on the opposite page plus five or more bumper stickers you have seen. Then try to group the bumper stickers into categories.

By creating categories of bumper stickers, you took the first steps in writing a research paper—synthesizing and condensing information from sources, in this case, a primary source. In Chapter 20 you learned how to plan a paper with sources and how to choose and evaluate useful information. Chapter 21 gave you advice on finding sources and taking notes. This chapter continues the research process by showing you how to organize, draft, revise, and document a paper using sources.

You will have numerous opportunities to write research papers in your college courses. Many jobs require research skills as well. You might, for instance, need to justify a proposed change in your company's vacation policy by citing the vacation policies of other companies, or you might need to research information about a company before going on a job interview. See the accompanying box for a few other examples of situations that would require research skills.

Think of a research paper as an opportunity to explore information about a topic, pull ideas from sources together, and present what you discover. This chapter will guide you through the process of writing a paper using sources. Figure 22.1 presents an overview of the process.

Organizing and Writing Your First Draft

After you conduct library and Internet research on your topic and take notes on your sources (as detailed in Chapter 21), you are ready to evaluate your work in preparation for writing a first draft. This stage of the research process involves evaluating your research and working thesis, developing an organizational plan, and drafting the research paper.

Evaluating Your Research and Synthesizing Information

Before you began researching your topic, you probably wrote a *working thesis*—a preliminary statement of your main point about the topic—and a list of research

---

SCENES FROM COLLEGE AND THE WORKPLACE

- For a *business* course, you are required to research a Fortune 500 company and write a report on its history and current profitability. At least two of your sources must be from the Internet.

- For a *social problems* course, you are asked to conduct your own field research (interviews or surveys) on a local or campus issue and to report your findings in a research paper.

- As *personnel director* of a publishing company, you are asked to research editorial salaries in the publishing industry and submit a report that your company will use to decide whether to change salary levels for editors.

FIGURE 22.1 Writing a Paper Using Sources

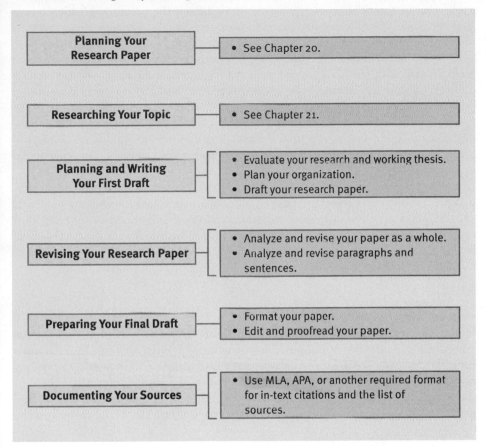

questions you hoped to answer. Then, as you researched your topic, you may have discovered new facts about your topic, statistics you were unaware of, or expert testimony that surprised you. In most cases the discoveries you make during the research process influence your thinking on the topic, requiring you to modify your working thesis. In some cases you may even need to rethink the direction of your paper.

As you evaluate your research notes and modify your thesis, keep the following questions in mind.

1. What research questions did I begin with?
2. What answers did I find to those questions?
3. What other information did I discover about my topic?
4. What conclusions can I draw from what I've learned?
5. How does my research affect my working thesis?

For more on writing a working thesis and research questions, see Chapter 20.

To answer these questions, you'll need to **synthesize** the information you gathered from sources. The word *synthesis* is formed from the prefix *syn-,* which means "together," and *thesis,* which means "main or central point." *Synthesis,* then, means "a pulling together of information to form a new idea or point."

You synthesize information every day. For example, after you watch a preview of a movie, talk with friends who have seen the film, and read a review of it, you then pull together the information you have acquired and come up with your own idea—perhaps that you do not want to see the movie because it is too juvenile.

You often synthesize information for your college courses as well. In a biology course, for instance, you might evaluate your own lab results, those of your classmates, and the data in your textbook to reach a conclusion about a particular experiment.

As you can see, synthesis involves putting together ideas to see how they agree, disagree, or otherwise relate to one another. When working with sources, you could ask the following questions: Does one source reinforce or contradict another? How do their claims and lines of reasoning compare? Do they make similar or dissimilar assumptions and generalizations? Is their evidence alike in any way? The remainder of this section shows several ways to synthesize information from sources.

Categorizing Information

One way to arrive at a synthesis is to condense the information into categories. For example, one student found numerous sources on and answers to this research question: What causes some parents to physically abuse their children? After rereading his research notes, the student realized he could synthesize the information by putting it into three categories—lack of parenting skills, emotional instability, and family history of child abuse. He then made this two-column list of the categories and his sources.

Category	*Sources*
Lack of parenting skills	Lopez, Wexler, Thomas
Emotional instability	Wexler, Harris, Thompson, Wong
Family history of child abuse	Thompson, Harris, Lopez, Strickler, Thomas

While evaluating his research in this way, the student also realized he needed to revise both his working thesis and the scope of his paper to include lack of parenting skills as a major cause of child abuse. Notice how he modified his working thesis accordingly.

WORKING THESIS

The main reasons that children are physically abused are their parents' emotional instability and family history of child abuse.

REVISED THESIS

Some children are physically abused because of their parents' emotional instability, family history of child abuse, and lack of parenting skills.

As you work on synthesizing information from sources, keep in mind that you can categorize many kinds of events or phenomena, such as types of life insurance, effects of education level on salary, and views on environmental problems.

Exercise 22.1

Imagine that you have done research on one of the following topics; write a list of some of the information you have found. Then, working with one or two classmates, discuss how you might categorize the information. Write a thesis statement that reflects your research.

1. The health hazards of children's toys
2. The fairness of college entrance exams
3. The advantages of college athletic programs

Drawing an Organizer for Multiple Sources

Using a graphic organizer is another way to synthesize information from sources. Your organizer may reveal patterns and show similarities and differences. It will also show you how main ideas and supporting details connect with each other.

Suppose you are writing an essay on voluntary simplicity—the idea that minimizing personal possessions and commitments leads to a happier, more manageable lifestyle. You have located three reliable and relevant sources that define voluntary simplicity, but each develops the idea somewhat differently. Source 1 (Walker) is a practical how-to article that includes some personal examples. Source 2 (Parachin) is a theoretical look at statistics about workloads and complicated lifestyles and the reasons that voluntary simplicity is appealing. Source 3 (Remy) also presents strategies for simplifying but emphasizes the values of a simplified lifestyle. Figure 22.2 presents a sample organizer for information from these three sources.

Depending on your sources and the type of information they contain, you can use a variety of organizer formats. If all your sources compare and contrast the same things, such as the functioning and effectiveness of two presidents, you could adapt one of the graphic organizers for comparison and contrast shown in Chapter 14, pages 348 to 350. If most of your sources focus on effects, such as the effects of a recession on retail sales and employment, you could adapt one of the cause-and-effect graphic organizers shown in Chapter 17, pages 452 to 455. Whatever style of organizer you use, be sure to keep track of the sources for each idea and to use them in your organizer (as shown in Figure 22.2).

Using a Pro-and-Con List to Synthesize Confirming and Conflicting Sources

As you research a topic, especially if it is controversial, you are likely to find sources from many sides of the issue. For example, some sources may favor gun control legislation, others may oppose it, and still others may present both viewpoints. Even sources that agree or disagree, however, often do so for different reasons. On the issue of gun control legislation, one source may favor it for national-security reasons: Gun control makes it harder for terrorists to acquire guns. Another source

Figure 22.2 GRAPHIC ORGANIZER FOR THREE SOURCES ON VOLUNTARY SIMPLICITY

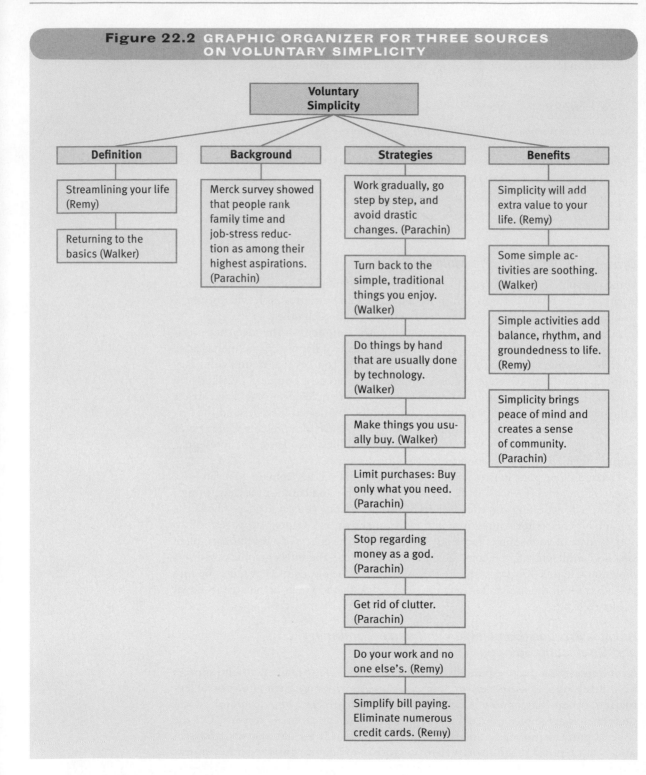

may favor legislation for a statistical reason: Statistics prove that owning a gun does not prevent crime.

As you encounter varying opinions in sources, a pro-and-con list may help you organize and synthesize your information. For the issue of gun control, you might create a two-column list such as the one shown in the box on page 606. Be sure to include the source of each entry.

Planning Your Organization

Your next step involves developing an organizational plan for your paper—deciding both what you'll say and the order in which you will say it. Think about whether you want to use chronological order, spatial order, most-to-least or least-to-most order, or one of the patterns of development discussed in Parts 3 and 4 of this text.

Following are some guidelines for organizing your research paper.

Arranging Your Information

If you used note cards, begin by sorting them into piles by subtopic or category. (You may already have developed categories when you evaluated your research and thesis and worked on synthesizing source information.) For example, note cards for the thesis "Prekindergarten programs provide children with long-lasting educational advantages" might be sorted by type of educational advantage, such as reading readiness, social skills, and positive self-image.

If you took notes on a computer, you may have arranged your research information by category as you went along. If not, this is the time to do it. As you move information within or among computer files, be careful to keep track of which material belongs to which source.

If you used photocopies of sources, attach self-stick notes to indicate the various subtopics each source covers.

Once your note cards, computer files, or photocopies are organized, you are ready to develop your outline or graphic organizer.

Developing an Outline or Graphic Organizer

Use an outline or a graphic organizer to show the divisions and subdivisions you intend for your paper. Preparing such a plan is especially important for a research paper because you are working with a substantial amount of information. Without something to follow, it is easy to get lost and write an unfocused paper.

For more on outlines and graphic organizers, see Chapter 6, pp. 122–24.

Pragmatic learners tend to prefer organizing in detail before beginning to write. If this is your tendency, make sure that you are open to change and new ideas as you write your draft. Creative learners, on the other hand, may prefer to start writing and try to structure the paper as they work. Most students should not take this approach, however; those who do should allow extra time for reorganizing and making extensive revisions.

Learning Style Options

Whatever your learning style, writing your outline or graphic organizer on a computer will help you reorganize material easily and test several different organizations.

PRO-AND-CON VIEWS ON GUN CONTROL LEGISLATION

Pro

Stronger federal regulations are necessary to increase homeland security following the September 11, 2001, terrorist attacks on the United States. (Melissa Robinson)

The crackdown on terrorism must close the loophole that allows many people to buy weapons at gun shows without background checks. (Fox Butterfield)

By 2000 violent crime had fallen for six consecutive years, due, in part, to mandating background checks, banning types of assault weapons, and limiting access for kids and criminals. (Brady Campaign)

A study by the Justice Department shows that background checks by the FBI and by state and local agencies have barred criminals from acquiring weapons hundreds of thousands of times. (*New York Times* editorial)

In the five years after the Brady Bill was passed (1994), background checks blocked 536,000 convicted felons and other illegal buyers from getting a gun. (Americans for Gun Safety)

Con

Stricter gun control creates vulnerable targets for enemies of a free society. (Phyllis Schlafly)

Gun control laws do not remove guns from the hands of criminals; they disarm victims. (Jack Duggan)

We should enforce the laws we have before creating new ones that may or may not provide any benefits. (Warren Ockrassa)

It is unrealistic to pass gun laws that prevent Americans from protecting themselves and their families. (Libertarian Party)

Existing laws preventing illegal purchase have proven to be effective in catching suspected terrorists, so new laws that target gun shows are not needed. (National Rifle Association)

Be sure to save your original outline or graphic organizer and any revised versions as separate files in case you need to return to earlier versions.

Research Paper in Progress 5

Using the research notes you developed for Research Paper in Progress 4 (p. 597), sort your source notes and information into several categories and evaluate your working thesis. Then prepare an outline or a graphic organizer for your paper.

Drafting Your Research Paper

The following guidelines will help you write the first draft of a research paper.

1. **Follow the introduction, body, and conclusion format.** A straightforward organization is usually the best choice for a research paper.

2. **Take a serious, academic tone and avoid using the first or second person.** Your credibility will be enhanced if you use the third person, which is more objective and gives you some distance from your topic.

3. **For most research papers, place your thesis in the introduction.** However, for papers analyzing a problem or proposing a solution, try placing your thesis near the end. For example, if you were writing an essay proposing stricter traffic laws on campus, you might begin by documenting the problem—describing accidents that have occurred and detailing their frequency. You might conclude your essay by suggesting that your college lower the speed limit on campus and install two new stop signs.

4. **Keep your audience in mind.** Although you now know a great deal about your topic, your readers may not. When appropriate, be sure to provide background information, explain concepts and processes, and define terms for your readers. For example, if you were writing a paper on recycling plastics for a chemistry class, your audience might already understand some of the technical terms and concepts in your paper. You wouldn't need to explain everything. But if you were writing on the same topic for a composition class, you would need to provide thorough explanations and use more nontechnical terms.

5. **Follow your outline or graphic organizer but feel free to make changes as you work.** You may discover a better organization, think of new ideas about your topic, or realize that a subtopic belongs in a different section. Don't feel compelled to follow your outline to the letter but be sure to address the topics you list.

6. **Determine the purpose and main point of each paragraph.** State the main point of each body paragraph in a topic sentence. Then use your sources to substantiate, explain, or provide detail in support of that main point.

7. **Use strong transitions.** Because a research paper may be lengthy or complex, strong transitions are needed to hold the paper together as a whole. In addition, transitions help your readers understand how you have divided the topic and how one point relates to another.

8. **Support your key points with evidence.** Be sure to identify your major points first, and support each major point with evidence from several sources. Keep in mind that relying on only one or two sources weakens your thesis, suggesting to readers that you did insufficient research. Bring together facts, statistics, details, expert testimony, and other types of evidence from a variety of sources to strengthen your thesis.

9. **Include source material only for a specific purpose.** Just because you discovered an interesting statistic or a fascinating quote, don't feel that you must use it. Information that doesn't support your thesis will distract your reader and weaken your paper.

10. **Refer to your source notes frequently as you write.** If you do so, you will be less likely to overlook an important piece of evidence. If you suspect that a note is inaccurate in some way, check the original source.

For more on organization, see Chapter 6, pp. 117–24.

For more on using transitions, see Chapter 6, pp. 124–26.

11. **Do not overuse sources.** Make sure your paper is not just a series of facts, quotations, and so forth taken from sources. Your research paper should not merely summarize what others have written about the topic; the basis of the paper should be your ideas and thesis.

12. **Use source information in a way that does not mislead your readers.** Even though you are presenting only a portion of someone's ideas, make sure you are not using information in a way that is contrary to the writer's original intentions.

13. **Incorporate in-text citations for your sources.** Whenever you paraphrase, summarize, or quote a source, be sure to include an in-text citation. (See pp. 608–11.)

Integrating Information from Sources

After you have decided what source information to use, you will need to build that information into your essay. The three methods for extracting information—paraphrasing, summarizing, or quoting—have been discussed in Chapter 21 (pp. 588–91). In general, try to paraphrase or summarize information rather than quote it directly. Use a quotation only if the wording is unusual or unique or if you want to provide the actual statement of an expert on the topic. Regardless of how you integrate sources, be sure to acknowledge and document all direct quotations as well as the paraphrased or summarized ideas of others. You must make it clear to your readers that you have borrowed ideas or information by citing the source, whether it is a book, a Web page, a journal article, a drawing, a DVD, or another type of source. The following section provides advice on what does and does not need to be documented as well as guidelines for writing in-text citations and using quotations appropriately.

Deciding What to Document

For more on what constitutes plagiarism, see Chapter 21, pp. 591–93.

You can use another person's material in your paper as long as you give that person credit. **Plagiarism** occurs when you present the ideas of others as your own. Whether intentional or not, plagiarism is a serious error that must be avoided. The accompanying box identifies the types of material that *do* and *do not* require documentation. If you are unsure about whether to document something, ask your instructor or a reference librarian.

In the last few years, deliberate plagiarism has become widespread, and unethical students have begun to exchange or sell papers over the Internet. To combat this problem, many instructors commonly use Internet tracking resources to check for plagiarized material. Be sure that all your sources are clearly documented. You do not want to plagiarize anyone's ideas, even inadvertently.

Writing In-Text Citations

Many academic disciplines have their own preferred format or style for documenting sources within the text of a paper. For example, in English and the humanities, the preferred documentation format is that of the Modern Language Association and is known as *MLA style*. In the social sciences, the guidelines of the American

WHAT DOES AND DOES NOT REQUIRE DOCUMENTATION

Documentation Required

Summaries, paraphrases, and quotations

Obscure or recently discovered facts (such as a little-known fact about Mark Twain or a recent discovery about Mars)

Others' opinions

Others' field research (results of opinion polls, case studies, statistics)

Quotations or paraphrases from interviews you conduct

Others' visuals (photographs, charts, maps, Web images)

Information from others that you use to create visuals (statistics or other data that you use to construct a table, graph, or other visual)

Documentation Not Required

Common knowledge (George Washington was the first U.S. president, the Earth revolves around the sun)

Facts that can be found in numerous sources (winners of Olympic competitions, names of Supreme Court justices)

Standard definitions of academic terms

Your own ideas or conclusions

Your own field research (surveys or observations)

Your own visuals (such as photographs you take)

Psychological Association, commonly called *APA style*, are often used. Many scientists follow a format used by the Council of Science Editors (CSE) (formerly the Council of Biology Editors, CBE). This format is now known as either *CSE style* or *CBE style*. The two most widely used formats—MLA and APA—are discussed in detail later in this chapter. (See pp. 618–34 for MLA style; see pp. 634–45 for APA style.)

When you paraphrase, summarize, or quote from a source in the text of your paper, you must provide an in-text citation—a brief reference to a source completely described that you provide in a list of sources at the end of the paper. The list is headed *Works Cited* in MLA style and *References* in APA style. Because this list includes only those sources you cite in your paper, it is different from a bibliography, which includes all the sources you consulted, whether or not you used them.

What Should I Include in an In-Text Citation?

An in-text citation usually includes the author's name and the page number(s) of the source information. Many writers put the author's name in an introductory phrase, called an **attribution**, and the page number(s) in parentheses at the end of the sentence. Sometimes, however, both the author and the page number(s) may appear in parentheses at the end of the sentence. The following examples, which are in MLA style, show several ways to write an in-text citation of a paraphrase.

> As Jo-Ellan Dimitrius observes, big spenders often suffer from low
> self-esteem (143).

Some behavioral experts claim that big spenders often suffer from low self-esteem (Dimitrius 143).

> Jo-Ellan Dimitrius, a jury-selection consultant whose book *Reading People* discusses
> methods of predicting behavior, observes that big spenders often suffer from low
> self-esteem (143).

As the last example shows, it is often a good idea to provide some background information about sources the first time you mention them, especially if the source is not commonly known. Such information helps readers understand that the source is relevant or important.

How Can I Integrate Sources Most Effectively?

To integrate most paraphrases and summaries and *all* quotations, use an introductory phrase or clause, such as "As Markham points out" or "Bernstein observes that," that allows information to flow smoothly to your readers. When you integrate a number of sources in a paper, try to vary both the structure of the phrase and the verb used. The following verbs are useful for introducing many kinds of source material.

advocates	contends	insists	proposes
argues	demonstrates	maintains	shows
asserts	denies	mentions	speculates
believes	emphasizes	notes	states
claims	explains	points out	suggests

When integrating paraphrases or summaries, you may sometimes decide not to use an introductory phrase. In these instances, be sure that the source material is clear to the reader. If an in-text citation is in the wrong spot, readers may not be able to tell whether an idea is yours or the source's.

When integrating quotations, you should *always* include a lead-in or introduction. Quotations should blend into your sentences and paragraphs; they should not simply be "dropped in" to your paper.

QUOTATION NOT INTEGRATED

Anecdotes indicate that animals experience emotions, but they are not considered scientifically valid. "Experimental evidence is given almost exclusive credibility over personal experience to a degree that seems almost religious" (Masson and McCarthy 3).

QUOTATION INTEGRATED

Anecdotes indicate that animals experience emotions, but they are not considered scientifically valid. Masson and McCarthy, who have done extensive field observation, comment, "Experimental evidence is given almost exclusive credibility over personal experience to a degree that seems almost religious" (3).

Using Quotations Appropriately

Although quotations can lend interest to your paper and support for your ideas, they need to be used appropriately. The following section answers some common questions about the use of quotations. The in-text citations in this section follow MLA style, as do the rules about changing quotations.

When Should I Use Quotations?

1. **Use quotations sparingly.** Do not use quotations to reveal ordinary facts and opinions. Look carefully at what you intend to quote: If a quotation does not achieve one of the following purposes, use a paraphrase instead.

   For more practice integrating quotations into your writing, visit www.bedfordstmartins .com/successfulwriting/ tutorials.

   • Quote when the author's wording is unusual, noteworthy, or striking. The quotation "Injustice anywhere is a threat to justice everywhere" from Martin Luther King Jr.'s "Letter from Birmingham Jail" is probably more effective than any paraphrase.
   • Quote when a paraphrase might alter or distort the statement's meaning.
   • Quote when the original words express the exact point you want to make.
   • Quote when the statement is a strong, opinionated, exaggerated, or disputed idea that you want to make clear is not your own.

2. **Use quotations to support your ideas.** Never use a quotation as the topic sentence of a paragraph. The topic sentence should state in your own words the idea you are about to explain or prove.

3. **Use quotations that are self-explanatory.** If a quotation needs to be restated or explained, paraphrase it instead.

What Format Do I Follow for Long Quotations?

In MLA style, lengthy quotations (more than three lines of poetry or more than four typed lines of prose) are indented in *block form*, ten spaces from the left margin. In APA style, the block format is used for quotations of more than forty words, and the block quotation is indented five spaces from the left margin. Both styles omit quotation marks and use a double-spaced format. Like a shorter quotation in the main text, a block quotation should always have an introduction; a colon is used at the end of the introduction if it is a complete sentence. Note that for a block quotation, the parenthetical citation appears *after* the final sentence period. This is different from the style for short quotations within the text, in which the parenthetical citation precedes the period.

BLOCK QUOTATION, MLA STYLE

Although a business is a profit-making organization, it is also a social organization. As Hicks and Gwynne note,

> In Western society, businesses are essentially economic organizations, with both the organizations themselves and the individuals in them dedicated to making as much money as possible in the most efficient way. But businesses are also social organizations, each of which has its unique culture. Like all social groups, businesses are made up of people of both sexes and a wide range of ages, who play different roles, occupy different positions in the group, and behave in different ways while at work. (174)

How Do I Punctuate Quotations?

There are specific rules and conventions for punctuating quotations. The most important rules follow.

1. **Use single quotation marks to enclose a quotation within a quotation.**

   Coleman and Cressey argue that "concern for the 'decaying family' is nothing new" (147).

2. **Use a comma after a verb that introduces a quotation.** Begin the first word of the quotation with a capital letter (enclosed in brackets if it is not capitalized in the source).

   As Thompson and Hickey report, "There are three major kinds of 'taste cultures' in complex industrial societies: high culture, folk culture, and popular culture" (76).

3. **Use a colon to introduce a quotation preceded by a complete sentence.** Note that in MLA style, the period *follows* a parenthetical citation for a short quotation that is integrated within the text.

   The definition is clear: "Countercultures reject the conventional wisdom and standards of the dominant culture and provide alternatives to mainstream culture" (Thompson and Hickey 76).

4. **When a quotation is not introduced by a verb, it is not necessary to use a comma or capitalize the first word.**

   Buck reports that "pets play a significant part in both physical and psychological therapy" (4).

5. **Place periods and commas inside quotation marks.**

   "The most valuable old cars," notes antique car collector Michael Patterson, "are the rarest ones."

6. **Place colons and semicolons outside quotation marks.**

   "Petting a dog increases mobility of a limb or hand"; petting a dog, then, can be a form of physical therapy (Buck 4).

7. **Place question marks and exclamation points inside quotation marks when they are part of the original quotation. No period is needed if the quotation ends the sentence.**

   The instructor asked, "Does the text's description of alternative lifestyles agree with your experience?"

8. **Place question marks and exclamation points that belong to your own sentence outside quotation marks.**

   Is the following definition accurate: "Sociolinguistics is the study of the relationship between language and society"?

How Can I Change Quotations?

1. When you use a quotation, the spelling, punctuation, and capitalization must be copied exactly as they appear in the original source, even if they are in error. (See item 5 on p. 614 for the only exception.) If a source contains an error, copy it with the error and add the word *sic* (Latin for "thus") in brackets immediately following the error.

   According to Bernstein, "The family has undergone rapid decentralization since Word [sic] War II" (39).

2. You can emphasize words by underlining or italicizing them, but you must add the notation *emphasis added* in parentheses at the end of the sentence to indicate the change.

   "In *unprecedented* and *increasing* numbers, patients are consulting practitioners of every type of complementary medicine" (emphasis added) (Buckman and Sabbagh 73).

3. You can omit part of a quotation, but you must add ellipsis points—three spaced periods (. . .)—to indicate that material has been deleted. You may delete words, sentences, paragraphs, or entire pages, as long as you do not distort the author's meaning by doing so.

   According to Buckman and Sabbagh, "Acupuncture . . . has been rigorously tested and proven to be effective and valid" (188).

   When an omission falls at the end of a quoted sentence, use the three spaced periods in addition to the sentence period.

   Thompson maintains that "marketers need to establish ethical standards for personal selling. . . . They must stress fairness and honesty in dealing with customers" (298).

   If you are quoting only a word or phrase from a source, do not use ellipse points before or after it because it will be obvious that you have omitted part of the original sentence. If you omit the beginning of a quoted sentence, you need not use ellipsis points unless what you are quoting still begins with a capitalized word and appears to be a complete sentence.

4. You can add words or phrases in brackets to make a quotation clearer or to make it fit grammatically into your sentence; be sure that in doing so you do not change the original sense.

> Masson and McCarthy note that the well-known animal researcher Jane Goodall finds that "the scientific reluctance to accept anecdotal evidence [of emotional experience is] a serious problem, one that colors all of science" (3).

5. You can change the first word of a quotation to a capital or lowercase letter to fit into your sentence. If you change it, enclose it in brackets.

> As Aaron Smith said, "The . . ." (32).
>
> Aaron Smith said that "[t]he . . ." (32).

> **Research Paper in Progress 6**
> Using your research notes, revised thesis, and the organizational plan you developed for your research paper, write a first draft. Be sure to integrate sources carefully and to include in-text citations. (See pp. 618–22 for MLA style guidelines for in-text citations; see pp. 634–37 for APA style.)

Revising Your Research Paper

For more on revision, see Chapter 8.

Revise a research paper in two stages. First focus on the paper as a whole; then consider individual paragraphs and sentences for effectiveness and correctness. If time allows, wait at least a day before rereading your research paper.

Analyzing and Revising Your Paper as a Whole

Begin by evaluating your paper as a unified piece of writing. Focus on general issues, overall organization, and the key points that support your thesis. Use Figure 22.3 to help you discover the strengths and weaknesses of your research paper as a whole. You might also ask a classmate to review your draft paper by using the questions in the flowchart.

Analyzing and Revising Paragraphs and Sentences

After evaluating your paper as a whole, check each paragraph to be sure that it supports your thesis and integrates sources appropriately. Then check your sentences for correct structure, transitions, and in-text citation format. Use your earlier work with Figure 22.3 to guide your analysis.

> **Research Paper in Progress 7**
> Using the questions in Figure 22.3, revise the first draft of your research paper.

Preparing Your Final Draft

After you have revised your paper and compiled a list of references or works cited, you are ready to prepare the final draft. Following are some guidelines to help you format, edit, and proofread your final paper. For an example, see the essay "Do Animals Have Emotions?" by Nicholas Destino on pages 646–52.

Formatting Your Paper

Academic papers should follow a standard manuscript format whether or not they use sources. The following guidelines are recommended by the Modern Language Association (MLA). If your instructor suggests or requires a different format, be sure to follow it. If your instructor does not recommend a format, these guidelines would probably be acceptable.

1. **Paper.** Use 8½- by 11-inch white paper. Separate the sheets if you use continuous-feed printer paper. Use a paper clip; do not staple or use a binder.
2. **Your name and course information.** Do not use a title page unless your instructor requests one. Position your name at the left margin about one inch from the top of the page. Underneath it, list your instructor's name, your course name and number, and the date. Use separate lines for each and double-space between the lines.
3. **Title.** Place the title two lines below the date. Center the title on the page. Capitalize the first word and all other words except articles, coordinating conjunctions, and prepositions. Double-space after the title and type your first paragraph. Do not underline or italicize your title or put quotation marks around it.
4. **Margins, spacing, and indentation.** Use one-inch margins. Double-space between all lines of your paper. Indent each paragraph five spaces.
5. **Numbering of pages.** Number all pages using arabic numerals (1, 2, 3) in the upper right corner. Place the numbers one-half inch below the top of the paper. (If your instructor requests a title page, do not number it and do not count it in your numbering.) Precede each with your last name, leaving a space between your name and the number.
6. **Headings.** The MLA does not provide any guidelines for using headings. However, the system recommended by the American Psychological Association (APA) should work for most papers. Main headings should be centered, and the first letter of key words should be capitalized. Subheadings—underlined—should begin at the left margin, with important words capitalized.
7. **Visuals.** You may include tables and figures (graphs, charts, maps, photographs, and drawings) in your paper. Label each table or figure with an arabic numeral (*Table 1, Table 2; Fig. 1, Fig. 2*) and give it a title. Place the title on a separate line above the table. Give each figure a number and title and place the figure number and title on a separate line below the figure.

Figure 22.3 Flowchart for Revising a Research Paper

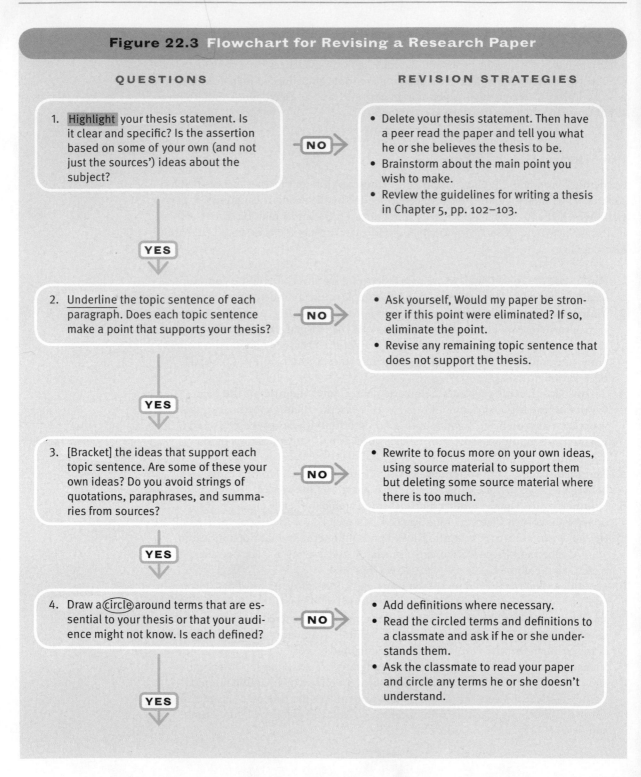

QUESTIONS

REVISION STRATEGIES

1. Highlight your thesis statement. Is it clear and specific? Is the assertion based on some of your own (and not just the sources') ideas about the subject?

NO

- Delete your thesis statement. Then have a peer read the paper and tell you what he or she believes the thesis to be.
- Brainstorm about the main point you wish to make.
- Review the guidelines for writing a thesis in Chapter 5, pp. 102–103.

YES

2. Underline the topic sentence of each paragraph. Does each topic sentence make a point that supports your thesis?

NO

- Ask yourself, Would my paper be stronger if this point were eliminated? If so, eliminate the point.
- Revise any remaining topic sentence that does not support the thesis.

YES

3. [Bracket] the ideas that support each topic sentence. Are some of these your own ideas? Do you avoid strings of quotations, paraphrases, and summaries from sources?

NO

- Rewrite to focus more on your own ideas, using source material to support them but deleting some source material where there is too much.

YES

4. Draw a circle around terms that are essential to your thesis or that your audience might not know. Is each defined?

NO

- Add definitions where necessary.
- Read the circled terms and definitions to a classmate and ask if he or she understands them.
- Ask the classmate to read your paper and circle any terms he or she doesn't understand.

YES

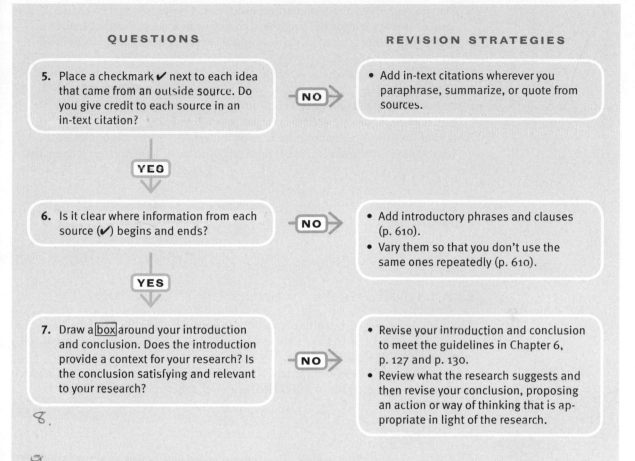

QUESTIONS

5. Place a checkmark ✔ next to each idea that came from an outside source. Do you give credit to each source in an in-text citation?

NO ▷

REVISION STRATEGIES

• Add in-text citations wherever you paraphrase, summarize, or quote from sources.

YES ▽

6. Is it clear where information from each source (✔) begins and ends?

NO ▷

• Add introductory phrases and clauses (p. 610).
• Vary them so that you don't use the same ones repeatedly (p. 610).

YES ▽

7. Draw a box around your introduction and conclusion. Does the introduction provide a context for your research? Is the conclusion satisfying and relevant to your research?

NO ▷

• Revise your introduction and conclusion to meet the guidelines in Chapter 6, p. 127 and p. 130.
• Review what the research suggests and then revise your conclusion, proposing an action or way of thinking that is appropriate in light of the research.

8.

9.

Editing and Proofreading Your Paper

As a final step, edit and proofread your revised paper for errors in grammar, spelling, punctuation, mechanics, and documentation style. In addition, be sure to check your error log for the types of errors you commonly make.

For more on editing and proofreading, see Chapter 9.

As you edit and proofread, watch out for the following common problems.

1. Does your paper contain any long, cumbersome sentences? If so, try splitting them into two separate sentences.
2. Do you use a consistent verb tense throughout your paper? Don't shift from present to past to future tense unless there is a good reason to do so.
3. Do you punctuate and style in-text citations correctly? Make sure that they conform to MLA style or that of another system of documentation.

4. Do you reproduce direct quotations exactly as they appear in the original source? In addition to checking the accuracy of individual words, be sure to check your use of quotation marks, capital letters, commas, and ellipses within quotations.

5. Do you avoid plagiarism by carefully quoting, paraphrasing, and summarizing the ideas of others?

6. Is your paper typed and spaced according to the format you need to follow? Be sure that block quotations are also typed appropriately.

7. Is your list of works cited or references complete? Make sure all sources cited in your paper are included in the list in the right order and are formatted correctly.

Research Paper in Progress 8

Edit and proofread your paper, paying particular attention to the questions in the preceding list.

Documenting Your Sources: MLA Style

The system described in this section is recommended by the Modern Language Association (MLA). If you are unsure whether to use the MLA system, check with your instructor.

The MLA style uses in-text citations to identify sources within the text of a research paper. A corresponding list of works cited appears at the end of the paper.

MLA Style for In-Text Citations

The MLA style for citing sources is commonly used in English and the humanities. Both in-text citations and a list of works cited are used to document sources, as the models in this chapter show. For more information, consult the following source.

MLA Handbook for Writers of Research Papers. 7th ed. New York: MLA, 2009. Print.

The student paper that appears later in this chapter uses MLA style (see pp. 646–52), as do all student papers in Chapters 6 to 15.

Your paper must include in-text citations for all material you borrow or quote from sources. There are two basic ways to write an in-text citation.

For more on attributions, see p. 609.

1. **Use an attribution.** Mention the author's name early in the sentence or paragraph and include only the page number(s) in parentheses. Use the author's full name the first time you mention the author. After the first mention, give only the author's last name in subsequent citations to the same source.

2. **Use only a parenthetical citation.** Include both the author's last name and the page number(s) in parentheses at the end of the sentence or paragraph. Do not separate the name and page number(s) with a comma.

Many instructors prefer that you use attributions rather than only parenthetical citations. For either type of citation, use the following rules.

- Do not use the word *page* or the abbreviation *p.* or *pp.*
- Place the sentence period after the closing parenthesis unless the citation follows a block quotation. (See p. 611.)
- If a quotation ends the sentence, insert the closing quotation marks before the parentheses.

The following section provides guidelines for formatting in-text citations in MLA style.

A single author

According to Vance Packard . . . (58).

. . . (Packard 58).

Two or three authors.
Include all authors' names, in either an attribution or a parenthetical citation.

Marquez and Allison assert . . . (74).

. . . (Marquez and Allison 74).

Four or more authors.
You may use all of the authors' last names or the first author's last name followed by either a phrase referring to the other authors (in an attribution) or *et al.,* Latin for "and others" (in a parenthetical citation). Whichever option you choose, apply it consistently within your paper.

Hong and colleagues maintain . . . (198).

. . . (Hong et al. 198).

Two or more works by the same author.
When citing two or more sources by the same author or group of authors in your paper, include the full or abbreviated title in the citation to indicate the proper work.

FIRST WORK

In *For God, Country, and Coca-Cola,* Pendergrast describes . . . (96).

Pendergrast describes . . . (*For God* 96).

. . . (Pendergrast, *For God* 96).

SECOND WORK

In *Uncommon Grounds,* Pendergrast maintains . . . (42).

Pendergrast maintains . . . (*Uncommon* 42).

. . . (Pendergrast, *Uncommon* 42).

Corporate or organizational author. When the author of the source is given as a corporation, an organization, or a government office, reference the organization's name as the author name. Use abbreviations such as *Natl.* and *Cong.* in parenthetical references of government authors.

> According to the National Institute of Mental Health . . . (2).
>
> . . . (Natl. Institute of Mental Health 2).

Unknown author. If the author is unknown, use the full title in an attribution or a shortened form in parentheses.

> According to the article "Medical Mysteries and Surgical Surprises," . . . (79).
>
> . . . ("Medical Mysteries" 79).

Authors with the same last name. Include the first initial of these authors in all parenthetical citations. Use the complete first name in an attribution or if both authors have the same first initial.

> John Dillon proposes . . . (974).
>
> . . . (J. Dillon 974).

Two or more sources in the same citation. When citing two or more sources of one idea in parentheses, separate the citations with a semicolon.

> . . . (Breakwater 33; Holden 198).

Entire work. To refer to an entire work, use only the author's name, preferably within the text rather than in a parenthetical reference; do not include page numbers. The title is optional.

> In *For God, Country, and Coca-Cola,* Pendergrast presents an unauthorized history of Coca-Cola--the soft drink--and the company that produces it.

Work within an anthology or textbook. An *anthology* is a collection of writings (articles, stories, poems) by different authors. In the in-text citation, name the author who wrote the work (not the editor of the anthology) and include the page number(s) from the anthology. The corresponding entry in the list of works cited begins with the author's last name; it also names the editor of the anthology.

IN-TEXT CITATION

According to Nora Crow . . . (226).

. . . (Crow 226).

WORKS-CITED ENTRY

Crow, Nora F. "Swift and the Woman Scholar." *Pope, Swift, and Women Writers.* Ed. Donald C. Mell. Newark: U of Delaware P, 1996. 222-38. Print.

Multivolume work. When citing two or more volumes of a multivolume work, indicate the volume number, followed by a colon and the page number.

> Terman indicates . . . (2: 261).
>
> . . . (Terman 2: 261).

Indirect sources. When quoting an indirect source (someone whose ideas came to you through another source, such as a magazine article or book), make this clear by adding, in parentheses, the last name and page number of the source in which the quote or information appeared, preceded by the abbreviation *qtd. in.*

> According to Ephron (qtd. in Thomas 33), . . .

Personal interviews, letters, email, conversations. Give the name of the person in your text.

> In an interview with Professor Lopez, . . .

Literature and poetry. Include information that will help readers locate the material in any edition of the literary work. Include page numbers from the edition you use.

- *For novels:* Cite page and chapter numbers.

  (109; ch. 5)

- *For poems:* Cite line numbers instead of page numbers; use the word *line* or *lines* in the first reference only.

  FIRST REFERENCE   (lines 12-15)

  LATER REFERENCES   (16-18)

- *For plays:* Give the act, scene, and line numbers in arabic numerals, separated by periods.

  (*Macbeth* 2.1.32-37)

  Include complete publication information for the edition you use in the list of works cited.

Internet sources. In general, Internet sources are cited like their printed counterparts. Give enough information in the citation so that readers can locate the source in your list of works cited. If the electronic source provides page numbers, you should provide them too. If the source uses another ordering system, such as paragraphs (*par.* or *pars.*), sections (*sec.*), or screens (*screen*), provide the abbreviation with the appropriate number.

> Brian Beckman argues that "centrifugal force is a fiction" (par. 6).
>
> . . . (Beckman, par. 6).

If the source does not have paragraphs or page numbers, which is often the case, then cite the work by author, title of the document or site, or sponsor of the site.

AUTHOR

Teresa Schmidt discusses . . .

. . . (Schmidt).

TITLE

The "Band of Brothers" section of the History Channel site . . .

. . . ("Band").

SPONSOR

According to a Web page posted by the Council for Indigenous Arts and Culture, . . .

. . . (Council).

MLA Style for the List of Works Cited

For more practice using the MLA style of documentation, visit www.bedfordstmartins .com/successfulwriting/ tutorials.

On a separate page at the end of your paper, you must include an alphabetical list of all the sources you cite. The list is headed *Works Cited*. Follow these general guidelines for preparing the list.

1. **List only the sources you cite in your paper.** If you consulted a source but did not cite it in your paper, do not include it in the list of works cited.
2. **Put the list on a separate page at the end of your paper.** The heading *Works Cited* should be centered an inch below the top margin of the page. Do not use quotation marks, underlining, or bold type for the heading.
3. **Alphabetize the list by authors' last names.** For works with multiple authors, invert only the first author's name.

    Kaplan, Justine, and Anne Bernays. *The Language of Names.* New York:
    Simon, 1997. Print.

4. **Capitalize the first word and all other words in a title except *a, an, the, to,* coordinating conjunctions, and prepositions.**
5. **Italicize titles of books and names of periodicals.**
6. **Give inclusive page numbers of articles in periodicals.** Do not use the word *page* or the abbreviation *p.* or *pp.*
7. **Indent the second and all subsequent lines five spaces.** This is known as the *hanging indent* style.
8. **Double-space the entire list.**

The following sections describe how to format works-cited entries for books, periodicals, Internet sources, and other sources.

Books

General guidelines and sample entries for books follow. Include the following elements, which you will find on the book's title page and copyright page. See Figure 22.4 on page 624 for an example.

1. *Author.* Begin with the author's last name, followed by the first name.

2. *Title.* Provide the full title of the book, including the subtitle. It should be capitalized and italicized.

3. *Place of publication.* Do not abbreviate city names (use *Los Angeles,* not *LA*). Unless the city is not easily recognizable, it is not necessary to include an abbreviation for the state. When you do need to include the state, use the two-letter postal style (e.g., AK, MT).

4. *Publisher.* Use a shortened form of the publisher's name; usually one word is sufficient (*Houghton Mifflin* is listed as *Houghton*). For university presses, use the abbreviations *U* for *University* and *P* for *Press* with no periods.

5. *Date.* Use the most recent publication date listed on the book's copyright page.

6. *Medium.* For books, the medium of publication is *Print.*

MLA FORMAT FOR CITING A BOOK

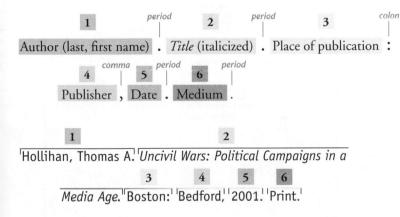

If applicable, also include the original publication date, editor, translator, edition, and volumes used; these should be placed immediately after the title of the work.

Book with one author

Rybczynski, Witold. *The Look of Architecture.* New York: Oxford UP, 2001. Print.

FIGURE 22.4 Where to Find Documentation Information for a Book

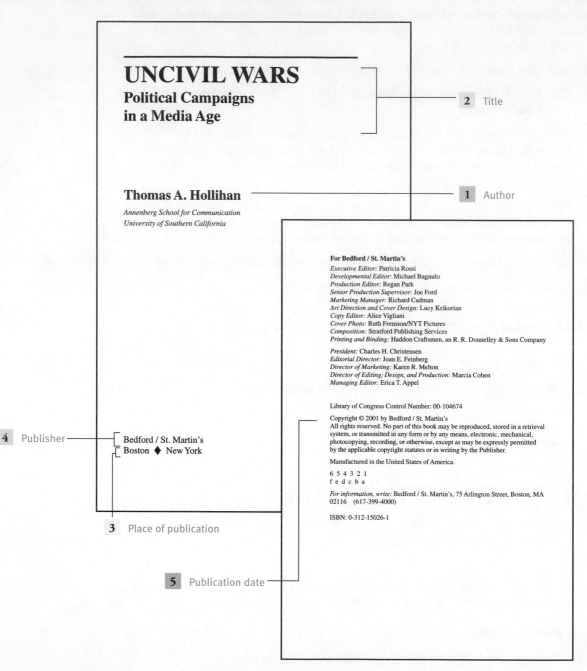

UNCIVIL WARS
Political Campaigns
in a Media Age

2 Title

Thomas A. Hollihan

Annenberg School for Communication
University of Southern California

1 Author

For Bedford / St. Martin's

Executive Editor: Patricia Rossi
Developmental Editor: Michael Bagnulo
Production Editor: Regan Park
Senior Production Supervisor: Joe Ford
Marketing Manager: Richard Cadman
Art Direction and Cover Design: Lucy Krikorian
Copy Editor: Alice Vigliani
Cover Photo: Ruth Fremson/NYT Pictures
Composition: Stratford Publishing Services
Printing and Binding: Haddon Craftsmen, an R. R. Donnelley & Sons Company

President: Charles H. Christensen
Editorial Director: Joan E. Feinberg
Director of Marketing: Karen R. Melton
Director of Editing, Design, and Production: Marcia Cohen
Managing Editor: Erica T. Appel

Library of Congress Control Number: 00-104674

Copyright © 2001 by Bedford / St. Martin's
All rights reserved. No part of this book may be reproduced, stored in a retrieval
system, or transmitted in any form or by any means, electronic, mechanical,
photocopying, recording, or otherwise, except as may be expressly permitted
by the applicable copyright statutes or in writing by the Publisher.

Manufactured in the United States of America.

6 5 4 3 2 1
f e d c b a

For information, write: Bedford / St. Martin's, 75 Arlington Street, Boston, MA
02116   (617-399-4000)

ISBN: 0-312-15026-1

4 Publisher

Bedford / St. Martin's
Boston ◆ New York

3 Place of publication

5 Publication date

Book with two or more authors. List the names in the order they appear on the title page of the book, and separate the names with commas. The second and subsequent authors' names are *not* reversed. For books with four or more authors, you can either list all names or list only the first author's name followed by *et al.*

TWO AUTHORS

Postel, Sandra, and Brian Richter. *Rivers for Life: Managing Water for People and Nature.*
    Washington: Island, 2003. Print.

FOUR OR MORE AUTHORS

Kelly, Rita Mae, et al. *Gender, Globalization, and Democratization.* Lanham.
    Rowman, 2001. Print.

Book with no named author. Put the title first and alphabetize the entry by title. (Do not consider the words *A, An,* and *The* when alphabetizing.)

The New Interpreter's Dictionary of the Bible. Nashville: Abingdon Press, 2006. Print.

Book by a corporation or organization. List the organization or corporation as the author, omitting any initial article (*A, An, The*).

American Medical Association. *American Medical Association Family Medical Guide.*
    Hoboken: Wiley, 2004. Print.

Government publication. If there is no author, list the government followed by the department and agency of the government. Use abbreviations such as *Dept.* and *Natl.* if the meaning is clear.

United States Dept. of Health and Human Services. Natl. Institute of Mental Health.
    Helping Children and Adolescents Cope with Violence and Disasters. Bethesda:
    NIMH, 2001. Print.

Edited book or anthology. List the editor's name followed by a comma and the abbreviation *ed.* or *eds.*

Frazier, Ian, and Jason Wilson, eds. *The Best American Travel Writing 2003.* Boston:
    Houghton, 2003. Print.

Work within an anthology. List the author and title of the work, followed by the title and editor of the anthology (*Ed.* is the abbreviation for "Edited by"); city, publisher, and date; and the pages where the work appears.

Tan, Amy. "Two Kinds." *The Story and Its Writer: An Introduction to Short Fiction.* Ed. Ann
    Charters. Boston: Bedford, 2003. 1278-86. Print.

Introduction, preface, foreword, or afterword

Aaron, Hank. Foreword. *We Are the Ship: The Story of Negro League Baseball.* By Kadir
    Nelson. New York: Jump at the Sun, 2008. Print.

Translated book. After the title, include the abbreviation *Trans.* followed by the first and last names of the translator.

> Houellebecq, Michel. *The Elementary Particles.* Trans. Frank Wynne. New York: Knopf, 2000.
> Print.

Two or more works by the same author(s). Use the author's name for only the first entry. For subsequent entries, use three hyphens followed by a period. List the entries in alphabetical order by title. List works for which the person is the only author before those for which he or she is the first coauthor.

> Covey, Stephen R. *Principle-Centered Leadership.* New York: Simon, 1991. Print.
>
> ---. *The Seven Habits of Highly Effective People: Restoring the Character Ethic.* New York:
> Simon, 1989. Print.
>
> Ehrenreich, Barbara. *Nickel and Dimed: On (Not) Getting By in America.* New York:
> Metropolitan, 2001. Print.
>
> Ehrenreich, Barbara, and Deirdre English. *For Her Own Good: Two Centuries of the Experts'*
> *Advice to Women.* New York: Anchor, 2005. Print.

Edition other than the first. Indicate the number of the edition following the title.

> Myers, David G. *Exploring Psychology.* 5th ed. New York: Worth, 2002. Print.

Multivolume work. Give the number of volumes after the title.

> Kazdin, Alan E., ed. *Encyclopedia of Psychology.* 8 vols. Washington: American
> Psychological Association, 2000. Print.

Encyclopedia or dictionary entry. Note that when citing well-known reference books, you do not need to give the full publication information, just the edition and year.

> "Triduum." *Merriam-Webster's Collegiate Dictionary.* 11th ed. 2003. Print.
>
> Levi, Anthony. "Maxim." *Encyclopedia of the Essay.* Ed. Tracy Chevalier. London: Fitzroy, 1997.
> Print.

One volume of a multivolume work. Give the volume number after the title, and list the number of volumes in the complete work after the date, using the abbreviations *Vol.* and *vols.*

> Kazdin, Alan E., ed. *Encyclopedia of Psychology.* Vol. 3. Washington: American
> Psychological Association, 2000. Print. 8 vols.

Article or chapter in a compilation. List the author and title of the article first and then the title of the anthology, the editor's name (introduced by the abbreviation *Ed.*, for "Edited by"), and the publication information.

> McGowan, Moray. "Multiple Masculinities in Turkish-German Men's Writing." *Conceptions of*
> *Postwar German Masculinity.* Ed. M. Kimmel. Albany: State U of New York P, 2001. 310-20.
> Print.

If more than one of these rules applies to a source, cite the necessary information in the order given in the preceding examples. For instance, to cite a reading from this textbook, treat it as a **work within an anthology (p. 625) in an edition other than the first (p. 626)**. To do this, list the author and title of the reading followed by the title of this book, the editor, the edition number, and all other publication information.

> Bernstein, Nell. "Goin' Gangsta, Choosin' Cholita: Claiming Identity." *Successful College*
>
> *Writing: Skills, Strategies, Learning Styles.* Ed. Kathleen T. McWhorter. 4th ed. Boston:
>
> Bedford, 2009. 292-95. Print.

Articles in Periodicals

General guidelines and sample entries for various types of periodical articles follow. Include the following elements, most of which you should find on the first page of the article. See Figure 22.5 for an example.

1. *Author.* Use the same format for listing authors' names as for books (see p. 623). If no author is listed, begin the entry with the article title and alphabetize the entry by its title.

2. *Article title.* The title should appear in double quotation marks; a period falls inside the ending quotation mark.

3. *Periodical title.* Italicize the title of the periodical. Do *not* include the word *A, An,* or *The* at the beginning: *Journal of the American Medical Association, New York Times.*

4. *Volume/issue and date.* For magazines and newspapers, list just the date in the following order: day, month, year; abbreviate the names of months except for *May, June,* and *July.* For scholarly journals, give the volume and issue numbers and then just the year in parentheses.

5. *Page(s).* If an article begins in one place, such as pages 19 to 21, and is continued elsewhere, such as on pages 79 to 80, just write *19+* for the page numbers (do *not* write 19–80).

6. *Medium.* For periodicals, the medium of publication is *Print.*

The basic format for citing a periodical article is as follows.

MLA FORMAT FOR CITING A PERIODICAL ARTICLE

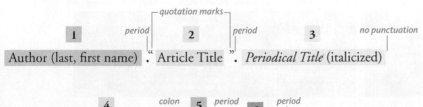

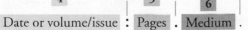

Magazine or newspaper article

1   **2**

Levy, Steven. "In the New Game of Tag, All of Us Are It."

3   **4**   **5** **6**

Newsweek 18 Apr. 2005: 14. Print.

FIGURE 22.5 Where to Find Documentation Information for an Article

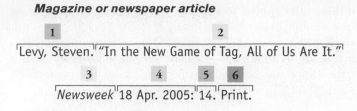

1 Author

2 Article title

5 Page

3 Periodical title

4 Date

Scholarly journal article

1   2   3

Prose, Francine. "Genocide without Apology." *American Scholar*

4   5   6

72.2 (2005): 39-43. Print.

Article in a scholarly journal when each issue begins with page 1. After the journal title, include the volume number, a period, and the issue number, followed by the year in parentheses, a colon, and the inclusive page numbers.

> Schug, Mark C., and J. R. Clark. "Economics for the Heart and the Head." *International Journal of Social Education* 16.1 (2001): 45-54. Print.

Article in a scholarly journal with issues paged continuously through each volume. Again, both the volume and issue numbers precede the year.

> Lawson, David M. "The Development of Abusive Personality: A Trauma Response." *Journal of Counseling and Development* 79.4 (2001): 505-09. Print.

Article in a newspaper

> Gay, Joel. "Glorious Wreck Rears Its Head." *Anchorage Daily News* 8 Sept. 2004, final ed.: A1+. Print.

Article in a monthly magazine

> Bethell, Tom. "Democracy: A Little Goes a Long Way." *American Spectator* Nov. 2003: 42-43. Print.

Article in a weekly magazine

> Henneberger, Melinda. "Tending to the Flock." *Newsweek* 13 Sept. 2004: 34-36. Print.

Editorial or letter to the editor. Cite the article or letter beginning with the author's name, and add the word *Editorial* or *Letter* followed by a period after the title. An author's name or a title may be missing.

> "The Search for Livable Worlds." Editorial. *New York Times* 8 Sept. 2004: A22. Print.

> Wolansky, Taras. Letter. *Wired* May 2004: 25. Print.

Book or film review. List the reviewer's name and title of the review. After the title, add the words *Rev. of* and give the title and author or director of the book or film reviewed. Include publication information for the review itself, not for the material reviewed.

> Gabler, Neal. "The Rise and Rise of Celebrity Journalism." Rev. of *The Untold Story: My Twenty Years Running the* National Enquirer, by Iain Calder, and *The Importance of Being Famous: Behind the Scenes of the Celebrity Industrial Complex,* by Maureen Orth. *Columbia Journalism Review* July/Aug. 2004: 48-51. Print.

Internet Sources

Citations for Internet sources should include enough information to enable readers to locate the sources. Because electronic sources change frequently, it is often necessary to provide more information than you do for print sources. MLA style does not require a network address or URL (uniform resource locator) for an online source, but your instructor may ask you to include one. If so, give the URL at the end of your citation, enclosed in angle brackets (< >). If a URL is too long to fit on one line, divide it only following a slash.

Citing Internet sources may not be as straightforward as citing print sources because Web sites differ in how much information they provide and where and how they provide it. As a general rule, give as many of the following elements as possible, and list them in the order shown.

1. *Author.* Include the name of the person or organization if it is available.

2. *Title of the work.* Enclose titles of articles in quotation marks; italicize the titles of longer works.

3. *Print publication information.* If the material was originally published in print, tell where and when it was originally published. Include volume and issue numbers, names of periodicals, names of publishers, dates, and so forth.

4. *Electronic publication information.* The information here will differ depending on the type of Web site.
  a. To cite an entire Web site or a document on a general Web site, provide as many of the following as are available: title of site (italicized); the sponsoring organization; and date of publication or last update.
  b. To cite an article in an online periodical, give all the information you would give for a print source: periodical title, volume/issue, and date.

5. *Medium.* For Internet sources, the medium of publication is *Web.*

6. *Access date.* Include the date you accessed the document (day, month, year).

Some sample citations for different kinds of Internet sources are given below.

MLA FORMAT FOR CITING INTERNET SOURCES

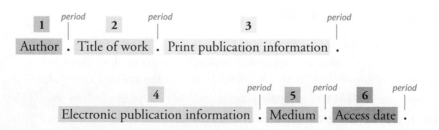

Entire Web site

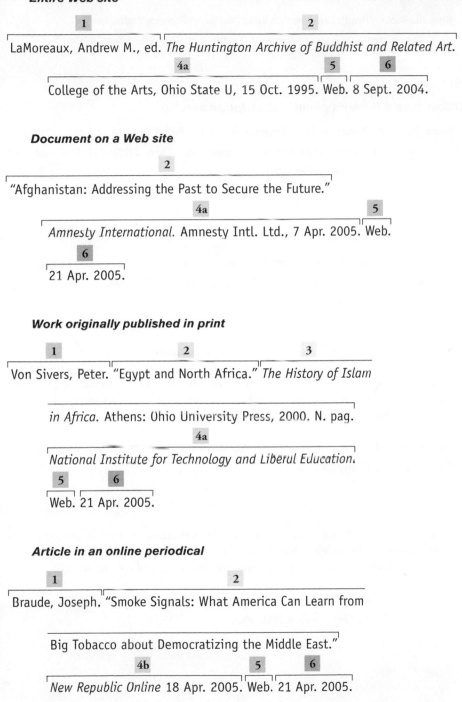

1 LaMoreaux, Andrew M., ed. **2** *The Huntington Archive of Buddhist and Related Art.*

4a College of the Arts, Ohio State U, 15 Oct. 1995. **5** Web. **6** 8 Sept. 2004.

Document on a Web site

2 "Afghanistan: Addressing the Past to Secure the Future."

4a *Amnesty International.* Amnesty Intl. Ltd., 7 Apr. 2005. **5** Web.

6 21 Apr. 2005.

Work originally published in print

1 Von Sivers, Peter. **2** "Egypt and North Africa." **3** *The History of Islam*

in Africa. Athens: Ohio University Press, 2000. N. pag.

4a *National Institute for Technology and Liberal Education.*

5 Web. **6** 21 Apr. 2005.

Article in an online periodical

1 Braude, Joseph. **2** "Smoke Signals: What America Can Learn from

Big Tobacco about Democratizing the Middle East."

4b *New Republic Online* 18 Apr. 2005. **5** Web. **6** 21 Apr. 2005.

Article from an online journal

Kimball, Bobbi. "Health Care's Human Crisis: Rx for an Evolving Profession."
Online Journal of Issues in Nursing 9.2 (2004): n. pag. Web. 8 Sept. 2004.

Article from a library's online subscription service

Wood, Robert A. "School as a Risk Environment for Children Allergic to Cats and a Site of
Transfer of Cat Allergen to Homes." *Pediatrics* 106.2 (Aug. 2000): 431. *Expanded
Academic ASAP.* Web. 4 Oct. 2001.

Online government document

United States, Federal Bureau of Investigation. *The Terrorist Threat to the U.S. Homeland.*
July 2007. *Off. of the Dir. of Natl. Intelligence.* Web. 18 Mar. 2008.

Posting to an online discussion group or newsgroup. For a discussion group,
include the author's name, the title or subject line enclosed in quotation marks, the
name of the Web site on which the group is found, the sponsor of the site, the date
of posting, the medium, and the date of access. If possible, cite an archived version.
If the posting has no title, label it *Online posting*.

McCarty, Willard. "Smart Medicines?" *Humanist Discussion Group.* Centre for Computing in
the Humanities, 10 May 2004. Web. 8 Sept. 2004.

Online book. Include the author's name; title (italicized); the name of any editor,
translator, or compiler; original publication information (if available); the name of the
Web site on which the online book appears; the medium; and date of access.

Twain, Mark. *A Connecticut Yankee in King Arthur's Court.* New York: Harper, 1889.
Electronic Text Center. Web. 8 Sept. 2004.

Other Sources

DVD-ROM or CD-ROM. Include the title, publication information, and the medium.

> *Mosby's Nursing Skills.* St Louis: Mosby, 2006. CD-ROM.

Personal communication (interview, letter, email). Indicate the name of the person, followed by the type of communication and the date. For interviews you conducted, indicate the type of interview (telephone, personal, email, and so forth). For a letter, include the designation *MS* for a manuscript (a letter written by hand) or *TS* for a typescript (a letter composed on a machine). For emails, include the subject line (if available) in quotation marks.

> Thompson, Alan. Telephone interview. 19 Jan. 2002.
>
> Chevez, Maria. Letter to the author. 14 July 2001. TS.
>
> Morales, Anita. "Antique China." Message to Ruth E. Thompson. 11 Jan. 2002. E-mail.

Published interview. List the person interviewed, and then list the title of the interview (if available) in quotation marks. If the interview has no title, label it *Interview.* Give the publication details for the source in which the interview was found.

> Everett, Percival. Interview. *Bomb* Summer 2004: 46-51. Print.

Published letter. If the letter was published, cite it as you would a selection in a book.

> Lewis, C. S. "To His Father (LPIII: 82)." 4 Sept. 1907. *The Collected Letters of*
> *C. S. Lewis, Vol. 1: Family Letters, 1905-1931.* Ed. Walter Hooper. San Francisco:
> Harper, 2004. 5. Print.

Film, video, or DVD. List the title, director, and key performer(s). Include the original release date before the name of the distributor, the year of distribution, and the medium.

> *The Big Sleep.* Dir. Howard Hawks. Perf. Humphrey Bogart and Lauren Bacall. 1946.
> Warner Home Video, 2000. DVD.

Television or radio program. List the title of the program (italicized), then give key names (narrator, producer, director, actors) as necessary and the title of the series (neither underlined nor in quotation marks). Identify the network, local station and city, and broadcast date. When citing a particular episode or segment, include its title in quotation marks before the title of the program.

> "Beyond Vietnam." *Alternative Radio.* Narr. David Barsamian. Natl. Public Radio. KUOW, Seattle, 25 Aug. 2004. Radio.

Music recording. List the composer or performer, the title of the recording or composition, the names of the artists, the medium (CD, audiocassette, LP, audiotape), the production company, and the date. Titles of recordings should be italicized, but titles of compositions identified by form (for example, Symphony No. 5) should not.

> Lloyd-Webber, Andrew. *Phantom of the Opera.* Perf. Michael Crawford, Sarah Brightman, and Steve Barton. Polydor, 1987. LP.

Documenting Your Sources: APA Style

APA style, recommended by the American Psychological Association, is commonly used in the social sciences. Both in-text citations and a list of references are used to document sources, as the following models show. For more information on citing print and other nonelectronic sources, consult the following reference work.

> American Psychological Association. *Publication Manual of the American Psychological Association.* 5th ed. Washington, DC: APA, 2001.

For more information and the latest APA guidelines on citing electronic sources, go to http://apastyle.apa.org/elecmedia.html. This page is excerpted from the *APA Style Guide to Electronic References*, an online publication that is available for purchase at http://books.apa.org/books.cfm?id=4210509 and that may also be available through your library; check with a reference librarian.

APA Style for In-Text Citations

Your paper must include in-text citations for all material you borrow or quote from sources. There are two basic ways to write an in-text citation.

1. **Use an attribution and a parenthetical citation.** Mention the author's name in a phrase or sentence introducing the material, and include the year of publication in parentheses immediately following the author's name. For quotations, include a page number at the end of the cited material.

2. **Use only a parenthetical citation.** Include both the author's last name and the year of publication in parentheses at the end of the sentence. Separate the name, year, and page number (if any) with commas.

Many instructors prefer that you use attributions rather than only parenthetical citations. For either type of citation, use the following rules.

- Place the sentence period after the closing parenthesis. When a quotation ends the sentence, insert the closing quotation mark before the opening parenthesis. Block quotations are an exception to these rules; see page 611.
- For direct quotations and paraphrases, include the page number after the year, separating it from the year with a comma. Use the abbreviation *p.* or *pp.* followed by a space and the page number.

ATTRIBUTION

Masson and McCarthy (1995) maintain that emotions of "captive wild animals are as real as those of wild animals" (7).

PARENTHETICAL CITATION

The emotions of "captive wild animals are as real as those of wild animals" (Masson & McCarthy, 1995, p. 7).

The following section provides guidelines for formatting in-text citations in the APA style.

A single author

According to Packard (1957), . . .

. . . (Packard, 1957).

Two authors.
Include both authors' last names and the year in an attribution or a parenthetical citation. In the latter case, use an ampersand (*&*) in place of the word *and*.

Masson and McCarthy (1995) assert . . .

. . . (Masson & McCarthy, 1995).

Three to five authors.
Include all authors' last names the first time the source is mentioned. In subsequent references to the same source, use the first author's last name followed by *et al.* (Latin for "and others").

FIRST REFERENCE

Hong, Kingston, DeWitt, and Bell (1996) have found . . .

. . . (Hong, Kingston, DeWitt, & Bell, 1996).

LATER REFERENCES

Hong et al. (1996) discovered . . .

. . . (Hong et al., 1996).

Six or more authors. Use the first author's last name followed by *et al.* in all in-text citations.

Two or more works by the same author in the same year. Add the lowercase letter *a* after the publication year for the first source as it appears alphabetically by title in your reference list. Add the letter *b* to the publication year for the source that appears next, and so forth. Include the years with the corresponding lowercase letters in your in-text citations. (See p. 640 for the corresponding reference entries.)

Gardner (1995a) believes that . . .

. . . (Gardner, 1995a).

Two or more works by the same author(s). Cite the works chronologically, in order of publication.

Gilbert (1988, 1993) believes that . . .

. . . (Gilbert, 1988, 1993).

Authors with the same last name. Use the authors' initials with their last names.

Research by F. P. Lopez (1997) demonstrated . . .

According to C. Lopez (1993), . . .

Unknown author. Use the title and year in the attribution or parenthetical citation. Give only the first two or three important words of a long title. Underline a book title; put the title of a journal article in quotation marks. Unlike the entry in the list of references, use standard capitalization in the in-text citation. (See p. 638.)

As noted in "Medical Mysteries" (1993), . . .

. . . ("Medical Mysteries," 1993).

Two or more sources in the same citation. When citing two or more sources in parentheses, put a semicolon between them and list them in alphabetical order.

(Breakwater, 1986; Holden, 1996)

Entire work. To refer to an entire work, give the author's name and the year. The title is optional; do not include page numbers.

Pendergrast (1997) presents an unauthorized history of Coca-Cola—the soft drink—and the company that produces it.

Work within an anthology. An *anthology* is a collection of writings by different authors. In the in-text citation, name the author who wrote the work (*not* the editor of the anthology) and give the year. The corresponding entry in the list of references begins with the author's last name; it also names the editor of the anthology.

IN-TEXT CITATION

As Kaul (1995) notes, . . .

. . . (Kaul, 1995).

REFERENCES ENTRY

Kaul, P. (1995). The unraveling of America. In L. Chiasson, Jr. (Ed.), *The press in times of crisis* (pp. 169–187). Westport, CT: Greenwood.

Multivolume work. When you cite one volume of a multivolume work, include the year of publication for that volume.

Terman (1990) indicates . . .

. . . (Terman, 1990).

When you cite two or more volumes of a multivolume work, give inclusive years for the volumes.

Terman (1990–1991) indicates . . .

Indirect sources. When you quote a source indirectly (rather than from the original source), include the abbreviation *qtd. in* along with the information for the source in which you found the quote.

According to Ephron, . . . (qtd. in Thomas, 1994, p. 33).

Personal interviews, letters, email, and conversations. Give the last name and initial of the person, the source of the communication, and the exact date. Do not include these sources in the list of references.

Professor B. Lopez (personal communication, October 30, 2001) asserts that . . .

Internet sources. For direct quotations, give the author, year, and page (if available) in the attribution or parenthetical citation. If paragraph numbers are available, cite them with the paragraph symbol (¶) or the abbreviation *para*. If the author is unknown, use the document title in place of the author. If the date is unknown, use the abbreviation *n.d.*

Stevens (1997) maintains . . .

. . . (Stevens, 1997).

*For more practice using the
APA style of documentation,
visit www.bedfordstmartins
.com/successfulwriting/
tutorials.*

APA Style for the List of References

On a separate page at the end of your paper, you must include an alphabetical list of all the sources you cite. The list is headed *References.* Follow these general guidelines for preparing the list.

1. **List only the sources you cite in your paper.** If you consulted a source but did not cite it in your paper, do not include it in the list of references.
2. **Put the list on a separate page at the end of your paper.** The heading *References* should be centered about an inch below the top margin of the page. Do not use quotation marks, underlining, or bold type for the heading.
3. **Alphabetize the list by authors' last names.** Give the last name first, followed by a comma and an initial or initials. Do not spell out authors' first names; use a space between initials: *Myers, D. G.* For works with multiple authors, list all authors' names in inverted order.

   Kaplan, J., & Bernays, A. (1997). *The language of names.* New York: Simon.

4. **Put the publication date in parentheses after the author's name.**
5. **Capitalize the first word of the titles of books and articles, the first word following a colon, and any proper nouns.** All other words are lowercase.
6. **Include the word *A, An,* or *The* at the beginning of titles.** The word *The* is dropped from the titles of journals, however.
7. **Italicize titles of books and names of journals.** If your instructors prefer, use underlining instead of italics. Do not italicize, underline, or use quotation marks with article titles.
8. **For magazine and journal articles, italicize the name of the publication and the volume number.** The punctuation and spaces between these elements are also italicized. Italicize the names of newspapers. Capitalize all important words in the names of periodicals.
9. **Indent the second and all subsequent lines five spaces.** This is the hanging-indent style, which the APA recommends for student papers.
10. **Double-space the entire list.**

The following sections describe how to format reference list entries for books, articles in periodicals, Internet sources, and other sources.

Books

The basic format for a book is as follows.

1 *Author.* Give the author's last name and initial(s). Do not spell out authors' first names; include a space between initials: *Myers, D. G.*

2 *Year.* Include the year of publication in parentheses following the author's name. Use the most recent copyright year if more than one is given.

3 *Title.* Italicize the title of the book. If you underline instead of italicize, be sure to underline the period that follows the title.

4 *Place of publication.* Give the city of publication followed by a colon. If the city is not well known, add the postal abbreviation for the state (*Hillsdale, NJ:*).

5 *Publisher.* Include the name of the publisher followed by a period. Use a short-ened form of the publisher's name: *Houghton Mifflin* would be listed as *Houghton,* for example. Do not omit the word *Books* or *Press* if it is part of the publisher's name: *Academic Press, Basic Books.*

APA FORMAT FOR CITING A BOOK

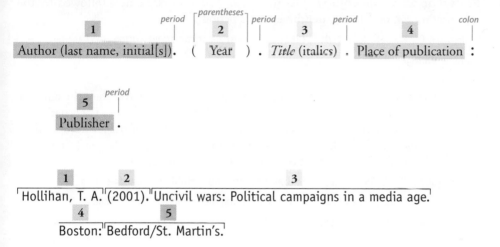

Book with one author

Rybczynski, W. (2001). *The look of architecture.* New York: Oxford University Press.

Book with two or more authors. List all authors' names in the order they appear on the book's title page. Use inverted order (*last name, initial*) for all authors' names. Separate the names with commas and use an ampersand (*&*) in place of the word *and.* Do not use *et al.* in the reference list unless the book has six or more authors.

Douglas, S., & Michaels, M. (2004). *The mommy myth: The idealization of motherhood and how it has undermined women.* New York: Free Press.

Postel, S., & Richter, B. (2003). *Rivers for life: Managing water for people and nature.* Washington, DC: Island Press.

Book with no named author. Give the full title first, and alphabetize the entry by title. (Do not consider the words *A, An,* or *The* when alphabetizing.)

The new interpreter's dictionary of the Bible. (2006). Nashville: Abingdon Press.

Book by an agency or a corporation. List the agency as the author. If the publisher is the same as the author, write *Author* for the name of the publisher.

Ford Foundation. (2003). *Celebrating Indonesia: Fifty years with the Ford Foundation, 1953–2003.* Jakarta: Author, 2003.

Government publication. List the agency as the author, followed by the date. Include the document or publication number if available.

> Environmental Protection Agency. (2001). *Providing solutions for a better tomorrow:*
> > *Reducing the risks associated with lead in soil.* EPA Publication No. EPA/600/F-01/014.
> > Washington, DC: U.S. Government Printing Office.

Edited book or anthology. List the editor's or editors' names, followed by the abbreviation *Ed.* or *Eds.* in parentheses and a period.

> Penzler, O., & Cook, T. H. (Eds.). (2004). *The best American crime writing.* New York:
> > Vintage.

Work within an anthology. List the author of the work first and then the date the work was published in the anthology. The title of the work follows. Then name the editor of the anthology (not in inverted order), give the title of the anthology (italicized), and include the inclusive page numbers in parentheses for the work (preceded by *pp.*). The publication information follows in normal order.

> Dachyshyn, D. (2006). Refugee families with preschool children: Adjustment to
> > life in Canada. In L. Adams (Ed.), *Global migration and education: Schools,*
> > *children and families* (pp. 251–262). London: Lawrence Erlbaum Associates.

Translated book. After the title, include the initial(s) and last name of the translator followed by a comma and *Trans.*

> Tolstoy, L. (1972). *War and peace.* (C. Garnett, Trans.). London: Pan. (Original work
> > published 1869)

Two or more works by the same author(s). Begin each entry with the author's name. Arrange the entries in chronological order of publication.

> Pollan, M. (2006). *The omnivore's dilemma: A natural history of four meals.* New York:
> > Penguin.
> Pollan, M. (2008). *In defense of food: An eater's manifesto.* New York: Penguin.

Two or more works by the same author in the same year. Arrange the works alphabetically by title; then assign a lowercase letter (*a, b, c*) to the year of publication for each source. (See p. 636 for the corresponding in-text citation.)

> Orman, S. (2003a). *The laws of money, the lessons of life: Keep what you have and*
> > *create what you deserve.* New York: Free Press.
> Orman, S. (2003b). *The road to wealth: A comprehensive guide to your money.* New York:
> > Riverhead.

Edition other than the first

Myers, D. G. (2002). *Exploring psychology* (5th ed.). New York: Worth.

Multivolume work. Give the inclusive volume numbers in parentheses after the title. If all volumes were not published in the same year, the publication date should include the range of years.

McAuliffe, J. D. (Ed.). (2001–2006). *Encyclopedia of the Qur'an* (Vols. 1–5). Leiden: Brill.

Article in a multivolume work. Include the author and title of the article, as well as the title, volume number, and publication information for the work.

Meerdink, J. E. (2006). Sleep. In *Encyclopedia of human development* (Vol. 3,

pp. 1180–1181). Thousand Oaks, CA: Sage.

If more than one of these rules applies to a source, cite the necessary information in the order given in the preceding examples. For instance, to cite a reading from this textbook, treat it as a **work within an anthology (p. 640) in an edition other than the first (above)**. To do this, list the author of the reading, the date the reading was published in the anthology, the title of the reading, the editor and the title of this book, the edition number, the pages where the reading appears, and all other publication information.

Bernstein, N. (2009). Goin' gangsta, choosin' cholita: Claiming identity. In K. T. McWhorter (Ed.),

Successful college writing: Skills, strategies, learning styles (4th ed., pp. 292–95).

Boston: Bedford/St. Martin's.

Articles in Periodicals

General guidelines and sample entries for various types of periodical articles follow.

1 *Author.* Follow the basic format for listing authors' names (see p. 638). If no author is listed, begin with the article title and alphabetize the entry by its title.

2 *Date.* The year of publication appears in parentheses following the author's name. For articles in newspapers and magazines, the issue month and day follow the year.

3 *Article title.* Do not enclose article titles in quotation marks, and do not use standard capitalization. Only the first word of an article title is capitalized, along with any proper nouns and the first word following a colon.

4 *Periodical title.* Italicize the name of the periodical. Use standard capitalization for the titles of periodicals.

5 *Volume/issue.* For scholarly journals only, give the volume number in italics; if needed, give the issue number in parentheses and roman type.

6 *Pages.* The abbreviation *p.* or *pp.* is used only in entries for newspaper articles.

APA FORMAT FOR CITING A PERIODICAL ARTICLE

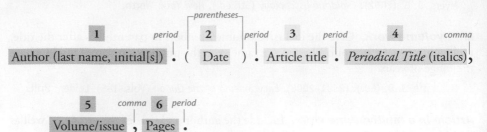

┌─ parentheses ─┐
1 *period* **2** *period* **3** *period* **4** *comma*
Author (last name, initial[s]) . (Date) . Article title . *Periodical Title* (italics) ,

5 *comma* **6** *period*
Volume/issue , Pages .

Magazine or newspaper article

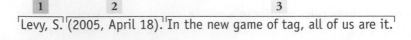

1   **2**   **3**
Levy, S. (2005, April 18). In the new game of tag, all of us are it.

4   **6**
Newsweek, 14.

Scholarly journal article

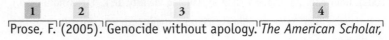

1   **2**   **3**   **4**
Prose, F. (2005). Genocide without apology. *The American Scholar,*

5   **6**
72(2), 39–43.

Article in a scholarly journal when each issue begins with page 1

Schug, M. C., & Clark, J. R. (2001). Economics for the heart and the head. *International Journal of Social Education, 16*(1), 45–54.

Article in a scholarly journal with issues paged continuously through each volume

Lawson, D. M. (2001). The development of abusive personality: A trauma response. *Journal of Counseling and Development, 79,* 505–509.

Article in a newspaper. Include the year, month, and day in parentheses following the author's name. Page numbers for newspaper articles should be preceded by a *p.* or *pp.*

Norris, F. (2001, September 13). A symbol was destroyed, not America's financial system. *The New York Times,* p. C1.

Article in a monthly magazine. Include the month of publication after the year.

Bethell, T. (2003, November). Democracy: A little goes a long way. *American Spectator*, 42–43.

Article in a weekly magazine. Give year, month, and day of publication.

Henneberger, M. (2004, September 13). Tending to the flock. *Newsweek*, 34–36.

Editorial or letter to the editor. Cite the editorial or letter beginning with the author's name (if available) and *Editorial* or *Letter to the editor* in brackets. If the author's name is not available, begin with the title.

The search for livable worlds [Editorial]. (2004, September 8). *The New York Times*, p. A22.

Wolansky, T. (2004, May) [Letter to the editor]. *Wired*, 25.

Book or film review. List the reviewer's name, the date, and the title of the review. In brackets, give a description of the work reviewed, including the medium (*book* or *motion picture*) and the title.

Gabler, N. (2004, July-August). Ephemera: The rise and fall of celebrity journalism.

[Review of the books *The untold story: My twenty years running the* National Enquirer

and *The importance of being famous: Behind the scenes of the celebrity-industrial*

complex]. *CJR*, 48–51.

Article with no author. Use the full title as the author.

The economy's bonus setback. (2002, January 14). *BusinessWeek*, 24.

Internet Sources

For Internet sources, include enough information to allow readers to locate the sources online. Guidelines for documenting Internet sources follow. For more help with formatting entries for Internet and other electronic sources in APA style, consult *Electronic Media and URLs* on the American Psychological Association's Web site at http://apastyle.apa.org/elecmedia.html.

1. Give the author's name, if available. If not, begin the entry with the name of the sponsor of the site or with the title of the document.

2. Include in parentheses the year of Internet publication or the year of the most recent update, if available. If there is no date, use the abbreviation *n.d.*

3. Capitalize the first word of the title of the document or subject line of the message, the first word following a colon, and any proper nouns. The other words are lowercase.

4. End with *Retrieved from* followed by the URL at which you accessed the source. The URL is not followed by a period.

The basic APA format for an Internet source is as follows.

APA FORMAT FOR CITING INTERNET SOURCES

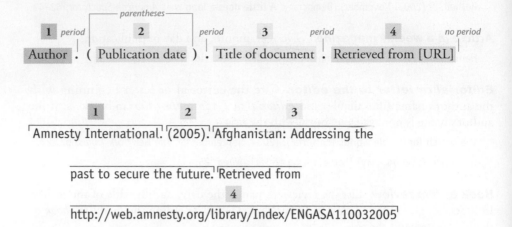

Document posted on an organization's Web site. If the document is not dated or the content could change, include a retrieval date.

> American Civil Liberties Union. (2004). Death penalty: A question of innocence.
>> Retrieved September 8, 2004, from http://www.aclu.org/DeathPenalty/DeathPenalty.
>> cfm?ID=9316&c=65

Article from an online journal. Provide page numbers if available. If the article has a Digital Object Identifier (DOI)—a unique letter/number combination that some journals assign to online articles—use the DOI instead of the URL. Look for the DOI in the database where you get the name and author of the article.

> Schubert, C. (2008). The need to consider the impact of previous stressors on current stress
>> parameter measurements. *Stress: The International Journal on the Biology of Stress,*
>> *11*(2), 85–87. doi:10.1080/10253890801895811

For articles with no DOI, give the full URL if the article is freely available. If the article requires a subscription to obtain it, use the URL for the journal's home page.

> Treharne, G. J., Lyons, A. C., & Tupling, R. E. (2001, December 17). The effects of
>> optimism, pessimism, social support, and mood on the lagged relationship between
>> daily stress and symptoms. *Current Research in Social Psychology, 7*(5). Retrieved
>> from http://www.uiowa.edu/~grpproc/crisp/crisp.7.5.htm

Online encyclopedia article

> Calef, S. (2008). Dualism and mind. In J. Fieser & B. Dowden (Eds.), *The Internet*
>> *encyclopedia of philosophy*. Retrieved May 6, 2008, from http://www.iep.utm.edu/

Online newspaper article

> Sullivan, P. (2008, May 6). Quiet Va. wife ended interracial marriage ban. *The*
> *Washington Post*. Retrieved May 6, 2008, from http://www.washingtonpost.com

Online government document

> Federal Bureau of Investigation. (2007). *The terrorist threat to the U.S. homeland.*
> Retrieved from http://www.dni.gov/press_releases/20070717_release.pdf

Other Sources

Film, video, or DVD

> Greenfield, L. (Director). (2006). Thin [Motion picture]. New York: Home Box Office.

Television program. Use the producer's name as the author unless you are citing a dramatic or fictional series. In that case, use the scriptwriter's name as the author, followed by the director. Give titles for individuals in parentheses after their names.

> Dochtery, N. (Producer). (2001, February 13). Hackers [Television series episode]. *Frontline.*
> Boston: WGBH.

Computer software. If a person has proprietary rights to the software, list that person's name. If not, use the format for a work with an unknown author.

> Mitterer, J. (1993). Dynamic concepts in psychology [Computer software]. Orlando, FL:
> Harcourt.

Research Paper in Progress 9

For the final paper you prepared in Research Paper in Progress 8, prepare a list of works cited or a reference list, following your instructor's preference.

Students Write

The following research paper was written by Nicholas Destino for his first-year writing course while he was a student at Niagara County Community College. Destino used the MLA style for formatting his paper and documenting sources. Notice his use of in-text citations and quotations to provide evidence in support of his thesis.

Destino 1

Nicholas Destino

Professor Thomas

English 101

10 November 2008

Double-spaced

Centered title

Do Animals Have Emotions?

Somewhere in the savannas of Africa a mother elephant is dying in the company of many other pachyderms. Some of them are part of her family; some are fellow members of her herd. The dying elephant tips from side to side and seems to be balancing on a thin thread in order to sustain her life. Many of the other elephants surround her as she struggles to regain her balance. They also try to help by feeding and caressing her. After many attempts by the herd to save her life, they seem to realize that there is simply nothing more that can be done. She finally collapses to the ground in the presence of her companions. Most of the other elephants move away from the scene. There are, however, two elephants who remain behind with the dead elephant--another mother and her calf. The mother turns her back to the body and taps it with one foot. Soon the other elephants call for them to follow and eventually they do (Masson and McCarthy, *Elephants* 95). These movements, which are slow and ritualistic, suggest that elephants may be capable of interpreting and responding to the notion of death.

In-text citation of a work with two authors; short title included because another work by these authors is cited later in the essay

The topic of animal emotions is one that, until recently, has rarely been discussed or studied by scientists. However, since the now-famous comprehensive field studies of chimpanzees by the internationally renowned primatologist Jane Goodall, those who study animal behavior have begun to look more closely at the notion that animals feel emotions. As a result of their observations of various species of animals, a number of these researchers have come to the conclusion that animals do exhibit a wide range of emotions, such as grief, sympathy, and joy.

Thesis statement

One of the major reasons that research into animal emotions was traditionally avoided is that scientists fear being accused of *anthropomorphism*--the act

Destino 2

of attributing human qualities to animals. To do so is perceived as unscientific (Masson and McCarthy, "Hope and Joy" xviii). Frans de Waal, of the Yerkes Regional Primate Research Center in Atlanta, believes that if people are not open to the possibility of animals having emotions, they may be overlooking important information about both animals and humans. He explains his position in his article "Are We in Anthropodenial?" The term *anthropodenial,* which he coined, refers to "a blindness to the humanlike characteristics of other animals, or the animal-like characteristics of ourselves" (52). De Waal proposes that because humans and animals are so closely related, it would be impossible for one not to have some characteristics of the other. He contends, "If two closely related species act in the same manner, their underlying mental processes are probably the same, too" (53). If de Waal is correct, then humans can presume that animals do have emotions because of the many similarities between human and animal behavior.

Grief has been observed in many different species. In many instances, their behaviors (and presumably, therefore, their emotions) are uncannily similar to the behaviors of humans. Birds, which mate for life, have been observed showing obvious signs of grief when their mates die. In *The Human Nature of Birds,* Theodore Barber includes a report from one Dr. Franklin, who witnessed a male parrot caring for his mate by feeding her and trying to help her raise herself when she was dying. Franklin observed the following scene:

> Her unhappy spouse moved around her incessantly, his attention
> and tender cares redoubled. He even tried to open her beak to give
> her some nourishment. . . . At intervals, he uttered the most plain-
> tive cries, then with his eyes fixed on her, kept a mournful silence. At
> length his companion breathed her last; from that moment he pined
> away, and died in the course of a few weeks. (qtd. in Barber 116)

Veterinarian Susan Wynn, discussing the physiological symptoms brought on by emotional trauma in animals, notes that "[a]nimals definitely exhibit grief when they lose an owner or another companion animal. . . . Signs of grief vary widely, including lethargy, loss of appetite, hiding . . ." (5). This observation re-

Marginal annotations:

Attribution of summaries and quotations within text

Page numbers follow quotations

Attributions of paraphrase and quotation

Clear topic sentence introduces first main point

Quotation longer than four lines indented ten spaces and not enclosed in quotation marks; period precedes citation

Citation for an indirect source

First letter of a quotation changed to lowercase to fit into sentence; ellipsis marks used to indicate omitted material

Destino 3

inforces de Waal's position that animals experience some of the same emotions as humans.

Perhaps the most extreme case of grief experienced by an animal is exemplified by the true story of Flint, a chimp, when Flo, his mother, died. In her book *Through a Window,* which elaborates on her thirty years of experience studying and living among the chimps in Gombe, Tanzania, Jane Goodall gives the following account of Flint's experience with grief.

> Flint became increasingly lethargic, refused most food and, with his immune system thus weakened, fell sick. The last time I saw him alive, he was hollow-eyed, gaunt and utterly depressed, huddled in the vegetation close to where Flo had died. . . . The last short journey he made, pausing to rest every few feet, was to the very place where Flo's body had lain. There he stayed for several hours, sometimes staring and staring into the water. He struggled on a little further, then curled up--and never moved again. (196-97)

Of course, animal emotions are not limited to despair, sadness, and grief. Indeed, substantial evidence indicates that animals experience other, more uplifting emotions, such as sympathy, altruism, and joy.

Many scientists who study animal behavior have found that several species demonstrate sympathy to one another. In other words, they act as if they care about one another in much the same way as humans do. It is probably safe to assume that no animal is more sympathetic, or at least displays more behaviors associated with the emotion of sympathy, than chimpanzees. Those who have studied apes in the wild, including de Waal, have observed that animals who had been fighting make up with one another by kissing and hugging. Although other primates also engage in similar behaviors, chimps even go so far as to embrace and attempt to console the defeated animal ("Going Ape"). Another striking example of one animal showing sympathy for another is the account cited by Barber of a parrot comforting its sick mate. It is not, however, the only example of this type of behavior, especially among birds. Barber cites several other instances as well. According to Barber, documented records show that responsible observers have seen robins trying to keep each other

Topic sentence introduces example

Source's credentials included within the text

Transitional paragraph to other main points

Clear topic sentence introduces next point

Information from a source paraphrased

Title used in citation since source does not indicate author; page number not given since the article is on only one page in the journal

Destino 4

alive. Also, terns have been known to lift a handicapped tern by its wing and
transport it to safety. Likewise, a jay has been known to successfully seek human
help when a newborn bird of a different species falls out of its nest. What makes
this latter example particularly noteworthy is that the newborn wasn't a jay but
an altogether different type of bird.

   Had the jay been helping another jay, it would be easy to assume that
the act of caring was the result of what scientists call *genetic altruism*--the
sociobiological theory that animals help each other to keep their own genes alive
so that they can reproduce and not become extinct. Simply put, scientists who
believe in genetic altruism assume that when animals of the same species help
each other out, they do so because there is something in it for them--namely,
the assurance that their species will continue. This theory certainly provides an
adequate, unbiased scientific explanation for why animals such as birds might
behave in a caring manner. However, if animals really help each other out only
when doing so will perpetuate their species, then the jay would have had no
genetic reason to help the newborn bird.

   There is another popular explanation for why a bird of one species might
help a bird of another species, however. Scientists who favor a related scientific
theory called *mutual altruism* believe that animals will help each other because
some day they themselves may need help, and then they will be able to count
on reciprocal help (Hemelrijk 479-81). This theory is a plausible, nonanthropo-
morphic explanation for why animals show sympathy, regardless of whether they
actually feel sympathy. This point is crucial because after all, humans can't actually observe how an animal feels; we can only observe how it behaves. It is then
up to the observer to draw some logical conclusion about why animals behave
in the ways they do. The mutual altruism theory, however, also can be disputed.
In many cases, animals have helped others even when the receiver of the help
would probably never be in a position to return the favor. For example, there
are many accounts of dolphins helping drowning or otherwise endangered swimmers. Phil Mercer, on the BBC Web site, reported that dolphins stopped a shark
from attacking swimmers off the coast of New Zealand. The animals surrounded

---

Information from a
source summarized

Transitional phrase refers
to incident reported in
preceding paragraph

Information in this
paragraph can be found
in many sources so
does not need to be
documented

Citation of Internet
source includes only
author's name and site's
sponsor; no page num-
bers available

Destino 5

the swimmers for about forty minutes while the great white shark circled. When the swimmers reached the shore, they remarked that they were sure that the dolphins acted deliberately to save them.

Not only do animals show sympathy, but they are also clearly able to express joy. For example, on many occasions primate experts have heard apes laugh while in the presence of other apes. These experts are sure that the noise they heard was laughter because of the clarity and tone of the sound. In their book, *Visions of Caliban,* Dale Peterson and Jane Goodall describe this laughter in detail.

> I'm not referring to a sort of pinched vocalization that might be roughly compared with human laughter, as in the "laughter" of a hyena. I'm referring to real laughter, fully recognizable laughter, the kind where you lie down on the ground and shake in a paroxysm of clear amusement and simple pleasure. (181)

According to Peterson and Goodall, only four species, in addition to humans, have the capacity to be amused and to show their amusement by laughing: chimpanzees, gorillas, bonobos, and orangutans.

Even the actions of animals who are not able to laugh uproariously indicate that they feel joy. Many animals engage in playful behavior that can emanate only

from a sense of joy. In "Hope and Joy among the Animals," Masson and McCarthy tell an amusing, yet true, story about an elephant named Norma.

> A traveling circus once pitched its tents next to a schoolyard with a set of swings. The older elephants were chained, but Norma, a young elephant, was left loose. When Norma saw children swinging, she was greatly intrigued. Before long, she went over, waved the children away with her trunk, backed up to a swing, and attempted to sit on it. She was notably unsuccessful, even using her tail to hold the swing in place. (45)

Geese, according to experts, have an "emotional body language which can be read: goose posture, gestures, and sounds can indicate feelings such as uncertain, tense, glad, victorious, sad, alert, relaxed or threatening." Additionally, birds can

Destino 6

sometimes be seen moving their wings back and forth while listening to sounds they find pleasant (McHugh).

In short, animals exhibit a large number of behaviors that indicate that they possess not only the capacity to feel but the capacity to express those feelings in some overt way, often through body language. If these are not proof enough that animals have emotions, people need look no further than their own beloved cat or dog. Pets are so frequently the cause of joy, humor, love, sympathy, empathy, and even grief that it is difficult to imagine that animals could elicit such emotions in humans without actually having these emotions themselves. The question, then, is not, Do animals have emotions? but, Which emotions do animals have, and to what degree do they feel them?

Transition to the conclusion of the essay

Destino presents his own conclusion about animal emotions

Destino 7

Works Cited

Barber, Theodore Xenophone. *The Human Nature of Birds: A Scientific Discovery with Startling Implications.* New York: St. Martin's, 1993. Print.

de Waal, Frans. "Are We in Anthropodenial?" *Discover* July 1997: 50-53. Print.

"Going Ape." *Economist* 17 Feb. 1997: 78. Print.

Goodall, Jane. *The Chimpanzees of Gombe: Patterns of Behavior.* Cambridge: Belknap Press, 1986. Print.

---. *Through a Window.* Boston: Houghton, 1990. Print.

Hemelrijk, Charlotte K. "Support for Being Groomed in Long-Tailed Macaques, Macaca Fascicularis." *Animal Behaviour* 48.2 (1994): 479-81. Print.

Masson, Jeffrey Moussaleff, and Susan McCarthy. "Hope and Joy among the Animals." *Utne Reader* July-Aug. 1995: 44-46. Print.

---. *When Elephants Weep: The Emotional Lives of Animals.* New York: Delacorte, 1995. Print.

McHugh, Mary. "The Emotional Lives of Animals." *Global:Ideas:Bank.* Global Ideas Bank, 1998. Web. 19 Dec. 2004.

Mercer, Phil. "Dolphins Prevent NZ Shark Attack." *BBC News.* BBC, 23 Nov. 2004. Web. 21 Jan. 2005.

Peterson, Dale, and Jane Goodall. *Visions of Caliban: On Chimpanzees and People.* New York: Houghton, 1993. Print.

Wynn, Susan G. "The Treatment of Trauma in Pet Animals: What Constitutes Trauma?" *Homeopathy Online* 5 (1998): n. pag. Web. 15 Dec. 2004.

PART 6

Academic Applications

The Bean Eaters
Gwendolyn Brooks

They eat beans mostly, this old yellow pair.
Dinner is a casual affair.
Plain chipware on a plain and creaking wood,
Tin flatware.

Two who are Mostly Good.   5
Two who have lived their day,
But keep on putting on their clothes
And putting things away.

And remembering . . .
Remembering, with twinklings and twinges,   10
As they lean over the beans in their rented back room that
    is full of beads and receipts and dolls and cloths,
        tobacco crumbs, vases and fringes.

CHAPTER 23

Reading and Writing about Literature

WRITING QUICK START

Suppose your American literature instructor asks you to read carefully the poem by Gwendolyn Brooks (1917–2000), a major American writer of poetry as well as fiction and nonfiction prose. Brooks was the first African American woman to win a Pulitzer Prize for poetry (for *Annie Allen*, 1949). "The Bean Eaters" was originally published in a collection of poems, *The Bean Eaters*, in 1960.

After reading Brooks's "The Bean Eaters," how can you describe the life of the elderly couple shown in the photo? Note that the elderly couple in the photo is not the couple described in the poem. Using information about the elderly lifestyle presented in "The Bean Eaters" as well as your own experience with elderly people, write a paragraph describing in your own words what you think the couple's relationship might be like.

Both Brooks's poem and the paragraph you just wrote paint a picture of an elderly couple. Through carefully selected details, the poem tells about the couple's daily activities, memories of the past, and current economic situation (for example, "They eat beans mostly," "Plain chipware," and "rented back room" reveal that the couple is poor). Brooks also suggests that routine is important to the couple ("But keep on putting on their clothes / And putting things away") and that their memories of the past are both good ("twinklings") and bad ("twinges").

Now think of an elderly couple you know, such as your grandparents or neighbors. Do some of the characteristics of Brooks's couple apply to the couple you know? How does Brooks's picture of one elderly couple help you understand other elderly people like the ones in the photo?

"The Bean Eaters" suggests an answer to the question many students ask: "Why should I read or write about literature?" This poem, like all literature, is about the experiences people share. Literature often deals with large issues: What is worthwhile in life? What is moral? What is beautiful? When you read and write about literature, you gain new insights into many aspects of human experience and thereby enrich your own life.

Understanding literature has practical purposes as well (see the accompanying box for a few examples). You may be asked to write about literature in many college courses—not only in English classes. Even in work situations, a knowledge of literature will make some tasks easier or more meaningful.

This chapter will help you read and respond to works of literature. The first half of the chapter offers a general approach to reading and understanding literature, including discussions of the language and other elements of short stories and poetry. The second half of the chapter focuses on the characteristics of literary analysis and helps you through the process of writing one in a Guided Writing Assignment. Although literature can take many forms—including poetry, short stories, biography, autobiography, drama, essays, and novels—this chapter concentrates on two literary genres: short stories and poetry.

SCENES FROM COLLEGE AND THE WORKPLACE

- Your *art history* professor asks you to read Ernest Hemingway's *For Whom the Bell Tolls* (a novel set in the time of the Spanish Civil War) and to write a paper discussing its meaning in conjunction with Picasso's *Guernica,* a painting that vividly portrays a scene from that war.

- In a *film* class, you watch the film *Romeo and Juliet,* directed by Franco Zeffirelli. Your instructor then asks you to read excerpts from Shakespeare's *Romeo and Juliet* and write a paper evaluating how successfully Juliet is portrayed in the film.

- You work for a *children's book store.* Your supervisor has asked you to read several children's books that she is considering featuring during story hour and to write an evaluation of each.

A General Approach to Reading Literature

Textbooks focus primarily on presenting factual information, but literature does not. Instead, *works of literature* are concerned with interpreting ideas, experiences, and events. They employ facts, description, and detail to convey larger meanings.

Use the following general guidelines to read a literary work effectively.

1. **Read with an open mind.** Be ready to respond to the work; don't make up your mind about it before you start reading.
2. **Preview the work before reading it.** Read background information about the author and the work and study the title. For a short story, read the first few and last few paragraphs and quickly skim through the pages in between, noticing the setting, the names of the characters, the amount of dialogue, and so forth. For a poem, read it through once to get an initial impression.

   For more on previewing, see Chapter 3, p. 47.

3. **Read slowly and carefully.** Works of literature use language in unique and creative ways, requiring you to read them slowly and carefully with a pen in hand. Mark interesting uses of language, such as striking phrases or descriptions, as well as sections that hint at the theme of the work.
4. **Note that literature often "bends the rules" of grammar and usage.** Writers of literature may use sentence fragments, ungrammatical dialogue, or unusual punctuation to create a particular *effect* in a short story or poem. When you see such instances in literature, remember that the writers bend the rules for a purpose.
5. **Establish the literal meaning first.** During the first reading of a work, try to establish its literal meaning. Who is doing what, when, and where? Identify the general subject, specific topic, and main character. What is happening? Describe the basic plot, action, or sequence of events. Establish where and during what time period the action occurs.
6. **Reread the work to focus on your interpretation.** To analyze a literary work, you will need to reread parts of the work or the entire work several times.
7. **Anticipate a gradual understanding.** Literary works are complex; you should not expect to understand a poem or short story immediately after reading it. As you reread and think about the work, its meanings will often come to mind gradually. Consider why the writer wrote the work and what message the writer is trying to communicate. Then ask, So what? to discover deeper meanings. Try to determine the work's view of, comment on, or lesson about the human experience.
8. **Interact with the work.** Jot down your reactions to it in the margins as you read. Include hunches, insights, and feelings as well as questions about the work. Highlight or underline key words, phrases, or actions that seem important or that you want to reconsider later.
9. **Identify themes and patterns.** Study your annotations to discover how the ideas in the work link together to suggest a theme. **Themes** are large or universal topics that are important to nearly everyone. For example, the theme of a poem or short story might be that death is inescapable or that aging involves a loss of the innocence of youth. Think of the theme as the main point a poem or short story makes. (Themes are discussed in greater detail later in the chapter.)

The Language of Literature

Many writers, especially writers of literary works, use figures of speech to describe people, places, or objects and to communicate ideas. In general, **figures of speech** are comparisons that make sense imaginatively or creatively but not literally. Three common types of figurative language are *similes, metaphors,* and *personification.* Writers often use another literary device, *symbols,* to suggest larger themes. Finally, writers use *irony* to convey the incongruities of life.

Similes, Metaphors, and Personification

For more on figures of speech, see Chapter 9, p. 193, and Chapter 11, p. 250.

Similes and metaphors are comparisons between two unlike things that have one common trait. A **simile** uses the word *like* or *as* to make a comparison, whereas a **metaphor** states or implies that one thing is another thing. If you say, "My father's mustache is a housepainter's brush," your metaphor compares two dissimilar things—a mustache and a paintbrush—that share one common trait: straight bristles. Such comparisons appeal to the reader's imagination. If you say, "Martha's hair looks like she just walked through a wind tunnel," your simile creates a more vivid image of Martha's hair than if you simply stated, "Martha's hair is messy." Here are examples from literary works.

SIMILE

My soul has grown deep like the rivers.

Langston Hughes, "The Negro Speaks of Rivers"

METAPHOR

Time is but the stream I go a-fishing in.

Henry David Thoreau, *Walden*

When writers use **personification**, they attribute human characteristics to objects or ideas. A well-known example of personification is found in an Emily Dickinson poem in which she likens death and immortality to passengers in a carriage: "Because I could not stop for Death— / He kindly stopped for me— / The carriage held but just Ourselves— / and Immortality." Like similes and metaphors, personification often creates a strong visual image.

Symbols

A **symbol** suggests more than its literal meaning. A flag, for instance, suggests patriotism; the color white often suggests innocence and purity. Because the abstract idea that a symbol represents is not stated but is left for the reader to infer, a symbol may suggest more than one meaning. A white handkerchief, for example, might symbolize retreat in one context but good manners in another. Some literary critics believe the white whale in Herman Melville's novel *Moby Dick* symbolizes evil, whereas others see the whale as representing the forces of nature.

To recognize symbols in a literary work, look for objects that are given a particular or unusual emphasis. The object may be mentioned often, may be suggested in the title, or may appear at the beginning or end of the work. Also be on the lookout for familiar symbols, such as flowers, doves, and colors.

Irony

Irony is literary language or a literary style in which actions, events, or words are the opposite of what readers expect. For example, a prizefighter cowering at the sight of a spider is an ironic action, a fire station burning down is an ironic event, and a student saying that she is glad she failed an important exam is making an ironic statement.

Exercise 23.1

Working with another student, make a list of common metaphors and similes; examples of personification; and symbols you have heard or seen in everyday life, in films or television programs, or in works of literature.

Analyzing Short Stories

A **short story** is a brief fictional narrative. It contains five key elements: setting, characters, point of view, plot, and theme. Short stories are shorter than novels, and their scope is much more limited. A short story, for example, may focus on one event in a person's life, whereas a novel may chronicle the events in the lives of an entire family. Like a novel, however, a short story makes a point about some aspect of the human experience.

Read the following short story, "The Secret Lion," before continuing with this section of the chapter. Then, as you continue with the chapter, you will discover how each of the key short-story elements works in "The Secret Lion."

The Secret Lion
Alberto Ríos

READING

Alberto Ríos (b. 1952), the son of a Guatemalan father and an English mother, was raised in Nogales, Arizona, near the Mexican border. His work has appeared in numerous national and international literature anthologies. In addition to fellowships from the Guggenheim Foundation and the National Endowment for the Arts, Ríos has won several awards: the Walt Whitman Award from the Academy of American Poets, the Arizona Governor's Arts Award, the PEN Beyond Margins Award, and the Western States Book Award for *The Iguana Killer: Twelve Stories of the Heart* (1984)—a collection of stories that includes the one reprinted here. Ríos is currently a Regents Professor of English at Arizona State University.

I was twelve and in junior high school and something happened that we didn't have   1
a name for, but it was there nonetheless like a lion, and roaring, roaring that way
the biggest things do. Everything changed. Just that. Like the rug, the one that gets
pulled—or better, like the tablecloth those magicians pull where the stuff on the
table stays the same but gasp! from the audience makes the staying-the-same
part not matter. Like that.

What happened was there were teachers now, not just one teacher, teach-erz, and we felt personally abandoned somehow. When a person had all these teachers now, he didn't get taken care of the same way, even though six was more than one. Arithmetic went out the door when we walked in. And we saw girls now, but they weren't the same girls we used to know because we couldn't talk to them anymore, not the same way we used to, certainly not to Sandy, even though she was my neighbor, too. Not even to her. She just played the piano all the time. And there were words, oh there were words in junior high school, and we wanted to know what they were, and how a person did them—that's what school was supposed to be for. Only, in junior high school, school wasn't school, everything was backward-like. If you went up to a teacher and said the word to try and find out what it meant you got in trouble for saying it. So we didn't. And we figured it must have been that way about other stuff, too, so we never said anything about anything—we weren't stupid.

But my friend Sergio and I, we solved junior high school. We would come home from school on the bus, put our books away, change shoes, and go across the highway to the arroyo.[1] It was the one place we were not supposed to go. So we did. This was, after all, what junior high had at least shown us. It was our river, though, our personal Mississippi, our friend from long back, and it was full of stories and all the branch forts we had built in it when we were still the Vikings of America, with our own symbol, which we had carved everywhere, even in the sand, which let the water take it. That was good, we had decided; whoever was at the end of this river would know about us.

At the very very top of our growing lungs, what we would do down there was shout every dirty word we could think of, in every combination we could come up with, and we would yell about girls, and all the things we wanted to do with them, as loud as we could—we didn't know what we wanted to do with them, just things—and we would yell about teachers, and how we loved some of them, like Miss Crevelone, and how we wanted to dissect some of them, making signs of the cross, like priests, and we would yell this stuff over and over because it felt good, we couldn't explain why, it just felt good and for the first time in our lives there was nobody to tell us we couldn't. So we did.

One Thursday we were walking along shouting this way, and the railroad, the Southern Pacific, which ran above and along the far side of the arroyo, had dropped a grinding ball down there, which was, we found out later, a cannonball thing used in mining. A bunch of them were put in a big vat which turned around and crushed the ore. One had been dropped, or thrown—what do caboose men do when they get bored—but it got down there regardless and as we were walking along yelling about one girl or another, a particular Claudia, we found it, one of these things, looked at it, picked it up, and got very very excited, and held it and passed it back and forth, and we were saying "Guythisis, this is, geeGuythis . . .": we had this perception about nature then, that nature is imperfect and that round things are perfect: we said "GuyGodthis is perfect, thisisthis is perfect, it's round, round and heavy, it'sit's the best thing we'veeverseen. Whatisit?" We didn't know. We just knew it was great. We just, whatever, we played with it, held it some more.

And then we had to decide what to do with it. We knew, because of a lot of things, that if we were going to take this and show it to anybody, this discovery, this best

2

3

4

5

6

---

[1] *arroyo:* A creek or stream in a dry part of the country.

thing, was going to be taken away from us. That's the way it works with little kids, like all the polished quartz, the tons of it we had collected piece by piece over the years. Junior high kids too. If we took it home, my mother, we knew, was going to look at it and say "throw that dirty thing in the, get rid of it." Simple like, like that. "But ma it's the best thing I" "Getridofit." Simple.

So we didn't. Take it home. Instead, we came up with the answer. We dug a hole   7
and buried it. And we marked it secretly. Lots of secret signs. And came back the next week to dig it up and, we didn't know, pass it around some more or something, but we didn't find it. We dug up that whole bank, and we never found it again. We tried.

Sergio and I talked about that ball or whatever it was when we couldn't find it. All   8
we used were small words, neat, good. Kid words. What we were really saying, but didn't know the words, was how much that ball was like that place, that whole arroyo: couldn't tell anybody about it, didn't understand what it was, didn't have a name for it. It just felt good. It was just perfect in the way it was that place, that whole going to that place, that whole junior high school lion. It was just iron-heavy, it had no name, it felt good or not, we couldn't take it home to show our mothers, and once we buried it, it was gone forever.

The ball was gone, like the first reasons we had come to that arroyo years earlier,   9
like the first time we had seen the arroyo, it was gone like everything else that had been taken away. This was not our first lesson. We stopped going to the arroyo after not finding the thing, the same way we had stopped going there years earlier and headed for the mountains. Nature seemed to keep pushing us around one way or another, teaching us the same thing every place we ended up. Nature's gang was tough that way, teaching us stuff.

When we were young we moved away from town, me and my family. Sergio's was   10
already out there. Out in the wilds. Or at least the new place seemed like the wilds since everything looks bigger the smaller a man is. I was five, I guess, and we had moved three miles north of Nogales where we had lived, three miles north of the Mexican border. We looked across the highway in one direction and there was the arroyo; hills stood up in the other direction. Mountains, for a small man.

When the first summer came the very first place we went to was of course the one   11
place we weren't supposed to go, the arroyo. We went down in there and found water running, summer rain water mostly, and we went swimming. But every third or fourth or fifth day, the sewage treatment plant that was, we found out, upstream, would release whatever it was that it released, and we would never know exactly what day that was, and a person really couldn't tell right off by looking at the water, not every time, not so a person could get out in time. So, we went swimming that summer and some days we had a lot of fun. Some days we didn't. We found a thousand ways to explain what happened on those other days, constructing elaborate stories about the neighborhood dogs, and hadn't she, my mother, miscalculated her step before, too? But she knew something was up because we'd come running into the house those days, wanting to take a shower, even—if this can be imagined—in the middle of the day.

That was the first time we stopped going to the arroyo. It taught us to look the   12
other way. We decided, as the second side of summer came, we wanted to go into the mountains. They were still mountains then. We went running in one summer Thursday morning, my friend Sergio and I, into my mother's kitchen, and said, well,

what'zin, what'zin those hills over there—we used her word so she'd understand us —and she said nothingdon'tworryaboutit. So we went out, and we weren't dumb, we thought with our eyes to each other, ohhoshe'stryingtokeepsomethingfromus. We knew adults.

We had read the books, after all; we knew about bridges and castles and wild- **13** treacherousraging alligatormouth rivers. We wanted them. So we were going to go out and get them. We went back that morning into that kitchen and we said, "We're going out there, we're going into the hills, we're going away for three days, don't worry." She said, "All right."

"You know," I said to Sergio, "if we're going to go away for three days, well, we **14** ought to at least pack a lunch."

But we were two young boys with no patience for what we thought at the time was **15** mom-stuff: making sa-and-wiches. My mother didn't offer. So we got out little kid knap-sacks that my mother had sewn for us, and into them we put the jar of mustard. A loaf of bread. Knivesforksplates, bottles of Coke, a can opener. This was lunch for the two of us. And we were weighed down, humped over to be strong enough to carry this stuff. But we started walking anyway, into the hills. We were going to eat berries and stuff otherwise. "Goodbye." My mom said that.

After the first hill we were dead. But we walked. My mother could still see us. And **16** we kept walking. We walked until we got to where the sun is straight overhead, noon. That place. Where that is doesn't matter; it's time to eat. The truth is we weren't any-where close to that place. We just agreed that the sun was overhead and that it was time to eat, and by tilting our heads a little we could make that the truth.

"We really ought to start looking for a place to eat." **17**

"Yeah. Let's look for a good place to eat." We went back and forth saying that for **18** fifteen minutes, making it lunchtime because that's what we always said back and forth before lunchtimes at home. "Yeah, I'm hungry all right." I nodded my head. "Yeah, I'm hungry all right too. I'm hungry." He nodded his head. I nodded my head back. After a good deal more nodding, we were ready, just as we came over a little hill. We hadn't found the mountains yet. This was a little hill.

And on the other side of this hill we found heaven. **19**

It was just what we thought it would be. **20**

Perfect. Heaven was green, like nothing else in Arizona. And it wasn't a cemetery **21** or like that because we had seen cemeteries and they had gravestones and stuff and this didn't. This was perfect, had trees, lots of trees, had birds, like we had never seen before. It was like The Wizard of Oz, like when they got to Oz and everything was so green, so emerald, they had to wear those glasses, and we ran just like them, laugh-ing, laughing that way we did that moment, and we went running down to this clearing in it all, hitting each other that good way we did.

We got down there, we kept laughing, we kept hitting each other, we unpacked our **22** stuff, and we started acting "rich." We knew all about how to do that, like blowing on our nails, then rubbing them on our chests for the shine. We made our sandwiches, opened our Cokes, got out the rest of the stuff, the salt and pepper shakers. I found this particular hole and I put my Coke right into it, a perfect fit, and I called it my Coke-holder. I got down next to it on my back, because everyone knows that rich people eat lying down, and I got my sandwich in one hand and put my other arm around the Coke in its holder. When I wanted a drink, I lifted my neck a little, put out my lips, and tipped my Coke a little with the crook of my elbow. Ah.

We were there, lying down, eating our sandwiches, laughing, throwing bread at each other and out for the birds. This was heaven. We were laughing and we couldn't believe it. My mother was keeping something from us, ah ha, but we had found her out. We even found water over at the side of the clearing to wash our plates with—we had brought plates. Sergio started washing his plates when he was done, and I was being rich with my Coke, and this day in summer was right.   23

When suddenly these two men came, from around a corner of trees and the tallest grass we had ever seen. They had bags on their backs, leather bags, bags and sticks.   24

We didn't know what clubs were, but I learned later, like I learned about the grinding balls. The two men yelled at us. Most specifically, one wanted me to take my Coke out of my Coke-holder so he could sink his golf ball into it.   25

Something got taken away from us that moment. Heaven. We grew up a little bit, and couldn't go backward. We learned. No one had ever told us about golf. They had told us about heaven. And it went away. We got golf in exchange.   26

We went back to the arroyo for the rest of that summer, and tried to have fun the best we could. We learned to be ready for finding the grinding ball. We loved it, and when we buried it we knew what would happen. The truth is, we didn't look so hard for it. We were two boys and twelve summers then, and not stupid. Things get taken away.   27

We buried it because it was perfect. We didn't tell my mother, but together it was all we talked about, till we forgot. It was the lion.   28

Setting

The **setting** of a short story is the time, place, and circumstance in which the story occurs. The setting provides the framework and atmosphere in which the plot develops and characters interact. For example, Charles Dickens's "A Christmas Carol" is set in nineteenth-century London. The setting of "The Secret Lion" is between the arroyo and the mountains just outside of Nogales, Arizona. The action occurs near the arroyo and on the golf course.

Characters

The **characters** are the actors in the story. They are revealed through their dialogue, actions, appearance, thoughts, and feelings. The **narrator**, the person who tells the story, may also comment on or reveal information about the characters. The narrator is not necessarily the author of the story. The narrator can be one of the characters in the story or an onlooker who observes but does not participate in the action. Therefore, you need to think critically about what the narrator reveals about the personalities, needs, and motives of the characters and whether the narrator's opinions may be colored by his or her perceptions and biases. "The Secret Lion" involves two principal characters: the narrator and his childhood friend, Sergio. Both twelve-year-old boys are playful, spirited, and inquisitive. They explore, disobey, and test ideas. The narrator's mother is a secondary character in the story.

Point of View

The **point of view** is the perspective from which the story is told. There are two common points of view: first person and third person. In the first-person (*I*) point of view, the narrator tells the story as he or she sees or experiences it ("*I* saw the crowd gather at the cemetery"). A first-person narrator may be one of the characters or someone observing but not participating in the story. In the third-person (*they*) point of view, the narrator tells the story as if someone else is experiencing it ("*Laura* saw the crowd gather at the cemetery"). A third-person narrator may be able to report only the actions that can be observed from the outside or may be able to enter the minds of one or more characters and tell about their thoughts and motives. An *omniscient*, or all-knowing, third-person narrator is aware of the thoughts and actions of all characters in the story.

To identify the point of view of a story, then, consider who is narrating and what the narrator knows about the characters' actions, thoughts, and motives. "The Secret Lion" is told by a first-person narrator who both participates in the action and looks back on the events to interpret them. For example, he says of their preparations for their trip to the mountains, "But we were two young boys with no patience for what we thought at the time was mom-stuff" (para. 15). He also uses a fast-talking narrative style characteristic of twelve-year-old boys, intentionally bending rules of spelling and grammar to achieve this effect. For example, he uses sentence fragments—"Lots of secret signs" (7), "Out in the wilds" (10)—and runs words together or emphasizes syllables to show how they are pronounced—"wildtreacherousraging alligatormouth rivers" (13), "sa-and-wiches" (15). He also uses slang words—"neat" (8)—and contractions to create an informal tone.

Plot

The **plot** is the basic story line—that is, the sequence of events and actions through which the story's meaning is expressed. The plot is often centered on a **conflict**— a problem or clash between opposing forces—and the resolution of the conflict. Once the scene is set and the characters are introduced, a problem or conflict arises. Suspense builds as the conflict unfolds and the characters wrestle with the problem. Near the end of the story, the events come to a **climax**—the point at which the conflict is resolved. The story ends with a conclusion.

In "The Secret Lion," two childhood friends, while playing near an arroyo, discover a grinding ball. They bury the ball but are unable to find it when they return. The narrator recollects an earlier time, when they had planned a trip to the mountains and stopped to have lunch on what they soon discovered was a golf course. The conflict, illustrated by several events, is between the boys' imaginations and adult realities.

Theme

The **theme** of a story is its central or dominant idea, the main point the author makes about the human experience. Readers do not always agree about a story's theme. Therefore, in a literary analysis of a short story, you must give evidence to support your interpretation of the theme. The following suggestions will help you uncover clues.

1. **Study the title.** What meanings does it suggest?
2. **Analyze the main characters.** Do the characters change? If so, how, and in response to what?
3. **Look for broad statements about the conflict.** What do the characters and narrator say about the conflict or their lives?
4. **Analyze important elements.** Look for symbols, figures of speech, and meaningful names (Young Goodman Brown, for example).

Once you uncover a theme, try expressing it in sentence form rather than as a single word or brief phrase. For example, to say the theme is "dishonesty" or "parent-child relationships" does not reveal the meaning of a story. When expressed as a sentence, however, a story's theme becomes clear: "Dishonesty sometimes pays" or "Parent-child relationships are often struggles for power and control."

One possible theme of "The Secret Lion" is that change is inevitable, that nothing remains the same. After the boys discover that they can't find the buried grinding ball, the narrator hints at this theme: "The ball was gone . . . like everything else that had been taken away" (para. 9). When the boys encounter the two men on the golf course, the narrator again comments on the theme of change: "Something got taken away from us that moment. Heaven. We grew up a little bit, and couldn't go backward" (26).

Another possible theme of Ríos's story is that perfection is unattainable. The boys are attracted to the ball because it is perfect: "GuyGodthis is perfect, thisisthis is perfect . . . it'sit's the best thing we'veeverseen" (5). But once the "perfect" ball is buried, it can never be found again. In much the same way, the boys cannot return to the "heaven" they once knew at the golf course.

Exercise 23.2

Working in groups of two or three, choose a television situation comedy and watch one episode, either together, if possible, or separately. After viewing the program, identify each of the following elements: setting, characters, point of view, and plot. Then consider whether you think the episode has a theme.

Use the questions in the box on page 666 to guide your analysis of short stories. As you read the story that follows, "The Story of an Hour" by Kate Chopin (p. 666), keep these questions in mind. You may choose to write an analysis of this story in response to the Guided Writing Assignment on page 674.

QUESTIONS FOR ANALYZING SHORT STORIES

Setting: Time
1. In what general time period (century or decade) does the story take place?
2. What major events (wars, revolutions, famines, political or cultural movements) occurred during that time, and what bearing might they have on the story?

Setting: Place
1. In what geographic area does the story take place? (Try to identify the country and the city or town, as well as whether the area is an urban or rural one.)
2. Where does the action occur? (For example, does it occur on a battlefield, in a living room, or on a city street?)
3. Why is the place important? (Why couldn't the story occur elsewhere?)

Characters
1. Who are the main characters in the story?
2. What are the distinguishing qualities and characteristics of each character?
3. Why do you like or dislike each character?
4. How and why do characters change (or not change) as the story progresses?

Point of View
1. Is the narrator a character in the story or strictly an observer?
2. Is the narrator knowledgeable about the motives, feelings, and behavior of any or all of the characters?
3. Does the narrator affect what happens in the story? If so, how? What role does the narrator play?

Plot
1. What series of events occurs? Summarize the action.
2. What is the conflict? Why does it occur? How does it build to a climax?
3. How is the conflict resolved?
4. Is the outcome satisfying? Why or why not?

Theme
1. What is the theme? What broad statement about life or the human experience does the story suggest?
2. What evidence from the story supports your interpretation of the theme?

READING

The Story of an Hour
Kate Chopin

Kate Chopin (1851–1904), a nineteenth-century American writer, is best known for her novel *The Awakening* (1899), which outraged early literary critics with its portrayal of a woman in search of sexual and professional independence. As you read the following short story, originally published in *Vogue* magazine in 1894, look for, highlight, and annotate the five primary elements of short stories discussed in this chapter.

Knowing that Mrs. Mallard was afflicted with a heart trouble, great care was taken to break to her as gently as possible the news of her husband's death. 1

It was her sister Josephine who told her, in broken sentences, veiled hints that revealed in half concealing. Her husband's friend Richards was there, too, near her. 2

It was he who had been in the newspaper office when intelligence of the railroad disaster was received, with Brently Mallard's name leading the list of "killed." He had only taken the time to assure himself of its truth by a second telegram, and had hastened to forestall any less careful, less tender friend in bearing the sad message.

3 She did not hear the story as many women have heard the same, with a paralyzed inability to accept its significance. She wept at once, with sudden, wild abandonment, in her sister's arms. When the storm of grief had spent itself she went away to her room alone. She would have no one follow her.

4 There stood, facing the open window, a comfortable, roomy armchair. Into this she sank, pressed down by a physical exhaustion that haunted her body and seemed to reach into her soul.

5 She could see in the open square before her house the tops of trees that were all aquiver with the new spring life. The delicious breath of rain was in the air. In the street below a peddler was crying his wares. The notes of a distant song which someone was singing reached her faintly, and countless sparrows were twittering in the eaves.

6 There were patches of blue sky showing here and there through the clouds that had met and piled one above the other in the west facing her window.

7 She sat with her head thrown back upon the cushion of the chair, quite motionless, except when a sob came up into her throat and shook her, as a child who has cried itself to sleep continues to sob in its dreams.

8 She was young, with a fair, calm face, whose lines bespoke repression and even a certain strength. But now there was a dull stare in her eyes, whose gaze was fixed away off yonder on one of those patches of blue sky. It was not a glance of reflection, but rather indicated a suspension of intelligent thought.

9 There was something coming to her and she was waiting for it, fearfully. What was it? She did not know, it was too subtle and elusive to name. But she felt it, creeping out of the sky, reaching toward her through the sounds, the scents, the color that filled the air.

10 Now her bosom rose and fell tumultuously. She was beginning to recognize this thing that was approaching to possess her, and she was striving to beat it back with her will—as powerless as her two white slender hands would have been.

11 When she abandoned herself a little whispered word escaped her slightly parted lips. She said it over and over under her breath: "Free, free, free!" The vacant stare and the look of terror that had followed it went from her eyes. They stayed keen and bright. Her pulses beat fast, and the coursing blood warmed and relaxed every inch of her body.

12 She did not stop to ask if it were not a monstrous joy that held her. A clear and exalted perception enabled her to dismiss the suggestion as trivial.

13 She knew that she would weep again when she saw the kind, tender hands folded in death; the face that had never looked save with love upon her, fixed and gray and dead. But she saw beyond that bitter moment a long procession of years to come that would belong to her absolutely. And she opened and spread her arms out to them in welcome.

14 There would be no one to live for during those coming years; she would live for herself. There would be no powerful will bending her in that blind persistence with which men and women believe they have a right to impose a private will upon a fellow creature. A kind intention or a cruel intention made the act seem no less a crime as she looked upon it in that brief moment of illumination.

15 And yet she had loved him—sometimes. Often she had not. What did it matter! What could love, the unsolved mystery, count for in face of this possession of self-assertion which she suddenly recognized as the strongest impulse of her being.

"Free! Body and soul free!" she kept whispering.   16

Josephine was kneeling before the closed door with her lips to the keyhole, implor-   17
ing for admission. "Louise, open the door! I beg; open the door—you will make yourself ill. What are you doing, Louise? For heaven's sake open the door."

"Go away. I am not making myself ill." No; she was drinking in a very elixir of life   18
through that open window.

Her fancy was running riot along those days ahead of her. Spring days, and summer   19
days, and all sorts of days that would be her own. She breathed a quick prayer that life
might be long. It was only yesterday she had thought with a shudder that life might be long.

She arose at length and opened the door to her sister's importunities. There was   20
a feverish triumph in her eyes, and she carried herself unwittingly like a goddess
of Victory. She clasped her sister's waist, and together they descended the stairs.
Richards stood waiting for them at the bottom.

Some one was opening the front door with a latchkey. It was Brently Mallard who en-   21
tered, a little travel-stained, composedly carrying his gripsack and umbrella. He had been far
from the scene of accident, and did not even know there had been one. He stood amazed at
Josephine's piercing cry; at Richards' quick motion to screen him from the view of his wife.

But Richards was too late.   22

When the doctors came they said she had died of heart disease—of joy that kills.   23

Analyzing Poetry

Poetry is written in lines and stanzas instead of in paragraphs. Because of poetry's
unique format, ideas in poems are often expressed in compact and concise language,
and reading and analyzing a poem may take as much time and effort as analyzing an
essay or a short story. To grasp the meaning of a poem, it is important to pay attention
to the sound and meaning of individual words and to consider how the words in the
poem work together to convey meaning.

Use the following general guidelines to read and analyze poetry effectively.

1. **Read the poem through once**, without any defined purpose. Read with an open
    mind; try to get a general sense of what the poem is about. If you come across an
    unfamiliar word or a confusing reference, keep reading.
2. **Use punctuation to guide your comprehension.** Although poetry is written in
    lines, each line may not make sense by itself. Meaning often flows from line to
    line, and a single sentence can be composed of several lines. Use the poem's punc-
    tuation to guide you. If there is no punctuation at the end of a line, read it with a
    slight pause at the end and with an emphasis on the last word. Think about how
    the poet breaks lines to achieve a certain effect.
3. **Visualize as you read.** Especially if you tend to be a spatial or an abstract learner,
    try to visualize or see what the poem is about.
4. **Read the poem several more times.** The meaning of the poem will become clearer
    with each successive reading. At first you may understand some parts but not others.
    If you tend to be a pragmatic or rational learner, you will probably want to work
    through the poem line by line, from beginning to end. With poetry, however, that
    approach does not always work. Instead you may need to use later stanzas to help

you understand earlier ones. If you find certain sections difficult or confusing, read these sections aloud several times. You might try copying them, word for word, on a piece of paper. Look up the meanings of any unfamiliar words in a dictionary.

5. **Check unfamiliar references.** A poet may make **allusions**—references to people, objects, or events outside of the poem. Understanding an allusion is often essential to understanding the overall meaning of a poem. If you see Oedipus mentioned in a poem, for example, you may need to use a dictionary or encyclopedia to learn that he was a figure in Greek mythology who unwittingly killed his father and unknowingly married his mother. Your knowledge of Oedipus would then help you interpret the poem.

6. **Identify the speaker and tone.** Poems often refer to an unidentified *I* or *we*. Try to describe the speaker's viewpoint or feelings to figure out who he or she is. Also consider the speaker's tone: Is it serious, challenging, sad, frustrated, or joyful? To help determine the tone, read the poem aloud. Your emphasis of certain words or the rise and fall of your voice may provide clues to the tone; that is, you may "hear" the poet's anger, despondency, or elation.

7. **Identify to whom the poem is addressed.** Is it written to a person, to the reader, to an object? Consider the possibility that the poet may be writing to work out a personal problem or to express strong emotions.

8. **Analyze the language of the poem.** Consider the *connotations,* or shades of meaning, of words in the poem. Study the poem's use of descriptive language, similes, metaphors, personification, and symbols (see p. 658).

For more on connotations, see Chapter 9, p. 191; for more on descriptive language, see Chapter 11, p. 236.

9. **Analyze the poem's theme.** Does its overall meaning involve a feeling, a person, a memory, or an argument? Paraphrase the poem; express it in your own words, and connect it to your own experience. Then link your ideas together to discover the poem's overall meaning. Ask yourself, What is the poet trying to tell me? and What is the theme?

Use the questions in the accompanying box to guide your analysis of poetry. As you read the following poem by Robert Frost, "Two Look at Two," keep these questions in mind.

QUESTIONS FOR ANALYZING POETRY

1. How does the poem make you feel—shocked, saddened, angered, annoyed, happy? Write a sentence or two describing your reaction.
2. Who is the speaker? What do you know about him or her? What tone does the speaker use? To whom is he or she speaking?
3. What is the poem's setting? If it is unclear, why does the poet not provide a setting?
4. What emotional atmosphere or mood does the poet create? Do you sense, for example, a mood of foreboding, excitement, or contentment?
5. How does the poet use language to create an effect? Does the poet use similes, metaphors, personification, or symbols?
6. Does the poem tell a story? If so, what is its point?
7. Does the poem express emotion? If so, for what purpose?
8. Does the poem rhyme? If so, does the rhyme affect the meaning? (For example, does the poet use rhyme to emphasize key words or phrases?)
9. What is the meaning of the poem's title?
10. What is the theme of the poem?

(READING)

Two Look at Two
Robert Frost

Robert Frost (1874–1963) is a major American poet whose work often focuses on familiar objects, natural scenes, and the character of New England. In his early life Frost was a farmer and teacher; later he became a poet in residence at Amherst College and taught at Dartmouth, Yale, and Harvard. Frost was awarded Pulitzer Prizes for four collections of poems: *New Hampshire* (1923), from which "Two Look at Two" is taken; *Collected Poems* (1930); *A Further Range* (1936); and *A Witness Tree* (1942). As you read the selection, use the questions in the box on page 669 to think critically about the poem.

> Love and forgetting might have carried them
> A little further up the mountain side
> With night so near, but not much further up.
> They must have halted soon in any case
> With thoughts of the path back, how rough it was   5
> With rock and washout, and unsafe in darkness;
> When they were halted by a tumbled wall
> With barbed-wire binding. They stood facing this,
> Spending what onward impulse they still had
> In one last look the way they must not go,   10
> On up the failing path, where, if a stone
> Or earthslide moved at night, it moved itself;
> No footstep moved it. "This is all," they sighed,
> "Good-night to woods." But not so; there was more.
> A doe from round a spruce stood looking at them   15
> Across the wall, as near the wall as they.
> She saw them in their field, they her in hers.
> The difficulty of seeing what stood still,
> Like some up-ended boulder split in two,
> Was in her clouded eyes: they saw no fear there.   20
> She seemed to think that two thus they were safe.
> Then, as if they were something that, though strange,
> She could not trouble her mind with too long,
> She sighed and passed unscared along the wall.
> "*This,* then, is all. What more is there to ask?"   25

But no, not yet. A snort to bid them wait.

A buck from round the spruce stood looking at them

Across the wall, as near the wall as they.

This was an antlered buck of lusty nostril,

Not the same doe come back into her place.   30

He viewed them quizzically with jerks of head,

As if to ask, "Why don't you make some motion?

Or give some sign of life? Because you can't.

I doubt if you're as living as you look."

Thus till he had them almost feeling dared   35

To stretch a proffering hand—and a spell-breaking.

Then he too passed unscared along the wall.

Two had seen two, whichever side you spoke from.

"This *must* be all." It was all. Still they stood,

A great wave from it going over them,   40

As if the earth in one unlooked-for favor

Had made them certain earth returned their love.

The poem takes place on a mountainside path, near dusk. A couple walking the path finds a tumbled wall. Looking beyond the wall, the couple first encounters a doe and then a buck. The doe and buck stare at the human couple and vice versa; hence the title "Two Look at Two." Neither the animals nor the humans are frightened; both couples observe each other and continue with their lives. The action is described by a third-person narrator who can read the thoughts of the humans. The speaker creates an objective tone by reporting events as they occur.

In "Two Look at Two," Frost considers the important relationship between humans and nature. The wall is symbolic of the separation between them. Beyond the wall the couple looks at "the way they must not go" (line 10). Although humans and nature are separate, they are also equal and in balance. These qualities are suggested by the title as well as by the actions of both couples as they observe each other in a nonthreatening way. The third-person point of view contributes to this balance in that the story is narrated by an outside observer rather than a participant. One possible theme of the poem, therefore, is the balance and equality between humans and nature.

As you read the following poem, "Filling Station," by Elizabeth Bishop, use the guidelines on pages 668 to 670 and the questions in the box on page 669 to help you analyze its elements and discover its meaning. You may choose to write an analysis of this poem in response to the Guided Writing Assignment on page 674.

(READING)

Filling Station
Elizabeth Bishop

Elizabeth Bishop (1911–1979) is an American poet who traveled most of her life. Much of her poetry recounts the places she visited and the intimate details of everyday things. She published several collections of poems, including *North and South* (1946); *Poems: North and South—A Cold Spring* (1956), for which she was awarded a Pulitzer Prize; *Questions of Travel* (1965); *The Complete Poems* (1969), for which she received the National Book Award; and *Geography III* (1976). The following poem was originally published in *Questions of Travel*. As you read, respond to the poem by making notes in the margin.

```
Oh, but it is dirty!
— this little filling station,
oil-soaked, oil-permeated
to a disturbing, over-all
black translucency,                        5
Be careful with that match!

Father wears a dirty,
oil-soaked monkey suit
that cuts him under the arms,
and several quick and saucy      10
and greasy sons assist him
(it's a family filling station),
all quite thoroughly dirty.

Do they live in the station?
It has a cement porch                      15
behind the pumps, and on it
a set of crushed and grease-
impregnated wickerwork;
on the wicker sofa
a dirty dog, quite comfy.             20
Some comic books provide
the only note of color —
of certain color. They lie
upon a big dim doily
draping a taboret*                           25
```

---

taboret: low cylindrical stool

(part of the set), beside
a big hirsute begonia.

Why the extraneous plant?
Why the taboret?
Why, oh why, the doily?   30
(Embroidered in daisy stitch
with marguerites, I think,
and heavy with gray crochet.)

Somebody embroidered the doily.
Somebody waters the plant,   35
or oils it, maybe. Somebody
arranges the rows of cans
so that they softly say:
ESSO**—SO—SO—SO

to high-strung automobiles,   40
Somebody loves us all.

**ESSO:* The mid-twentieth-century name for a petroleum products company that began in the late nineteenth century as Standard Oil Trust and continues today as ExxonMobil.

Now that you have a better understanding of the elements of poetry and short stories, you are ready to write about a literary work. In English and humanities courses, you will often be asked to read and analyze works of literature and then write literary analyses. The following sections will discuss this type of essay and take you step by step through a Guided Writing Assignment.

What Is Literary Analysis?

A **literary analysis** essay, sometimes called *literary criticism* or a *critique,* analyzes and interprets one or more aspects of a literary work. As with other types of essays, writing a literary analysis involves generating ideas through prewriting, developing a thesis, collecting supporting evidence, organizing and drafting, analyzing and revising, and editing and proofreading.

Keep in mind that a literary analysis does *not* merely summarize the work; rather, it focuses on *analysis* and *interpretation* of the work. Therefore, in a literary analysis, you take a position on some aspect of the work and support your position with evidence. In other words, you assume the role of a critic, in much the same way that a film critic argues for his or her judgment of a film rather than simply reporting its plot. For this chapter's assignment, your literary analysis should focus on *one* element of the work, even though some literary analyses cover multiple elements or more than one work.

Characteristics of Literary Analysis

A literary analysis has the following characteristics.

- It makes a point about one or more elements of a literary work.
- It includes and accurately documents evidence from the work. (It may also include evidence from outside sources.)
- It assumes that the audience is somewhat familiar with the work but not as familiar as the writer of the analysis.
- It has a serious tone and is written in the present tense.

A GUIDED WRITING ASSIGNMENT

The following guide will help you write a literary analysis of a poem or short story. Depending on your learning style, you may find some of the suggested strategies more suitable than others. Social or verbal learners, for instance, may prefer to generate ideas about the poem or short story through discussion with classmates. Spatial or creative learners may decide to draw a character map. Independent or concrete learners may choose to draw a time line or write a summary. This Guided Writing Assignment will provide you with alternatives.

The Assignment

Write a literary analysis of a poem or short story. Choose one of the following works reprinted in this chapter, a work you select on your own, or a work assigned by your instructor. Your classmates are your audience.

1. Gwendolyn Brooks, "The Bean Eaters" (p. 654)
2. Alberto Ríos, "The Secret Lion" (p. 659)
3. Kate Chopin, "The Story of an Hour" (p. 666)
4. Robert Frost, "Two Look at Two" (p. 670)
5. Elizabeth Bishop, "Filling Station" (p. 672)

For more on illustration, comparison and contrast, and cause and effect, see Chapters 12, 14, and 17.

As you develop your literary-analysis essay, you will probably use one or more patterns of development. You will use illustration, for instance, to cite examples from the poem or short story that support your analysis of it. In addition, you might compare or contrast two main characters or analyze a plot by discussing causes and effects.

Generating Ideas

The following guidelines will help you explore the short story or poem you have selected and generate ideas for writing about it.

1. **Highlight and annotate as you read.** Record your initial impressions and responses to the work in marginal annotations as you read. For recording lengthy comments, use a separate sheet of paper. Look for and highlight figures of speech, symbols, revealing character descriptions, striking dialogue, and the like. Here is a sample annotated portion of Frost's "Two Look at Two."

Learning Style Options

For more on annotating, see Chapter 3, p. 53.

SAMPLE ANNOTATED PASSAGE

Love and forgetting might have carried them

A little further up the mountain side

With night so near, but not much further up. ◄———————— *limitations of humans*

They must have halted soon in any case

With thoughts of the path back, how rough it was ◄———— *road of life?*
difficulty of life

With rock and washout, and unsafe in darkness;

When they were halted by a tumbled wall ◄——————— *separates man and*
nature — Why is it
With barbed-wire binding. They stood facing this, ◄——— *tumbled?*

Spending what onward impulse they still had *sharp, penetrating*

In one last look the way they must not go, ◄———————— *prohibited from*
crossing

Robert Frost, "Two Look at Two"

2. **Discuss the literary work with classmates.** Discussing the short story or poem with others will help you generate ideas about it. Plan your discussion, moving from the general meaning of the work to a more specific paragraph-by-paragraph or line-by-line examination. Then consider your interpretation of the work's theme.

3. **Write a summary.** Especially when you draw a blank about a work, try writing a summary of it in your own words. You may find yourself raising and answering questions about the work as you summarize it. Jot down ideas as they occur to you, either on your summary page or on a separate sheet of paper.

For more on writing a summary, see Chapter 3, p. 63.

4. **Draw a time line.** For a short story, especially one with a complex plot that flashes back or forward in time, draw a time line of the action in chronological sequence on paper or on a computer. Here is a sample time line for Ríos's "The Secret Lion."

Sample Time Line: "The Secret Lion"

Age 5 ————————————→ Main character moves three miles north of Nogales.

   First half of summer ————→ He visits the arroyo with Sergio; goes swimming,
                               mother suspects.

   Second half of summer ————→ Boys visit mountains; think they have found heaven
                               but learn it is a golf course.

                           ——→ They return to the arroyo; try to have fun.

Age 12 (junior high school)——→ They visit the arroyo.

                           ——→ They shout dirty words and yell about girls.

   One Thursday ————————→ They find grinding ball.

                       --------→ They bury grinding ball.

                           ——→ They can't find the buried ball; stop going to the arroyo.

5. **Draw a character map.** To explore the connections and interactions among the characters in a story, draw a character map. In the center of a blank piece of paper, put a main character's name inside a circle. Then add other characters' names, connecting them with lines to the main character. On the connecting lines, briefly describe the relationships between characters and the events or other factors (such as emotions) that affect their relationship. You might use a drawing or symbol to represent some aspect of a character or relationship (for instance, *$* for "wealthy" or a smiley face for "happy"). Here is a sample character map for Ríos's "The Secret Lion."

Sample Character Map: "The Secret Lion"

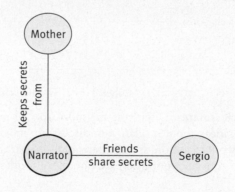

For more on finding sources, see Chapter 21.

6. **Investigate the background of the work and the author.** Research the historical context of the work as well as biographical information about the author. Look for connections among the work; the author's life; and the social, economic, and political events of the time. Investigating the background of a work and its author can give you valuable insights into the writer's meaning (or theme) and purpose. For example, an interpretation of Charles Dickens's "A Christmas Carol" might be more meaningful if you understood how the author's difficult childhood and the conditions of the poor in nineteenth-century England contributed to his portrayal of the Cratchit family.

7. **Use a two-column response journal.** Divide several pages of your journal into two vertical columns. Label the left column *Text* and the right column *Response*. In the left column, record five to ten quotations from the poem or short story. Choose only quotations that convey a main point or opinion, reveal a character's motives, or say something important about the plot or theme. In the right column, describe your reaction to each quotation. You might interpret, disagree with, or question the quotation. Try to comment on the language of the quotation and to relate it to other quotations or elements in the work. Here is a sample two-column journal response to Frost's "Two Look at Two."

For more on journal writing, see Chapter 2, p. 30, and Chapter 3, p. 67.

Sample Two-Column Response to "Two Look at Two"

Text	*Response*
"With thoughts of the path back, how rough it was" (line 5)	The couple's past has been difficult; returning to daily life may be difficult, too. Nature is rough and challenging.
"'This is all,' they sighed, / 'Good-night to woods.'" (lines 13–14)	The couple will soon come to the end -- of their relationship or their lives.

8. **Discover parallel works or situations.** You can often evoke a response to a work by comparing it to other literary works, another narrative form (such as a film or television show), or a familiar situation. For example, after reading the poem "On His Blindness" by John Milton, one student connected it to the movie *Scent of a Woman*, in which one central character is blind. By comparing the literary work to the more familiar film, the student was better able to analyze the meaning of the poem.

9. **Use prewriting.** Prewriting helps you generate ideas for all types of essays, including a literary analysis. Try freewriting, brainstorming, sketching, questioning, or any of the other prewriting strategies discussed in Chapter 4.

> **Essay in Progress 1**
> Use one or more of the preceding techniques to generate ideas about the short story or poem you have chosen for your analysis.

Evaluating Your Ideas

Once you generate sufficient ideas about the work, begin your evaluation by reviewing your notes and prewriting. Look for a perspective or position that reflects your understanding of some aspect of the work. Here are several possible approaches you might take in a literary analysis.

1. **Evaluate symbolism.** Discuss how the author's use of images and symbols creates a particular mood and contributes to the overall meaning of the work.
2. **Analyze conflicts.** Focus on their causes, effects, or both.

3. **Evaluate characterization.** Discuss how characters are presented, whether a particular character's actions are realistic or predictable, or what the author reveals or hides about a character.
4. **Interpret characters or relationships among them.** Analyze how the true nature of a character is revealed or how a character changes in response to circumstances.
5. **Explore themes.** Discover the important point or theme the work conveys, and back up your ideas with examples from the work.

Developing Your Thesis

After evaluating your ideas and choosing an aspect of the work to focus on, it is time to write a thesis statement. Your thesis should indicate the element of the work you will analyze (its theme, characters, or use of symbols, for example) and state the main point you will make about that element, as in the following sample thesis statements.

- Flannery O'Connor's short story "A Good Man Is Hard to Find" uses color to depict various moods throughout the story.
- In Susan Glaspell's play *Trifles,* the female characters are treated condescendingly by the males, and yet the women's interest in so-called trivial matters leads them to interpret the "trivial" pieces of evidence that solve the murder mystery.

For more on thesis statements, see Chapter 5, p. 101.

Be sure your thesis statement focuses on your interpretation of one specific aspect of the work. As in other types of essays, the thesis for a literary analysis should identify your narrowed topic.

Essay in Progress 2

Using the preceding guidelines, write a working thesis for your literary-analysis essay. Then review the poem or short story and your notes to make sure you have enough evidence to support your thesis. In the body paragraphs of your essay, you will need to cite examples from the work that show why your thesis is valid. You might, for example, include relevant descriptions of characters or events, snippets of dialogue, examples of imagery and figures of speech, or any other details from the work that confirm or explain your thesis.

As you review the work and your notes about it, try to meet with one or two classmates who are working on the same poem or short story. They may have noticed evidence that you have overlooked or offer insights into the work that enrich your own reading of it. No two readers will have the same interpretation of a literary work, however, so don't be alarmed if their ideas differ from yours.

Trying Out Your Ideas on Others

Working in a group of two or three students, discuss each other's thesis and supporting evidence for this chapter's assignment. Encourage your peers to ask questions about your work and suggest improvements.

Essay in Progress 3
Use your own analysis and the feedback you received from peer reviewers to evaluate your thesis and supporting evidence. Gather additional examples from the work if necessary, and delete any examples that do not support your thesis.

Organizing and Drafting

Use the following guidelines to organize and draft your literary analysis.

1. **Choose a method of organization.** See Chapter 6 for more detailed suggestions about organizing an essay.
2. **Focus your essay on ideas and not on events.** Remember that your literary analysis should not merely summarize the work or the plot but focus on your ideas and interpretations.
3. **Write in the present tense.** Treat the events in the work as if they are happening now rather than in the past. For example, write "Brooks describes an elderly couple . . . ," not "Brooks described . . ."
4. **Include sufficient examples from the work and cite them correctly.** Use enough examples to support your thesis but not so many that your essay becomes one long string of examples with no clear main point. In addition, provide in-text citations (including paragraph or page numbers for a short story, or line numbers for a poem) in parentheses immediately after any quotations from the work. Include a works-cited entry at the end of your paper indicating the edition of the work you used.

   For help with citing examples from a literary work, see Chapter 22, p. 621.

5. **Write an effective introduction.** The introduction for a literary analysis should engage readers, name the author and title of the work, present your thesis, and suggest why your analysis of the work is useful or important. For example, to engage your readers' interest, you might include a meaningful quotation from the work, comment on the universality of a character or theme, or briefly state your response to the work.
6. **Write a satisfying conclusion.** To conclude your essay, you can use techniques similar to those just described for introductions. Your purposes are to give the essay a sense of closure as well as to reaffirm your thesis. You may want to tie your conclusion directly to your introduction, offering a final word or comment on your main point.

   For more on writing effective introductions and conclusions, see Chapter 6, p. 126.

Essay in Progress 4
Using the preceding guidelines for organizing and drafting along with the thesis you developed in Essay in Progress 2 (p. 678), draft your literary-analysis essay.

Analyzing and Revising

If possible, set aside your draft for a day or two before rereading and revising it. Then, as you reread your draft, concentrate on your ideas and organization, not on grammar or mechanics. Use Figure 23.1 to guide your evaluation. You might also ask a classmate to review your draft by using the questions in the flowchart.

For more on the benefits of peer review, see Chapter 8, p. 162.

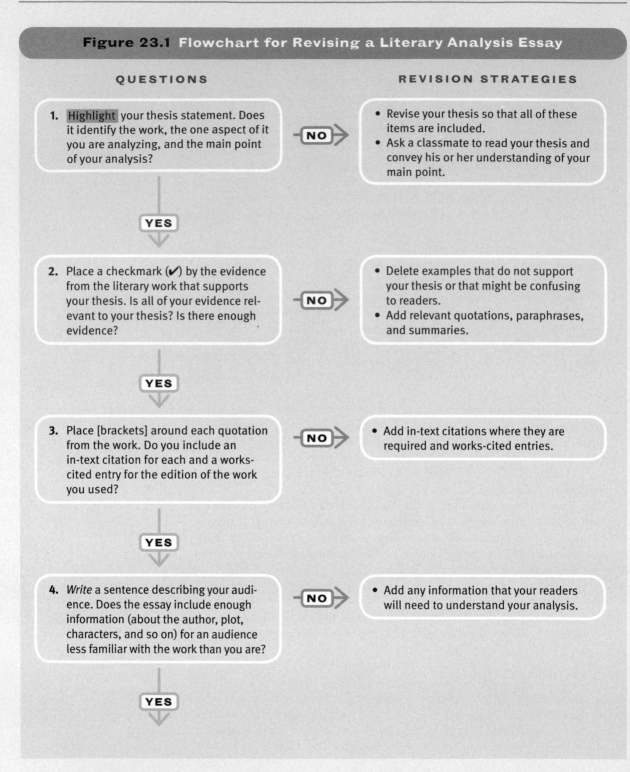

Figure 23.1 Flowchart for Revising a Literary Analysis Essay

QUESTIONS

REVISION STRATEGIES

1. Highlight your thesis statement. Does it identify the work, the one aspect of it you are analyzing, and the main point of your analysis?

   NO →
   - Revise your thesis so that all of these items are included.
   - Ask a classmate to read your thesis and convey his or her understanding of your main point.

   YES ↓

2. Place a checkmark (✔) by the evidence from the literary work that supports your thesis. Is all of your evidence relevant to your thesis? Is there enough evidence?

   NO →
   - Delete examples that do not support your thesis or that might be confusing to readers.
   - Add relevant quotations, paraphrases, and summaries.

   YES ↓

3. Place [brackets] around each quotation from the work. Do you include an in-text citation for each and a works-cited entry for the edition of the work you used?

   NO →
   - Add in-text citations where they are required and works-cited entries.

   YES ↓

4. *Write* a sentence describing your audience. Does the essay include enough information (about the author, plot, characters, and so on) for an audience less familiar with the work than you are?

   NO →
   - Add any information that your readers will need to understand your analysis.

   YES ↓

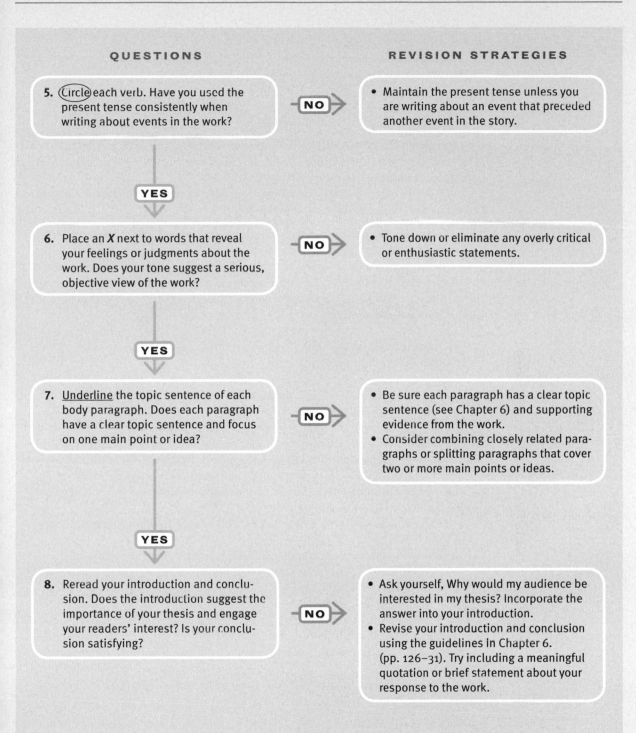

QUESTIONS

REVISION STRATEGIES

5. Circle each verb. Have you used the present tense consistently when writing about events in the work?

NO →

- Maintain the present tense unless you are writing about an event that preceded another event in the story.

YES

6. Place an *X* next to words that reveal your feelings or judgments about the work. Does your tone suggest a serious, objective view of the work?

NO →

- Tone down or eliminate any overly critical or enthusiastic statements.

YES

7. Underline the topic sentence of each body paragraph. Does each paragraph have a clear topic sentence and focus on one main point or idea?

NO →

- Be sure each paragraph has a clear topic sentence (see Chapter 6) and supporting evidence from the work.
- Consider combining closely related paragraphs or splitting paragraphs that cover two or more main points or ideas.

YES

8. Reread your introduction and conclusion. Does the introduction suggest the importance of your thesis and engage your readers' interest? Is your conclusion satisfying?

NO →

- Ask yourself, Why would my audience be interested in my thesis? Incorporate the answer into your introduction.
- Revise your introduction and conclusion using the guidelines in Chapter 6. (pp. 126–31). Try including a meaningful quotation or brief statement about your response to the work.

For more on keeping an error log, see Chapter 9, p. 196.

Essay in Progress 5

Revise your draft essay using Figure 23.1 and the comments you received from peer reviewers.

Editing and Proofreading

The last step is to check your revised essay for errors in grammar, spelling, punctuation, and mechanics. In addition, be sure to check your error log for the types of errors you tend to make.

As you edit and proofread your literary analysis, watch out for the following errors that are often found in this type of writing.

1. **Use the literary present tense.** Even though the poem or short story was written in the past, as a general rule you should write about the events in it and the author's writing of it as if they were happening in the present. This is called the *literary present tense.* An exception to this rule occurs when you are referring to a time earlier than that in which the narrator speaks, in which case a switch to the past tense is appropriate.

   - Keats in "Ode on a Grecian Urn" ~~referred~~ *refers* to the urn as a "silent form" (line 44).

   - In "Two Look at Two," it is not clear why the couple *decided* to walk up the mountainside path.

   The couple made the decision before the action in the poem began.

2. **Punctuate quotations correctly.** Direct quotations from a literary work, whether spoken or written, must be placed in quotation marks. Omitted material is marked by an ellipsis mark. The lines of a poem are separated by a slash (/).

   - In "Two Look at Two," Frost concludes "that the earth in one unlooked-for

   favor / Had made them certain earth returned their love" (lines 41–42).

   Periods and commas appear within quotation marks. Question marks and exclamation points go within or outside of quotation marks, depending on the meaning of the sentence. Here the question mark goes inside the closing quotation marks because it is part of Frost's poem (line 32). Notice, too, that double and single quotation marks are required for a quotation within a quotation.

   - The buck seems "to ask, 'Why don't you make some motion' "? (line 32).

Essay in Progress 6

Edit and proofread your literary analysis essay, paying particular attention to verb tense and punctuation of quotations.

Students Write

Andrew Decker was a student at Niagara County Community College when he wrote the following literary analysis of Ríos's "The Secret Lion" in response to an assignment in his first-year writing class. As you read the essay, notice the one aspect of the literary work that Decker focuses on, his thesis, and the evidence he uses to support it.

READING

The Keeping of "The Secret Lion"

Andrew Decker

Alberto Ríos's "The Secret Lion" charts the initiation of a young boy into adolescence. During this climactic period of growth, the narrator experiences several shifts in perception that change him from a child to an adolescent by teaching him the value of secrets. [1]

Within the first paragraph, the author introduces the reader to the new and perplexing feelings of the main character during his junior high years. His impression of what happened during those years remains nameless, "but it was there nonetheless like a lion, and roaring, roaring that way the biggest things do. Everything changed. Just that" (paragraph 1). It is as if the boy is being swept away by a great swell, the wave of anticipation traditionally associated with the child's entry into adolescence. [2]

He finds that these changes are confusing and yet enticing. Evident within the context of the first page is the boy's newfound curiosity about and fascination with the opposite sex. He is also bewildered by the use of profanity and delights in the opportunity to verbally (and very loudly) explore his own feelings with respect to the use of such words. [3]

Although adults scold him when he questions them about the meaning of these words, their dismay does not discourage him from saying the words privately. He and his friend Sergio like to hide away from such authoritarian voices, and so they cross the highway to the arroyo where they are not supposed to play. In the arroyo, they "shout every dirty word we could think of, in every combination we could come up with, and we would yell about girls, and all the things we wanted to do with them, as loud as we could" (4). Of course, they take great pleasure in this youthful audacity for "it just felt good and for the first time in our lives there was nobody to tell us we couldn't" (4). All is new. All is fresh. Opportunity abounds, and possibilities remain infinite, for time has not yet become an enemy. [4]

One day when the two boys are playing and cussing in the arroyo, they find a perfectly round iron ball. It is heavy and smooth, and to them it is the perfect object. In the eyes of the two children, the world is formless and pure, as is the ball. Similarly, they consider the arroyo to be the perfect place--their perfect place. When faced with deciding what to do with the ball, they choose to bury it so that nobody can take it away--if only in a less literal sense. [5]

Introduction: Decker gives a one-sentence synopsis, assuming his audience is familiar with the work. In his thesis statement, he indicates that he will focus on a specific aspect of it.

Decker gives background for the essay, quoting the "secret lion" passage and associating it with adolescence. He identifies quotations with paragraph numbers. Clear topic sentences identify main point of each body paragraph.

Note Decker's use of present tense and transitions.

Quotations as supporting evidence

Decker discusses the iron ball as a symbol of the purity of childhood. Note that he organizes his essay by presenting events from the work in chronological order, since his thesis focuses on changes in perception over time.

Their minds are still free of the narrow vision of an adult. They are free to roam and roar   6
and echo the spirit of the lion, which is for Sergio and the narrator the spirit of that time.
In their own words, when they talk of that ball, they speak of "how much that ball was like
that place, that whole arroyo: couldn't tell anybody about it, didn't understand what it was,
didn't have a name for it. It just felt good. It was just perfect in the way it was that place,
that whole going to that place, that whole junior high school lion" (8). They know that once
they bury the grinding ball (they only learn later what it is), it will be gone forever and yet
thereby preserved.

The two boys are applying a lesson they have already learned. They understand that an   7
experience can be stolen or changed by a shift in perception so that the original feeling, the
original reality, ceases to exist in its more pure and innocent form. The boys had experienced
disillusion before; when they were very young, they had also played in the arroyo and gone
swimming in the stream. It was a time of naiveté, but their naiveté had been challenged when
they learned that the water was at times filled with the waste flushed downstream by a local
sewage plant.

Decker uses more transitional phrases to move to the final events in the story and to the conclusion of his essay.

Another shift in perception happened later that same summer, when the boys think   8
they have found a new haven beyond some small hills near their houses. On the other
side of a hill they find a green clearing, and they declare its lush beauty their "heaven."
They learn, however, that this heaven is merely a product of their unworldly imagination; the boys have youthfully glorified a simple golf course, in which they were unwelcome visitors.

Conclusion: Decker offers a final interpretation of the work by making reference to its title and reflecting the introduction of the essay.

These events and others teach the boys to protect a new experience, to keep new feelings   9
safe and virginal so as not to lose them to the ravages of time and change. When they return
to the arroyo several years later, when they are twelve and experiencing the exuberance and
excitement of adolescence, they know enough not to share or expose their experiences. The
grinding ball is a symbol of that age, that sense of newness, and as they say, "when we buried
it we knew what would happen" (27). Burying the ball is an attempt on their part to crystal-
lize a certain time, a certain perception, "because it was perfect" (28). "It was the lion" (28),
and the lion was the "roaring" of both that time and that place, and they bury it so that it
might never truly be lost.

Work Cited

Edition of "The Secret Lion" that Decker used

Ríos, Alberto. "The Secret Lion." *The Iguana Killer: Twelve Stories of the Heart.* Lewiston: Blue
    Moon, 1984. Print.

Analyzing the Writer's Technique

1. Does Decker provide sufficient evidence to support his thesis? Choose one example Decker offers and evaluate its effectiveness.
2. Evaluate Decker's introduction and conclusion. In what ways could they be improved?
3. Which paragraphs are particularly well developed? Which, if any, need further development?

Reacting to the Essay

1. How does Decker's interpretation of "The Secret Lion" compare with yours?
2. Evaluate Decker's perception of childhood and adolescence. Write a journal entry comparing his perception to your own.

"... IN THE FUTURE, PLEASE REFRAIN FROM ANSWERING 'DUH' ON THE EASIER QUESTIONS."

CHAPTER 24

Essay Examinations, Portfolios, and Oral Presentations

WRITING QUICK START

The cartoon on the opposite page humorously comments on the process of taking tests. No doubt you've been taking tests throughout school, and they are an important part of college classes as well.

Assume you are taking a short timed writing test. You have been asked to write about your experience taking tests. You might write about how you prepare for exams or share test-taking tips, for example. You have fifteen minutes to complete the writing test.

In completing the timed writing test, did you feel pressured by the fifteen-minute limit? How did you decide which assignment to complete? Did you have as much time as you would have liked to organize, plan, develop, and revise your ideas? Probably not.

Many college instructors use timed writings, essay exams, portfolios, or oral presentations to assess students' knowledge and skills. As you progress through college, you will be required to take many essay exams, especially in advanced courses. In some courses you may be asked to collect and present samples of your work in a portfolio or to give a talk to your instructor and classmates. In the workplace, too, you may be asked to make an oral presentation or produce a memo, report, or proposal and have it on your supervisor's desk "by five o'clock." See the accompanying box for a few examples.

You may ask, Why do instructors give essay exams and other kinds of timed writing assignments? In many college courses, essay exams allow instructors to determine how well students have grasped important concepts and whether they can organize and integrate key concepts with other material. In addition, instructors realize that an essay exam requires students to use different and more advanced thinking skills than they use when taking a more objective type of exam, such as a multiple-choice test. For instance, an essay exam for a history course would require you to pull ideas together and focus on larger issues, perhaps analyzing historical trends or making comparisons between two political figures. Timed writing assignments serve a similar purpose in a composition course. When you are given forty-five minutes to write a brief process analysis of something you know how to do, a short comparison of two television shows, or a description of someone you admire, your instructor wants to make sure you are learning how to write various types of essays and can do so quickly and efficiently. Finally, some colleges require students to demonstrate their writing expertise in a competency test given shortly after admission to the college, at the end of a writing course, or at the completion of a program of study.

This chapter will help you prepare for the timed essay writings you will encounter in college and in your career. Developing good study skills is a key to success on such exams. You will learn how to anticipate the types of questions instructors ask, how to organize your ideas quickly and efficiently, and how to work within the time constraints of essay exams. Although the chapter focuses on essay exams, the skills you learn here also apply to other kinds of timed writing assignments.

SCENES FROM COLLEGE AND THE WORKPLACE

- For a *business communication* class, you are asked to assemble a portfolio that illustrates your mastery of the six course objectives.

- For the midterm exam in your *philosophy of religion* course, you have one hour to complete the following essay: "Contrast the beliefs of Islam with those of either Judaism or Christianity."

- As a *sales representative* for a Web site design company, you are required to create and give an oral presentation to a group of owners of restaurant chains that demonstrates how creating a Web site for a chain could increase profitability.

You may also wonder why instructors require oral presentations. Speaking to a live audience provides a window into your ability to structure and present ideas in a significantly different way from doing so in a written text. In this chapter you will learn how to plan, organize, draft, and deliver an effective presentation. You will also learn how to create a writing portfolio and write a reflective essay that introduces it.

ESSAY EXAMINATIONS

Preparing for Essay Exams

Because essay exams require you to produce a written response, the best way to prepare for them is by organizing and writing. The following guidelines will help you prepare for such exams.

Write Study Sheets That Synthesize Information

Most essay exams require you to *synthesize*, or pull together, information. To prepare for this task, try to identify the key topics in a course, and write a study sheet for each main topic. Study sheets help you organize and consolidate complex or detailed information and give you brief topic outlines to study. To prepare a study sheet, draw on information from your textbook as well as from your class notes, in-class handouts, papers (note key topics), previous exams (look for emphasized topics), and assigned readings.

For more on synthesizing information, see Chapter 22, p. 601.

You can organize a study sheet in a variety of ways. For example, you might draw a graphic organizer to create a visual study sheet, create a time line to connect historical events, write an outline to organize information, or construct a comparison-and-contrast chart to see relationships between different topics. Whatever method of organization you use for your study sheet, be sure to include key information about topics: definitions, facts, principles, theories, events, research studies, and the like.

Here is part of one student's study sheet for a speech communication course on the topic *audience analysis.*

SAMPLE STUDY SHEET

Topic: Audience Analysis

1. Demographic characteristics
   — Age and gender
   — Educational background (type and level of education)
   — Group membership (people who share similar interests or goals)
   — Social activities
   — Religious activities
   — Hobbies and sports

2. Psychological characteristics
   — Beliefs (about what is true or false, right or wrong)
   — Attitudes (positive or negative)
   — Values (standards for judging worth of thoughts and actions)

Exercise 24.1

Use the preceding guidelines to prepare a study sheet on a general topic that you expect will be covered on an upcoming exam in one of your courses.

Predict Essay Exam Questions

Once you prepare study sheets for a particular course, the next step is to predict questions that might be asked on an essay exam. Although essay exam questions usually focus on general topics, themes, or patterns, you will probably need to supply details in your response. For example, an essay question on an economics exam might ask you to compare and contrast the James-Lange and Cannon-Bard theories of motivation. Your answer would focus on the similarities and differences between these key theories, incorporating relevant details where necessary.

Use the following strategies to help you predict the types of questions you might be asked on an essay exam.

1. **Group topics into categories.** Review your textbook, class notes, and study sheets. Look to see how you can group topics into general subject areas or categories. For example, if you find several chapters that deal with kinship in your anthropology textbook, a question on kinship is likely to appear on one or more essay exams for the course.
2. **Study your course syllabus and objectives.** These documents contain important clues about what your instructor expects you to know at various points during the course.
3. **Study previous exams.** Notice which key ideas are emphasized in previous exams. If you had to explain the historical significance of the Boston Tea Party on your first American history exam, you can predict that you will be asked to explain the historical significance of other events on subsequent exams.
4. **Listen to your instructor's comments.** When your instructor announces or reviews material for an upcoming essay exam, pay close attention to what is said. He or she may reveal key topics or suggest areas that will be emphasized on the test.
5. **Draft some possible essay questions.** Use Table 24.1 (on p. 695) to help you draft possible essay questions using key verbs. The verb in a question affects the way you answer it. It takes time to learn how to predict exam questions, so don't get discouraged if at first you predict only one question correctly. Even if you predict none of the questions, the attempt to do so will help you learn the material.

Exercise 24.2

Suppose your business marketing textbook includes a chapter with the following headings. Using the preceding guidelines for predicting essay exam questions and the key verbs in Table 24.1 (p. 695), write three possible questions that the course instructor might ask about the chapter material.

Textbook: *Marketing*, by William G. Nickels and Marian Burk Wood
Chapter: "Consumer Buying Behavior"
Headings:
    Marketing, Relationships, and Consumer Behavior
        Real People, Real Individuals
        Consumers as Moving Targets
    How Consumers Buy
        The Need-Recognition Stage
        The Information-Seeking Stage
        The Evaluation Stage
        The Purchase Stage
        The Postpurchase Evaluation Stage
        Involvement and the Purchase-Decision Process
    External Influences on Consumer Behavior
        Family and Household Influences
        Opinion Leaders and Word of Mouth
        Reference Groups
        Social Class
        Culture, Subculture, and Core Values
        Situational Influences
    Internal Influences on Consumer Behavior
        Perception
        Motivation
        Attitudes

Essay in Progress 1

For an upcoming essay exam in one of your courses, predict and write at least three possible questions your instructor might ask about the course material.

Draft Answers in Outline Form

Once you predict several possible essay exam questions, the next step is to write a brief, rough outline of the information that answers each question. Be sure each outline responds to the *wording* of the question—that is, it should *explain, compare, describe,* or do whatever else the question asks (see Table 24.1 on p. 695). Writing a rough outline will strengthen your recall of the material. It will also save you time during the actual exam because you will have already spent some time thinking about, organizing, and writing about the material.

Here is a sample essay question and an informal outline written in response to it.

ESSAY QUESTION

Explain the ways in which material passes in and out of cells by crossing plasma membranes.

INFORMAL OUTLINE

Types of Transport

1. Passive—no use of cellular energy; random movement of molecules
   a. Diffusion—movement of molecules from areas of high concentration to areas of low concentration (example: open bottle of perfume, aroma spreads)
   b. Facilitated diffusion—similar to simple diffusion; differs in that some kinds of molecules are moved more easily than others (helped by carrier proteins in cell membrane)
   c. Osmosis—diffusion of water across membranes from area of lower to area of higher solute concentration

2. Active—requires cellular energy; usually movement against the concentration gradient
   a. Facilitated active transport—carrier molecules move ions across a membrane
   b. Endocytosis—material is surrounded by a plasma membrane and pinched off into a vacuole
   c. Exocytosis—cells expel materials

Essay in Progress 2

For one of the questions you predicted in Essay in Progress 1, prepare a brief informal outline in response to the question.

Reduce Informal Outlines to Key-Word Outlines

To help you recall your outline answer at the time of the exam, reduce it to a brief key-word outline or list of key topics. Here is a sample key-word outline for the essay question about cells.

KEY-WORD OUTLINE

Types of Transport

1. Passive
   — Diffusion
   — Facilitated diffusion
   — Osmosis

2. Active
   — Facilitated active transport
   — Endocytosis
   — Exocytosis

Essay in Progress 3
Reduce the outline answer you wrote in Essay in Progress 2 to a key-word outline.

Taking Essay Exams

Once you have done some preparation, you should be more confident about taking an essay exam. Although the time limit for an essay exam may make you feel somewhat pressured, remember that your classmates are working under the same conditions.

Some General Guidelines

Keep the following general guidelines in mind when you take essay exams.

1. **Arrive at the room where the exam is to be given a few minutes early.** You can use this time to collect your thoughts and get organized.
2. **Sit in the front of the room.** You will be less distracted and better able to see and hear the instructor as last-minute directions or corrections are announced.
3. **Read the directions carefully.** For example, some exams may direct you to answer only one of three questions, whereas other exams may ask you to answer all questions.
4. **Preview the exam and plan your time carefully.** Get a complete picture of the task at hand and then plan how you will complete the exam within the allotted time. For example, if you are given fifty minutes to complete an essay exam, spend roughly ten minutes planning, thirty minutes writing, and ten minutes editing, proofreading, and making last-minute changes. If an exam contains both objective and essay questions, do the objective questions first so that you have the remaining time to concentrate on the essay questions.
5. **Notice the point value of each question.** If your instructor assigns points to each question, use the point values to plan your time. For example, you would spend more time answering a thirty-point question than a ten-point question.
6. **Choose topics or questions carefully.** Often you will be given little or no choice of topic or question. If you do have a choice, choose the topics or answer the questions that you know the most about. If you are given a broad topic, such as a current social issue, narrow the topic to one you can write about in the specified amount of time.
7. **Answer the easiest question first.** Answering the easiest question first will boost your confidence and allow you to spend the remaining time working on the more difficult questions.
8. **Consider your audience and purpose.** For most essay exams, your instructor is your audience. Since your instructor is already knowledgeable about the topic, your purpose is to demonstrate what *you know* about the topic. Therefore, you should write thorough and complete answers, pretending that your instructor knows only what you tell him or her.

9. **Remember that your first draft is your final draft.** Plan on writing your first draft carefully and correctly so that it can serve as your final copy. You can always make minor changes and additions as you write or while you edit and proofread.

10. **Plan and organize your answer.** Because time is limited, your first response may be to start writing immediately. However, planning and organizing are especially important first steps because you will not have the opportunity to revise your essay. (If you usually write whatever comes to mind and then spend a great deal of time revising, you will need to modify your approach for essay exams.) Begin by writing a brief thesis statement. Then jot down the key supporting points and number them in the order you will present them. Leave space under each supporting point for your details. If the question is one you predicted earlier, write down your key-word outline. If an idea for an interesting introduction or an effective conclusion comes to mind, jot it down as well. As you write your answers, be sure to reserve enough time to reread your essay and correct surface errors.

Analyzing Essay Exam Questions

Essay exam questions are often concise, but if you read them closely, you will find that they *do* specifically tell you what to write about. Consider the following sample essay question from a sociology exam.

Choose a particular institution, define it, and identify its primary characteristics.

The question tells you exactly what to write about—*a particular institution.* In addition, the key verbs *define* and *identify* tell you how to approach the subject. For this essay question, then, you would give an accurate definition of an institution and discuss its primary characteristics.

Table 24.1 lists key verbs commonly used in essay exam questions along with sample questions and tips for answering them. As you study the list, notice that many of the verbs suggest a particular pattern of development. For example, *trace* suggests using a narrative sequence, and *justify* suggests using argumentation. For a more vague key verb such as *explain* or *discuss,* you might use a combination of patterns.

Writing Essay Answers

Since your first-draft essay exam is also your final draft, be sure to write in complete and grammatically correct sentences, to supply sufficient detail, and to follow a logical organization. For essay exams, instructors do not expect your writing to be as polished as it might be for an essay or research paper assignment. It is acceptable to cross out words or sentences neatly and to indicate corrections in spelling or grammar. If you

TABLE 24.1 Responding to Key Verbs in Essay Exam Questions

Key Verb	Sample Essay Question	Tips for Answering Questions
Compare	Compare the poetry of Judith Ortiz Cofer to that of Julia Alvarez.	Show how the poems are similar as well as different; use details and examples.
Contrast	Contrast classical and operant conditioning.	Show how they are different, use details and examples.
Define	Define biofeedback and describe its uses.	Give an accurate explanation of the term with enough detail to demonstrate that you understand it.
Discuss	Discuss the halo effect and give examples of its use.	Consider important characteristics and main points; include examples.
Evaluate	Evaluate the accomplishments of the feminist movement over the past fifty years.	Assess its merits, strengths, weaknesses, advantages, or limitations.
Explain	Explain the functions of amino acids.	Use facts and details to make the topic or concept clear and understandable.
Illustrate	Illustrate with examples from your experience how culture shapes human behavior.	Use examples that demonstrate a point or clarify an idea.
Justify	Justify laws outlawing smoking in federal buildings.	Give reasons and evidence that support an action, decision, or policy.
List	List the advantages and disadvantages of sales promotions.	List or discuss one by one; use most-to-least or least-to-most organization.
Summarize	Summarize Maslow's hierarchy of needs.	Briefly review all the major points.
Trace	Trace the life cycle of a typical household product.	Describe its development or progress in chronological order.

think of an idea to add, write the sentence at the top of your paper and draw an arrow to indicate where it should be inserted.

Essay exam answers tend to have brief introductions and conclusions. The introduction, for instance, may include only a thesis statement. If possible, include any necessary background information on the topic and write a conclusion only if the question seems to require a final evaluative statement.

If you run out of time on an essay exam, jot the unfinished portion of your outline at the end of the essay. Your instructor may give you partial credit for your ideas.

Writing Your Thesis Statement

For more on thesis statements, see Chapter 5.

Your thesis statement should be clear and direct, identify your subject, and suggest your approach to the topic. Often the thesis rephrases or answers the essay exam question. Consider the following examples.

Essay Exam Question	*Thesis Statement*
Explain how tides are produced in the earth's oceans. Account for seasonal variations.	The earth's gravitational forces are responsible for producing tides in the earth's oceans.
Distinguish between bureaucratic agencies and other government decision-making bodies.	Bureaucratic agencies are distinct from other government decision-making bodies because of their hierarchical organization, character and culture, and professionalism.

For some essay exam questions, your thesis should also suggest the organization of your essay. For example, if you are asked to explain the differences between primary and secondary groups, your thesis might be stated as follows: "Primary groups differ from secondary groups in their membership, purpose, level of interaction, and level of intimacy." Your essay, then, would be organized accordingly, discussing membership first, then purpose, and so forth.

Exercise 24.3

Write thesis statements for two of the following essay exam questions.

1. Define and illustrate the meaning of the term *freedom of the press.*
2. Distinguish between the medical care provided by private physicians and that provided by medical clinics.
3. Choose a recent television advertisement and describe its rational and emotional appeals.
4. Evaluate a current news program in terms of its breadth and depth of coverage, objectivity, and political and social viewpoints.

Developing Supporting Details

For more on topic sentences, see Chapter 7, p. 141.

Write a separate paragraph for each of your key points. In an essay answer distinguishing primary from secondary groups, for example, you would devote one paragraph to each distinguishing feature: membership, purpose, level of interaction, and level of intimacy. The topic sentence for each paragraph should identify and briefly explain a key point. For example, a topic sentence for the first main point about groups might read like this: "Membership, or who belongs, is one factor that distinguishes primary from secondary groups." The rest of the paragraph would explain membership: what constitutes membership, what criteria are used to decide who belongs, and who decides. Whenever possible, supply examples to make it clear that you can apply the information you have learned. Keep in mind that on an essay exam your goal is to demonstrate your knowledge and understanding of the material.

Rereading and Proofreading Your Answer

Be sure to leave enough time to reread and proofread your essay answer. Begin by rereading the question to make sure you have answered all parts of it. Then reread your answer, checking it first for content. Add missing information, correct vague or unclear sentences, and add facts or details. Next, proofread for errors in spelling, punctuation, and grammar. Before taking an essay exam, check your error log and then evaluate your answer with those errors in mind. A neat, nearly error-free essay makes a positive impression on your instructor and identifies you as a serious, conscientious student. An error-free essay may also improve your grade.

For more on proofreading and on keeping an error log, see Chapter 9, p. 196.

> ### Essay in Progress 4
> For the essay question you worked on in Essay in Progress 3, use the preceding guidelines to write a complete essay answer.

Students Write

The following model essay exam response was written by Ronald Robinson for his sociology course. As you read Ronald's essay, note that it has been annotated to identify key elements of its organization and content.

Essay Exam Response

Essay Exam Question
Distinguish between fads and fashions, explaining the characteristics of each type of group behavior and describing the phases each usually goes through.

Fashions and fads, types of collective group behavior, are distinct from one another in terms of their duration, their predictability, and the number of people involved. Each type follows a five-stage process of development.

Thesis statement

A fashion is a temporary trend in behavior or appearance that is followed by a relatively large number of people. Although the word *fashion* often refers to a style of dress, there are fashions in music, art, and literature as well. Trends in clothing fashions are often engineered by clothing designers, advertisers, and the media to create a particular "look." The hip-hop look is an example of a heavily promoted fashion. Fashions are more universally subscribed to than fads. Wearing athletic shoes as casual attire is a good example of a universal fashion.

Definition and characteristics of *fashion*

Definition and characteristics
of *fad*

A fad is a more temporary adoption of a particular behavior or look. Fads are in-group behaviors that often serve as identity markers for a group. Fads also tend to be adopted by smaller groups, often made up of people who want to appear different or unconventional. Unlike fashions, fads tend to be shorter-lived, less predictable, and less influenced by people outside the group. Examples of recent fads are bald heads, tattoos, and tongue piercings. Fads are usually harmless and have no long-range effects.

Description of 5-phase
process

Fashions and fads each follow a five-phase process of development. In the first phase, latency, the trend exists in the minds of a few people but shows little evidence of spreading. In the second phase, the trend spreads rapidly and reaches its peak. After that, the trend begins a slow decline (phase three). In the fourth phase, its newness is over and many users drop or abandon the trend. In its final phase, quiescence, nearly everyone has dropped the trend, and it is followed by only a few people.

Thinking Critically about Essay Exams

Read essay exam questions critically, approaching them from the viewpoint of the instructor. Try to discover the knowledge or skill that your instructor is attempting to assess by asking the question. Then, as you write your answer, make sure your response clearly demonstrates your knowledge or skill. For example, in posing the question "Discuss the issue of sexual behavior from the three major sociological perspectives," the instructor is assessing two things—how well you *understand* the three sociological perspectives and how successfully you can *apply* them to a particular issue (sexual behavior). First you would need to give a clear, complete, but brief definition of each perspective. Then you would explain how each of the three sociological perspectives approaches the issue of sexual behavior.

PORTFOLIOS

Creating a Writing Portfolio

A portfolio is a collection of materials that is representative of a person's work. It often demonstrates or exemplifies skill, talent, or proficiency. Architects create portfolios that contain drawings and photographs of buildings they have designed. Sculptors' portfolios may include photographs of their work, as well as copies of reviews, awards, or articles about their work. Similarly, your writing instructor may ask you to create a portfolio that represents your skill and proficiency as a writer. Think of your portfolio as a picture of your development as a writer over time.

Purposes of a Writing Portfolio

Usually a writing portfolio is assigned by your writing instructor to achieve one or more purposes. One purpose is assessment. Your instructor may use your collection of writing to evaluate your mastery of the objectives outlined in the course syllabus. That evaluation will become a part of your final grade in the course.

The second purpose is learning and self-assessment. Building a portfolio makes you think about yourself as a learner and as a writer. By building a writing portfolio, you can learn a great deal about the writing process, assess your strengths and weaknesses as a writer, and observe your own progress as you build writing proficiency. Think of building your writing portfolio as an opportunity to present yourself in the best possible way—highlighting the work you are proud of and demonstrating the skills you have mastered. It is also an opportunity, as you track your progress, to realize that your hard work in the course has paid off.

Deciding What to Include

Instructors often specify what their students' portfolios should include. If you are uncertain about what to include, be sure to ask your instructor for clarification. You might ask to see a sample of a portfolio that meets your instructor's expectations. Be sure you can answer each of the following questions.

- How many pieces of writing should I include? Are there limits?
- Should all writing done in the course be included, or am I allowed to choose what to include?
- What version(s) should be included—drafts, outlines, and revisions or just the final essay?
- What types of writing should be included? Should essays be based on personal experience, library or Internet research, or field research?
- Is the portfolio limited to essays, or can research notes, downloaded Web pages, or completed class exercises be included?
- Can writing from other courses or pieces of writing for nonacademic audiences (email, work-related correspondence, or service learning projects, for example) be included?
- How should the portfolio be organized?
- What type of introductory letter or essay is required? What length and format are appropriate?
- How much does the portfolio count in my grade?
- What is the due date, or is the portfolio to be submitted at various intervals throughout the term?
- How will it be graded? That is, is the grade based on improvement or only on the quality of the work included?

Using Your Course Syllabus as a Guide

Your course syllabus is an important guide that can help you decide what to include in your portfolio—especially if your instructor has given you choices in structuring and organizing it. Your course syllabus contains objectives. These are statements of what your instructor expects you to learn from the course. You can use several or all

For a sample syllabus, see Chapter 2, p. 26.

of these to structure your portfolio. Suppose one objective states, "Students will develop prewriting strategies that accommodate their learning style." In your portfolio, then, you might include a copy of the results of the Learning Style Inventory (p. 33) and then show examples of your use of two or more prewriting strategies. If another objective states, "Students will demonstrate control over errors in sentence structure, spelling, and punctuation," you would want to include examples of essays in which you identified and corrected these types of errors. You might also include a copy of your error log and a list of exercises you completed using Exercise Central or other online resources.

Organizing Your Portfolio

Begin collecting materials for your portfolio as soon as you know it is required. If you wait until the due date to assemble what you need, you may have discarded or misplaced important prewriting, revision materials, or drafts of essays.

Begin by deciding whether you will keep track of materials for your portfolio using printed copies or electronic copies. If you are using printed copies, use a file folder or accordion folder divided into sections to separate your work. Keep everything associated with each writing assignment you complete. This includes the original assignment, prewriting, outlines, graphic organizers, and all drafts. If you are using sources, keep your notes, photocopies, or printouts of sources. Be sure to keep peer-review comments as well as papers with your instructor's comments.

If you are using an electronic system to collect materials for your portfolio, create a file system that will make it easy for you to locate all of your work. Be sure to make backup copies of your files on a CD. Keep a paper file for hard copies of materials such as research notes or peer-review comments that are not on your computer.

Your portfolio represents you. Be sure it is neat, complete, and carefully assembled. Use the following suggestions to present a well-organized portfolio that demonstrates that you have taken care in its preparation.

- Include a cover or title page that gives your name, course number, instructor's name, and date.
- Include a table of contents that identifies the elements in the portfolio and the page number on which each piece begins. Number the portfolio consecutively from beginning to end. Since your essays may already have page numbers, put the new page numbers in a different position or use a different color of ink.
- Attach earlier drafts of papers behind the final draft, clearly labeling each draft.
- Be sure each piece is dated so that your instructor can identify its place within your growth process.
- Label each piece, indicating what it is intended to demonstrate. For example, if an essay demonstrates your ability to use narration, be sure to label it as such.
- Plan the sequence of your portfolio. If your instructor has not expressed a preference, choose a method of organization that presents your work and skill development in the best possible way. If you are including two essays to demonstrate your effective use of narration, for example, you might present the better one first, thereby making the strongest possible first impression. If, on the other hand,

you are trying to show the growth in your ability to use narration, you might present the weaker one first.

Choosing Pieces to Include

One key to creating a successful portfolio is choosing the *right* pieces to include, assuming that you have a choice. The right pieces depend on what your portfolio is intended to demonstrate. If you are supposed to demonstrate growth, it is a mistake to include only your best papers. If you are supposed to demonstrate your ability to write for a variety of purposes and audiences, it would be a mistake to include only argumentative essays. If the length is unlimited, do not include everything; be selective and choose pieces that illustrate what your instructor wants you to evaluate. Use Table 24.2 to guide your selection.

TABLE 24.2 Guidelines for Building a Writing Portfolio

If You Are Asked to . . .	What to Include
Demonstrate your growth as a writer	• Include weak papers from early in the semester and conclude with your best papers written toward the end of the semester. • You might also include an essay that demonstrates major changes from first to final draft.
Demonstrate your ability to approach writing as a process	• For several essays, include work you did for topic selection, generating ideas, drafting, revising, and proofreading. • Choose pieces that show your essay gradually developing and evolving as you worked; they should also show major changes in revised drafts. • Avoid pieces that were well developed in your early stages of writing and that required only final polishing.
Feature your best work of the semester	• Choose essays that solidly exemplify the method of organization you are using. • Use the revision flowcharts and the Evaluating Your Progress boxes in Chapters 10–17 and 19 to guide your selection.
Demonstrate your ability to write for a variety of audiences and purposes	• Review the section on audience and purpose in Chapter 4, p. 82. • Select pieces that are widely different. • Include non-course-related and nonacademic pieces, if allowed.
Demonstrate your ability to use library and Internet sources	• Review the appropriate sections of Chapters 20–22. • Choose an essay that uses both library and Internet sources rather than one or the other.

Writing the Introductory Letter or Essay

Most instructors expect you to include an essay or a letter that introduces your portfolio. It is often called a *reflective essay* or *letter* because in it you reflect on your development as a writer. This letter or essay is crucial to an effective portfolio, and you should spend a good amount of time composing it. In fact, you might begin thinking and making notes about it long before the portfolio is due, observing trends, problems, and patterns in your writing.

This essay is the key to the portfolio, since it reflects on and explains its contents. It should explain how your portfolio is organized and give an overview of what it includes. It also should explain *how* various items that you have placed in the portfolio demonstrate what you intend them to demonstrate. For example, if you have included two essays to illustrate your ability to write for a variety of audiences and purposes, then explain for whom and for what purpose each essay was written.

Your reflective letter may also include some or all of the following:

- An appraisal of what you have learned in the course, referring to specific materials included in the portfolio as evidence.
- A discussion of your strengths and weaknesses as a writer, again referring to portfolio materials that illustrate and explain your points.
- A discussion of your progress or development as a writer. Explain how you have changed, giving examples of new strategies you have learned. Point out examples of them in the portfolio.

Here are a few things to avoid when building your portfolio. Make sure you write about what you learned about *your* writing, not about writing in general. That is, do not repeat points from the book about the writing process. Instead, explain how you have used that information to become a better writer. Also, do not exaggerate your progress or try to say what you think the instructor wants to hear. Instead, be honest and forthright in assessing your progress. Finally, avoid flattery or praise of the instructor or the course. Most instructors will give you a separate opportunity to evaluate them and the courses they teach.

Here is a sample reflective essay written by Bryan Scott, a nursing student and former Marine, for his first-year writing course.

Students Write

The Portfolio Assignment

For your final assignment you will submit a portfolio containing the following.

- A table of contents listing the titles and page numbers of all included writing pieces
- A reflective essay that introduces your portfolio
- One series of writing pieces (prewriting, outlines, drafts) that demonstrates your ability to move successfully through the steps in the writing process

- At least two pieces of writing that demonstrate your growth as a writer
- One piece of writing done this term for another class
- Essays that demonstrate your ability to use various methods of organization
- A limited number of materials of your own choice

In your reflective essay, you are expected to include answers to the following questions.

1. What are your current strengths and weaknesses as a writer?
2. What specific writing skills have you developed?
3. How have you changed as a writer?
4. In what ways has your awareness of learning style improved your ability to write?
5. What critical reading and thinking skills have you learned, *or* in what ways have you strengthened your critical reading and thinking skills?

Sample Reflective Essay

TABLE OF CONTENTS

Bryan Scott

May 5, 2008

Final Portfolio

English 109

From the Marines to the Writing Classroom

I enrolled in this course because it was a required course in my nursing   1
curriculum, but I can now say that I am glad that it was required. As a former
Marine, I had little experience with writing, other than writing letters home
to my wife and parents. Now, as I prepare for a career as a nurse, I realize that
writing is an important communication skill. Writing reports about patients, such
as "Nursing Care Plan: Patient 4," requires me to present clear, precise,

and accurate information about patients and their care. Through this
course I have learned to do so. Although I improved in almost every area
of writing, my greatest improvements were in approaching writing as a process,
moving from personal to informative writing, and developing an awareness
of audience.

Through this course I have learned to view writing as a process rather than a   2
"write-it-once-and–I–am-done" activity. As shown in the packet of writing for "The
Wall at Sunset," I have discovered the value of prewriting as a way of coming up
with ideas. Before I started writing this essay, I knew that visiting the Vietnam
Veterans Memorial had been an emotional experience for me, but I found that
mapping helped me define and organize my feelings. Since I am a spatial learner,
I could visualize the wall and map my responses to seeing the names of other
soldiers. My first draft in the packet demonstrates my ability to begin with a
thesis statement and build ideas around it. My second draft shows how I
added detail and arranged my impressions into an organized essay.
My final draft shows my ability to catch most errors in spelling, grammar,
and punctuation.

Moving from personal writing to informative writing was a valuable   3
learning experience that is essential for my career. My first essay, "The Wall at
Sunset," was a very personal account of my visit to the Vietnam Veterans
Memorial, as was the essay "How the Marines Changed My Life," a personal
account of life in the U.S. Marine Corps. While I had a lot to say about my
own experiences, I found it difficult to write about topics that did not directly
involve me. I found that learning to use sources, especially Internet sources,
helped me get started with informative writing. By visiting news Web sites,
doing Internet research, and reading blogs, I learned to move outside of
myself and begin to think about and become interested in what other
people were saying and thinking. My essay "Miracle in the Operating Room"
demonstrates my ability to use sources, both print and Internet, to learn
how kidney transplants are done.

As I moved from personal to informative writing, I found that the patterns of   4
development provided a framework for developing and organizing informative
writing. Process seemed to be an effective way to present information for the
essay "Miracle in the Operating Room." My essay "Emotional Styles of Athletes"
initially contained a lot of my own personal impressions (see the first draft that

I have included), but by using classification, I was able to focus on characteristics of athletes rather than on my opinions of them.

Before I took this course, I had no idea that I should write differently for different audiences. My essay "How the Marines Changed My Life" was written for my classmates, many of whom had no military experience. I found I had to explain things about chain of command, regimentation, and living conditions--all things that I and other Marines are familiar with. In my case report for my nursing class, "Nursing Care Plan: Patient 4," my audience was other nurses and medical staff, even doctors. Because I was writing for a specialized audience, I could mention medical terms, procedures, and medications freely without defining them. However, in "Miracle In the Operating Room," I was writing for a general, nonspecialized audience, so I realized it was necessary to explain terms such as *dialysis*, *laparoscopy*, and *nephrectomy*. This essay and my nursing case report demonstrate my ability to write in a clear, direct, and concise manner in my chosen field for different audiences.

5

While I developed many strengths as a writer, I am still aware of many weaknesses. I have difficulty with descriptive writing; I just cannot come up with words to paint a visual picture as effectively as I would like. Fortunately, nursing will not require much creative description. I also have difficulty choosing a topic. Although I found the suggestions in our textbook helpful, I still feel as if I am overlooking important or useful topics. Finally, I have not benefited from peer review as much as others have. I still find myself uncomfortable when accepting criticism and revision ideas from other students. Perhaps my military training to look to authority for direction is still getting in the way.

6

As I developed strengths as a writer, I also became a more critical reader and thinker. I am enclosing my annotations for the professional essay "Bad Conduct, by the Numbers." These annotations demonstrate my ability to ask questions and challenge the author. I also found enlightening discussions in the text on connotative language, bias, and fact and opinion. These are things I had never thought much about, and now I find myself being aware of these things as I read.

7

Overall, by taking this course, I have become a more serious and aware writer and have come to regard writing as a rewarding challenge.

8

Note that Bryan organized his reflective essay using the principles of good writing he learned in the course. Within this organization, he was able to identify his strengths and weaknesses as a writer, discuss learning styles, and analyze his essays. Notice that Bryan identifies his strengths and weaknesses as a writer throughout the essay.

ORAL PRESENTATIONS

Giving Oral Presentations

Oral presentations are an important part of many college classes. In an ecology class, you may be asked to report on a local environmental problem. In a sociology class, you may have to summarize your findings from a survey about a campus issue. Presentations vary in type: You may express your own ideas, inform, or persuade. These purposes are similar to those you have learned for writing essays.

Effective presentations are important in academic situations and also in many jobs and careers. By learning to speak before groups, you will gain self-confidence and become a more effective communicator. As you work through this section, you will see that the steps you take in giving an oral presentation parallel the steps required in writing an essay: planning, organizing and drafting, rehearsing (similar to revising), and delivering (similar to the final submission of your essay).

Planning Your Presentation

The more carefully you plan your presentation, the more comfortable you will be in delivering it. Use the following steps.

Select Your Topic

Choosing a topic is as important for making a presentation as it is for writing an essay. The topic you choose should depend on the assignment. Make sure you understand the assignment and the type of speech you are to give. Is it to be informative or persuasive? Are visual aids permitted, encouraged, or required? Are you allowed to speak from an outline or note cards? What is the time limit? Also consider your audience, as you do when writing essays. What topics are important to your listeners and will sustain their interest? Here are a few suggestions for choosing a topic.

- **Choose a topic that is appropriate for your audience.** You might be interested in choosing a day-care center, but if your audience is mostly young college students, you may have difficulty sustaining their interest with a speech titled "How to Choose the Best Day-Care Center."
- **Choose a topic of value.** Your topic should be worthwhile or meaningful to your audience. Trivial topics such as how to create a particular hairstyle or a report about characters on a soap opera may not have sufficient merit for college classrooms.

- **Choose a narrow topic.** As in writing, if you choose a topic that is too broad, you will have too much to say in the allotted time or may resort to generalities that lack supporting evidence.
- **Choose a topic that you find interesting or know something about.** You will find it easier to exude and generate enthusiasm if you are speaking about a topic that is familiar and that you enjoy.

Identify Your Purpose

As when you are writing, first determine if your purpose is to inform or persuade. Then more carefully define your purpose. For an informative speech, what information do you want to convey? If your topic is wrestling, do you want to explain its popularity, demonstrate several wrestling holds, or discuss it as a collegiate sport? If your purpose is to persuade, do you want to argue values, encourage action, or change your audience members' thinking or beliefs?

Research Your Topic

As you would for an essay, unless your presentation is to be based on your personal knowledge or experience, you will need to research your topic. As you give your speech, be sure to mention your sources. You might mention the author, the work, or both—whatever is meaningful and adds credibility to your presentation. If you use quotations, avoid tedious expressions such as "I quote here" or "I want to quote an example." Instead, integrate your quotations into your speech as you would quotations into an essay.

For more information on researching, see Chapters 20 and 21.

For more information on integrating quotations, see Chapter 22, p. 610.

Organizing and Drafting Your Presentation

Develop a Thesis and Identify Supporting Ideas

Once you have read about your topic, you are ready to draft a thesis statement and collect information that supports it. Again, these processes parallel those you have been using to write an essay. Be sure to include a variety of evidence, considering the types that would appeal to your audience. When you write an essay, your readers can reread if they miss a point. When you give an oral presentation, your listeners do not have that option, so reiterate your thesis frequently to make your presentation easier to follow.

Organize Your Speech

Using a method of organization will make your speech easier to follow and easier for you to present. By grouping your ideas together, you will be able to remember them better. If you are using classification to organize a speech titled "Types of Procrastinators," you can remember that you have four main categories, with descriptive details to explain each. Be sure to use plenty of transitions that signal your organization to ensure that your listeners don't get lost.

Use Appropriate Visuals

Visuals add interest to your presentation and can be used to reinforce your message and make your ideas clear and concrete. You may also find that using a visual aid builds your confidence and lessens apprehension. Presentation aids seem to relax speakers and distract them from thinking about themselves and how they look. A wide range of presentation aids are available, including related objects (if you are giving a speech about in-line skating, bring your skates), charts, maps, photographs, tapes, CDs, videotapes, flip charts, and Microsoft PowerPoint presentations. Ask your instructor what is permissible and what media are available for classroom use.

Plan Your Introduction and Conclusion

For more information on introductions, see Chapter 6, p. 126.

Your introduction should grab your audience's attention, introduce your topic, and establish a relationship between you and your audience. You can capture your reader's interest and introduce your topic in many of the same ways you do when you write essays. To build a relationship with your audience, try to make connections with them. You might mention others who are present; refer to a shared situation (a previous class or another student's speech); or establish common ground by referring to a well-known event, personality, or campus issue.

Your conclusion is a crucial part of your presentation because it is often the most memorable. It is the final impression with which you leave your audience. Your conclusion should summarize your speech, but it should also let your audience know your presentation is ending. You might also end your presentation with a statement that leaves a lasting final impression.

Rehearsing Your Presentation

Practicing your speech is the key to comfortable and effective delivery. Once you have drafted and organized your ideas, you need to prepare an outline or note cards that you can use to guide your presentation. Use the following rehearsal tips.

- **Practice giving the entire speech, not just parts.** Rehearse at least three or four times. Try to improve your speech during each rehearsal.
- **Time yourself.** If you are over or seriously under the time limit, make necessary cuts or additions.
- **If possible, rehearse the speech in the room in which you will give it.**
- **Rehearse in front of an audience of a few friends or classmates.** Ask them for constructive criticism. Some students videotape their presentations to build their confidence and look for areas that need improvement.

Overcoming Apprehension

Many students are nervous or afraid to make oral presentations to their classmates. Often called "stage fright," this apprehension is normal and natural but also easily overcome. The first step to overcoming apprehension is to understand its causes.

Some speakers are apprehensive because they feel conspicuous—at the center of attention. Others feel they are competing with other, better speakers in the class. Still others are apprehensive because the task is new and they have never done it before. You can often overcome these feelings using the following suggestions.

- If you feel conspicuous, try to imagine that you are talking to one friend or one friendly and supportive classmate.
- To reduce the newness of the task, be sure to practice your speech. (See the previous section on rehearsal.)
- Preparation—knowing you have put together a solid, interesting presentation—can build your self-confidence and lessen your sense of competition.

Use Visualization to Enhance Your Performance

Many athletes, actors, and musicians use the technique of visualization to enhance their performances. Performance visualization involves imagining yourself successfully completing a task. For an oral presentation, visualize yourself successfully making the presentation. Create a mental videotape. It should begin with your arrival at the classroom and take you through each step: confidently walking to the front of the room, beginning your speech, engaging your audience, handling your notes, and so on. Be sure to visualize the presentation positively; avoid negative thoughts. Now you have the image of yourself as a successful speaker. You know what it looks and feels like to give an effective presentation. Review your "videotape" often, especially on the day of your presentation. As you give your presentation, try to model the look and feel of your videotape.

Use Desensitization

Desensitization is a method of overcoming fears by gradually building up your tolerance of the feared situation or object. If someone is afraid of snakes, for example, a desensitization therapist might begin by showing the person a photograph, then a videotape, then a small snake at a distance, and so forth, gradually building up the person's exposure time and tolerance. You can do the same thing to overcome your apprehension of oral presentations by gradually building up to making presentations. Begin by asking a question in class. When you are comfortable with that, move to answering questions in class. Then you might move toward speaking in front of small groups (practicing your speech on a group of friends, for example). Each step you take makes the next one easier. Eventually you will become more comfortable with public speaking and ready to make a presentation to the class.

Delivering an Effective Presentation

The delivery of your presentation ultimately determines its effectiveness. Use the following suggestions, as well as Table 24.3, to improve the delivery of your presentation.

- **Avoid using too many notes or a detailed outline.** Instead, construct a key-word outline that will remind you of major points in the order you wish to present them.
- **Make eye contact with your audience.** Make them part of your presentation.

- **Move around a little rather than standing stiffly.** Use gestures to add an expressive quality to your presentation.
- **Speak slowly.** It is a common mistake to speak too fast. Your audience may miss your main points and lose interest in your presentation.

TABLE 24.3 Frequently Asked Questions for Making Presentations

Question	Suggested Solutions
What should I do if I go blank?	• Refer to your notes or index cards. • Ask if there are any questions. Even if no one asks any, the pause will give you time to regroup your ideas.
What should I do if classmates are restless, uninterested, or even rude?	• Make eye contact with as many members of the class as possible as you speak. • For a particularly troublesome person, you might lengthen your eye contact. • Change the tone or pitch of your voice. • Try to make your speech more engaging by asking questions or using personal examples.
What should I do if I skip over or forget to include an important part of the presentation?	• Go back and add it in. Say something like, "I neglected to mention . . . " and present the portion you skipped.
What if I realize that my speech will be too short or too long?	• If you realize it will be too short, try to add examples, anecdotes, or more detailed information. • If you realize it will be too long, cut out examples or summarize instead of fully explaining sections that are less important.

Dorothy Allison. "Panacea" from *The New York Times Magazine,* October 28, 2007. Copyright © 2007 by The New York Times Company. Reprinted with permission. Screenshot from Bartleby.com. Courtesy Bartleby.com.

Greg Beato. "Amusing Ourselves to Death: Is *The Onion* Our Most Intelligent Newspaper?" from *Reason,* November 2007. Copyright © 2007 by Greg Beato. Reprinted with permission of the author.

Nell Bernstein. "Goin' Gangsta, Choosin' Cholita: Claiming Identity" from *West* (1994). Copyright © 1994 by Nell Bernstein. Reprinted with the permission of the author.

Elizabeth Bishop. "Filling Station" from *The Complete Poems: 1927–1979.* Copyright © 1979, 1983 by Alice Helen Methfessel. Reprinted with the permission of Farrar, Straus & Giroux, LLC.

David Bodanis. "A Brush with Reality: Surprises in the Tube" from *The Secret House.* Copyright © 1986 by David Bodanis. Reprinted with the permission of the Carol Mann Agency.

Cat Bohannon. "Shipwreck" from *The Best American Nonrequired Reading 2006,* edited by Dave Eggers. Copyright © 2005 by Cat Bohannon. Originally published in *The Georgia Review,* Spring 2005. Reprinted with the permission of the author.

Gwendolyn Brooks. "The Bean Eaters" from *Blacks.* Copyright © 1991 by Gwendolyn Brooks. Reprinted by consent of Brooks Permissions.

Mike Crissey. "Linguist Deciphers Uses of Word 'Dude'" (December 8, 2004). Copyright © 2004 by Associated Press. Used with permission of The Associated Press. All rights reserved.

Joseph A. DeVito. "Territoriality" from *Human Communications, Seventh Edition,* published by Allyn & Bacon, Boston, MA. Copyright © 1997 by Pearson Education. Reprinted by permission of the publisher.

Susan Douglas. "Remote Control: How to Raise a Media Skeptic" from *Utne Reader* (January/February 1997). Copyright © 1997 by Susan Douglas. Used with the permission of the author.

Sarah Dowdey. "Freegans." Original title "How Freegans Work" From HowStuffWorks.com. http://people .HowStuffWorks.com/freegan/htm. Copyright © 1998–2007 by HowStuffWorks, Inc. Courtesy of HowStuffWorks.com.

Barbara Ehrenreich. Excerpt from "Selling in Minnesota" from *Nickel and Dimed: On (Not) Getting By in America.* Copyright © 2001 by Barbara Ehrenreich. Reprinted with the permission of Henry Holt and Company, LLC.

Curt Franklin. "How Internet Search Engines Work" from HowStuffWorks.com. http://computer .howstuffworks.com/search-engine.htm. Copyright © 1998–2007 by HowStuffWorks, Inc. Courtesy of HowStuffWorks.com.

Ian Frazier. "Dearly Disconnected." From *Mother Jones Wire* (January/February 2000). Copyright © 2000 by the Foundation for National Progress. Reprinted with permission.

Robert Frost. "Two Look at Two" from *The Poetry of Robert Frost,* edited by Edward Connery Lathem. Copyright 1923, © 1969 by Henry Holt and Company, LLC. Copyright 1951 by Robert Frost. Reprinted with the permission of Henry Holt and Company, LLC.

Tim Gideon and Jeff Pearlman. "Geeks in the Clubhouse" from www.pcmag.com, August 16, 2006. Copyright © 2006 Ziff Davis Publishing Holdings Inc. Reprinted with permission. All Rights Reserved.

Daniel Goleman. "His Marriage and Hers: Childhood Roots" from *Emotional Intelligence.* Copyright © 1995 by Daniel Goleman. Used by permission of Bantam Books, a division of Random House, Inc.

Martin Gottfried. "Rambos of the Road" from *Newsweek* (September 8, 1986). Copyright © 1986 by Martin Gottfried. Used with the permission of the author.

Riverbend. "Bloggers without Borders . . ." (October 22, 2007) from Baghdad Burning blog, http://riverbendblog.blogspot.com. Reprinted by permission of The Feminist Press at the City University of New York, www.feministpress.org. All rights reserved.

William Safire. "Abolish the Penny" from *The New York Times* (June 2, 2004). Copyright © 2004 by The New York Times Company. Reprinted with permission.

Peter Scott. "Selling Civility" Originally published in *The Wall Street Journal* (June 29, 2001). Copyright © 2001 by Dow Jones & Company, Inc. Used by permission of the author.

Carolyn Foster Segal. "The Dog Ate My Disk, and Other Tales of Woe." Originally from *The Chronicle of Higher Education* (August 11, 2000). Copyright © 2000 by Carolyn Foster Segal. Used by permission of the author.

Andrew Simms. "Would You Buy a Car That Looked Like This?" from *New Statesman* 133, no. 4176 (November 29, 2004). Copyright © New Statesman. Reprinted by permission of the publisher. All rights reserved.

Brent Staples. "Black Men and Public Space" from *Harpers* (1987). Originally titled "Just Walk On By: A Black Man Ponders His Power to Alter Public Space," from *Ms.* magazine, September 1986. Reprinted by permission of the author.

Ilan Stavans. "A Latin Lingo." from *The Boston Globe*, September 14, 2003. Copyright © 2003 by Ilan Stavans. Reprinted by the permission of the author.

Laurence Steinberg. "Part-Time Employment Undermines Students' Commitment to School" from *Beyond the Classroom: Why School Reform Has Failed and What Parents Need to Do*. Copyright © 1996 by Laurence Steinberg. Reprinted with the permission of Simon & Schuster Adult Publishing Group.

Lynn Steirer. "When Volunteerism Isn't Noble" from *The New York Times*, April 22, 1997. Copyright © 1997 by The New York Times Company. Reprinted with permission.

Gary M. Stern. "Hitting the 'Granite Wall'" from *Hispanic* (December 2004). Copyright © 2004 by Gary M. Stern. Used with the permission of the author.

Amy Tan. "Inferior Decorating" from *The Opposite of Fate* (New York: Putnam, 2003). Originally published (as "Tête-à-Tête") in *Elle Décor* (1992). Copyright © 1992 by Amy Tan. Reprinted by permission of the author and Sandra Dijkstra Literary Agency.

Jutka Terris. "Sprawl Is Harmful to Wildlife." Originally titled "Unwelcome (Human) Neighbors: The Impacts of Sprawl on Wildlife." From Natural Resources Defense Council, www.nrdc.org, August 1999. Copyright © 2003 by the Natural Resources Council, Inc. Reproduced by permission.

Kathleen Vail. "Words That Wound" from *American School Board Journal* (September 1999). Copyright © 1999 by the National School Boards Association. Reprinted with permission. All rights reserved.

Alton Fitzgerald White. "Right Place, Wrong Face" from *The Nation* (October 11, 1999). Originally titled "Ragtime, My Time." Reprinted with permission. For subscription information, call 1–800–333–8536. Portions of each week's *Nation* magazine can be accessed at http://www.thenation.com.

Abigail Zuger. "Defining a Doctor, with a Tear, a Shrug, and a Schedule" from *The New York Times*, November 2, 2004. Copyright © 2004 by The New York Times Company. Reprinted with permission.

Pictures
2: Bill Vance/Corbis; **20:** (top) Phil Boorman/Getty Images, (middle) David Young Wolff/Photo Edit, (bottom) Bruce Lawrence/Getty Images; **29:** By permission. From Bartleby.com; **42:** David Wells/The Image Works; **60:** Robert Beck/Sports Illustrated; **76:** Elaine Sulle/Image Bank/Getty Images; **98:** © Tee and Charles Addams Foundation; **114:** (top left) Jeff Greenberg, (top right) Silka Reents/The Image Works, (bottom) Michael Keller/CORBIS; **138:** Daniel Garcia/Getty Images; **154:** Logan Mock/Getty Images; **176:** (top) Gaerano/CORBIS, (bottom) © The New Yorker Collection 1987 Michael Maslin from cartoonbank.com. All Rights Reserved; **200:** Rick Wilking/Reuters/Corbis; **232:** De Agostini/Getty Images; **268:** Getty Images; **302:** (all) Courtesy of Sauder Woodworking Co., Archbold, Ohio; **338:** (top) Steve C.

Mitchell/Corbis, (bottom) Herbert Neubauer/Corbis; **374:** © The New Yorker Collection 1994 Bernard Schoenbaum from cartoonbank.com. All Rights Reserved; **408:** A. Ramey/Photo Edit; **411:** Stan Honda/ Getty Images; **444:** © Nigel Cooke/Daytona Beach News/Corbis; **482:** A. Ramey/Photo Edit; **552:** Craig Lovell/CORBIS; **572:** Chuck Nacke/Woodfin Camp Associates; **577, 578:** Images used with permission of Seattle Pacific University; **598:** Bill Horsman/Stock Boston; **628:** © 2005 Newsweek, Inc. All rights reserved. Reprinted by permission; **654:** John and Yva Momatiuk/The Image Works; **686:** Dave Carpenter/ Cartoon Stock.

patterns of development
  argument essays, 514–50
  arguments, 484–511
  cause-and-effect essay, 446–80
  classification and division, 375–407
  comparison and contrast, 340–73
  descriptions, 234–67
  to explore topics, 91–93
  extended definition, 410–43
  illustrations, 270–301
  narratives, 202–31
  process analysis, 303–37
Pearlman, Jeff, "Geeks in the Clubhouse," 277–79
Pechter, Kerry, "Pet Therapy for Heart and Soul," 110–12
peer review, 162–66
  example of, 170–72
  finding reviewer, 164
  tips for writers/reviewers, 164–65
periodical articles
  APA *References*
    online sources, 644
    print articles, 641–43
  MLA *Works Cited*
    online articles, 632
    print articles, 627–29
periodical indexes
  EBSCO, 580
  general, 580
  searching, 579–81
  specialized, 581
periodicals, contents of, 579
periodic sentences, 185
periods, with quotation marks, 612, 682
person. *See also* first-person; second-person; third-person
  shifts, avoiding, 285
personal correspondence
  APA in-text citations, 637
  MLA in-text citations, 621
  MLA *Works Cited*, 633
personification
  defined, 193, 239
  in descriptions, 239
"Pet Therapy for Heart and Soul" (Pechter), thesis statement/evidence, 110–12
phrases
  commas with, 394
  as modifiers, 184
  parallelism, 187
  unnecessary, avoiding, 179, 180
pity, appeal to, 500
plagiarism
  avoiding, 592
  cyberplagiarism, 592
  defined, 591, 608
  and paraphrasing, 589–90
  types of, 592
plain folks appeal, 500
planning, types of plans, 7
plays, MLA in-text citations, 621
plot, short stories, 664
poetry, 668–73
  allusions in, 669
  analysis, questions for, 669
  examples of, 670–73
  lines, separating with (/), 682
  MLA in-text citations, 621
  reading guidelines, 668–69
point-by-point organization
  comparison and contrast, 340–43, 357, 364–65
  defined, 340
  examples of, 341–45, 350–52
  graphic organizer, 348
point of view. *See also* first-person; second-person; third-person
  bias, recognizing, 567–68
  choosing, 85
  defined, 85
  short stories, 664
  and thesis statement, 103
popular diction, 190
portfolios. *See* writing portfolio
positive attitude, about writing, 25–26
post hoc, ergo propter hoc, 461, 502
pragmatic learners
  and active reading, 71
  characteristics of, 37, 41
  and outlines, 124, 605
  summary writing, 498
  and thesis statement, 101
preface, MLA *Works Cited*, 625
prepositional phrases, unnecessary, 180
present tense
  literary, 682
  literary analysis, 679
  in narratives, 216
previewing, reading assignments, 47–50
prewriting, 78–97
  audience, considering, 83–85
  idea generation, 86–95, 677
  point of view, choosing, 85
  purpose for writing, 82–83
  topic selection, 78–82
primary sources, types of, 554
problems, as evidence, 105
problem-solving, and writing skills, 15
process, explaining, as evidence, 105
process analysis, 303–37
  audience/purpose for writing, 318
  characteristics of, 308–10
  critical thinking about, 328–29
  defined, 304
  details in, 310, 318–19
  drafting, 320–21
  editing/proofreading, 321, 324
  examples of, 305–8, 312–14, 329–31, 333–35
  graphic organizers, 311, 315
  graphics in, 310, 320
  headings in, 309, 320
  how-it-works essays, 304
  how-to essays, 304
  idea generation, 92
  integrating in essay, 316, 333–35
  introduction/conclusion, 321
  point of view, 318
  reading, 328
  response paper to, 328
  revision, 321–23
  steps in process, organizing, 309, 319, 320
  student example, 325–27
  thesis statement, 318
  topic selection, 317–18
  troubleshooting content in, 310
  writing, guided assignment, 317–24
procrastination, avoiding, 7
pronouns
  antecedents, explicit, 537
  relative, 183
proofreading. *See also* specific types of essays
  errors, eliminating, tips for, 195–96
  literary analysis, 682
  research paper, 617–18
  student example, 196–98
purpose for reading, elements of, 50–55

purpose for writing, 82–83. *See also* specific
    types of essays
    main purposes, 82–83
    questions to ask, 83
    revising, 159
"Purse Snatching" (Lopiano)
    annotations, 54–55
    graphic organizer for, 59
    previewing, 48–49
    purpose for reading, 51–53
    response essay to, 72–73

qtd. in (quoted in), 621, 637
question marks, with quotation marks,
    613, 682
questions
    for audience analysis, 84
    class participation, 15–16
    for concrete supporting details, 148
    critical, for analysis essay, 66–67
    end-of-assignment, 48
    to guide reading assignments, 50
    for idea generation, 90
    in introduction, 128
    to narrow topic, 81–82, 96
    purpose for writing, 83
    research questions, 560
    for revising, 159
    survey questions, 594–95
    in title of essay, 131
    W questions, 81–82, 162
quotation marks
    in dialogue, 220
    with direct quotations, 612–13
    in keyword searches, 576
    with other punctuation, 612–13
    single, 612
quotations
    added information, brackets for, 614
    in arguments, 532
    block quotations, 611–12
    changing, methods for, 613–14
    in conclusion, 130
    deleted elements, ellipsis for, 591, 613
    direct, recording, 591
    as evidence, 105
    integrating in paper, 610–11
    in introduction, 128
    punctuation of, 612–13, 682
    within quotations, 612, 682

in research papers, 611–14
use, guidelines for, 611

radio programs, MLA *Works Cited*, 633
"Rambos of the Road" (Gottfried), as
    illustration, 271–72, 275
rational learners
    and active reading, 71
    characteristics of, 38, 41
    and revising, 169
reading, 44–74
    annotations, 53–55, 64, 491–92
    and college success, tips for, 45
    critical reading, 46
    difficult, reading strategies, 56
    graphic organizer for, 44, 55–59
    key points, highlighting, 53, 55, 64, 492
    and learning style, 69–71
    of literature. *See* literature, reading
    myths about, 46
    online sources, 571
    versus passive reading, 48
    response paper based on, 62–69
    scanning and skimming, 570–71
    source materials, 570–71
    steps in, 46–55
    visuals, 57
"Reality of Real TV, The" (Lee)
    editing/proofreading, 196–98
    first draft, 132–33
    paragraph development, 152–53
    peer review of, 170–72
    revision of, 171–75
    supporting details, 109–10
    thesis statement, 109
    topic selection, 96–97
reasoning
    deductive, 521–22, 533
    inductive, 520–21, 533
reasoning errors
    circular reasoning/begging the
        question, 501
    correlation versus causation, 461
    either-or fallacy, 502
    false analogy, 501
    hasty generalization, 501
    non sequitur, 501
    post hoc, ergo propter hoc, 461, 502
    red herring, 501
    sweeping generalization, 501

reasons
    in arguments, 487–88, 519, 534
    defined, 488
Rebensdorf, Alicia, "The Animal Kingdom
    Storms Reality TV and the Docu-
    mentary Industry," 438–41
recommendations, in conclusion, 130
red herring, 501
redundancy, avoiding, 179
reference desk, online, 29
References. See APA style
reference works, online, 29–30, 582
reflective essay/letter, with writing
    portfolio, 702–6
refutation
    of argument, 485, 489–90, 522, 532
    defined, 489, 522
rehearsing, oral presentations, 708
relative pronouns
    in dependent clauses, 183
    list of, 183
"Remote Control: How to Raise a Media
    Skeptic" (Douglas), as process
    analysis, 329–31
repetition, words, as transition, 126
research
    for arguments, 530, 534
    field research, 593–96
    literary works, 676
    to narrow topic, 94
    for oral presentations, 707
research paper, 555–61, 600–652. *See also*
    sources
    assignment, defining, 557
    audience, 607
    categories, 602–3
    drafting, 607–8
    editing/proofreading, 617–18
    evidence, 607
    formatting, 615
    graphic organizers, 605
    in-text citations, 608–10
    organizational patterns, 605–6
    plagiarism, 608
    quotations, 611–14
    research questions, 560
    revising, 616–17
    sources, integrating, 610–11
    student example, 646–52
    synthesizing information, 602–5

Because each person has a unique style of learning new skills and information—some people learn more from listening, for example, while others prefer reading—understanding your own unique learning style will help you in your writing course as well as other college work. This book includes a Learning Style Inventory (pp. 33–36) that will help you discover characteristics of the way you learn and how you can apply this discovery to your writing. The list below explains these characteristics, and the chart on the facing page explains how each characteristic relates to your strengths as a writer. As you work through the assignments in the book, look for the Learning Style Options icons in the margins that call your attention to suggestions for how students with different learning styles can approach particular writing tasks.

1. Independent or Social

This characteristic indicates the level of interaction with others that you prefer. *Independent* learners prefer to work and study alone. They focus on the task at hand rather than on the people around them and are often goal oriented and self-motivated. *Social* learners are more people oriented and prefer to learn and study with classmates. They often focus their attention on those around them and see a task as an opportunity for social interaction.

2. Pragmatic or Creative

This characteristic suggests how you prefer to approach learning tasks. *Pragmatic* learners are practical and systematic. They approach tasks in an orderly, sequential manner. They like rules and learn step by step. *Creative* learners, in contrast, approach tasks imaginatively. They prefer to learn through discovery or experiment. They enjoy flexible, open-ended tasks and tend to dislike following rules.

3. Verbal or Spatial

This characteristic indicates the way you prefer to take in and process information. *Verbal* learners rely on language, usually written text, to acquire information. They are skilled in the use of language and can work with other symbol systems as well. *Spatial* learners prefer to take in information by studying graphics such as drawings, diagrams, films, or videos. They can visualize in their minds how things work or how things are positioned in space.

4. Rational or Emotional

This characteristic suggests your preferred approach to decision making and problem solving. *Rational* learners are objective and impersonal; they rely on facts and information when making decisions or solving problems. Rational learners are logical, often challenging or questioning a task. They enjoy prioritizing, analyzing, and arguing. In contrast, *emotional* learners are subjective; they focus on feelings and values. Emotional decision makers are socially conscious and often concerned with what others think. In making a decision, they seek harmony and may base a decision in part on the effect it may have on others. Emotional decision makers are often skilled at persuasion.

5. Concrete or Abstract

This characteristic indicates how you prefer to perceive information. *Concrete* learners pay attention to what is concrete and observable. They focus on details and tend to perceive tasks in parts or steps. Concrete learners prefer actual, tangible tasks and usually take a no-nonsense approach to learning. *Abstract* learners look at a task from a broader perspective. They tend to focus on the "big picture" or an overview of a task. Abstract learners focus on large ideas, meanings, and relationships.